Regulating Mergers and Acquisitions of U.S. Electric Utilities: Industry Concentration and Corporate Complication

To George Spiegel, Harry Trebing and David Penn:
Teachers, mentors, leaders

Regulating Mergers and Acquisitions of U.S. Electric Utilities: Industry Concentration and Corporate Complication

Scott Hempling

Edward Elgar
PUBLISHING

Cheltenham, UK • Northampton, MA, USA

Published by
Edward Elgar Publishing Limited
The Lypiatts
15 Lansdown Road
Cheltenham
Glos GL50 2JA
UK

Edward Elgar Publishing, Inc.
William Pratt House
9 Dewey Court
Northampton
Massachusetts 01060
USA

A catalogue record for this book
is available from the British Library

Library of Congress Control Number: 2020944306

This book is available electronically in the **Elgar**online
Law subject collection
http://dx.doi.org/10.4337/9781839109461

ISBN 978 1 83910 945 4 (cased)
ISBN 978 1 83910 946 1 (eBook)

Printed and bound by CPI Group (UK) Ltd, Croydon, CR0 4YY

Contents

Extended contents

About the author

Scott Hempling has taught the law of public utilities to a generation of regulatory practitioners, appearing throughout the United States and in Australia, Canada, Central America, Germany, India, Italy, Jamaica, Mexico, New Zealand, Nigeria, Peru and Vanuatu. He has advised clients from all industry sectors—regulators, utilities, consumer organizations, independent competitors, labor unions and environmental organizations. As an expert witness, he has testified before committees of the United States Congress; before the state commissions of the District of Columbia, Hawai'i, Illinois, Indiana, Kansas, Louisiana, Maryland, Minnesota, Mississippi, New Jersey, North Carolina, Oklahoma, Texas, Vermont and Wisconsin; and before the state legislatures of Arkansas, California, Connecticut, Maine, Maryland, Minnesota, Nevada, North Carolina, South Carolina, Vermont and Virginia.

His book on the law of regulation, *Regulating Public Utility Performance: The Law of Market Structure, Pricing and Jurisdiction* (American Bar Association 2013), has been described as a "comprehensive regulatory treatise [that] warrants comparison with Kahn and Phillips." His book of essays on the art of regulation, *Preside or Lead? The Attributes and Actions of Effective Regulators* (2d ed. 2013), has been described as "matchless" and "timeless." The essays continue monthly at www.scotthemplinglaw.com.

His articles have appeared in the *Energy Law Journal*, *The Electricity Journal*, *Energy Regulation Quarterly*, *Public Utilities Fortnightly*, *ElectricityPolicy.com* and in publications of the American Bar Association, covering such topics as mergers and acquisitions, the introduction of competition into formerly monopolistic markets, corporate restructuring, ratemaking, utility investments in non-utility businesses, transmission planning, renewable energy and state–federal jurisdictional issues.

Hempling is an adjunct professor at Georgetown University Law Center. From 2006 to 2011, he was the Executive Director of the National Regulatory Research Institute. He received a B.A. *cum laude* in (1) Economics and Political Science and (2) Music from Yale University; and a J.D. *magna cum laude* from Georgetown University Law Center. He is a member of the District of Columbia and Maryland Bars.

More detail is available at www.scotthemplinglaw.com.

Preface

This book describes what happens when electric utility monopolies pursue their acquisition interests—undisciplined by competition, and insufficiently disciplined by the regulators responsible for replicating competition.

Since the mid-1980s, a stream of mergers and acquisitions has cut the number of local, independent electric retail utilities in the U.S. by more than half. Nearly eighty transactions, mostly debt-financed, have converted retiree-suitable investments into subsidiaries of geographically scattered conglomerates—multi-layered, multi-state and multinational holding company systems that mix lower-risk utilities in with higher-risk ventures. The utilities in today's consolidated, complicated electric industry are no longer your grandparents' nest eggs.

No one—no legislator, no regulator, no utility CEO, no bond analyst, no investment banker—intended this result. No commissioner voting twenty years ago to allow her local utility to sprout a simple shell holding company intended that utility to end up in a holding company conglomerate reaching from Indiana to Florida (Duke) or from Illinois to Delaware (Exelon). No objective analyst ever recommended that the U.S. electric utility industry look like it does now. And no thinking citizen would find comfort with these five facts:

- Control of a public privilege—the government-granted, monopoly utility franchise—is sold and re-sold by the private franchisee to the highest bidder, in multi-billion-dollar transactions undisciplined by normal competitive market forces.
- The gain extracted from these sales goes mostly to the acquired utility's shareholders and executives, even though the economic value underlying that gain comes not from shareholder risk-taking or executive decision-making, but from customers—customers made captive by state laws that protect the utility from competition.
- The purpose commonly claimed by the merging companies—"synergies"—is non-factual because they create their efficiencies estimates only after they sign their merger agreements.
- The regulators responsible for deciding who should control these franchises have no plan or procedures for finding the most cost-effective provider. Instead they let their utility choose—knowing that the utility will

base its choice on gain to its shareholders rather than performance for its customers.

• While the merging companies seek to maximize return for their shareholders, the regulators seek mostly to avoid harm to the customers—a passion gap that produces predictably lopsided results.

The Harms

Three decades of concentration and complication have brought four harms.

Economic waste: When companies undisciplined by competition choose their partners based on price instead of performance, they preclude more cost-effective couplings. They waste the economy's resources.

Misallocated value: A utility's franchise is not its private asset. Unlike corporate stock, buildings or trucks, the franchise was not bought with dollars; unlike a baseball star's ten-year contract, it was not earned through merit. The franchise is a privilege, not an asset; so the utility has no logical or legal claim to the gain from its sale. Yet the merging companies keep that gain all for themselves, leaving none for their customers—the customers whose captivity creates the value underlying the gain.

Weakened competition: Horizontal mergers reduce the number of competitors; vertical mergers get the merged entity control of essential inputs. By enabling anticompetitive conduct and vesting unearned advantages, mergers can weaken competition in traditional electricity markets. In emerging product markets—renewable energy, storage, microgrids and other distributed resources—mergers can create first-mover advantages: advantages based not on merit but on government-protected incumbency. Mergers are concentrating these markets at the same time that policymakers are seeking to diversify them.

Customer risk from parent-utility conflict: Between the holding company's business objectives and its utility subsidiaries' service obligations, conflicts are unavoidable. Those conflicts cause harms: overcharging customers to pay off acquisition debt, diverting utility funds to support non-utility affiliates, raising electricity rates to cover capital costs inflated by the holding company's higher risks.

Merger advocates say their transactions exploit economies of scale, improve access to capital, diversify investment risk and spread best practices. The economies-of-scale argument, presented as a generic, automatic fact, finds no support in any objective study—or in reality, because the small Madison Gas & Electric thrives alongside the huge Exelon Corporation. The capital-raising argument fails because small utilities access capital routinely, as long as their regulators set rates properly. Shareholders can diversify their own investments; they don't need a holding company to do it for them. And "best practices" are an obligation of every franchise-holding utility; high-paid executives don't need mergers to learn best practices. Merger supporters also argue, accurately, that no merger has gone sour. That's the wrong standard for a multi-trillion-dollar, infrastructural industry on which our economy and lives depend. The right standard is not failure-avoidance but maximum performance. Electricity mergers fail that test.

How Does it Happen?

How does the utility franchise, a legal device created by state governments to bring public benefits, become a source of private gain—an earnings stream for acquisitive holding companies, a cash-out opportunity for target shareholders?

Monetizing a government privilege: Any market position has value. A utility's market position has special value, because it is a monopoly position—a position created and protected by state government. The acquirer buys that monopoly position by paying the utility's shareholders a price reflecting that government-created value. The merging parties—private parties—monetize a public franchise.

Transacting without the discipline of competition: In fully competitive markets, mergers can advance the public interest. The acquirer will offer, and its target will expect, an acquisition price no higher than what the acquirer can recover from its customers—customers free to shop elsewhere. Under competitive conditions, then, which bidder will offer the highest price? The bidder most able to reduce costs and improve quality—because under competition, reducing costs and improving quality are the only ways to earn the extra profit needed to recover the acquisition price. Competition in the ultimate service market disciplines competition in the merger market. All interests are aligned: the target gets a good price, the acquirer gets a profitable market position and the merged company's customers get the most cost-effective service.

Retail electric service doesn't occur in a competitive market, because the utility has a state-protected monopoly. So competition doesn't discipline the offer price. Instead the acquirer offers, and the target utility seeks, a price reflecting what they can persuade the utility's regulators to approve. Under these non-competitive conditions, the shareholder and customer interests are not aligned, because the highest bidder will not necessarily be the best performer. Any competitor seeks to exploit its advantages. If its advantages come from merit—the soccer player's stamina, the pianist's technique, the architect's inventiveness—the competition will reward merit. A utility's main advantage is its government-protected franchise. Its value is unrelated to merit. The competition to acquire utilities does not reward merit.

The Regulatory Lapses

Why do utility regulators, charged by law to replicate the discipline of competition, routinely defer to mergers undisciplined by competition? Why do they allow their utility to sell its government-protected privilege for profit? Why do regulators allow the gain from these sales to go almost entirely to the utility's shareholders? Why has no regulatory agency paused to consider how its individual approval will increase the nation's cumulative costs—of economic waste, reduced competition, misallocated gain and customer risk? Four reasons stand out.

Checklists instead of vision: No regulatory commission, state or federal, has described a vision for the electric industry—in terms of ownership type, asset concentration, corporate structure, financial structure and business activities. From 1935 to 2005, the Public Utility Holding Company Act supplied a vision—the "integrated public-utility system." Utilities and their holding companies had to be local, conservatively financed, uninvolved in non-utility ventures, their electricity assets interconnected or capable of interconnection. In 2005 Congress repealed that vision, leaving states to create their own. No state did. No commission established standards that distinguish optimal mergers from suboptimal ones. Instead of visions, commissions have only checklists—issue folders that applicants fill with claims that suit their strategies.

Passion gap: The dozens of regulatory approvals display a disparity in determination—a passion gap between merger promoters and merger regulators. The promoters seek to maximize gain, the regulators seek to avoid harm. Merger promoters have affirmative objectives: increase shareholder value, grow market share, add to earnings, discourage competitors. And they have affirmative strategies: acquire assets, leverage a monopoly position in one market to gain advantage in another, channel ratepayer-funded resources to new competitive businesses. Merger regulators, in contrast, lack affirmative objectives and strategies, so they focus on avoiding negatives. Their requests are few and small—intentionally small, so as not to upset the applicants. They tell merging entities, in effect: "Execute your strategies, keep the gains, maintain market dominance; just don't raise rates, don't degrade service, don't fire workers immediately, don't act anticompetitively." Deference to a merger can be logical when the merger comes from, and improves, a competitive market. Mergers of electric utility monopolies don't qualify.

Systematic mental errors: In official proxy statements, target utilities tell their shareholders the real story: "We sought and got the highest possible price." In applications for regulatory approval, they tell regulators a different story: "We're merging to benefit our customers." Why do commissions so often ignore the real story? Possible answers come from the fields of decisional psychology and behavioral economics. Nobel Prize winners Daniel Kahneman and Richard Thaler, along with their colleague Amos Tversky, have proven that the human mind has two "systems": an automatic, instinctive system; and an effortful, analytical system. The automatic system exerts power over the effortful system, causing our initial impressions to harden into beliefs. The automatic system's power—a power that affects everyone's decisions daily—causes a variety of mental errors. Applying their insights to electricity mergers raises this question: When regulators address mergers, which force is more powerful—instinct or analysis?

No retrospective studies: Despite nearly eighty electricity monopoly mergers over thirty-five years, no regulatory agency has paused to examine, objectively, whether these transactions have produced the benefits their proponents claimed, or have avoided the harms their opponents predicted.

Solutions

Electricity's concentration and complication continue. Prospective targets want the gains gotten by prior targets. Prospective acquirers want to get larger because their neighbors have gotten larger. As energy conservation flattens sales, and as large coal and nuclear generation is replaced by local renewable generation, utilities seek new revenue sources. Some choose acquisitions.

To channel these urges in productive directions, regulators need to replace passivity with planning. They need first to ask the basic questions: What resource mix do we want? What services do customers need? Who should supply those services—incumbent utilities or new competitors? For the old-world activities of generation, transmission and physical distribution, what are our standards for performance? For the new distributed resource space, what market structures, what mix of monopoly and competition, will attract the most cost-effective providers? Is the incumbent utility, as currently owned or as merged or acquired, part of our future or not?

Without answering these questions, without creating their own electric industry visions, regulators cannot assess a merger proposal objectively. The typical regulatory approach—letting the target choose its acquirer based on price instead of performance, then trying to induce the post-acquisition company to meet the commission's standards for performance—does things backwards. Approving a merger that brings risks of overcharges, business risk and debt-constrained decision-making, then hoping that the commission's under-resourced staff will spot the risks and impose consequences for the harms, is also doing things backwards.

The right commission vision requires best-in-class performance, low risks and no business distractions—mergers motivated by customer service rather than revenue streams. With that vision in place, a commission can develop its must-haves and must-not-haves—the screens that distinguish mergers that satisfy the vision from those that don't. Commissions need detailed merger filing requirements that cause applicants to tell the full story—and how that story satisfies the commission's standards. Those steps, along with evidentiary procedures that emphasize issues over parties, perspectives over positions, will cause regulators to rely less on instinct, more on analysis.

Two more necessities: the regulatory decisions assessed in this book have all been issued under decades-old regulatory statutes. While the principles advanced here are consistent with those statutes, the better course is to clarify statutory language so that commissions can apply the principles free of appellate challenge. Finally, commission staff veterans, many hired in the 1970s and 1980s, are retiring. Commissions need to rebuild—by hiring the continuously varying skill sets necessary to confront the concentration and complexity that mergers have brought.

That one's work involves challenging mergers does not mean one opposes mergers. Discouraging uneconomic couplings opens the door to economic ones. Discouraging mergers based on price opens the door to mergers based on performance. Underlying Senator Truman's criticism of military waste was a patriotic commitment to military efficiency.[1] Underlying criticism of uneconomic mergers is a commitment to economic performance. That commitment is the reason for this book.

---

[1] *See Harry S. Truman*, U.S. SENATE, www.senate.gov/artandhistory/history/minute/Harry_S_Truman.htm (last visited Jan. 10, 2020): "Waste and corruption in the construction of army posts in preparation for World War II led [Senator Truman] to propose and then to chair the Senate Special Committee to Investigate the National Defense Program. During the three years of his chairmanship, the 'Truman Committee' held hundreds of hearings here and throughout the nation. This role made him a respected national figure."

Author's note: Why write a book on electricity mergers?

In 2013, the American Bar Association published my *Regulating Public Utility Performance: The Law of Market Structure, Pricing and Jurisdiction*. With that book I aimed to fill a gap: there was no single, modern volume explaining the unified legal principles by which we regulate, and bring competition into, our major public utility industries—electricity, gas, telecommunications and water. Due to the publisher's page limits, that book could not cover the crucial subject of corporate structure, mergers and acquisitions. The present book provides that coverage. With it, I hope to fill three other gaps.

Education: The regulatory profession has no objective, comprehensive text presenting the legal, economic, financial and accounting issues that commissions must confront when addressing electric utility mergers. A regulator hearing her first merger case has to learn things on the fly—from warring parties unlikely to present matters objectively.

Evaluation: While each merger has its critics, the merger movement itself has lacked critical attention. Each commission decision focuses only on a single transaction; no commission decision addresses the cumulative effects. Three decades of concentration and complication, insufficiently disciplined by competition or regulation, has received insufficient attention.

Recommendation: Despite hundreds of electricity merger decisions at the federal and state levels, we have no consistent set of principles that promoters, customers, competitors, regulators and legislators can use to guide these private transactions toward public interest outcomes. Policy debate, such as it is, happens only in the heat of litigation—litigation that focuses narrowly on the transacting companies' immediate, self-interested proposal rather than on the long-term, public-interest questions: What mix of services do customers need and want? What market structures and corporate structures will most cost-effectively produce that mix? For the various utility functions, what are the real economies of scale and scope? How do we prevent a merged company's unearned advantages—advantages gained through government protection rather than managerial skill—from distorting competition? How do we avoid a tragedy of the commons—each state approving a merger to gain minor benefits for itself, while ignoring the cumulative harms to all?

When I've raised these questions with regulators, when I've advised them to create a merger policy, I've gotten one of two answers: "We have no merger pending, so we don't care about it"; or "We have a merger pending, so we can't talk about it." This book is for those who care about electric utility mergers and want to talk about them.

Tutorial

To make this book useful for industry newcomers without burdening veterans, I have created a Tutorial on electric industry basics: physical functions, market structures, transactions, pricing, types of ownership, types of corporate forms and legal jurisdiction. The Tutorial appears after the main text.

Terminology

I use several verbal shorthands common in the electric utility industry.

When describing corporate couplings, practitioners tend to use generic terms—*merger, acquisition, consolidation, combination* and *change in control*. I use those terms interchangeably for any transaction causing two utilities previously not owned and controlled in common to be owned and controlled in common. I distinguish among those terms when technically necessary to describe a particular transaction.

Utility and *public utility* refer to companies having an exclusive retail franchise granted by state law. Different state and federal statutes define those terms differently.

For the term *holding company*, a still-useful definition is that offered by Bonbright and Means in 1932: "Any company, incorporated or unincorporated, which is in a position to control, or materially to influence, the management of one or more other companies by virtue, in part at least, of its ownership of securities in the other company or companies."[1] As with *utility* and *public utility*, different statutes define the term differently.

Acquirer and *target* refer to the corporations that, in an acquisition, are, respectively, buying a company or being bought by a company. Even in transactions that are technically mergers rather than acquisitions, one company is usually the acquirer and the other the target. The exception—an unusual one—is a stock-for-stock exchange with no implicit acquisition premium. Practitioners call such a transaction a "merger of equals"—a term that becomes

---

[1]   JAMES C. BONBRIGHT & GARDINER C. MEANS, THE HOLDING COMPANY: ITS PUBLIC SIGNIFICANCE AND ITS REGULATION 10 (A.M. Kelley 1969) (1932).

non-factual when referring to a transaction in which one company is paying for the other, and post-closing will control the other.

Merger applicants refers to the acquirer and target, or the two merging companies, when they are asking a commission to approve their transaction. Statutes vary, however, on whether the official applicant—the entity obligated to get commission permission—is the acquirer, the target or both.

Technically, a merger, acquisition or other change in control need not result in one company wholly owning the other. An acquirer can buy less than 100 percent of the target. But in nearly every electric utility transaction discussed in this book, the acquirer bought 100 percent of the target's stock or assets; or, the stock-for-stock exchange involved 100 percent of one company's stock.

In the U.S., state-level utility regulatory agencies have similar-sounding names—public service commission, public utility commission, public service board, department of public utilities. I use a shorthand, coupling the state with the capitalized term Commission, as in New York Commission or Hawaii Commission.

Footnote Practices

The footnotes mostly follow Bluebook conventions, amended for clarity and brevity.

When citing merger decisions by FERC, the FCC or state commissions, I use a short-form title that names the merging firms separated by a hyphen; e.g., *Oncor Electric Delivery-NextEra Energy Merger*. This short-form name is more informative than the long list of parent companies and temporary shell entities that usually appears in official case names.

On FERC citations I use the legal profession's convention, which can be confusing to newcomers. For all FERC decisions, the number preceding "F.E.R.C." identifies the volume in the official FERC Reports, while the paragraph sign (¶) identifies the decision's paragraph location within the Reports. For decisions on or after June 26, 2002, a capital "P" refers to the decision's internal paragraph number in which the cited or quoted material appears. (Prior FERC decisions did not use internal paragraph numbers.) For decisions preceding that date, a small "p." identifies the page number, within the FERC Reports, on which the cited or quoted material appears.

Where a commission has addressed the same transaction in multiple proceedings (such as when a rejection is followed by an approval), I differentiate the case names by adding a Roman numeral to the abbreviated title.

For state commission materials: I cite to Lexis or to Public Utility Reports (P.U.R.4th) when possible. For Lexis materials, I abbreviate the cite, using the material's title, the commission's name and the decision year.

For decisions unavailable from either of those sources, I provide a docket number, an order number (if available) and a decision date.

In each chapter, footnote numbering starts anew.

Merger and Acquisitions Experience

Utility merger decision-making is litigious. Billions of dollars turn on how a handful of regulators vote. Given the stakes, readers are entitled to know, to put it colloquially, whose water I'm carrying. The answer is no one's. Over thirty-six years, I have acted as advisor and opinion-writer for regulatory commissions; and as trial counsel, appellate counsel and expert witness for intervenors, both public-sector and private-sector. Some of my clients supported the transactions; others opposed them. The list below identifies my public presentations; it does not include transactions where I acted as advisor to litigants or commissions. I hope readers will find that I base this book's analyses on facts and logical reasoning; and that when values matter, I explain my values and the weights I give them. Only with these tools can those who pursue, support, oppose, approve or reject mergers find their way toward what we lack today: a merger policy that puts the public interest first.

Testimony before Commissions and Courts

California Public Utilities Commission (affiliate relations and mixing of utility and non-utility businesses, 1989).

Vermont Public Service Board (cost allocation and inter-affiliate pricing among service company and utility affiliates, 1991).

Public Service Commission of Wisconsin (effect of inter-affiliate transactions on state regulatory authority, 1998).

Illinois Commerce Commission (affiliate relations and mixing of utility and non-utility businesses, 1998).

North Carolina Utilities Commission (Florida Progress-Carolina Power & Light Merger, 2000).

U.S. District Court for the Western District of Wisconsin (Alliant's challenge to Wisconsin's Holding Company statute, 2002).

Maryland Public Service Commission (Exelon-Constellation Merger, 2011).

Mississippi Public Service Commission (International Transmission Company-Entergy transaction, 2013).

District of Columbia Public Service Commission (Exelon-PHI Merger, 2014).

Maryland Public Service Commission (Exelon-PHI Merger, 2014).

Hawaii Public Utilities Commission (NextEra-Hawaiian Electric Merger, 2015).

Louisiana Public Service Commission (private equity acquisition of Central Louisiana Electric, 2015).

Kansas Corporation Commission (Great Plains Energy-Kansas City Power & Light Merger, 2016).

District of Columbia Public Service Commission (AltaGas-Washington Gas Light Merger, 2017).

Maryland Public Service Commission (AltaGas-Washington Gas Light Merger, 2017).

Testimony before Legislative Bodies

U.S. Senate Committee on Energy and Natural Resources (analyzing proposed amendment to the Public Utility Holding Company Act of 1935 (PUHCA)) (Nov. 1989).

U.S. Senate Committee on Energy and Natural Resources (analyzing proposed amendment to PUHCA) (Mar. 1991).

U.S. Senate Committee on Banking, Housing, and Urban Affairs (analyzing proposed amendment to PUHCA) (Sept. 1991).

U.S. Senate Committee on Energy and Natural Resources (analyzing bill to transfer PUHCA functions from SEC to FERC) (May 1993).

U.S. House Subcommittee on Energy and Power, Energy and Commerce Committee (July 1994).

U.S. House Subcommittees on Energy and Power and Telecommunications and Finance, Energy and Commerce Committee (discussing regulation of public utility holding companies) (Oct. 1995).

U.S. Senate Committee on Energy and Natural Resources (analyzing bill to amend PUHCA) (Feb. 2002).

U.S. Senate Committee on Energy and Natural Resources (addressing the adequacy of state and federal regulation of electric utility holding company structures) (May 2008).

Court of Appeals Cases

Wisconsin's Environmental Decade v. SEC, 882 F.2d 523 (D.C. Cir. 1989) (holding company restructuring of Wisconsin Power & Light).

Environmental Action v. SEC, 895 F.2d 1255 (9th Cir. 1990) (holding company restructuring involving Sierra Pacific Resources and various contractors).

Environmental Action v. FERC, 939 F.2d 1057 (D.C. Cir. 1991) (merger of PacifiCorp and Utah Power & Light).

Madison Gas & Electric v. SEC, 168 F.3d 1337 (D.C. Cir. 1999) (merger of utilities in Wisconsin and Iowa).

National Association of Regulatory Utility Commissioners v. SEC, 63 F.3d 1123 (D.C. Cir. 1995) (rulemaking addressing holding company control of wholesale generating companies).

National Rural Electric Cooperative Ass'n v. SEC, 276 F.3d 609 (D.C. Cir. 2002) (merger of American Electric Power and Central and Southwest).

Articles

"Inconsistent with the Public Interest: FERC's Three Decades of Deference to Electricity Consolidation," *Energy Law Journal* (Fall 2018).

"Corporate Structure Events Involving Regulated Utilities: The Need for a Multidisciplinary, Multijurisdictional Approach," 19-7 *Electricity Journal* 7 (Aug.–Sept. 2006).

"Electric Utility Holding Companies: The New Regulatory Challenges," *Land Economics* (Aug. 1995).

"Preserving Fair Competition: The Case for the Public Utility Holding Company Act," 3-1 *Electricity Journal* 51 (Jan.–Feb. 1990).

"Corporate Restructuring and Consumer Risk: Is the SEC Enforcing the Public Utility Holding Company Act?" 1 *Electricity Journal* 1 (July 1988).

Acknowledgements

Early in my career, I learned much about how market structure and corporate structure affect the public interest from George Spiegel and Harry Trebing, both of blessed memory; and from David Penn. Their devotion to facts, logic and community has inspired me for thirty-six years.

I received essential advice from Peter Carstensen and John Kwoka on competition issues; and from Justin Grady, Stephen Hill and Ralph Smith on finance issues. I also owe thanks to the many colleagues who shared material and insights, including Robin Allen, Keith Berry, Peter Bradford, Nicholas Brown, Jorge Camacho, Robert Fleishman, Robert Frank, Adam Gatewood, Ignacio Herrera-Anchustegui, David Hsu, David Hudson, Alisa Lacey, Robert Lande, William Massey, Jeff McClanahan, Gabriella Passidomo, Ari Peskoe, Rob Rains, Harvey Reiter, Alan Richardson, Christina Simeone, Steven Salop, John D. Wilson, John W. Wilson and Edward Yim. Providing special inspiration, each in her own way, were Debra Knopman, Jane Stewart and Ann Turpin. All errors are mine alone.

Candis Miller, a true treasure, formatted every draft of every table, list and chapter, all while studying for a PhD in health care management. Health care will be lucky to have her. Daniel Passon, Tyler Pierce and Xiaoyang Wang checked citations and sources expertly, helping with substantive research too. Alejandra Vides-Austin, following in her mother's and grandmother's footsteps, excelled at proofreading. As with my 2013 book, Elizabeth Watson was a dream of a diagram-maker. Dominic Gallucci's stamina, patience and meticulousness bordered on the superhuman.

Three nonprofit organizations unhesitatingly permitted me to use material from my prior writings. Those organizations are: the American Bar Association (for my *Regulating Public Utility Performance: The Law of Market Structure, Pricing and Jurisdiction* (2013)); *Energy Law Journal* (for my articles "Litigation Adversaries and Public Interest Partners: Practice Principles for New Regulatory Lawyers" (Spring 2015) and "Inconsistent with the Public Interest: FERC's Three Decades of Deference to Electricity Consolidation" (Fall 2018)); and the National Regulatory Research Institute (for my table displaying the FERC-state jurisdictional relationship, first published in *Effective Regulation: Guidance for Public Interest Decisionmakers* (NRRI 2011)).

My commissioning editor, Stephen Gutierrez, along with the dedicated professionals at Edward Elgar Publishing, including Katia Williford, Sarah

Brown, Rose Campbell, Wendy Telfer, Sally Philip and Margaret McCormack, consistently demonstrated why this company has won so many awards.

Maggi, my wife, deserves thanks not only for improving this book but for giving me so much, every day for thirty-eight years.

Figures

Tables

Acronyms

AMI	Advanced metering infrastructure
ARPU	Average revenue per user
ARR	Annual revenue requirement
ATC	Available transmission capacity
BATs	Business area teams
BOCs	Bell Operating Companies
BTU	British thermal unit
CEO	Chief executive officer
CFO	Chief financial officer
COO	Chief operating officer
DSM	Demand-side management
EWG	Exempt wholesale generator
FCC	Federal Communications Commission
FERC	Federal Energy Regulatory Commission
FPA	Federal Power Act
FPC	Federal Power Commission
FTC	Federal Trade Commission
GHG	Greenhouse gas
HHI	Herfindahl-Hirschman Index
ICC	Interstate Commerce Commission
IOU	Investor-owned utility
ISO	Independent system operator
KWH	Kilowatthour
LBO	Leveraged buyout
LDC	Local distribution company
LEC	Local exchange company
LSE	Load-serving entity

MWH	Megawatthour
NEPOOL	New England Power Pool
NLRB	National Labor Relations Board
NOL	Net operating loss
O&M	Operations and maintenance
PANS	Pretty amazing new stuff
POTS	Plain old telephone service
PUHCA	Public Utility Holding Company Act
PURPA	Public Utility Regulatory Policies Act
QF	Qualifying facility
R&D	Research and development
ROE	Return on equity
ROFR	Right of first refusal
RTO	Regional transmission organization
SEC	Securities and Exchange Commission
SPE	Special purpose entity
SQI	Service quality index
USDOJ	U.S. Department of Justice
WYSIATI	What you see is all there is

Table of legal authorities

FEDERAL COURT CASES

STATE COURT CASES

FEDERAL ADMINISTRATIVE RULES AND DECISIONS

OTHER FEDERAL ADMINISTRATIVE PUBLICATIONS

FEDERAL STATUTES, CONSTITUTION AND LEGISLATIVE MATERIALS

STATE ADMINISTRATIVE RULES AND DECISIONS

OTHER STATE ADMINISTRATIVE PUBLICATIONS

STATE STATUTES

PART I

The transactions: sales of public franchises for private gain, undisciplined by competition— producing a concentrated, complicated industry no one intended

A utility's market position is a monopoly position—created, granted and protected by state law. This fact makes utility mergers different from competitive market mergers, in three ways. Chapter 1 explains that a utility merger not only transfers ownership of a private company; it transfers control of a government-protected market position. The acquirer gets the monopoly position; the target gets what the acquirer pays. A utility merger transfers a public franchise for private gain. Chapter 2 shows that because a monopoly utility faces no competition, these merger transactions are not disciplined by competition. That means the target utility, unlike target companies serving competitive markets, can keep the acquisition gain mostly for itself rather than share it with its customers. The absence of competitive discipline also means that mergers do not achieve economic efficiency. The cumulative result of these transactions, Chapter 3 explains, is an electric industry whose consolidation and complication no one intended.

1. Diverse strategies, common purpose: selling public franchises for private gain

A utility's earnings are made possible by its unique market position—a monopoly position embodied in and protected by a government-granted franchise. Controlling that franchise has value. Selling that control brings gain to the seller; buying that control brings new earnings to the buyer. Each utility merger is a sale of a public franchise for private gain. Acquirers, especially conglomerates, have additional goals, like balancing business portfolios and diversifying regulatory risk. Then there are supporting stimuli, such as "everyone does it," and low interest rates. After illustrating these concepts, this chapter describes how customer benefits—the proper purpose of mergers in competitive markets—are nearly missing from mergers in utility monopoly markets.

1.1 THE TRANSACTION'S ESSENCE: TRANSFERRING CONTROL OF A GOVERNMENT-PROTECTED FRANCHISE

A corporate acquisition is an acquisition of control—control of stock, for starters. In a cash buyout, the acquirer buys the target shareholders' stock for cash; the target shareholders leave with cash. In a stock-for-stock merger, the acquirer buys the target shareholders' stock by paying those target shareholders merged company stock. In both models, the acquirer acquires the target's stock. The reasons are many.[1]

---

[1] *See, e.g.*, VICTOR BRUDNEY & WILLIAM W. BRATTON, BRUDNEY AND CHIRELSTEIN'S CASES AND MATERIALS ON CORPORATE FINANCE 651 (4th ed. 1993) ("A firm which acquires another company … does so ideally for exactly the same reason that it purchases a new piece of machinery."); DAVID J. RAVENSCRAFT & F.M. SCHERER, MERGERS, SELL-OFFS, AND ECONOMIC EFFICIENCY 210, 211–15 (1987) ("There are surely more opinions on why mergers are made than there are economists who have written on the subject.") (listing merger motivations, including: operational efficiencies, market power, access to under-valued assets, executive empire-building,

The acquirer also gets the target's market position. That market position has value to the acquirer because it will produce a stream of future earnings—the expected revenue from sales less the cost of making those sales.[2] All acquirers acquire a market position. But that market position's value differs, depending on whether the target is a competitive company or a utility monopoly. In an effectively competitive market, the target has gained its market position by merit. Its investment decisions, assets, executive leadership, employee knowledge and customer service activities, all funded with dollars risked by investors, combine to provide a service that its customers prefer over its competitors' services. That market position comes with no guarantees; to keep it, the company must continue beating its competitors.

Contrast a utility's market position—a monopoly position granted and guaranteed by an exclusive franchise.[3] The incumbent utility got this monopoly market position not through performance merit and not through cash purchase, but through government favor. In return for providing nondiscriminatory service that satisfies the government's requirements, the utility has an exclusive right to provide the service at rates set by regulators, under legal standards that guarantee the utility a reasonable opportunity to earn a fair return on its prudent, used-and-useful investments.[4]

---

executive hubris, speculation and access to new earnings streams to fund more acquisitions).

[2] *See* STEPHEN A. ROSS ET AL., CORPORATE FINANCE 87–90, 894–95 (11th ed. 2016) (describing how analysts value mergers and acquisitions by calculating the net present value of discounted cash flows); WILLIAM T. ALLEN ET AL., COMMENTARIES AND CASES ON THE LAW OF BUSINESS ORGANIZATIONS 119–29 (3d ed. 2009) (same).

[3] A franchise is a special privilege, granted by state government to the utility, to provide defined services subject to defined obligations. *See* New Orleans Gas Co. v. La. Light Co., 115 U.S. 650, 669 (1885) (describing a franchise as "belonging to the government, to be granted, for the accomplishment of public objects, to whomsoever, and upon what terms it pleases"); Bank of Augusta v. Earle, 38 U.S. (13 Pet.) 519, 595 (1839) (describing franchises as "special privileges conferred by government upon individuals, and which do not belong to the citizens of the country generally of common right"). Some jurisdictions describe the privilege as a "concession" or as a "certificate of public convenience and necessity." Some jurisdictions use the term "franchise" to refer only to a utility's right, granted by a municipality, to lay wires or pipes under city streets. This book uses "franchise" to mean the state-granted right to provide a service protected from competition.

[4] *See* Tutorial § 4. I have explained elsewhere that the typical utility franchise has seven dimensions:

1. *Exclusive retail franchise:* the utility's right to be the sole provider of a government-prescribed service within a state-defined service territory.
2. *Obligation to serve:* the utility's obligation to serve, and to plan to serve, all customers in its service territory, without undue discrimination.
3. *Consent to regulation:* the utility's consent to all reasonable regulation.

Comparing the competitive company with the utility monopoly, their market position values differ because the source of those values differs. The utility serves customers made captive by regulatory decisions, at prices set not by unsympathetic markets but by regulators applying sympathetic legal principles. The competitive company's market position has no such solidity. Its customers can leave for competitors, and its prices must bow to market pressures. And a competitive company gets its market position by investing at risk, while a utility gets its position by government grant. (The utility must invest to carry out its obligation to serve, but regulators must recognize those investments when setting rates—rates that compensate for risk.[5])

True, a utility's market position can soften. Exclusivity is typically guaranteed by statute or regulatory order,[6] but legislatures can authorize retail competition and allow customers to self-generate, while technology can empower customers to reduce consumption. But even in those situations, policymakers usually provide the utility a reasonable opportunity to recover stranded costs—investments previously made in the exclusivity era but not readily recoverable in the competitive era.[7]

Most utility franchises have no express term limit. Others have very long terms,[8] with revocation possible only for serious service failure or misconduct, which the utility first has an opportunity to cure.[9] So while variations on exclu-

---

4.   *Quality of service:* the utility's obligation to meet the regulator's service quality standards.

5.   *Power of eminent domain:* the utility's power to take private property when necessary to satisfy its public service obligation, while paying the property owner just compensation.

6.   *Limit on liability:* the utility's protection from lawsuits for ordinary negligence.

7.   *Just and reasonable rates:* the utility's right to charge rates set by the regulator, designed to provide a reasonable opportunity to earn a fair return on equity investment.

For additional detail, see Scott Hempling, Regulating Public Utility Performance: The Law of Market Structure, Pricing and Jurisdiction, chs. 2, 6 (American Bar Association 2013).

[5]   *See* Tutorial § 4.1.

[6]   A clear example is South Dakota's statute: "Each electric utility has the exclusive right to provide electric service at retail at each and every location where it is serving a customer as of March 21, 1975, and to each and every present and future customer in its assigned service area." S.D. Codified Laws § 49–34A-42.

[7]   For a detailed discussion of stranded cost, see Hempling, *supra* note 4, at chs. 3.C.1 and 3.C.3.

[8]   Nevada's statute, for example, prescribes franchise terms of up to 50 years. *See* Nev. Rev. Stat. § 709.210.

[9]   For a detailed discussion of legal criteria for franchise revocation, see Hempling, *supra* note 4, at 30–32. Even when Pacific Gas & Electric was convicted of five federal felonies and fined by its state commission $1.6 billion for a gas pipeline explosion

sivity exist in theory and law, the typical retail utility monopoly faces no practical risk of replacement or competition—at least no risk that publicly traded companies disclose in their financial reports to the Securities and Exchange Commission, under rules requiring disclosure of all material risks.

These factors produce this conclusion: the acquirer of a utility acquires control of stock, of a company and of a market position—a position whose solidity and stability come from government policy rather than performance merit.

1.2　THE TRANSACTION'S PURPOSE: MONETIZE THE GOVERNMENT-GRANTED FRANCHISE

Any for-profit firm's board aims to increase shareholder value. For a utility's board, one way is to sell control of the utility's franchise. In a cash buyout, the target shareholders sell all their stock to the acquirer for a premium paid in cash, then depart. In a stock-for-stock merger, they receive stock in the acquirer and stay on, hoping that the combined company will increase the value of the target's current market position, help the target expand into new market positions, or both. Whether vertical, horizontal, conglomerate, or pure-play; international or domestic; going private or staying public; cash buyout or stock-for-stock; long distance or adjacent—each merger represents a melding of the two companies' independent strategies, each aimed at what analysts call "unlocking" the franchise's value.

1.2.1　Target's Goal: Sell Franchise Control for Gain

When a target's board seeks acquirers, it has a fiduciary duty, imposed by state corporate law, to get the highest price. No longer "defenders of the corporate bastion," the board's directors become "auctioneers charged with getting the

---

that caused eight deaths and destroyed a neighborhood, the California Public Utilities Commission raised no possibility of revoking the utility's franchise. More recently, the Commission asked parties to address whether the Commission should establish a "periodic review" of PG&E's certificate of convenience and necessity. Ruling on Proposals to Improve the Safety Culture of Pacific Gas & Elec. Co. and PG&E Corp., Investigation No. 15-08-019 (Cal. Pub. Util. Comm'n June 18, 2019) (interim order). In that proceeding, the author advised the California Public Advocates Office.

best price for the stockholders."[10] In electric utility acquisitions, auctioneering is precisely what target CEOs do. Consider four examples:[11]

Exelon-PHI Holdings[12]

PHI's CEO Joseph Rigby had meetings with outside legal and financial advisors to discuss "different possible approaches . . . to seek to *take advantage of the significant competition* between Exelon and Bidder D to permit PHI to obtain *the best possible price* and the greatest transaction certainty."

Mr. Rigby informed Mr. Crane [Exelon's CEO] that "Bidder D *had raised its bid* and asked Mr. Crane for Exelon's best and final price. In response, Exelon raised its bid to $27.25 per share in cash."

"During the morning of April 29, 2014 … Mr. Rigby updated the Board with respect to the increased bids made by each of Exelon and Bidder D. Mr. Rigby noted that each such counterparty had indicated to Mr. Rigby that its increased bid was its best and final offer on price, and that *based on the higher price being offered by Exelon* and the other terms in the Merger Agreement draft that Exelon had agreed to, that the purpose of the meeting was for the Board to discuss and consider a proposed transaction with Exelon."

Great Plains Energy-Westar[13]

By early 2015, Westar's CEO Mark Ruelle had informed his Board that "terms may have been shifting *in favor of shareholders of selling companies* in utility transactions announced in the last half of 2014 and first few months of 2015. Specifically, he noted that, in these transactions, there seemed to have been a greater willingness

---

[10]   *See* ARTHUR FLEISCHER, JR. & ALEXANDER R. SUSSMAN, DIRECTORS' FIDUCIARY DUTIES IN TAKEOVERS AND MERGERS 23, 79 n.iv (2004), https://www.friedfrank.com/siteFiles/ffFiles/sri_directors_duties.pdf (citing Revlon, Inc. v. MacAndrews & Forbes Holdings, Inc., 506 A.2d 173, 182 (Del. 1986)) (describing the board's duty "to obtain the highest value reasonably available for the stockholders under the circumstances"). In *Revlon*, the Delaware Supreme Court held that the company's board had breached its duty of loyalty to shareholders when it acted to benefit a bidder that included Revlon's management. "[I]f a sale of control is in question, at least in Delaware, *Revlon* principles will apply." FLEISCHER & SUSSMAN at 10.

[11]   Each of the following excerpts comes from a "proxy statement" filed with the Securities and Exchange Commission by one or both of the merging entities. Technically called a Form DEF 14A, or a Form DEFM 14A, a proxy statement provides shareholders with essential information about a transaction before they vote on it. Each proxy statement contains a narrative describing the chronology of the merger negotiations. The merging parties use this narrative to show how they arrived at their price. All emphases in these excerpts are added.

[12]   Pepco Holdings, Inc., Definitive Proxy Statement (Form DEFM 14A) at 30 Great Plains Energy Inc 31 (Aug. 12, 2014).

[13]   Great Plains Energy Inc., Amendment No. 1 to Registration Statement (Form S-4/A) at 52, 58, 63 (Aug. 17, 2016).

of buyers to take regulatory risk, and they reflected stronger price/earnings multiples and *robust takeover premia*."

During that same period, Mr. Ruelle told Mr. Bassham [GPE's CEO] that if Westar "were to pursue a consolidating transaction, management would be more likely to recommend the route of *being acquired at a premium*" (as opposed to being the acquirer or merging as equals).

In its meeting on February 22, 2016, the Westar Board "concluded that to *ascertain maximum potential value*, it wished to solicit indications of interest from several potential counter-parties … No decision to pursue a strategic transaction was made."

"Mr. Ruelle's decision was based on the price and other terms proposed by Great Plains Energy as well as his judgment that it was *unlikely that Westar would be able to obtain as high or a higher price from any of the other bidders within the next few days*, and that if Westar did not act quickly to execute a merger agreement with Great Plains Energy, the opportunity to enter into a transaction with Great Plains Energy *on the terms then proposed* could be lost."

"The Transaction is *the result of a competitive process*."[14] That competitive process was designed to achieve the Westar Board's central goal: "to provide long-term value to [Westar] shareholders."[15]

Macquarie, et al.-Central Louisiana Electric Company[16]

June 22, 2014: "[T]he Board directed senior management and representatives of the financial advisors to *contact nine potential counterparties on the list (which consisted of five industry and four financial counterparties)*."

June 24, 2014: "The standstill provision [executed by seven entities expressing interest] included in each draft contained a provision … intended to *incentivize potential counterparties to put forth their best and highest offer for Cleco* …*"

July 22, 2014: "The proposal from the MIP III consortium provided for an acquisition of Cleco in an all cash transaction at an indicative price of $55.25 per share. The proposal from Party C provided for an acquisition of Cleco in an all cash transaction at an indicative price of $59.25 per share. … The proposal from Party E and its

---

[14] Direct Testimony of Terry Bassham at 3, Great Plains Energy-Westar Energy Merger I, Docket No. 16-KCPE-593-ACQ (Kan. Corp. Comm'n filed June 28, 2016).

[15] Great Plains Energy Inc., *supra* note 13, at 52. This Proxy Statement, and the events quoted in it, arose from the original negotiations between the two companies. The merger agreement emerging from those discussions was rejected by the Kansas Commission. Great Plains Energy-Westar Energy Merger I, 2017 Kan. PUC LEXIS 1142. The two companies then negotiated a new agreement to merge, using a stock-for-stock exchange that reflected no premium. The Kansas Commission approved that transaction. Great Plains Energy-Westar Energy Merger II, 2018 Kan. PUC LEXIS 899.

[16] Cleco Corp., Definitive Proxy Statement (Form DEFM 14A) at 34–40 (Jan. 13, 2015).

potential co-investors provided for an acquisition of Cleco in an all cash transaction at an indicative price between $57.00 and $59.00 per share."

September 19, 2014: "The Board decided that it was in the best interest of Cleco and its shareholders to continue exploring a potential business combination transaction with the MIP III consortium, *but that senior management should continue to seek an increase in the MIP III consortium's price.*"

September 30, 2014: "[T]he Board instructed Locke Lord [financial advisors] and senior management to *seek more favorable terms with respect to the terms and conditions of the transaction and to reiterate Cleco's request for a price increase from the MIP III consortium.*"

October 16, 2014: "Mr. Williamson [President and Chief Executive Officer of Cleco] and the chief executive officer of MIP III discussed the remaining issues in the merger agreement. The MIP III consortium *agreed to increase its purchase price from $55.25 to $55.37 per share.*"

REASONS FOR THE MERGER; RECOMMENDATION OF OUR BOARD: "the Board's belief, following discussions with Goldman Sachs and TPH and based on knowledge of the industry and the operations of Cleco, that *it was unlikely that any other buyer would be willing to pay more than the per share Merger Consideration payable in the Merger; . . . the Board's belief that Parent will continue Cleco's strategy of providing safe and reliable electric service to Cleco's utility customers and has the platform and expertise required to maintain Cleco's existing relationships with regulators, employees and customers.*"

Central Louisiana Electric Company (CLECO) sought this gain-producing acquisition for three reasons: first, having "recently completed a multi-year generation construction and [resource] acquisition effort that left it with excess generating capacity," CLECO had no near-term prospect of increasing earnings by adding assets to rate base. Second, its customer base was "entering a phase of limited growth." Third, it "face[d] pressure to reduce its rates"—then Louisiana's highest.[17]

NextEra-Hawaiian Electric[18]

While this transaction was a stock-for-stock exchange (with some cash) rather than a full cash buyout, the target company still sought the highest value for its shareholders:

July 21, 2014: "Since the amount of the merger consideration was a gating issue for the HEI Board, the HEI Board determined at the July Board Meeting only that the amount of the merger consideration was unacceptable."

September 5, 2014: After meeting with management and advisors, the HEI Board concluded, "in light of the proposed merger consideration and the regulatory approvals required to complete a transaction, that *the likelihood of securing*

---

[17]   *Id.* at 33.
[18]   Hawaiian Elec. Indus., Inc., Definitive Proxy Statement (Form DEFM 14A) at 32–35, 45 (Mar. 26, 2015).

a superior proposal was low, from both a financial and a deal certainty perspective. ... [T]he HEI board authorized management to enter into further due diligence and negotiations with NEE *to seek enhanced value* and to negotiate the terms of a potential merger agreement with NEE."

September 11, 2014: "NEE communicated a revised proposal to HEI, in which NEE would pay HEI shareholders $25.00 per share of HEI common stock and HEI's bank business would be spun off to HEI's shareholders. NEE further agreed that it would bear the full expected corporate tax liability resulting from the bank spin-off." (As distinct from NextEra's late August offer, which capped its tax absorption at $130 million.)

October 16, 2014: "Following discussion [at an NEE board meeting of Oct. 16, 2014], the NEE board of directors authorized NEE management to proceed with the proposed transaction at a valuation of up to $25.50 per HEI share."

Through the end of November: "Following further discussions ... NEE indicated that it was unwilling to increase the proposed merger consideration above $25.00 in NEE stock per HEI common share in light of its acceptance of HEI's proposed special cash dividend to HEI shareholders of $0.50 per share."

December 2, 2014: The parties agreed on "a fixed exchange ratio of 0.2413 shares of NEE common stock for each outstanding share of HEI common stock, which was derived by dividing the agreed upon $25.00 per HEI common share merger consideration by the volume weighted average price of NEE common stock for the twenty trading days ended December 2, 2014." The exchange ratio assumed spinoff of American Savings Bank (an HEI subsidiary) and the $0.50/share cash dividend to HEI shareholders.

1.2.2 Acquirer's Goal: Buy Franchise Control to Increase Earnings

When a competitive company's acquirer buys a market position, it gets only a chance to compete. Other than existing contracts, it gets no guarantees. The acquirer's offer price will reflect its risks: the risks of losing existing customers, failing to attract new ones and making investments that earn no return. A regulated monopoly's acquirer faces fewer risks. Its existing customer base is assured by law. In setting the utility's rates the regulator must comply with statutory and constitutional principles, so the likelihood of recovering prudent investments and earning a reasonable return is high. Even better, most of the risks get reflected in the authorized return on equity.[19]

Along with this stream of relatively secure earnings, the acquirer gets a chance at four additional streams of earnings: earnings from increasing the value of generation assets, gaining new market positions, increasing the acquired utility's rate base and gaining advantages in competitive markets.

---

[19] *See* Tutorial § 4.1.

And for an acquirer owning higher-risk non-utility businesses, one more benefit: balancing that higher-risk portfolio with the relatively low-risk monopoly franchise. Each of these opportunities, discussed next, supports the acquirer's offer price.

1.2.2.1 Increase the value of generation assets

A merger of two vertically integrated utilities in the same geographic market has both horizontal and vertical aspects. A horizontal merger—acquiring an existing generation competitor—increases the merged company's market share and reduces competition. If the transaction reduces competition enough, the merged entity can exercise market power—the ability to raise its price above competitive levels, for a significant period of time, without an unacceptable loss of sales.[20] Early examples were the proposed mergers of Northern States Power and Wisconsin Electric Power;[21] and of Exelon and Public Service Electric & Gas.[22] In both cases, protesting parties presented evidence that the transaction would allow the merged company to increase earnings by exercising generation market power.

With a vertical merger—like one combining a generation owner with a transmission owner—the merged company can use its transmission highway to advantage its own generation over its competitors'. An early example was PacifiCorp's 1988 proposal to buy Utah Power & Light (UP&L). UP&L's transmission system linked low-cost hydroelectric power in the Northwest

---

[20] More detailed explanations of horizontal and vertical mergers, and market power appear in Chapter 6, and in the Tutorial §§ 2, 6.3.

[21] *Northern States Power-Wisconsin Electric Power Merger*, 79 F.E.R.C. ¶ 61,158, at pp. 61,699–700 (1997) (conditioning merger approval on merged company's divesting generation assets to avoid increases in merged entity's market power). Following FERC's order, the merger applicants withdrew their transaction.

[22] In December of 2004, Exelon Corp. and the Public Service Enterprise Group (PSEG) agreed to a $12 billion merger plan to create what then would have been the nation's largest U.S. electric company, serving in Illinois, New Jersey and Pennsylvania. Rebecca Smith, *Exelon to Buy PSEG for $12 Billion*, Wall St. J. (Dec. 21, 2014), https://www.wsj.com/articles/SB110355278733904712. FERC approved the transaction in July 2005, after the parties negotiated several mitigation terms, including a divestiture of 6,600 megawatts of generation. *FERC Clears Exelon-PSEG Merger*, Nat. Gas Intelligence (July 5, 2005), https://www.naturalgasintel.com/articles/69103-ferc-clears-exelon-pseg-merger. But state regulators still had concerns. After nineteen months of review and negotiation in the proceeding before the New Jersey Board of Public Utilities, the companies withdrew their proposal. *PSEG and Exelon Announce Termination of Proposed Utility Merger; Companies cite insurmountable gaps with New Jersey Board of Public Utilities*, Bus. Wire (Sept. 14, 2006), https://www.businesswire.com/news/home/20060914006047/en/PSEG-Exelon-Announce-Termination-Proposed-Utility-Merger.

with high-cost, thirsty markets in the Southwest. The merged company hoped to generate and buy Northwest power at a low price, then resell it in the Southwest at a high price. By excluding Northwest competitors from UP&L's transmission highway, the merged company could keep these lucrative opportunities for itself.[23]

Strategies aimed at increasing the value of generation, whether through a horizontal, vertical, or horizontal-and-vertical merger, have produced a long line of FERC decisions, rules and policy statements aimed at detecting and preventing competitive harm. We will discuss FERC's efforts, and the debates over their effectiveness, in Chapter 6.4.4.

1.2.2.2 Buy a new market position

The above-described strategy—increasing the merging companies' generation value—involves one or both companies serving their existing markets. Another acquisition goal is to buy positions in other markets. Acquirers have done so for at least three reasons.

Compensate for flat sales: A utility suffering flat sales can grow by buying another company's sales. NextEra, the holding company owner of Florida Power & Light, tried to acquire both Hawaiian Electric and the Texas utility Oncor during the same period, 2015–2016. Explaining his efforts, NextEra's CEO used the term "grow" four times in two sentences:

> [T]his industry is at best, nationwide, a flat growth industry in terms of electric usage. ... We're in Florida and we're getting terrific growth and we're going to grow at [only] 1.5 percent ... What I tell my team is, is our challenge is, how do you

---

[23] FERC allowed the merger, but in a landmark opinion required the merged company to share its transmission with competitors nondiscriminatorily. *Utah Power & Light-PacifiCorp Merger*, 45 F.E.R.C. ¶ 61,095 (1988). The merging companies accepted the condition. In that FERC proceeding, the author represented Environmental Action and the United Mine Workers. Transmission conditions proposed by his witness, Whitfield Russell, were cited by FERC as a basis for its decision. *Id.* at 61,291 n.164. Like PacifiCorp's merger with Utah Power & Light, Northeast Utilities' acquisition of Public Service of New Hampshire also involved a strategy of marrying generation with transmission. And as with the PacifiCorp-UP&L transaction, FERC conditioned its approval on the merged company's sharing its transmission facilities with others. *Northeast Utilities-Public Service of New Hampshire Merger*, 56 F.E.R.C. ¶ 61,269 (1991), *aff'd on reh'g*, 59 F.E.R.C. ¶ 61,042 (1992), *upheld sub nom.* Northeast Utils. Serv. Co. v. FERC, 993 F.2d 937 (1st Cir. 1993). In that proceeding the author represented the Connecticut Municipal Electric Energy Cooperative and the Connecticut Office of Public Utility Counsel.

grow at 8 percent a year in a 1 percent world? So, that is the challenge for anyone in the industry who is hoping to continue to grow going forward.[24]

Gain a position in someone else's existing market: The Canadian holding company AltaGas acquired Washington Gas Light Holdings, the holding company for Washington Gas Light (WGL), because it wanted a "foothold" in the Washington, D.C. area.[25] Berkshire Hathaway, already owning utilities in Iowa, bought utilities in Washington State and Nevada. Exelon, in 2013 the holding company for several utilities, told its shareholders that "[m]anagement continually evaluates growth opportunities aligned with Exelon's existing businesses in electric and gas distribution, electric transmission, generation, customer supply of electric and natural gas products and services, and natural gas exploration and production activities, leveraging Exelon's expertise in those areas."[26] This market-entering category has included non-U.S. holding companies that specialize in acquiring regulated monopolies—holding com-

---

[24]   Direct Testimony of Charles S. Griffey at 345, Oncor Electric Delivery-NextEra Energy Merger, PUC Docket No. 46238 (Tex. Pub. Util. Comm'n filed Jan. 11, 2017) (quoting NextEra's CEO's response to Texas Industrial Energy Consumers' interrogatory 3–10). The Commissions of Hawai'i and Texas rejected each of NextEra's proposals. More detail on those rejections appears in Chapter 11.2.

[25]   *See* Direct Testimony of David M. Harris at 10, AltaGas-Washington Gas Light Merger, Case No. 9449 (Md. Pub. Serv. Comm'n filed April 24, 2017) (describing AltaGas's intent to "establish[] a significant foothold in areas with growth potential"). *See also,* in the same case, Applicants' Response to Office of People's Counsel Discovery Request 10–21(a) (defining "foothold" to mean a "position usable as a base for further advance"). In that proceeding, the author was an expert witness for the Maryland Office of People's Counsel.

[26]   Exelon Corp., Annual Report (Form 10-K) at 88 (Feb. 14, 2014).

panies like National Grid (United Kingdom),[27] Iberdrola (Spain),[28] and Macquarie (Australia).[29]

The acquisitions by AltaGas, Berkshire Hathaway, Exelon and the three foreign acquirers all involved geographic expansion. Other acquisitions aim at product expansion. By combining an electric utility's name recognition, customer base and service territory knowledge with a target company's expertise in some other service market, the merged company can gain a competitive advantage in that other market. Western Resources (now called Westar) acquired Protection One, a holding company for monitored security alarm businesses.[30] Duquesne Light Co. sold off some of its electric generation plants, using the proceeds to buy water and sewer utilities. It planned to use its executives' "experience with billing and customer service procedures, their background in utility operations and their expertise in regulatory compliance

---

[27] As of the time of writing, National Grid's portfolio consists of twenty-six "Principal Group" companies, many of which act as holding companies for dispersed subsidiaries in the UK and the northeast United States. In total, National Grid's portfolio consists of 158 subsidiaries, along with five joint ventures. National Grid, Annual Report and Accounts 2018/19, at 174–75 (2019), https://www.nationalgrid .com/document/124642/download. National Grid's corporate structure resulted from "acquisitions as well as regulatory requirements to have certain activities within separate legal entities." *Id.* at 174. Its "business development activities and the delivery of [its] growth ambition include acquisitions, disposals, joint ventures, partnering and organic investment opportunities, such as development activities relating to changes to the energy mix and the integration of distributed energy resources and other advanced technologies." *Id.* at 214.

[28] As of December 31, 2018, Iberdrola owned twenty-three holding companies. Those companies held subsidiaries in Europe, North America and South America. Iberdrola, S.A., Annual Financial Report 32–33 (2019), https://www.iberdrola .com/wcorp/gc/prod/en_US/corporativos/docs/FinancialStatements_AuditorsReport _Individual2018.pdf.

[29] Macquarie has assets in six continents and multiple industries. Macquarie Group Ltd., 2019 Annual Report 7, 13 (2019), https://static.macquarie.com/ dafiles/Internet/mgl/global/shared/about/investors/results/2019/Macquarie-Group -FY19-Annual-Report.pdf?v=9. Macquarie began investing in utilities in the 2000s with a "broad and varied sector and geographic focus." *Id.* at 6. The Macquarie Group includes at least sixty different subsidiaries. *Id.* at 165. In 2019, the Macquarie Group invested over $5 billion in renewable energy projects alone. *Id.* at 32.

[30] *See* Western Resources, Inc., Statement by Holding Company Claiming Exemption Under Rule 2 from the Provisions of the Public Utility Holding Company Act of 1935 (Form U-3A-2) (Mar. 2, 1998), http://services.corporate-ir.net/SEC .Enhanced/SecCapsule.aspx?c=89455&fid=500285 (describing multiple alarm-related subsidiaries).

[to] consolidate operations of a host of small, privately owned water companies and achieve economies of scale."[31]

Buy a position in a new market: While Western Resources and Duquesne Light used acquisitions to enter existing product markets, some acquisitions seek first-mover advantages in new product markets. A convergence merger joins providers whose different services, when combined, create a new service. Non-merging companies can achieve product convergence contractually (e.g., a restaurant and a theatre offering a movie and dinner at a discount); a merger can add efficiency to the arrangement by integrating administration, strategy planning, marketing, delivery and billing. In the 1990s, some utilities combined their fiber networks, transmission towers, customer bases and rights-of-way with wireless companies' telecommunications expertise, to offer combined energy and telecommunications services. In the same period, electricity-gas mergers became a "key strategic theme"[32] as industry strategists felt that "customers want to go to one source for both gas and electricity needs."[33]

Some utilities even entered the real estate market, hoping to lock in customer relationships before families hooked up their houses. Mid-American Energy Holdings Co., then a holding company for several Iowa utilities (now owned by Berkshire Hathaway), bought AmerUS Services, the nation's third largest real estate company. Said MidAmerican's CEO: "when a person buys a home, that decision triggers others—from purchasing cable television to subscribing to the local newspaper. Already, we offer products such as home security, appliance warranty and home connections services that can build customer relationships and help us become the gateway to the home." The goal, again, was first-mover advantage: "[u]ltimately, when competition comes to the energy marketplace, this will allow us to support sales of our core products, electricity and natural gas."[34]

---

[31] *DQE Leaving Electricity, Plans to Invest in Water & Sewer Companies*, PITT. POST-GAZETTE (Nov. 25, 1998), http://old.post-gazette.com/businessnews/19981125dqe2.asp.

[32] *EEI Reports on Electric Industry Key Trends*, FOSTER NAT. GAS REPORT, Jan. 14, 1999 (citing trade association report stating that from 1993 to 1998, the percentage of electric utilities affiliated with gas companies rose from 39 percent to 48 percent and could rise to 54 percent with the consummation of then-pending mergers).

[33] *CP&L Wants in on Gas Service*, ELECTRICITY DAILY, Apr. 3, 1998. *See also Convergence on a Small Scale: Ohio Coop Buys IOU Gas Co.*, ELECTRICITY DAILY, May 28, 1998 (Ohio electric cooperative purchased an investor-owned gas distribution company because, according to the cooperative's vice president, "customers want 'one-stop shopping'").

[34] *MidAmerican Does Real Estate*, ELECTRICITY DAILY, Apr. 10, 1998. *See also It's Not Just About Energy Anymore: Utilities Add Roles*, OMAHA WORLD-HERALD, Sept. 10, 1998, at 1 (describing the company's Home Connect Service, allowing new home-

1.2.2.3 Increase the acquired utility's rate base

The acquirer pays a premium to get the target utility's earnings stream. Under conventional cost-based ratemaking, that earnings stream depends on rate base.[35] The acquirer therefore hopes to increase its earnings by increasing the target's rate base, in two distinct ways—through existing services and new services.

Increase target's rate base needed for existing franchised services: Utilities continuously need new infrastructure. Demand grows, plants retire and new technologies appear. Unless its commission requires competitive bidding,[36] the utility expects to be the sole provider of the new infrastructure, and get the earnings from it. AltaGas made its motivation plain: it wanted Washington Gas because the utility "will have opportunities to rate-base new investments in its infrastructure."[37]

---

owners to sign up for "gas, electricity, long-distance telephone, newspaper, a security system, lawn care and cable television" with a single call. The spokesperson drew the line at dog-walking services.).

[35] *See* the Tutorial § 4.1.

[36] FERC Order No. 1000 required Regional Transmission Organizations (RTOs) to delete contract provisions granting incumbent transmission owners a right of first refusal to build regional transmission facilities. *See* Order No. 1000, *Transmission Planning and Cost Allocation by Transmission Owning and Operating Public Utilities*, 136 F.E.R.C. ¶ 61,051, 76 Fed. Reg. 49842, 49842, 49973 (2011), *order on reh'g*, Order No. 1000-A, 139 F.E.R.C. ¶ 61,132, *order on reh'g and clarification*, Order No. 1000-B, 141 F.E.R.C. ¶ 61,044 (2012), *aff'd sub nom.* S.C. Pub. Serv. Auth. v. FERC, 762 F.3d 41 (D.C. Cir. 2014).

Since Order No. 1000's issuance, some states have blocked the Order's effect by prohibiting non-utilities from building transmission within their states, or by granting incumbent utilities a right of first refusal over transmission construction opportunities. *See* MINN. STAT. § 216B.246 (granting a right of first refusal to incumbent electric transmission owners for new transmission line construction in Minnesota despite Order No. 1000); NEB. REV. STAT. § 70-1028 (same but in Nebraska); N.D. CENT. CODE § 49-03-02 (same but in North Dakota); OKLA. STAT. tit. 17, § 292 (same but in Oklahoma); S.D. CODIFIED LAWS § 49-32-20 (same but in South Dakota); TEX. UTIL. CODE §§ 37.051, 37.056, 37.057, 37.151, 37.154 (same but in Texas). Non-utility companies have challenged some of these measures on Commerce Clause grounds, so far unsuccessfully. For Minnesota, *see* LSP Transmission Holdings, LLC v. Lange, 329 F. Supp. 3d 695 (D. Minn. 2018), *upheld*, LSP Transmission Holdings v. Sieben, No. 18-2559 (8th Cir. Mar. 25, 2020), https://statepowerproject.files.wordpress.com/2020/03/mn-8th-cir-decision.pdf. For Texas, *see* NextEra Energy Capital Holdings, Inc. v. Walker, Civ. No. 1:19-CV-626-Y (W.D. Tex. Feb. 26, 2020), https://statepowerproject.files.wordpress.com/2020/02/tx-district-ct-decision.pdf. As of the date of publication, the author is unaware of any challenge to the Nebraska, Oklahoma, North Dakota or South Dakota law.

[37] Applicants' Response to Office of People's Counsel Discovery Request 10-39 at 2, AltaGas-Washington Gas Light Merger, Case No. 9449 (Md. Pub. Serv. Comm'n

Increase target's rate base by providing new franchised services: New service options bring new earnings opportunities. Interactive metering, smart thermostats, solar panels, microgrids and energy efficiency services all represent new services requiring new investments. Rate-basing the associated investments, and gaining first-mover advantage in these new product markets, are additional acquirer motivations.

1.2.2.4 Gain advantages in competitive markets

Due to its longstanding government-protected status, a target utility has name recognition, customer loyalty and access to relatively low-cost capital. These features enable the acquirer to enter competitive markets with advantages over its less-established competitors. Those advantages create two distinct earnings flows.

The first earnings flow would come from selling non-utility services to the target utility's current customers. Early examples of this strategy were energy efficiency services (e.g., performing energy audits, installing insulation); home alarm systems; and heating, ventilation and air conditioning services, including sales, installation and maintenance. The utility's competitors will not have the utility's name recognition (displayed throughout the region on trucks, advertisements, the downtown headquarters building and monthly energy bills); or its customer lists, computer systems and service territory knowledge. These competitive advantages have value to the utility's acquirer.[38] The distributed energy resources space presents more recent examples. Renewable energy, advanced meters, storage, electric vehicle charging stations, microgrids, community solar, energy efficiency and demand aggregation all can be inputs to the bundled electricity product traditionally sold by the utility. A utility looking to protect or increase its franchise value will consider merging with, being acquired by or acquiring companies that provide these services.[39]

The second earnings flow would come from providing these same non-utility services to customers outside the utility's service territory but within its name recognition area. Having already provided these services within the target's service territory, the merged company will have gained experience and

---

2018). *See also*, in the same case, Applicants' Response to Office of People's Counsel Discovery Request 10-42 ("To the extent [OPC's question] is asking whether AltaGas took into consideration Washington Gas's projected returns on investments in its distribution infrastructure, then yes, AltaGas considered that factor.").

[38]   Whether this business strategy strengthens competition by stimulating innovation, or weakens competition by giving the merged company unearned advantages, is discussed in Chapters 6.3.3, 6.4.3 and 6.4.5.

[39]   These efforts raise market structure concerns, discussed in Chapters 6.3.3 and 6.4.5.

strengthened its reputation in the new product market. Expanding the business to adjacent territories is a natural next step.

1.2.2.5 Balance business portfolios, diversify regulatory risk

Acquirers see value in reducing their existing risks by acquiring revenue streams that have lower risks. These diversification strategies take two forms.

Balancing business portfolios: Protected from competition and entitled to government-set rates, regulated utilities have lower risks than most unregulated companies. That feature makes them attractive to holding companies with higher-risk portfolios. The most prominent example is Berkshire Hathaway, which has acquired multiple utilities to balance the risks associated with over sixty non-utility businesses.[40] Holding companies that are primarily energy companies also buy utilities to balance their portfolios. In 2016 Exelon already owned three utilities—Commonwealth Edison, PECO Energy Company and Baltimore Gas & Electric.[41] But it also owned nearly $47 billion worth of assets in merchant generation, a business riskier than monopoly utilities.[42] (In November 2017, Exelon's merchant generation subsidiary in Texas entered bankruptcy.[43]) Among Exelon's reasons for acquiring the utility monopolies Potomac Electric Power, Delmarva Power and Atlantic City Electric in 2016

---

[40] As of December 31, 2018, Berkshire Hathaway owned sixty-two non-utility companies across the insurance, manufacturing, railroad and service and retailing industries. Warren E. Buffet, Berkshire Hathaway Inc., 2018 Annual Report, at A-1, K-26 (2019), https://www.berkshirehathaway.com/2018ar/2018ar.pdf. Also as of that date, Berkshire Hathaway owned these utility or utility-related companies: PacifiCorp, MidAmerican Energy, NV Energy, Northern Powergrid, Northern Natural Gas, Kern River Gas, AltaLink, BHE Renewables, BHE U.S. Transmission, CalEnergy Philippines and MidAmerican Energy Services. These utility-related holdings span multiple industries including natural gas, coal, wind, solar, hydroelectric, nuclear and geothermal. *Id.* In 2018, Berkshire Hathaway received approximately $20 billion in revenue from Berkshire Hathaway Energy Company, accounting for about 8.1 percent of its yearly operating revenue. *Id.* at K-106.

[41] *See* Exelon Corp., Exelon Corporation 2016 Annual Report 7–8 (2017), https://www.exeloncorp.com/newsroom/events/Event%20Documents/Exelon%20Corporation%20Annual%20Report%202016.PDF.

[42] *Id.* at 313. *See also Exelon, PSEG Have Highest Business Risk Among 34 Utilities in Moody's Report*, Util. Dive (Nov. 8, 2018), https://www.utilitydive.com/news/exelon-pseg-have-highest-business-risk-among-34-utilities-in-moodys-repor/541751/ (noting that "merchant generation and energy trading businesses have a significantly higher risk exposure" than monopoly utilities).

[43] *Exelon Puts Texas Plants Totaling 3,500 MW into Bankruptcy*, Am. Pub. Power Ass'n (Nov. 7, 2017), https://www.publicpower.org/periodical/article/exelon-puts-texas-plants-totaling-3500-mw-bankruptcy.

was lowering its overall risk.[44] Similarly, while NextEra in 2016 owned the regulated monopoly Florida Power & Light, it also owned higher-risk generation businesses in Texas. Its 2016 proposal to acquire the Texas utility Oncor would have reduced its overall risk.[45]

Diversifying regulatory risk: Multi-utility acquirers sometimes talk of reducing "regulatory risk": the shareholder risk that a commission's decisions will reduce earnings below expectations, such as by disallowing imprudent costs from rates or imposing penalties for poor performance. Owning utilities in multiple states reduces the impact of disallowance or a penalty imposed by a single state. But what shareholders gain in risk reduction, customers can lose in attention reduction. Served by a utility whose holding company owns utilities in multiple states, a customer has no influence over the quality of regulation in those other states: no influence over the commissioners' qualifications, the staff's resources, or the quality of legislative oversight. All those factors can affect the holding company's financial condition, with consequences for the customer's own utility.

* * *

This chapter has described the major ways companies use utility mergers to increase shareholder value. Target utility shareholders can cash out. Then there is market positioning: (a) buying a direct competitor to increase market share (horizontal merger); (b) buying a company that provides an indispensable input, so the acquirer can exclude competitors from accessing that input (vertical merger); and (c) buying a remote monopoly to gain a "foothold" in a new market (extension merger). Separate from cashing out and market positioning is financial positioning: balancing a high-risk portfolio with government-protected monopolies, and reducing the risk that performing poorly in any one state will hurt the financial condition of the holding system as a whole.[46]

---

[44]   EXELON CORP., *supra* note 41, at 8. After Exelon's acquisition of Potomac Electric Power, Delmarva Power and Atlantic City Electric, its merchant generation assets dropped from 48.8 percent to 40.9 percent of its total assets. *Id.* at 313.

[45]   *NextEra Energy Reaches Definitive Agreement to Acquire Energy Future Holdings' Interest in Oncor Electric Delivery Company*, NEXTERA ENERGY (July 29, 2016), http://newsroom.nexteraenergy.com/news-releases?item=123402. As detailed in Chapter 11.2, that NextEra-Oncor transaction was rejected by the Texas Commission. *Texas Regulators Reject $18B NextEra-Oncor Deal*, UTIL. DIVE (Apr. 13, 2017), https://www.utilitydive.com/news/texas-regulators-reject-18b-nextera-oncor -deal/440468/.

[46]   John Reed, a frequent witness for merger applicants, offers another way to categorize merger goals: "strategic" vs. "financial." Direct Testimony of John Reed at 10,

These strategies benefit shareholders but do nothing to improve utility operations. The utility has no need for holding company diversification. As long
as the utility acts prudently, regulatory decisions that comply with ratemaking
law will keep it financially healthy.[47] Shareholders can diversify their own
investments; they don't need the holding company to do it for them. In sum,
it is difficult to connect acquirers' motivations with public interest benefits.[48]

AltaGas-Washington Gas Light Merger, Case No. 9449 (Md. Pub. Serv. Comm'n filed
Apr. 24, 2018). Strategic acquisitions, he explains, fall into two categories:

> (1) operational integration, in which management and operational functions are
> merged; and (2) confederation, in which the utilities largely maintain their own
> operational status. … Mergers built around the confederation model tend to
> produce benefits through diversification of markets and regulatory jurisdictions,
> and economies of scale. Mergers built around operational integration tend to be
> more transformative for the acquired entity, and derive most of their benefits
> through merger synergies and expense reductions.

Financial acquisitions, he says, are

> driven by private equity or institutional capital entities with an interest in
> having a portfolio position filled by a utility equity holding. Such acquisitions
> by financial acquirers have often been accomplished through shorter holding
> periods, multiple levels of leverage, and complex structures intended to enhance
> shareholder returns.

Reed's distinctions are analytically valid, but they understate each strategy's potential
conflict with the public interest. His distinctions can lull a commission into seeing
mergers as natural, innocuous events creating no risk and causing no harm.

[47] *See* Tutorial § 4.1.

[48] As one commentator has written:

> The premise of contemporary merger policy is that merger among firms is
> basically a desirable event. But disappointing results are, however, consistent
> with the repeated observation that many motivations for merger are largely
> disconnected from achieving economic efficiency despite what the promoters
> may assert in securities filings and press briefings. The publicly held corporation
> faces very substantial agency problems. The shareholders are largely powerless
> when ownership is widely dispersed. The board of directors, the agent of the
> shareholders, is usually under the control of management, which in turn can
> shape both buying and selling decisions to serve its strategic interests. Moreover,
> third parties, takeover funds, legal and financial advisers, can and do reap ben-
> efits from promoting such transactions even when the result for the enterprise
> is negative. Hence, many major mergers arise from motivations unrelated to
> increased efficiency.

Peter C. Carstensen, *The* Philadelphia National Bank *Presumption: Merger Analysis
in an Unpredictable World*, 80 Antitrust L.J. 219, 257 (2015) (footnotes omitted).

1.3   SUPPORTING STIMULI

This chapter has addressed two acquisition purposes—monetizing the franchise and diversifying risk. These purposes find additional support in two stimuli: "everyone's doing it," and low interest rates.

1.3.1   "Everyone's Doing It"

Scholars have described mergers as "information cascades"—events that, if profitable, "inform[] agents in similar circumstances about the profitability of similar actions."[49] If a merger succeeds—at least for those who planned it—more will follow. This logic has applied to electricity mergers. Consider three reasons.

Shareholders pressure executives to replicate gains received by other targets: NextEra and Central Louisiana Electric worried about "flat sales" and "flat earnings."[50] When shareholders of low-growth utilities see shareholders of other utilities getting large gains from cash buyouts, they can pressure their boards to seek similar results. CEOs and boards otherwise unwilling to cede control to an acquirer will get the message—not only from their shareholders, but from their financial advisors (who estimate the gains from sale) and their legal advisors (who stress the board's fiduciary obligation to consider acquisition offers).[51]

Merger applicants argue that larger company size brings lower-cost financing: Washington Gas Light's Chief Financial Officer supported his company's buyout by arguing that the merged company's larger size would expand the gas utility's equity sources.[52] The argument came without evidence that WGL lacked sufficient access to equity.

"Deregulation" pressures management to preserve or grow market share: How does an information cascade begin? One possible cause is a "shock" to industry structure—the obvious example being when legislatures loosen

---

[49]   Gregor Andrade et al., *New Evidence and Perspectives on Mergers*, 15 J. Econ. Persp. 103, 107 n.6 (2001).

[50]   As detailed in Chapter 1.2.2.2.

[51]   For more on how state corporate law's fiduciary duty affects the merger trend, see Chapter 1.2.1.

[52]   Rebuttal Testimony of Vincent L. Amman, Jr. at 6, AltaGas-Washington Gas Light Merger, Case No. 9449 (Md. Pub. Serv. Comm'n filed Sept. 11, 2017). In that proceeding, the author was an expert witness for the Maryland Office of People's Counsel. *See also* Central Vermont Public Service-Gaz Metro Merger, 2012 Vt. PUC LEXIS 279, at *44, Finding 29 (finding, among other things, that the acquirer, Gaz Metro, "is financially strong and would have the ability to support the capital needs" of the acquired utility).

an industry's longstanding entry restrictions.[53] These legal adjustments also "potentially remove[] long-standing barriers to merging and consolidating, which might have kept the industry artificially dispersed."[54]

The electric industry's cascade had its own stimuli. First came statutory changes. The Public Utility Regulatory Policies Act of 1978 (PURPA) and the Energy Policy Act of 1992 eliminated PUHCA 1935's integrated public-utility system requirement for qualifying facilities and exempt wholesale generators, respectively, so that they could enter wholesale markets in any location.[55] Retail utility monopolies that historically had built and owned their own generation then faced regulatory pressure (and in the case of PURPA qualifying facilities, a federal legal obligation) to buy from these wholesale generators if their costs were lower than the utility's avoidable costs. Then came FERC's Order No. 888, requiring utilities to share their transmission highways with generation competitors. The third factor came in the mid-to-late 1990s, when some states authorized competition in retail electricity sales. The fourth factor was the SEC's administrative loosening of PUHCA 1935's acquisition restrictions, followed by the Act's repeal in 2005. (PUHCA section 10(c)(2) had prohibited acquisitions of utilities unless the transaction "tended towards the economical and efficient development of an integrated public-utility system.")[56]

---

[53] Andrade et al., *supra* note 49, at 104 (referring to industry "deregulation" as an example of a cascade-causing shock). Why the quote marks? Your author views "deregulation" as a term carrying a surplus of political baggage and a deficit of verbal precision. A single word cannot usefully describe a complex series of statutory and regulatory changes that attempt to introduce competition into historically monopolistic markets. For a multi-chapter explanation of those statutory and regulatory changes, see HEMPLING, *supra* note 4, at chs. 3, 4 and 5.

[54] Andrade et al., *supra* note 49, at 108. Andrade cites these industries: "airlines (1978), broadcasting (1984 and 1996), entertainment (1984), natural gas (1978), trucking (1980), banks and thrifts (1994), utilities (1992) and telecommunications (1996)." *Id. See also* Jim Chen, *The Echoes of Forgotten Footfalls: Telecommunications Mergers at the Dawn of the Digital Millennium*, 43 HOUS. L. REV. 1311, 1318 (2007) ("The 1996 [Telecommunications] Act may have provided precisely the sort of institutional spur to a telecommunications industry whose preexisting oligopolistic structure inherently favored mergers by raising the benefits from increased concentration relative to free-riding gains accrued by nonmerging firms.").

[55] For background on PUHCA 1935, see Chapters 4.2.2 and 8.2, and Tutorial § 2.

[56] In 1997, midway through these events, observers confirmed that electricity mergers were indeed reactions to the market pressures produced by those four stimuli. "Strength through union" was, in the words of Richard Cudahy, "a natural response." *FERC's Policy on Electric Mergers: A Bit of Perspective*, 18 ENERGY L.J. 113, 115 (1997). Judge Cudahy added: "At least two dozen electric utilities have announced plans to merge in the past few years. Forty-five percent of utility executives and power marketers report being involved in merger activities. And two-thirds of utility executives do not expect their companies to remain 'intact' over the next decade." *Id.*

1.3.2   Low Interest Rates

Paying cash for a target's stock requires transaction financing.[57] The acquirer gets that financing from retained earnings, proceeds from assets sales, issuances of new equity and issuances of new debt. Debt plays a large role. Consider these two electricity examples:

* *Exelon-PHI:* The companies projected total cash paid to target shareholders to be $6.826 billion ($27.25/share, $1.6 billion premium over market value of stock). Financing fees and costs were projected at $514 million. The sources for the $7.3 billion total were $6.3 billion of new securities and $1.0 billion from the sale of generating assets. The $6.3 billion in securities, in turn, consisted of $3.5 billion of new Exelon debt, $1.84 billion in new Exelon common equity and $1.0 billion of mandatory convertible debt. Exelon would also assume $6.197 billion of PHI's consolidated outstanding debt.[58]
* *GPE-Westar (the original proposal):* GPE would pay $8.6 billion for all of Westar's equity—$51 per share in cash, $60 per share in total consideration.[59] GPE would have financed that price with $4.4 billion in debt and the remainder in newly issued equity.[60]

Where acquisition debt plays a large role, so do interest rates. Utility acquirers are like home buyers: the lower the interest rate, the bigger the purchase.[61] This logic led Westar's CEO to consider selling his company:

> [U]tilities ... are trading at pretty high values. The reason for that is low interest rates. That meant that the value for our shareholders is good. ... Maybe those

---

Judge Cudahy, a treasured colleague of the author, was a Chair of the Public Service Commission of Wisconsin, a judge on the U.S. Court of Appeals for the Seventh Circuit and a prolific contributor to the regulatory profession and its journals. He passed away in 2015.

[57]   In contrast, a stock-for-stock exchange requires upfront cash only for transaction costs—advisory fees, filing fees, parachute payments and regulatory costs. For more detail on transaction costs, see Chapter 4.3.1.

[58]   Direct Testimony of John W. Wilson at 8, Exelon-PHI Merger, Formal Case No. 1119 (D.C. Pub. Serv. Comm'n filed Nov. 3, 2017).

[59]   Joint Application at 5, Great Plains Energy-Westar Energy Merger I, Docket No. 16-KCPE-593-ACQ (D.C. Pub. Serv. Comm'n Apr. 19, 2017).

[60]   *See* Great Plains Energy Inc., *supra* note 13, at 170.

[61]   Any homebuyer knows that for a given lifetime cost (the sum of principal and interest over the entire period of residence), the lower the interest rate, the more she can afford to pay in principal. The more she can pay in principal, the larger the house.

conditions will persist, maybe they won't, but we felt it important to capture those advantages.[62]

Similarly, GPE's (Westar's acquirer) acquisition finance plan would "rel[y] on substantial debt financing in the current unprecedented low-cost interest rate environment, enabl[ing] the creation of an energy company with much larger scale."[63] And PHI's Board "believe[d] that the time to execute a sale for cash is advantageous because utility trading multiples are at historic highs due in part to the low interest rate environment and the resulting attractiveness of utility dividend yields."[64] Low interest rates stimulate mergers.

1.4 MISSING FROM THE TRANSACTION'S PURPOSE: CUSTOMER BENEFITS

1.4.1 Acquirers Compete on Price, Not on Performance

This first chapter has described the acquirer's and target's common purpose—transferring a public franchise for private gain. Missing from that purpose are customer benefits. Using auction-like procedures, the target causes prospective acquirers to compete on shareholder price only. The GPE-Westar narrative illustrates the point. GPE first offered Westar a control premium of 20–25 percent and a cash-to-stock ratio of 30:70. Westar invited other bidders to move the prices up. GPE's final offer had a control premium of 36 percent and cash-to-stock ratio of 85:1.[65] That was the offer "necessary to win the competitive bidding process."[66] No one bargained over consumer benefits.

That customer benefits do not affect acquirer-target bargaining finds additional proof in the "material factors"—the detailed list targets give their shareholders as reasons to vote for the transaction. The Exelon-PHI Proxy Statement declared that PHI "had conducted a competitive process and that Exelon was the highest bidder in such process." The Proxy Statement then lists these positive factors, among others: the premium of 29.5 percent, the implied valuation multiple of 22.7 x earnings per share, the 20 percent increase from

---

[62] Direct Testimony of Mark A. Ruelle at 16, Great Plains Energy-Westar Energy Merger I, Docket No. 16-KCPE-593-ACQ (Kan. Corp. Comm'n filed June 28, 2016) (discussing the original agreement by which Great Plains Energy would buy out Westar's shareholders for cash).

[63] Rebuttal Testimony of Kevin E. Bryant at 6, Great Plains Energy-Westar Energy Merger I, Docket No. 16-KCPE-593-ACQ (Kan. Corp. Comm'n filed Feb. 9, 2017).

[64] Pepco Holdings, Inc., *supra* note 12, at 32.

[65] Great Plains Energy Inc., *supra* note 13, at 54–58, 61, 67.

[66] Response to KCC Staff Interrogatory 218, Great Plains Energy-Westar Energy Merger I, Docket No. 16-KCPE-593-ACQ (Kan. Corp. Comm'n filed Oct. 24, 2016).

Exelon's original offer, the benefits of an all-cash offer, PHI's termination rights and PHI's right to consider superior unsolicited proposals factors. The Proxy Statement also identified "a variety of risks and potentially negative factors": the possibility of the merger's being delayed or withdrawn; the inability of PHI shareholders, having cashed out, to participate in future Exelon gains; the expense of regulatory approvals; management attention diverted to implementing the merger; adverse effects on PHI's relations with regulators, employees, contractors and others if the transaction is not completed; the taxes PHI shareholders will owe on their gain; and the possibility that PHI's executives might have personal financial interests that conflict with the shareholders' interest.[67] No factor, positive or negative, touches on customer benefits. They played no role in the bargaining or in the decision.

If utility targets intended to choose acquirers based on utility performance, their advisors would be experts on utility performance. Instead they are experts on utility valuation. PHI hired Lazard, Westar hired Guggenheim Securities—companies expert in stock prices and earnings multiples. Operations experts get involved only after the targets have chosen their acquirers. In the Exelon-PHI transaction, PHI admitted that "[m]embers of the Integration Office, the Core Teams and the BATs did not participate in negotiations between PHI and Exelon over the acquisition price."[68] And Exelon had agreed to buy PHI and its three utilities without "undertak[ing] an in-depth review of local priorities."[69]

Targets do conduct a "due diligence" investigation of prospective bidders (and vice versa).[70] But a due diligence investigation assesses minimum competence only. It neither compares bidders based on performance nor causes bidders to compete based on performance. And since due diligence analysis is performed only on the survivors of prior bidding rounds based on price, it excludes prospective acquirers that might offer lower prices but better performance. A "due diligence" review confirms that the bidding and selection are based on price.

Most emphatically confirming the preeminence of price is a standard provision in merger agreements allowing the target to withdraw, before the

---

[67] Pepco Holdings, Inc., *supra* note 12, at 33.

[68] Applicants' Responses to GRID2.0 Data Request 1-97, Exelon-PHI Merger, Formal Case No. 1119 (D.C. Pub. Serv. Comm'n filed Nov. 3, 2014) (referring to the direct testimony of Exelon witness Carim Khouzami in the same proceeding).

[69] Applicants' Responses to Office of the People's Counsel Data Request 4-23, Exelon-PHI Merger, Formal Case No. 1119 (D.C. Pub. Serv. Comm'n filed Nov. 3, 2014). Even as of October 2014, months after the parties came to an agreement, "Exelon has not yet undertaken an in-depth review of local priorities in PEPCO's service territory." *Id.*

[70] Pepco Holdings, Inc., *supra* note 12, at 31 (describing PHI's review of bidders' "regulatory relationships, reliability, operating track records and employee matters").

shareholder vote and subject to penalties, if the target receives a "Superior Company Proposal." A superior proposal is one that is "more favorable to the holders of [the target's] Common Stock."[71] No comparable provision authorizes the target to withdraw if another acquirer offers more customer benefits. A superior proposal could in fact produce fewer customer benefits, because superiority depends solely on the perspective of the target shareholders. KCP&L described this provision as "commonplace[,] ... permit[ting] the members of the board of directors to satisfy their fiduciary obligations under state law";[72] but that statement confirms the primacy of purchase price over customer benefit. A board's fiduciary obligations under state corporate law are subject to the utility's obligations under state utility law. Utility law puts the public interest first. The public interest does not allow a government-protected utility to place shareholder gain before customer benefit.

1.4.2 Customer Benefits Serve Regulatory Strategy, Not Transactional Purpose

While customer benefits are missing from the selection process, merger applicants make them central to the regulatory process. Consider these examples:

- Westar CEO Ruelle asserted that "[p]ooling resources with another company would allow Westar to be part of a more efficient company and spread costs over a larger platform to the benefit of customers in the form of reduced future rate increases."[73]

---

[71] Joint Application, *supra* note 59, at 42–43. Here is the full definition of "Superior Company Proposal," from section 5.03(f)(ii) of the GPE-Westar Merger Agreement:
"Superior Company Proposal" means a *bona fide* written Company Takeover Proposal (provided that for purposes of this definition, the applicable percentage in the definition of Company Takeover Proposal shall be "50.1 percent" rather than "20 percent or more"), which the Company Board determines in good faith, after consultation with outside legal counsel and a financial advisor, and taking into account the legal, financial, regulatory, timing and other aspects of such Company Takeover Proposal, the identity of the Person making the proposal and any financing required for such proposal, the ability of the Person making such proposal to obtain such required financing and the level of certainty with respect to such required financing, and such other factors that are deemed relevant by the Company Board, is more favorable to the holders of Company Common Stock than the transactions contemplated by this Agreement (after taking into account any revisions to the terms of this Agreement that are committed to in writing by Parent (including pursuant to section 5.03(c))).
[72] Response to KCC Staff Interrogatory 238, Great Plains Energy-Westar Energy Merger I, Docket No. 16-KCPE-593-ACQ (Kan. Corp. Comm'n filed Oct. 24, 2016).
[73] Direct Testimony of Mark A. Ruelle, *supra* note 62, at 9–10.

- Duke Energy and Progress Energy "estimated fuel and joint dispatch savings of ~$700 million" between 2012 and 2016.[74]
- NextEra argued that its "significantly larger market capitalization," "wide geographic reach" and its "excellent credit rating, strong liquidity profile, long history of success with its Applicants' banking partners, and carefully managed capital structure" would lead to lower borrowing costs for Hawaiian Electric because "the major credit rating agencies consider the financial strength and geographic diversity of a company as essential to its picture of their credit and generally view larger size as a sign of greater creditworthiness."[75]

We will address the quality and credibility of these generic claims in Chapter 4.4. The point for now is that none of these items were bargained over, quantified, or committed to during the target's acquirer-selection process. Appearing for the first time in the companies' application for approval, they serve regulatory strategy, not transactional purpose.

Are customer benefits completely irrelevant to the selection process? No. Due diligence requires boards to pick merger partners that are at least capable of performing obligatory utility functions. (Though some financial acquirers, like Berkshire Hathaway and the hedge fund KKR, make no pretense of bringing new utility expertise.) But requiring minimum competence is not basing a competition on merit. Targets do not select acquirers based on performance merit.

* * *

This first chapter has described a utility merger's essence. An acquirer buys control of the target's government-protected franchise. That franchise has value because it grants and protects a monopoly market position. The acquirer can use that market position to increase its earnings—in the home monopoly market and in competitive markets. Where the acquirer has other business risks, the acquired utility's stable earnings help to diversity those risks. These opportunities have value. The acquirer pays for that value by paying the target shareholders a premium over the current stock price.

Common to the acquirer and the target is this goal: monetize the government franchise. Missing from that purpose is customer benefits. The target selects its acquirer based on gain to its shareholders, not performance for its custom-

---

[74] Duke Energy & Progress Energy, Presentation to the 46th Edison Electric Institute Financial Conference: Transforming Our Future (Nov. 8, 2011).

[75] Applicants' Response to State Office of Planning Information Request 77 at 1–4, Hawaiian Electric-NextEra Merger, Docket No. 2015-0022 (Haw. Pub. Util. Comm'n filed Nov. 19, 2015).

ers. In competitive market mergers, shareholder benefits depend on customer satisfaction. And as Chapter 2 now will explain, utility monopoly mergers are not disciplined by competitive market forces. In utility monopoly mergers, shareholder gain is primary, customer benefit incidental.

2. Missing from utility merger markets: competitive discipline

Chapter 1.2 described merging parties' goals—highest price for the target, expansion opportunities for the acquirer. These goals would not necessarily create conflict with the public interest if the merged company faced competition. Competition's discipline aligns private behavior with the public interest, forcing merging companies to focus on customer benefits. But utility mergers lack competitive discipline, because one or both entities have a monopoly. This chapter contrasts the competitive merger model with the monopoly merger model. The absence of competitive pressure on electricity mergers makes customer benefits subordinate.

2.1 MERGER DISCIPLINE UNDER COMPETITIVE MARKET CONDITIONS

Economists distinguish markets based on their level of competitiveness. The two theoretical poles are hard monopoly and perfect competition. Hard monopoly is what it sounds like: a single seller selling to captive customers an indispensable product with no reasonable substitutes. In hard monopoly, the seller prices at will. Perfect competition has four key features: (1) standardized products, (2) many buyers and sellers, (3) perfect information, and (4) no barriers to new entrants.[1] In perfect competition, no single seller can affect the market price; the market price emerges from the actions of numerous buyers and sellers.

---

[1]   Darren Bush & Carrie Mayne, *In (Reluctant) Defense of Enron: Why Bad Regulation Is to Blame for California's Power Woes (or Why Antitrust Law Fails to Protect Against Market Power When the Market Rules Encourage its Use)*, 83 OR. L. REV. 207, 233 (2007). The authors explain:
> (1) [T]he product sold must be uniform across all sellers, or, in other words, consumers are not compelled to choose one producer's output over the other based on product differentiation; (2) there must be many buyers and sellers, such that no one seller's or buyer's actions alone will change the prevailing market price; (3) all agents participating in the market must have perfect information; and (4) no barriers of entry may exist for sellers considering entering the market.

Somewhere between those theoretical markets lie real-world markets. An oligopolistic market has a small number of sellers. They compete, but not vigorously, because their small number allows each seller to know that "its decision about how much to produce would affect the market price."[2] A monopolistically competitive market has "large numbers of competing producers, differentiated products, and free entry into and exit ... in the long run." Differentiated products mean that customers view the products as "close substitutes," but "somewhat distinct." In a single food court, individual sellers (burgers, sushi, wok dishes, fish fry) compete monopolistically. The products are imperfect substitutes, allowing sellers to charge different prices according to customers' preferences.

The sweet spot is effective competition. Effective competition is not mere rivalry—a struggle among competitors to collect and keep customers. Effective competition is a market structure in which competition is based on merit.[3] In that market structure, no company has "market power"—a term defined variously as the "power to control prices or exclude competition";[4] "the ability profitably to maintain prices above competitive levels for a significant period of time";[5] and the ability to "lessen competition on dimensions other than price, such as product quality, service, or innovation."[6]

How does effective competition discipline mergers? If the merged company's customers can shop freely among suppliers, the acquirer will be buying an uncertain revenue stream—one that will run dry if the customers leave for a lower-pricing, better-serving performer. That uncertainty disciplines the acquirer's offer price. Competition among sellers for the target's customers disciplines competition among acquirers for the target's shareholders. Market pressures align all three interests—acquirer, target shareholders and customers.

Here's a simple example: You own an apartment building in a city with vacancies; you want to sell it. The prospective buyer will offer you a price no greater than what the buyer can recover through rent levels set by the competitive market. The price will reflect a premium over current market value only if the buyer can (a) improve quality, so she can raise rents; or (b) reduce operating costs, so she can increase profit. The highest bid offer will come from the most quality-enhancing, cost-effective bidder. Competition in the

---

[2]   PAUL KRUGMAN & ROBIN WELLS, MICROECONOMICS 420 (4th ed. 2015).

[3]   For a more detailed explanation of different levels of competitiveness, see Chapters 6.1, 6.2 and 6.3.

[4]   United States v. E.I. du Pont de Nemours & Co., 351 U.S. 377, 391 (1956).

[5]   DEP'T OF JUSTICE & FED. TRADE COMM'N, HORIZONTAL MERGER GUIDELINES § 0.1 (1992, rev. 1997).

[6]   *Id.* § 1.11.

rental market disciplines competition in the acquisition market. All interests—building seller, building buyer and tenants—are aligned.

2.2   THE ABSENCE OF COMPETITIVE DISCIPLINE IN UTILITY MONOPOLY MERGERS

2.2.1   The Absence of Competitive Conditions

A target subject to effective competition will receive offer prices disciplined by that competition. The highest acquisition price will come from the best performer. The interests of acquirer, target and consumers converge.

When the target has a retail franchise monopoly, two things don't change. The target will still seek the highest price, and the acquirer's offer will still reflect its expected post-merger earnings. But three things do change. First, the customers are captive, so the earnings stream is relatively certain; second, there is no competition to discipline the price of retail service. Those two facts increase the acquisition's value to the acquirer, producing a higher offer price. Third and most important: because a monopoly market doesn't penalize suboptimal performance the way a competitive market does, the highest offer price will not necessarily come from the best performer. In a monopoly market, the merging parties' interests do not align with the customers' interests.

An acquisition process does involve rivalry among acquirers. When the target serves a competitive market, that rivalry benefits customers because the highest offer will come from the most cost-effective performer. But when the target serves a monopoly market, that same acquirer rivalry does not benefit the customer. Because the competition is based on price, the higher the price paid by the acquirer, the fewer dollars it has to benefit customers. By insisting on a higher price, therefore, the target deprives its customers of benefits. It violates its duty to serve at "lowest feasible cost."[7]

Commissions could solve this problem by setting merger standards that replicate competitive forces. But they don't. As Chapters 4, 10 and 11 will show, commissions allow target utilities to select their acquirers based on price instead of performance; then they routinely fail to require customer benefit levels matching what competition would have produced. Commissions focus on preventing harm instead of maximizing benefits. Each transaction's benefits stay largely with the merging companies, divided between them as

---

[7]   Potomac Elec. Power Co. v. Pub. Serv. Comm'n, 661 A.2d 131, 137 (D.C. 1995) (quoting Potomac Elec. Power Co., 150 P.U.R.4th 528 (D.C. Pub. Serv. Comm'n 1994)).

they wish, rather than being shared with customers in the proportions that competition would require.

2.2.2 The Absence of Arm's-length Bargaining

When merger applicants describe their negotiations as "arm's-length," they imply that the terms resemble a competitive result. This description has two defects—the first applicable to mergers generally, the second applicable to mergers of regulated monopolies.

Defect #1: Merger negotiations are not arm's-length where the parties have a common purpose. True arm's-length transactions involve "business adversaries," each seeking to "further their own [individual] economic interests."[8] The parties negotiate "rigorously, selfishly and with an adequate concern for price."[9] In contrast, when two companies have a "common economic interest in the outcome," they don't negotiate as adversaries, so they don't bargain at arm's-length.[10] Their convergent interests "compromise the market discipline inherent in arm's-length bargaining."[11] Two companies destined to become accountable to the same shareholders cannot be adversaries.

Defect #2: Competitive market assumptions do not apply in a monopoly market context. Under competition, when two entities negotiate as adversaries one's gain is the other's loss. The acquirer that overpays loses money; the target that over-demands loses the deal. Each bargains hard against the other. But in a monopoly market, one entity's gain is not necessarily the other's loss. The high price demanded by the target will not diminish the acquirer's wealth if the merged entity can recover the price from its captive customers. So in the utility merger context, acquirer and target don't bargain against each other as business adversaries; they collaborate on regulatory strategies. They focus on their common purpose: recovering the transaction's costs from the merged company's captive customers.[12] Their mutual success depends not on an objective competitive market but on a subjective regulatory process.

---

[8] Santomenno v. Transamerica Life Ins. Co., No. CV 12-02782 DDP MANX, 2013 U.S. Dist. LEXIS 22354, at *19 n.3 (C.D. Cal. Feb. 19, 2013) (quoting A.T. Kearney, Inc. v. Int'l Bus. Machs. Corp., 73 F.3d 238, 242 (9th Cir. 1995)), *rev'd, on other grounds*, 883 F.3d 833 (9th Cir. 2018).

[9] *Id.* (quoting Jeanes Hosp. v. Sec'y of Health & Human Servs., 448 F.App'x 202, 206 (3d Cir. 2011)).

[10] *Northwest Central Pipeline Corp.*, 44 F.E.R.C. ¶ 61,200, at p. 61,719 (1988).

[11] *Delmarva Power & Light Co.*, 76 F.E.R.C. ¶ 61,331, at p. 62,583 (1996).

[12] For a discussion of how merging utilities try to persuade regulators to set prices above cost, see Chapter 5.3.2.

Absent competition, claims of arm's-length bargaining depend on circular reasoning. Here's how an AltaGas merger witness described the AltaGas-Washington Gas Light Holdings (WGLH) negotiation: a "willing buyer and willing seller settled on a price and other transaction terms that satisfied their respective interests, reflecting the reasonable market value of the company."[13] But where the to-be-acquired utility company faces no competition, the agreed-upon price cannot logically reflect its "reasonable market value." A utility's true "market value" depends on its projected earnings. Those projected earnings are determined not by a market but by regulatory decisions—especially rate decisions.[14] AltaGas and WGLH based their agreed-on price not on "reasonable market value" as determined by a competitive market, but on their expectations of how Washington Gas's regulators would set its post-acquisition rates. Then in the merger proceeding they sought regulatory policies that would satisfy those expectations. That is the essence of circularity.

2.3   THE ABSENCE OF COMPETITIVE DISCIPLINE LEADS TO INSUFFICIENT CUSTOMER BENEFITS

Companies with competitors choose acquirers that help them serve customers better than their competitors. The more cost-effective the acquirer, the more benefits for the customers. Meanwhile, a prospective acquirer will pursue a given acquisition only if the cost of providing those benefits, along with its other acquisition costs, does not cause its projected return to fall below its required return—the return available from its other investment options.

Companies without competitors think differently, because they face no risk of losing customers.[15] Instead of choosing the acquirer that maximizes customer benefits, they choose the acquirer that maximizes price; then they design a benefits package sufficient to persuade their regulators. As Chapters 4.4 and 10.4 will detail, regulators don't require the benefit level that competition would require; they accept the benefits that applicants propose. That gap,

---

[13]   Rebuttal Testimony of John Reed at 60, AltaGas-Washington Gas Light Merger, Case No. 9449 (Md. Pub. Serv. Comm'n filed Apr. 24, 2017).

[14]   As explained in the Tutorial § 4.1.

[15]   *Cf.* The Structure of Equality, NEW YORKER (Dec. 31, 2018), https://www .newyorker.com/magazine/2019/01/07/the-philosopher-redefining-equality ("If one person's supposed freedom results in someone else's subjugation, that is not actually a free society in action. It's hierarchy in disguise.") (describing the reasoning of political philosopher Elizabeth Anderson).

between what competition would produce and what regulators accept, is a gain to the merger parties but a loss to consumers.

If regulation replicated competition's pressures, each utility merger would create new economic value, then allocate that value objectively between shareholders and customers. The acquisition price paid to the target would reflect an earnings stream consistent with that value and allocation. Regulatory policies that defer to merger proposals, where competition does not discipline those proposals, produce mergers with less economic value and less objective allocations. Chapter 5 will explain how this difference affects the acquisition price, and how the gain produced by that price gets allocated between shareholders and customers. Readers can guess the conclusion: in utility mergers, the acquisition price is not disciplined by the cost of providing competitive-level benefits; and the allocation of transaction gain favors shareholders disproportionately. How do these uneconomic results happen? Chapter 9 will explain that merger applicants use means of persuasion sometimes unharnessed from the facts, while Chapter 10 will explain that merger regulators use means of decision-making that don't sufficiently consider the facts.

3. The structural result: concentration and complication no one intended

Madison Gas & Electric (MG&E) serves the Madison, Wisconsin area. It is the sole utility subsidiary of the publicly-traded holding company MGE Energy. The utility owns 92 percent of the holding company system's total assets and contributes most of its revenues and earnings. Its seven small subsidiaries all exist to support the local utility, which provides only local service.[1]

Baltimore Gas & Electric (BG&E) serves the Baltimore, Maryland area. It is one of several hundred subsidiaries owned by the publicly-traded holding company Exelon Corp. BG&E has only 8 percent of Exelon's assets and 9 percent of its revenues. It is one of Exelon's six monopoly utility subsidiaries; the others serving captive customers in the District of Columbia, Delaware, Illinois, New Jersey and Pennsylvania. Besides its six utility companies, Exelon owns around 300 other companies, including subsidiaries, and subsidiaries of subsidiaries, invested in fossil, nuclear, solar and wind generation, making wholesale and retail sales in over thirty states.[2] Figures 3.1 and 3.2 display each system's corporate structure.

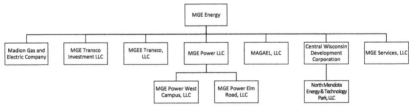

Source: A version of this diagram appears in MGE Energy, Inc., 2019 Q2 Earnings Call Slides, SEEKING ALPHA (Aug. 12, 2019), https://seekingalpha.com/article/4284926-mge -energy-inc-2019-q2-results-earnings-call-slides.

Figure 3.1   MG&E corporate structure

[1]   MGE Energy, Inc. Annual Report (Form 10-K) at 7, 54–60 (Feb. 22, 2019). Two of the holding company's subsidiaries, MGE Transco Investment LLC and MGEE Transco, LLC, merely hold the utility's small interest in a regional transmission facility used for the utility's core service.
[2]   Exelon Corp., Annual Report (Form 10-K) at 7, 10 (Feb. 8, 2019); Exelon Corp., Annual Report (Form 10-K) at 11 (Feb. 9, 2018). According to Exelon's 2018

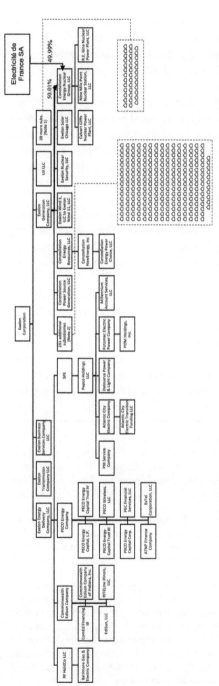

Notes: 1. The number 38, representing Exelon Corporation affiliates not shown here, was derived as follows: Exelon has a total of 340 subsidiaries. *See* Exhibit 21.1 of Exelon Corp., Annual Report (Form 10-K for calendar year 2018). From that total of 340, subtract 273 (Generation and its subsidiaries), 5 (ComEd and its subsidiaries), 9 (PECO and its subsidiaries), 2 (BG&E & holding company), 9 (PHI and its holding company and subsidiaries), and 4 (EEDC, Transmission, EBSC, UII LLC), so 340-273-5-9-2-9-4 = 38 subsidiaries not shown. 2. The number 251, representing Exelon Generation subsidiaries not shown here, was derived as follows: Exelon Generation has a total of 272 subsidiaries. *See* Exhibit 21.2 of Exelon Corp., Annual Report (Form 10-K for calendar year 2018). The diagram shows 21, so 272-21=251 subsidiaries not shown.

Source: This diagram is based on two sources: Exelon's 2018 Form 10-K, and a diagram produced in discovery by Exelon in the 2012 regulatory proceedings relating to its acquisition of Constellation Energy. The diagram incorporates Exelon's discussion on how it has restructured PHI and its utility subsidiaries (Potomac Electric, Delmarva Power & Light, and Atlantic City Electric). Exelon Corp., Annual Report, at 8. The diagram also includes known subsidiaries for each Exelon entity, as listed in Exhibits 21.1 to 21.9 in Exelon's 2018 Form 10-K. Because Exelon's 10-K disclosed only the names of its non-utility subsidiaries, the diagram cannot always show accurately where in the multiple corporate layers each non-utility subsidiary resides. Finally, because the 2018 Exelon Form 10-K sometimes referred to an entity using a generic phrase like "special purpose entity," the diagram may be missing the names of certain entities.

Figure 3.2   Exelon corporate structure

Until the early 1980s, BG&E looked like MG&E. So did most electric utilities—each one a stand-alone, local company serving a compact territory, a few minor affiliates supporting its primary operations. Today, most electric utilities look like BG&E—one subsidiary among many, surrounded by dozens, or hundreds, of non-utility businesses.

Over the last three decades, nearly eighty electricity mergers have concentrated the control of state-granted, exclusive retail franchises. They have concentrated control of the generation, transmission and distribution assets that service those franchises. And they have complicated the holding company systems that control those franchises—in terms of business activity, corporate structure and financial structure. This final chapter in Part I describes the changes. Part II will describe the harms they cause.

Why focus on the last three decades? Though utility mergers go back a century,[3] the period beginning in the mid-1980s has three distinguishing factors. First, the prominent merger proposals that opened this era—such as PacifiCorp-Utah Power & Light, Southern California Edison-San Diego Gas & Electric and Northeast Utilities-Public Service of New Hampshire—were much larger, affecting bigger geographic markets, than prior transactions.[4] Second, during this period Congress created exceptions to, then repealed, the Public Utility Holding Company Act (PUHCA) of 1935.[5] For 50 years, the Act's "integrated public-utility system" test had limited the geographic area and type-of-business scope that electric and gas holding company systems could cover.[6] Third, these three decades of consolidation and complication have coincided with an industry-wide debate over whether and how to intro-

---

Form 10-K, the generation sales occur in the Mid-Atlantic (Pennsylvania, New Jersey, Maryland, Virginia, West Virginia, Delaware, the District of Columbia and North Carolina); the Midwest (North Dakota, South Dakota, Nebraska, Minnesota, Iowa, Wisconsin, Illinois, Indiana, Michigan, Ohio, Montana, Missouri and Kentucky); New England (Connecticut, Maine, Massachusetts, New Hampshire, Rhode Island and Vermont); New York; and Texas.

[3]   In 1920 investor-owned utilities numbered around 2000; in 1957 there were 465 and in 1991 there were around 230. John S. Moot, *Electric Utility Mergers: Uncertainty Looms over Regulatory Approvals at FERC*, 12 ENERGY L.J. 1, 4, 5 n.18 (1991) (quoting FERC TRANSMISSION TASK FORCE, ELECTRICITY TRANSMISSION: REALITIES, THEORY AND POLICY ALTERNATIVES 6–7 (1989)).

[4]   *Id.* at 5 (explaining that the recent mergers "dwarfed previous mergers in size").

[5]   Public Utility Holding Company Act of 1935, Pub. L. No. 74-333, 49 Stat. 803, *repealed by* Energy Policy Act of 2005, Pub. L. No. 109-58, § 1263, 119 Stat. 594, 974.

[6]   We will explain PUHCA 1935 and its profound effects in Chapters 4.2.2 and 8.2. In 1992, Congress exempted acquisitions of "exempt wholesale generators" from the Act's "integrated public-utility system" requirement. In 2005, Congress eliminated the integration requirement entirely by repealing the statute, thereby allowing unlimited acquisitions of utilities by anyone, regardless of the acquired utility's location.

duce competition into historically monopolistic markets. This coinciding is not coincidence, because whether the competition is for wholesale generation, retail sales, transmission construction, or the new distributed energy products—local solar and wind, storage, demand aggregation, energy efficiency and microgrids—a natural reaction of incumbents is to merge.[7]

3.1   CONCENTRATION: CHRONOLOGICAL AND GEOGRAPHICAL

3.1.1   Concentration Defined

For this book, concentration refers to a reduction in the number of independent corporations controlling monopoly retail electric service franchises. Conversely, it refers to an increase in the number of formerly independent utilities now controlled by other entities. A utility corporation is independent if it is not owned by, commonly owned with, or affiliated with, another utility corporation. Concentration occurs when two or more independent utility corporations become owned in common—such as when one utility corporation (or its holding company owner) acquires or merges with another utility corporation (or its holding company owner).

One can view the concentration trend chronologically and geographically.

3.1.2   Chronological View: Three Decades of Mergers

Since the mid-1980s, mergers of retail utility monopolies have been continuous. Table 3.1 lists the independent retail utilities joined by these transactions. Some transactions were mergers, some were acquisitions, some joined independent utilities and some joined holding companies of utilities. The dates refer to FERC's approvals. The italics signal the few transactions that were, after FERC's approval, either withdrawn by the parties or rejected by a state commission. The parentheticals listing holding company subsidiaries include only electric utilities.

---

[7]   *See* William S. Lamb & Michael Didriksen, *Electric and Gas Utility Mergers and Acquisitions: Trends in Deal Terms, Contract Provisions, and Regulatory Matters,* 38 ENERGY L.J. 133, 134 (2017) (describing the "current wave of consolidation [as] appear[ing] to have begun relatively slowly in the late 1980s, and gain[ing] momentum during the 1990s, driven in part by the Energy Policy Act of 1992 and electric industry restructuring initiatives that were taking place in many states"). See also the discussion in Chapter 1.3.1, *supra* of "information cascades" and industry responses to structural "shocks."

Table 3.1   FERC merger approvals

1986	Toledo Edison and Cleveland Electric Illuminating (forming the holding company Centerior)
1988	Georgia Power (owned by Southern Company) and Savannah Electric
1988	Duke Power and Nantahala Power & Light
1988	Utah Power & Light and PacifiCorp
1990	Central Vermont Public Service and Allied Power & Light
1991	Northeast Utilities (holding company for Connecticut Light & Power, Western Massachusetts Electric and Holyoke Water Power) and Public Service of New Hampshire
1991	Kansas Power & Light and Kansas Gas & Electric
1992	Iowa Public Service and Iowa Power & Light (forming the holding company Midwest Power Systems)
1993	Cincinnati Gas & Electric and Public Service of Indiana (forming the holding company Cinergy)
1993	Entergy (holding company owner of Arkansas Power & Light, Louisiana Power & Light, Mississippi Power & Light and New Orleans Public Service) and Gulf States
1994	*El Paso Electric Company and Central & Southwest*
1995	Midwest Power Systems (consisting of Iowa Public Service and Iowa Power & Light) and Iowa-Illinois Gas & Electric (forming the holding company MidAmerican)
1997	Public Service of Colorado and Southwestern Public Service (forming the holding company New Century Energies)
1997	Union Electric and Central Illinois Public Service (forming the holding company Ameren)
1997	*Baltimore Gas & Electric and Potomac Electric Power*
1997	Duke Power and PanEnergy
1997	IES Utilities, Interstate Power, Wisconsin Power & Light, South Beloit Water, Gas & Electric (forming the holding company Alliant)
1997	Enron and Portland General
1997	Centerior (holding company owner of Toledo Edison and Cleveland Electric Illuminating), Ohio Edison Company, Pennsylvania Power Company (forming the holding company FirstEnergy)
1997	Atlantic City Electric and Delmarva Power & Light (becoming Conectiv Power Delivery)
1998	Louisville Gas & Electric and Kentucky Utilities
1998	Scottish Power and PacifiCorp (which owns Utah Power & Light)
1999	New England Electric System (holding company for New England Electric Power, Massachusetts Electric and Narragansett Electric) and National Grid
1999	Eastern Utility Associates (holding company for Montaup Electric, Blackstone Valley Electric, Eastern Edison and Newport Electric) and New England Electric System and National Grid
1999	MidAmerican Energy (holding company for Iowa Public Service, Iowa Power & Light and Iowa-Illinois Gas & Electric) and Berkshire Hathaway
1999	Boston Edison and Commonwealth Energy
1999	AES and Central Illinois Light
1999	Consolidated Edison of New York and Orange & Rockland

1999	Sierra Pacific Power and Nevada Power
1999	Dynegy and Illinois Power
2000	American Electric Power and Central & South West
2000	*Sierra Pacific Power, Nevada Power and Portland General Electric*
2000	New Century Energies (holding company for Southwestern Public Service and Public Service of Colorado), Northern States Power (Minnesota) and Northern States Power (Wisconsin) (forming Xcel Energy)
2000	New York State Electric & Gas and Central Maine Power
2000	Commonwealth Edison and PECO Energy (forming Exelon)
2000	PowerGen (UK) acquires Louisville Gas & Electric and Kentucky Utilities
2000	Carolina Power & Light and Florida Progress (holding company for Florida Power)
2000	UtiliCorp United, St. Joseph Light & Power and Empire District Electric
2000	*Consolidated Edison and Northeast Utilities*
2001	AES and Indianapolis Power & Light (UK)
2001	E.ON (Germany) acquires Louisville Gas & Electric and Kentucky Utilities from PowerGen
2001	FirstEnergy (holding company for Toledo Edison, Cleveland Electric Illuminating, Ohio Edison Company and Pennsylvania Power Company) and General Public Utilities (holding company for Metropolitan Edison, Jersey Central Power & Light and Pennsylvania Electric)
2001	Energy East (holding company for New York State Electric & Gas and Central Maine Power) and RGS Energy Group (holding company for Rochester Gas & Electric)
2001	Potomac Electric Power and Conectiv Power Delivery (the result of the Atlantic City Electric-Delmarva merger) (forming Pepco Holdings)
2002	Ameren (holding company for Union Electric and Central Illinois Public Service) and Central Illinois Light
2004	Ameren (holding company for Union Electric, Central Illinois Public Service and Central Illinois Light) and Illinois Power
2005	Cinergy (holding company for Cincinnati Gas & Electric and PSI Energy) and Duke Energy
2007	Texas Holdings Limited Partnership acquires Oncor Electric Delivery
2005	MidAmerican Energy Holdings acquires PacifiCorp from Scottish Power
2007	Great Plains Energy (holding company for Kansas City Power & Light) acquires Aquila's Missouri operations
2007	Black Hills acquires Aquila's Colorado electric operations
2007	Iberdrola (Spain) acquires Energy East (holding company for New York State Electric & Gas, Central Maine Power and Rochester Gas & Electric)
2010	PPL Electric (holding company for Pennsylvania Power & Light) acquires Louisville Gas & Electric and Kentucky Utilities from E.ON
2010	FirstEnergy Corp. (holding company for Pennsylvania Power, Ohio Edison, Cleveland Electric Illuminating, Toledo Edison, Pennsylvania Electric, Metropolitan Edison and Jersey Central Power & Light) and Allegheny Energy (holding company for Monongahela Power, Potomac Edison and West Penn Power)

2011	Northeast Utilities (holding company for Connecticut Light & Power, Western Massachusetts Electric and Public Service of New Hampshire—it had sold off Holyoke) and NSTAR Electric (consisting of what were Cambridge Electric Light, Commonwealth Electric, Canal Electric and Boston Edison)
2011	Duke Energy (holding company for Duke Energy Carolinas, Duke Energy Indiana, Duke Energy Ohio and Duke Energy Kentucky) and Progress Energy (holding company for Carolina Power & Light and Florida Power Corp)
2011	AES (owner of Indianapolis Power & Light) and Dayton Power & Light
2012	Exelon Corporation (holding company for Commonwealth Edison and PECO Energy) and Constellation Energy Group (holding company for Baltimore Gas & Electric)
2012	Fortis (Canada) acquires Central Hudson Gas & Electric
2013	MidAmerican (holding company for Iowa Public Service, Iowa Power & Light, Iowa-Illinois Gas & Electric and PacifiCorp) and Nevada Power and Sierra Pacific
2014	Fortis (Canada) acquires UNS Energy (holding company for Tucson Electric and UNS Electric)
2015	Wisconsin Energy (holding company for Wisconsin Electric Power) merges with Integrys Energy Group (holding company for Wisconsin Public Service and Upper Peninsula Power)
2015	Macquarie et al. acquires Central Louisiana Electric
2015	Exelon (holding company for Commonwealth Edison, PECO Energy and Baltimore Gas & Electric) acquires Pepco Holdings (holding company for Potomac Electric Power, Delmarva and Atlantic City Electric)
2015	*NextEra and Hawaiian Electric*
2015	Iberdrola (Spain, renamed Avangrid) (holding company for New York State Electric & Gas, Rochester Gas & Electric and Central Maine Power) acquires United Illuminating
2016	Emera (Canada) and Tampa Electric
2016	Empire District Electric and Liberty Utilities
2017	*Oncor and NextEra (holding company for Florida Power & Light)*
2017	Oncor and Sempra (holding company for San Diego Gas & Electric)
2018	*Hydro One (Canada) and Avista*
2018	Great Plains Energy (holding company for Kansas City Power & Light) and Westar (holding company for Kansas Gas & Electric and Kansas Power & Light)
2018	Vectren (holding company for Southern Indiana Gas & Electric) and Centerpoint Energy
2018	Dominion Energy (holding company for Virginia Electric & Power) and SCANA (holding company for South Carolina Gas & Electric)
2018	NextEra and Gulf Power
2020	ENMAX and Emera Maine

3.1.3 Geographical View: Intra-regional, Inter-regional, International

The early mergers in this period were intra-regional. They involved either adjacent utilities, or non-adjacent utilities connected to a common transmission network and sufficiently close to each other to allow them to plan and share power sources. Their limited geographic scope stemmed from PUHCA 1935's central principle: utility couplings had to "serve the public interest by tending toward the economical and efficient development of an integrated public-utility system."[8] To meet that test, a consolidation had to produce a more economical, efficient company.[9] Adjacency, or proximity plus transmission interconnection, characterized many of the early mergers: Toledo Edison and Cleveland Electric Illuminating; Kansas Power & Light and Kansas Gas & Electric; Northeast Utilities and Public Service of New Hampshire; Iowa Public Service Company, Iowa Power Inc. and Midwest Power Systems; Entergy and Gulf States; and Cincinnati Gas & Electric Company and Public Service of Indiana among them.[10]

More recent transactions have been inter-regional and international. Toward the end of the 1990s, the SEC applied PUHCA 1935's integration requirement

---

[8]   PUHCA § 10(c)(2), 15 U.S.C. § 79j(c)(2). An "integrated public-utility system," for an electric company, was

> a system consisting of one or more units of generating plants and/or transmission lines and/or distributing facilities, whose utility assets, whether owned by one or more electric utility companies, are physically interconnected or capable of physical interconnection and which under normal conditions may be economically operated as a single interconnected and coordinated system confined in its operations to a single area or region, in one or more States, not so large as to impair (considering the state of the art and the area or region affected) the advantages of localized management, efficient operation, and the effectiveness of regulation …

Id. § 2(a)(29)(A).

[9]   *See, e.g.,* Wisconsin's Envtl. Decade, Inc. v. SEC, 882 F.2d 523, 528 (D.C. Cir. 1989) (reversing SEC approval of an acquisition that made no improvement in utility operations). *See also* Nat'l Rural Elec. Coop. Ass'n v. SEC, 276 F.3d 609, 610, 615-16 (D.C. Cir. 2002). In the latter case, the court remanded to the SEC its approval of the merger between American Electric Power Company and Central & South West Corporation, because the agency failed to determine whether, post-merger, the inter-company electrical flow would be bidirectional—a feature that the court viewed as essential to the statutory definition of "integrated public-utility system." The court also held that the SEC cannot "interpret the phrase 'single area or region' [in the definition of 'integrated public-utility system'] so flexibly as to read it out of the Act." *Id.* at 618. For three years after the 2002 remand, the SEC took no action against the newly formed holding company. The transaction's lawfulness became a non-issue with PUHCA 1935's repeal in 2005. In both of the above cases, the author was appellate counsel for the successful petitioners. In the AEP case, the argument on bidirectionality came from his then associate, David Lapp.

[10]   Some electric utility systems did consist of non-adjacent, non-proximate utilities. These systems fell outside of PUHCA 1935 because they did not involve the holding company form. Each utility was a division of a single corporation rather than a subsidiary of a holding company. Examples were Citizens Utilities, which had utility divisions in Arizona, Hawai'i, Vermont and other states; and PacifiCorp, which had utility divisions in seven Western states.

less literally than did its predecessors. It allowed long-distance, non-integrating transactions like those involving the American Electric Power Company and Central & South West Corp.; Florida Progress (the holding company for Florida Power Corp.) and Carolina Power & Light; and National Grid (UK) and New England Electric System.[11] With the 2005 repeal of PUHCA 1935, mergers and acquisitions soon produced utility holding company systems with

Table 3.2   Inter-regional holding company systems

Holding company	Locations of utility subsidiaries
Berkshire Hathaway	Washington State, Nevada, Oregon, California, Utah, Wyoming and Iowa
Exelon	Illinois, Maryland, District of Columbia, Delaware and New Jersey
American Electric Power	Ohio, Indiana, Michigan, Kentucky, West Virginia, Virginia, Texas, Louisiana, Arkansas and Oklahoma
Duke	Florida, North Carolina, Ohio, Indiana and Kentucky
Xcel	Minnesota, Colorado, New Mexico and Texas

Table 3.3   International holding company systems

Holding company	Utilities
Fortis (Canada)	Tucson Electric, Unisource Energy and Central Hudson Electric & Gas
Emera (Canada)	Bangor-Hydro and Tampa Electric
Iberdrola (Spain)	United Illuminating, New York State Electric & Gas, Rochester Gas & Electric and Central Maine Power
National Grid (UK)	New England Electric System (consisting, before the 1980s, of New England Power, Massachusetts Electric and Narragansett Electric); EUA (consisting, before the 1980s, of Montaup Electric, Blackstone Valley Electric, Eastern Edison and Newport Electric); Niagara Mohawk
Gaz Metro (Canada)	Green Mountain Power and Central Vermont Public Service

---

[11]   The wisdom of those SEC decisions (some of which this author contested—*see Wisconsin's Envtl. Decade* and *Nat'l Rural Elec. Coop. Ass'n, supra* note 9; and Envtl. Action, Inc. v. SEC, 895 F.2d. 1255 (9th Cir. 1990)) is outside this chapter's scope. The historically inclined can consult LEONARD S. HYMAN, AMERICA'S ELECTRIC UTILITIES: PAST, PRESENT AND FUTURE 102 (1994) (asserting that the SEC "seems to have lost interest in enforcing the letter of the law … and now approves the formation of holding companies that comply with the law in the most far-fetched ways"); and Richard D. Cudahy & William D. Henderson, *From Insull to Enron: Corporate (Re)Regulation After the Rise and Fall of Two Energy Icons*, 26 ENERGY L.J. 35, 103–104 (2005) (stating that before 2002, "it had become commonplace for the SEC to approve merger activity with virtually no regard for the Act's geographic strictures"). For a critique of the SEC's actions, see Scott Hempling, *Corporate Restructuring and Consumer Risk: Is the SEC Enforcing the Public Utility Holding Company Act?*, ELECTRICITY J., July 1988.

utilities whose remoteness precluded physical integration. Tables 3.2 and 3.3 display, respectively, examples of inter-regional and international mergers.

At least twenty electric utilities are now owned by five foreign companies.

3.1.4 Acceleration: Mergers of the Previously Merged

Several previously merged utilities have merged with each other, intra-regionally and inter-regionally. Three prominent examples are displayed in Table 3.4 as equations, the parentheses and brackets signaling prior mergers.

Table 3.4   Mergers of the merged

2001	FirstEnergy + GPU = [(Cleveland Electric + Toledo Edison) + Ohio Edison + Pennsylvania Power] + [(Jersey Central Power & Light Company, Metropolitan Edison Company and Pennsylvania Electric Company)]
2011	Duke Energy + Florida Progress = [Duke + (Cincinnati Gas & Electric + Public Service of Indiana)] + [(Florida Power Corp. + Carolina Power & Light)]
2015	Exelon + PHI = [(Commonwealth Edison + PECO) + BG&E)] + [(Delmarva + Atlantic City Electric) + Pepco].

With mergers of the previously merged, the ten most active acquirers now own what used to be sixty-four independent utilities—over half the United States total (see Table 3.5).[12]

Adding to those ten holding companies three of the multi-utility holding company systems that pre-dated the 1980s shows a concentration that is even more marked (Table 3.6).

Adding those three systems to our totals, we see that eighty-three formerly independent utilities are now owned by thirteen holding companies.[13]

---

[12] For National Grid and Eversource, some of the utilities listed were already in a holding company prior to the 1980s.

[13] The various sources recording the merger trend cite different numbers—because they use different definitions of utility, different definitions of merger, and different time periods. But they all support the existence of a trend. Consider the following five examples.

- In 2000, the U.S. Energy Information Agency reported that "[b]y the end of 2000, the 10 largest IOUs (investor-owned electric utilities) will own approximately 51 percent of all IOU-owned power production capacity (up from about 36 percent in 1992) and the 20 largest IOUs will own approximately 73 percent (up from about 36 percent in 1992)." Stephen Paul Mahinka & Theodore A. Gebhard, *Preclosing Cooperation in Energy Mergers: Antitrust Issues and Practical Concerns*, 13 ELECTRICITY J. 68 (2000) (quoting U.S. Energy Information Agency and other sources).

Table 3.5   Ten acquirers own over half of the U.S. utilities

National Grid owns ten	New England Electric System (consisting, before the 1980s, of New England Power, Massachusetts Electric, Granite State Electric, Narragansett Electric, Nantucket Electric); EUA (consisting, before the 1980s, of Montaup Electric, Blackstone Valley Electric, Eastern Edison, Newport Electric); Niagara Mohawk
Great Plains Energy owns eight	UtiliCorp United, St. Joseph Light & Power, Empire District Electric, Kansas City Power & Light, Aquila, Black Hills, Kansas Power & Light and Kansas Gas & Electric
Duke Power Company owns seven	Duke Power, Nantahala Power & Light, Cincinnati Gas & Electric, Public Service of Indiana, PanEnergy, Florida Power & Light and Carolina Power & Light
Berkshire Hathaway owns seven	Iowa Public Service, Iowa Power & Light, Iowa-Illinois Gas & Electric, PacifiCorp, Utah Power & Light, Nevada Power and Sierra Pacific Power
Northeast Utilities (now called Eversource) owns seven	Connecticut Light & Power, Western Massachusetts Electric Power (those two already owned by NU before the 1980s), Public Service of New Hampshire, Boston Edison, Commonwealth Energy, Cambridge Electric Light and Canal Electric
FirstEnergy owns seven	Cleveland Electric Illuminating, Toledo Edison, Ohio Edison, Pennsylvania Power, Monongahela Power Company, Potomac Edison Company and West Penn Power
Exelon owns six	Commonwealth Edison, Philadelphia Electric, Baltimore Gas & Electric, Potomac Electric Power, Delmarva Power & Light and Atlantic City Electric
Ameren owns four	Union Electric, Central Illinois Public Service, Central Illinois Light (acquired from AES in 2003) and Illinois Power (acquired from Dynegy in 2004)
Xcel Energy owns four	Northern States Power-Minnesota, Northern States Power-Wisconsin, Public Service Company of Colorado and Southwestern Public Service
Iberdrola (now called Avangrid) owns four	New York State Electric & Gas, Central Maine Power, United Illuminating and Rochester Gas & Electric

Table 3.6   AEP, Southern and Entergy

American Electric Power owns ten	Appalachian Power, Kingsport Power, Indiana Michigan Power, Kentucky Power, Ohio Power, Columbus and Southern (all from the prior AEP family that pre-dated the 1980s-forward merger trend and some of which have merged into a single company); Central Power & Light, West Texas Utilities, Public Service Company of Oklahoma and Southwestern Electric Power Company (all from the prior Central & Southwest family that pre-dated the post-1985 merger trend and some of which have merged into a single utility)
Southern Company owns four	Alabama Power, Georgia Power, Gulf Power and Mississippi Power
Entergy owns five	Entergy Arkansas, Entergy Mississippi, Entergy Louisiana, New Orleans Public Service and Entergy Texas (formerly Gulf States)

Mergers of the previously merged mean larger transaction sizes. As one author noted in 2012:

> For most of the past 12 years, major M&A activities were very limited among the top 10 largest utilities with virtually no mergers among them until recently.

- In 2000, FERC referred to "the more than 50 merger cases filed" since its 1996 Merger Policy Statement. Order No. 642, *Revised Filing Requirements Under Part 33 of the Commission's Regulations*, F.E.R.C. Stats. & Regs. ¶ 31,111, 65 Fed. Reg. 70,984 (2000), *order on reh'g*, Order No. 642-A, 94 F.E.R.C. ¶ 61,289, 66 Fed. Reg. 16,121 (2001).
- A 2012 survey found that from 1995 to 2012, "the number of shareholder-owned electric utility holding companies has declined by 48 percent." Jack Azagury et al., *The Race to Consolidate*, Pub. Util. Fortnightly (Sept. 2012), https://www.fortnightly.com/fortnightly/2012/09/race-consolidate.
- In a 2015–16 merger case before the Hawaii Public Utilities Commission, where NextEra (the holding company for Florida Power & Light) sought to acquire HEI (the holding company for Hawaiian Electric Company's two utility affiliates and a bank), a witness for the applicants testified that the number of investor-owned electric utilities had declined from ninety-eight companies in December 1995 to forty-nine companies as of December 2013. Direct Testimony of John Reed at 10, Hawaiian Electric-NextEra Merger, Docket No. 2015-0022 (Haw. Pub. Util. Comm'n filed Apr. 13, 2015).
- According to the Edison Electric Institute, there were, at the end of 2016, fifty remaining utility systems: forty-four publicly traded on U.S. stock exchanges and six owned by either independent power producers or foreign companies. Edison Elec. Inst., 2016 Financial Review: Annual Report of the U.S. Investor-Owned Electric Utility Industry 101 (2017), http://www.eei.org/resourcesandmedia/industrydataanalysis/industryfinancialanalysis/finreview/Documents/FinancialReview_2016.pdf.

In 2011 and 2012, we saw a departure from this trend, driven primarily by the Exelon-Constellation and Duke-Progress mergers. These changes in concentration within the industry, particularly among the larger players, support the hypothesis that a new pattern of more active mergers and acquisitions is emerging.[14]

One last way to see the national picture is to count the unmerged. Of several hundred independent investor-owned utilities from the early 1980s, only the fourteen listed in Table 3.7 remain uncoupled with some other franchised utility.

Table 3.7   Electric utilities remaining unmerged

Arizona Public Service (owned by Pinnacle West)
Black Hills
Detroit Edison
El Paso Electric
Idaho Power
Madison Gas & Electric
Montana Dakota Utilities
NorthWestern Energy (formerly Montana Power)
Oklahoma Gas & Electric
Otter Tail
Pacific Gas & Electric
Portland General Electric
Public Service Electric & Gas (New Jersey)
Southern California Edison

Some of these fourteen utilities are subsidiaries of holding companies; but unlike the holding companies in the preceding lists, these holding companies own no electric utilities, and usually no other major businesses, other than the listed utility company.[15] These are relatively simple companies.

---

[14]   Jack Azagury et al., *supra* note 13.
[15]   The author developed this list by (1) identifying, from the Edison Electric Institute's Financial Review's 2016 list of all utilities, those that were not part of a multi-utility holding company system; then (2) checking the list against each company's public information.

3.2 COMPLICATION: BUSINESS ACTIVITIES, CORPORATE STRUCTURE, FINANCIAL STRUCTURE

3.2.1 Complication Defined

The typical 1980s electric utility was a single corporation. Vertically integrated, it owned generation, transmission and distribution—and little else. It earned most of its revenues by providing retail service under a single monopoly franchise subject to a single state's jurisdiction; the rest from wholesale sales subject to FERC jurisdiction. Some of these companies also earned minor revenues from non-utility businesses.[16] The industry also had thirteen so-called "registered holding companies," each owning multiple utilities in adjacent states.[17] Section 11(b)(1) of PUHCA 1935 prohibited these registered holding companies from owning any non-utility businesses unrelated to their utility subsidiaries.[18]

For this book, complication occurs when a utility's corporate family departs from that prior model. We next discuss the three main dimensions of departure: business activities, corporate structure and financial structure.

3.2.2 Business Activities

A utility's corporate family becomes complicated to the extent it includes business activities other than providing franchised electric services within one or

---

[16] Each "exempt" holding company (a category consisting mostly of intrastate systems and exempt from most of PUHCA 1935) was limited to a single integrated system. But under PUHCA section 3(a), 15 U.S.C § 79c(a) (repealed 2005), that exempt holding company could own unrelated non-utility businesses unless doing so became "detrimental to the public interest or the interest of investors or consumers."

[17] U.S. Gov't Accountability Office, GAO-05-617, Public Utility Holding Company Act: Opportunities Exist to Strengthen SEC's Administration of the Act (2005). By 2004, mergers and acquisitions had increased this number to twenty-nine. U.S. Sec. & Exch. Comm'n, Holding Companies Registered Under the Public Utility Holding Company Act of 1935 (2004), https://www.sec.gov/divisions/investment/regpucacompanies.htm.

[18] Section 11(b)(1) of PUHCA 1935 limited "registered" holding companies (a category consisting mostly of multi-state systems) to "a single integrated public-utility system" plus "such other businesses as are reasonably incidental, or economically necessary or appropriate to the operations of such integrated public-utility system." Section 11(b)(2) directed the SEC to simplify registered holding companies' corporate structures.

more state-defined, operationally integrated service territories. Business complication can occur across two dimensions: geography and type-of-business.

3.2.2.1　Geographic complication

Geographic expansion has four stages, described here in order of increasing complexity.

Stage 1—Merger of adjacent utilities: This action causes no regulatory complication, if the purpose and result are to adjust a decades-old service territory boundary to reflect modern economies of scale.[19] If instead the purpose and result is to weaken competition, such as by giving the merged company a high market share or control of inputs needed by competitors, regulatory problems do arise, as Chapter 6 on competition will discuss.

Stage 2—Merger of utilities that are non-adjacent but capable of physical integration: Non-adjacent integration can happen if the merging utilities lie within a region or sub-region whose transmission capacity and generation dispatch procedures allow the merging companies to plan and operate as a single system, with each company's resources available to serve both companies' customers continuously using what engineers call single-system dispatch. Consider the 1991 acquisition of Public Service of New Hampshire by Northeast Utilities (now called Eversource). Both companies lay within the New England Power Pool (NEPOOL), which at the time conducted integrated transmission planning and single-system dispatch within its six-state footprint. (Today, non-adjacent utilities that lie within a regional transmission organization (RTO) often can integrate their resources without merging. A merger of such utilities therefore is not likely to have power supply integration as its purpose.)

Stage 3—Mergers of non-adjacent utilities that are not capable of single-system integration but capable of some resource-sharing: These mergers involve utilities that are not in the same integrated region or sub-region, so single-system dispatch is not possible. But their service territories are sufficiently close, with enough transmission capacity between them, that some of one company's generation capacity can support some of the load of the other, though not continuously. Examples are the merger of Pepco (D.C. and Maryland), Atlantic City Electric (New Jersey) and Delmarva (Delaware, Maryland and Virginia), creating the holding company Conectiv, and now part of the holding company Exelon; and the merger of Commonwealth Edison and Philadelphia Electric (also now part of Exelon).

---

[19]　Economies of scale exist when, for a particular product or service, long-run average cost per unit declines as output increases. Paul Krugman & Robin Wells, Microeconomics 348 (4th ed. 2015).

Stage 4—Mergers where no resource-sharing of generation or transmission is physically feasible: An early example was the merger of MidAmerican (which owned utilities in the Midwest) and PacifiCorp (which owned utilities in the West). NextEra (the holding company for Florida Power & Light) tried to acquire both Hawaiian Electric and the Texas utility Oncor; in neither situation would any integration be feasible. (These NextEra efforts were rejected by the Hawaii and Texas Commissions, respectively, for reasons discussed in Chapter 11.2.) Any of the acquisitions by non-North American companies, such as Scottish Power's acquisition of PacifiCorp or National Grid's (U.K.) acquisition of New England Electric System, fit into this fourth category.

3.2.2.2   Type-of-business complication

Type-of-business complication refers to the presence in the utility's corporate family of non-core activities—activities other than (i) selling retail service within the utility's state-franchised service territory, and (ii) selling wholesale electric service to customers within or near that territory. Non-core businesses can be electric or non-electric.

Electric businesses: The holding company creates or buys wholesale generating businesses. These wholesale businesses could own generating units physically near the original retail utility, selling the output at wholesale (i) to the original retail utility, or (ii) to unaffiliated retail utilities in the same region. Or the wholesale businesses could own generating units physically remote from the original retail utility, selling the output at wholesale to other retail utilities in that remote region.

Non-electric businesses: Business complication involving non-electric businesses can comprise at least eight activities:

1. Holding company subsidiaries sell services to the affiliated utility, services like (a) inputs specific to utility operations (e.g., a coal-mining or gas pipeline subsidiary selling coal or gas to a utility affiliate that owns coal-fired or gas-fired power plants); or (b) general overhead services (e.g., accounting, legal and real estate services).
2. The subsidiaries described in Activity #1 expand their customer bases by selling the same services to non-affiliated utilities (e.g., a coal-mining affiliate selling coal to other utilities).
3. Using the affiliated utility's service territory knowledge, name recognition and customer loyalty, an affiliate sells energy-related services to the utility's customer base. Those services could include energy efficiency improvements; home energy audits; and heating, ventilation and air conditioning installation, maintenance and repair.
4. The affiliate in Activity #3 expands its energy-related business to other service territories.

5. As with Activity #3, a subsidiary uses the affiliated utility's service territory knowledge, name recognition and customer loyalty to sell non-energy products first to the utility's customer base and then to others. Examples are home energy alarm systems and real estate services.
6. The affiliate in Activity #5 expands its non-energy businesses into other geographic areas.
7. The holding company creates or buys subsidiaries to engage in unrelated non-utility businesses, like banking, real estate development, or furniture sales, within the affiliated utility's service territory.
8. The subsidiaries described in Activity #7 enter unrelated non-utility businesses outside the affiliated utility's service territory.

Paths to business-mixing: These non-core businesses can become part of the utility's corporate family by one of three paths:

• An existing utility or utility holding company, directly or through a subsidiary, enters a non-utility market. In the 1990s, Constellation Energy (then the holding company for Baltimore Gas & Electric) entered the global commodities trading business. And Exelon has described its generation business as "continuously look[ing] to invest in new business initiatives and actively participate in new markets. These include, but are not limited to, unconventional oil and gas exploration and production, residential power and gas sales, solar and wind generation, and managed load response."[20]
• An existing utility or utility holding company acquires a non-utility business. Western Resources (then the holding company for Kansas Power & Light and Kansas Gas & Electric—later renamed Westar and acquired in 2018 by Great Plains Energy (the holding company for KCP&L and other utilities and now named Evergy)) acquired companies selling home alarm systems. In 1988, Hawaiian Electric's holding company bought American Savings Bank.
• A holding company owning non-utility businesses acquires a utility or a utility holding company. Berkshire Hathaway, a conglomerate, has bought three utilities or utility holding companies: MidAmerican Energy Holding Company (the holding company for MidAmerican Energy Company, which provides electric and gas utility services in Iowa, Illinois, South Dakota and Nebraska); PacifiCorp (which serves in several Western states); and Nevada Power (the product of a prior merger of Sierra Pacific Resources and Nevada Power). KKR and other private hedge funds bought

---

[20] Exelon Corp., Annual Report (Form 10-K) at 63 (Feb. 14, 2014).

Oncor (a retail utility in Texas—now owned by Sempra, the holding company for San Diego Gas & Electric).

These non-core activities usually occur within an affiliate, corporately separate from the utility but owned by the utility's holding company.

3.2.3   Corporate Structure

Corporate structure refers to the ownership relationships within a utility's holding company system. It involves these questions: How many subsidiaries does the top holding company have? Which subsidiaries own which assets? Which subsidiaries conduct which businesses with whom? Who controls what decisions? Which executives plan, finance and operate the utility businesses, and how?

When electric utilities were pure-play companies, their ownership structure resembled other single-activity corporations; they issued millions of shares to diverse entities: individual people, trust funds, philanthropic funds, pension funds, mutual funds and hedge funds. Today the typical electric utility is owned not by numerous individual shareholders but by a single holding company, which in turn might be owned by another holding company owning other companies.[21] At the end of this chain are still the ultimate owners— individuals, philanthropic funds, pension funds, mutual funds and hedge funds. But the mix of those ultimate owners, their corporate distance from the original utility business and the strategies of the utility's holding company owner, all differ from the model of independent, pure-play utilities.

We can describe variations of corporate structure through three frames: the utility's relationship to its shareholders, the types of ultimate shareholders and the types of inter-affiliate relationships.

3.2.3.1   The utility's relationship to its shareholders
The utility-shareholder relationship can take one of the following forms:

- The utility is owned directly by the ultimate shareholders (e.g., individuals, mutual funds and pension funds). This was the common model before the modern merger trend.
- The utility is owned by a holding company, which in turn is owned by the ultimate shareholders.
- The utility is owned by a holding company that itself is owned by another holding company, which in turn is owned by the ultimate shareholders—

---

[21]   For example, see the corporate structures of MGE Energy and Exelon in Figures 3.1 and 3.2, respectively.

with multiple corporate layers separating the core utility from the ultimate shareholders.
- The utility resides within the top-level holding company, as a division rather than a subsidiary. That top-level holding company owns one or more subsidiaries.

3.2.3.2   The types of ultimate shareholders

Complicating the corporate family's business mix necessarily complicates its shareholder mix. Consider an independent, pure-play utility, providing only electric service within a single state. It will attract (and historically did attract) conservative investors seeking to buy and hold shares for stable dividends and slow-but-steady value growth. A holding company bent on making multiple, debt-financed acquisitions of entities unconnected to the core utility service—like NextEra seeking to buy Hawaiian Electric and the Texas utility Oncor at nearly the same time—will attract a different set of shareholders: those willing to take higher risks, for higher returns and faster value growth.

These differences in shareholder goals can produce differences in corporate leadership. That leadership then determines business priorities and strategies, such as whether to

- have the utilities build new generation capacity, or instead to buy output from others;
- expand trading boundaries and trading partners (such as by forming or joining a regional transmission organization), or instead create trade barriers so as to maintain market dominance over the utility's historic service region;
- make acquisitions, be acquired, or remain pure-play;
- pay out dividends to shareholders, or instead save cash for future acquisitions; or
- propose or oppose policies that introduce more competition into historically monopolistic utility markets.

The mix of holding company activities can affect the mix of shareholders, which in turn can affect the mix of holding company activities.

How shareholder mix affects utility performance is subject to debate. Some assert that diverse ownership "provide[s] adequate capital at the lowest cost"; makes the utility system "more robust (less susceptible to systemic risk)," more able to "withstand … financial collapse"; and "bring[s] more diversity of management and technologies."[22] Others raise concerns, as did intervenors

---

[22]   Markian M.W. Melnyk & William S. Lamb, *PUHCA's Gone: What Is Next for Holding Companies?*, 27 ENERGY L.J. 1, 21 (2006).

in the Washington State Commission's review of Macquarie's (an Australian holding company) proposal to acquire Puget Sound Energy. The Commission itself saw no problem:

> [T]he source of the equity behind the Investor Consortium, including the Macquarie investors, is overwhelmingly government and private pension funds and endowments. It is not hedge funds, venture capital, "corporate raiders" and other sources of capital often thought of in the context of "highly leveraged private equity buyouts." The Investor Consortium represents very large pools of "patient capital" that invest in utility companies like Puget Energy expecting relatively stable long-term returns that are a good fit with the relatively long-term liabilities of pension funds and endowments. There is no evidence in our record that the Consortium intends or desires to "flip" its investment in Puget Energy in the near term or at any particular point in time.[23]

Shareholder type was also an issue when another Australian holding company, Babcock & Brown, sought to buy NorthWestern Energy, the company providing retail electric service in Montana, South Dakota and Nebraska. NorthWestern had recently emerged from a bankruptcy caused by its failed non-core investments. That drama led the Montana Commission to declare a preference for a stand-alone utility and for acquirers that demonstrated "[c]ommitment to long-term ownership of the utility."[24] Recognizing that its acquisition proposal conflicted with the Commission's preference, Babcock & Brown tried to change the Commission's mind. Its witness warned that if the Commission rejected Babcock & Brown's bid, short-term investors would find another buyer: "[The] hedge funds or 'merger arbitragers' … who bought stock after the sale announcement in anticipation of a short-term return … will pressure NorthWestern to find a way to recover their investments if this merger is denied."[25] Unimpressed, the Commission rejected the acquisition. The possibility of short-term owners did not "have any bearing one way or the other on the merits of the proposed acquisition at issue in [the] proceeding."[26] NorthWestern remains a stand-alone utility.

3.2.3.3 The types of inter-affiliate relationships
Inter-affiliate relationships involve transactions between a holding company and its subsidiaries and among the subsidiaries. These transactions can accom-

---

[23] Puget Sound Energy-Macquarie Merger, 2008 Wash. UTC LEXIS 1023, at *15–16. One Commissioner dissented.

[24] Statement of Factors for Evaluating Proposals to Acquire NorthWestern Energy, Docket No. N2004.10.166, slip op. at 2 (Mont. Pub. Serv. Comm'n Oct. 2004).

[25] NorthWestern-Babcock & Brown Merger, 2007 Mont. PUC LEXIS 54, at *116 (Commission paraphrasing of Babcock & Brown's testimony).

[26] *Id.*

modate efficient resource-sharing; they can also harm customers or weaken competition. When a monopoly utility sells to a competitive affiliate (i.e., an affiliate that sells in a competitive market), the holding company will want the utility to undercharge (to give the affiliate a competitive advantage). When the monopoly buys from an affiliate, the holding company will want the affiliate to overcharge the utility (to increase the holding company's earnings). The many possible transactions fall into two main categories: sales of services and financial transactions. This subsection illustrates these various relationships; we discuss the risk of harms, and the regulatory protections from those harms, in Chapter 6.5.5.

3.2.3.3.1 Sales of services: three types

Sale by utility to non-utility affiliates: The utility provides to its non-utility affiliates marketing advice, customer information, management assistance, office space and equipment, branding, and advertising.

Sale by non-utility affiliate to the utility: The non-utility affiliate sells to its utility affiliate generation capacity or energy, land, buildings, or fuel—all essential inputs for the utility's business.

Service company: A utility holding company with multiple businesses typically creates a central service company, sometimes called a "Servco." The Servco provides general business services—human resources, accounting, legal advice and information technology—to the various business affiliates, utility and non-utility. The Servco recovers its costs in two ways: (a) by charging an affiliate directly for services provided uniquely to that affiliate, and (b) by allocating common costs (costs not uniquely attributable to a particular affiliate, like the CEO's salary and the headquarters building) among the affiliates according to some allocation formula. Either type of charge is usually based on the Servco's cost rather than a market price.

3.2.3.3.2 Financial transactions: four types

Direct loans and other forms of credit support: An affiliate with surplus cash, or with access to low-cost external credit, might make direct loans to other affiliates. Or it might pledge its assets or revenues as collateral for another affiliate's loans.

Dividends: When a subsidiary has earnings (revenues exceeding its costs), it can either retain those earnings to finance its own investments, or it can pay those earnings out to its holding company shareholder as dividends.

Money pools: A money pool is an agreement among multiple affiliates, allowing them to share cash for short-term needs, like working capital. Each member puts some of its spare cash into a central fund, from which each member can borrow and then repay. (Otherwise, affiliates would have to arrange separate bilateral loans whenever they needed short-term cash.) If the interest rate charged to the temporary borrowers is less than what those borrowers would have paid to external lenders, the holding company system saves money. (This statement assumes each participant does not have other, more profitable ways to invest its spare cash.) Any borrower from the pool is deemed to be borrowing pro rata from each contributor to the pool, at some interest rate specified in the money pool agreement. The typical money pool agreement requires all loans to be repaid within a year. A central administrator keeps track of the inflow and outflow, places surplus funds in liquid investments and pays out any earnings to participating companies in proportion to their contributions.

Factoring: Every utility has accounts receivable—money owed by customers who have received their electricity bills but have not yet paid. Accounts receivable reflect a time lag, between when the utility incurs a cost in providing a service and when it receives payments for that service. During that time lag, the utility might need cash. Factoring can provide that cash. The holding company creates a factoring subsidiary, funded with the holding company's equity and debt. The factoring subsidiary buys the utility's receivables at a discount—the utility receiving the cash it needs sooner than if it waited for the customer's payment. The factoring subsidiary makes a profit if its revenue from collecting the receivables exceeds what it paid the utility for them, less the factoring subsidiary's financing and administrative costs.

3.2.4   Financial Structure

Financial structure (also called capital structure) refers to the types and sources of a corporate family's financing, within each family member and for the family as a whole. The types of financing are equity, debt and equity-debt hybrids like preferred stock. Internal financing occurs when the holding company puts equity into a subsidiary, or an affiliate lends to another affiliate. External financing occurs when the holding company issues new stock, or when the holding company or a subsidiary issues external debt. (Wholly-owned subsidiaries of the holding company do not issue stock externally; they issue stock to the holding company.)

To understand a merger's effects on the merged entity's capital structure, financial analysts ask these questions:

*   What is the debt-equity ratio for the holding company and each affiliate?
*   What are the maturity dates for the corporate family's loans?
*   Which affiliates have obligations to pay dividends to which companies, under what terms and at whose direction?
*   Which companies are responsible for issuing debt or equity to which companies, under what terms and at whose direction?

- Which affiliates, if any, are legally responsible for the debts of other affiliates?
- Which affiliates, if any, have had their stock or assets pledged as collateral, or otherwise encumbered, for their own debts or for debts incurred by other affiliates?

When assessing and guiding financial structure, utility regulators aim to minimize the utility's long-term cost of capital. A key focus is the ratio of equity to debt. The equity share must be large enough to make lenders confident of repayment (and therefore willing to accept relatively low interest rates). The equity share must be small enough so that its higher cost (equity costs more than debt because shareholders receive no contractual guarantee of repayment) does not raise the total cost unnecessarily. Mergers and acquisitions always change a corporate family's debt-equity mix, for either or both of two reasons: (a) each merging company had a different equity-debt ratio, so the merged company's combined ratio will necessarily differ from each pre-merger ratio; or (b) the acquirer has financed the purchase price with a debt-equity mix different from the target utility's pre-acquisition mix, thereby changing the mix of the whole.

A holding company's capital structure affects utility performance. There are two distinct concerns, one for each direction of the fund flow. First, funds need to flow into the utility. A pure-play utility, owned by the ultimate shareholders, accesses the equity markets directly. But once the utility is wholly acquired by a holding company, it becomes a subsidiary—so its only source of equity is its holding company owner. The utility's dependence on the holding company for equity puts the utility at risk if the holding company has competing investment priorities, like buying other businesses. Second, funds flow out of the utility to its holding company owner. Because the utility's income stream is predictable, the holding company has an incentive—and because of its 100 percent control, the opportunity—to extract from the utility the dividends it wants, or to pledge the utility's assets or stock as collateral to support debt incurred by the holding company or its other subsidiaries. When the utility's resources are diverted or pledged to other purposes, they become unavailable to support the utility business.

These examples assume that pressure on the utility comes from the holding company that directly owns the utility. But influence can come from indirect ownership, as the Maryland Commission found. A Maryland statute prohibits any transaction by which a company "acquire[s], directly or indirectly, the power to exercise ... substantial influence over the policies and actions" of a utility, unless the transaction receives Commission approval.[27] An affiliate

---

[27]   MD. CODE ANN., PUB. UTIL. § 6-105(e)(1).

of Electricité de France (EDF) sought to buy a 49.99 percent share in a nuclear subsidiary owned by Constellation Energy Group (CEG), the top-level holding company for Baltimore Gas & Electric. Once EDF bought that 49.99 percent, it would control the flow of dividends from the nuclear affiliate to CEG. The Maryland Commission found that with that control, EDF could influence CEG's decisions about when, and at what cost, to support BG&E's finances. That influence, in turn, "could affect substantially the decisions CEG and BGE make as to the financing and financial structure of the utility."[28]

* * *

We have described complication's three dimensions: business activities, corporate structure and financial structure. Merger strategists can combine these structures in various ways. Adding non-utility businesses to a utility's corporate family can occur vertically (they become subsidiaries of existing companies), or horizontally (they become siblings of existing companies that are commonly owned by one or more holding companies). Adding higher-risk non-utility businesses can induce a holding company to balance its portfolio by seeking more lower-risk utility businesses. Conversely, the utility's steady income and productive assets allow the holding company to incur new debt to buy or start other businesses.

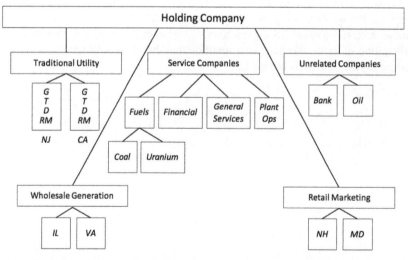

Figure 3.3   Permissible corporate structure, post-PUHCA

---

[28]   Baltimore Gas & Elec. Co., 2009 Md. PSC LEXIS 39, at *2. The Commission ultimately approved the transaction, with conditions.

Figure 3.3 displays this complexity in simplified form. This theoretical holding company, made possible by the repeal of PUHCA 1935, owns five sub-holding companies, each playing a different commercial role. Traditional Utility owns retail utilities in California and New Jersey, each one performing for captive customers the traditional functions of generation, transmission, distribution and retail marketing. Wholesale Generation owns generating companies that sell in diverse wholesale markets. Retail Marketing owns retail electric marketing companies that sell in states that allow retail competition. Unrelated Companies owns a bank and an oil company. Service Companies has subsidiaries that provide fuel purchasing, financing, plant operations and general services to the other subsidiaries. This holding company system mixes utility and non-utility businesses, monopoly and competitive businesses.

A holding company system's post-acquisition picture—business activities, corporate structure and financial structure—affects the affiliated utilities' performance. Chapters 1 and 2 addressed the transaction's birth: how buyer and seller choose each other and decide the transaction price, in a monopoly context undisciplined by competition. This chapter has described some effects of that birth, when repeated dozens of times over thirty years: the concentration of franchise ownership and the complication of the business structure. Concentration and complication affect utility performance. Injecting non-utility businesses into the utility's family, vesting control over utility finance decisions in executives with potentially conflicting priorities, expecting that the utilities will provide predictable cash to fund other activities—all these factors combine to create risks of economic waste, disproportionate allocation of gains, weakened competition and direct customer harm. We will address those concerns in Part II.

PART II

The harms: economic waste, misallocation of gain, competitive distortion, customer risks and costs

Part I explained the transactions: sales of public franchises for private gain, undisciplined by effective competition, leading to a concentrated, complicated industry that no one intended. Thirty years of these transactions have brought four major harms.

Permanent economic waste: Effective competition aligns price with performance. Because franchised utilities don't face competition, they choose acquirers based on price instead of performance. Chapter 4 explains that mergers undisciplined by competition necessarily under-produce value compared to couplings disciplined by competition. Non-competitive mergers preclude competitive mergers, causing permanent economic waste. Regulators accept this inefficiency when they require only no net harm rather than best benefit-cost ratio. They then define harm incorrectly—most importantly by ignoring opportunity cost.

Diversion of gain from ratepayers to shareholders: The acquirer pays a premium to buy control of the target utility's franchise. Chapter 5 shows that although the franchise's value comes largely from state government decisions mandating customer captivity, the premium goes largely to the target's shareholders.

Distorted competition: Horizontal combinations increase the merging companies' market share while reducing the number of competitors. Vertical combinations enable the combined companies to control inputs that non-merging competitors need. Chapter 6 explains that both merger types enable the combined company to act anticompetitively, by discriminating against or excluding competitors. But even without acting anticompetitively, the merged company will have unearned advantages over their competitors—government-granted advantages that prevent competition on the merits.

Hierarchical conflict, causing harm to customers: A multi-utility, multi-business holding company has strategic objectives that conflict with its utilities' obligation to serve. Seated atop the corporate hierarchy, the holding company has the power and incentive to align the utility's major decisions with the holding company's business purposes. Chapter 7 describes the risks: rates exceeding the reasonable cost of service, utility subsidiaries weakened by the acquirer's acquisition debt, and contagion from the non-utility affiliates' business risks. Among the solutions: limits on business risks, ring-fencing, separation of utility from non-utility businesses, guardrails against holding company interference in utility decisions, service quality metrics and enforcement tools.

4. Suboptimal couplings cause economic waste

Franchised monopoly utilities face no competition for customers. So in choosing acquirers, they elevate price over performance. Better performers lose out to higher payers. Regulators accept this misplaced priority; instead of insisting on the most cost-effective coupling they focus on avoiding harm. Their harm analysis is wrong as well, because they treat merger costs inconsistently while counting customer benefits incorrectly. These practices—corporate and regulatory—waste economic resources.

4.1 BY CHOOSING ACQUIRERS BASED ON PRICE, TARGET UTILITIES LEAVE PERFORMANCE GAINS BEHIND

Where a target sells services in a competitive market, its rational acquirer will pay no more than the net present value of the earnings expected from that market. The highest offer will come from the most cost-effective acquirer. The interests of acquirer, target and customers align; the economy gains. A utility monopoly faces no similar competitive discipline. The acquisition price will reflect the parties' prediction of earnings not from market prices but from commission-set prices—prices they hope to keep above the normal cost of service. The acquirer's and target's interests diverge from the customers' interests. This result wastes economic resources in three ways.

4.1.1 Opportunity Cost

Selecting an acquirer based on price means ignoring acquirers that could perform better. The decision diverts resources from more productive uses. It causes opportunity cost. "[T]he opportunity cost of an item—what you must give up in order to get it—is its true cost."[1] Opportunity cost is opportunity lost—a permanent loss to the economy. It is waste. And the waste includes not only the foregone benefits from a more productive transaction, but also the excess dollars paid by the acquirer to win the target—dollars the acquirer could

---

[1]   PAUL KRUGMAN & ROBIN WELLS, MICROECONOMICS 7 (4th ed. 2015).

have invested more productively. The waste occurs because the transacting parties' self-interests, undisciplined by competition, diverge from the public interest. For the target, choosing the highest offer was rational. From a public interest perspective, the decision was irrational.

4.1.2   Economic Rent vs. Dynamic Efficiency

Under effective competition, a company that incurs opportunity cost loses out to competitors that don't. But a utility target faces no competition, so it doesn't lose out. When the target merges suboptimally, the opportunity cost falls on customers because they forgo the benefits of a more efficient coupling. They forgo those benefits because regulators set post-merger rates based on the merged company's costs, rather than on the costs of that more efficient coupling. Because the approved rate exceeds that lower cost, because it exceeds the cost level that competition would have produced, the approved rate is an excessive rate.

When a price exceeds a competitive price, economists call the excess "economic rent": technically, a "return to a factor of production in excess of what would be needed to keep [that factor] in the market"; alternatively, "excessive returns to market activity that would have occurred anyway in their absence."[2] Translation: economic rent arises from activity that is both economically inefficient and competitively unsustainable. Because the rent is competitively unsustainable, the target can seek and receive this rent only because of its monopoly position. Economic rents are "statically unproductive"—they produce nothing good. Worse, "the allocation of time and energy to the pursuit of rents ... hurts productivity by diverting that capital away from more innovative pursuits."[3] So even reducing the post-merger rates to reflect the economic loss, thereby causing the post-acquisition company to bear the opportunity cost it caused, does not eliminate the waste.[4]

---

[2]   Jason Furman & Peter Orszag, *A Firm-Level Perspective on the Role of Rents in the Rise in Inequality, in* TOWARD A JUST SOCIETY: JOSEPH STIGLITZ & TWENTY-FIRST CENTURY ECONOMICS 19, 21 (Martin Guzman ed., 2018), http://gabriel-zucman.eu/files/teaching/FurmanOrszag15.pdf.

[3]   *Id.*

[4]   *See, e.g.*, Robert S. Pindyck, *Sunk Costs and Real Options in Antitrust Analysis*, 1 ISSUES COMP. L. & POL'Y 619, 626–27 (2008) ("When a firm makes an irreversible investment expenditure, it exercises its option to invest. It gives up the possibility of waiting for new information to arrive that might affect the desirability or timing of the expenditure; it cannot disinvest should market conditions change adversely. This lost option value is an opportunity cost that must be included as part of the total cost of the investment. As a result, the [net present value] rule 'Invest when the value of a unit of capital is at least as large as its purchase and installation cost' must be modified. The

Now suppose the target utility monopoly changed its priorities, choosing acquirers based on performance instead of price. Competing acquirers would lower their offer prices, because they would have to devote more resources to competing on performance. The economy would gain, because dollars would flow toward productivity rather than rent. The target utility might still receive rent, but

> rents can be dynamically efficient: for example, our patent system effectively promises monopoly rents to innovators should they successfully bring a new technology to market. While the patent-protected rent is not necessary to encourage a producer to sell, it is designed to encourage the initial innovation that leads to the product in the first place, with benefits for aggregate productivity.[5]

A utility merger involves no inventor or innovator, no one risking career and capital to create some benefit deserving a patent. A utility merger involves only a franchised monopoly, awarded by government decades ago for reasons unconnected to performance. Acquisitions of utility monopolies, when based on price instead of performance, transfer economic rent but produce no necessary gain in dynamic efficiency.

4.1.3 Portfolio Risk

By selecting their acquirers based on price, target utilities become members of higher-risk holding company systems. Exelon bought PHI, and NextEra sought to buy the Texas utility Oncor, in part to balance their higher-risk generation holdings with lower-risk utility franchises. This private portfolio benefit—using the target utility as an investment hedge against other risks—is a value to the acquirer. The acquirer reflects that value in its acquisition price offer. So the more risks the acquirer has before the acquisition—and the more risks it intends to take on after the acquisition—the more it will value the hedge, the more it will raise its price offer and thus the more attractive the acquirer will be to the target. Selling control of their low-risk utility to a higher-risk acquirer benefits the target's shareholders while causing new risks to the target's customers.[6]

---

value of the unit must exceed the purchase and installation cost, by an amount equal to the value of keeping the investment option alive.").

[5] Furman & Orszag, *supra* note 2, at 19–21.
[6] We will describe those customer risks in Chapters 7.3 and 7.4.

4.1.4   Selection Based on Price: a Violation of Legal Duty

A utility has an obligation to serve at "lowest feasible cost";[7] to "operate with all reasonable economies";[8] and to use "all available cost saving opportunities."[9] By selecting its acquirer based on price instead of performance, the target violates those duties. It denies its customers what they pay for: service at a quality and cost that replicates competitive market outcomes.

Target companies say they seek the highest price to satisfy their fiduciary obligation. But as Chapter 1.2.1 explained, that "auctioneer" obligation exists only when the board has actually decided to sell the company. A board has no fiduciary obligation to sell the company just to produce shareholder gain. Even if a fiduciary duty did exist, that duty is subject to other statutory and regulatory duties. Otherwise companies could spill hazardous waste, trade with forbidden countries and hire children, all to comply with an asserted fiduciary duty to maximize profit. Whatever corporate law duty a target board has to maximize its shareholders' wealth is constrained by its utility law duty to provide customers with the most cost-effective service. Bidding out the franchise based on price instead of performance violates that obligation.

In competitive markets, a target's urge to get the highest price meets a competitive reality: paying an excessive price leaves the acquirer unable to serve its customers without raising prices or cutting quality. Market competition constrains fiduciary responsibility. Regulation must do the same.

Won't the highest offer price necessarily come from the most efficient company?[10] The answer could be yes, for three possible reasons. First, the bidder able to cause the most cost reductions—assuming it can keep the savings—would expect the highest stream of future earnings. Second, the bidder with the best history of operational efficiencies might have the largest cash reserve. Third, the bidder with the best performance reputation might be able to attract debt and equity financing at the lowest cost. Each of these factors could

---

[7]   Potomac Elec. Power Co. v. Pub. Serv. Comm'n, 661 A.2d 131, 137 (D.C. 1995).

[8]   El Paso Nat. Gas Co. v. FPC, 281 F.2d 567, 573 (5th Cir. 1960).

[9]   *Midwestern Gas Transmission Co. v. East Tenn. Nat. Gas Co.*, 36 F.P.C. 61, 70 (1966), *aff'd sub nom.* Midwestern Gas Transmission Co. v. FPC, 388 F.2d 444 (7th Cir. 1968).

[10]   This argument—and it is only an argument—appeared in the Rebuttal Testimony of John Reed at 18–19, 35, Great Plains Energy-Westar Energy Merger I, Docket No. 16-KCPE-593-ACQ (Kan. Corp. Comm'n filed Jan. 10, 2017) (stating, as support for GPE's initial offer for Westar, that "the acquirer that is most likely to be able to create sustainable value and remain financially strong, is able to bid the highest"; and that "as a general matter, a high price reveals a greater degree of confidence by GPE's Board of Directors and shareholders that the merged company will be able to generate synergies that will benefit both customers and shareholders").

support the highest offer price. This reasoning is worth considering conceptually, but no merger applicant has proven it factually. Counter-explanations are equally plausible. The acquirer could be basing its high-price offer on its expectation of persuading regulators to set rates above its actual costs—in ways Chapter 5.3.2 will explain. The acquirer's cash reserves could have come not from its performance skills but from the government-assisted revenues it gets from its other utility subsidiaries. Or the cash could have come from its non-utility subsidiaries—companies that had unearned competitive advantages due to their association with their holding company's other retail monopolies. These factors have no necessary connection to performance.

* * *

Competitive markets align price with performance. Monopoly markets don't. Utility acquisitions based on price consolidate the industry in the hands of the best financed rather than the most skilled. No commission has commented on, let alone corrected, the target utility's practice of placing price before performance.

4.2   "NO HARM": THE WRONG BENEFIT-COST RATIO

A utility merger results from three distinct decisions: the target's decision to sell, the acquirer's decision to buy and the regulator's decision to approve. Each entity considers benefits and costs. But they do it differently. Whereas acquirer and target seek for their shareholders the highest possible ratio of benefit to cost, commissions require for the customers only that benefits not be less than cost. This lower, "no-harm" standard conflicts with regulation's central purpose: to produce results comparable to competition.

Commissions address a merger's benefits and costs at two distinct stages: at the merger approval stage, to see if the transaction satisfies the statute; and at the ratemaking stage, to decide whether and when to reflect the benefits and costs in rates. We discuss the approval stage here; the ratemaking stage in Chapter 7.2.

4.2.1   The Investors' Standard: Highest Possible Return

Investment advisors don't recommend deals that cause no harm. Instead they ask: Will this investment yield a return on investment (i.e., a benefit-cost ratio) at least as large as alternative investments with comparable risks? The same reasoning applies to corporate acquisitions. The highest possible return standard applies to both sides of the transaction. The target looks for the highest possible price; the acquirer looks for the highest possible return. No investor, no acquirer of utilities, no target shareholder assesses a transaction using a no-harm standard.

4.2.2   The Commissions' Standard: No Harm, with Variations

In utility mergers, no regulatory commission seeks biggest bang for buck. The dominant standard is no harm, with three modest variations: no harm plus a defined benefit, no harm plus some undefined benefit, and some harm if outweighed by benefit. Here are examples of each type.

4.2.2.1 No harm

The Federal Power Act (FPA) requires mergers to be "consistent with the public interest."[11] FERC interprets this phrase to mean no "adverse effects" on wholesale ratepayers, on transmission customers, or on the Commission's authority to regulate.[12] FERC conditions its merger approvals "only when needed to address specific, transaction-related harm."[13]

What is harm? FERC sees three possible types: "unnecessary rate increases," "inhibit[ion of] rate reductions," and the merged entity's failure to "operate economically and efficiently." To offset these harms, FERC requires merger applicants to offer "ratepayer protection mechanisms": short-term rate freezes or rate reductions. While some applicants refer to these mechanisms as merger benefits, their explicit purpose is to offset harm.[14]

---

[11]   Federal Power Act § 203(a)(4), 16 U.S.C. § 824b(a)(4).

[12]   Order No. 592, *Inquiry Concerning the Commission's Merger Policy Under the Federal Power Act; Policy Statement*, F.E.R.C. Stats. & Regs. ¶ 31,044, 61 Fed. Reg. 68,595, 68,595-601 (1996) [hereinafter *1996 Merger Policy Statement*], *reconsideration denied*, Order No. 592-A, 79 F.E.R.C. ¶ 61,321, 62 Fed. Reg. 33,341 (1997).

[13]   *Entergy Gulf States-Calcasieu Power Merger*, 121 F.E.R.C. ¶ 61,182 at P 71 (2007). *See also Duke Energy-Cinergy Merger*, 113 F.E.R.C. ¶ 61,297 at P 82 (2005) (stating that the Commission "will only condition merger approval when there would otherwise be harm to competition").

[14]   *1996 Merger Policy Statement*, *supra* note 12, at text accompanying nn. 39–40 and at text following n.44 (describing the ratepayer protection mechanisms as protections against rate increases). For a detailed critique of FERC's approach to merger harm, see generally Scott Hempling, *Inconsistent with the Public Interest: FERC's Three Decades of Deference to Electricity Consolidation*, 39 Energy L.J. 233 (2018).

Turning to states: Like FERC, Missouri has required only that mergers be "not detrimental to the public."[15] Illinois's statute requires the Commission to find that the transaction will not, among other things,

> diminish the utility's ability to provide adequate, reliable, efficient, safe and least-cost public utility service;

> result in the unjustified subsidization of non-utility activities by the utility or its customers; ...

> significantly impair the utility's ability to raise necessary capital on reasonable terms or to maintain a reasonable capital structure; ...

> likely ... have a significant adverse effect on competition in those markets over which the Commission has jurisdiction; [or]

> likely ... result in any adverse rate impacts on retail customers.[16]

Meanwhile, the Texas Commission has held that a merger must not cause a "concentration of market power," "impede competition," or be "used as a means to evade regulation" or cause ratepayers costs unrelated to benefits.[17] Like the Illinois statute, the now-repealed Public Utility Holding Company Act (PUHCA) of 1935 identified the harms to prohibit. It required the SEC to reject a transaction if

> such acquisition will tend towards interlocking relations or the concentration of control of public-utility companies, of a kind or to an extent detrimental to the public interest or the interest of investors or consumers;

> in case of the acquisition of securities or utility assets, the consideration, including all fees, commissions, and other remuneration, to whomsoever paid, to be given, directly or indirectly, in connection with such acquisition is not reasonable or does not bear a fair relation to the sums invested in or the earning capacity of the utility assets to be acquired or the utility assets underlying the securities to be acquired; or

> such acquisition will unduly complicate the capital structure of the holding-company system of the applicant or will be detrimental to the public interest or the interest of investors or consumers or the proper functioning of such holding-company system.[18]

---

[15] In *Great Plains Energy-Kansas City Power & Light Merger*, 2008 Mo. PSC LEXIS 693, the Commission referred to a regulation using this language. The regulation has since been rescinded. Mo. CODE REGS. ANN. tit. 4, § 240-3.115(1)(D) (rescinded 2019).

[16] 220 ILL. COMP. STAT. 5 / 7-204.

[17] Southwestern Public Service-PSColorado Merger, 1997 Tex. PUC LEXIS 4, at *6.

[18] Public Utility Holding Company Act of 1935 § 10(b)(1)–(3), 15 U.S.C. § 79j(b)(1)-(3) (repealed 2005).

PUHCA 1935 section 10(c)(1) also prohibited any transaction that was "detrimental to the carrying out of the provisions of section 11."[19] Section 11, in turn, limited every holding company system to a "single integrated public-utility system" and certain types of related businesses.[20]

4.2.2.2 No harm plus a defined benefit

The repealed PUHCA 1935 required utility acquisitions to have a specific benefit; namely, to "serve the public interest by tending towards the economical and efficient development of an integrated public-utility system."[21]

4.2.2.3 No harm plus an undefined benefit

Along with prohibiting harm, some states require benefits but do not define the type.

Maryland's statute requires each merger to be "consistent with the public interest, convenience, and necessity, including benefits and no harm to consumers."[22] The Commission must consider eleven statutory factors, plus a catchall:

(i)   the potential impact of the acquisition on rates and charges paid by customers and on the services and conditions of operation of the public service company;

(ii)   the potential impact of the acquisition on continuing investment needs for the maintenance of utility services, plant and related infrastructure;

(iii) the proposed capital structure that will result from the acquisition, including allocation of earnings from the public service company;

(iv)   the potential effects on employment by the public service company;

(v)   the projected allocation of any savings that are expected to the public service company between stockholders and rate payers;

(vi)   issues of reliability, quality of service and quality of customer service;

(vii) the potential impact of the acquisition on community investment;

(viii) affiliate and cross-subsidization issues;

(ix)   the use or pledge of utility assets for the benefit of an affiliate;

(x)   jurisdictional and choice of law issues;

---

[19]   *Id.* § 10(c)(1).

[20]   *Id.* § 11(b)(1).

[21]   *Id.* § 10(c)(2). Technically, the restriction of section 10(c)(2) was triggered when a person (such as a holding company) already owning one utility subsidiary sought to acquire a second. *Id.* § 9(a)(2). *See* Wisconsin's Envtl. Decade, Inc. v. SEC, 882 F.2d 523 (D.C. Cir. 1989) (invalidating SEC's approval of a corporate reorganization that placed a new holding company above two existing utilities, where the transaction would produce no changes in the operations or functioning of an already integrated system). The author represented the petitioner. On remand, the SEC found benefits in the form of financing flexibility.

[22]   MD. CODE ANN., PUB. UTIL. § 6-105(g).

(xi) whether it is necessary to revise the Commission's ring fencing and code of conduct regulations in light of the acquisition; and

(xii) any other issues the Commission considers relevant to the assessment of the acquisition in relation to the public interest, convenience and necessity.[23]

The Maryland Commission has distilled these twelve factors into three elements: (a) consistency with the public interest, convenience and necessity; (b) receipt by the utility's retail customers of "certain and direct benefits from the transaction, in their capacity as customers rather than members of the general public"; and (c) no harm to the utility's retail customers.[24]

The Pennsylvania Commission requires "some affirmative benefit to the public," along with the "lack of any adverse effect on the public."[25] Similarly, the D.C. Commission requires that mergers "'benefit the public rather than merely leave it unharmed." There must be "direct and traceable financial benefits to ... ratepayers."[26] The Texas Commission requires that the transaction, besides "not unduly harm[ing] or act[ing] as a detriment to the public interest," must also "at a minimum, anticipate and guarantee specific levels of cost savings and service improvements." The merging companies must "do more than promise cost savings"; the transaction should "result in improvement of service."[27]

4.2.2.4 Harm is permissible if outweighed by benefit

While the above-described jurisdictions prohibit harm, the FCC allows harm if outweighed by benefits. It "employ[s] a balancing test weighing any potential public interest harms of the proposed transaction against any potential public interest benefits."[28]

* * *

These regulatory approaches have a common feature: benefits must at least equal cost, but they need bear no particular positive relationship to cost. This

---

[23] *Id.* § 6-105(g)(2).

[24] FirstEnergy-Allegheny Energy Merger, 2011 Md. PSC LEXIS 5, at *2.

[25] UGI Utilities-PPL Gas Merger, 2008 Pa. PUC LEXIS 58, at *10–11 (citing City of York v. Pub. Util. Comm'n, 295 A.2d 825 (Pa. 1973)).

[26] Pepco-New RC Merger, 2002 D.C. PUC LEXIS 375, at *21, *27 (interpreting D.C. Code § 34-504).

[27] Southwestern Public Service-PSColorado Merger, 1997 Tex. PUC LEXIS 4, at *7–8.

[28] AT&T-Cellco Merger, 25 FCC Rcd. 8704, 8716 ¶ 22 (2010) (applying sections 214(a) and 310(d) of the Communications Act).

lack of specificity contrasts with investors' insistence on the highest feasible ratio of benefit to cost.

4.2.3   Regulatory Error: Merger Competition Discouraged, Regulatory Principles Violated

Comparing the investor approach with the regulatory approach reveals two differences: the benefit-cost ratio, and the elements compared in that ratio.

The benefit-cost ratio: The no-harm standard means a benefit-cost ratio of 1:1, or slightly better than 1:1 (with no guidance on how much better). For an investor, a benefit-cost ratio of 1:1 means a gain of exactly zero. Zero gain satisfies commissions; it would get any money manager fired.[29]

The comparison: The no-harm standard looks only inward; it compares only the costs and benefits of the transaction itself. The investor's maximum-return standard looks outward; it compares the transaction's benefit-cost ratio to the ratio of all feasible alternatives. Looking outward induces objectivity. Looking inward relies on subjectivity, because it looks only at the companies proposing the transaction.

The no-harm standard also conflicts with elementary principles of both competition and regulation.

Competition: Effective competition forces continuous improvement, from horses to stage coaches to street cars to buses to jet engines; from telegrams to telephones to faxes to cell phones to the internet to the world wide web. The $1500 paid for a computer thirty years ago[30] buys a better one today. In competition, no company succeeds by saying it will make the customer no worse off—not when its competitors promise customers the best deal for their money. The no-harm standard denies customers that commonplace benefit.

---

[29]   This difference was captured in a back-and-forth FERC had with American Electric Power. As Chapter 4.2.2.1 explained, merger applicants seeking to satisfy FERC's requirement of "ratepayer protection mechanisms" had to offer wholesale customers only modest rate freezes or rate reductions, and those only for a few years. FERC proposed to prohibit applicant-imposed time limits on these offers. AEP resisted, arguing that a prohibition would "put the Commission back in the position of weighing the costs and benefits of mergers." Agreeing with AEP, the Commission allowed merger applicants to impose time limits. *Policy Statement on Hold Harmless Commitments*, 155 F.E.R.C. ¶ 61,189 at P 74 (2016) [hereinafter *2016 Policy Statement*] (FERC paraphrasing AEP's position).

[30]   The author's first computer, bought in 1987 for $1500, was the Toshiba 1100T+: two 3½-inch disk drives, no hard drive, no color, no modem. To that portable Toshiba, along with WordPerfect 4.2 (may it rest in peace) and Neil Larson's miraculous Maxthink, the author owes his career.

If commissions required merger applicants to act like competitive companies—to prove that their transaction will produce for customers a higher benefit-cost ratio than all feasible transactions—target utilities would have to select acquirers based on performance rather than price. Competing for the target's favor, each contestant would bid more customer benefits, up to the point where its own benefit-cost ratio fell below the return available from other investments. Mergers designed to produce maximum benefit to customers would replace those designed to produce maximum gain to shareholders. Regulation would replicate competition.

A regulatory standard that replicates competition helps shareholders as well as customers. Suppose that as a condition of merger approval, a commission required the impossible: (a) trim all trees monthly, (b) hire customer care reps who speak three languages fluently, but (c) don't raise rates for ten years. The unfairness is obvious—because no competitive market would demand those results. The public interest standard protects the utility from supra-competitive obligations. Symmetry requires that it protect the consumer from sub-competitive outcomes.

As for commissions that require some benefit: by leaving "some" undefined, these commissions set no standard by which to judge the applicants' offer. When a commission approves a transaction with some benefits, what is it saying? Only three answers are possible: (a) any amount of benefit is sufficient, regardless of how small; (b) a benefit's sufficiency is defined by the applicant's willingness to offer it; or (c) a benefit is sufficient whenever the Commission says it is sufficient. Option (a) is arbitrary, option (b) is abdication, and option (c) is circular. None of the three serves the public interest.

Regulation: Under conventional cost-based ratemaking, rates must reflect only prudent costs—the least-costly, reliable means of achieving a given objective. Prudence review substitutes for competitive forces.[31] A prudent utility doesn't merely avoid harm; it uses the most economical means. Suppose a utility had to replace a widget whose operating cost was $10/hour. Suppose it then buys a $10/hour widget when an $8/hour widget of equal quality was

---

[31] *See* Tutorial § 4.1. *See also Midwestern Gas Transmission Co. v. East Tenn. Nat. Gas Co.*, 36 F.P.C. 61, 70 (1966), *aff'd sub nom.* Midwestern Gas Transmission Co. v. FPC, 388 F.2d 444 (7th Cir. 1968) ("Managements of unregulated business subject to the free interplay of competitive forces have no alternative to efficiency. If they are to remain competitive, they must constantly be on the lookout for cost economies and cost savings. Public utility management, on the other hand, does not have quite the same incentive."). The Commission later rescinded its decision on unrelated grounds. *Knoxville Utils. Bd. v. East Tenn. Nat. Gas Co.*, 40 F.P.C. 172 (1968). For a detailed discussion of prudence, see SCOTT HEMPLING, REGULATING PUBLIC UTILITY PERFORMANCE: THE LAW OF MARKET STRUCTURE, PRICING AND JURISDICTION, ch. 6.C (American Bar Association 2013).

available. If the utility said, "We were prudent because we caused no harm," it would be laughed out of the hearing room. The commission would disallow $2/hour in costs. Prudence is not "no harm"; prudence is economically efficient conduct. Applied to mergers, the prudence standard requires merger applicants to prove that the merger's cost is the least-cost means of achieving a guaranteed benefit. No-harm doesn't cut it.

Recall the concept of opportunity cost. Disregarding opportunity cost necessarily leads to inefficient outcomes. The no-harm standard disregards opportunity cost—the benefits forgone by not requiring maximum benefits. It does so by mis-defining "harm" to exclude opportunity cost. This error should come as no surprise: "Even economists have trouble equating opportunity costs with out-of-pocket costs. ... Opportunity costs are vague and abstract when compared to handing over actual cash."[32]

4.2.4   Judicial Error: Misunderstanding "Public Interest"

The preceding subsection reasoned that the statutory public interest standard requires regulators to replace no-harm with biggest-bang-for-buck. FERC and the courts have said otherwise. Early in the current merger era, FERC held that merger applicants need show only that the "probable merger benefits ... add up to substantially more than the costs of the merger."[33] And an old Ninth Circuit decision held that the Federal Power Act's merger standard, "consistent with the public interest," does not "connote a public benefit to be derived or suggest the idea of a promotion of the public interest. The thought conveyed is merely one of compatibility."[34]

These decisions ignore a central principle: that the public interest served by regulation is the interest in protecting consumers from suppliers who face no competition. That protection has meaning only if it produces results that

---

[32]   RICHARD H. THALER, MISBEHAVING: THE MAKING OF BEHAVIORAL ECONOMICS 17 (2015).

[33]   *Northeast Utilities-Public Service of New Hampshire Merger*, 56 F.E.R.C. ¶ 61,269, at p. 61,994 (1991) (quoting *Utah Power & Light-PacifiCorp Merger*, 47 F.E.R.C. ¶ 61,209, at p. 61,750 (1989)), *aff'd on reh'g*, 59 F.E.R.C. ¶ 61,042 (1992), *upheld sub nom.* Northeast Utils. Serv. Co. v. FERC, 993 F.2d 937 (1st Cir. 1993). *See also* 47 F.E.R.C. ¶ 61,209, at p. 61,750 and n. 93 ("[A]pplicants need not show a positive benefit of the merger. Rather, they need only show that the merger is compatible with the public interest."); Boston Gas-Essex Gas Merger, 2010 Mass. PUC LEXIS 46, at *34 ("Given the level of anticipated savings and the assurance that none of the merger-related costs will be borne by ratepayers, we conclude that it is not unreasonable for the Companies to have foregone a formal cost-benefit analysis.").

[34]   Pac. Power & Light Co. v. FPC, 111 F.2d 1014, 1016 (9th Cir. 1940) (reversing a Commission decision requiring a showing of benefit).

replicate competition. Competition produces constant improvement—positive benefit. The Ninth Circuit's decision makes a distinct error. Interpreting "consistent with the public interest" as requiring no improvement, the court focused on the term "consistent" rather than the phrase "public interest." True, "consistent" can mean "no better than"—as when a baseball pitcher's earned run average of 3.85 this year is "consistent" with his 3.85 last year.[35] But in the Federal Power Act, section 203 pairs the adjectival phrase "consistent with" with the noun phrase "public interest." In the context of utility regulation, the term "public interest" doesn't mean "no worse than last year." If regulation strives to emulate effective competition, then "consistent with the public interest" cannot mean "no harm." It must mean results consistent with effective competition—specifically, all cost-effective improvement over the status quo. FERC has statutory discretion to determine what cost-effective improvements the public interest requires. But it does not have statutory discretion to say that "public interest" requires no improvement.[36]

* * *

Merger applicants describe their transactions as causing no harm while improving the status quo. But neither effective competition nor effective regulation stops at the status quo. Both aim to produce the most cost-effective performance. Because a merger transaction necessarily precludes some other transaction, because $300 million spent on an acquisition premium is $300 million not spent on energy efficiency or labor productivity, because the target company will choose the coupling that pays its shareholders the most rather

---

[35] For non-baseball fans: earned run average, for a given time period, is the average number of runs a pitcher allows per nine innings. Arithmetically: (earned runs/innings pitched) x 9.

[36] The Commission need not be "forever bound" by *Pacific Power & Light*. It can declare and explain a new interpretation if the statute's language supports that interpretation and if it considers how affected parties legitimately relied on the prior interpretation. *See* Verizon v. FCC, 740 F.3d 623, 636 (D.C. Cir. 2014) (holding that FCC "need not remain *forever* bound by" its prior statutory interpretation) (emphasis in original); Chevron U.S.A., Inc. v. Nat. Res. Def. Council, Inc., 467 U.S. 837 (1984) (requiring judicial deference to reasonable agency interpretations of statutes susceptible to multiple interpretations); Nat'l Cable & Telecomms. Ass'n v. Brand X Internet Servs., 545 U.S. 967 (2005) (holding that an agency interpretation valid under *Chevron* may not be invalidated by the court of appeals based on stare decisis). Less attractive, but available, is nonacquiescence, at least outside the Ninth Circuit. *See* Samuel Estreicher & Richard L. Revesz, *Nonacquiescence by Federal Administrative Agencies*, 98 YALE L.J. 679, 743 (1989) ("[E]ven if an agency must conform its administrative proceedings to the case law of the court of appeals to which review would lie, where this case law is inconsistent with the agency's policy, the agency can continue to press that policy in other circuits if it chooses to do so.").

than the one that benefits its customers the most, the no-harm standard denies customers what competition promises.

Moving forward: to apply their no-harm standard, and any of the other benefit-cost relationships just described, regulators must identify and assess the benefits and costs. The next two sections explain and assess how commissions make those decisions. It turns out that they treat merger costs inconsistently, and count customer benefits incorrectly.

4.3   COMMISSIONS TREAT MERGER COSTS INCONSISTENTLY

In assessing merger costs, commissions usually focus on only two categories: transaction costs and transition costs. We explain those concepts first. But there are bigger costs. Acquisition cost is the largest quantifiable cost; yet when commissions assess a transaction's benefit-cost relationship they usually ignore it. Five types of less quantifiable costs receive similarly short shrift.

4.3.1   Transaction Costs

Transaction costs are the costs to consummate—to reach agreement and get regulatory approvals. FERC defines this category to include the costs of

> securing an appraisal, formal written evaluation, or fairness opinions related to the transaction; structuring the transaction, negotiating the structure of the transaction, and obtaining tax advice on the structure of the transaction; preparing and reviewing the documents effectuating the transaction (e.g., the costs to transfer legal title of an asset, building permits, valuation fees, the merger agreement or purchase agreement and any related financing documents); the internal labor costs of employees and the costs of external, third-party, consultants and advisors to evaluate potential merger transactions, and once a merger candidate has been identified, to negotiate merger terms, to execute financing and legal contracts, and to secure regulatory approvals; obtaining shareholder approval (e.g., the costs of proxy solicitation and special meetings of shareholders); professional service fees incurred in the transaction (e.g., fees for accountants, surveyors, engineers, and legal consultants); and installation, integration, testing, and set up costs related to ensuring the operability of facilities subject to the transaction.[37]

---

[37]   *2016 Policy Statement, supra* note 29, at P 21. *See also* GTE-Bell Atlantic Merger, 2000 Cal. PUC LEXIS 398 (describing transaction costs as including legal and regulatory costs and investment banking fees—including the "costs for performing due diligence in connection with the merger, of preparing regulatory filings, and developing retention agreements with key management personnel to assure continuity of management throughout merger implementation").

Some commissions deny, or approve settlements denying, recovery of these costs, on the grounds that they provide no utility service.[38] Other states allow recovery up to the level of proven merger benefits, reasoning that recipients of merger benefits should bear the costs of achieving those benefits. This latter reasoning repeats the error of the no-harm standard, because making customers bear costs equal to the benefits wipes out those benefits. The economically rational approach would be to charge these costs to customers up to the amount that causes the transaction's benefit-cost ratio to fall below the ratio of the most efficient alternative.

4.3.2   Transition Costs

If transaction costs consummate the merger, transition costs implement it. To knit separate companies into one, the merged entity retains consultants, meshes information systems, consolidates headquarters, buys out some employees and relocates others, and pays for departing executives' parachutes. For FERC, the category includes costs

> incurred after the transaction is consummated, often over a period of several years. These costs include both the internal costs of employees spending time working on transition issues, and external costs paid to consultants and advisers to reorganize and consolidate functions of the merging entities to achieve merger synergies. These costs may also include both capital items (e.g., a new computer system or software, or costs incurred to carry out mitigation commitments accepted by the Commission in approving the transaction to address competition issues, such as the cost of constructing new transmission lines) and expense items (e.g., costs to eliminate redundancies, combine departments, or maximize contracting efficiencies).[39]

---

[38]   *See, e.g.*, CalPeco-Algonquin Merger, 2012 Cal. PUC LEXIS 259, at *49 (approving agreement not to recover transaction costs from customers, because the costs were "not related to the provision of electric service"); Northeast Utilities-NSTAR Merger, 2012 Conn. PUC LEXIS 47, at *28 (accepting settlement agreement that "[n]o transaction costs incurred to negotiate, draft, or execute the merger agreement, or to obtain the regulatory approvals required to consummate [the] transaction," will be recorded on the books of any Connecticut utility subsidiary); Conn. Light & Power Co., 1991 Conn. PUC LEXIS 115 (denying recovery of legal fees and expenses associated with regulatory approval of merger); Exelon-Constellation Energy Group Merger, 2012 Md. PSC LEXIS 12, at *153 (holding that merger will cause utility customers no "transaction-related harm" because all transaction costs will remain at the holding company level).

[39]   *2016 Policy Statement, supra* note 29, at P 23.

As with transaction costs, some commissions disallow them; others link their recovery to proven benefits.[40]

4.3.3   Acquisition Cost

4.3.3.1   Acquisition price vs. acquisition cost

Acquisition price and acquisition cost are two different things. Acquisition price is the price paid for the target's equity—the amount target stockholders receive for selling their stock. Acquisition cost—the total cost to the acquirer—is different, and higher. The 100 percent acquirer buys the entire enterprise. Since all utilities have debt, buying the entire enterprise means buying the stock plus taking on the debt. The sum of the two—the amount paid for the stock and the amount of debt taken on—is the "enterprise value." It is the acquirer's total acquisition cost.[41]

As with merger costs generally, the acquisition cost is relevant to commissions at two stages. At the acquisition stage, commissions assess the transaction's benefit-cost relationship for purposes of approval or disapproval. At the ratemaking stage, commissions determine whether and how to reflect the various acquisition costs in rates. We deal with each topic in turn.

4.3.3.2   Treatment of acquisition cost in merger approval decisions

Whether a commission uses the investor standard (highest possible ratio of benefit to cost) or the no-harm standard (benefit-cost ratio not less than 1:1), the "cost" variable must include acquisition cost. No one buys a rental property if the expected rent revenue just covers operating costs. If the rents don't also recover, and produce a return on, the acquisition cost over some reasonable time, the purchase makes no economic sense. Similarly, when a prospective acquirer determines a transaction's benefit-cost ratio, it will compute cost as total acquisition cost (acquisition price paid to target shareholders, plus debt assumed, plus transaction cost, plus transition cost).

---

[40]   *See, e.g.,* Cinergy-Duke Energy Merger, 2006 Ind. PUC LEXIS 91, at *13 (capping recovery of implementation costs for the first two post-merger years and requiring the utility to show that the costs were "prudent, reasonable and recurring").

[41]   Here's an illustration. In the originally proposed GPE-Westar transaction, GPE had agreed to give Westar shareholders, for each share of Westar stock, $51 in cash and about $9 in GPE common stock. That $60 in payment, multiplied by the 143.3 million Westar shares then outstanding, equals the total value paid to Westar shareholders, $8.6 billion. But Westar also had an outstanding debt of $3.6 billion. By paying Westar's shareholders $8.6 billion and taking on Westar's debt of $3.6 billion, GPE would incur a total purchase cost of $12.2 billion. That $12.2 billion was Westar's enterprise value.

Yet when comparing benefits to costs, commissions ignore acquisition cost. The likely reason: merger applicants normally don't seek, explicitly, to recover the purchase price from their customers.[42] Commissions therefore view acquisition cost as the acquirer's problem, not the customers' problem. But regulation's purpose is broader than just protecting customers from excess costs; regulation's purpose is to produce cost-effective performance. Only by including in the benefit-cost ratio all costs—along with applying the correct benefit-cost test—can a commission know whether a transaction is cost-effective.

4.3.3.3 Distinct issue: rate treatment of the acquisition premium

Having addressed how to treat acquisition cost at the approval stage, we turn to the ratemaking stage: Should commissions let the merged entity recover its acquisition cost in rates? The case law on this question focuses on the portion of the acquisition cost known as the control premium: the excess of purchase price paid to the target's shareholders over the market price of the target's shares. Those dollars do not represent capital expenditures made to provide utility service; they represent only a wealth transfer, from the acquirer's owners to the target's owners. Should ratepayers pay that cost?

4.3.3.3.1 Consistent principle: exclude the premium from rates

In paying a premium, the acquirer makes an investment. But charging ratepayers for that investment would detach rates from reality:

> If a utility were allowed to revalue its assets each time they changed hands, it could artificially inflate its rate base by selling and repurchasing assets at a higher cost, while recovering those costs from its ratepayers. Thus, ratepayers would be required to pay for the same utility plant over and over again. The sale of assets to artificially inflate rate base was an abuse that was prevalent in the 1920s and 1930s and such abuses could still occur.[43]

To prevent this abuse, regulators usually base rates on book value (original cost of the utility's assets, less accumulated depreciation); not on the purchase price paid by the acquirer. This conservative practice goes back to regulation's earliest days.[44] As the Louisiana Commission explained: "Because the premium

---

[42] Not directly, that is. Chapter 5.3.2 will explain how the post-acquisition company seeks to recover the acquisition cost indirectly.

[43] UtiliCorp United-St. Joseph Light & Power Merger, 2004 Mo. PSC LEXIS 233, at *5 (footnote omitted).

[44] *See, e.g.*, FED. TRADE COMM'N, UTILITY CORPORATIONS, S. DOC. No. 70-92, pt. 72-A (electric utilities) and pts. 84 A, B and C (gas utilities) (1st Sess. 1935); American Tel. & Tel. Co. v. United States, 299 U.S. 232 (1936); General Tel. Co. of the Midwest,

over book value adds nothing to the value of the plant serving ratepayers, the excess of the acquisition cost over the original cost in no way benefits the consumer and should not be included in rates."[45] Allowing rate recovery of the acquisition premium, "regardless òf the cost, [would] create[] a disincentive for the purchasing utility to minimize the amount of such premium."[46]

Though commissions' reasons for excluding the premium from rates are consistent, their actual treatment is not, as discussed next.

4.3.3.3.2 Variations in rate treatment

No recovery: Most commissions allow in rate base "only the original cost of utility plant to the first owner devoting the property to public service, adjusted for depreciation."[47]

Recovery depends on merger savings: Some states allow recovery of the premium up to some specified level of merger-caused cost reductions. The 1991 merger of Kansas Power & Light and Kansas Gas & Electric had a premium of $388 million. The Kansas Commission allowed rate recovery of $312 million, representing the level of reasonably anticipated merger savings.[48] And under the Natural Gas Act, FERC allows recovery, subject to

---

3 P.U.R.4th 113, 119–20 (Iowa Commerce Comm'n 1974); Dayton Power & Light Co., 21 P.U.R.4th 376, 381 (Ohio Pub. Util. Comm'n 1977); Southwestern Bell Tel. Co., 19 P.U.R.4th 1, 11 (Kan. Corp. Comm'n 1977); Rate-Making Treatment of Capital Gains Received from the Sale of a Public Utility, 104 P.U.R.4th 157 (Cal. Pub. Util. Comm'n 1989); Intrastate Access Charges and Subscriber Line Charges, 110 P.U.R.4th 376, 386 (Alaska Pub. Util. Comm'n 1990).

[45] Techne Electric-CLECO Merger, 1997 La. PUC LEXIS 200, at *39 (citing *General Tel. Co. of the Midwest*, 3 P.U.R.4th at 119). *See also* Consolidated Edison-Northeast Utilities Merger, 2000 Conn. PUC LEXIS 325, at *173 (explaining that if rates recovered the premium, "the buying and selling of utilities could escalate rates without benefit to ratepayers").

[46] *Consolidated Edison-Northeast Utilities Merger*, 2000 Conn. PUC LEXIS 325, at *173. *See also Locust Ridge Gas Co.*, 29 F.E.R.C. ¶ 61,052, at p. 61,114 (1984) ("A change in ownership alone does not increase the service value of a facility and so provides no basis for increasing the associated rate base and depreciation.").

[47] Great Plains Energy-Kansas City Power & Light Merger, 2008 Mo. PSC LEXIS 693, at *470 (*quoting* UtiliCorp *United-St. Joseph Light & Power Merger*, 2004 Mo. PSC LEXIS 233, at *4). *See also Consolidated Edison-Northeast Utilities Merger*, 2000 Conn. PUC LEXIS 325, at *173 ("The Department has not allowed recovery of acquisition premium costs through rates when utilities merge.").

[48] Kansas City Power & Light-Kansas Gas & Electric Merger, Consolidated Docket Nos. 172,745-u, 174,155-D (Kan. Corp. Comm'n Nov. 18, 1991). *See also* UtiliCorp United Inc., 127 P.U.R.4th 75 (Kan. Corp. Comm'n 1991) (noting that the utility agreed not to seek recovery of merger-related costs and acquisition premium except to the extent it can demonstrate and quantify savings in cost of service result-ing from the acquisition). The author advised the Kansas Commission in those two pro-

a "heavy" burden of proof: the pipeline must prove consumer benefits that are "tangible, non-speculative, and quantifiable in monetary terms."[49]

What is the rationale for allowing any recovery? Proponents argue that unless the acquirer pays a premium, no target will sell, so there would be no merger and thus no merger savings. They also argue that ratepayers should cover the cost necessary to produce the savings.[50] And the rationale for limiting the recovery to merger-caused savings? It disciplines the merging parties to find those savings, and then to make those savings happen.

Vermont's clawback of prior bailout: In 2007, the Northern New England Energy Corporation proposed to buy Green Mountain Power, a Vermont utility, for a $62 million premium. Seven years earlier, the Vermont Public Service Board had found Green Mountain Power's purchased power costs imprudent. To keep the company solvent, the Board allowed the imprudent costs in rates, but reserved the option of returning those dollars to customers should a later acquirer buy the utility at a premium. Northern New England Energy's proposal presented that opportunity. The Board approved the acquisition, conditioned on a "windfall sharing mechanism" that required the post-merger entity to spend $9.3 million of the premium on an Efficiency Fund whose projects would provide customer benefits.[51] And in a later merger, the Board viewed a $197 million premium as "unjust enrichment" of the target's shareholders, unless the merged entity contributed $20.9 million to a fund for energy efficiency, renewable and clean energy programs, demand resources and new technologies.[52]

---

ceedings. *See also* National Grid-KeySpan Merger, 2010 Mass. PUC LEXIS 28, at *42 (citing policy that "merger-related costs, such as acquisition premiums and transaction costs, may be recovered to the extent that there are savings resulting from the merger"). *Cf.* U.S. West Communications, 149 P.U.R.4th 416 (Colo. Pub. Util. Comm'n 1994) (denying recovery of premium due to lack of offsetting savings).

[49] Mo. Pub. Serv. Comm'n v. FERC, 601 F.3d 581, 584 (D.C. Cir. 2010) (quoting *Kansas Pipeline Co.*, 81 F.E.R.C. ¶ 61,005, at p. 61,018 (1997)).

[50] *See, e.g.*, Guidelines and Standards for Acquisitions and Mergers of Utilities, D.P.U. 93-167-A, 155 P.U.R.4th 320 (Mass. Dep't of Pub. Utils. 1994) (stating that regulators will consider rate recovery of the premium if disallowance would deter a merger that serves the public interest); Attorney General v. Dep't of Telecomms. & Energy, 780 N.E.2d 33, 39 (Mass. 2002) (recognizing regulators' policy of evaluating premiums case-by-case, given that the "theoretical basis ... for allowing a premium is that a transaction otherwise in the public interest would not occur" (quoting commission decision)).

[51] Green Mountain Power-New England Energy Merger, 2007 Vt. PUC LEXIS 74, at *4 n.4.

[52] Central Vermont Public Service-Gaz Metro Merger, 2012 Vt. PUC LEXIS 279, at *7–8, *85, *94.

Regulatory timing: If a commission does allow the post-acquisition company to recover the premium up to merger-created savings, at what point in time should the commission set the recoverable amount? In the Kansas Gas & Electric-Kansas Power & Light transaction, the Kansas Commission set the amount in the merger proceeding. The Iowa Board, in contrast, waited until the merged utility's first rate case, so it would have a complete record and more public participation.[53] Which procedure is better? My answer is neither. Kansas's procedure—deciding the recoverable amount in the merger case—reduces uncertainty but requires the Commission to estimate savings without sufficient information. Iowa's approach—deciding premium recovery post-consummation—leaves the merging parties uncertain about their financial fate. That uncertainty might cause some acquirers to keep the premium low, so as to limit their risk. But other acquirers might buy high, intending to argue in the later rate case that disallowance would weaken the company.[54]

I recommend a third approach: combine the merger case with a rate case. First determine whether the transaction satisfies the statutory standard. If the answer is yes, then hold a full rate case, where the to-be-merged entity presents full information on its cost structures with and without the merger. The rate case's rigor will strengthen the savings estimates, allowing a better-informed decision on the premium. Knowing then the premium's treatment, the companies can decide whether to complete the transaction.

4.3.3.3.3 Does disallowing the premium from rates protect customers sufficiently?

Though regulators disallow or limit premia, acquirers pay them anyway.[55] If the premium is excluded from rates, is it still a problem? The Montana and Missouri Commissions came out differently.

---

[53] MidAmerican Energy-Berkshire Hathaway Merger, 2000 Iowa PUC LEXIS 1558, at *9–10 (explaining that "[i]n a [merger] proceeding, only projected benefits are available"; also, general rate cases draw interventions from consumer groups, who are "not usually active in [merger] proceedings because rate issues are not being decided"). *See also* Aquila-Black Hills Merger, 2007 Iowa PUC LEXIS 341, at *28–29 (approving merger but reserving power to decide the premium recovery question in the future rate cases, unconstrained by the parties' settlement of the issue); Central Illinois Public Service-Union Electric Merger, 1997 Ill. PUC LEXIS 546 (deferring Applicants' proposed merger cost recovery plan to the next general rate proceeding and directing the utility to submit, within 12 months of the merger, a rate case filing reflecting all merger costs (including the premium) and merger cost savings).

[54] A tactic otherwise known as "Better to seek forgiveness than permission."

[55] *See, e.g., ITC Holdings Corp.,* 139 F.E.R.C. ¶ 61,112 (2012) (noting that ITC paid a premium of $330 million to buy transmission assets from Interstate Power and Light Company despite the certainty of non-recovery).

Montana: The Australian holding company Babcock & Brown Infrastructure, Ltd. (BBIL) sought to acquire NorthWestern Energy (the utility serving in Montana, South Dakota and Nebraska). BBIL would pay NorthWestern's shareholders a premium of $700 million. Because the Montana Commission prohibited premium recovery through rates, BBIL planned to recover the premium by making NorthWestern pay BBIL dividends. But the projected dividend payments would exceed NorthWestern's projected net earnings. The Commission rejected the transaction:

> No prudent business owner would make such a sizeable investment unless it could recover its costs. The obvious question is: How does BBIL plan to recover the acquisition premium? ... Ratepayers, as the source of NorthWestern's revenues, will foot the bill.[56]

And even if ratepayers didn't foot the bill, the dividending plan was "inappropriate and risky because having insufficient reserves on hand could adversely affect the utility's ability to provide adequate service."[57] Once NorthWestern paid all its retained earnings to BBIL, its only source of equity capital for new infrastructure would be BBIL. Given the financial needs of BBIL's many other subsidiaries, there was no guarantee that NorthWestern would get what it needed.

Missouri: UtiliCorp and St. Joseph's Power proposed to recover their $92 million premium to the extent they proved merger-related cost savings. In its 2000 order approving that merger, the Missouri Commission deferred the premium's rate treatment to the next general rate case—the Iowa approach described above.[58] But because the 2000 Order had made no finding about the premium's reasonableness, the Missouri Supreme Court remanded, holding that the premium's reasonableness was "relevant and critical" to whether the merger would be "detrimental to the public"—the statutory standard, and a concern independent of the rate treatment.[59] On remand the Commission revised its merger order in two ways. It denied rate recovery of the premium, but it found the premium reasonable because the merging companies had negotiated at arm's length.[60]

---

[56] NorthWestern Energy-Babcock & Brown Merger, 2007 Mont. PUC LEXIS 54, at *93–96 (citing expert testimony of John W. Wilson).

[57] *Id.*

[58] UtiliCorp United-St. Joseph Light & Power Merger, 2004 Mo. PSC LEXIS 233 (summarizing the Commission's 2000 reasoning).

[59] State *ex rel.* AG Processing, Inc. v. Pub. Serv. Comm'n, 120 S.W.3d 732, 736 (Mo. 2003).

[60] *UtiliCorp United-St. Joseph Light & Power Merger*, 2004 Mo. PSC LEXIS 233.

The Missouri decision had two problems. First, as Chapter 2.2.2 explained, when two monopoly utilities plan a merger they do not negotiate at arm's length. They are acting jointly, not adversarially. Second, the Missouri Commission did not address the problems identified by the Montana Commission: whether absorbing the premium rather than recovering it from ratepayers would weaken the combined company, or cause the holding company to drain the target company's retained earnings.

If acquirers don't recover the premium in rates explicitly, can they recover it implicitly? The answer is yes, by persuading the commission to allow excess earnings. Chapter 5.3.2 will describe several applicant strategies. One approach is to use low-cost debt to buy the target's equity, then persuade the commission to allow an equity-level return on that debt-financed equity. Recovering the premium indirectly creates problems no less serious than recovering it directly. Besides encouraging the acquirer to take on excess acquisition debt, the practice disconnects purchase price from true transactional economies.

The premium represents no physical equipment; it produces no electricity. It is an intangible asset, a line labeled "goodwill" on the asset side of the acquirer's balance sheet.[61] But to remain on that balance sheet, it must have economic value equal to the stated amount. That economic value, if any, is the expected increase in earnings from the acquisition. Expected does not mean earned. If expectations dim, if the expected earnings don't appear, accounting rules require the company to treat the goodwill asset as "impaired."[62] That means

---

[61] Officially, goodwill "represents the excess of cost over fair market value of identifiable net assets acquired through business purchases." AMERICAN INST. OF CERTIFIED PUB. ACCTS., U.S. GAAP FINANCIAL STATEMENTS: BEST PRACTICES IN PRESENTATION AND DISCLOSURE 51 (67th ed. 2013). *See also* FIN. ACCOUNTING STANDARDS BD., ACCOUNTING STANDARDS UPDATE: INTANGIBLES—GOODWILL AND OTHER (TOPIC 350), at 6–9 (2019); ROBERT LIBBY ET AL., FINANCIAL ACCOUNTING 421 (6th ed. 2009) ("For accounting purposes, goodwill is defined as the difference between the purchase price of a company as a whole and the fair market value of its net assets.").

[62] To detect and report impairment, accountants review goodwill at least annually, by applying a fair-value-based test. ... Goodwill is evaluated using a two-step impairment test at the reporting unit level. ... The first step compares the book value of a reporting unit, including goodwill, with its fair value, as determined by its discounted cash flows. If the book value of a reporting unit exceeds its fair value, we complete the second step to determine the amount of the goodwill impairment loss that we should record. In the second step, we determine an implied fair value of the reporting unit's goodwill by allocating the fair value of the reporting unit to all of the assets and liabilities other than goodwill (including any unrecognized intangible assets). The amount of impairment loss is equal to the excess of the book value of the goodwill over the implied fair market value of goodwill.

revising the acquirer's balance sheet—downwards. Consider these examples of goodwill impairments connected to utility acquisitions:

Qwest-U.S. West:	$41 billion	(2002)
AOL-Time Warner:	$54 billion	(2002)
Scottish Power-PacifiCorp:	£922 million	(2005)
AES-Dayton Power & Light Company:	$1.7-2.0 billion	(2012)[63]

4.3.4   Hard-to-quantify Costs

We have discussed transaction costs, transition costs and acquisition costs. There are four other types of cost, less quantifiable but no less important.

Diminution in management attention: As the holding company's acquisitions grow, its executives become responsible for more businesses, more assets, more debt and more risk. The attention they pay to each utility necessarily diminishes.

Risk-seeking investors: As the corporate family invests in ventures less financially secure than regulated monopoly service, the investor portrait can change. For conservative investors—those who buy-and-hold patiently, those who forty years ago invested in "utilities"—the holding company's stock is no longer an optimal investment. New investors can enter: those seeking higher-risk, higher-return opportunities. These new investors can pressure the holding company's leadership for more growth requiring more risks, worsening the attention-diminution problem.

Bond rating uncertainty: When the holding company has non-utility holdings, the utility can no longer count on consistently stable bond ratings. The traditional, predictable factors supporting those ratings—the utility's opera-

---

AM. INST. OF CERTIFIED PUB. ACCTS., *supra* note 61, at 51; *see also* FIN. ACCOUNTING STANDARDS BD., *supra* note 61, at 9–12. One treatise recommends testing goodwill for impairment no later than two years after the merger acquisition, if at the time of the transaction one of the following factors are present:
- A significant premium was paid over the market capitalization of the acquiree prior to its going into play or being acquired.
- The acquisition involved a clearly visible auction or bidding war.
- The amount of goodwill recorded is significant in relation to the purchase price.
- The purchase consideration was primarily in the form of the acquirer's stock.

JOSEPH M. MORRIS ET AL., MERGERS AND ACQUISITIONS: BUSINESS STRATEGIES FOR ACCOUNTANTS 171–72 (2d ed. 2000).

[63]   These examples come from Direct Testimony of Ralph C. Smith, Exhibit RCS-3, at 3-4, 6, 11, Iberdrola-UIL Holdings Merger, Docket No. 15-03-45 (Conn. Pub. Utils. Reg. Auth. filed May 11, 2015). The Scottish Power-PacifiCorp impairment related to discontinued PacifiCorp operations. *Id.* at 6. For the AES-Dayton Power & Light merger, total goodwill was about $2.6 billion. *Id.* at 13.

tional performance and its regulatory treatment—will be mixed in with the holding company's other risks.

Resistance to pro-competitive policy initiatives: Acquisition debt makes the holding company more dependent on stable utility earnings. That dependency can lead holding company executives to resist regulators' efforts to introduce competition, including removing entry barriers—such as incumbents' unearned advantages—that distort competition.[64]

Each of these factors causes costs; costs affect a transaction's benefit-cost ratio. But commissions don't weigh these costs systematically. Some commissions don't weigh them at all. Analysts can reasonably disagree over their magnitude, but that magnitude is not zero. Why commissions weigh them insufficiently is a subject for Part III.

4.4 REGULATORS COUNT CUSTOMER BENEFITS INCORRECTLY

We have contrasted two benefit-cost ratios. The investor approach requires the highest feasible ratio. The typical regulatory approach requires only that benefits marginally exceed cost, or at least not fall below cost. We then addressed how commissions treat and ought to treat costs: transaction costs, transition costs, acquisition costs and four less quantifiable costs—costs arising from diminished management attention, risk-seeking investors, uncertain bond ratings and incumbents' resistance to competition. We turn now to the benefits.

The key question is this: Are the benefits applicants claim uniquely attributable to their merger? That is, are they unachievable without the merger? If so, they should count in the benefit-cost ratio—if they are verifiable and guaranteed. But if the claimed benefits are achievable without the merger they should be excluded from the ratio. A benefit achievable without a merger is one that the target utility should have achieved already. To count that benefit as an offset to merger cost means the customers in effect bear that cost.

As with acquisition costs, merger benefits matter at two different stages. At the merger approval stage, commissions must decide whether benefits justify the cost—whether the merger is "worth it." A mistake at the approval stage means approving an uneconomic transaction or rejecting an economic transaction. At the ratemaking stage, commissions decide how and when to reflect the benefits in rates. A mistake at the ratemaking stage means charging ratepayers too much or too little. The remainder of this chapter addresses these issues.

---

[64] We will detail the harms to competition in Chapter 6.

4.4.1 Benefits Dependent on the Merger: Appropriate when Verified

By changing physical or administrative operations, a corporate combination can cause two companies to perform more cost-effectively together than apart. Typically labeled "merger efficiencies" or "merger synergies," these benefits can arise from multiple factors, including

> economies of scale or scope, technological complementarity, reduced transportation or other distribution costs, reduced capital costs, product line specialization, the deployment of scarce managerial talent across a wider portfolio of assets, and positive innovation effects due to the combination of research and development laboratories or intellectual property portfolios.[65]

By lowering rates or improving service, merger efficiencies help customers directly; they can help customers indirectly by spurring competitors to improve their performance.[66]

A merger-dependent benefit should count only if quantifiable and verifiable. Skepticism is appropriate: as scope expands, management control can decline; larger firms require more hierarchical layers, adding costs while reducing accountability; some acquirers replace experienced managers with inexperienced ones; and the integration of two companies can cause costs without necessarily increasing efficiency.[67] Commissions must distinguish between aspirations and commitments, while establishing clear consequences for non-achievement of the commitments. We discuss those matters now.

4.4.1.1 Difficulties quantifying and verifying benefits
Lacking a history of joint operation, two merging companies cannot predict merger savings with certainty. They often fall back on generic claims about

---

[65] Daniel A. Crane, *Rethinking Merger Efficiencies*, 110 Mich. L. Rev. 347, 355 (2011).

[66] Dep't of Justice & Fed. Trade Comm'n, Horizontal Merger Guidelines §10 (2010) [hereinafter 2010 Horizontal Merger Guidelines] (explaining that "two ineffective competitors [can] form a more effective competitor").

[67] Mark W. Frankena & Bruce M. Owen, Electric Utility Mergers: Principles of Antitrust Analysis 150-51 (1994) (citing numerous sources, including D. Ravenscraft & F.M. Scherer, *The Profitability of Mergers*, 7 Int'l J. Indus. Org. 101 (1989); D. Mueller, *Mergers and Market Share*, 67 Rev. Econ. & Stat. 259 (1985); A.M. Louis, *The Bottom Line on Ten Big Mergers*, Fortune, May 1982; Oliver E. Williamson, Markets and Hierarchies: Analysis and Antitrust Implications, chs. 2, 7 (1975); Raymond S. Hartman, *The Efficiency Effects of Utility Mergers: Lessons from Statistical Cost Analysis*, 17 Energy L.J. 425 (1996)) (explaining that expanding service territories without increasing the intensity of a system's use will not necessarily produce economies).

"synergies," "shared services," and "best practices." Commissions should reject these claims, because they lack (a) specific plans involving specific assets, operations and personnel; (b) metrics for achievement; and (c) methods for verifying achievement. The Maryland Commission called such claims "inherently speculative." The claimed cost savings, if any, are "likely [to] benefit ratepayers only as 'forgone requests for rate relief,' which we have previously held to be too intangible to qualify as a benefit."[68]

Commissions are especially skeptical of distant future benefits: "we believe the Legislature shared our recognition that the clearest of available crystal balls become translucent and eventually opaque as we look further into the future."[69] Regulators therefore should discount otherwise credible savings estimates to reflect the risk of non-achievement.[70] Distant future benefits also can cause intergenerational inequity. Mergers causing long-term costs—like management distraction, financial weakness and damage to competition—must offset those costs with long-term benefits. But if long-term benefits are unreliable, later customers lose out, while today's customers at least get the short-term benefits of rate reductions or rate freezes.

To solve the long-term problem in the Exelon-Constellation acquisition, the Maryland Commission sought to "provide an essentially even balance ($112 million v. $113.5 million) between short-term and long-term benefits to ratepayers." The "long-term benefits" included a required $113.5 million spent on energy efficiency and low-income energy assistance.[71] And the California Commission, applying a statute that expressly required long-term benefits, defined "long-term" to mean the utilities' "normal planning horizons." So in 1991 when Southern California Edison and San Diego Gas & Electric claimed future savings from deferring generation construction, the California

---

[68]   Exelon-Constellation Energy Group Merger, 2012 Md. PSC LEXIS 12, at *164 (quoting FirstEnergy-Allegheny Energy Merger, 2011 Md. PSC LEXIS 5, at *78).

[69]   Southern California Edison-San Diego Gas & Electric Merger, 1991 Cal. PUC LEXIS 253, at *23. *See also* AT&T-Bellsouth Merger, 22 FCC Rcd. 5662, 5770 ¶ 217 (2007) (finding that "benefits that are to occur in the distant future may be discounted or dismissed because, among other things, predictions about the more distant future are inherently more speculative than predictions about events that are expected to occur closer to the present"). *See also* Great Plains Energy-Westar Energy Merger I, 2017 Kan. PUC LEXIS 1142, at *44–47 ¶ 50–51 (rejecting Applicants' assumption that $344 million in annual savings would last forever).

[70]   FRANKENA & OWEN, *supra* note 67, at 150 (analogizing to financial assets, whose risks are reflected in interest rates; and explaining that "[d]iscount rates somewhat higher than a utility's cost of capital are not unreasonable, since there is a greater risk inherent in the estimates of cost savings than in a utility's regulated profit stream").

[71]   *Exelon-Constellation Energy Group Merger*, 2012 Md. PSC LEXIS 12, at *9, *165.

Commission required credible forecasts of savings "for at least several years into the next century."[72]

In evaluating merger efficiencies, commissions face information asymmetry. The merging firms control the information about their existing costs and capabilities, and about their plans for joint operations.[73] Commissions don't always know what they don't know. This asymmetry assists a specific applicant strategy: first persuade commissions to approve post-merger rates based on conservative savings estimates, then beat those estimates to produce extra earnings. But game-playing has risks. Project savings too conservatively, and risk losing the commission's support. Project savings too optimistically, and risk later rate disallowances for failing to achieve them.[74]

4.4.1.2 Common benefit claims and their challenges
Most merger efficiency claims fall into the six main categories described here. Each category has its uncertainties. Before crediting these claims, commissions need hard data.

1. Exploiting economies of scale: Merger applicants cite their ability to spread fixed costs over a larger customer base. No one disputes that combining companies can reduce duplicative administrative costs—billing, accounting, shareholder relations and fuel procurement—operations and maintenance.[75] But studies supporting these claims, usually performed by an applicant-paid consultant, have at least five problems.

First, working under tight deadlines (merger negotiations have drop-dead dates), the consultant does not gather data independently; he uses assumptions and numbers provided by the companies. The Great Plains Energy (GPE) consultant acknowledged that he based his savings estimates on data provided by Westar—the company whose shareholders would receive a $2.3 billion,

---

[72] *Southern California Edison-San Diego Gas & Electric Merger*, 1991 Cal. PUC LEXIS 253, at *23 (applying Cal. Pub. Util. Code § 854 (b)(1), (2) to require both short-term and long-term benefits). The Commission rejected the transaction, for multiple reasons, as discussed in Chapter 11.2.

[73] 2010 Horizontal Merger Guidelines, *supra* note 66, §10 (explaining that "much of the information relating to efficiencies is uniquely in the possession of the merging firms").

[74] *See, e.g., Great Plains Energy-Westar Energy Merger I*, 2017 Kan. PUC LEXIS 1142, at *40–41 ¶ 87 (expressing concern that a shortfall in claimed savings could cause the merged company to cut vegetation management and defer maintenance and system improvements).

[75] *See, e.g.,* Central Vermont Public Service-Gaz Metro Merger, 2012 Vt. PUC LEXIS 279, at *81–85, Findings 160–73 (finding that by merging, adjacent utilities can integrate field and support operations while eliminating redundant technology, audits, regulatory activities and support of corporate board and shareholders).

36 percent control premium.[76] He also had no access to the Westar executives responsible for achieving the claimed savings; and he had only "indirect access through the descriptions by GPE executives of the management briefings by Westar that they attended." There were no joint meetings at which managers of both companies questioned each other's savings assumptions or methodically assessed their magnitude.[77] Moreover, the applicants developed their savings estimates only after they signed the merger agreement: "No specific data or quantifications of savings were provided [by GPE] to the Westar board."[78]

Second, merger applicants calculate the savings from a base of status quo costs. These projections assume, unrealistically, that neither company would reduce its costs without a merger.

Third, generic assumptions about economies of scale ignore the possibility of diseconomies of scale.[79]

Fourth, some utility-side witnesses justify their savings estimates by comparing them favorably to other merging entities' pre-merger estimates—a comparison both subjective and circular.

Fifth, the savings estimates usually come from consultants paid by the merging companies to persuade. The Kansas Commission thus criticized one consultant's estimates because the company gave him "targets ... designed to make the transaction work."[80]

In the dozens of merger proceedings reviewed for this book (over twenty of which the author participated in), in not one did applicants present an economies of scale study that (a) was performed by someone not paid by one or both merging companies, or that (b) accounted for cost reductions likely to occur without the transaction.

---

[76] Supplemental Direct Testimony of Kevin E. Bryant at 8, Great Plains Energy-Westar Energy Merger I, Docket No. 16-KCPE-593-ACQ (Kan. Corp. Comm'n filed Nov. 2, 2016) (Attachment A to Joint Applicants' Motion for Leave to Final Supplemental Direct Testimony).

[77] Response to KCC Staff Interrogatory 252, Great Plains Energy-Westar Energy Merger I, Docket No. 16-KCPE-593-ACQ (Kan. Corp. Comm'n filed Oct. 24, 2016).

[78] *Id.*, Response to KCC Staff Interrogatory 221. *See also Entergy Services-Gulf States Merger*, 65 F.E.R.C. ¶ 61,332, at p. 62,486 (1993) (rejecting estimates of nonfuel operations and maintenance savings as "overstated and speculative" because, among other reasons, "Entergy had limited access to Gulf States' records, and, in fact, did not have access to Gulf States' accounting practices, i.e., Entergy had inadequate knowledge of Gulf States").

[79] *See, e.g.*, Southern California Edison-San Diego Gas & Electric Merger, 1991 Cal. PUC LEXIS 253, at *25 (rejecting generalized claims of "economies of scale" because "applicants have not accounted for administrative inefficiencies that may result as the merged company becomes even larger").

[80] Great Plains Energy-Westar Energy Merger I, 2017 Kan. PUC LEXIS 1142, at *53–60 ¶ 59–66.

2. *Improving performance through "best practices":* Acquirers say they will bring to the target more efficient business practices.[81] These assertions have three weaknesses.

First, they usually omit specifics.[82] Exelon made its best practices claim without having identified or analyzed a single practice.[83]

Second, "best practices" implies some innovation unique to the acquirer. But what often emerges under questioning are mundane business procedures. Exelon said it would bring to Pepco a corporate-wide "Management Model," but the Model comprised commonsense steps: "monitoring," "assessment," "goals," "tracking and reporting," "programs," "compliance with regulatory requirements," "benchmarking," "best practices," "technology," "performance of required regulatory activities," "clear lines of reporting," "formal processes for sharing knowledge," "participat[ing] in benchmarking studies and industry meetings and internal reviews," "cross-company communities of practice (or peer groups)," and executive compensation based on achieving objectives.[84]

Third, the target already has a duty of using best practices. An acquirer that replaces the target's quill pens and Roman numerals with computers and Arabic numbers is merely bringing competence to the incompetent.[85] No merger is necessary. Seeking approval to acquire PHI, Exelon promised to improve Pepco's reliability problems. Exelon's commitment to specific reliability metrics influenced the Maryland Commission's decision to approve the transaction.[86] But nothing prevented the Commission from addressing Pepco's reliability problems directly, without a merger, by establishing clear

---

[81] *See, e.g.,* UGI Utilities-PPL Gas Merger, 2008 Pa. PUC LEXIS 58, at *22–23 (finding benefits from the acquisition of a small electric and gas company by a larger one with "substantial expertise and experience in managing natural gas distribution systems," while allowing the transferor to "concentrate its expertise" on electricity).

[82] *See, e.g.,* Exelon-Constellation Energy Group Merger, 2012 Md. PSC LEXIS 12, at *162–63 (finding the best practices claim "too intangible to qualify as a benefit").

[83] Applicants' Responses to Office of the People's Counsel Data Requests at DR 5-39, Exelon-PHI Merger, Formal Case No. 1119 (D.C. Pub. Serv. Comm'n filed Nov. 3, 2014) [hereinafter Responses to OPC Data Requests for Formal Case No. 1119] (admitting that Exelon "has not yet determined which best practices will be implemented at Pepco as no analysis has been completed at this time regarding which processes and procedures are most beneficial and best suited for implementation at Pepco").

[84] Responses to OPC Data Requests for Formal Case No. 1119, *supra* note 83, at DR 4-3, DR 5-33, DR 5-39, DR 5-46, DR 5-47.

[85] This fine analogy comes from Dan Davidson of blessed memory, who used it against the applicants' merger savings witness in the 1988 FERC proceeding on the merger of PacifiCorp and Utah Power & Light.

[86] *See, e.g.,* Exelon-PHI Merger, Case No. 9361, Order No. 86990, slip op. at 3 (Md. Pub. Serv. Comm'n May 15, 2015) (finding that the merger "will enable

metrics and penalties for non-achievement. The Commission never explained why Pepco was inherently incapable of improving reliability on its own—or why that incapability, if it existed, warranted its shareholders receiving an acquisition premium. The purpose of merger benefits is to justify merger costs. Attributing to the merger an improvement to mere competence means making customers bear extra costs—merger costs—to get performance they should be receiving already.

3. Improving financial condition: Some acquirers say they will improve the target's financial condition—increase its bond ratings, expand its access to capital, or reduce its marginal cost of debt. Beware of free lunches. A financially healthy acquirer buying a less healthy target risks its own downgrade. Indeed some transactions have the opposite goal: using the low-risk target's financial strength to improve the high-risk acquirer's financial condition. Also, maintaining a sufficient financial condition, like using best practices, is a utility and regulatory obligation independent of a merger.[87] When NextEra said it would make sure Oncor had sufficient capital, the Texas Commission was unimpressed; Oncor was doing fine without NextEra's help: "Oncor has made $6 to $7 billion in capital investments over the past five years, funding the equity portion of these investments using Oncor's retained earnings, and there is no evidence even suggesting that Oncor would be unable to continue to do so in the future."[88] AltaGas's CFO said Washington Gas Light's small size meant it needed AltaGas's help raising equity.[89] But he presented no evidence suggesting Washington Gas Light was having trouble raising equity on its own. If Washington Gas Light was having trouble, it could have and would have asked regulators to do their legal duty—setting rates sufficient to allow the utility to raise the necessary capital.[90] No acquisition was necessary.

4. Diversifying load and coordinating generation: Utilities with different load shapes—one's peak matching another's trough—can share generation to save each other money. Even companies with similar load shapes can lower costs. They can (a) coordinate their generation dispatch, substituting in each hour one company's lower-cost units for the other company's higher-cost

---

Delmarva and Pepco in Maryland to improve their reliability performance more quickly than they would without the merger").

[87] *See* Tutorial § 4.

[88] Oncor Electric Delivery-NextEra Energy Merger, PUC Docket No. 46238, slip op. at text accompanying n.25 (Tex. Pub. Util. Comm'n Apr. 13, 2017).

[89] Rebuttal Testimony of Vincent L Amman, Jr. at 7, AltaGas-Washington Gas Light Merger, Case No. 9449 (Md. Pub. Serv. Comm'n filed Sept. 11, 2017).

[90] *See* Tutorial § 4.1.

units;[91] and (b) defer construction of new capacity, by using one company's surplus to serve the other company's growing load.[92] Another example: a renewables-heavy utility can merge with one owning gas-fired generation to "firm up" the renewable units' variable output.[93] Other examples of generation coordination economies include density economies (reducing per-unit costs by using the same infrastructure to serve more customers); maintenance economies (having more units available to substitute for those taken off line for maintenance, thereby avoiding expensive replacement power); and reliability and emergency economies (sharing of generation reserves within a merged company, thereby reducing the reserves required by each pre-merger company).[94]

This category of benefits, frequently asserted by merger applicants in the late 1980s and 1990s, has less value today. Why? Because regional transmission organizations now serve most of the nation's customers, providing regional transmission service and administering capacity and energy markets. These activities enable unaffiliated companies to share reserves and coordinate dispatch over large regions—without merging.[95]

5. Combining purchasing power to get better prices: Some merger applicants say that their larger, merged company will get volume discounts on supplies. This author has never seen in utility merger cases any actual evidence for this—no surprise since each applicant is, by itself, already

---

[91] Generating units' hour-by-hour operating costs can vary, depending on each unit's fuel cost and heat rate (the latter a form of operating efficiency, calculated as Btu/kWh). Individual utilities always seek to use, in each hour, the set of generating units costing the least to operate. Multiple utilities can agree to "pool" their units, thereby increasing the opportunities to substitute higher-cost units for lower-cost ones. *See* FRANKENA & OWEN, *supra* note 67, at 151–52 (describing a merger's potential for "dispatch economies" by increasing a system's mix of baseload, intermediate and peaking plants, providing more opportunities to substitute, hour-by-hour, low-cost units for higher-cost units).

[92] *See, e.g., Utah Power & Light-PacifiCorp Merger*, 45 F.E.R.C. ¶ 61,095, at text accompanying nn.193–96 (1988) (accepting Applicants' assertions that by combining the summer-peaking UP&L and the winter-peaking PacifiCorp, the merged company will reduce reserve requirements, dispatch generation more efficiently and defer generation construction).

[93] Gas units with fast "ramping" capability can raise or lower their output rapidly in response to changes in the sun and wind. The combination helps to make power flow firm, i.e., uninterrupted.

[94] *See* FRANKENA & OWEN, *supra* note 67, at 151–52.

[95] See Chapter 4.4.2, on efficiencies achievable without a merger. *See also* Great Plains Energy-Westar Energy Merger I, 2017 Kan. PUC LEXIS 1142, at *50–52 ¶ 55–56 (rejecting general claims about savings from accelerating generation retirement, because applicants identified no specific generators).

a multi-billion-dollar company. And volume discounts will serve the public interest only if cost-based (i.e., if the merger company's size moves it to a lower step in the supply seller's cost function). Otherwise, the discount would reflect the merged company's buyer market power, converting "synergies" into "pecuniary economies," where "the gains to the merged firm exactly match losses to the input suppliers."[96]

6. Bringing outsourced inputs in-house: A vertical merger enables the downstream company to self-provide, at cost, what it used to buy externally at prices reflecting cost plus profit. Economists call this cost-saving effect "avoiding double-marginalization."[97] The downstream firm, if subject to effective competition, will reflect its savings in lower prices.[98] Self-providing inputs internally also can reduce the "barriers and friction" that accompany negotiations among unaffiliated companies.[99] But these savings reach the merged utility's customers only if the regulator lowers the downstream company's rates. Otherwise, the prior input provider's profit goes to the merged company's shareholders. And a vertical merger can actually increase the downstream customer's costs if the input provider's inter-affiliate price to the downstream exceeds the price offered by nonaffiliated sellers. Vertical acquisitions also can harm competition in the input market, by foreclosing unaffiliated companies from competing for the downstream utility's business.[100]

* * *

---

[96]   Gregory J. Werden, *Essays on Consumer Welfare and Competition Policy* 9 (March 2, 2009), https://papers.ssrn.com/sol3/papers.cfm?abstract_id=1352032.

[97]   *See, e.g.*, Dennis W. Carlton & Randal C. Picker, *Antitrust and Regulation, in* ECONOMIC REGULATION AND ITS REFORM 25, 45 (Nancy L. Rose ed., 2014) (explaining that "when regulated firms must interconnect, the price of interconnection will typically be regulated to be above marginal cost. If so, there will be an efficiency motivation for a firm to vertically integrate to avoid double marginalization."). *See also* NBC Universal-Comcast Merger, 26 FCC Rcd. 4238, 4335 ¶ 237 (2007) (explaining the "well accepted" economic theory that "when both an upstream and a downstream firm set their [pre-merger] prices above their marginal costs, ... [a vertical merger] will lead to lower prices (or higher quality goods)," because the "combined firm will no longer treat the marginal cost of the upstream product (e.g., programming) as the price the downstream firm previously paid but as the lower amount it actually costs to produce it").

[98]   Carlton & Picker, *supra* note 97, at 45. In assessing the proposed Qwest-Century-Tel merger, the Iowa Board found that by "putting 'off-net' traffic in the legacy CenturyLink markets onto the Qwest long-haul network," the merged company would reduce or eliminate its costs of purchasing transport functions from unaffiliated carriers. Qwest-CenturyTel Merger, 2010 Iowa PUC LEXIS 387, at *69–70.

[99]   *NBC Universal-Comcast Merger*, 26 FCC Rcd. at 4333 ¶ 231 (recognizing the benefit but questioning its magnitude).

[100]   A detailed discussion of the harms to competition appears in Chapter 6.

In the many merger cases participated in or reviewed by the author, no appli-cant has supported these six generic benefit claims with company-specific evi-dence. No applicant has produced objective studies showing that prior mergers produced savings in those categories. Nor have the rating agencies been impressed: "With some mergers years have passed and we are still looking for the cost savings that were promised. The market will be more skeptical about realizing those synergies."[101] The few objective studies that do exist express skepticism. One found that "efficiency gains from market restructuring are due to factors other than mergers."[102] Another found that the larger the merger, the less likely is it to create the savings anticipated:

> All of the studies find significant increasing returns to scale in electricity for smaller utilities and constant or decreasing returns to scale for large utilities. Minimum efficient firm size (MES) for the bulk of the studies is in the range of 2,000–4,000 MW of capacity; 9,000–30,000 GWH of net generation; and 10,000–35,000 GWH of sales.[103]

And then there's Judge Posner: "I wish someone would give me some exam-ples of mergers that have improved efficiency. There must be some."[104] This combination of evidentiary gap and analyst skepticism supports the need for more studies, as Chapter 13 will recommend.

4.4.1.3 Aspirations vs. commitments
Instead of quantifying and committing to merger benefits, merger applicants usually offer only aspirations. Consider six aspirational statements made by Exelon in its application to acquire PHI. As explained here, each statement dissolved in discovery:

1. Distribution improvements: Exelon said it would improve Pepco's physi-cal distribution practices, but then admitted having no specifics:

> Specific changes to Pepco's vegetation management program have not been identi-fied to date. Exelon ... plans to look for opportunities to accelerate [Pepco's exist-ing] work where possible and to improve the performance of the system through

---

[101] Michael T. Burr, *Squeezing Synergies*, Pub. Util. Fortnightly, Oct. 2004, at 50 (quoting Peter N. Rigby, a director for Standard and Poor's).

[102] Mark J. Niefer, *Explaining The Divide Between DOJ and FERC on Electric Power Merger Policy*, 33 Energy L.J. 505, 512 n.30 (2012) (citing J. Dean Craig & Scott J. Savage, *Market Restructuring, Competition and the Efficiency of Electricity Generation: Plant-level Evidence from the United States 1996 to 2006*, 34 Energy J. 1, 23 (2013)).

[103] Hartman, *supra* note 67, at 443.

[104] Philadelphia National Bank *at 50: An Interview with Judge Richard Posner*, 80 Antitrust L.J. 205, 216 (2015) (referring to mergers generally).

the application of best practices and processes as part of the Exelon Management Model.[105]

Asked specifically about distribution feeders and undergrounding, again Exelon had no specifics.[106]

2. Employment savings: Exelon talked of employment savings, but then admitted "it is too early in the integration process to estimate the reduction in employment in Pepco's DC operations and the associated savings subsequent to the two-year moratorium [on employee layoffs]. … The details of the actual consolidations have not yet been determined."[107]

3. Capital expenditures: Exelon said it could produce savings on capital expenditures, but then admitted it "has not completed any analysis projecting the estimated cost savings in future capital expenditure budgets at PHI's utilities."[108] And, "[t]here have not yet been any plans identified that would abandon, scale down or defer capital projects if this merger is completed."[109]

4. Mutual support structure: PHI's CEO, Joseph Rigby, testified that a "mutual support structure will enhance performance and lower costs." But then he admitted he had no studies to support this statement.[110] Similarly, Exelon's CEO, C.M. Crane, said BG&E and Pepco's adjacency will create "robust mutual support capabilities and substantially greater combined resources to respond promptly and effectively to major storms and other emergencies." But the company then admitted it "has not performed a quantitative analysis as to the benefits derived from the geographic proximity of its utilities and PHI's utilities."[111]

5. More resources: Mr. Rigby said the Exelon-PHI transaction will give Pepco "access to greater resources available from a larger enterprise."[112] But then Mark Alden, Exelon's Vice President of Utility Oversight and Integration,

---

[105]   Responses to OPC Data Requests for Formal Case No. 1119, *supra* note 83, at DR 3-34. And as explained previously in the text, Exelon's Management Model contained only obvious, conventional management practices.

[106]   *Id.* at DR 3-35, DR 3-36, DR 3-41.

[107]   *Id.* at DR 6-6.

[108]   *Id.* at DR 6-31.

[109]   *Id.* at DR 3-24(C).

[110]   *Compare* Direct Testimony of Joseph M. Rigby at 9, Exelon-PHI Merger, Formal Case No. 1119 (D.C. Pub. Serv. Comm'n filed June 18, 2014), *with* Responses to OPC Data Requests for Formal Case No. 1119, *supra* note 83, at DR 4-22.

[111]   *Compare* Direct Testimony of C.M. Crane at 11, Exelon-PHI Merger, Formal Case No. 1119 (D.C. Pub. Serv. Comm'n filed June 18, 2014), *with* Applicants' Responses to GRID 2.0 Data Requests at DR 1-32, Exelon-PHI Merger, Formal Case No. 1119 (D.C. Pub. Serv. Comm'n filed Nov. 3, 2014) [hereinafter Responses to GRID 2.0 Data Requests for Formal Case No. 1119].

[112]   Direct Testimony of Joseph M. Rigby, *supra* note 110, at 10.

admitted that the Applicants had made no "determination" about what type or amount of resources Pepco will have "greater access to."[113]

6. *Bargaining power and economies of scale:* Exelon CEO Crane talked of "increased bargaining power" and "economies of scale." But Exelon admitted it "has not made its own explicit study of the benefits of increased bargaining power and economies of scale as a general matter."[114]

* * *

Admissions like Exelon's cause the value of benefit claims to approach zero; they confirm that operational improvement is not these mergers' purpose.[115] Two companies merging to create efficiencies will have an efficiencies-creating plan, specified and quantified, especially if the acquirer is paying billions for the privilege. The merging companies have no operational efficiency plan because operational efficiency is not their purpose.

4.4.1.4   Consequences of non-achievement
Claims of merger benefit would gain credibility if accompanied by five things: specific metrics, a plan for achieving those metrics, enforceable commitments, a list of responsible individuals, and clear consequences—to the merged company and the individuals—for non-achievement. But in no merger

---

[113] *See* Responses to OPC Data Requests for Formal Case No. 1119, *supra* note 83, at DR 4-25.

[114] *Compare* Direct Testimony of C.M. Crane, *supra* note 111, at 6, *with* Responses to GRID 2.0 Data Requests for Formal Case No. 1119, *supra* note 111, at DR 1-24(B).

[115] The DOJ/FTC Horizontal Merger Guidelines view merger efficiency projections with "skepticism, particularly when generated outside of the usual business planning process. ..." The Guidelines add that applicant-touted efficiencies "relating to procurement, management, or capital cost, are less likely to be merger-specific or substantial." 2010 HORIZONTAL MERGER GUIDELINES, *supra* note 66, § 10 & n.13. *See also* NYNEX-Bell Atlantic Merger, 12 FCC Rcd. 19,985 (1997) ("Efficiencies that can be achieved through means less harmful to competition than the proposed merger ... cannot be considered to be true pro-competitive benefits of the merger.").

Much scholarly and regulatory ink has been spilt over whether merger applicants over-promise on merger efficiencies to justify anticompetitive transactions. *See, e.g.,* Robert Pitofsky, *Efficiency Considerations and Merger Enforcement: Comparison of U.S. and EU Approaches,* 30 FORDHAM INT'L L.J. 1413, 1415 (2007) (noting efficiency skeptics' view that efficiencies of scope or scale "can be achieved by internal expansion of a single firm, or by less restrictive alternatives like joint ventures"); Crane, *supra* note 65, at 356–57 (arguing that the DOJ guidelines "implicitly treat efficiencies and anticompetitive risks asymmetrically by insisting that efficiencies be proven to a very high degree of certainty in order to justify a merger whereas risks need not be proven with great certainty in order to block a merger").

case participated in or studied by this author were all five factors present.[116] Aspirations without accountability invite excess optimism. As the Kansas Commission declared, merging companies "obviously have every reason to present overly optimistic estimates."[117]

Consider GPE's original application to acquire Westar. William Kemp, GPE's savings consultant, testified that "GPE senior executives ... took ownership for achieving the targeted benefits."[118] "Took ownership" is business-buzzspeak, never defined by Mr. Kemp.[119] He was asked to "explain precisely how executive management will be held accountable, and how consequences will be assigned, to those who have taken 'ownership for achieving the targeted benefits.'" He was also asked to "explain the career consequences, in terms of compensation or promotion, that are associated with taking ownership." The answer revealed nothing: "This would be decided on a case-by-case basis."[120]

Outside of mergers, commissions don't typically credit aspirations without accountability. When a utility proposes a new purchased power agreement or a new generating unit, regulators require year-by-year projections comparing the proposal's costs to the costs of feasible alternatives. Accompanied by alternative scenarios and sensitivity studies, those numbers come from the mouths of specific witnesses who risk their reputations, because later facts will make their projections right or wrong. Merger witnesses face no similar fate because they make few enforceable promises.

---

[116] In the Exelon-PHI merger, the applicants' final proposal on reliability did include metrics and penalties for the merged company. But there was no list of responsible individuals or consequences to them. Exelon-PHI Merger, Case No. 9361, Order No. 86990, slip op. app. A at 13 (Md. Pub. Serv. Comm'n May 15, 2015). And in approving the merger of Southwestern Public Service and Public Service of Colorado, the Texas Commission reserved the power to penalize the merged company's rate of return if the claimed merger efficiencies did not occur. Southwestern Public Service-PSColorado Merger, 1997 Tex. PUC LEXIS 4, at *39 (stating that "in calculating a rate of return in a future rate case, the Commission will examine whether the merger has indeed resulted in an improvement of service to SPS ratepayers and, if not, take appropriate action").

[117] Kansas City Power & Light-Kansas Gas & Electric Merger, Consolidated Docket Nos. 172,745-u, 174,155-D, slip op. at 59 (Kan. Corp. Comm'n Nov. 18, 1991).

[118] Direct Testimony of William J. Kemp at 18, Great Plains Energy-Westar Energy Merger I, Docket No. 16-KCPE-593-ACQ (Kan. Corp. Comm'n filed June 28, 2017).

[119] Indeed, Mr. Kemp used the same phrase—"took ownership"—nearly ten years earlier when testifying before the Missouri Public Service Commission in favor of the merger of KCP&L and Aquila. *See* Great Plains Energy-Kansas City Power & Light Merger, 2008 Mo. PSC LEXIS 693, at *190 n.371.

[120] Response to KCC Staff Interrogatory 213, Great Plains Energy-Westar Energy Merger I, Docket No. 16-KCPE-593-ACQ (Kan. Corp. Comm'n filed Oct. 24, 2016).

4.4.1.5 Appropriate treatment: certainty, commitment and consequences

Regulators should credit only commitments, not aspirations; otherwise advertising replaces accountability.[121] Evidence on benefits should have the rigor of rate case data, with applicants bearing the risk of non-achievement. Seller accountability produces customer benefits. Then proposed mergers will more resemble what competitive markets produce.

The FCC and the Department of Justice apply that principle routinely. The FCC requires merger applicants "to provide sufficient evidence supporting each benefit claim so that the Commission can verify the likelihood and magnitude of the claimed benefit."[122] The Department of Justice, when weighing a merger's benefits against its anticompetitive effects, requires evidence sufficient to verify "the likelihood and magnitude of each asserted efficiency, how and when each would be achieved (and any costs of doing so), how each would enhance the merged firm's ability and incentive to compete, and why each would be merger-specific."[123] Both agencies use a sliding scale: the greater and more certain a merger's harms, the greater and more certain must be the evidence of benefits.[124]

4.4.2 Crediting Benefits Achievable Without the Merger: Violations of Logic and Law

The FCC has stated:

> [T]he claimed benefit must be transaction- or merger-specific. This means that the claimed benefit "must be likely to be accomplished as a result of the merger but unlikely to be realized by other means that entail fewer anticompetitive effects."[125]

---

[121] *See* Great Plains Energy-Westar Energy Merger I, 2017 Kan. PUC LEXIS 1142, at *60 ¶ 66 ("trust" does not substitute for evidence).

[122] AT&T-Bellsouth Merger, 22 FCC Rcd. 5662, 5761 ¶ 202 (2007) (citing, among other sources, DEP'T OF JUSTICE & FED. TRADE COMM'N, HORIZONTAL MERGER GUIDELINES § 4 (1992, rev. 1997)).

[123] 2010 HORIZONTAL MERGER GUIDELINES, *supra* note 66, § 10.

[124] AT&T-Deutsche Telekom Merger, 26 FCC Rcd. 16,184, 16,248 ¶ 127 (2011) ("As the harms to the public interest become greater and more certain, the degree and certainty of the public benefits must also increase commensurately."); 2010 HORIZONTAL MERGER GUIDELINES, *supra* note 66, § 10 ("The greater the potential adverse competitive effect of a merger, the greater must be the cognizable efficiencies, and the more they must be passed through to customers, for the Agencies to conclude that the merger will not have an anticompetitive effect in the relevant market.").

[125] *AT&T-Bellsouth Merger*, 22 FCC Rcd. at 5761 ¶ 202 & n. 554 (quoting EchoStar Communications-Hughes Electronics Merger, 17 FCC Rcd. 20,559, 20,630 ¶ 189 (2002)) ("Public interest benefits also include any cost saving efficiencies arising

Measuring merger benefits means comparing the merged case to the stand-alone case. But the stand-alone case is not the status quo case. The stand-alone case must assume prudence: that the non-merged companies not only act prudently at present, but will continue to act prudently, making the improvements that any prudent utility would.[126] Commissions violate this principle routinely. They credit applicants' offers of "best practices," cash payments to customers and actions unrelated to the merger. Counting these offers as merger benefits commits a series of errors, discussed next.

4.4.2.1 "Best practices"

Merger applicants do not distinguish "best practices" from normal, prudent utility practices. Take Exelon's proposal to improve Pepco's reliability. No applicant witness suggested that achieving the proposed metrics actually depended on joining the two companies. Exelon would simply teach Pepco to perform better. But learning and improving is what ratepayers pay utilities to do; it is not a merger benefit.[127] And at the time of its proposal to acquire Pepco, Exelon already owned the adjacent Baltimore Gas & Electric (BG&E). So the Maryland Commission, with jurisdiction over both BG&E and Pepco, could have ordered BG&E to share its reliability practices with Pepco—making Exelon's "merger benefit" superfluous. Exelon also said Pepco would have

---

from the merger if such efficiencies are achievable only as a result of the merger." (citing Ameritech-SBC Communications Merger, 14 FCC Rcd. 14,712, 14,825 ¶ 255 (1999))). *See also* Comcast-AT&T Merger, 17 FCC Rcd. 23,246, 23,313 ¶ 173 (2002) (Commission considers whether benefits are "merger-specific"); 2010 HORIZONTAL MERGER GUIDELINES, *supra* note 66, § 10 (stating that the antitrust agencies will count "only those efficiencies likely to be accomplished with the proposed merger and unlikely to be accomplished in the absence of either the proposed merger or another means having comparable anticompetitive effects"). And under the Bank Merger Act of 1966, 12 U.S.C. § 1828(c), applicants must show that the merger benefits are not reasonably achievable through other means. United States v. Third Nat'l Bank of Nashville, 390 U.S. 171, 189–90 (1968); United States v. Phillipsburg Nat'l Bank & Trust Co., 399 U.S. 350, 372 (1970).

   126 FRANKENA & OWEN, *supra* note 67, at 149.

   127 That Exelon's offers added nothing to Pepco's capabilities was confirmed by Pepco's Senior Vice President for Strategic Initiatives. He acknowledged that Pepco "already had programs, procedures, and standards in place similar to those" Exelon offered. And Pepco already had "hired consultants to advise its utility subsidiaries on best reliability practices. For example, the Company has hired Accenture regarding cost containment and the Company participates in the PA Consulting Group's annual studies on best practices in the utility industry." *See* Responses to OPC Data Requests for Formal Case No. 1119, *supra* note 83, at DR 3-12; Responses to GRID 2.0 Data Requests for Formal Case No. 1119, *supra* note 111, at DR 1-66.

access to Exelon's utility crews during major storm events.[128] But inter-utility agreements for storm-crew-sharing are a prudent—and common—utility practice. And this offer was zero-sum, since making Exelon crews preferentially available to Pepco would make them less available to other utilities.

Treating prudent practices as merger benefits produces a counterintuitive result: the poorer the target's pre-merger performance, the more "benefits" the acquirer can bring; then the more merger costs it can incur and recover from customers.[129] Distilled: the poorer the target's performance, the more merger costs customers absorb. The irrationality is obvious.

4.4.2.2 Cash payments

Many merger applicants propose cash payments to the target utility's customers. Here are some recent examples:

- Exelon-Constellation: $100 to each Maryland customer.[130]
- Exelon-PHI: $100 to each Maryland customer.[131]
- Macquarie Partners-Central Louisiana Electric: total rate credits of $136 million.[132]
- AltaGas-Washington Gas Light: $50 to each Maryland customer.[133]

Cash offers based on valid predictions of true merger savings should count as merger benefits, because by definition they depend on the merger, and because the applicants bear the risk of non-achievement. But if the payments come from the acquirer's treasury rather than true merger savings, they are merely persuasion payoffs. Counting them as merger benefits favors acquirers with

---

[128] Joint Application ¶ 41, Exelon-PHI Merger, Formal Case No. 1119 (D.C. Pub. Serv. Comm'n filed June 18, 2014).

[129] One more example: the FCC Staff viewed AT&T and T-Mobile's proposed improvements to business functions as achievable without a merger. Fed. Commc'ns Comm'n, Staff Analysis and Findings on Applications of AT&T Inc. and Deutsche Telekom Ag for Consent to Assign or Transfer Control of Licenses and Authorizations, WT Docket No. 11-65 ¶ 241 (2011), http://www.wirelessestimator.com/publicdocs/ATT-TMO-FCC.pdf. After issuance of the Staff report the parties withdrew the merger. The FCC Staff's document is not an official Commission document; nor was it part of the official record in the named Docket. It was a draft report prepared by the Staff and released to the public by the FCC Chairman. The FCC issued no order because the applicants withdrew their proposal.

[130] Exelon-Constellation Energy Group Merger, 2012 Md. PSC LEXIS 12, at *163–64.

[131] Exelon-PHI Merger, Case No. 9361, Order No. 86990, slip op. app. A at 1 (Md. Pub. Serv. Comm'n May 15, 2015).

[132] Cleco Power-Macquarie Merger, 2016 La. PUC LEXIS 95, at *11.

[133] AltaGas-Washington Gas Light Merger, Case No. 9449, Order No. 88631, slip op. app. A at 2 (Md. Pub. Serv. Comm'n Apr. 4, 2018).

extra cash over acquirers with more merit. They lead to industry consolidation unsupported by operational efficiencies. A student should get an "A" for excelling at her schoolwork, not for donating to the teachers' retirement fund.

4.4.2.3 Offers unrelated to the merger

This category's boundaries are limited only by the intervenors' goals. Two merger orders illustrate the diverse possibilities.

In acquiring PacifiCorp, MidAmerican Energy Holdings Company (MEHC) promised that the merged company would, among other things,

1. "gather outside input on environmental matters, such as through the Environmental Forum";
2. "continue to have environmental management systems in place that are self-certified to ISO 14001 standards at all PacifiCorp operated thermal generation plants";
3. "maintain at least the existing level of PacifiCorp's community-related contributions" and "continue to consult with regional advisory boards to ensure local perspectives are heard regarding community issues";
4. not reduce employee benefits unilaterally for a specified number of years;
5. continue to produce integrated resource plans and select generation resources using formal requests for proposals;
6. use best efforts to complete specified transmission projects and reliability improvements;
7. initiate a process to collaboratively design short-term transmission products;
8. continue a transmission tariff provision "that allows transmission customers to alter pre-scheduled transactions up to 20 minutes before the hour as long as such provision is consistent with established scheduling practices and does not jeopardize system reliability";
9. acquire specified amounts and types of renewable resources, including "community renewable energy projects in Oregon";
10. establish a "global warming working group" and file with the Commission a "strategy" for reducing its contribution to global warming;
11. conduct a study on "third party market potential" for demand side management and energy efficiency;
12. continue the utility's "existing economic development practices and use MEHC's experience to maximize the effectiveness of these efforts"; and

13. hire, with shareholder funding, "a consultant to study and design for possible implementation of an arrearage management project for low-income customers" and create a working group to study low-income problems.[134]

And to eliminate most intervenors' objections to their merger, Exelon and Constellation agreed to

1. invest $113.5 million over three years in a "Customer Investment Fund for the purpose of providing energy efficiency and low-income energy assistance to BGE [Baltimore Gas & Electric] customers";
2. construct a headquarters building in Baltimore;
3. provide an average of $7 million in annual charitable contributions to Maryland recipients;
4. build or buy specified quantities and types of renewable energy; and
5. contribute specified amounts to various low-income and other local programs.[135]

Like cash payments unconnected to real savings, offers unrelated to the merger don't come from the merger; they come from the merging companies' pre-existing resources—resources often made possible by their government-franchised status. Commissions that count these offers as merger benefits discourage potential acquirers that might be better performers.

4.4.2.4 Violation of merger statutes

Under every merger statute, what must satisfy the public interest is the merger. The D.C. statute requires that "the *consolidation* ... be in the public interest."[136] Under Federal Power Act section 203, what must be consistent with the public interest is the "proposed disposition, consolidation, acquisition, or control."[137] And FERC's Merger Policy Statement requires that a merger with detrimental effects has "countervailing benefits that *derive from the merger*."[138] If what must satisfy the public interest is the "merger or consolidation" itself—the act of coupling the companies—then inducements to win support can play no legal role. What must satisfy the public interest is the merger, not

---

[134] This list is not exhaustive. For more, *see* MidAmerican Energy-PacifiCorp Merger, 2006 Ore. PUC LEXIS 74, at *68–74, *77–79, *81, *102, *106.

[135] *Exelon-Constellation Energy Group Merger*, 2012 Md. PSC LEXIS 12, at *8–9.

[136] D.C. Code § 34-504 (emphasis added).

[137] FPA § 203(a)(4), 16 U.S.C. § 824b(a)(4).

[138] *1996 Merger Policy Statement*, *supra* note 12, at text accompanying n.21 (emphasis added).

the merger persuasion strategy.[139] If FERC finds merger harm, then approves the merger because the applicants offer a three-year rate reduction unrelated to the merger, FERC violates the statute because that three-year payoff is not "derived from the merger." Whether used to approve detrimental mergers or to over-condition satisfactory mergers, unrelated conditions conflict with best performance.

* * *

Motivated by gain and undisciplined by competition, mergers of franchised utility monopolies cause economic waste. Targets choose their acquirers based on price instead of performance, depriving their customers of the benefits from competition based on performance. Commissions could prevent this waste by requiring merger applicants to show and commit to a benefit-cost ratio that matches or exceeds the most efficient alternatives. Commissions instead focus on avoiding harm. Even when commissions insist on benefits exceeding costs, they require only minor benefits, they ignore acquisition cost and they count as benefits operational improvements that a prudent utility would achieve without a merger. They also treat as benefits items unrelated to the merger, thereby discouraging merger applicants that could perform better. By making performance incidental, dozens of mergers approvals have caused economic waste.

---

[139] *See* AT&T-Bellsouth Merger, 22 FCC Rcd. 5662, 5674–75 ¶ 22 (2007) (FCC may impose conditions "only to remedy harms that arise from the transaction … and that are related to the Commission's [statutory] responsibilities"); AT&T Wireless-Cingular Merger, 19 FCC Rcd. 21,522, 21,546 ¶ 43 (2004) (declining to "impose conditions to remedy pre-existing harms or harms that are unrelated to the transaction"). In the NBCU-Comcast transaction, merger opponents called out Comcast's labor practices, along with applicants' shortcomings on diversity hiring. The Applicants reached agreements with minority groups, but asked the FCC not to convert agreements into approval conditions, because the matters covered were "not related to the transaction"—and also dealt with matters outside the Commission's authority. The FCC agreed. NBC Universal-Comcast Merger, 26 FCC Rcd. 4238, 4329–30 ¶ 223 (2011) (stating that "these matters are enforced by agencies of government other than the Commission: the NLRB has jurisdiction over issues related to compliance with the laws concerning union matters, and the Equal Employment Opportunity Commission, along with relevant state authorities, oversees the laws on workforce discrimination and diversity").

5. Merging parties divert franchise value from the customers who created it

Utility mergers waste economic resources, but they bring their backers gains. Most acquirers pay a control premium—the excess of purchase price over stock market price. The merging parties allocate nearly the entire excess to the target's shareholders, little to customers. Regulators routinely approve that outcome unquestioningly.

This chapter critiques that regulatory treatment. The control premium represents the value of control. But the sources of that value are largely unconnected to the target utility's merit. So there is no logical, statutory or constitutional basis for letting the target shareholders keep the entire premium. Under principles of regulation and competition, the control premium should go to those who created its underlying value, in proportion to their contribution. Whether the value-creators are the shareholders or the customers, and in what proportion, is a question of fact that each merger decision must address.[1]

5.1 THE CONTROL PREMIUM EXPLAINED

5.1.1 The Value of Control: Maximizing the Utility's Earnings

An individual investor tells her broker, "Buy me some shares at the market price." Because she buys only a sliver of the company—an entitlement to a small share of the company's future earnings and future value—she pays only the market price. She owns passively, because her sliver gives her no influence. She is buying stock and only stock.

A corporation's acquirer is buying stock and control. Control allows the acquirer to increase earnings in ways ordinary investors cannot. Consider

---

[1]   This chapter thus seeks to make a small contribution toward solving our national problem of inequality. *See* JOSEPH E. STIGLITZ, THE PRICE OF INEQUALITY 7 (2012) ("[M]uch of America's inequality is the result of market distortions, with incentives directed not at creating new wealth but at taking it from others.").

three categories of control, exercised through twelve distinct levers. First, the acquirer can *control the acquired utility's decisions*

1. on budgeting, production processes, infrastructure spending and service quality;
2. on the timing and substance of rate increase requests, including whether and when to keep merger savings or instead pass them on to customers;
3. on the pace of utility innovation (taking into account whether innovation helps maintain the utility's dominant market position or instead increases the likelihood of competitive entry by others);[2] and
4. on how to influence regulatory decisions affecting rates, market entry and the allocation of risk, as between shareholders and customers.

Second, the acquirer can *influence the markets within which the acquired utility and its affiliates operate*, by

1. influencing regulatory decisions about whether and when to introduce competition into services historically controlled by the utility; and
2. executing strategies to gain market power, including blocking prospective competitors from entering markets the acquirer hopes to dominate.

Third, the acquirer can *establish the business priorities* for the utility's entire corporate family, by

1. setting the consolidated enterprise's direction, then appointing board members and executives to carry it out;
2. deciding when to change the consolidated corporation's business mix, including adding or reducing risk;
3. deciding when to provide equity to various affiliates;
4. deciding how much debt the consolidated system should take on;
5. deciding when to use the target utility's franchise as a platform for buying new businesses or entering new markets; and
6. deciding when to use the utility's financial strength to support other affiliates.

Using these twelve levers, the acquirer exercises control. The control premium reflects the acquirer's expectation of the extra earnings that will come with control.

---

[2]   For a discussion of how innovation can have both effects, see Chapter 6.4.3.

Reflecting these purposes, AltaGas's CEO explained his reasons for acquiring the holding company for Washington Gas Light:

> The combined company will harness the strength of the platform that WGL has built in Maryland, Virginia and Washington, D.C. to continue to grow our presence in each of these jurisdictions, and to further invest in the region. We ... are excited to pursue growth opportunities in the region. ...
>
> WGL's management and employees will play important roles within the combined company. Not only will they continue to be the leaders of WGL's existing businesses, but they will also assist with the management of our other U.S. utility businesses by providing strategic oversight and guidance. ...
>
> [W]e believe a combined portfolio provides us with insight into developments in the broader energy sector, which benefits all of our subsidiary companies and their customers going forward.[3]

5.1.2   Control Premium: the Price Paid for Control

To calculate the control premium—the excess of purchase price over market price—analysts use the unaffected market price. The unaffected market price is the price published on public stock exchanges before that price was affected by news of the acquisition. (News can come from the parties' official announcement, or from a leak.) Some analysts use the market price published on the day immediately preceding the announcement or leak; others view any single-day price as arbitrary, so they prefer the volume-weighted average of the daily prices for the thirty days preceding the announcement or leak. One can express the premium as a percentage over the market price, or as total dollars.[4]

Control premium or acquisition premium—which phrase to use? Market analysts often refer to the control premium as the "acquisition premium." Confusion can arise because in the ratemaking context, accountants define "acquisition premium" differently—as the excess of purchase price over book value, not market value. They do so because the basis for cost-based rates

---

[3]   Direct Testimony of David M. Harris at 7–10, AltaGas-Washington Gas Light Merger, Case No. 9449 (Md. Pub. Serv. Comm'n filed Apr. 24, 2017).

[4]   In the Exelon-PHI transaction, for example, Exelon described the control premium as "19.6% [above] the closing price of our common stock on April 29, 2014, the last trading day prior to the public announcement of the proposed Merger"; and as "29.5% [above] our 20-day volume-weighted average share price as of April 25, 2014, the third business day prior to the public announcement." Pepco Holdings, Inc., Definitive Proxy Statement (Form DEFM 14A) at 9 (Aug. 12, 2014). Exelon estimated the control premium at $1.2 billion. Applicants' Responses to Office of the People's Counsel Data Requests at DR 3-7, Exelon-PHI Merger, Formal Case No. 1119 (D.C. Pub. Serv. Comm'n filed Nov. 3, 2014).

is book value, not market value.[5] For publicly-traded utilities, book value is usually lower than market price.[6] The accountants' acquisition premium—purchase price less book value—therefore consists of two layers. The lower layer is the excess of unaffected stock price over book value; the upper layer is the excess of purchase price over unaffected stock price—the control premium.

Cash buyout vs. stock-for-stock exchange: A control premium can exist in both cash buyouts and stock-for-stock exchanges. In cash buyouts, the premium is paid in cash: the target shareholders sell their stock for a cash amount exceeding market price. In stock-for-stock exchanges with a premium, the premium is paid with stock: the target shareholders exchange their target stock for merged company stock of higher value.

Not every utility acquisition involves a premium. Two companies bargaining as equals might value a transaction equally. The target would have no reason to demand a premium because doing so would endanger the transaction it wanted; and with the target demanding no premium the acquirer would have no reason to offer one. A recent example comes from Kansas. After the Kansas Commission rejected Westar's acquisition by Great Plains Energy

---

[5]   *See* Tutorial § 4.1 (explaining how regulators set utility rates). *See also Central Illinois Light-Central Illinois Public Service Merger (Ameren Corp.)*, 140 F.E.R.C. ¶ 61,034 at P 1 n.1 (2012) (defining "acquisition premium" as "the difference between the total acquisition cost of assets and the historical basis of the net assets acquired"); *Entergy Services-Gulf States Merger*, 65 F.E.R.C. ¶ 61,332, at p. 62,535 (1993) (explaining that the acquisition premium is the difference between purchase price and net book value). Because the acquisition premium does not represent a physical asset, accountants treat it as an intangible asset, recording it on the merged company's books as "goodwill." *See* 140 F.E.R.C. ¶ 61,034 at P 1 n.1 (explaining that goodwill is "an accounting concept and represents the excess cost of the acquired company over the sum of the amounts assigned to all identifiable assets acquired and liabilities assumed").

[6]   For multiple reasons. One obvious reason is that book value reflects accumulated book depreciation; market value does not. A second reason, disputed by some, is that utility stock trades above book value when investors expect that regulators will set rates using an authorized return on equity that exceeds the real cost of equity—the latter being the return investors actually require if they are going to invest in the company. A third reason would be that investors expect the utility's actual earnings to exceed its authorized earnings—due to the utility making more sales, or experiencing lower costs, than the levels assumed by the regulators when setting the utility's rates. A fourth reason is that if the utility's holding company also owns non-utility businesses, investors might expect those businesses to earn a return on equity exceeding the utility's authorized return on equity. The point here is not to engage in the longstanding dispute over why utility stock prices exceed book values, but to make clear that the difference between market and book exists, thereby causing the need to distinguish the two common usages of the phrase "acquisition premium."

(GPE)—because the premium was too high—the two companies agreed to a stock-for-stock exchange with no premium.[7]

5.1.3 Other Influences on the Acquisition Price

Affecting the acquisition price will be the merger agreement's many non-price features. Here are some prominent ones.

Cash or stock? The acquirer's payment to the target shareholders can take three forms: cash, acquirer stock, or a combination of cash and stock. These forms vary in attractiveness. The value of cash is certain, but the target shareholders lose their connection to their company; plus they likely will owe tax on the gain. The value of the acquirer's stock is not certain, because the merged company's operational success and regulatory treatment are not certain; but the shareholders retain their connection to the company.[8]

Termination fee: A merger agreement does not guarantee a merger. The target might find a more attractive acquirer; the acquirer might dislike the commission's approval conditions. Or a commission might reject the transaction entirely. For each of these outcomes, the typical merger agreement assigns financial consequences to one or both parties. The parties reflect these risks in the agreed price.

Compensation for departing executives: The merged company does not need two CEOs, two COOs and two CFOs. Corporate boards typically promise their top executives attractive departure payments—in part to reduce the executives' resistance to takeovers that benefit shareholders but end careers. Buying out high-level executives is costly. The anticipated cost can affect the acquisition price.

Other possibilities: Might acquisition premia have other explanations? The corporate takeover literature has offered several theories. When acquirers suffer no penalty in their stock price, some observers argue that premia reflect value-creation—exploiting economies of scale and scope, meshing skill sets, replacing under-performing executives. Others argue that premia are imprudent overpayments, associated with wasteful transactions pursued by unaccountable executives who use internal cash to expand their empires instead

---

[7]   *See* Great Plains Energy-Westar Energy Merger II, 2018 Kan. PUC LEXIS 899, at *30, *33–40.

[8]   *See, e.g.*, the discussion in Westar's proxy statement of a special Board meeting on November 19, 2015: "The Westar Board concluded that in addition to the price to be received by Westar's shareholders, other important factors would be the type of consideration and certainty of value to be received by Westar shareholders." Great Plains Energy Inc., Amendment No. 1 to Registration Statement (Form S-4/A) at 56 (Aug. 17, 2016).

of paying out dividends.[9] Professor Lynn Stout rejected both explanations. If the premia created value, accounting evidence and stock price studies would show that value. They don't. And if the premia represented overpayment, the market would punish premium-paying acquirers by lowering their share prices. It doesn't. Acquirers pay premia, Professor Stout reasoned, because they face a downward-sloping demand curve, and an upward-sloping supply curve, for the target's stock. The downward-sloping demand curve exists because different target shareholders value their shares differently: pessimists view their shares as less valuable than the market price; optimists view their shares as more valuable than the market price. The upward-sloping supply curve means that the more shares that are sought by the acquirer, the higher the price it must pay; that is, to buy all the target's shares at once (the usual practice), the acquirer must pay to all shareholders the price demanded by the most optimistic shareholder. This reasoning, she concludes, suggests that "[t]he phenomenon of takeover premiums, alone, ... tells us almost nothing about whether takeovers produce gains or losses for society in general or target shareholders in particular."[10]

5.2   TYPICAL ALLOCATION OF THE CONTROL PREMIUM: 100 PERCENT TO TARGET SHAREHOLDERS

Utility merger applicants always assign the entire control premium to the target company's shareholders, zero to the target's customers. The applicants do offer customer benefits, as Chapter 4.4 described, but compared to the premia their size is small. The Exelon-PHI and the HEI-NextEra proposals, for example, had control premia of twelve and nine times the promised ratepayer benefits, respectively.[11] One can quarrel with the specific calculations, but one cannot disagree that in electric utility mergers with premia, the target shareholders'

---

[9]   Lynn A. Stout, *Are Takeover Premiums Really Premiums? Market Price, Fair Value, and Corporate Law*, 99 YALE L.J. 1235, 1259–74 (1990). Technically, the acquirer need not pay the price demanded by *the* most optimistic shareholder, because to sell the company the target's board doesn't need the votes of all the shares. That necessary percentage of shares will depend on state law, but it will exceed 50% and will likely be at a point on the supply curve that produces a purchase price higher than the pre-merger market price.

[10]   *Id.*

[11]   These figures were the author's calculations presented in testimony before the state commissions. *See* Direct Testimony of Scott Hempling at 38, Exelon-PHI Merger, Formal Case No. 1119 (D.C. Pub. Serv. Comm'n filed Nov. 3, 2014); Direct Testimony of Scott Hempling at 166, NextEra-Hawaiian Electric Merger, Docket No. 2015-0022 (Haw. Pub. Util. Comm'n filed July 5, 2015).

gain overwhelms the target customers' benefits. Nearly every commission has accepted this lopsidedness without question.

This differential in benefit arises from the differentials in standards and strategies. As Chapter 4.2 explained, the target shareholders insist on the highest possible price, while commissions require only no "harm"—with harm defined as ignoring opportunity cost. The target acts as an auctioneer, actively seeking the highest price; the target's commission sits back, waiting to receive what the merger applicants offer as benefits. A competitive market would produce no such lopsidedness. Effective competition would both discipline the control premium and allocate the transaction's value between the target and its customers objectively. For utility monopoly mergers, the absence of competition leaves the premium undisciplined and lets the merging entities allocate it according to their self-interests. Lopsidedness prevails.

In accepting these differentials, commissions commit an analytical error. An effectively competitive market would allocate a transaction's value to those who created the value. As the next section explains, an acquisition's value to the acquirer comes from multiple sources—most having no connection to target shareholder actions. Allocating 100 percent of the control premium to target shareholders disconnects transactional gain from value creation.

5.3   SOURCES OF THE CONTROL PREMIUM'S VALUE: UNCONNECTED TO THE TARGET UTILITY'S MERIT

The control premium reflects the acquirer's valuation of control. What are the inputs to that valuation? This section considers two: (1) the target utility's government-granted franchise, supported by captive ratepayers; and (2) the acquirer's expectation that regulators will allow the target to keep excess earnings. The latter category includes four ways the utility can earn a return exceeding its actual cost of equity. A final reason for paying the control premium is the target's operational performance for customers—performance so good that the acquirer will pay a premium to own the company responsible for it. After analyzing these possibilities, the section concludes that only this last reason—performance merit—is a logical basis for allocating the control premium to the target shareholders.

5.3.1   Captive Ratepayers' Support of the Target's Government-granted Franchise

Buying all the target utility's shares gets the acquirer two distinct things: (a) the ordinary ingredients of the utility's business—assets, business processes, intellectual property, executive team, knowledgeable employees; and

(b) control of the utility's state-granted franchise. The ordinary business ingredients, by themselves, do not justify paying a control premium. Why? Before the acquisition, those other ingredients supported a revenue requirement based on the utility assets' book value.[12] After the acquisition, that book value will be the same. Because the book value will not change, it will produce the same stream of commission-authorized earnings as before. That stream, considered alone, will have the same value to the acquirer that it had to the target—the value reflected in the target's unaffected market price.

So if the acquirer were buying only those utility business ingredients, and had no plans to change any of those ingredients or use them for other business purposes, it would have no cause to pay a control premium. It would pay the market price like any ordinary investor. But the acquirer does pay a control premium. It pays that control premium because it places extra value on control—controlling an exclusive market position protected by government. The franchise's direct value is the earnings stream from selling franchised service—a revenue stream determined and protected by the statutory just and reasonable standard[13] and the Constitution's assurance of just compensation.[14] The franchise's indirect value is the value of controlling all those decisions described in Chapter 1.2.2—decisions on products, management, finance, strategy and policy. The acquirer can use that control to create earnings above those enabled by statute and protected by the Constitution.

None of these franchise values comes from the target utility's actions. Consider three analogs in the competitive sector: a New York City taxi medallion, a McDonald's franchise and a wireless company's spectrum.[15] Entering each of these markets requires paying big dollars, upfront, to some entity—the City cab regulator, McDonald's headquarters, the Federal Communications Commission. Paying upfront, these market entrants risk their investment's value-diminution;[16] and the taxi driver and the McDonald's franchisee work long hours to attract and keep customers. So when they resell their asset they

---

[12]   As discussed in the Tutorial § 4.1.

[13]   *See* Farmers Union Cent. Exch., Inc. v. FERC, 734 F.2d 1486, 1504-05 (D.C. Cir. 1984) (quoting the legislative history of the Interstate Commerce Act—the first economic regulatory statute in the U.S. using the "just and reasonable" phrase—to demonstrate Congress's intent that sellers earn a "fair profit").

[14]   U.S. Const. amend. V ("[N]or shall private property be taken for public use, without just compensation.").

[15]   For detail on the FCC's spectrum auctions, see Fed. Commc'ns Comm'n, *Conducting Auctions*, https://www.fcc.gov/auctions/conducting-auctions; Peter Cramton, *The Efficiency of the FCC Spectrum Auctions*, 41 J.L. & Econ. 727, 728 (1998).

[16]   In May 2019, the New York Times reported dramatic declines in taxi medallion values. *See* Brian M. Rosenthal, *"They Were Conned": How Reckless Loans Devastated*

expect to keep the gain. But electric utilities did not buy their franchises; they got them for free[17] in return for accepting the obligation to serve—the cost of which they recover through commission-set rates. Nor did target utilities win their franchises through merit-based competition. Because the target utility didn't pay for its franchise, and because it didn't win its franchise competitively, it cannot accurately argue that the control premium portion attributable to controlling the franchise represents value it created.

But doesn't the target's unaffected market price already reflect the franchise's value? If so, then the acquirer's offer of a premium would reflect not the value of controlling the franchise but the additional value created by the acquisition—thus entitling the target shareholders to that value. This argument ignores the value of franchise *control*—the difference between the target stock's value in the hands of an ordinary shareholder (represented by the unaffected market price) and the value in the hands of the 100 percent acquirer. Control allows the acquirer to exercise the twelve levers described in Chapter 5.1.1, from populating the utility's board to using the target's stable assets and predictable revenues to support more acquisitions. Control also enables the acquirer to expand the target utility's current market position by expanding horizontally and vertically, and by buying new market positions in existing and new markets.[18] Certainly the unaffected market price reflects, to some extent, the value to the target of having an exclusive franchise. Certainly if the state legislature repealed retail exclusivity in favor of retail competition, the target utility's market price would drop. A market position protected by government is worth more than a market position subject to competition. But that same repeal statute would also change the acquirer's control premium, because controlling an unstable market position is less attractive than controlling a guaranteed position. The control premium represents the value of controlling something. That something is the franchise.

That acquirers routinely pay control premia for competitive companies changes none of this reasoning. In both contexts—competitive market and

---

a Generation of Taxi Drivers, N.Y. Times (May 19, 2019), https://www.nytimes com/2019/05/19/nyregion/nyc-taxis-medallions-suicides.html?module=inline.

[17] WGL Holdings acknowledged that Washington Gas Light got its utility franchise for free: "Except for potential application fees or the posting of bonds and deposits with various county and municipal franchisors, Washington Gas did not provide payment to any government entity to acquire its right to provide gas distribution service in Maryland." Applicants' Response to Office of People's Counsel Discovery Request 10–17, AltaGas-Washington Gas Light Merger, Case No. 9449 (Md. Pub. Serv. Comm'n 2018). Utilities do pay annual franchise fees, but those fees become part of the revenue requirement used to set rates; so those fees are not upfront, at-risk investments. Nor do the fees bear any mathematical relationship to the franchise's commercial value.

[18] As discussed in Chapter 1.2.2.

franchised monopoly—the acquirer is buying control of a market position. The competitive target earned that market position with investment, effort, risk-taking and skill—although luck plays a role, too; the target then has maintained that market position with more of the same. The utility target got its franchise through government favor, decades ago for reasons no one remembers; it has maintained that position because the government invites no one else to compete for it. A utility's acquirer pays a premium to control a market position whose value derives not from risk-taking, effort and skill, but from government decisions unrelated to those values. Analogizing to competitive markets doesn't work.

Confirming that government protection adds value to the premium is a finding by the Connecticut regulators. In 2000, Northeast Utilities offered Consolidated Edison an acquisition premium of $1.5 billion. Recent statutory and regulatory actions had compelled ratepayers to pay for certain legacy generation costs incurred by Connecticut Light & Power (CL&P), a Northeast Utilities subsidiary. The Connecticut Department of Public Utility Control found that absent that statutory compulsion, the Connecticut utility would have had only "an opportunity, not a guarantee, to recover costs between rate cases," and thus would have borne "operational risks and the risk of … regulatory disallowance." The statutory compulsion "convert[ed] … the opportunity to recover [an income stream] into an unassailably certain stream of income"—a stream "unrelated to the operational performance of CL&P." The Department concluded: "ratepayers have to some degree influenced the size of the acquisition premium."[19]

In sum: the acquirer pays a control premium because it values control—of the target's market position made exclusive by government action that the target neither bought nor earned.

5.3.2   The Acquirer's Expectation that Regulators Will Set the Target's Rates above the Target's Reasonable Costs

We have explained that the acquirer pays a premium in part because it can use the target's franchise to provide existing and new services to existing and new customers. Also influencing the premium is the acquirer's expectation of success in persuading the target utility's regulators to approve rate treatments

---

[19]   Consolidated Edison-Northeast Utilities Merger, 2000 Conn. PUC LEXIS 325, at *176-177, *179. This transaction did not go forward.

that produce returns exceeding the acquirer's cost of capital. This subsection describes four examples of those expectations; specifically expectations of

1. earning equity-level returns on acquisition debt;
2. receiving authorized returns exceeding the acquirer's "required" return;
3. earning excess returns by charging rates based on commission-approved cost projections that exceed the acquirer's own projections; and
4. monetizing net operating losses.

As discussed next, none of these additions to earnings occurs because target shareholders take unusual risks or because target executives make unusually effective decisions. Each occurs because the acquirer persuades the regulator to make ratepayers pay more than the appropriate cost of service. That fact leads to this conclusion: these contributors to the control premium do not justify allowing target shareholders to keep the entire control premium.

5.3.2.1 Equity-level returns on acquisition debt

To buy a company is to buy its equity. The acquirer pays for its purchase with some combination of internal cash, proceeds from issuance of new stock and proceeds from the issuance of new debt. That new debt creates an opportunity for excess earnings.

Debt costs less than equity because the lender's risk is lower than the shareholder's risk. Loan contracts require the borrower to repay the principal with interest; but a company issuing common equity has no obligation to pay the equity investor anything. Since equity investors bear more risk, they demand higher returns. Now assume an acquirer uses a combination of debt and equity to buy the target utility. Assume that the interest on the debt portion is 5.00 percent, but that the commission recently authorized a return on the equity portion of the utility's rate base of 9.00 percent. What result? The acquirer's actual return on its equity investment (i.e., the non-debt-financed portion of the acquisition price) will exceed 9.00 percent—for each year in which the target's rate base reflects that debt-financed equity. It is the expectation of this excess return that makes the acquirer willing to pay for the target's equity a price exceeding the current stock price. Financial analysts call this technique "double-leveraging," because it reflects debt at the holding company level and the utility level. They also describe it as "financial engineering," because the extra earnings come not from performance merit but finance technique.[20]

---

[20]   *See, e.g.*, Letter from Ryan Wobbrock, Vice President of Moody's, to Lori Wright of Great Plains Energy (May 18, 2016) (provided in discovery in Kan. Corp. Comm'n Docket No. 16-KCPE-593-ACQ) (describing a particular acquisition finance

The point is not to criticize double-leveraging, though it has its critics.[21] The point is this: the acquirer's willingness to pay a premium, to the extent attributable to double-leveraging, owes nothing to the target shareholders' risk-taking or the target executives' decision-making. The willingness results solely from the interaction of five factors: (a) the financial market's standard differential between interest cost and equity cost; (b) the acquirer's decision to finance the acquisition in part with debt; (c) the target utility's decision to seek an equity-level return on the equity portion of its rate base financed with that debt; (d) the regulator's decision to allow an equity-level return on all the target utility's book equity, including the portion financed with debt; and (e) the target utility's franchised monopoly position, which leaves ratepayers with no choice but to pay the commission-set rates.

Buying stock with borrowed funds—known as "buying on margin"—is not new. When individual stockholders do it, the rate-setting process doesn't care. Commissions award equity returns on the full equity portion of rate base, regardless of how that equity was financed. So individual investors buying on margin earn leverage-inflated returns. This fact leads double-leveraging's defenders to ask this question: If regulators regularly ignore the source of funds when the equity purchaser is an individual, why should they act differently when the equity purchaser is a corporate acquirer? The situations are not comparable. An individual's margin buy does not affect the utility's health, because the individual's financial condition is irrelevant to the utility's financial condition. If he suffers financial difficulty and defaults on his loan, the utility, its customers and its other investors are unaffected. And before

---

scenario as "financial engineering"). This document is a confidential document, but no confidential information is revealed here.

[21]   Rejecting Great Plains Energy's original proposal to acquire Westar, the Kansas Corporation Commission described double-leveraging as allowing the utility to charge rates exceeding cost:

> [I]f the Joint Applicants are allowed to use a capital structure for ratemaking purposes that is not representative of the financing for the transaction, the ratepayers are actually subsidizing the acquisition premium. ... Such a financial structure allows the Joint Applicants to recover the acquisition premium by taking advantage of the difference between the higher returns paid to the operating utilities and the low cost of debt. ... Rather than refund the difference to the ratepayers, GPE is retaining those funds to pay the acquisition premium. Essentially, GPE is using the ratepayers as its bank.

Great Plains Energy-Westar Energy Merger I, 2017 Kan. PUC LEXIS 1142, at *44 (footnotes omitted). The Kansas Commission's order on reconsideration invited a revised application at a lower price with less debt. The two companies then reached a new agreement under which they would merge via a non-cash, stock-for-stock exchange with no premium. The Commission approved this revised agreement. Great Plains Energy-Westar Energy Merger II, 2018 Kan. PUC LEXIS 899.

financial troubles arise, he can reduce his margin risk by selling his stock. That sale, and the identity of the buyer, will make no difference to the utility's customers or to the public. But when the leveraging acquirer is a holding company buying 100 percent of the utility, those simple facts don't apply. If financial difficulties arise the acquirer can't simply sell off the utility's stock with no public consequence; the identity of the new owner matters to the consumers and the public. And the acquirer's financial difficulties matter to the utility. If the holding company acquirer cannot repay its acquisition loan, it will face ratings downgrades, resulting in higher costs for debt and equity. It will have less ability to support the utility financially. Unlike the individual stockholder, who has no control over the utility, the corporate owner can cut utility expenditures, seek rate increases, or force the utility to pay dividends with funds the utility otherwise needed for its own performance. A corporate acquirer's acquisition debt causes customers risk but brings them no benefit.

The added effect of low interest rates: Double-leveraging's value to the target's shareholders is increased by low interest rates. As Chapter 1.3.2 explained, just as low interest rates allow people to pay more for a house, they can cause corporate acquirers to offer higher prices. Like double-leveraging itself, the presence of low interest rates owes nothing to the target utility's shareholders' risk-taking or its executives' decision-making.

5.3.2.2 Authorized returns exceeding the acquirer's "required" return

A prospective acquirer has a "required" return (also called its "hurdle rate"). It is the projected return on a prospective investment below which the acquirer would not make that investment, because the acquirer has more attractive uses for its funds.[22] Put another way, the required return is the return sufficient to

---

[22] A firm's hurdle rate is

the rate of return [on investment] that managers expect a new project to earn before they are willing to undertake it. ... This distinguishes the hurdle rate from the cost of capital, the rate of return before corporate taxes that the firm must earn on new investments to provide shareholders and bondholders with the returns they demand. ... A firm's hurdle rate includes the cost of capital and also an internal risk premium considered applicable by management to the particular project at that particular time.

BD. ON SCI., TECH., AND ECON. POLICY, NAT'L RESEARCH COUNCIL, INVESTING FOR PRODUCTIVITY AND PROSPERITY 24 (1994), https://www.nap.edu/read/9075/chapter/6. Arithmetically, the hurdle rate is a fraction whose denominator is the acquisition cost and whose numerator is annual income. Synonyms for hurdle rate include internal cost of equity, required return on equity and opportunity cost of equity.

Here's a simple example. Assume the prospective acquirer's hurdle rate for prospective investments is 5%. Assume the assets of the to-be-acquired utility have a total book value of $450 million. Assume that the regulator authorizes a total return on book value of 10%, thereby providing a simple return of $45 million a year. The investor will be

attract the to-be-invested funds. A company's hurdle rate will at least equal the return available from alternative investments of comparable risk.

Suppose a prospective acquirer sees that the target utility's regulatory commission recently authorized a return on equity of 10 percent, while the acquirer's hurdle rate is only 8 percent. The acquirer will be willing to pay a premium for the opportunity to earn that higher authorized return. In GPE's original proposal to acquire Westar, a Kansas Commission staff witness concluded that the "differential between GPE's expectation of allowed equity returns in Westar's rates, compared to the real cost of equity (required return on equity) estimated by [GPE's financial advisor] Goldman," was "the most significant contributing factor for GPE's decision to pay nearly $5 billion more for Westar's equity than it is allowed to recover through rates."[23] And since the authorized return applies to the target's entire rate base, the acquirer will be willing to pay even more premium if it thinks it can persuade the regulator to allow the acquirer to increase the rate base.

Now to the main question: For that portion of the premium—the portion attributable to the acquirer's perceived opportunity to receive an authorized return exceeding its hurdle rate—what caused this value? Not any action taken by the target, its shareholders, or its executives. The value comes from regulation's inherent imperfections (setting authorized returns higher than necessary to attract capital) and from the ratepayers' status as captives (they have no choice but to pay the commission-set rates, right or wrong). In a competitive market, a seller that charged prices higher than necessary to produce a reasonable return would soon find itself undersold—so it would lower its price. But in the monopoly utility context, price correction occurs only if the regulator discovers the excess and corrects the rates. Because that correction must be prospective only, the utility can profit from the imperfection until correction

---

willing to pay up to $900 million for assets, because the $45 million return authorized by the regulator, on a $900 million investment, will satisfy the investor's 5% hurdle rate ($45/900 = 5\%$). In this example, the investor will have paid $900 million to buy book value of $450 million—a premium of 100%—all because the authorized return was double the investor's required return.

This same logic explains why bond prices rise when interest rates drop. As a Kansas Corporation Commission staff witness explained: "The financial theory and calculation mechanics supporting this conclusion are the same facts that cause a 30-year corporate bond with a $1,000 face value and annual 10% coupon payments to trade at $1770 in an environment where the true market required interest rate is only 5%." Direct Testimony of Justin Grady at 77, Great Plains Energy-Westar Energy Merger I, Docket No. 16-KCPE-593-ACQ (Kan. Corp. Comm'n filed Dec. 16, 2016).

[23]   Direct Testimony of Justin Grady, *supra* note 22, at 30.

occurs.[24] Because a situation of authorized returns exceeding required returns does not result from target shareholder risk-taking or target management decision-making, the target utility's shareholders have no logical claim on the associated portion of the premium.

Caution: The market's expectation that authorized returns will exceed required returns might already be "baked into" the target's market price. In that case, the expectation would not affect the premium. But if the acquirer expects to grow that excess, it will be willing to pay a control premium to receive those extra returns. And the acquirer could grow the excess by using rate case strategies that (a) increase the periods of regulatory lag, or (b) persuade the regulator to set rates based on cost levels higher than appropriate or sales levels lower than appropriate.

5.3.2.3 Rates based on commission-approved cost projections that exceed the acquirer's own projections

What if the acquirer expects to persuade the target utility's commission to set rates based on cost projections exceeding the acquirer's own projections? All else equal, that regulatory error will produce an actual return exceeding the acquirer's authorized return.[25] And if that authorized return exceeds the acquirer's required return, then the earned return will exceed the required return. For that extra return, an acquirer will be willing to pay a premium.

Again, this possibility of regulatory error might already be baked into the target stock's market price—especially if the stock is trading above book value. But if the utility's prospective acquirer expects to increase the probability and magnitude of regulatory error, it will be willing to pay a premium. Why might an acquirer have that expectation? Great Plains Energy's CFO testified that his company would earn an extra $65–$200 million by cutting utility operating costs post-merger, while continuing to charge rates based on cost levels set pre-merger. While future rate cases would align rates with costs prospectively, this interim cash would allow GPE "to service and repay debt and fund the incremental dividends."[26]

---

[24] Due to the prohibition on retroactive ratemaking. *See* SCOTT HEMPLING, REGULATING PUBLIC UTILITY PERFORMANCE: THE LAW OF MARKET STRUCTURE, PRICING AND JURISDICTION, ch. 10 (American Bar Association 2013).

[25] As explained in the Tutorial § 4.1. A related error would be if the commission based the rate on sales projections lower than what the acquirer expected.

[26] *See* Direct Testimony of Kevin E. Bryant at 16–17, Great Plains Energy-Westar Energy Merger I, Docket No. 16-KCPE-593-ACQ (Kan. Corp. Comm'n filed June 28, 2016). Mr. Bryant made this statement in the context of GPE's original proposal to buy Westar for cash. As explained in note 21, *supra*, the Kansas Commission rejected this proposal. The two companies then received approval of, and consummated, a stock-for-stock merger without a premium.

That these extra earnings owe nothing to target shareholders becomes clear on examining two of acquirers' most frequent cost-reduction claims: economies of scale and best practices.

Economies of scale: Economies of scale refers to a particular service's cost function. A cost function describes how production cost per unit changes with the quantity produced. A given service has a declining cost function if the per-unit cost declines as production increases. A product's cost function is inherent in that product; it does not come from investor risk-taking or managerial skill. If a bakery's per-loaf cost is lower at 1000 loaves per day than at 400, the reason is not risk-taking or skill; the reason is bread-making's inherent cost function: spreading the fixed costs of space and ovens over a larger number of loaves lowers the cost-per-loaf. To use a common merger example: if the shareholder relations function can be carried out as effectively through one office rather than two, eliminating one office post-merger will reduce the per-kWh cost. The savings come from the cost function, not from the target shareholders. Target shareholders deserve no premium attributable to cost-cutting made possible by a cost function.[27]

Best practices: Best practices are prudent practices—the practices that any successful competitor, and any prudent utility, must engage in to attract and retain customers. Regulation does not require perfection, but it does require cost-effectiveness. Hiring consultants, observing other utilities, sharing ideas with professional peers, overseeing contractors, recruiting capable managers and employees, compensating personnel based on merit—these are normal practices, not best practices. A target utility that has failed to use those practices deserves no control premium just because its acquirer will introduce them.

5.3.2.4 Monetization of net operating losses

GPE's original proposal to acquire Westar included one more contributor to the control premium: monetizing GPE's net operating losses (NOLs). Non-utility affiliates previously acquired by GPE had suffered losses of around $400 million. Losses reduce federal taxable income. GPE's net income could absorb some of the NOLs but not all; and some of the NOLs had an imminent tax law deadline, after which they could no longer shelter GPE's income from tax. The acquisition would enable GPE to apply the remaining NOLs against Westar's

---

[27] A contrasting opinion says that shareholders ought to receive some portion of the premium relating to these cost savings because mergers are not risk-free to the shareholders. They can distract management away from their normal jobs, cause the departure of good employees who fear losing their prior status, and involve financial risks associated with acquisition debt. These points are more persuasive in a context where acquirers compete based on merit instead of price.

taxable income, sooner than GPE could have used them without Westar. And because the Kansas Commission had set rates based on Westar's higher tax level (higher because there were no NOLs), a post-merger tax reduction without a rate reduction would increase the merged company's after-tax earnings and thus its value to GPE. That extra value justified a premium.[28] While in the GPE-Westar transaction the NOLs made only a minor contribution ($10.98 million)[29] to a large control premium ($2.3 billion), utility holding companies with affiliates heavily invested in generation might see more value.

As with the preceding contributors to the control premium, the acquirer's ability to use NOLs to shelter income from tax owes nothing to target shareholders' risk-taking or target management's decision-making. The NOLs arise from failed business decisions made by the acquirer's pre-existing subsidiaries, not from any innovations created by the target utility.

5.3.3   The Target's Performance Merits

We have described five likely contributors to the premium. One was the dominant market position embodied in the state-granted franchise. The remaining four were ways the merged company could influence the regulatory process to produce excess earnings: (a) applying equity-level returns to equity financed with debt; (b) receiving authorized returns exceeding the acquirer's required return; (c) earning excess returns by charging rates based on Commission-approved cost projections exceeding acquirer's own projections; and (d) monetizing net operating losses. All these contributors to the premium have their source in government actions, ratepayer captivity, regulatory imperfection and acquirer strategy. Because these contributors owe nothing to actions by target shareholders, they provide no basis for allocating the control premium to those shareholders.

There is one possible basis: the target's performance merits. A poorly financed, indifferently led, sloppily managed utility is a poorly performing utility: frequent outages, surly employees, high operating costs, unreliable

---

[28]   As GPE's CFO explained: "GPE has approximately $400 million in non-regulated net operating loss carry-forwards ... that provide a source of cash GPE plans to use to service debt and pay dividends. As a result of these NOLs, GPE does not expect to pay cash income taxes until approximately 2022." Direct Testimony of Kevin E. Bryant, *supra* note 26, at 17. *See also*, in that same case, Applicants' Response to Grady Interrogatories at DR 357 (filed Nov. 10, 2016) ("GPE expects that taxable income of Westar generated after the acquisition will allow GPE to use a large amount of its tax attributes a year or two sooner than it would have without the transaction.").

[29]   Direct Testimony of Justin Grady, *supra* note 22, at 79–80 (explaining that by using Westar's net income to accelerate use of the NOLs, the merged entity would save $10.98 million).

infrastructure and undisciplined money management. The result—low customer loyalty and high regulatory penalties—will push earnings and value down. Problems will worsen over time: the utility's service territory will become less attractive to new load, the utility will have trouble attracting and keeping top talent, and finance costs will rise—all those factors leading to deferred maintenance, more outages, more customer complaints and more regulatory penalties. Excellent management, in contrast, produces high-quality service at reasonable prices, higher customer loyalty and greater regulatory satisfaction. Because those conditions signal a long-lasting stream of stable earnings and rising value, they will cause a prospective acquirer to raise its price offer. That company's shareholders deserve some portion of the premium.

With this caveat: normal shareholder risk-taking and prudent performance already receive appropriate compensation through commission-set rates. So absent evidence of unique shareholder risk-taking, or of target performance exceeding obligatory prudent performance, the control premium is logically attributable not to performance merit but to one or more of the other five factors.

* * *

This subsection has focused on logic, explaining that the target's value to the acquirer owes much to government decisions and customer captivity; much less to target performance. Logic aside, what about law? The next section explains that no statutory or constitutional principle grants target shareholders an automatic right to the control premium. That legal conclusion leads to this solution: commissions should allocate the control premium between target shareholders and target customers according to the value each group contributed.

5.4 THE LAW: SHAREHOLDERS HAVE NO AUTOMATIC RIGHT TO THE ENTIRE CONTROL PREMIUM

In markets that are effectively competitive and economically efficient, cost-causers bear the costs and value-creators get the value. For regulation to emulate those results, commissions should allocate the control premium to those who create its associated value. But they don't. Most commissions accept the merging companies' decision to grant the full control premium to the target shareholders.

Defending this treatment, some merger applicants insist that making the target share the premium with customers would violate constitutional principles. They make three main arguments: (a) the franchise is an asset—the target utility's asset—so like any privately owned asset its owner is entitled to the full gain on sale; (b) owning the target's stock means having an automatic right to all value received when selling that stock; and that therefore (c) denying shareholders that value is a taking without just compensation, prohibited by the Fifth Amendment of the U.S. Constitution.

This section explains the errors in those arguments. Briefly: first, the franchise is a conditional privilege; it is not a private asset to sell for gain. Second, under no legal principle does stock ownership confer an automatic exemption from regulatory decisions that reduce stock value. Third, under longstanding case law, the compensation constitutionally due shareholders is a fair return on "capital embarked in the [public utility] enterprise";[30] the control premium does not fit that definition. Since a utility's rates already provide just compensation—through rate-setting's authorized return on equity associated with prudent, used-and-useful infrastructure—the control premium is over-compensation.

5.4.1 The Utility Franchise: a Conditional Privilege, Not a Private Asset

Chapter 5.1 explained that the target utility's acquirer is buying two things: ownership of the utility's business assets and control of the utility's franchise. While the assets are owned by the target utility, the franchise is not. The franchise is not an asset, so it is not owned by anyone.

The franchise is a conditional privilege. It has two main features: (a) a right to provide an essential service free from competition—that right conditioned on its holder complying with standards that replicate competitive service; and (b) a right to charge rates calculated to produce a fair return on prudent, used-and-useful investments made to provide that service. This privilege is not an asset. Its holder didn't buy it, so the holder cannot resell it. The franchise is not like a McDonald's franchise or a New York City taxi medallion. It is not like corporate stock, or buildings, or trucks, or power plants. It is not a private property whose owner can sell it to the highest bidder. The franchise is created by state government; it belongs to its creator. Its rights and responsibilities go, conditionally and temporarily, to whichever company the government chooses

---

[30]   Missouri *ex rel.* Southwestern Bell Tel. Co. v. Pub. Serv. Comm'n, 262 U.S. 276, 290 (1923) (Brandeis, J., dissenting).

based on criteria the government designs.[31] The franchise is not a private asset because it never loses its public character.

Because the franchise is a privilege created by government, it cannot have been created by the shareholders; nor was it purchased by shareholders. Contrast a wireless company that buys an FCC-auctioned spectrum. Having risked its money on the spectrum's value, the company can resell the spectrum for gain.[32] A utility did not buy the franchise. It took no risk on its value, so it has no reasonable expectation of selling it for gain.

The franchise does have value, because the right to provide exclusive service at government-set rates has value. But as Chapter 5.3 explained, that value comes not from actions by shareholders or executives, but from actions by government—actions prohibiting competition and guaranteeing reasonable rates. That the acquirer views the franchise as something worth paying for does not entitle the target to keep what the acquirer wants to pay.

Opposing this reasoning, one utility witness analogized the utility's franchise to the utility's "other licenses or permits, e.g., its environmental permits, and its corporate charter."[33] Since selling a business at a gain includes transferring those licenses for gain, he reasoned, so may a target utility transfer its franchise privilege for gain. This comparison fails because competitive markets are not like franchised monopoly markets. Those ordinary licenses and permits provide only an opportunity to compete. They allow market entry, but they guarantee no market position, no product price, no revenue flow. They do not ensure business success; they provide only a chance to seek success. An exclusive utility franchise, in contrast, guarantees a dominant market position and a government-assisted revenue flow. By buying control of that market position and that revenue flow, the acquirer not only avoids competition in the utility's product market; it gains advantages to win competitions in other product markets. A utility's franchise privilege is not like an ordinary business permit.

5.4.2   Target Stock Ownership: No Automatic Legal Entitlement to the Control Premium

Target utilities also argue that they deserve the premium because they owned the stock whose sale produced the premium. This argument reasons in

---

[31]   *See* New Orleans Gas Co. v. La. Light Co., 115 U.S. 650, 669 (1885) (describing a franchise as "belong[ing] to the government, to be granted, for the accomplishment of public projects, to whomsoever, and upon what terms [the government] pleases").

[32]   *See* Fed. Commc'ns Comm'n, *supra* note 15.

[33]   Rebuttal Testimony of John Reed at 68, AltaGas-Washington Gas Light Merger, Case No. 9449 (Md. Pub. Serv. Comm'n filed Sept. 11, 2017).

a circle. The relevant question is: "Are the owners of target stock entitled to the premium?" The answer cannot be: "Yes, because they are owners of the stock." In the utility business as in all businesses, the benefits from owning stock are always subject to diminution by government decisions. Anyone who invests in a business, whether formally regulated or not, impliedly accepts the risk that government action will devalue the investment. That has been the law since medieval times, memorialized in modern times by the U.S. Supreme Court in *Munn v. Illinois.*[34]

Attempts to equate stock ownership with premium entitlement confuse what target shareholders own (the company and its assets) with what they do not own (the government-granted franchise). As Chapter 5.1 explained, the acquirer's purchase price buys not only ownership of the utility target's stock (which is what ordinary stock purchasers buy); it also buys control of the franchise. The portion of the purchase price equal to unaffected market price buys what ordinary market purchasers buy—the stock. That amount goes to the target shareholders; if they bought their stock at a lower price, the gain represented by the higher market price is indisputably theirs. The control premium pays for something beyond mere stock; it pays for control of the franchise. Because the franchise is a conditional privilege granted to the utility rather than an asset owned by the utility, the utility's shareholders have no necessary right to the portion of the purchase price associated with it.

It is true that "what is sold in a utility merger is not public property, … but 'stocks and properties [that] are the private property of their owners.'"[35] This statement, true as a matter of contract law, clarifies nothing about regulatory law. And it concisely repeats the argument's circularity. Under a merger agreement, the target shareholders sell what they own—their target stock. Since they

---

[34]   94 U.S. 113 (1877). In *Munn*, an Illinois statute capped the prices charged by grain elevators and warehouses. Their owners argued that the cap violated the Constitution's Fifth and Fourteenth Amendments by "taking" their property—that property being the profits associated with uncapped prices. The owners lost. It had been "customary in England from time immemorial, and in this country from its first colonization, to regulate ferries … hackmen, bakers, millers, wharfingers, [and] innkeepers." *Id.* at 125. (Also mentioned were chimney-sweeping, hackney carriages, hauling by cartmen, wagoners, carmen, draymen and auctioneers.) The Court continued:

> [When someone][devotes his property to a use in which the public has an interest, he, in effect, grants to the public an interest in that use, and must submit to be controlled by the public for the common good, to the extent of the interest he has thus created. He may withdraw his grant by discontinuing the use; but, so long as he maintains the use, he must submit to the control.

Id. at 126.

[35]   *See* Respondents' [Merger Applicants'] Reply Brief at 3, Md. Office of People's Counsel v. Md. Pub. Serv. Comm'n, 192 A.3d 744 (Md. filed Aug. 30, 2017) (quoting Elec. Pub. Utils. Co. v. Pub. Serv. Comm'n, 154 Md. 445, 451 (1928)).

don't own the franchise privilege, they don't sell the franchise privilege. And since the acquirer's offer price reflects the acquirer's valuation of both the stock and franchise privilege, while what is sold is only the stock, the target shareholders cannot keep the portion of the purchase price associated with the franchise. That the transaction transfers both stock and franchise does not mean the seller gets the value of the stock and the value of the franchise.

All shareholders, of a regulated and unregulated companies, have hopes of being bought out for a premium. A government decision denying them that premium will cause disappointment. But mere hopes and disappointment are not the Constitution's concern; only just compensation, in the form of a fair return on prudent, used-and-useful investment, is. As discussed next, shareholders already receive just compensation through the authorized return on the utility's prudent, used-and-useful investment. The control premium, unless based on performance merit, is overcompensation.

5.4.3 Target Shareholders Receive their Just Compensation through the Commission-authorized Return on Equity

Target utility shareholders have a right to just compensation. As discussed, that right comes from two legal sources: the statutory requirement that rates be "just and reasonable",[36] and the constitutional standard, inscribed in the Fifth Amendment's Takings Clause (as applied to the states through the Fourteenth Amendment's Due Process Clause), stating: "nor shall private property be taken without just compensation." Satisfying the statute necessarily satisfies the Constitution.[37]

Conventional cost-based ratemaking satisfies both standards. Regulators compute an annual revenue requirement by summing reasonable expenses (including operating expenses, depreciation expense,[38] and taxes) and the

---

[36] The "just and reasonable" standard first appeared in U.S. law in the Interstate Commerce Act of 1887. Congress wanted rates that "would permit … carriers to earn a fair return while protecting … shippers and the public from economic harm." Farmers Union Cent. Exch., Inc. v. FERC, 734 F.2d 1486, 1504-05 (D.C. Cir. 1984) (quoting Senator Elkins' statement that rates should allow "the shipper and producer [to] make a fair profit on their products, the [carrier to receive] a fair return for the service rendered, and the consumer [to] get what he buys at a fair price").

[37] FPC v. Hope Nat. Gas Co., 320 U.S. 591, 607 (1944) ("Since there are no constitutional requirements more exacting than the standards of the [Natural Gas] Act, a rate order which conforms to the latter does not run afoul of the former.").

[38] In ratemaking, depreciation expense is the means by which the utility recovers from its customers the original cost of an asset that will last for multiple years. If an asset costs $450 million and will last for 30 years, commissions typically will include in the annual revenue requirement $15 million (1/30 of 450 million). Depreciation

cost of capital. The cost of capital is calculated by multiplying (a) a rate base, consisting of the reasonable capital expenditures necessary to provide a utility service (technically, the original cost of those expenditures less accumulated depreciation) by (b) a weighted rate of return reflecting contractual interest rates and a regulator-estimated cost of equity.[39] As Justice Brandeis famously explained: "The thing devoted by the investor to the public use is not specific property, tangible and intangible, but capital embarked in the enterprise. Upon the capital so invested the Federal Constitution guarantees to the utility the opportunity to earn a fair return."[40] The "capital embarked in the enterprise" is the rate base:

> The adoption of the amount prudently invested as the rate base and the amount of the capital charge as the measure of the rate of return would give definiteness to these two factors involved in rate controversies which are now shifting and treacherous, and which render the proceedings peculiarly burdensome and largely futile. Such measures offer a basis for decision which is certain and stable. The rate base would be ascertained as a fact, not determined as matter of opinion. It would not fluctuate with the market price of labor, or materials, or money.[41]

Justice Brandeis's explanation forms the basis for our modern understanding of how the Constitution applies to ratemaking. When commissions set cost-based rates, utility shareholders receive the compensation required by statute and Constitution.

5.4.4 The Control Premium is Not "Capital Embarked in the Enterprise"

In Justice Brandeis's terms, the "capital embarked in the enterprise" is what the utility spends to buy trucks and build generating plants. The control premium is different money. It is not money spent by the utility to buy trucks; it is money spent by the acquirer to gain control of the franchise. It reflects the acquirer's bet that controlling the franchise will increase its value by at least the amount of the premium. The acquirer's willingness to bet the premium gives the target shareholders no automatic right to receive the premium. The Constitution

---

expense allows the utility to recover its original cost from ratepayers proportionally over the asset's life. The portion of the original cost that remains unrecovered (say, $420 million after the first year, $390 million after the second year and so on) remains in rate base to earn a return.

[39] *See* Tutorial § 4.1.

[40] Missouri *ex rel.* Southwestern Bell Tel. Co. v. Pub. Serv. Comm'n, 262 U.S. 276, 290 (1923) (Brandeis, J., dissenting).

[41] *Id.* at 306–307.

protects "capital embarked in the enterprise"; it does not guarantee gain from the acquirer's bet.[42]

That target shareholders have no automatic right to the premium is confirmed by commonsense scenarios. A legislative body wishing to discourage debt-leveraged acquisitions with high premia could impose a tax on the associated gain. It could even prohibit, or tax heavily, entire classes of acquisitions—such as acquisitions that involved remote utilities; or acquisitions that subordinated the utility to a holding company system more than, say, three times the utility's size; or exposed the utility to international currency risk; or mixed higher-risk, non-utility businesses with lower-risk utility businesses.[43] These measures would shrink the universe of potential acquirers bidding to buy targets. Doing so would lower the premia paid, thereby reducing target shareholders' gain. Yet these measures raise no constitutional questions. Statutes taxing capital gains are common. And value-lowering prohibitions are constitutional; they were central to the Public Utility Holding Company Act 1935, which the U.S. Supreme Court upheld against Fifth Amendment attack.[44] In short, rational government action to reduce shareholders' hoped-for gain does not violate the Constitution—especially when it advances valid public interest goals such as (1) preventing transactions that burden the merged company with debt (as in the case of a cash buyout), or burden the acquirer's shareholders with stock dilution (as in the case of a stock-for-stock exchange);

---

[42]   Caution: If in granting the franchise, the government entity promised, either by statute or contract, that the target could keep the gain, the target's constitutional claim to that gain would be strong, under either the Takings Clause or the Contract Clause. *See* New Orleans Water-Works Co. v. Rivers, 115 U.S. 674, 681 (1885) (holding that the city's grant of an exclusive franchise to a water company was a contract, which even a later-enacted state constitutional amendment banning utility monopolies could not impair).

[43]   *See, e.g.*, Wisconsin Utilities Holding Company Act, WIS. STAT. § 196.795(6m) (b). This feature of the Act was upheld by the Seventh Circuit on Commerce Clause grounds in Alliant Energy Corp. v. Bie, 330 F.3d 904, 919 (7th Cir. 2003). The author was a witness for the Wisconsin Attorney General in the District Court case leading to the Seventh Circuit decision.

[44]   *See* North American Co. v. SEC, 327 U.S. 686, 708, 710 (1946) (holding that the divestiture requirement in PUHCA § 11(b)(1) did not deprive shareholders of constitutionally protected just compensation, since Congress could decide that "the benefit alleged to flow from efficient, common management of diversified interests" was "clearly outweighed by the actual and potential damage to the public, the investors and the consumers resulting from the use made of pooled investments"); Am. Power & Light Co. v. SEC, 329 U.S. 90, 106-07 (1946) (applying reasoning from *North American Co.* to uphold PUHCA section 11(b)(2), which required the SEC to simplify corporate structure).

and (2) discouraging target companies from seeking acquirers based on gain rather than customer welfare.

In competitive markets, shareholders who sell their businesses for a gain do keep the gain—subject to gain-reducing taxation. That fact does not affect the constitutional analysis here. In the competitive context, the acquirer's willingness to pay a control premium, and the target shareholders' expectation of receiving that premium, are both disciplined by competition in the target's product market. And the target company receives neither government protection from competition nor government assurance of reasonable prices for its products. Competition in the merged entity's product market will lower the premium that target shareholders receive, while forcing the merged company to share any merger-created value with the customers. So when regulation limits either the premium or the target shareholders' gain, it is doing what competition does. There is no basis for constitutional concern.

Because the control premium is not capital embarked in the public utility enterprise, the target shareholders' expectation of receiving gain comes from their decision to bet on stocks, not from the utility's decision to invest in obligatory service assets. Nothing in Justice Brandeis's seminal formulation, or any constitutional case, protects bets on utility stock prices. Rate base is where government honors its constitutional obligations; stock value is where shareholders bet their money. The dollars shareholders spend to buy stock are constitutionally distinct from the dollars a utility spends to acquire utility assets.

Another way to understand the point: accompanying the franchise is the obligation to provide the franchise service. That obligation includes investing in the necessary assets. By imposing on the utility this obligation to invest, the government has, in the Fifth Amendment's words, "taken" private property for which the Constitution requires "just compensation." Government provides that just compensation by allowing gradual recovery of the investment through depreciation expense and by allowing a return on the not-yet-depreciated amount. Those steps provide the utility with Justice Brandeis's "opportunity to earn a fair return." So the constitutionally required "just compensation" relates only to the utility's investment in utility assets—"capital embarked in the enterprise." A shareholder's purchase of stock involves no obligation imposed by government; it is a voluntary act, taken in hopes of increasing the shareholder's wealth. The Fifth Amendment promises compensation for takings—involuntary actions like making capital expenditures to carry out the obligation to serve, not voluntary actions like buying stock.

5.4.5 The Control Premium Exceeds the Target Shareholders' Legally Required Compensation

If lawfully set rates already give target shareholders just compensation, then giving them the control premium necessarily produces overcompensation.[45] The control premium does not compensate the target shareholders for any costs incurred or risks undertaken to carry out the target's obligation to serve, because (a) the compensation for those costs and risks is included already in the target's rates, and because (b) the target's investment in the franchise privilege itself was zero.[46] The control premium is gain beyond the just compensation provided by lawful ratemaking.

Target shareholders might argue that they are entitled to the control premium's value because they elected the board that hired the executive team that created the value, and because they risked the dollars that financed the executive team's decisions that led to that value. Addressing this argument requires careful attention to the term "value." As Chapter 5.1.2 explained, the target's unaffected stock price usually exceeds its book value. That excess reflects the market's expectation that actual returns will exceed required returns. And that excess ordinarily belongs to shareholders, because in buying stock they risked their dollars hoping that the utility's board and executives would run the company so as to produce that excess. Commissions do not make shareholders pay ratepayers the excess of unaffected stock price over book value—just as they do not make ratepayers pay shareholders when the stock price falls below book value. The control premium is a different story. For the reasons explained in Chapter 5.3, the control premium, unlike the excess of market value over book value, exists for reasons mostly unrelated to target company management decisions. And because shareholders already receive, through ratemaking, the legally required compensation for those decisions, the extra compensation from the control premium is over-compensation.

* * *

Chapter 5.3 explained that absent extraordinary target utility performance, there is no policy justification for allowing target utility shareholders to keep

---

[45]   I refer, of course, to only that portion of the control premium properly attributable to the target utility's obligation to serve. Part of the premium could be attributable to the acquirer's valuation of the target utility's non-utility affiliates. Except to the extent the non-utility affiliates' profitability depended on support from the utility, that portion of the premium belongs entirely to the target shareholders.

[46]   Chapter 5.3.1 explained that, unlike wireless spectrum or taxi medallions, franchises go to utilities for free, except for annual franchise fees—and those fees are recovered from customers because they are included in the utility's revenue requirement.

the control premium. The current subchapter has just explained that those shareholders have no constitutional entitlement to the control premium either. What then should regulators do about the control premium? We address that question next.

5.5   THE CORRECTION: ALLOCATE THE CONTROL PREMIUM'S VALUE TO THE VALUE-CREATORS AND BURDEN-BEARERS

Under economic theory and regulatory law, society is best off when costs go to the cost-causers; and when gains go to the risk-takers, benefit-creators and burden-bearers. Applying this principle to the control premium means allocating it between the target utility shareholders and customers according to each group's contribution to the premium's value.

Regulation applies the benefit-follows-burden principle when a utility sells off assets previously used for utility service. If customers had historically borne the asset's costs and risks (if, for example, the asset had been in the utility's rate base), they get the gain on sale:

> It is well settled that utility investors are entitled to recoup from consumers the full amount of their investment in depreciable assets devoted to public service. ...
>
> [Since customers] have shouldered these burdens, ... it is eminently just that consumers, whose payments for service reimburse investors for the ravages of wear and waste occurring in service, should benefit in instances where gain eventuates—to the full extent of the gain.[47]

---

[47]   Democratic Central Committee of D.C. v. Washington Metro. Area Transit Comm'n, 485 F.2d 786, 808, 810–11 (D.C. Cir. 1973) (footnotes omitted). *See also id.* at 808 ("[I]f the land no longer useful in utility operations is sold at a profit, those who shouldered the risk of loss are entitled to benefit from the gain."); Separation of Costs of Regulated Telephone Service from Costs of Nonregulated Activities, 2 FCC Rcd. 6283, 6295 ¶ 114 (1987) (order on reconsideration) (observing that "[t]he equitable principles identified in [*Democratic Central Committee*] have direct application to a transfer of assets out of regulation that produces gains to be distributed"; and requiring "that ratepayers receive the gains on assets when the market value of the assets exceeds net book cost"); N.Y. Water Serv. Corp. v. Pub. Serv. Comm'n, 12 A.D.2d 122, 129 (N.Y. App. Div. 1960) (allocating gain on sale to ratepayers when ratepayers bore the risk of a loss in value of the assets); N.Y. State Elec. & Gas, 1996 N.Y. PUC LEXIS 671, at *8 (memorandum opinion) (finding that reserving the net gains on the sale of land for ratepayers is "equitable and reasonable"); N.Y. Tel. Co. v. N.Y. Pub. Serv. Comm'n, 530 N.E.2d 843 (N.Y. 1988) (ratepayers entitled to benefits on sale of Yellow Pages advertisements).

See also Kansas Power & Light Co. v. State Corp. Comm'n, 620 P.2d 329, 341 (Kan. Ct. App. 1980) (holding that in allocating a utility's capital gain between shareholders and ratepayers, the Commission "should consider" five guidelines: (1) "the risk of

If the asset had not been in rate base, the gain would go to the shareholders because they would have borne the economic burden.[48]

While the gain-on-sale cases use the benefit-follows-burden principle, their outcomes do not resolve the control premium question directly. In those cases, someone—shareholders or ratepayers—bore the cost of the asset being sold. But no one—neither target shareholders nor ratepayers—paid for the franchise whose value supports the control premium. So the necessary focus must be not on burden borne but on value created. As between ratepayers and shareholders, who created the franchise's value? While a utility-specific answer must depend on utility-specific facts, here are some general arguments on either side.

Arguments for ratepayers: As Chapters 1.2.2 and 5.3 explained, the acquirer sees value in controlling a franchise that produces stable revenue. The source of that value is the customers. Their captivity comes from the government's decision to exclude competition. So the premium should go to the customers, the government, or both. Merger applicants might respond that (a) ratepayers got what they paid for—utility service, and (b) the government got what it wanted—a healthy economy served by a viable electric company; therefore, neither ratepayers nor the government deserve anything more. That is a fair argument—but it tells us only that ratepayers do not *automatically* get the entire control premium. It does not tell us that their roles entitle them to zero and that the shareholders get everything. The argument also ignores this point: the acquirer pays a control premium because it expects its control to create economic value in the future—value that depends on customers remaining captive in the future. To the acquirer's perceived future value, the customers' past satisfaction is irrelevant.

Arguments for shareholders: Without shareholders' investment, there would be no service for ratepayers to buy and no business for the acquirer to buy; therefore, the control premium's value comes from target shareholders. But just as the ratepayers received service in return for paying rates, shareholders have received compensation in return for making their investment. One cannot say, therefore, that the target shareholders contributed any more to the premi-

---

loss of investment capital"; (2) "contribution by the ratepayers to the value of the property, such as maintenance, upkeep and improvements"; (3) "financial integrity of the company, and the effect of the allocation on the price of the stock and the ability of the company to attract adequate capital"; (4) "increases in the value of the property due to inflation"; and (5) "increased value of the property due to improvements in the neighborhood of the facilities sold as a result of special assessments ... which were paid in whole or in part by the ratepayers").

[48]   *See, e.g.*, Boise Water Corp. v. Idaho Pub. Utils. Comm'n, 578 P.2d 1089, 1092–93 (Idaho 1978) (distinguishing *Democratic Central Committee* because, in the water asset sale at issue, shareholders had borne the asset's cost).

um's value than the ratepayers did. And because the target shareholders did not have to pay for the franchise (unlike taxi medallion owners and wireless spectrum holders), they get no help from the gain-on-sale precedent.[49] They bore no burden justifying a benefit.

One point is not debatable: to the extent we can attribute the control premium to the target's non-utility affiliates, the target shareholders deserve the premium, because that value comes neither from captive ratepayers' payments nor the government's exclusion of competition (except to the extent the non-utility affiliates' success depended on the utility's support). The shareholders also must receive the portion of the purchase price that is not the control premium; that is, the portion equal to the excess of unaffected market value over book value. That amount has nothing to do with the acquisition because it pre-dated the acquisition.

What if the shareholder and ratepayer arguments have equal weight (or weightlessness)? What if, for example, a commission finds that the control premium is, technically, a windfall—a lucky value to which no one actually contributed? In these situations, logic and neutrality call for a default result of 50-50. If two friends simultaneously discovered a cashier's check of $1 million, they would split it in half. Back to target shareholders and ratepayers: absent either party demonstrating a relative contribution exceeding 50 percent, the logical result is equal sharing. There is no logic to granting 100 percent to the shareholders, any more than there is logic to granting 0 percent to the shareholders.

In the only judicial opinion relating to these arguments, the Maryland Court of Appeals (the state's highest court) held that the Maryland Commission was not "required to regard [the] acquisition premium ... as a harm to consumers or as inconsistent with the public interest."[50] Applying a deferential standard of review, the Court held as follows:

- Because the statute made no explicit mention of the control premium, the Commission had discretion over whether and how to address it.

---

[49]   But if the current shareholders had previously bought the company at a premium, could they not argue that they in fact did pay for the franchise? No, for the reasons already given. The franchise is a government-granted privilege; it is not for sale. When these hypothetical shareholders paid a premium, they were not buying the franchise; they were buying stock, betting their payments on the possibility of receiving future earnings from controlling the franchise.

[50]   Md. Office of People's Counsel v. Md. Pub. Serv. Comm'n, 192 A.3d 744, 754 (Md. 2018). This case was the appellate review of the Commission's approval of Exelon's acquisition of PHI (the holding company for Pepco, Atlantic City Electric and Delmarva Power & Light). The author was a witness for the Maryland Office of People's Counsel on the control premium issue.

- In not finding the premium harmful, the commission had not deviated from its prior treatment of mergers—treatment which included both comparing the premium to that paid in prior mergers and prohibiting rate recovery.
- Given that the Commission had no statutory obligation to consider the issue, its decision to disregard concerns about the premium was not an abuse of discretion. It was "difficult to see how consumers are necessarily worse off as a result of the payment of a premium, or would necessarily be better off if an acquiring company paid a smaller premium."
- The gain-on-sale precedent did not apply, because unlike utility property, the control premium had not been placed in rate base and therefore was not a cost borne by ratepayers.

The Court did not address constitutional arguments. It also cautioned that nothing in its reasoning "suggest[s] that an acquisition premium can never be considered by the Commission, either as a potential harm or as contrary to the public interest." The Commission could find, for example, that the premium could harm consumers if it was so large as to cause the layoff of essential employees, or if it was based on "unrealistic expectations about future profits that risk consumer harm."[51]

* * *

To buy control, the acquirer pays a control premium. The typical merger agreement, and the typical commission approval, assigns that control premium entirely to the target shareholders, none to the customers. But the most likely sources of value supporting the premium don't come from the target shareholders. The most likely source of value is the target's monopoly market position—a position granted by government, not paid for or earned by shareholders. The next most likely source of value is the acquirer's earnings expectation; specifically, the expectation that regulators will allow the merged company to have earnings exceeding competitive levels. Both these sources of value result from the state government's decision to make customers captive. A third source of value is the target's unique performance merits. To the extent those merits reflect performance exceeding what captive customers already pay for in their rates, the target shareholders do deserve the associated portion of the premium.

By missing these distinctions, commissions allow the merging companies to divert the entire premium to the shareholders, leaving none for customers. The correct approach is to allocate the premium between shareholders and customers in proportion to what they've contributed to its associated value.

---

[51]   *Id.* at 758.

6. Mergers can distort competition: market power, anticompetitive conduct and unearned advantage

When two utilities serve the same or nearby markets, or might do so someday, their merger affects competition. The effects can range from positive to negative, from minimal to dramatic.

To understand a merger's effects on competition, one first must understand competition. Competition is both a market structure and a process. Market structures range from hard monopoly to perfect competition. A market's structure affects its sellers' conduct; those sellers' conduct affects the market's performance. Since the goal of regulatory policy is performance, policymakers must understand these influences on performance. When a market's structure is not effectively competitive—when sellers have market power, or act anticompetitively or exploit unearned advantages—the sellers' conduct will not produce cost-effective performance—the performance customers would receive were the market effectively competitive. We will not have competition on the merits.[1]

This focus on market structure leads us to mergers, because mergers change market structures. This chapter explains horizontal mergers—mergers that reduce the number of competitors—and vertical mergers—mergers that give the merged company control of important inputs. Either type, under certain facts, can harm customers by weakening competitive forces. The chapter closes by describing and assessing the tools and remedies regulators use to detect and deter—or at least dilute—a merger's competitive harms.

Running through this chapter are two distinct sources of legal authority by which policymakers can address competitive harm. Antitrust law addresses

---

[1]   Readers of a certain age may recall humorist Art Buchwald's 1966 prediction of the U.S. economy in 1978, when only two companies remained: Samson Securities and the Delilah Company. The full column, reprinted at the end of this chapter, originally appeared in *The Washington Post* on June 2, 1966 at p. A21. Eleven days later, the first of many reprints appeared as an appendix to Justice Douglas's concurrence in *United States v. Pabst Brewing Co.*, 384 U.S. 546, 593–94 (1966). Buchwald's columns, along with Charles Schultz's comic strips and Russell Baker's essays, were among the few things that made my late father laugh.

anticompetitive conduct—conduct that weakens competition. Its enforcers are the Federal Trade Commission and the Department of Justice applying federal antitrust law, state attorneys general applying federal and state antitrust law, and private plaintiffs at both levels. While antitrust law addresses only anticompetitive conduct,[2] regulatory law can cause pro-competitive conduct. Regulatory law—carried out in the electricity space by state utility commissions and the Federal Energy Regulatory Commission (FERC)—recognizes that competitive forces can be weakened by factors other than anticompetitive conduct—factors like entry barriers, sellers' unearned advantages and insufficient customer information. Recognizing antitrust law's limits, while appreciating regulatory law's breadth, is essential to creating and carrying out merger policies that benefit consumers.[3]

6.1 COMPETITION: A MARKET STRUCTURE AND A PROCESS

After explaining markets and market structure, this section describes how a market's structure affects its competitiveness.

6.1.1 Markets and Market Structures

A market is a medium through which sellers and buyers exchange goods or services for value.[4] Every market, properly defined, has two dimensions:

---

[2] *See* DANIEL A. CRANE, THE INSTITUTIONAL STRUCTURE OF ANTITRUST ENFORCEMENT, at iv (2011) ("Unless a plaintiff can describe the defendant's conduct as harming the process of economic rivalry in a way that harms consumers, she probably does not have an antitrust claim.").

[3] *See* Concord v. Boston Edison Co., 915 F.2d 17, 22 (1st Cir. 1990) (Breyer, J.) ("'[R]egulation' and 'antitrust' typically aim at similar goals—i.e., low and economically efficient prices, innovation, and efficient production methods—but they seek to achieve these goals in very different ways. Economic regulators seek to achieve them *directly* by controlling prices through rules and regulations; antitrust seeks to achieve them *indirectly* by promoting and preserving a process that tends to bring them about."); CRANE, *supra* note 2, at iv ("[A]ntitrust is really a 'residual regulator' that comes into play when other legal and regulatory mechanisms are not in play.") (citing HERBERT HOVENKAMP, THE ANTITRUST ENTERPRISE 13 (2005)).

[4] *See, e.g.,* JOHN B. TAYLOR & AKILA WEERAPANA, PRINCIPLES OF ECONOMICS 3 (6th ed. 2010) ("A market is simply an arrangement by which buyers and sellers can interact and exchange goods and services with each other."); N. GREGORY MANKIW, PRINCIPLES OF ECONOMICS 64 (3d ed. 2004) ("A market is a group of buyers and sellers of a particular good or service. The buyers as a group determine the demand for the product, and the sellers as a group determine the supply of the product."); THOMAS D. MORGAN, CASES AND MATERIALS ON MODERN ANTITRUST LAW AND ITS ORIGINS 7–8

a product dimension and a geographic dimension. The product dimension describes the specific product a customer seeks, plus all products that the customer views as reasonable substitutes.[5] The geographic dimension describes the area within which the customer is willing and able to shop for the product. That geographic area will include all sellers willing and able to reach the customer economically.[6] We experience product and geographic dimensions in everyday life: vegetarian restaurants in downtown Baltimore, wireless service in rural Iowa. Electricity examples include firm wholesale electric capacity in the upper Midwest, non-firm wholesale electric energy in New England, renewable energy in coastal Virginia.

A market can also have a time element, when time is important to the customer. Examples from everyday life are bakeries open after Sunday church, taxi service after late-night concerts, airplane seats the day after Christmas. In

---

(4th ed. 2009) ("The 'market' described in economic theory and in antitrust cases ... has neither a street address, website, nor a FAX number. What is critical for purposes of economic theory is that sometimes people can realistically deal with one another, and sometimes they cannot. Those that can deal are said to be participating in a market.").

[5] *See* Sunshine Cellular v. Vanguard Cellular Sys., Inc., 810 F. Supp. 486, 493 (S.D.N.Y. 1992) (explaining that the product dimension includes "those commodities or services that are reasonably interchangeable by consumers for the same purposes"); FTC v. Staples, Inc., 970 F. Supp. 1066, 1074 (D.D.C. 1997) ("The general rule when determining a relevant product market is that '[t]he outer boundaries of a product market are determined by the reasonable interchangeability of use [by consumers] or the cross-elasticity of demand between the product itself and substitutes for it.'" (quoting Brown Shoe v. United States, 370 U.S. 294, 325 (1962)); Order No. 642, *Revised Filing Requirements Under Part 33 of the Commission's Regulations*, F.E.R.C. STATS. & REGS. ¶ 31,111, 65 Fed. Reg. 70,984, 70,991 (2000) [hereinafter Order No. 642] ("[I]t is important to define relevant products from the perspective of the consumer, i.e., including in a product group those products considered by the consumer to be good substitutes."), *order on reh'g*, Order No. 642-A, 94 F.E.R.C. ¶ 61,289, 66 Fed. Reg. 16,121 (2001).

[6] *See* Sunshine Cellular, 810 F. Supp. at 493 (explaining that the geographic dimension encompasses "the area in which sellers of the relevant product effectively compete"); Am. Key Corp. v. Cole Nat'l Corp., 762 F.2d 1569, 1580 (11th Cir. 1985) ("[T]he geographic market consists of the area from which sellers of [substitute goods or services] derive their customers and the area within which purchasers of [those substitutes] can practically turn for such products or services."); DEP'T OF JUSTICE & FED. TRADE COMM'N, HORIZONTAL MERGER GUIDELINES § 4.2 (2010) [hereinafter 2010 HORIZONTAL MERGER GUIDELINES] ("The arena of competition affected by the merger may be geographically bounded if geography limits some customers' willingness or ability to substitute to some products, or some suppliers' willingness or ability to serve some customers. Both supplier and customer locations can affect this."). For a summary of how the *Horizontal Merger Guidelines* have changed since 1968, see JOHN KWOKA, MERGERS, MERGER CONTROL, AND REMEDIES: A RETROSPECTIVE ANALYSIS OF U.S. POLICY 13–16 (2015).

electricity, time is important because power must be available the instant we demand it. Generation capacity available at 2 a.m. is not necessarily available at 2 p.m.—at least not until we have widespread storage.

Having defined a market's dimensions—product, geographic and time— one can describe its structure. A market's structure has these elements: (a) the number of sellers and buyers and their market shares; (b) the sellers' competitive strengths and weaknesses, evidenced by their financial resources, asset control, customer loyalty and other factors; and (c) the ease with which prospective competitors can enter or leave the market.[7]

6.1.2   How Market Structure Affects Market Competitiveness

A market's structure affects its competitiveness. When competition is insufficient, one or more companies can have market power—the "power to control prices or exclude competition."[8] For a seller, market power is "the ability profitably to maintain prices above competitive levels for a significant period of time"; along with the ability to "lessen competition on dimensions other than price, such as product quality, service, or innovation."[9] For a buyer, market power is the ability "to depress the price paid for a product to a level that is below the competitive price and thereby depress output."[10] Besides controlling prices, a firm with market power can exclude its competitors: the seller, by denying its competitors access to essential inputs; the buyer, by denying its competitors adequate supplies by forcing its suppliers to deal exclusively with that buyer.[11] Market power can be exercised unilaterally; or in coordination with others, implicitly or explicitly.

---

[7]   *See* Joseph E. Stiglitz & Carl E. Walsh, Economics, at A6 (3d ed. 2002) (describing market structure as a "term used to describe the organization of the market, such as whether there is a high degree of *competition*, a *monopoly*, an *oligopoly*, or *monopolistic competition*") (emphasis in original).

[8]   United States v. E.I. du Pont de Nemours & Co., 351 U.S. 377, 391 (1956).

[9]   Dep't of Justice & Fed. Trade Comm'n, Horizontal Merger Guidelines § 0.1 (1992, rev. 1997) [hereinafter 1997 Horizontal Merger Guidelines]. *See also Portland Gen. Exch., Inc.*, 51 F.E.R.C. ¶ 61,108, at p. 61,244 n.47 (1990) (seller market power includes the ability to "hold a price constant and offer an inferior service while excluding competitors").

[10]   1997 Horizontal Merger Guidelines, *supra* note 9, § 0.1.

[11]   *See, e.g.*, Ignacio Herrera Anchustegui, Buyer Power in EU Competition Law, ch. 7.3 (2017) (describing exclusive supply obligations); Peter C. Carstensen, Competition Policy and the Control of Buyer Power (2017). For examples of buyer market power in electricity, see Chapter 6.4.2 below (discussing how a vertically merged company can damage competition in the upstream market by discriminating against non-affiliate sellers of inputs).

This brief explanation of market power displays its two key harms: exploitation and exclusion. Exploitation is direct harm: the seller overcharging its customers; the buyer underpaying its suppliers. Exclusion is harm to the competitive process—a firm with market power preventing its rivals from competing, or raising its rivals' costs so that they have trouble competing.[12]

To understand how market structures affect competitiveness, consider four market structures, sequenced in rising levels of competitiveness.

a. No competition: A market having no competition is a monopoly market. Its single seller has market power—the ability to control price and supply. Why might a monopoly market exist? Here are four possible reasons.

Patent: A patent is a government-protected monopoly, granted to the product's creator for a statutorily set period. If consumers have no reasonable substitute for the patented product, the patent holder will have a monopoly in that product market. (Remember: A product market includes the named product plus all reasonable substitutes. So one could have a monopoly over one's patented product, but not have a monopoly in that product market if the patented product has reasonable substitutes.)

Natural monopoly: Every product or service has a cost function—the rate at which its per-unit cost of production rises or falls as quantity increases. (A product's cost function will vary among firms depending on their efficiency; but for any given firm the product will have its own cost function.) For a geographic market, a product is a natural monopoly product if its cost function declines over the total quantity demanded by customers in that market. Because of that declining cost function, the cost of serving that total quantity will be lower with a single seller than with multiple sellers. As Richard Posner explained, the term "natural monopoly"

> does not refer to the actual number of sellers in a market but to the relationship between demand and the technology of supply. If the entire demand within a relevant market can be satisfied at lowest cost by one firm rather than by two or more, the market is a natural monopoly, whatever the actual number of firms in it.[13]

---

[12] *See generally* Thomas G. Krattenmaker & Steven C. Salop, *Anticompetitive Exclusion: Raising Rivals' Costs to Achieve Power over Price*, 96 YALE L.J. 209 (1986).

[13] Richard A. Posner, *Natural Monopoly and Its Regulation*, 21 STAN. L. REV. 548, 548 (1969).

Legal prohibition against competition: Historically, governments have prohibited competition for services they assume are natural monopolies. As the U.S. Supreme Court explained, discussing local distribution of natural gas,

> [B]y the time natural gas became a widely marketable commodity, the States had learned from chastening experience that public streets could not be continually torn up to lay competitors' pipes, that investments in parallel delivery systems for different fractions of a local market would limit the value to consumers of any price competition, and that competition would simply give over to monopoly in due course. It seemed virtually an economic necessity for States to provide a single, local franchise with a business opportunity free of competition from any source, within or without the State, so long as the creation of exclusive franchises under state law could be balanced by regulation and the imposition of obligations to the consuming public upon the franchised retailers.[14]

A majority of states prohibit competition in the retail sale of electricity; nearly all states prohibit competition in the physical distribution of electric current.

Market forces: A monopoly market structure can arise, ironically, from competitive market forces. Competitors naturally strive to win. Through skill, effort and luck, a company can lower its costs or increase its quality so effectively as to attract away its competitors' customers. Those competitors can become discouraged, less well-financed, less able to attract the best employees and ultimately unable to compete.

b. Oligopolistic competition: An oligopolistic market has a small number of competitors.[15] The competition among those competitors—oligopolistic competition—is characterized by (a) "interdependence among the sellers because each is large relative to the size of the market," (b) "substantial economies of scale," and (c) "high entry barriers into the market."[16] In an oligopolistic market, "each firm is affected by the decisions of its rivals and must take those decisions into account in determining its own price and output."[17] To exercise oligopoly power—that is, to maintain prices above competitive levels—the sellers must be able to agree on price, monitor each other's prices and detect and punish deviations from the agreement.[18] While the group's members try avoid competing with each other on price (so as to keep price above competitive levels), they do compete by differentiating their products.[19]

---

[14]   GMC v. Tracy, 519 U.S. 278, 289–90 (1997).

[15]   PAUL KRUGMAN & ROBIN WELLS, MICROECONOMICS 420 (4th ed. 2015).

[16]   JAMES D. GWARTNEY ET AL., ECONOMICS: PRIVATE & PUBLIC CHOICE 551 (10th ed. 2002).

[17]   CAMPBELL R. MCCONNELL & STANLEY L. BRUE, ECONOMICS: PRINCIPLES, PROBLEMS, AND POLICIES 400 (17th ed. 2008).

[18]   PHILLIP E. AREEDA ET AL., ANTITRUST ANALYSIS 205 (6th ed. 2004).

[19]   MCCONNELL & BRUE, *supra* note 17, at 400.

c. Monopolistic competition: Whereas oligopolistic competition involves only a few sellers, monopolistic competition involves many sellers, none with a large market share. Each seller sells a differentiated product—products that "differ in their design, dependability, location, [and] ease of purchase," among other factors. Market entry and exit are relatively easy. The phrase "monopolistic competition" can be confusing because "there is nothing 'monopolistic' about these markets."[20] A classic example? Competition among law firms, each seeking to differentiate itself by displaying unique client lists, hiring star partners, publicizing major victories and getting quoted in the media. Monopolistically competitive firms do face competition, because the quantity each firm can sell and the price it can charge depend on what its competitors sell and charge.[21] But that competition is imperfect competition, because by differentiating its product a seller gains market power—an ability to raise and sustain prices above competitive levels—over customers desiring that differentiated product.[22]

d. Perfect competition: Perfect competition exists when "the number of firms selling a homogeneous commodity is so large, and each individual firm's share of the market is so small, that no individual firm itself is able to influence appreciably the commodity's price by varying the quantity of output it sells."[23] A perfectly competitive market has four main characteristics:

1. "Sellers and buyers are so numerous that no one's actions can have a perceptible impact on the market price, and there is no collusion among buyers or sellers."
2. "Consumers register their subjective preferences among various goods and services through market transactions at fully known market prices."
3. "All relevant prices are known to each producer, who also knows of all input combinations technically capable of producing any specific combination of outputs and who makes input-output decisions solely to maximize profits."

---

[20] GWARTNEY ET AL., *supra* note 16, at 526.
[21] KRUGMAN & WELLS, *supra* note 15, at 449.
[22] As an economist once told the author—in front of the author's 60 seminar attendees—"You have a monopoly over your personality." It was not clear he intended a compliment.
[23] FREDERIC M. SCHERER & DAVID R. ROSS, INDUSTRIAL MARKET STRUCTURE AND ECONOMIC PERFORMANCE 16 (3d. ed. 1990). *See also* STIGLITZ & WALSH, *supra* note 7, at A7 (defining perfect competition as "a situation in which each firm is a price taker—it cannot influence the market price; at the market price, the firm can sell as much as it wishes, but if it raises its price, it loses all sales").

4. "Every producer has equal access to all input markets and there are no artificial barriers to the production of any product."[24]

Under these conditions, any seller that raised its price would lose its customers to sellers that didn't.

These four market structures—monopoly, oligopoly, monopolistic competition and perfect competition—are theoretical points on a spectrum. A cello string can produce an infinitude of pitches; markets span an infinitude of competitiveness. Most competitive markets are imperfectly competitive, some more imperfect than others. A given market's competitiveness depends on facts: the number of buyers and sellers, their relative shares of the sales made, their control of resources essential to competition (such as raw materials and transportation), buyers' access to alternatives, and the ease with which sellers can enter and exit.

* * *

Up to now, we have focused on market structure. But competition is both a market structure and a process. The competitive process involves competitor conduct. Laypeople—and many businesses—tend to see competition only in terms of conduct. For them, competition is mere rivalry—"a conscious striving against other business firms for patronage perhaps on a price basis but possibly also (or alternatively) on non-price grounds."[25] But mere rivalry is not effective competition, because in a market with few viable competitors (like an oligopoly market), or one with product differentiation (like a monopolistically competitive market), each rival can exercise market power unilaterally. And if the product is homogenous and the number of sellers small, they can exercise market power jointly, through explicit agreements or through conscious parallel behavior. Economists therefore evaluate a market's competitiveness in terms of both structure and conduct. Market structure influences seller conduct, and seller conduct influences market performance. Since the purpose of regulation is to improve market performance, alert regulators focus on both structure and conduct.[26]

To prepare for our analysis of how mergers affect competition, we have two remaining tasks: explain the concept of effective competition; then contrast it with ineffective competition.

---

[24]   AREEDA ET AL., *supra* note 18, at 5.

[25]   SCHERER & ROSS, *supra* note 23, at 16.

[26]   For a defense of structure-conduct-performance analysis, see Peter C. Carstensen, *Antitrust Law and the Paradigm of Industrial Organization*, 16 U.C. DAVIS L. REV. 487 (1983).

6.2 EFFECTIVE COMPETITION: COMPETITION ON THE MERITS

Effective competition is competition on the merits—a market structure and seller conduct that together yield "greater efficiency or enhanced consumer appeal."[27] Competition on the merits affects more than price. It can produce "greater responsiveness to consumer demands," while "generat[ing] more potent incentives for the frugal use of resources.[28] It can produce performance that is "positively good—efficient, progressive, risk-taking, innovative."[29] One can also view effective competition as a progression of breakthroughs, as

> a mechanism by which new ideas emerge and the best ones survive, only to be superseded by other still better ones. ... When the Berlin Wall came down, West Germans were not amazed at how high prices were in the East; they were amazed at the extraordinary lack of choice and poor quality of the products that were available, suggesting that this had been the real, enduring benefit of a competitive market economy.[30]

A market is effectively competitive if (a) the number of sellers is sufficiently large, and their market shares sufficiently small, such that no seller, or group of sellers coordinating, can exercise market power; and if (b) no seller can exclude competitors, such as by denying them access to goods or facilities essential to competing. Scherer and Ross describe an effectively competitive market as having specific structural and conduct features that produce specific performance results, all quoted fully here:

Structural Features

1. The number of traders [will] be at least as large as scale economies permit.
2. There [will] be no artificial inhibitions on mobility and entry.

---

[27] United States v. Microsoft Corp., 253 F.3d 34, 59 (D.C. Cir. 2001), *cert. denied*, 534 U.S. 952 (2001).

[28] SCHERER & ROSS, *supra* note 23, at 54.

[29] 2 ALFRED E. KAHN, THE ECONOMICS OF REGULATION: PRINCIPLES AND INSTITUTIONS 18 (MIT Press 1970, 1988) (emphasis omitted).

[30] Stephen Littlechild, *The Nature of Competition and the Regulatory Process*, in "EFFECTIVE COMPETITION" IN TELECOMMUNICATIONS, RAIL AND ENERGY MARKETS 1, 13 (Intereconomics Forum 2011) (quoting Derek Morris, *Dominant Firm Behaviour Under UK Competition Law*, presented to Fordham Corporate Law Institute, Thirtieth Annual Conference on International Antitrust Law and Policy (Oct. 23–24, 2003)), https://webcache.googleusercontent.com/search?q=cache:1T8YqbqB21QJ:https://archive.intereconomics.eu/downloads/getfile.php%3Fid%3D761+&cd=1&hl=en&ct=clnk&gl=us.

   3. There [will] be moderate and price-sensitive quality differentials in the products offered.

Conduct Features

1. Some uncertainty should exist in the minds of rivals as to whether one rival's price moves will be followed by the others.
2. Firms should strive to attain their goals independently, without collusion.
3. There should be no unfair, exclusionary, predatory or coercive tactics.
4. Inefficient suppliers and customers should not be shielded from competition.
5. Sales promotion should be informative or at least not be misleading.
6. There should be no persistent, harmful price discrimination.

Performance Results

1. Firms' production and distribution operations should be efficient and not wasteful of resources.
2. Output levels and product quality (i.e., variety, durability, safety, reliability and so forth) should be responsive to consumer demands.
3. Profits should be at levels just sufficient to reward investment, efficiency and innovation.
4. Prices should encourage rational choice, guide markets toward equilibrium and not intensify cyclical instability.
5. Opportunities for introducing technically superior new products and processes should be exploited.
6. Success should accrue to sellers who best serve consumer wants.[31]

An effectively competitive market structure produces pro-competitive conduct, which in turn produces efficient, innovative performance. Each seller strives to succeed, making other sellers strive harder to succeed. Costs decline, quality improves. Breakthroughs happen. The market's performance aligns with the customers' needs. Effective competition is competition on the merits.

---

[31] SCHERER & ROSS, *supra* note 23, at 53–54. *See also* Stephen G. Breyer, *Antitrust, Deregulation, and the Newly Liberated Marketplace*, 75 CALIF. L. REV. 1005, 1006 (1987) (describing these benefits of effective competition: "(1) prices close to incremental costs, leading to buying and production decisions that minimize economic waste, (2) efficient production processes, and (3) innovation as to both product and production process").

6.3   INEFFECTIVE COMPETITION: MARKET POWER, ANTICOMPETITIVE CONDUCT AND UNEARNED ADVANTAGE

Effective competition produces winners and losers. Competition policy protects effective competition, not inefficient competitors.[32] But when losers lose for reasons other than merit, competition is ineffective. Mergers can make competition ineffective by affecting market structure and seller conduct. They can produce market structures that give the merged company market power, enable it to act anticompetitively, or allow it to use unearned advantages. This section explains these three concepts, using examples from various industries. Chapter 6.4 will apply these concepts to electricity mergers.

6.3.1   Market Power: Unilateral and Coordinated

Market power, recall, is a seller's ability to raise price or withhold supply for a significant period of time, without an unacceptable loss of sales. A seller's market power arises from the market's structure. A seller can exercise market power unilaterally or in coordination with others.

Unilateral exercise: Consider the proposed merger of AT&T and T-Mobile. At pre-merger prices, a "non-trivial fraction" of AT&T's wireless customers viewed T-Mobile's services as a close second choice. Other firms' services (and forgoing service entirely) were "more distant choices." So post-merger, these customers would likely stay with AT&T even if AT&T raised its prices, whereas if unmerged AT&T raised its prices they would switch to T-Mobile. Raising prices without losing customers: that's market power, merger-created. And market power harm can spread, because if the merged company could

---

[32]   *See* Brown Shoe Co. v. United States, 370 U.S. 294, 320 (1962) (holding that Congress enacted antitrust laws for "the protection of competition, not competitors"). *See also* Guidelines on the Assessment of Non-horizontal Mergers Under the Council Regulation on the Control of Concentrations Between Undertakings, 2008 O.J. (C 265) 6, 8 ¶16 [hereinafter Guidelines on Assessment of Non-horizontal Mergers] ("[T]hat rivals may be harmed because a merger creates efficiencies cannot in itself give rise to competition concerns."); Concord v. Boston Edison Co., 915 F.2d 17, 21–22 (1st Cir. 1990) ("[A] practice is not 'anticompetitive' simply because it harms competitors. After all, almost all business activity, desirable and undesirable alike, seeks to advance a firm's fortunes at the expense of its competitors. Rather, a practice is 'anticompetitive' only if it harms the competitive process. It harms that process when it obstructs the achievement of competition's basic goals—lower prices, better products, and more efficient production methods." (citations omitted)).

raise its prices without losing sales, its competitors would feel more confident about raising theirs.[33]

Coordinated exercise: Under conditions of coordinated market power, competitors "recogniz[e] their interdependence," then "take actions 'that are profitable for each of them only as a result of the accommodating reactions of others.'"[34] Coordinated action can take at least three forms:

1. "explicit negotiation of a common understanding of how firms will compete or refrain from competing. Such conduct typically would itself violate the antitrust laws."
2. "a similar common understanding that is not explicitly negotiated but would be enforced by the detection and punishment of deviations that would undermine the coordinated interaction."
3. "parallel accommodating conduct not pursuant to a prior understanding, [including] situations in which each rival's response to competitive moves made by others is individually rational, and not motivated by retaliation or deterrence nor intended to sustain an agreed-upon market outcome, but [which] nevertheless emboldens price increases and weakens competitive incentives to reduce prices or offer customers better terms."[35]

This last form of coordinated interaction, "parallel accommodating conduct" (sometimes called "tacit coordination"), is "'feared by antitrust policy even more than express collusion' as it is harder to detect and to prevent." In highly concentrated markets (such as markets concentrated by horizontal mergers),

---

[33] AT&T-Deutsche Telekom Merger, 26 FCC Rcd. 16,184, 16,212–15 ¶¶ 50, 51, 54–55 (2011). This citation and these quotes come from the Report issued by the Federal Communications Commission Staff. After the Report was issued, the companies withdrew their merger. There was no FCC decision.

[34] EchoStar Communications-Hughes Electronics Merger, 17 FCC Rcd. 20,559, 20,619 ¶ 152 (2002) (quoting 1997 HORIZONTAL MERGER GUIDELINES, *supra* note 9, § 2.1). *See also* 2010 HORIZONTAL MERGER GUIDELINES, *supra* note 6, § 7 ("Coordinated interaction involves conduct by multiple firms that is profitable for each of them only as a result of the accommodating reactions of the others.").

[35] 2010 HORIZONTAL MERGER GUIDELINES, *supra* note 6, § 7. *See also* Order No. 642, *supra* note 5, at 71,004 n.89 ("'Anticompetitive coordination' refers generally to the exercise of market power through the concurrence of other (non-merging) firms in the market or [through the] coordinated responses by those firms."); *Atlantic City Electric-Delmarva Power & Light Merger*, 80 F.E.R.C. ¶ 61,126, at p. 61,412 (1997).

coordination "need not be explicit, and typically is not."[36] Nor does coordination necessarily violate antitrust laws.[37]

Back to AT&T and T-Mobile. The FCC Staff found that the pre-merger wireless market already had few competitors. Those competitors were likely coordinating already, because across multiple geographic markets their prices and service plans were both transparent (making coordination easy) and similar (making coordination visible). Prospective market entrants couldn't easily lure customers away with price cuts, because many were stuck in two-year contracts with early termination fees, giving the incumbents time to respond with their own price cuts. Under these circumstances, the merger would make the incumbents' coordination more likely and more effective. The AT&T-BellSouth merger, in contrast, posed no coordinated interaction risks, at least not for wholesale "special access services," because the post-merger market would still have many competitors. Purchasers of those services, moreover, were sophisticated companies that chose suppliers through competitive bidding or individual negotiations.[38]

Firms with market power can not only charge excess prices; they can reduce output, operate inefficiently, weaken system reliability by under-investing in infrastructure,[39] and eschew product development and innovation.[40] Reduced competition also hampers a regulator's ability to "benchmark"—to compare price, quality and innovation among multiple regulated entities.[41]

* * *

Market power enables a seller both to exploit consumers and exclude competitors. A seller can exploit market power by raising prices above, or lowering quality below, competitive levels. The seller can also exclude its rivals from

---

[36] *AT&T-Deutsche Telekom Merger*, 26 FCC Rcd. at 16,226 ¶ 74 (quoting FTC v. H.J. Heinz Co., 246 F.3d 708, 725 (D.D.C. 2011)).

[37] 2010 HORIZONTAL MERGER GUIDELINES, *supra* note 6, § 7 ("Coordinated interaction includes conduct not otherwise condemned by the antitrust laws.").

[38] AT&T-BellSouth Merger, 22 FCC Rcd. 5662, 5693 ¶ 58 (2007).

[39] *See, e.g.*, TABORS CARAMANIS & ASSOCIATES, HORIZONTAL MARKET POWER IN WISCONSIN ELECTRICITY MARKETS: A REPORT TO THE PUBLIC SERVICE COMMISSION OF WISCONSIN 8 (2000), http://www.utilityregulation.com/content/reports/WImktstudy .pdf.

[40] *See, e.g., AT&T-Deutsche Telekom Merger*, 26 FCC Rcd. at 16,195 ¶ 14.

[41] *AT&T-BellSouth Merger*, 22 FCC Rcd. at 5755 ¶ 188 (first citing GTE-Bell Atlantic Merger, 15 FCC Rcd. 14,032, 14,101-03 ¶¶ 132-37 (2000); and then citing Ameritech-SBC Communications Merger, 14 FCC Rcd. 14,712, 14,770–80 ¶¶ 125–43 (1999)) (expressing concern that mergers reduce benchmarks, especially those relating to the "introduction of new technologies and services").

essential inputs, or raise their costs of acquiring those inputs. These forms of anticompetitive conduct, and others, are discussed next.

6.3.2   Anticompetitive Conduct

Aggressive, pro-competitive conduct becomes anticompetitive conduct when the seller acts to weaken competition rather than win the competition. Pro-competitive behavior yields competition on the merits. Anticompetitive behavior undermines competition on the merits.

The incentive and opportunity to behave anticompetitively is especially strong when a firm, directly or through affiliates, sells in two distinct markets: one where it has market power and one where it does not. Using its market power in one market it can undermine competition in the other. The first four types of anticompetitive conduct discussed next—refusal to deal, tying, price squeeze and cross-subsidization—all illustrate that strategy. In the fifth type, predatory pricing, a firm selling in a single product market tries to drive out its competitors by selling at a loss. All five are versions of exclusionary conduct—conduct aimed at excluding competitors—as distinct from exploitative conduct—conduct aimed at raising prices to consumers (although the ultimate goal of exclusionary conduct is to raise prices to customers after excluding the competitors). Cross-subsidization is both exclusionary (because it gives the seller an artificial cost advantage over its unaffiliated competitors) and exploitative (because it raises prices to the seller's monopoly customers).

6.3.2.1   Refusal to deal

In unregulated capitalism, every seller is free to deal with others, or not. But suppose a seller of a downstream product controls an input that is both essential to that product and not economically duplicable by the seller's competitors. Refusing to sell the input to those competitors blocks their entry completely; selling the input to the competitors at a discriminatorily high price forces them to raise their prices, lowering their sales. If their sales drop enough, they will need to raise their price a second time to cover their fixed costs—losing more sales. And so on—until their competitor's revenues fall below their costs, and they leave.[42]

In this scenario, we label the essential, non-duplicable input a "bottleneck facility" (sometimes called an "essential facility"). Common examples are electricity transmission and distribution facilities; gas pipelines and distribution systems; and in the early days of wireline telephone competition, what

---

[42]   Guidelines on Assessment of Non-horizontal Mergers, *supra* note 32, at 24 ¶ 112.

practitioners call the "last mile"—the wires and central office equipment necessary to connect customers' phones with the local and long-distance networks. Some courts have held that these refusals to deal violate antitrust law's prohibition against monopolizing.[43] More recent decisions, however, have placed this behavior outside antitrust law's reach, at least where other statutes authorize a regulatory agency to address the facility owner's conduct.[44]

---

[43] Section 2 of the Sherman Antitrust Act, 15 U.S.C. § 2, makes it unlawful for any person to "monopolize, or attempt to monopolize, or combine or conspire with any other person or persons, to monopolize any part of the trade or commerce among the several States, or with foreign nations." *See* United States v. Terminal R.R. Ass'n, 224 U.S. 383, 394–97 (1912) (holding that "the unification of substantially every terminal facility by which the traffic of St. Louis is served resulted in a combination which is in restraint of trade" because the unified terminal made it practically "impossible for any railroad company to pass through, or even enter St. Louis ... without using the facilities entirely controlled by the terminal company."); Alaska Airlines, Inc. v. United Airlines, Inc., 948 F.2d 536, 542 (9th Cir. 1991) ("[T]he essential facilities doctrine imposes liability when one firm, which controls an essential facility, denies a second firm reasonable access to a product or service that the second firm must obtain in order to compete with the first."); Robert Pitofsky et al., *The Essential Facilities Doctrine Under United States Antitrust Law*, 70 ANTITRUST L.J. 443, 446 (2002) ("The [bottleneck] facility doctrine has been articulated as a subset of the so-called 'refusal to deal' cases which place limitations on a monopolist's ability to exclude actual or potential rivals from competing with it.").

A bottleneck facility need not be a physical facility. Non-physical examples have included a newspaper publishing association, Associated Press v. United States, 326 U.S. 1 (1945); newspaper advertising space, Lorain Journal Co. v. United States, 342 U.S. 143 (1951); a fruit and vegetable warehouse, Gamco, Inc. v. Providence Fruit & Produce Bldg., Inc., 194 F.2d 484 (1st Cir. 1952); a football stadium, Hecht v. Pro-Football, Inc., 570 F.2d 982 (D.C. Cir. 1977); downhill ski services under special conditions, Aspen Skiing Co. v. Aspen Highlands Skiing Corp., 472 U.S. 585 (1985); and telephone central office services, AT&T Co. v. N. Am. Indus., Inc., 772 F. Supp. 777 (S.D.N.Y. 1991).

[44] *See, e.g.*, Verizon Commc'ns Inc. v. Law Offices of Curtis V. Trinko, LLP, 540 U.S. 398, 410–11 (2004) (describing the essential facilities doctrine as a "doctrine crafted by some lower courts," stating that the Court has "never recognized such a doctrine," and finding "no need either to recognize it or to repudiate it" in a context where the FCC and the New York Commission had already penalized Verizon for its exclusionary conduct). Signaling its skepticism of the doctrine, the Court then quoted a major treatise's view that "essential facility claims should ... be denied where a state or federal agency has effective power to compel sharing and to regulate its scope and terms." *Id.* at 411 (citing PHILLIP E. AREEDA & HEBERT HOVENKAMP, ANTITRUST LAW 150 ¶ 773e (2d ed. Supp. 2003)).

Some critics of the bottleneck facility doctrine argue that "it represents a government 'taking' of private property," that "it will be likely to reduce incentives to innovate," and that it is not worth the administrative expense of enforcing and supervising the alleged monopolist. *Id.* at 443. *See also* Abbott B. Lipsky, Jr. & J. Gregory Sidak, *Essential Facilities*, 51 STAN. L. REV. 1187, 1195 (1999) (asserting that the doctrine

And regulators have done so, stepping in where antitrust law is uncertain or unavailable. In electricity, gas and telecommunications specifically, regulators have established rules that require incumbents to share these essential, not-economically-duplicable facilities with their competitors on a nondiscriminatory basis.[45]

Despite regulatory actions addressing transmission and distribution, the potential for refusals to deal remains. Consider two hypotheticals.

Interconnection of storage: Suppose a company wishes to offer a retail electric storage service in the incumbent utility's service territory. The company needs inputs available only from the utility: data on the locations and shapes of neighborhood-level loads, electricity flow diagrams showing the best locations for the storage, interoperability protocols and timely interconnection. If the utility competes in the storage market, it has the incentive and ability to refuse to provide these inputs, or to increase its competitors' uncertainty and cost by dragging out negotiations. The storage company's financing dries up and it departs. The utility has leveraged its existing, legitimate monopoly over the inputs into an illegitimate monopoly over storage service.

Neighborhood-level solar: Suppose a neighborhood needs a new distribution feeder to accommodate growing load. Before installation, a non-utility company offers to satisfy that load with neighborhood-level solar facilities that obviate the feeder. Like the storage company, the solar company aggregator will need data on customer load and location—data that only the utility has. Because the utility profits by installing distribution feeders but not by buying solar output from a third party,[46] it will have incentive and opportunity to withhold the information so that the solar company leaves town. Then the utility can install the feeder, at a profit.[47]

6.3.2.2 Price squeeze

A refusal to deal involves the vertically integrated incumbent refusing to sell Input M (a monopoly product) to its downstream competitor in Product Market C. In price squeeze, the incumbent sells Input M, but at an inflated price

---

"do[es] not fit comfortably within antitrust law"); Gregory J. Werden, *The Law and Economics of the Essential Facility Doctrine*, 32 Sᴛ. Lᴏᴜɪs U. L.J. 433, 480 (1987) (arguing that "courts should reject the doctrine").

[45] *See* Tutorial § 2.2.

[46] Under standard cost-based ratemaking, a utility profits when it makes capital expenditures but not when it buys services from others. *See* Tutorial § 4.1.

[47] For a detailed study of possible refusals to deal in the smart grid and distributed resource space, see Jᴏʜᴀɴɴ J. Kʀᴀɴᴢ & Aʀɴᴏʟᴅ Pɪᴄᴏᴛ, Nᴀᴛ'ʟ Rᴇɢᴜʟᴀᴛᴏʀʏ Rᴇsᴇᴀʀᴄʜ Iɴsᴛ., Tᴏᴡᴀʀᴅ ᴀɴ Eɴᴅ-ᴛᴏ-Eɴᴅ Sᴍᴀʀᴛ Gʀɪᴅ: Oᴠᴇʀᴄᴏᴍɪɴɢ Bᴏᴛᴛʟᴇɴᴇᴄᴋs ᴛᴏ Fᴀᴄɪʟɪᴛᴀᴛᴇ Cᴏᴍᴘᴇᴛɪᴛɪᴏɴ ᴀɴᴅ Iɴɴᴏᴠᴀᴛɪᴏɴ ɪɴ Sᴍᴀʀᴛ Gʀɪᴅs (2011), https://pubs .naruc.org/pub/FA865F09-934E-F89E-5141-7E766D260068.

that leaves the competitor unable to price its Product C competitively. Like refusal to deal, price squeeze distorts competition in the downstream market for Product C. As FERC has explained: "Price discrimination becomes 'price squeeze' when the disparity between wholesale and retail rates causes an anti-competitive effect, i.e., the wholesale customer loses or is likely to lose retail load, thereby 'squeezing' the wholesale customer out of the retail market."[48]

As with refusals to share bottleneck facilities, courts have held that price squeeze does not necessarily violate antitrust law. Linkline sold digital sub-scriber line (DSL) service—an early method of accessing the Internet over telephone lines. Pacific Bell owned the lines—the only ones available to Linkline—and also sold DSL at retail in competition with Linkline. Linkline accused Pacific Bell of monopolizing the retail DSL market by raising its wholesale DSL price to Linkline while cutting its own retail DSL price. The Court disagreed. Pacific Bell had no antitrust law obligation to provide the wholesale DSL service in the first place; its obligation arose from an FCC order. And, "if a firm has no antitrust duty to deal with its competitors at wholesale, it certainly has no duty to deal under terms and conditions that the rivals find commercially advantageous."[49]

Price squeeze may not always violate antitrust law, but as with control of essential facilities it can make competition ineffective. Regulatory law steps in where antitrust law steps back.

6.3.2.3 Tying

A seller ties when it refuses to sell monopoly Product M unless the customer also buys from the seller competitive Product C. Product M is the tying product, Product C is the tied product. The tying weakens competition in the market for Product C by diverting customers away from competing suppliers. As the Supreme Court has explained,

> the essential characteristic of an invalid tying arrangement lies in the seller's exploitation of its control over the tying product to force the buyer into the purchase of a tied product that the buyer either did not want at all, or might have preferred to purchase elsewhere on different terms. When such "forcing" is present, competition

---

[48] *Southern California Edison Co.*, 40 F.E.R.C. ¶ 61,371, at p. 62,151 (1987), *reh'g granted in part*, 50 F.E.R.C. ¶ 61,275 (1990). *See also* Cities of Anaheim v. FERC, 941 F.2d 1234, 1237 (D.C. Cir. 1991) (describing price squeeze as "an unjustified dispar-ity between a public utility's wholesale and retail electric power rates ... that harms the ability of wholesale customers to compete with the utility in the retail market").

[49] Pacific Bell Tel. Co. v. Linkline Commc'ns, 555 U.S. 438, 454 (2009) (summa-rizing the holding of *Trinko*, 540 U.S. 398).

on the merits in the market for the tied item is restrained and the Sherman Act is violated.[50]

Tying is monopolizing, a *per se* violation of antitrust law, if four factors are present:

> (1) the tying and tied goods are two separate products; (2) the defendant has market power in the tying product market; (3) the defendant affords consumers no choice but to purchase the tied product from it; and (4) the tying arrangement forecloses a substantial volume of commerce.[51]

Prior to FERC Order No. 888, many utilities that owned both transmission (a monopoly product) and generation (a potentially competitive product) refused to provide wholesale customers transmission service (the tying product) unless the customer also bought the utility's generation service (the tied product). This practice weakened generation competition by depriving non-incumbent generators of customers.[52] Prior to the Telecommunications Act of 1996, incumbent phone companies could monopolize local telephone service—a potentially competitive service—by tying that service to their control of the monopoly "last mile"—the physical line connecting telephones

---

[50]   Jefferson Parish Hosp. Dist. No. 2 v. Hyde, 466 U.S. 2, 12 (1984). The hospital required that patients purchasing the hospital's surgical services also buy the hospital's contracted-for anesthesiology services. Surgery was the tying product, the anesthesiology service was the tied product. Reiterating its longstanding view that tying was a *per se* violation of antitrust law, the Court stated: "It is far too late in the history of our antitrust jurisprudence to question the proposition that certain tying arrangements pose an unacceptable risk of stifling competition and therefore are unreasonable '*per se*.'" *Id.* at 9. But the Court found that no unlawful tying had occurred: Jefferson Parish's patients were not forced to buy the tied anesthesiology service because they could get their surgeries elsewhere.
[51]   United States v. Microsoft Corp., 253 F.3d 34, 85 (D.C. Cir. 2001), *cert. denied*, 534 U.S. 952 (2001). *See also* Guidelines on Assessment of Non-horizontal Mergers, *supra* note 32, at 23 ¶ 101 ("[W]here a supplier of complementary goods has market power in one of the products (product A), the decision to bundle or tie may result in reduced sales by the non-integrated suppliers of the complementary good (product B). … [W]here entry into the market for the complementary product is contemplated by potential entrants, the decision to bundle by the merged entity may have the effect of deterring such entry. The limited availability of complementary products with which to combine may, in turn, discourage potential entrants to enter market A.").
[52]   Until Order No. 888, FERC had not universally prohibited transmission-owning utilities' practice of denying access to their transmission facilities, or of providing that access only on terms less favorable than the terms on which the transmission owner itself used its facilities. Decades earlier, the Supreme Court had held that under certain circumstances, this exclusionary practice constituted unlawful monopolizing. Otter Tail Power Co. v. United States, 410 U.S. 366 (1973).

to the central switched network. Prior to FERC's Order No. 636, interstate pipelines could monopolize wholesale natural gas sales by tying those sales to their monopoly pipeline transportation service.

Tying can take two forms. In contractual tying, the seller ties the two products with a contract. In technology tying, the seller ties with technology: it designs the tying product to work only with that seller's tied product and not with any competitor's product.[53] Technology tying weakens competition in the tied market if the tying product is essential for competition and not duplicable by the tied market competitor. But tying can also be pro-competitive, or at least pro-consumer. Microsoft Windows had bundled its operating system (Windows, the alleged tying product) with its browser (Internet Explorer, the alleged tied product) under a single price. A customer forced to buy Microsoft's browser (because she wanted to use Windows) would not likely also buy a competitor's browser.[54] The Department of Justice accused Microsoft of, among other things, using Windows to monopolize the market for browsers. The court of appeals disagreed, giving two reasons. First, with bundling common in competitive platform software markets, courts should pause before condemning it in less competitive markets. Second, "because of the pervasively innovative character of platform software markets, tying in such markets may produce efficiencies that courts have not previously encountered."[55] Though *Jefferson Parish* reiterated that tying is a *per se* violation,[56] the *Microsoft* court held that when tying arrangements involve platform software products, a rule of reason (i.e., balancing anticompetitive harm against pro-competitive benefit) should apply.[57] Adds one author:

> Many technology products run on a common platform. The more individuals that buy that particular platform, the more products will be produced and available to

---

[53] Guidelines on Assessment of Non-horizontal Mergers, *supra* note 32, at 22 ¶ 97. *See also* Sarita Frattaroli, Note, *Dodging the Bullet Again: Microsoft III's Reformulation of the Foremost Technological Tying Doctrine*, 90 B.U. L. REV. 1909, 1916 (2010) (citing Daniel E. Gaynor, *Technological Tying* 1 (FTC Bureau of Econ., Working Paper No. 284, 2006)) (explaining that in technology tying, "a firm designs a product so that it functions only when used with a complementary product").

[54] Netscape was a popular browser in the 1990s. Know anyone who uses it now?

[55] *Microsoft Corp.*, 253 F.3d at 93.

[56] 466 U.S. 2 (1984).

[57] *Microsoft Corp.*, 253 F.3d at 84 ("While every 'business relationship' will in some sense have unique features, some represent entire, novel categories of dealings. As we shall explain, the arrangement before us is an example of the latter, offering the first up-close look at the technological integration of added functionality into software that serves as a platform for third-party applications. There being no close parallel in prior antitrust cases, simplistic application of per se tying rules carries a serious risk of harm.").

the consumer. Technology markets therefore have network effects, where the value of a product to an individual consumer increases with the number of consumers that adopt that same product. The integration of two products may provide other efficiency benefits, such as convenience to the consumer or increased functionality. Given rapid innovation and shifting understanding of consumer preferences in the technology industry, technological integration may be particularly likely to foster efficiencies and increase consumer welfare.[58]

Not all bundling is anticompetitive tying, because not all bundling involves a monopoly product. Bundling can lower customer costs and increase customer convenience.[59] But some forms of bundling, even if not anticompetitive tying, can weaken competition by giving the incumbent utility an unearned advantage—a problem that can be addressed only through regulatory law. We will address that problem in Chapter 6.3.3.

6.3.2.4 Cross-subsidization

We opened this section by explaining that the risk of anticompetitive conduct is especially high when a firm has market power in one market and also sells in a competitive market. Electric utility mergers have created holding company systems that have that very feature: utilities selling monopoly services (transmission, distribution, retail electricity in the non-competition states); and affiliates selling competitive services (wholesale generation, storage, demand aggregation, retail electricity in competition states). These corporate entities have incentive and opportunity to cross-subsidize: over-charge for the monopoly services, then under-charge for the competitive services.[60] This practice is both exploitative and exclusionary: it abuses the utility's captive customers

---

[58]   Frattaroli, *supra* note 53, at 1916–17 (citing Pietro Crocioni, *Leveraging of Market Power in Emerging Markets: A Review of Cases, Literature, and a Suggested Framework*, 4 J. Competition L. & Econ. 449, 450 (2008)).

[59]   *See, e.g.*, Guidelines on Assessment of Non-horizontal Mergers, *supra* note 32, at 22 ¶ 93 (explaining that bundling can "provide ... customers with better products or offerings in cost-effective ways").

[60]   *See, e.g.*, Computer & Commc'ns Indus. Ass'n v. FCC, 693 F.2d 198, 205 n.25 (D.C. Cir. 1982) ("Cross-subsidization occurs when a carrier misattributes costs incurred in the provision of unregulated services to the provision of regulated services. Because rates for regulated services are based partially upon the cost of providing those services, misattribution of costs results in the carrier's monopoly ratepayers having to bear a part of the cost of unregulated services.").

Technically, a company cross-subsidizes when it raises the price for its monopoly product above that product's stand-alone (fully distributed) cost, then uses the excess to charge purchasers of the competitive product a price below that product's incremental cost. I emphasize this technical definition because the term "subsidy" has acquired usages that are imprecise, ideological and often inaccurate. In the electricity field, many people, including even experts, define cross-subsidizing to include allocating sunk

while undermining competition.[61] Eighty-five years ago, Congress described the harms:

1. "paper profits from intercompany transactions"
2. "excessive revenues from subsidiary public-utility companies"
3. utility subsidiaries being "subjected to excessive charges for services, construction work, equipment, and materials"
4. "transactions in which evils result from an absence of arm's-length bargaining or from restraint of free and independent competition"
5. "service, management, construction, and other contracts involv[ing] the allocation of charges among subsidiary public-utility companies in different States so as to present problems of regulation which cannot be dealt with effectively by the States ..."[62]

Cross-subsidizing's risks grow as the number and scope of a utility holding company's non-utility activities increase.[63]

As with the other examples of anticompetitive conduct, cross-subsidizing does not necessarily violate antitrust law. When a firm with a lawfully gained monopoly charges monopoly prices, antitrust has no role. And when that company uses the proceeds to subsidize its competitive product prices, antitrust again has no role, provided the prices are not predatorily low (see the next subsection). But the practice does undermine competition on the merits. So what antitrust law cannot reach, regulatory law must.

6.3.2.5 Predatory pricing

Predatory pricing is "pricing below an appropriate measure of cost for the purpose of eliminating competitors in the short run and reducing competition in the long run."[64] It violates antitrust law's prohibition against monopolizing.

---

costs disproportionately to load responsibility. Disproportionate allocations can raise questions of discrimination, but technically they are not necessarily cross-subsidies.

[61] Standards of Conduct Governing Relationships Between Utilities and Their Affiliates, 1997 Cal. PUC LEXIS 1139, at *20–21 (explaining that cross-subsidizing "skews the [competitive] market to the detriment of other potential entrants").

[62] Public Utility Holding Company Act of 1935 § 1(b)(1)-(2), 15 U.S.C. § 79a(b) (1)–(2) (repealed 2005).

[63] Southwestern Public Service Co., Case No. 2678, 1997 WL 78696, at *34–35 (N.M. Pub. Util. Comm'n 1997) (citing concerns that the proposed merger would increase the number of non-utility affiliate transactions, causing customers to subsidize unregulated activity).

[64] Cargill, Inc. v. Monfort of Colorado, Inc., 479 U.S. 104, 117 (1986). *See also* Brooke Group Ltd. v. Brown & Williamson Tobacco Corp., 509 U.S. 209, 222 (1993) (explaining that predatory pricing occurs when "[a] business rival has priced its products in an unfair manner with an object to eliminate or retard competition and thereby

What distinguishes anticompetitive, predatory pricing from pro-competitive, aggressive pricing is the predator's intent to recoup its losses by raising prices after its competitors depart: "Recoupment [of the profits lost from price-cutting] is the ultimate object of an unlawful predatory pricing scheme; it is the means by which a predator profits from predation."[65]

Courts today hesitate to find a company guilty of predatory pricing, for fear of prohibiting legitimate, pro-consumer price-cutting. Pricing below competitors' costs does not necessarily equal predation, even if the practice kills competitors off. The low price could "either reflect[] the lower cost structure of the alleged predator, and so represent[] competition on the merits, or is beyond the practical ability of a judicial tribunal to control without courting intolerable risks of chilling legitimate price-cutting."[66]

6.3.3   Unearned Advantage

Anticompetitive conduct is active conduct, intended and designed to weaken competition, to succeed for reasons other than merit. As the prior subsections explain, some anticompetitive conduct violates antitrust law; some does not, thus requiring solutions from regulatory law.

Unearned advantage is different. Today's electricity markets include both traditional monopoly services and new, potentially competitive services. Incumbent utilities want to provide both types. But in the newly competitive markets, utilities with decades of government protection will have advantages that non-utility competitors lack—advantages unearned through merit. Those advantages distort competition. And because unearned advantage, like good luck, does not trigger antitrust law, regulation must step in. This subsection describes the salient sources of unearned advantage, and the regulatory solutions.

---

gain and exercise control over prices in the relevant market"). What is "an appropriate measure of cost"? The question has no certain answer. *See id.* at 222–24 (citing conflicts among lower courts over the appropriate measure of costs). One oft-discussed option is average variable cost.

[65]   *Brooke Group Ltd.*, 509 U.S. at 223–26 ("[T]o recoup their losses, [predators] must obtain enough market power to set higher than competitive prices, and then must sustain those prices long enough to earn in excess profits what they earlier gave up in below-cost prices.") (quoting Matsushita Elec. Indus. Co. v. Zenith Radio Corp., 475 U.S. 574, 590–91 (1986)).

[66]   *Id.* at 223–24 ("Even if the ultimate effect of the cut is to induce or reestablish supracompetitive pricing, discouraging a price cut and forcing firms to maintain supracompetitive prices, thus depriving consumers of the benefits of lower prices in the interim, does not constitute sound antitrust policy.").

6.3.3.1 Today's market structures: an unstable mix of monopoly and competition

Until the late twentieth century, most customers bought their electricity from a vertically integrated utility monopoly. Each utility used its generation, transmission and distribution facilities to produce and deliver a single bundled service—firm electricity service—to retail customers located within an exclusive franchised territory defined by state law. Many of these utilities also had wholesale customers, such as cities, towns and cooperatives. These wholesale customers would buy "bulk power" (generation and transmission) from the utilities, then handle physical distribution and customer relations themselves. Beginning in the 1980s, electricity policymakers at the state and national level gradually introduced competition at various levels: wholesale electricity sales, retail sales, demand aggregation and energy efficiency; and more recently, renewable energy, transmission construction, storage, and electric vehicle charging stations.

For most of this latter period, the distinction between monopoly services and competitive services has been clear: transmission and distribution are monopoly services, generation and retail sales are competitive services. Today, those distinctions are blurring. A combination of technology and regulatory policy is producing substitutes for transmission and distribution.

Transmission: The interconnected transmission networks have natural monopoly characteristics. For a given geographic area, a single operator controls and monitors power flows, because customer loads and generation resources must be equal continuously. The benefits of everyone using the same network, and the costs to reliability if unregulated usage causes imbalances, justify our relying on that single operator. And because the transmission network also is a bottleneck facility—essential for generation competition and not economically duplicable by competitors—we require its operator and its owners to grant access non-discriminatorily. So transmission service remains largely a monopoly service, provided in some multistate regions by a regional transmission organization (RTO) and in non-RTO regions by traditional utilities; with all providers subject both to FERC Order No. 888 and to reliability rules established by the North American Electric Reliability Corporation.[67]

Though the transmission service remains a monopoly service, transmission facility construction need not be. FERC therefore has declared that incumbent utilities have no automatic right—known as a right of first refusal—to build and own new regional transmission facilities (i.e., facilities crossing multiple utility service territories). So when a regional transmission organization identifies a need for new regional facilities, non-incumbents can compete to build

---

[67] For more detail, see the Tutorial § 2.

and own them.[68] It also is feasible, and permissible, for non-incumbents to buy capacity on existing transmission networks and resell it competitively.

Distribution: Physical distribution remains largely a monopoly service, provided by the state-franchised utility monopolies. But utility proposals for new physical distribution facilities can now face competition from providers of storage, demand response,[69] and solar and wind energy, all at the neighborhood and residential levels. California, the District of Columbia and New York, among other states, are testing whether and how to bring competition into these spaces.[70]

---

[68]   *See* Order No. 1000, *Transmission Planning and Cost Allocation by Transmission Owning and Operating Public Utilities*, F.E.R.C. STATS. & REGS. ¶ 31,323, 136 F.E.R.C. ¶ 61,051 at PP 256–57 (2011) [hereinafter Order No. 1000] (eliminating, under certain conditions, incumbents' contractual rights of first refusal to build regional transmission facilities, due to the benefits of allowing non-incumbents to propose and carry out alternative solutions), *order on reh'g*, Order No. 1000-A, 139 F.E.R.C. ¶ 61,132, *order on reh'g and clarification*, Order No. 1000-B, 141 F.E.R.C. ¶ 61,044 (2012), *aff'd sub nom.* S.C. Pub. Serv. Auth. v. FERC, 762 F.3d 41 (D.C. Cir. 2014).
     The road to transmission competition has had some bumps. Transmission-owning utilities challenged FERC's deletion of the right-of-first-refusal clauses from existing contracts. The court of appeals rejected this general challenge while preserving the utilities' right to challenge specific contract changes. *See S.C. Pub. Serv. Auth.*, 762 F.3d at 72–76. Also, some states have banned non-utility companies from building transmission in competition with incumbent utilities. For detail on legal challenges to these states, see Chapter 1, n.36.
[69]   "Demand response" means a reduction in the consumption of electric energy by customers from their expected consumption in response to an increase in the price of electric energy or to incentive payments designed to induce lower consumption of electric energy. 18 C.F.R. § 35.28(b)(4).
[70]   *California:* The California Commission has approved a competitive solicitation framework and a utility regulatory incentive mechanism pilot so that distributed energy resources can displace or defer distribution capital expenditures. *Integrated Distributed Energy Resources*, CAL. PUB. UTIL. COMM'N (Dec. 15, 2016), https:// www.cpuc.ca.gov/General.aspx?id=10710 (explaining this plan, adopted by decision D16.-12-036). *See also* CAL. PUB. UTIL. COMM'N, CALIFORNIA'S DISTRIBUTED ENERGY RESOURCES ACTION PLAN: ALIGNING VISION AND ACTION 1–2 (2016), https://www .cpuc.ca.gov/uploadedFiles/CPUC_Public_Website/Content/About_Us/Organization/ Commissioners/Michael_J._Picker/2016-09-26%20DER%20Action%20Plan %20FINAL3.pdf (describing the four goals of the plan: (1) "Provide a long-term vision for DER [distributed energy resources] and supporting policies"; (2) "Identify continuing efforts in support of the long-term vision"; (3) "Assess and direct further near-term action needed to support long-term vision"; and (4) "Establish a DER steering committee responsible for sustained coordination of DER activities.").
     District of Columbia: The D.C. Public Service Commission has created a docket, originally called Modernizing the Energy Delivery System for Increased Sustainability (MEDSIS). The goal is to explore and assess "non-wires" alternatives to traditional distribution investments. The originating order directed a working group to compile

This instability—technological advances blurring the competition-monopoly boundaries, accompanied by regulatory decisions—or lack of decisions—about what roles incumbent utilities may play—can give those utilities unearned advantages in the newly competitive markets. We address that problem now.

6.3.3.2 Unearned advantage: a result of government protection

A decades-long, government-protected provider of monopoly services has advantages when providing competitive services. Those advantages come from four main sources: customer behavior, the utility's internal characteristics, the utility's own actions and simple luck. Because these advantages arise not from risk-taking or skill, but from the utility's historic status, they are unearned.

6.3.3.2.1 Customer behavior

Customer behavior advantages utilities and their non-utility affiliates in four ways: brand, government imprimatur, halo effect and inertia.

Brand: For decades, electricity customers have known only one provider. Its name is pervasive: on trucks, monthly bills, employee uniforms, economic development projects, the headquarters building; even sports stadiums, convention centers and concert halls. If the utility has served reasonably well, customers will associate it with a century of solid service. The utility's name

---

recommendations on rate design, customer impact, microgrids and pilot projects. *See* SMART ELEC. POWER ALLIANCE., FINAL REPORT v1.0 OF THE MEDSIS STAKEHOLDER WORKING GROUPS (2019), https://dcpsc.org/PSCDC/media/PDFFiles/Final-Report .pdf. The Report came with multiple dissents. *See What's the Path Forward for DC's Grid Mod? After Nearly a Year of Study, the City is Still Finding Out,* UTIL. DIVE (June 10, 2019), https://www.utilitydive.com/news/whats-the-path-forward-for-dcs-grid -mod-after-nearly-a-year-of-study/556165/. The MEDSIS has moved into an initial implementation phase called Power Path. Investigation into Modernizing the Energy Delivery System for Increased Sustainability, Formal Case No. 1130, Order No. 19432 (D.C Pub. Serv. Comm'n Aug. 9, 2018), https://dcpsc.org/PSCDC/media/PDFFiles/ FC1130-OrderNo19432.pdf.

New York: The New York Public Service Commission has opened proceedings to "activat[e] markets for distributed energy resources." Order Adopting Regulatory Policy Framework and Implementation Plan, Case 14-M-0101, at 30 (N.Y. Pub. Serv. Comm'n Feb. 26, 2015), http://documents.dps.ny.gov/public/Common/ViewDoc.aspx ?DocRefId=%7B0B599D87-445B-4197-9815-24C27623A6A0%7D. The order seeks "to achieve optimal system efficiencies, secure universal, affordable service, and enable the development of a resilient, climate-friendly energy system." *Id.* at 3. Among the topics is the creation of a distributed system platform provider: "an intelligent network platform that will provide safe, reliable and efficient electric services by integrating diverse resources to meet customers' and society's evolving needs." *Id.* at 31. The goal is to view DER providers "as customers and partners, rather than competitors, of traditional grid service." *Id.* at 41.

and reputation have economic value—value the utility heightens with seasonal public service announcements about saving energy and reducing bills. And with advertising. Advertising seeks to "'impregnate the atmosphere of the market with the drawing power of a congenial symbol[,]' . . . rather than to communicate information as to quality or price." The goal is to introduce "economically irrational elements . . . into consumer choices[, so that. the product] is insulated from the normal pressures of price and quality competition."[71]

In the mid-1990s, Southern California Edison created an affiliate, ENvest<SCE>, to enter the performance contracting market.[72] The California Commission's consultants found that ENvest<SCE> could establish its market presence without expensive advertising; it could use "SCE's name recognition, reputation, and image without cost." To overcome a brand advantage SCE "had been establishing for decades," competitors would have to spend big advertising dollars—"a risky expenditure considering the level of customer loyalty that appears to exist for SCE."[73] The consultants' report described the affiliate's "home field advantage":

> [T]he biggest advantage that SCE/ENvest<SCE> had in the existing market was its name recognition, reputation, and image. ENvest<SCE> was not perceived as a fly-by-night or self-interested business. It in fact had all of the features that most

---

[71]   Smith v. Chanel, Inc., 402 F.2d 562, 566–67 (9th Cir. 1968) (quoting Mishawaka Rubber & Woolen Mfg. Co. v. S.S. Kresge Co., 316 U.S. 203, 205 (1942)) (finding that due to advertising, "the competitive system fails to perform its function of allocating available resources efficiently"). *See also* S. Pac. Commc'ns Co. v. AT&T Co., 740 F.2d 980, 1002 (D.C. Cir. 1998) (describing competitors' "need to overcome brand preference established by the defendant's having been first in the market or having made extensive 'image' advertising expenditures").

[72]   Energy performance contracting is a "turnkey service, sometimes compared to design/build construction contracting[,] which provides customers with a comprehensive set of energy efficiency, renewable energy and distributed generation measures and often is accompanied with guarantees that the savings produced by a project will be sufficient to finance the full cost of the project." ICF INT'L & NAT'L ASS'N OF ENERGY SERV. COS., INTRODUCTION TO ENERGY PERFORMANCE CONTRACTING 1 (2007), https://www.energystar.gov/ia/partners/spp_res/Introduction_to_Performance_Contracting.pdf.

[73]   Rules and Procedures Governing Utility Demand-side Management, 1997 Cal. PUC LEXIS 760, at *39. Another example: In the 1960s, Procter & Gamble sought to acquire Clorox. Because all liquid bleach is chemically identical, "[t]he major competitive weapon ... is advertising." When advertising Clorox bleach, the giant Procter could use volume discounts, raising the entry barrier to smaller competitors. FTC v. Procter & Gamble Co., 386 U.S. 568, 579 (1967). *But see* Southern California Gas Co., 2012 Cal. PUC LEXIS 596, at *36, *50 (finding that Southern California Gas's access to 5.9 million captive customers does not give it an unearned advertising advantage over competitors in the natural gas compression business; the utility had acquired its

traditional ESCOs [energy service companies] have had difficulty getting potential customers to perceive. In short, ENvest<SCE> brought a large competitor into the market, which could differentiate itself from other providers by its unique affiliation with SCE and [which] had a powerful motivation to be successful.[74]

Government imprimatur: The government we rely on to educate our children, pave our streets and protect our property has endorsed the incumbent utility, trusting it to provide a service necessary for life. That exclusive endorsement distinguishes the utility from all other competitors. Granted in the monopoly context, the endorsement becomes an advantage in the competitive context. The advantage is unearned because it comes from the utility's franchised status, not from the competitive affiliate's own risk-taking or skill.[75]

Halo effect: A utility's electricity operation is awesome, literally. It runs the baby's incubator and the grandparent's heart monitor. Flip a switch, 500 miles away a puff of smoke goes up and your light goes on. Though electric power engineering was invented a century ago, by inventors unconnected with the local utility, customers give their utility some of the credit. Behavioral psychologists call this the halo effect: viewing two things (electricity's physical characteristics and the utility's worthiness) as closely related when they are not.[76] The utility's philanthropic efforts—its sponsorship of the local orchestra, its support for soup kitchens and community colleges—also have no connection to its operational competence, but they make the halo brighter.

Customer inertia: When the familiar is adequate, why risk change? Changing suppliers requires research and risk—research about alternative companies, their services and terms; risks about their quality and viability. Inertia keeps customers. Increasing inertia's force is customer inexperience. People who

---

"brand equity" by providing services "in a responsible way," while other utilities have managed to provide services in a way that reduced their brand equity).

[74] Rules and Procedures Governing Utility Demand-side Management, *supra* note 73, at *34–35. *See also id.* at *39 ("The ability of ENvest<SCE> to differentiate itself based on its affiliation with SCE meant that it did not need to spend substantial funds trying to establish its identity in the market. Rather, it was able to market using SCE's name recognition, reputation, and image without cost. Competitors, including new entrants, face the expenditure of substantial sums of money to attempt to overcome this advantage which SCE had been establishing for decades. This would undoubtedly be a risky expenditure considering the level of customer loyalty that appears to exist for SCE.").

[75] *See id.* at *49 ("Government subsidies provided only to one firm can be a definite barrier to new entry. The ability of ENvest<SCE> to use its affiliation with a regulated utility to create an 'indirect' franchise in the federal performance contracting sector is an example.").

[76] DANIEL KAHNEMAN, THINKING, FAST AND SLOW 82 (2011). Chapter 11.3.3.10 will address how the halo effect affects regulators.

for decades passively bought plain vanilla electric service at a government-set rate can easily become paralyzed by confusing choices. Facing a complex mix of new pricing plans, renewable energy offers and energy efficiency bundles, many stay with the name they've always known.[77]

6.3.3.2.2 Utility's internal characteristics

Incumbent utilities gain unearned advantages from their internal characteristics: economies of scale and scope, service territory knowledge, technical expertise, predictable earnings, sunk costs and surplus capacity.

Economies of scale: The economies of scale concept has a firm-specific meaning and a market-specific meaning. A firm achieves economy of scale if its production capacity, and its actual production, reach a level that minimizes total cost. Firms subject to competition pursue economies of scale by growing their customer base. These pursuits benefit the competitive process, because to add customers firms must lower their costs and increase their quality.[78] A franchised utility is different. Its economies of scale do not come from competitive effort. They exist—if they exist[79]—because the utility (a) provides a service

---

[77] "Apathy is one of the characteristic responses of any living organism when it is subjected to stimuli too intense or too complicated to cope with." JOHN DOS PASSOS, THE PROSPECT BEFORE US 10 (1950). *See also* United States v. AT&T Co., 524 F. Supp. 1336, 1348 (D.D.C. 1981) (finding that AT&T's monopoly position was protected in part by "entrenched customer preferences").

[78] *See, e.g.,* NBC Universal-Comcast Merger, 26 FCC Rcd. 4238, 4303 ¶ 154 (2007) (finding that the NBCU-Comcast merger could improve competition in the online advertising market, because "packaging advertising across multiple platforms may provide an efficiency that reduces the effective price of advertising").

[79] In none of the two dozen mergers the author has participated in has a witness for the merging companies presented technical, objective, verifiable evidence showing that either of the merger applicants had not already exhausted economies of scale in any of its major functions. In none of the merger decisions studied for this book has FERC or a state commission cited such evidence. Certainly savings are possible from eliminating overlapping functions like shareholder relations and power supply planning. But these potential savings come largely from labor costs—small costs for these multi-billion-dollar entities. As to the large costs—the infrastructure costs associated with generation, transmission and distribution—at least since the era of regional transmission organizations no one has provided evidence of merger-induced economies of scale. Perhaps for that reason, merger applicants have been turning to other, similarly non-quantified claims, such as from dynamic efficiencies, quality benefits and vertical economies. For an analysis of those types of claims, and antitrust agencies' response to them, see John Kwoka, *The Changing Nature of Efficiencies in Mergers and Merger Analysis*, ANTITRUST BULL., Sept. 2015, at 1–19 (describing how antitrust agencies' expertise on conventional claims of efficiencies "may have lagged behind the capabilities of merging parties to make credible claims of efficiencies, resulting in undue deference to such claims"; adding that as merging firms claim new forms of efficiencies,

that has, inherently, a declining cost function; and (b) has received from the government an exclusive service territory large enough to make economical use of that cost function. The cost advantage does not come from competitive effort; it comes from government action.

A market achieves economies of scale when total customer demand reaches the level at which each of the market's suppliers achieves its own economy of scale. Suppose an efficient firm achieves economies of scale at 1500 widgets per year. If the market has a total demand of 2500 widgets, it can accommodate only one efficient competitor producing 1500 widgets.[80] Because any other competitors will produce fewer than 1500, they will not achieve the larger company's scale economy. So their costs will be higher, translating into higher prices or lower profits. Over time, customers of the smaller competitors will likely migrate to the first—not because the first company performs better but because its lower production cost—a result of scale economies inherent in widget production—allows it to charge lower prices. If that larger company is the incumbent utility, it has achieved its cost-minimizing size not from competitive merit but from the combination of the electric service's inherent cost function and the service territory size defined by the government-granted franchise. Its competitive advantage is unearned.

A related source of unearned advantage is economies of scope—a firm's ability to reduce costs by "producing two or more products jointly, rather than in [separate] specialized firms."[81] Recall Southern California Edison's affiliate, ENvest<SCE>. It competed to provide energy performance contracting to federal buildings. Its affiliation with the utility gave it advantages over competitors: "(1) special access to SCE's billing system, customer information, and customer representatives, (2) access to financing from SCE and having customers repay financing on the utility bill; and (3) the use of SCE's name recognition, reputation, and image for marketing."[82] These advantages more resemble economies of scope than economies of scale, because their source is the mix of different products, rather than the amount produced of a single product. A non-affiliate would have not these advantages.

"the agencies may once again lag behind firms' capabilities and once again give unwarranted deference to such claims").

[80]   SCHERER & ROSS, *supra* note 23, at 424 (explaining that for a particular product or service, scale economies limit the number of firms that can operate in an industry at minimum cost).

[81]   *Id.* at 361 (describing an incumbent's economies of scope, and multiproduct cost subadditivity generally, as entry barriers).

[82]   Rules and Procedures Governing Utility Demand-side Management, *supra* note 73, at *37 (findings by the Commission's consultant).

Service territory knowledge and technical expertise, ratepayer-funded:
Competitive success requires market information. Operating in one territory
for decades, the incumbent utility acquires detailed technical knowledge:
of residential load and consumption patterns; large customers' expansion
plans; weather; available sites for generation, transmission and distribution
facilities; and customers' payment histories. The utility also has gained technical expertise in engineering, finance, accounting, economics and law. It has
developed economic, professional, social and political relationships with local
banks, manufacturers, and local and state government officials. It has become
a fixture in the local economy. Most of this knowledge the utility gained at no
cost to itself because ratepayers paid for it.[83]

The incumbent utility can use this knowledge to design, test and market
new products—such as green power, remote-controlled thermostats, advanced
meters, pricing plans and gas-electric-efficiency convergence products.
Besides bringing the utility more data on customer preferences, these efforts
strengthen the utility's brand, giving it a first-mover advantage in these new
product markets. Competitors cannot readily use this information and experience; what they can replicate will require their shareholders to incur costs that
the utility has already recovered from its customers. This advantage, like the
others, comes not from the utility's skill but from its incumbency.

Predictable earnings: A utility that performs consistently with its regulators' expectations has predictable earnings.[84] That predictability allows the
utility, and its affiliates, to finance business expansion at lower cost than its
competitors, because lenders will have higher confidence in being repaid.
Non-utility competitors have no similar government-advantaged cash flow.[85]

---

[83]   *See, e.g.*, Rules and Procedures Governing Utility Demand-side Management,
supra note 73, at *41 (finding that Southern California Edison's energy performance
contracting affiliate "had its learning curve experience paid out of ratepayer funds. This
cost was not reflected in prices to customers. … While other firms may acquire such
skills, there will be a cost that must be collected from customers, or else fall upon shareholders."); Standards of Conduct Governing Relationships Between Utilities and Their
Affiliates, 1997 Cal. PUC LEXIS 1139, at *20–21 (explaining that "customer-specific
information can become quite valuable to businesses in a competitive environment");
Competitive Opportunities Regarding Electric Service, 1997 N.Y. PUC LEXIS 450, at
*24 (finding that "access to usage data is a critical component of an effective competi-
tive retail market").

[84]   As Tutorial § 4.1 explains, statutory and constitutional law requires utility regulators to set rates that provide the utility with a reasonable opportunity to earn a fair
return on its prudent, used-and-useful investments. That legal fact, coupled with the key
market fact—customer captivity—makes earnings predictable.

[85]   *See, e.g.*, Rules and Procedures Governing Utility Demand-side Management,
supra note 73, at *49 (describing ENvest<SCE>'s "ability to use ratepayer funds
to make its projects more attractive to customers and to provide some protection to

Sunk cost: To carry out its obligation to serve, a utility makes major capital expenditures. The utility also spends to recruit and train top talent. Once made, those expenditures become sunk costs. If those expenditures were prudent and the associated assets used and useful, the utility's customers must pay for them. What if a competitor then offers a substitute service at a lower cost? Too late. To avoid uneconomic bypass, most regulatory commissions require a customer wishing to substitute a new supplier to pay its pro rata share of the utility's sunk cost; otherwise the departing customer's cost-share would shift to the customers left behind.[86] The sum of sunk cost charge plus the new option's cost will likely exceed what the customer would pay by staying with the utility. The sunk cost becomes the utility's competitive advantage:

> [W]e can think of no more effective exclusion [of competitors] than progressively to embrace each new opportunity as it opened, and to face every [competitive] newcomer with new capacity already geared into a great organization, having the advantage of experience, trade connections and the elite of personnel.[87]

The electric utility's sunk costs represent costs incurred to satisfy its monopoly franchise function, not its affiliates' competitive activities. But when a prospective entrant wishes to provide a substitute for the utility's monopoly product—such as wind, solar, storage, or microgrids substituting for the incumbent conventional generation, transmission or distribution—sunk cost is an entry barrier.

Surplus capacity: A species of the sunk cost problem arises from the utility's surplus capacity. A franchised retail utility has an obligation to serve. It must stand ready to serve all loads, including peak loads, at all hours. Having sufficient capacity on-peak means having surplus capacity off-peak. Even

---

shareholders for credit losses. These subsidies either gave ENvest<SCE> a preferred position in a market or allowed it to underprice competitors because it had access to ratepayer funds which need not be repaid.").

[86] Uneconomic bypass occurs when the incumbent utility's customer departs to an alternative seller, if the alternative seller's charge to the customer (reflecting that seller's fixed cost and variable cost) is (a) less than the rate the customer pays to the utility, making the choice positive for the customer; but (b) greater than the utility's variable costs, making the result negative for society. The problem occurs if the customer, by leaving the utility, can avoid the sunk cost normally recovered in the utility's rates. The standard technique for preventing uneconomic bypass is to make the customer responsible for its share of that sunk cost. Then the customer will compare the alternative's seller's total charge (reflecting its fixed and variable cost) to the utility's fixed and variable cost. This apples-to-apples comparison promotes economic efficiency. On this topic, legitimate arguments are less about setting up the apples-to-apples framework and more about determining the costs.

[87] United States v. Aluminum Co. of Am., 148 F.2d 416, 431 (2d Cir. 1945).

during peak periods most utilities have surplus capacity—capacity exceeding required reserves. Why? A new generator's economic size—the size that minimizes cost per megawatt—is usually larger than the utility's need for new capacity at the time the generator enters service. As a result, generating capacity often comes on line in large lumps rather than small increments; customer load then grows into the installed capacity.[88] When this surplus arises from prudent planning, the utility's customers pay for it in their rates. But the utility's competitors can't afford surplus, because they have no captive ratepayers to pay for it. These competitors can afford to build only the amount of capacity that customers will contract for today—usually smaller generating units that have higher per-unit costs. So in markets for firm energy, interruptible energy and short-term capacity, the utility can sell from its surplus capacity, paid for by captive ratepayers, at prices lower than its competitors. That competitive advantage comes not from merit but from the utility's state law obligation to serve. And these prices need not be predatorily low—a violation of antitrust law[89]—to damage competition on the merits. That these lower prices don't violate antitrust law warrants their attention from utility regulators.

* * *

This subsection has described how a utility's internal characteristics, arising from its franchised status, can give unearned advantages in competitive markets. The consultant's report on ENvest<SCE>'s market position sums up the problem well:

> The potential economies of scale in the ENvest<SCE> pilot arose from: (1) special access to SCE's billing system, customer information, and customer representatives; (2) access to financing from SCE and having customers repay financing on the utility bill; and (3) the use of SCE's name recognition, reputation, and image for marketing. The special access to utility and customer billing information reduced transaction costs to develop and target marketing strategies. The potential use of SCE's billing system could avoid the need to create a billing system and to develop and input the customer and other information needed. Simply, the fact that information is collected and systems are in place avoids the time, resources, and hassle to develop those necessary items. Not having to pay for these costs creates a competitive advantage.[90]

---

[88]   Rough analogy: Parents don't buy their young children new clothes every few months; they buy pants long, then the child grows into them.

[89]   *See* Chapter 6.3.2.5 (defining predatory pricing as charging prices below some measure of cost, with the intent of driving competitors from the market and then charging supracompetitive prices to recoup the losses).

[90]   Rules and Procedures Governing Utility Demand-side Management, *supra* note 73, at *37–38. Of course, no market position is guaranteed. As the Commission's consultants explained:

6.3.3.2.3 *The utility's actions*

The previous subsections discussed two sources for utilities' unearned advantages: customer behavior, and the utility's internal characteristics. A third source is the utility's own actions. The four actions discussed below help the utility and its affiliates defeat their competitors. The opportunities to take these actions exist because of the franchise, not because of merit.

Sending monthly bills: The utility's monthly bills provide twelve-per-year opportunities to build and cement loyalty and to advertise new products. With mailing list, envelopes and stamps all paid for by customers, the incremental cost of adding promotional material is near zero. The non-utility competitor incurs all those costs from scratch. And while every customer has to open the utility's monthly bill, no one has to open the competitors' mailing.

Tying up large customers in long-term contracts: Long-term contracts can be pro-competitive and pro-consumer. By ensuring stable revenues, they allow the seller to finance equipment at lower cost. By obviating annual renegotiations while creating a history of satisfactory performance, they reduce transaction costs. A buyer's willingness to sign a long-term contract can reflect the seller's merits. But if the utility can use its ratepayer-funded knowledge to tie up the most attractive customers, its advantage comes from incumbency rather than merit. This advantage then discourages newcomers from entering the market: with few attractive customers to gain, their risks will be greater, their financing costs will be higher and therefore their prices will be higher—lowering their chances for success.

Using captive customer revenues to fund aggressive pricing: Aggressive price-cutting damages competition if based on unearned advantage rather than merit. Antitrust law bans predatory pricing, but predatory pricing does not include a utility's competitive affiliate pricing below fixed cost but above variable cost, then covering its fixed costs with the utility's profits earned from its monopoly customers. If the non-utility competitors lack access to a comparable profit stream, they cannot meet the utility affiliate's low price and still cover their own fixed costs. When they fail and leave the market,

---

An open question is whether future competitors to ENvest<SCE> will create a more intense competitive market. If industry restructuring proceeds as it appears it will, there is an increasing likelihood that other well-capitalized firms with solid reputations will enter the Southern California market. These firms could include unregulated utility affiliates from around the country and consolidated ESCOs [energy service companies] partnered with independent power producers or equipment manufacturers. The issue will be whether these new entrants could influence customer decisionmaking to the same extent as SCE/ENvest<SCE>.

Id. at *35.

the utility's competitive affiliate can raise prices to recover the fixed costs it did not previously recover. The affiliate wins the competition not because of its competitive merits but because of its pre-existing wealth, gained from its government-protected franchise.

Bundling: A utility ties anticompetitively when it refuses to sell monopoly Product M unless the buyer also buys competitive Product C.[91] What if the utility (or its competitive affiliate) bundles two products, neither of which is a monopoly product? Mere bundling is not anticompetitive tying.[92] Bundling can be economically efficient if it exploits economies of scope—when the total cost of producing two items together is lower than producing them separately.[93] Economically efficient bundling can be pro-competitive, by causing competitors to find their own economies of scope; and pro-consumer, because one-stop shopping reduces transaction costs.[94] But if the utility's bundle includes a product paid for by captive customers, the utility will have an unearned advantage over competitors, because they will have to produce or procure their version of that product from scratch. Consider distributed energy resources. Suppliers seeking to sell a package of firm renewable energy will need to bundle solar panels, installation service, distribution interconnection, storage, billing services and backup energy. The utility, due to its franchised status, can provide all these services by itself. The non-utility competitors will need to collect these items from various sources, paying a profit to each one; so its bundle will cost more. Only if the utility shares those components on terms comparable to its own costs will its unearned advantage disappear.

---

[91]   As explained in Chapter 6.3.2.3.

[92]   *See* Jefferson Parish Hosp. Dist. No. 2 v. Hyde, 466 U.S. 2, 12 ("[I]f one of a dozen food stores in a community were to refuse to sell flour unless the buyer also took sugar it would hardly tend to restrain competition [in sugar] if its competitors were ready and able to sell flour by itself.") (quoting N. Pac. Ry. Co. v. United States, 356 U.S. 1, 7 (1958)). *See also* Guidelines on Assessment of Non-horizontal Mergers, *supra* note 32, at 23 ¶ 104 (explaining that offering a bundle is not acting anticompetitively).

[93]   Consider tax preparation software. The CD-ROM "usually contains several other modules, including a link to a Web page, government documents, and a tax preparation manual. ... [T]he different modules can be more inexpensively produced, packaged, and used together than separately." PAUL A. SAMUELSON & WILLIAM D. NORDHAUS, ECONOMICS 116–17 (19th ed. 2010). Another example: Toshiba makes the iPod's hard drive. Because the company makes other hard drives and related products, it can produce the iPod drive at a lower cost than if the iPod drive were its only product. MICHAEL PARKIN, ECONOMICS 243 (10th ed. 2012).

[94]   *See, e.g.*, Guidelines on Assessment of Non-horizontal Mergers, *supra* note 32, at 23 ¶ 104.

6.3.3.2.4 *Luck*

"[O]ne should not underemphasize plain luck as a way to stay on top. ... [O]ne cannot explain dominance entirely on the basis of superior product, superior management, or even predatory practices."[95] Firms might start out with equal attributes and equal opportunities, but some "will inevitably enjoy a run of luck, experiencing several years of rapid growth in close succession."[96] And when luck leads to dominance, the market structure does not reflect competition on the merits.[97] Especially when the market structure is fragile—when its competitiveness has not reached full vigor—luck can distort competition by entrenching the lucky.[98] Indeed, "[o]nce the most fortunate enterprises climb well ahead of the pack it is difficult for laggards to rally and rectify the imbalance."[99]

6.3.3.3 Unearned advantage: entry barrier to prospective competitors

The previous subsection discussed four sources of utility advantage: customer behavior (brand loyalty, government's imprimatur, halo effect and inertia); the utility's internal characteristics (economies of scale, service territory knowledge, predictable earnings, sunk cost, surplus capacity and financing advantage); the utility's actions (sending monthly bills, tying up legacy customers in long-term contracts, using captive customer revenues to fund aggressive pricing and bundling); and luck. None of these advantages arises from merit—shareholder risk-taking or managerial excellence. Each derives from, and depends on, the government's decision to grant an exclusive franchise.

Individually and combined, these unearned advantages create entry barriers. An entry barrier is a difference, between incumbent and newcomer, in the cost to enter a market—a cost difference large enough to matter competitively. A cost difference matters competitively if it is large enough (a) to deter a newcomer's entry; or, if the newcomer enters, (b) to render the new entrant

---

[95] Stephen G. Breyer, *The Problem of the Honest Monopolist*, 44 ANTITRUST L.J. 194, 195–96 (1975).

[96] SCHERER & ROSS, *supra* note 23, at 141.

[97] *See* Robin Mordfin & Toni Shears, *Regulation and Market Power*, BECKER FRIEDMAN INST. NEWS (May 28, 2015), http://bfi.uchicago.edu/news/feature-story/regulation-and-market-power (attributing to Nobel Prize recipient Jean Tirole the view that if a firm "dominates simply because of luck of circumstance, that skews competition unfairly").

[98] *See, e.g.*, Peter C. Carstensen & Robert H. Lande, *The Merger Incipiency Doctrine and the Importance of "Redundant" Competitors*, 2018 WIS. L. REV. 781, 830 (2018) (citing Yossi Sheffi & Barry C. Lynn, *Systemic Supply Chain Risk*, THE BRIDGE 22 (Fall 2014)).

[99] SCHERER & ROSS, *supra* note 23, at 141.

unable to take customers from the incumbent despite performing better.[100] By deterring or disadvantaging prospective competitors, entry barriers enable the incumbent to succeed for reasons other than merit, and then to charge supra-competitive prices.[101]

While all entry barriers affect competition, not all cause customers harm. Professional licensing for lawyers and doctors protects clients and patients from the unqualified. Patents attract risk-taking inventors who bring society new products. Exclusive franchises for natural monopoly services protect consumers from the costs of uneconomic redundancy. These government-created entry barriers make sense where the gains from professionalism (licensing), innovation (patents) and scale economies (utilities) exceed any economic losses caused by preventing competition. And all vigorous competitors seek to build their own entry barriers, by differentiating their products and creating hard-to-beat reputations. Where the entry barriers result from competitive merit, the efforts to create them actually strengthen competition and benefit consumers.[102] Furthermore, unearned advantage is inherent in human society. People born to wealthy families, tall people, people of ethnicities or races not

---

[100] *See, e.g.*, Rebel Oil Co. v. Atlantic Richfield Co., 51 F.3d 1421, 1439 (9th Cir. 1995) (describing entry barriers as "additional long-run costs [to enter a new market] that were not incurred by incumbent firms but must be incurred by new entrants") (quoting L.A. Land Co. v. Brunswick Corp., 6 F.3d 1422, 1427–28 (9th Cir. 1993)). The economic literature offers more sophisticated definitions. Here are three: "the extent to which, in the long run, established firms can elevate their selling prices above minimal average costs of production and distribution ... without inducing potential entrants to enter the industry" (Joe Bain); "a cost of producing (at some or every rate of output) which must be borne by firms which seek to enter an industry but is not borne by firms already in the industry" (George Stigler); and "socially undesirable limitations to entry of resources which are due to protection of resource owners already in the market" (Carl von Weizsäcker). Each definition is discussed in W. KIP VISCUSI, JOSEPH E. HARRINGTON & JOHN M. VERNON, ECONOMICS OF REGULATION AND ANTITRUST 168 (4th ed. 2005).

[101] *Rebel Oil Co.*, 51 F.3d at 1439 (9th Cir. 1995). *See also* Breyer, *supra* note 31, at 1014 (explaining that entry barriers allow the incumbent to "raise prices from competitive levels *up to* the height of the entry barrier, up to the point where potential competitors will step in") (emphasis added).

[102] SCOTT HEMPLING, REGULATING PUBLIC UTILITY PERFORMANCE: THE LAW OF MARKET STRUCTURE, PRICING AND JURISDICTION 178–79 (American Bar Association 2013) (explaining that "longstanding, outstanding performance builds customer loyalty, discouraging competitors unwilling to spend comparable effort. Entry barriers are not inherently anti-competitive; the prospect of erecting them is what attracts competitors to begin with."). Indeed, "the opportunity to charge monopoly prices—at least for a short period—is what attracts 'business acumen' in the first place; it induces risk taking that produces innovation and economic growth." Verizon Commc'ns Inc. v. Law Offices of Curtis V. Trinko, LLP, 540 U.S. 398, 407 (2004).

subject to systemic discrimination, people born with gratification-deferral wiring, people needing only four hours of sleep, hockey players born early in the year, people whose 1960s-era middle schools had an unused computer[103]— all have advantages not attributable to merits. The same goes for companies. Because we will never have markets in which no company has an unearned advantage, we will never have competition purely on the merits.

But entry barriers created, assisted or protected by regulatory action still deserve our attention. Brand loyalty, government imprimatur, halo effect and inertia all increase the likelihood that customers choosing a competitive service supplier will choose the utility or its affiliate over a better-performing but less familiar newcomer. To overcome this preference, to change the customer's mind, new entrants need to spend money that the incumbent doesn't need to spend. That extra cost—for advertising, product differentiation or direct contact—is an entry barrier. Economies of scale, service territory knowledge, predictable earnings, sunk costs, surplus capacity, financing advantage—these elements are not readily replicable by competitors, because their source is the government-granted franchise. The newcomer can spend some money on gaining service territory knowledge—again a cost difference; but replicating the utility's full knowledge is impossible. Finally, the utility's actions—using the customer-funded monthly bills to deepen loyalty and promote new products, tying up legacy customers in long-term contracts, using captive customer revenues to fund aggressive pricing, and bundling—most of these actions are not available to the non-franchised newcomer. Unearned advantage undermines competition on the merits.

6.3.3.4 Unearned advantage: outside antitrust law's reach
Exploiting unearned advantage does not necessarily mean exercising market power—the ability to control price or output. Nor does it necessarily involve exclusionary conduct—refusing to deal, creating entry barriers, tying, price squeezing or pricing predatorily. So utilities' unearned advantages, and their efforts to exploit those advantages, will usually fall outside antitrust's reach. Antitrust law prevents anticompetitive conduct in competitive markets; it does not remove pre-existing defects—like unearned advantages—in those

---

[103] The last two items come from MALCOM GLADWELL, OUTLIERS: THE STORY OF SUCCESS (2008). Gladwell found that a disproportionate percentage of Canadian professional hockey players were born early in the year. At age four, which is when they started league play, the older ones were bigger and stronger than their later-born peers, so received more coaching attention. In the late 1960s, Bill Gates's middle school had a spare computer.

markets.[104] Anticompetitive conduct is conduct by the competitor. In the franchised utility context, unearned advantage usually comes from conduct by the government.

Even if unearned advantages did trigger antitrust law, federal antitrust courts cannot readily remove them. Bounded by a single plaintiff-specific complaint, a court cannot remove advantages that distort an entire market, let alone the entire industry.[105] Different federal trial courts will produce different standards and principles, with those differences resolved by the Supreme Court only rarely. Detecting and fixing cross-subsidies between the monopoly and competitive businesses takes industry-specific expertise, and involves "political decisions about levels of service and the rate of return to capital needed to provide those services."[106] Federal judges lack both the necessary expertise and the political accountability.[107]

Regulatory agencies, in contrast, can

> push forward on all parts of the economic system at the same time. Agencies can change a number of policies simultaneously and can do so sharply—moving from the existing framework to a substantially different spot in a process of punctuated equilibria—while courts have little control over agendas, can only decide the issues directly before them, and are normally limited to smaller moves consistent with judicial precedent.[108]

To have effective competition, eliminating market power and anticompetitive conduct is necessary but not sufficient. We must eliminate unearned advan-

---

[104] *See, e.g., Trinko,* 540 U.S. at 407 (2004) ("[T]he possession of monopoly power will not be found unlawful unless it is accompanied by an element of anticompetitive *conduct*"); Scott Hempling, *No Anticompetitive Conduct, No Unearned Advantage: Effective Competition Depends on Merit,* Scott Hempling Law (Aug. 2018), https://www.scotthemplinglaw.com/essays/no-anticompetitive-conduct-no-un earned-advantage-effective-competition-depends-on-merit.

[105] *Cf.* Scott Hempling, *Commissions Are Not Courts; Regulators Are Not Judges,* Scott Hempling Law (Mar. 2019), https://www.scotthemplinglaw.com/essays/ commissions-are-not-courts-regulators-are-not-judges.

[106] Dennis W. Carlton & Randal C. Picker, *Antitrust and Regulation, in* Economic Regulation and Its Reform 26 (Nancy L. Rose ed., 2014).

[107] *But see* Crane, *supra* note 2, at 96–97 ("Whereas regulation tends to concentrate power in a few powerful hands, adjudication disperses decision-making power: horizontally, among the many different judges who may draw a case; and vertically, as decisions of a lower court can be appealed to a higher court. Generalist judges may avoid the tunnel vision, power-aggrandizing tendencies, and agency-capture problems of administrative agencies.") (citing Peter H. Schuck, *Mass Torts: An Institutional Evolutionist Perspective,* 80 Cornell L. Rev. 941, 974–76 (1995); and Caleb Nelson, *Statutory Interpretation and Decision Theory,* 74 U. Chi. L. Rev. 329, 351 (2007)).

[108] *Id.* at 32.

tages. And to eliminate unearned advantages, we cannot rely on antitrust law; we must turn to regulatory law.[109]

This chapter has explained, in sequence, how market power, anticompetitive conduct and unearned advantages can harm electricity competition. We can now turn to how electric utility mergers contribute to these harms.

6.4 ELECTRICITY MONOPOLY MERGERS: RISKS TO COMPETITION ON THE MERITS

Every market has a structure. That structure is described by its product and geographic dimensions; by the sellers' and buyers' identities, market shares and other characteristics; and by the entry barriers, if any, between incumbents and new entrants. A merger affects a market's structure by changing one or more of those features. The structural effects vary with the merger type— horizontal, vertical, convergence or conglomerate (or some combination). Changes to market structure cause changes in competitor conduct; and changes in competitor conduct affect market performance. A merger's effect on performance can be positive or negative:

> The preponderant case for the mergers is that they will improve efficiency. The preponderant case against them is their possible impairment of competition, for two reasons: first, the merging companies are typically actual or potential competitors in some parts of their business, and, second, they may be enabled by joining together to deny outside firms a fair opportunity to compete.[110]

This section describes the two most common types of electricity mergers: horizontal and vertical. As with the preceding discussion of market power, anticompetitive behavior and unearned advantage, both antitrust law and general regulatory law apply.

6.4.1 Horizontal Mergers: Reducing the Number of Competitors

Horizontal mergers can "advance the potential for procompetitive effects, including the achievement of otherwise unattainable efficiencies." But they

---

[109] *See* Breyer, *supra* note 31, at 1007 (1987) (describing how classical regulation is most appropriate where antitrust laws are inadequate to police market defects); Southern California Edison-San Diego Gas & Electric Merger, 1991 Cal. PUC LEXIS 253, at *61 (holding that under California's utility merger statute, the Commission's "decisionmaking authority over this merger, and its broad public interest aspects, is not so limited that it must be premised on whether the acquisition violates federal antitrust statutes").

[110] 2 KAHN, *supra* note 29, at 282.

also "eliminate competition between competitors far more surely than does any agreement in restraint of trade—and the elimination of competition may be permanent."[111] By reducing customers' choices, horizontal mergers give sellers, acting unilaterally or in coordination, the incentive and opportunity to raise prices and lower quality.[112]

Horizontal mergers affect structure. Besides reducing the number of competitors, they can eliminate mavericks and potential competitors. Structural effects aside, analysts look also at competitive effects: Does the merger change the seller's conduct in ways that weaken competition? Finally, mergers of adjacent utilities have unique effects; they can weaken head-to-head competition, yardstick competition and franchise competition. After defining horizontal mergers, we look at these effects on structure and conduct.

6.4.1.1 Horizontal mergers defined

A horizontal merger joins competitors—companies that sell the same or similar services within the same geographic area. Common examples: mergers between utilities that sell a generation service to wholesale or retail customers in the same region; between national long-distance telephone companies; and between regional wireless telephone providers.

The category includes mergers of companies selling different products, if consumers view the products as reasonable substitutes. Consider a merger of a gas utility with an electric utility. If electricity and gas are satisfactory substitutes (say, for industrial customers with fuel-switching capability, or for residential customers using those sources for cooking or heating), regulators

---

[111] JOHN SHENEFIELD & IRWIN STELZER, THE ANTITRUST LAWS: A PRIMER 61–62 (4th ed. 2001).

[112] AT&T Wireless-Cingular Merger, 19 FCC Rcd. 21,522, 21,552 ¶ 57 (2004). *See also* 2010 HORIZONTAL MERGER GUIDELINES, *supra* note 6, § 1 ("A merger enhances market power if it is likely to encourage one or more firms to raise price, reduce output, diminish innovation, or otherwise harm customers as a result of diminished competitive constraints or incentives."); Order No. 642, *supra* note 5, at 70,989–90 (explaining that FERC's competition analysis aims to "determine whether the merger will result in higher prices or reduced output in electricity markets. This may occur if the merged firm is able to exercise market power, either alone or in coordination with other firms."). *See also* Jim Chen, *The Echoes of Forgotten Footfalls: Telecommunications Mergers at the Dawn of the Digital Millennium*, 43 HOUS. L. REV. 1311, 1338 (2007) ("Reducing the number of [Bell Operating Companies] from seven to three and eliminating the two largest, independent LECs [local exchange companies] in the United States have increased the likelihood of collusion, eroded regulatory benchmarks, and aggravated the loss of actual potential competitors who might challenge these carriers and other established (and entrenched) telecommunications companies.") (citing Jim Chen, *The Magnificent Seven: American Telephony's Deregulatory Shootout*, 50 HASTINGS L.J. 1503, 1505 (1999)).

will view a gas-electricity merger as horizontal, then test whether it will reduce interfuel competition. The Vermont Public Service Board approved a gas-electric merger only after making three findings: (a) in the affected geographic market, end uses of the two fuels differed, so the two products were not complete substitutes; (b) price disparity between gas and electricity offered more evidence of non-substitutability; and (c) the merged entity would operate the gas and electric subsidiaries separately.[113] Similarly, when wireless and wireline companies merge, the FCC assesses the effects on intermodal competition by measuring product substitutability.[114]

Because a horizontal merger involves companies that are, or could be, competing with each other, the category excludes mergers of companies selling the same product in different geographic markets. A merger of a Maine utility with a California utility is a geographic extension merger, not a horizontal merger, because electricity produced in California cannot substitute for electricity produced in Maine.

---

[113] Green Mountain Power-New England Energy Merger, 2007 Vt. PUC LEXIS 74, at *54–56. *See also* Puget Sound Power & Light-Washington Natural Gas Merger, 1997 Wash. UTC LEXIS 6, at *52 (imposing conditions on a gas-electric merger to reduce the risk of anticompetitive cost-shifting that would advantage one fuel type over another). The Vermont Board's third finding—that the two subsidiaries would operate separately—does not align well with reality, because affiliates of a holding company do not compete with each other:

> A parent and its wholly owned subsidiary have a complete unity of interest. Their objectives are common, not disparate; their general corporate actions are guided or determined not by two separate corporate consciousnesses, but one. They are not unlike a multiple team of horses drawing a vehicle under the control of a single driver.

Copperweld Corp. v. Independence Tube Corp., 467 U.S. 752, 771 (1984). The Vermont Board did reserve its power to restrict the merged company's conduct if the two subsidiaries combined.

[114] Consider the Cingular-AT&T merger. Cingular was a wireless company, itself a joint venture between two regional wireline incumbent local exchange carriers. AT&T at the time was the largest wireless company not affiliated with an incumbent local exchange carrier. Because customers in the early aughts were just starting to substitute wireless for wireline service, the FCC examined whether the merger would reduce competition between those two services. *AT&T Wireless-Cingular Merger*, 19 FCC Rcd. at 21,552–53 ¶ 59 & n.225 (imposing conditions relating to horizontal concentration in individual wireless markets).

6.4.1.2 Harm analysis: structural concentration

By eliminating a competitor, will the merger give the merged company market power? To answer that question, analysts first measure the extent to which the merging pair, unmerged, compete with each other—or might:

> The level of competition depends on what products or services are substitutes for each other (product market), where those substitute products are available (geographic market), what firms produce them (market participants), and what other firms might be able to produce substitutes if the price were to rise (market entry).[115]

Having determined the extent to which the merging companies compete with each other pre-merger, analysts then ask whether eliminating that competition—reducing consumers' choices—will cause them harm. Answering that question involves six steps, in sequence:

1. Define the products and geographic markets affected by the merger.
2. Determine whether, within those defined markets, the merger-caused concentration will give the merged entity undue market power.[116]
3. Assess the likelihood, timeliness and sufficiency of entry by other competitors—entry that would constrain the merged company from exercising its market power.
4. Determine if the merger will produce for the customers efficiencies that will offset customer harm from the reduced competition.
5. Design, if possible, conditions to mitigate the merged company's market power.
6. If efficiencies are insufficient and mitigating conditions unavailable, reject the merger.[117]

The following four subsections address these steps. This six-step analysis focuses on structure, on the grounds that adverse effects on competition can be

---

[115] *Id.* at 21,552 ¶ 57. *See also* AT&T-Deutsche Telekom Merger, 26 FCC Rcd. 16,184, 16,196 ¶ 15 (2011).

[116] This second step produces a conclusion about the merger's structural effect. Some analysts argue that an adverse structural effect is sufficient either to reject the merger or impose mitigation remedies. Other analysts argue that a structural determination alone is insufficient; before proceeding to remedies one must determine whether the adverse effect on structure is likely to have an adverse effect on competition, such as exploitation of consumers or suppliers, exclusion of competitors, or harm to innovation.

[117] These steps constitute the horizontal component of the "competitive analysis screen" in FERC's merger policy, otherwise known as the Appendix A screen. *See* Order No. 642, *supra* note 5, at 70,985. FERC based its approach on the 1997 *Horizontal Merger Guidelines*. Those Guidelines are commonly relied on by the courts. *See, e.g.*, FTC v. H.J. Heinz Co., 246 F.3d 708, 716 (D.C.C. 2001).

inferred from changes in structure. An alternative, or supplemental, approach is to inquire into the likelihood of competitive effects directly, rather than inferring competitive effects from structural analysis. We will discuss competitive effects analysis in Chapter 6.4.1.4.[118]

6.4.1.2.1 Relevant product markets

The product markets affected by a merger include all products that the merging companies intend to sell, plus those products' reasonable substitutes.[119] Determining which products are reasonable substitutes involves the "hypothetical monopolist" test: For what group of products would a hypothetical, profit-maximizing firm, a firm that was "the only present and future seller of those products," likely be able to "impose at least a small but significant and non-transitory increase in price" (i.e., an increase above the competitive price)? The firm could impose and sustain that increase only if it had market power; i.e., if it expected that the revenue gained from the higher price would exceed the revenue forgone from customers cutting their purchases or shifting to other suppliers. The test prevents the analyst from making the product market too small; it would be too small if "competition from products outside that group is so ample that even the complete elimination of competition within the group would not significantly harm either direct customers or downstream consumers."[120]

---

[118] For a metastudy providing evidence that supports structure-based inferences, see generally KWOKA, *supra* note 6. Some have argued that structural analysis, by itself, risks mis-predicting a merger's effects because, among other reasons, (a) some mergers have had effects different from what structural analysis predicted; (b) non-structural factors like degree of product substitution have affected outcomes; and (c) causation can be unclear—e.g., industry concentration might reflect the dominant firms' merits. *Id.* at 40–41 (summarizing, without endorsing, criticisms of structural analysis).

[119] *See* United States v. E.I. du Pont de Nemours & Co., 351 U.S. 377, 395 (1956) (explaining that the relevant product market includes "commodities reasonably interchangeable by consumers for the same purposes"); Order No. 642, *supra* note 5, at 70,991 (emphasizing that a relevant product group includes only those products consumers consider "good substitutes").

[120] 2010 HORIZONTAL MERGER GUIDELINES, *supra* note 6, § 4. Frankena and Owen describe the hypothetical monopolist test usefully:

> Suppose one firm gained control of all supplies of a product (or group of products) sold in a specified geographic area. Could that hypothetical monopolist increase its profits by raising prices above the levels that would otherwise prevail? ... If the answer to [this] question[] is affirmative, then an antitrust market [i.e., a relevant market] has been identified.

MARK W. FRANKENA & BRUCE M. OWEN, ELECTRIC UTILITY MERGERS: PRINCIPLES OF ANTITRUST ANALYSIS 69 (1994). They also provide a straightforward, three-part test:

1. "[I]dentify a specific set of customers that might be victimized by an increase in the price of ... Service X."

How does product market analysis apply to electricity? As discussed next, some electricity services have reasonable substitutes; some do not.

Electric current: Like liquid bleach, electric current is a commodity, physically identical regardless of its source. It makes equipment work. But this product category does include distinct sub-products that are not commodities. Some customers prefer renewable-sourced electricity over fossil-sourced electricity. Customers operating sensitive equipment require electric current at special levels of power quality.[121] And absent storage, electricity available in the middle of the night is not necessarily available in the middle of the afternoon.

Wholesale electricity: This category includes several distinct, non-substitutable products: non-firm energy (also called interruptible energy), firm energy, short-term capacity and long-term capacity.[122] Energy is the electric current. Non-firm energy comes with no guarantee; the customer gets it only if, when, and to the extent that the supplier has the capacity available to produce and deliver it. Non-firm energy is not a reasonable substitute for firm energy. Firm energy comes with a guarantee: it is energy available to the customer whenever desired, without interruption, for whatever is the contractual period—weeks, months or years. For energy to be firm, it must be backed by capacity. Capacity is the physical capability to produce energy on demand. When determining the amount of capacity in the relevant geographic market, FERC counts only "available economic capacity," a concept having three components: (a) it is the capacity that "remains after native load requirements and firm contractual

---

2.   "Identify other products or services that are substitutes for Service X from the point of view of these customers. Customers cannot be victimized by an increase in the price of Service X if enough of them can switch to some other product or service (Service Y) without suffering significant adverse effects. If enough customers can switch, suppliers of Service X will not find a price increase profitable."

3.   "Identify suppliers that can respond to the increase in the price of Service X by beginning to supply either Service X or Service Y. Customers cannot be victimized by current suppliers increasing the price of Service X if enough customers can switch to a new supplier that is not currently producing Service X but that would do so if it could sell its output."

Id. at 68. Dr. Frankena was a sturdy, supportive colleague of the author's in the early 1990s—when the electricity merger trend was just getting its boots on. Sadly, he passed away in 2017.

[121]   *See Power Quality*, IEEE STANDARD DICTIONARY OF ELECTRICAL AND ELECTRONICS TERMS (defining power quality as "the concept of powering and grounding sensitive electronic equipment in a manner that is suitable to the operation of that equipment").

[122]   Order No. 642, *supra* note 5, at 70,991, text accompanying n.33.

commitments are subtracted";[123] (b) it is capable of "produc[ing] energy at a competitive cost"; and (c) it is "available to compete in the short-term energy market (or short-term capacity market)."[124] Short-term capacity is not a reasonable substitute for long-term capacity: "purchasing a 20-year commitment to meet power needs that exist for a few days or years would be prohibitively expensive. Conversely, relying on relatively short-term annual contracts to meet a long-term power requirement is likely to involve excessive risk of price volatility and availability."[125]

Ancillary services: Wholesale customers buy transmission service separately from generation service. They buy transmission from a monopoly provider—either the local utility or the regional transmission organization.[126] Most then buy their generation from competing companies or from organized power supply markets. By FERC rule, the transmission service that customers

---

[123] Native load refers to the customers' demand which the utility has an obligation— by franchise or contract—to satisfy. *See* Order No. 888-A, *Promoting Wholesale Competition Through Open Access Non–Discriminatory Transmission Services by Public Utilities*, F.E.R.C. STATS. & REGS. ¶ 31,048, 62 Fed. Reg. 12,274, 12,299 n.129 (1997) (defining native load to mean "wholesale and retail power customers of the Transmission Provider on whose behalf the Transmission Provider, by statute, franchise, regulatory requirement or contract, has undertaken an obligation to construct and operate the Transmission Provider's system to meet the reliable electric needs of such customers"), *order on reh'g*, Order No. 888-B, 81 F.E.R.C. ¶ 61,248 (1997), *order on reh'g*, Order No. 888-C, 82 F.E.R.C. ¶ 61,046 (1998), *aff'd in relevant part sub nom.* Transmission Access Policy Study Grp. v. FERC, 225 F.3d 667 (D.C. Cir. 2000), *aff'd sub nom.* New York v. FERC, 535 U.S. 1 (2002).

[124] Stephen Paul Mahinka & Theodore A. Gebhard, *Deregulation and Industry Restructuring: Antitrust Issues in Electric Utility Mergers and Alliances*, 12 ANTITRUST 38, 42 (1998) (explaining FERC Order No. 592, *Inquiry Concerning the Commission's Merger Policy Under the Federal Power Act; Policy Statement*, F.E.R.C. STATS. & REGS. ¶ 31,044, 61 Fed. Reg. 68,595 (1996) [hereinafter *1996 Merger Policy Statement*], *reconsideration denied*, Order No. 592-A, 79 F.E.R.C. ¶ 61,321, 62 Fed. Reg. 33,341 (1997)). This definition of available economic capacity excludes three types of capacity: (a) capacity already committed to other customers (due to native load obligations and contractual obligations); (b) capacity that cannot physically reach customers in the geographic market because of transmission constraints; and (c) uneconomic capacity—capacity whose high cost of operation makes it an unlikely competitor. (Capacity is uneconomic if the marginal cost of delivered power from that capacity exceeds 105 percent of the competitive market price.) In merger analysis, FERC excludes these products from the relevant product market because the sellers, including the to-be-merged company, cannot use them as competitive weapons. *See also* Order No. 642, *supra* note 5, at 70,991 (describing the "delivered price test," which determines which suppliers can reach a market economically).

[125] *Northeast Utilities-Public Service of New Hampshire Merger*, 56 F.E.R.C. ¶ 61,269, at p. 62,003, text accompanying n.157 (1991) (footnote omitted).

[126] *See* Tutorial § 2.

must buy (or in some cases, self-supply) includes six "ancillary services," all necessary to stabilize the transmission system.[127] In analyzing a merger's effect on competition, FERC analyzes ancillary services separately from the other products, because their technical requirements "may be more stringent than those for providing energy, and there may be fewer potential suppliers than in energy markets."[128]

---

[127]　The six ancillary services are:
- *Scheduling, System Control and Dispatch Service:* "This service is required to schedule the movement of power through, out of, within, or into a Control Area."
- *Reactive Supply and Voltage Control from Generation Sources Service:* "In order to maintain transmission voltages on the Transmission Provider's transmission facilities within acceptable limits, generation facilities (in the Control Area where the Transmission Provider's transmission facilities are located) are operated to produce (or absorb) reactive power."
- *Regulation and Frequency Response Service:* "Regulation and Frequency Response Service is necessary to provide for the continuous balancing of resources (generation and interchange) with load and for maintaining scheduled Interconnection frequency at sixty cycles per second (60 Hz). Regulation and Frequency Response Service is accomplished by committing on-line generation whose output is raised or lowered (predominantly through the use of automatic generating control equipment) as necessary to follow the moment-by-moment changes in load."
- *Energy Imbalance Service:* "Energy Imbalance Service is provided when a difference occurs between the scheduled and the actual delivery of energy to a load located within a Control Area over a single hour."
- *Operating Reserve-Spinning Reserve Service:* "Spinning Reserve Service is needed to serve load immediately in the event of a system contingency. Spinning Reserve Service may be provided by generating units that are on-line and loaded at less than maximum output."
- *Operating Reserve-Supplemental Reserve Service:* "Supplemental Reserve Service is needed to serve load in the event of a system contingency; however, it is not available immediately to serve load but rather within a short period of time. Supplemental Reserve Service may be provided by generating units that are on-line but unloaded, by quick-start generation or by interruptible load."

Order No. 888, *Promoting Wholesale Competition Through Open Access Non–Discriminatory Transmission Services by Public Utilities*, F.E.R.C. Stats. & Regs. ¶ 31,036, 61 Fed. Reg. 21,540, 21,722 (1996) [hereinafter Order No. 888], *order on reh'g*, Order No. 888-A, 78 F.E.R.C. ¶ 61,220, *order on reh'g*, Order No. 888-B, 81 F.E.R.C. ¶ 61,248 (1997), *order on reh'g*, Order No. 888-C, 82 F.E.R.C. ¶ 61,046 (1998), *aff'd in relevant part sub nom.* Transmission Access Policy Study Grp. v. FERC, 225 F.3d 667 (D.C. Cir. 2000), *aff'd sub nom.* New York v. FERC, 535 U.S. 1 (2002).

[128]　Order No. 642, *supra* note 5, at 70,992, text accompanying n.34.

Metering and billing services: In some retail competition states, metering and billing services are sold competitively, unbundled from physical distribution services and from electric current.[129]

Total energy service: In some retail competition states, utilities have created energy service subsidiaries. They sell a package of energy services, such as electricity, gas and energy efficiency. From these efforts emerged the phrase "BTU convergence"—BTU-measured energy products sold to end users by a single energy provider. The energy service company (ESCO) gathers and analyzes customer consumption data, procures and provides energy supplies, negotiates terms of service, installs and reads meters, then issues invoices and collects payments. In these efforts, utilities and their affiliates have two advantages over their non-utility competitors. They already control the production, transportation and delivery of the key components; and they have immediate access to knowledge of a large and largely captive customer base.[130] That customer base has years of familiarity with and trust in the utility.

6.4.1.2.2 Relevant geographic markets
For a given product, the relevant geographic market is the area within which the seller's customers can "practicably turn for supplies."[131] More technically,

---

[129] *See, e.g.*, Kinder Morgan, Inc., 2007 WL 1201539, at *47 (Wyo. Pub. Serv. Comm'n 2007) (discussing third-party customer service and billing function companies used by competitive providers of retail gas service); Unlicensed Independent Entities Offering Billing Services Affecting Electric Retail Choice, 2001 WL 942591 (Pa. Pub. Util. Comm'n 2001) (discussing billing aggregators).

[130] *See, e.g.*, Sam I. Bratton, Commissioner, Arkansas Public Service Commission, Statement to U.S. Senate Committee on Energy and Natural Resources (June 24, 1997), *included in* COMM. ON ENERGY AND NAT. RES., 105TH CONG., COMPETITIVE CHANGE IN THE ELECTRIC POWER INDUSTRY 257 (Comm. Print 1997) (defining BTU convergence as "BTU-measured energy products sold to end-users by a single energy provider. The marketing goal appears to be to concentrate, within one provider, the task of gathering and analyzing information, providing energy supplies, negotiating terms of service, and providing customer service functions such as metering and bill payment."). A treasured colleague and client of the author's, Chairman Bratton not only had immense intelligence and acute political skills; he was a person of extraordinary wisdom and integrity, one who despite his stature and erudition did not take himself too seriously. Sadly, he passed away in 2014. *See also BTU Convergence Spawning Gas Market Opportunities in North America*, OIL & GAS J. (June 29, 1998), https://www.ogj.com/home/article/ 17226262/btu-convergence-spawning-gas-market-opportunities-in-north-america; *NGC/Destec Merger Latest in BTU Convergence*, OIL & GAS J. (Feb. 24, 1997), https:// www.ogj.com/general-interest/companies/article/17242646/ngcdestec-merger-latest -in-btu-convergence.

[131] Tampa Elec. Co. v. Nashville Coal Co., 365 U.S. 320, 327 (1961) (defining relevant geographic market as "the market area in which the seller operates, and to which the purchaser can practicably turn for supplies").

it is "the smallest geographic area in which a hypothetical monopolist could profitably and permanently impose a small but significant price increase."[132] To draw the geographic market's boundaries, the analyst identifies two things: the customers affected, and the suppliers to which they can practicably turn for supplies.

(a) Customers in the relevant geographic market: Under FERC precedent, the customers affected by a horizontal merger—the "destination market"—fall into three categories: (i) all customers directly or indirectly interconnected to either of the merger applicants; (ii) all customers who have purchased wholesale power from one of the merging companies in the two years preceding the merger application; and (iii) all customers having the same supply alternatives as the customers in the first two categories. FERC treats the entire PJM territory as a single destination market because "customers in PJM trade largely with the same set of suppliers."[133] FERC also includes in the relevant geographic market all areas which the merging companies might enter in the future. Doing so allows one to assess whether the merger would eliminate a potential competitor (meaning, one of the merging companies)—one whose entry "can have a salutary effect" on competition.[134]

(b) Suppliers in the relevant geographic market: Analysts draw the geographic market's boundaries to include all sellers that can practicably compete for customers in that market, i.e., those that can reach the destination market physically and economically.

(i) Reaching the destination market physically: An electricity supplier can compete in the destination market only if it has access to transmission capacity sufficient to carry its output to that market. The transmission tariffs required by FERC promise legal access,[135] but if capacity is unavailable the tariffs provide no practical access.[136] Capacity must be available both physically (e.g., the necessary transmission capacity is not off-line for maintenance or repairs) and commercially (e.g., the capacity is not already committed to other customers).[137]

---

[132] Western Wireless-ALLTEL Merger, 20 FCC Rcd. 13,053, 13,069 ¶ 34 (2005). *See also* AT&T Wireless-Cingular Merger, 19 FCC Rcd. 21,522, 21,562 ¶ 86 (2004).

[133] Order No. 642, *supra* note 5, at 70,992 (citing *Atlantic City Electric-Delmarva Power & Light Merger*, 80 F.E.R.C. ¶ 61,126 (1997)).

[134] *Id.*

[135] As required by FERC Order No. 888. *See* Tutorial § 2.2.

[136] *See, e.g., Wisconsin Electric Power-Northern States Power Merger*, 74 F.E.R.C. ¶ 61,069, at p. 61,193 (1996) (expressing concern "about how transmission constraints may affect the analysis of [generation] market power even with non-discriminatory open access transmission tariffs in place").

[137] Order No. 642, *supra* note 5, at 70,993 text accompanying nn.37–38, 70,996, 71,016 (measuring transmission capability as the sum of (a) "available transmission

Due to changes in customer demands, weather and maintenance, transmission availability varies by hour, day, week and year. Transmission capacity available to a seller during non-peak periods may be unavailable during peak periods. If so, the relevant geographic market will include that seller for the non-peak periods but will exclude the seller for the peak periods. This exclusion, by reducing the number of sellers, could reveal that during those peak periods the to-be-merged company will have market power.[138]

A merger can reduce a market's size by causing transmission congestion. Like downtown city congestion, transmission congestion reduces sellers' access to customers. Suppose the merging companies intend to use their combined generation to serve their combined loads. Doing so will change power flows on the region's transmission network. Those new flows can cause congestion on paths competitors would use to reach the merged company's customers. If the congestion excludes those sellers from the destination market, the merged company could have market power over the customers.[139] FERC therefore requires merger applicants to show how their post-merger operations will affect transmission line loadings. For this analysis, though, FERC looks only at whether congestion affects the to-be-merged company's markets. If the power flows cause concentration in other markets, FERC has expressed no concern.[140]

(ii) Reaching the destination market economically: Recall that the relevant product market includes the merged company's products plus all reasonable substitutes. What if a competitor's generation product can reach a merged company's customer physically, but the sum of the competitor's generation price and transmission cost exceeds what customers want to pay? That competitor's

---

capacity" and (b) "firm transmission rights" held by the supplier and not committed to long-term transactions).

[138] *Id.* at p. 70,993 ("[M]arkets analyzed during peak load levels are often smaller because transmission links are full at those load levels.").

[139] *See, e.g., UtiliCorp United-St. Joseph Light & Power Merger*, 92 F.E.R.C. ¶ 61,067, at p. 61,232 (2000) (finding that "the loading of the Applicants' generation post-merger could change flows on adjacent systems, which might hamper competitors' ability to reach certain customers") (citing *American Electric Power-Central & Southwest Merger*, 85 F.E.R.C. ¶ 61,201, at p. 61,819 n.79 (1998), *reh'g denied*, 87 F.E.R.C. ¶ 61,274 (1999)); *Ohio Edison-Pennsylvania Power Merger*, 81 F.E.R.C. ¶ 61,110, at p. 61,401 (1997) (expressing concern that "the altered usage of internal transmission that may result from the joint dispatch of the system, creates uncertainty about how Applicants will, in the future, ensure an open and competitive market within and into [the merged company]'s service area").

[140] *Northern States Power-New Century Energies Merger*, 90 F.E.R.C. ¶ 61,020, at p. 61,133 (2000) ("We are not generally concerned about increases in market concentration exceeding the thresholds in cases where neither NSP or SPS is a supplier in the relevant market or when the market share of one Applicant decreases.").

product will not be a reasonable substitute for the merged company's product. To address these situations—to avoid including in the geographic market products that customers would not buy—FERC includes in the relevant geographic market only those sellers that pass a "delivered price test." The test excludes from the market those suppliers whose delivered price exceeds 105 percent of the pre-merger competitive market price. To estimate a seller's likely delivered price, FERC adds (a) the seller's short-term variable production cost, plus (b) the seller's delivery cost (specifically, the costs of transmission and ancillary services needed to move the power from generator to customer),[141] plus (c) any congestion charges imposed on the transmission customer.[142]

FERC requires merger applicants to provide transmission availability data for different periods of the year.[143] Why? Geographic market boundaries change with the seasons—and even with the times of the day and days of the week—because changes in electricity demand and supply change power flows; changes in power flows then change the amount and cost of available transmission capacity. When transmission availability or cost shrinks the market's

---

[141] *See Duke Energy-Progress Energy Merger I*, 136 F.E.R.C. ¶ 61,245 at P 40 n.66 (2011) (explaining the delivered price test).

[142] *Atlantic City Electric-Delmarva Power & Light Merger*, 80 F.E.R.C. ¶ 61,126, at 61,407 (1997) ("[W]here there is congestion pricing, supplies from entities transacting along a congested transmission path would become more expensive relative to supplies from entities transacting along uncongested paths. A congestion charge could conceivably alter the amount of energy that could be delivered at a price lower than 5 percent above the market-clearing price."). Two authors explain congestion and congestion charges well:

> Transmission congestion occurs when there is not enough transmission capability to support all requests for transmission services, and in order to ensure reliability, transmission system operators must re-dispatch generation or, in the limit, deny some of these requests to prevent transmission lines from becoming overloaded. In other words, transmission congestion does not refer to deliveries that are simply held up or delayed (as in traffic congestion); it refers to requests for deliveries (transactions) that cannot be physically implemented as requested. The cost of transmission congestion, assuming that demand is fixed and must be met, is the net cost of the replacement power that must be supplied by other means (e.g., from generators located closer to the loads to be served) to make up for deliveries that cannot be executed as requested.

BERNARD C. LESIEUTRE & JOSEPH H. ETO, ERNEST ORLANDO LAWRENCE BERKELEY NAT'L LAB., ELECTRICITY TRANSMISSION CONGESTION COSTS: A REVIEW OF RECENT REPORTS 1 (2003), https://www.energy.gov/sites/prod/files/oeprod/DocumentsandMedia/review _of_congestion_costs_october_03.pdf. Congestion costs arise "when, in order to respect transmission constraints, some higher-cost generation is dispatched in favor of lower-cost generation that would otherwise be used (in the absence of the constraint)." *Id.* at vi. Congestion prices charge customers for congestion costs.

[143] *See 1996 Merger Policy Statement*, *supra* note 124, app. A at 68,808–809.

geographic boundaries, consumers must shop closer to home, reducing their choices.[144] Reducing their choices increases the likelihood of merged company market power.

6.4.1.2.3 *Measuring and assessing market concentration*

The prior two steps describe how analysts define the product and geographic boundaries of the to-be-merged company's markets. The analyst then measures how much the merger concentrates those markets. Concentration means reducing the number of suppliers and increasing their market shares. Concentration can reduce competitiveness, because the fewer the sellers the more easily they can coordinate to raise prices or reduce output. Scherer and Ross explain this effect by describing its opposite:

> [A]s the number of sellers increases and the share of industry output supplied by a representative firm decreases, individual producers are increasingly apt to ignore the effect of their price and output decisions on rival reactions and the overall level of prices.

> [A]s the number of sellers increases, so also does the probability that at least one will be a maverick, pursuing an independent, aggressive pricing policy. And if market shares are sensitive to price differentials, even one such maverick of appreciable size can make it hard for other firms to hold prices near monopoly levels.[145]

To measure a merger's concentrating effect, merger analysts use the Herfindahl-Hirschman Index (HHI). A market's HHI is the sum of the squares of each seller's market shares, with the shares measured in percentages.[146] A monopoly market has the maximum HHI of 10,000, which is 100^2; a market with five equal-share (20 percent) sellers has an HHI of 2000 ($20^2 = 400$, times 5). For each market, the analyst compares the pre-merger and post-merger HHIs to determine the change in HHI caused by the merger. Under FERC precedent, those calculations place the merger in one of three categories defined by two variables—the merger-induced change in the HHI, and the post-merger HHI:

1. *Unconcentrated:* If the post-merger HHI is below 1000, the merger will not likely have adverse competitive effects, regardless of the change in HHI caused by the merger.

---

[144] Order No. 642, *supra* note 5, at 70,992 n.36, 70,993 (explaining that "markets analyzed during peak load levels are often smaller because transmission links are full at those load levels").

[145] SCHERER & ROSS, *supra* note 23, at 277–78.

[146] *See, e.g.*, 2010 HORIZONTAL MERGER GUIDELINES, *supra* note 6, § 5.3.

2. *Moderately concentrated:* If the post-merger HHI is between 1000 and 1800, and the merger-caused change exceeds 100, the merger "potentially raises significant competitive concerns."

3. *Highly concentrated:* If the post-merger HHI exceeds 1800, and the merger-caused change exceeds 50, "the merger potentially raises significant competitive concerns; if the change in HHI exceeds 100, it is presumed that the merger is likely to create or enhance market power."[147]

That an HHI signals concern does not determine outcomes, because a merger can increase a market's concentration without affecting competition adversely.[148] Merger applicants with alarm-setting HHIs could try to show, for example, that new competitors will enter the market within two years of the merger (though during that two-year period the merged company must have other mitigating actions in place).[149] But entry evidence must be solid. Analyzing the proposed merger of AT&T and T-Mobile, the FCC Staff doubted that smaller regional providers could enter successfully against the merged national firm. The smaller companies had "considerably less spectrum, much smaller footprints, and lower ARPU (average revenue per user) than T-Mobile." They also "fac[ed] difficulties with respect to various inputs (e.g., roaming and handsets …)." T-Mobile, in contrast, had "more spectrum, an extensive existing network and infrastructure, a larger scale that enables lower input costs and greater access to handsets, and a national brand."[150]

More generally, a high HHI does not necessarily mean low competition. The HHI measures concentration only at merger-time—a time when market leaders might have only a "random, temporary advantage." Over time, an industry's leaders—those whose high market shares make the market concentrated—can change, even though the market-wide HHI does not change. Frequent turnover at the top can signal a "competitive struggle for position"—a struggle that benefits consumers even though the industry remains concentrated.[151]

---

[147]   Order No. 642, *supra* note 5, at 70,999 n.62.

[148]   2010 HORIZONTAL MERGER GUIDELINES, *supra* note 6, § 2.1.3 (stating that an HHI's presumption of adverse effect "can be rebutted by persuasive evidence showing that the merger is unlikely to enhance market power"). The Commonwealth Edison-PECO Energy merger produced high concentrations in ComEd's destination market, but FERC found no merged company market power because "most of its capacity was nuclear, which is difficult to ramp up or down in order to withhold output"— withholding output being a way to raise prices. Order No. 642, *supra* note 5, at 70,990–991 & n.31 (citing *Commonwealth Edison-PECO Energy Merger*, 91 F.E.R.C. ¶ 61,036 (2000)).

[149]   Order No. 642, *supra* note 5, at 71,001.

[150]   AT&T-Deutsche Telekom Merger, 26 FCC Rcd. 16,184, 16,221 ¶ 62 (2011).

[151]   SCHERER & ROSS, *supra* note 23, at 89.

"Coverage" vs. competition: HHI analysis prevents merger applicants from understating—by oversimplifying—their transaction's structural effects. AT&T and T-Mobile argued that post-merger, other sellers' "coverage" would preserve customer choice. As the FCC Staff paraphrased this point, "approximately three-quarters of Americans live in areas where they may choose among at least five facilities-based wireless providers ... such that the [merger] would 'at most' reduce the number to four or more facilities-based providers." But presence does equal competitiveness—the ability to constrain other market sellers. Market share analysis, in contrast, "reflect[s] each provider's competitive significance ... because smaller shares often reflect limited facilities or spectrum footprint, targeted service offerings, or brand recognition that could not be expanded in a timely or sufficient manner in response to [a merged company's] anticompetitive price increase."[152]

If a proposed merger does exceed the HHI thresholds, FERC applicants have a choice: propose "mitigation measures," or show "countervailing considerations."[153] Three countervailing considerations include (a) operational efficiencies caused by the merger and not achievable without the merger;[154] (b) the threat of new entry if the merged company raises prices or reduces output;[155] and (c) the benefit from saving a failing firm that otherwise would exit the market.[156]

The HHI measures how the merger concentrates the relevant market as a whole. FERC also calculates the merger's "unilateral effect"—the change in the merged company's own share of the post-merger market.[157] Unilateral effect matters because by eliminating pre-merger competition between the merging firms, the transaction can harm consumers even if the market as a whole is not highly concentrated. What if the customers of Company A viewed Company B as their next best choice, were Company A to raise its

---

[152] *AT&T-Deutsche Telekom Merger*, 26 FCC Rcd. at 16,208–209 ¶ 42 n.127 (citing Annual Report and Analysis of Competitive Market Conditions with Respect to Commercial Mobile Services, 25 FCC Rcd. 11,407 (2010); then citing Applications of AT&T Inc. and Deutsche Telekom AG for Consent to Assign or Transfer Control of Licenses and Authorizations, file no. 0004669383 (filed April 21, 2011)).

[153] Order No. 642, *supra* note 5, at 70,999–71,000, text accompanying nn.62 & 65.

[154] *See, e.g.*, NBC Universal-Comcast Merger, 26 FCC Rcd. 4238, 4303 ¶ 154 (2011) (finding that "packaging advertising across multiple platforms may provide an efficiency that reduces the effective price of advertising").

[155] *See, e.g.*, United States v. Penn-Olin Chem. Co., 378 U.S. 158, 174 (1964) ("The existence of an aggressive, well equipped and well financed corporation engaged in the same or related lines of commerce waiting anxiously to enter an oligopolistic market [is] a substantial incentive to competition which cannot be underestimated.").

[156] *See* 2010 HORIZONTAL MERGER GUIDELINES, *supra* note 6, §§ 10, 11.

[157] Order No. 642, *supra* note 5, at 70,999.

prices? A merged company A-B could then raise its price with less loss of sales.[158] Customers would be worse off.

If the merging companies don't compete in the same market, is market share analysis still necessary? Early in the modern merger era, FERC exempted Duke Power and PanEnergy from a full market share analysis because PanEnergy's generating facilities were minor, and remote from Duke's market.[159] Today, if the merger applicants compete in different geographic markets, or if their geographical overlap is minor, FERC requires of applicants only an abbreviated submission rather than a full HHI analysis.[160] But no overlap does not mean no competitive effect, if either firm is a prospective competitor in the other's market, because a prospective competitor "may exert a salutary influence on behavior in a market without actually competing in it." In those situations, FERC will require the full HHI analysis—but only if an intervenor has raised the possibility of "salutary influence."[161] In effect, the Commission applies a rebuttable presumption that merging firms in different geographic markets are not potential competitors; intervenors must rebut the presumption.

6.4.1.2.4   What about product markets that don't yet exist?

Some merger applicants aim for first-mover status in new product markets—to gain a favorable foothold before regulators establish competitive discipline.[162] While effective competition should reward early birds, if this early bird gets its worm not through merit but through resources accumulated from its franchised position—resources like access to low-cost capital and information on customer preferences—competition will not be effective.

---

[158] 2010 HORIZONTAL MERGER GUIDELINES, *supra* note 6, § 6.1.

[159] *Duke Power-PanEnergy Merger*, 79 F.E.R.C. ¶ 61,236 (1997). *See also* Order No. 642, *supra* note 5, at 71,001–71,002.

[160] Order No. 642, *supra* note 5, at 71,002 ("[W]e will not require a merger applicant to provide the full competitive analysis screen if: (1) The applicant demonstrates that the merging entities do not currently operate in the same geographic markets, or if they do, that the extent of such overlapping operation is de minimis; and (2) no intervenor has alleged that one of the merging entities is a perceived potential competitor in the same geographic market as the other.").

[161] *Id.* at 71,002 n.76 (citing FTC v. Procter & Gamble Co. 386 U.S. 568 (1967); and U.S. v. Falstaff Brewing Corp., 410 U.S. 426 (1973)).

[162] *See* Mahinka & Gebhard, *supra* note 124 (describing competitive concerns with gas-electric mergers); Richard D. Cudahy, *The FERC's Policy on Electric Mergers: A Bit of Perspective*, 18 ENERGY L.J. 113, 124 n.53 (1997) (arguing that "[t]he FERC takes notice of these new cross-industry mergers in the [1996 Merger] Policy Statement, but offers little detail on its contemplated approach to assessing them").

To address the first-mover problem, merger concentration analysis should cover emerging product markets along with existing ones.[163] In the mid-1990s, some utility commissions missed that boat. At the very time states were considering whether to allow head-to-head retail electricity competition, utilities were proposing mergers of companies that would have competed head-to-head.[164] Commissions had to assess these mergers' effects on competitive retail electric markets that didn't yet exist. Consider the three following examples.

FERC and Maryland: In 1996, the adjacent Baltimore Gas & Electric and Potomac Electric Power (Pepco) proposed a merger. FERC found that if the relevant states authorized retail competition, the merged company would control "100 percent of the market for firm energy and between 80–88 percent of the market for non-firm energy."[165] The Commission acknowledged that "concerns [about retail competition] merit consideration," but deferred the issue to the state commissions.[166] In other words, FERC approved as "consistent with the public interest"—the standard in Federal Power Act section 203—a merger that it knew would be inconsistent with the public interest, if Maryland, the District of Columbia or Virginia adopted retail competition. (All three states did.) At least FERC did the analysis. The Maryland Commission didn't, saying that the record could not be made "adequate enough to make the necessary assessments and findings." The Maryland Commission instead "retain[ed] full jurisdiction to mitigate, by whatever lawful means available, including divestiture of assets, impacts on retail competition arising from the merger that are not consistent with the public interest."[167]

Missouri: The Missouri Commission found that if Union Electric and Central Illinois Public Service merged, the new company would dominate generation and control transmission in a future competitive retail services market. The Commission approved the merger anyway, requiring only that the merged company perform a horizontal market power study—after the

---

[163] *See* Richard J. Pierce, *Mergers in the Electric Power Industry, in* COMPETITION POLICY AND MERGER ANALYSIS IN DEREGULATED AND NEWLY COMPETITIVE INDUSTRIES 8, 15–16 (Peter C. Carstensen & Susan Beth Farmer eds., 2008) (explaining why the regulator must look at "the future environment in which the potentially merged firm is likely to operate").

[164] Table 3.1 in this book shows that between 1995 and 2000, twenty-nine mergers were approved and consummated.

[165] *Baltimore Gas & Electric-Pepco Merger*, 79 F.E.R.C. ¶ 61,027, at p. 61,115 (1997).

[166] *Id.* at 61,115 & n.51 (citing *1996 Merger Policy Statement, supra* note 124).

[167] Baltimore Gas & Electric-Pepco Merger, 1997 Md. PSC LEXIS 205, at *32. The parties ended up withdrawing their merger.

merger.[168] The Commission did not explain what action it would take if the merger it approved adversely affected retail competition. (Missouri never authorized retail competition.)

Pennsylvania: The Pennsylvania Commission found that the merger of Philadelphia Electric Company (PECO) and Public Service Electric & Gas of New Jersey (PSEG) would not produce market power in retail markets because (a) the applicants were located in different (albeit adjacent) states, (b) Exelon (PECO's owner) did no retail marketing in Pennsylvania or New Jersey, and (c) PSEG did no retail marketing anywhere.[169] The Commission did not address the possibility that either company might enter these retail markets in the future. (Both states later authorized retail competition.)

In contrast to these state commissions, FERC has recognized that by focusing only on current markets, a regulator can miss a merger's very purpose—to control future markets:

> Recognizing that energy companies are entering new product markets and that the effect of a merger could be to eliminate one of the merged companies as a perceived potential competitor in such new product markets, we will also require applicants to identify product markets in which they may be reasonably perceived as potential competitors.[170]

6.4.1.3 Harm analysis: mavericks and potential competitors

Besides increasing concentration, mergers can eliminate mavericks and potential competitors. Mavericks matter competitively. They can:

1. "threaten[] to disrupt market conditions with a new technology or business model";
2. "take the lead in price cutting or other competitive conduct";
3. "discipline prices based on [their] ability and incentive to expand production rapidly using available capacity"; or
4. "resist[] otherwise prevailing industry norms to cooperate on price setting or other terms of competition."[171]

---

[168] Union Electric-Central Illinois Public Service Merger, 1997 Mo. PSC LEXIS 1, at *25–26.

[169] PECO Energy-Public Service Electric & Gas Merger, 2006 Pa. PUC LEXIS 33, at *31.

[170] Order No. 642, *supra* note 5, at 70,991 (footnote omitted). *See also* Southern California Edison-San Diego Gas & Electric Merger, 1991 Cal. PUC LEXIS 253, at *60 ("[E]ven if the merging firms are not now in competition in a particular market, if there is evidence showing that one is a potential competitor of the other, the elimination of the potential competitor constitutes an adverse effect on competition.").

[171] 2010 HORIZONTAL MERGER GUIDELINES, *supra* note 6, § 2.1.5.

A merger that eliminates a maverick can reduce actual or potential competition.[172] Back to the merger of AT&T and T-Mobile. The FCC Staff viewed T-Mobile as a maverick in the competitive wireless market. The company differentiated itself through its broad coverage, tiered pricing, unlimited data plans, prepaid plans and month-to-month post-paid plans (instead of the typical two-year contracts). It offered family plans for shared voice, text and data limits. The merger would eliminate these pro-competitive stimuli.[173]

Whereas mavericks are already in the market, potential competitors hover outside the market. Their entry threat can discipline the incumbents. So a potential competitor's acquisition of a target could weaken competition if

> the target market is substantially concentrated; the acquiring firm has the characteristics, capabilities and economic incentive to render it a perceived potential *de novo* entrant; and the acquiring firm's pre-merger presence on the fringe of the target market (as a potential entrant) in fact tempered oligopolistic behavior on the part of existing participants in the market.[174]

The potential competitor can be the target or the acquirer; it can be a competitor in an existing product market or in some future market. To protect potential competition, FERC requires merger applicants to "identify product markets in which they may be reasonably perceived as potential competitors."[175]

---

[172] *Id.*

[173] AT&T-Deutsche Telekom Merger, 26 FCC Rcd. 16,184, 16,196–201 ¶¶ 17–24 (2011).

[174] *Duke Energy-Cinergy Merger*, 113 F.E.R.C. ¶ 61,297 at P 40 (2005) (describing the "potential competition" doctrine).

See also Order No. 642, *supra* note 5, at 71,002 n.76 ("A firm may exert a salutary influence on behavior in a market without actually competing in it."); John Kwoka & Evgenia Shumilkina, *The Price Effect of Eliminating Potential Competition: Evidence from an Airline Merger*, 58 J. Indus. Econ. 767, 770–72 (2010) (analyzing gain in pricing power from 1987 merger between USAir and Piedmont, and finding statistically significant price increases in markets where the two firms had been potential competitors); Jonathan Baker, *Comcast/NBCU: The FCC Provides a Roadmap for Vertical Merger Analysis*, 25 Antitrust 36, 38 n.30 (2011) ("The FCC can often address potential competition issues more easily than the antitrust agencies because it can be particularly hard to prove a potential competition case in court."); AT&T-BellSouth Merger, 22 FCC Rcd. 5662, 5687 ¶ 51 (2007) (finding that "existing competitive collocations and the threat of competitive entry through collocation allow for special access competition in BellSouth's in-region wire centers where AT&T competes today"). *See generally* William J. Baumol, John C. Panzar & Robert D. Willig, Contestable Markets and The Theory of Industry Structure 2 (1982) (providing a "formal analytic structure" to support the insight that "potential competition, that is, the mere threat of entry, can ... affect the behavior of firms significantly and beneficially").

[175] Order No. 642, *supra* note 5, at 70,991, text accompanying n.33 (recognizing that "energy companies are entering new product markets and that the effect of a merger

Caution: If the merging companies lack physical proximity, if no sales history exists between each other's service territory and if the market each serves is unconcentrated, FERC will reject as speculative claims of potential competition, as well as assertions of "general trends" toward concentration.[176]

6.4.1.4 Harm analysis: competitive effects

Merger regulators address concentration because concentration affects competitiveness, and competitiveness affects performance. But concentration—a feature of structure—affects competitiveness and performance only indirectly. Market structure affects seller conduct; seller conduct affects market performance. So structural analysis—HHI measures, and identification of mavericks and potential competitors—infers changes in conduct from changes in market structure. But to assess competitive effects, one can also look at seller conduct directly—such as whether sellers are withholding output to raise prices.[177] The 2010 *Horizontal Merger Guidelines* therefore recommends collecting evidence of post-merger price increases. But the *Guidelines* caution that the absence of price increases does not mean the merger has not weakened competition; the merged firm "may be aware of the possibility of post-merger antitrust review and [is] moderating its conduct."[178]

6.4.1.5 Special concern: horizontal mergers of adjacent companies

Adjacent electricity mergers affect competition uniquely. Most people think of competition as head-to-head competition—two or more rivals seeking to sell

---

could be to eliminate one of the merged companies as a perceived potential competitor in such new product markets").

[176] *Duke Energy-Cinergy Merger*, 113 F.E.R.C. ¶ 61,297 at PP 78–79.

[177] *See* FTC v. Indiana Federation of Dentists, 476 U.S. 447, 460–61 (1986) (holding that "proof of actual detrimental effects, such as a reduction of output," makes a structural market power inquiry unnecessary, because market power is but a "surrogate for detrimental effects") (quoting 7 PHILLIP E. AREEDA, ANTITRUST LAW 429 ¶ 1511 (1986)); Todd v. Exxon Corp., 275 F.3d 191, 206 (2d Cir. 2001) (holding that evidence indicating that "a defendant's conduct exerted an actual adverse effect on competition … arguably is more direct evidence of market power than calculations of elusive market share figures"); Michael L. Katz & Howard A. Shelanski, *Merger Analysis and the Treatment of Uncertainty: Should We Expect Better?*, 74 ANTITRUST L.J. 537, 567 (2007) (citing numerous courts and agencies for the proposition that "market definition [i.e., structural analysis] is an indirect way of showing a merger's effects"; market definition "should not stand in the way of considering direct evidence of competitive harm"); Michael G. Cowie & Paul T. Denis, *The Fall of Structural Evidence in FTC and DOJ Merger Review*, ANTITRUST SOURCE, Feb. 2013 ("Competitive effects analysis—not inferences from market structure—is the primary rationale for the agencies' decision to clear visible, heavily investigated transactions.").

[178] 2010 HORIZONTAL MERGER GUIDELINES, *supra* note 6, § 2.1.1.

the same product to the same set of customers. While all competition is about winning a customer, not all electricity competition is head-to-head competition; the industry also has yardstick competition and franchise competition. This subsection explains how mergers of adjacent utilities can damage all three forms.

6.4.1.5.1 Head-to-head competition

Some states allow retail electricity competition; most do not.[179] If in non-competition states two adjacent utilities merge horizontally, might the transaction reduce competition? Some say no: if two utilities don't compete head-to-head, their merger cannot reduce competition. This argument misses four factors.

First, if the merging companies both own generation, they compete in wholesale generation markets. If they are located within a regional transmission organization—where each generation owner sells all its output into the RTO's energy market and buys all its energy from that market—then the two firms' generating units compete continuously.[180] Outside RTOs, generation owners compete in bilateral markets, selling and buying surplus capacity, economy energy and reserves. Second, since we know from a dozen states that head-to-head retail competition is physically and economically feasible, either of the merging utilities' states could authorize retail competition in the future. Merger policy must consider both existing and potential competition. Third, some states that have not authorized head-to-head retail competition are physically near states that have.[181] A merger of companies in a non-competition state would eliminate competition between them for customers in the competition states—competition in which each merging company would be a formidable competitor to the other, given each one's size, name recognition, employee

---

[179] *See* Tutorial § 2.

[180] As one RTO explains:

PJM operates a wholesale electricity market that spans all or part of Delaware, Illinois, Kentucky, Maryland, Michigan, New Jersey, North Carolina, Ohio, Pennsylvania, Tennessee, Virginia, West Virginia and the District of Columbia. Acting as a neutral, independent party, PJM operates electricity "spot markets" in which generators sell and utilities or electricity providers buy energy for immediate delivery. These energy markets operate every day, and participants in the market establish a price for electricity by matching supply (what generators want to sell) and demand (what utilities and customers want to buy).

Market for Electricity, PJM LEARNING CENTER, https://learn.pjm.com/electricity -basics/market-for-electricity.aspx.

[181] Examples: Kentucky and Indiana (no retail competition) adjoin Illinois and Ohio (retail competition); Vermont (no retail competition) adjoins New Hampshire and Massachusetts (retail competition).

experience and regional knowledge. Fourth, even when adjacent utilities don't compete with each other door-to-door, they do compete to attract and retain industrial and commercial customers. Existing industrial customers needing to modernize or expand their factories, and new industrial customers considering a move to the region, compare the prices and quality of adjacent utilities.[182]

In these four ways, adjacent mergers can affect head-to-head competition. They deserve merger regulators' attention.

6.4.1.5.2 Yardstick competition

Yardstick competition, along with its cousins benchmark competition and across-the-fence rivalry, rests on comparisons: "Regulators, competitors, and even incumbent carriers themselves have learned to set baselines according to the performance of existing regulated monopolists."[183] If mergers reduce an industry's diversity, regulators can "lose the ability to compare performance between similar carriers that have made different management or strategic choices."[184]

In electricity, regulators and customers of adjacent companies compare notes on prices and service quality. Then they make decisions: regulators, about cost disallowances and service quality penalties; customers (especially large industrial customers), about location. Residents write letters to the editor and to their elected officials, urging their municipal government to buy out a poorly performing utility or pressuring decision-makers to order improvements.[185] Public accountability backstops inevitably imperfect reg-ulation.[186] Among the California Commission's reasons for rejecting the

---

[182]   *See, e.g.*, Conway Corp. v. FPC, 510 F.2d 1264, 1268 (D.C. Cir. 1975) (stating that wholesale competitors "seek to maintain customer satisfaction with the quality and price of their service in order to attract new industries and to retain existing custom-ers"), *aff'd*, 426 U.S. 271 (1976).

[183]   Jim Chen, *The Echoes of Forgotten Footfalls*, *supra* note 112, at 1327.

[184]   NYNEX-Bell Atlantic Merger, 12 FCC Rcd. 19,985, 19,994 ¶ 16 (1997). *See also* California v. FCC, 39 F.3d 919, 927 (9th Cir. 1994) ("[R]egulators ... [can] use the seven [Bell operating companies (BOCs)] as benchmarks ... to detect predatory pricing."); United States v. W. Elec. Co., 993 F.2d 1572, 1580 (D.C. Cir. 1993) ("[T]he existence of seven BOCs increases the number of benchmarks that can be used by reg-ulators to detect discriminatory pricing ... in evaluating compliance with equal access requirements.").

[185]   *See, e.g.*, Opinion No. 57, *Florida Power & Light Co.*, 8 F.E.R.C. ¶ 61,121, at p. 61,455 (1979) (noting the importance of "significant" yardstick competition and franchise competition between Florida Power & Light (FPL) and its municipal whole-sale customers, and explaining that this competition is vulnerable should the utility use its "wholesale monopoly power ... to maintain or enhance [its] retail market position").

[186]   *See generally* Harvey L. Reiter, *Implications of Mergers and Acquisitions in Gas and Electric Markets: The Role of Yardstick Competition in Merger Analysis*, NAT'L

Southern California Edison-San Diego Gas & Electric (SDG&E) merger was the prospective loss of the companies' longstanding across-the-fence rivalry. That rivalry produced "proximate comparative data," spurring SDG&E to study the reasons for its higher rates. Losing that rivalry would diminish the Commission's "ability to regulate the merged utility effectively."[187] And when District-of-Columbia-based Pepco suffered numerous outages during storms, Maryland's Governor sent the holding company's CEO a letter with this comparative passage:

> Why can't Pepco perform as its fellow utilities do? To date, [Baltimore Gas & Electric (BG&E)] has restored service to 227,800 of the 233,500, or 98 percent, of its customers affected by the storm. Pepco still has 27,500 customers in Maryland without electricity, a restoration rate of a dismal 80 percent.[188]

Any CEO receiving this letter, comparing her company's performance unfavorably to its neighbor's, would find ways to improve. But now that BG&E and Pepco are part of the same holding company,[189] they are no longer rivals.

REGULATORY RESEARCH INST. Q. BULL., Summer 1999 (citing Alfred Kahn's statement that regulators "are essentially incapable of assuring that performance will be positively good," as a reason why they should use yardstick competition to supplement their efforts).

[187] *Id.*

[188] Letter from Martin O'Malley, Governor, State of Maryland, to Joseph Rigby, Chairman, Pepco Holdings Inc. (Jan. 29, 2011), https://maryland-politics.blogspot.com/2011/01/governors-letter-to-pepco.html?m=0.

[189] Due to a transaction approved by Governor O'Malley's appointees (and opposed by the author, as an expert witness for the Maryland Office of People's Counsel). *See* Exelon-PHI Merger, Case No. 9361, Order No. 86990 (Md. Pub. Serv. Comm'n May 15, 2015).

Utilities can't credibly argue against the usefulness of yardstick competition, because they regularly offer public comparisons to their neighbors—when those comparisons are favorable. Seeking a rate increase in 2016, Florida Power & Light made these arguments: "For more than a decade, FPL has attained the best overall transmission and distribution system reliability among all Florida investor-owned utilities (IOU), as measured by the System Average Interruption Duration Index (SAIDI). For 2015, the Florida major IOU SAIDI average was 50 percent higher than FPL's." Letter Accompanying Petition for Rate Increase, Florida Power & Light, Docket No. 160021-EI (Fla. Pub. Serv. Comm'n filed Mar. 15, 2016). "FPL … maintain[s] a typical residential 1,000 kilowatt hour (kWh) customer bill that today is 20 percent lower than the state average …" FPL Opening Brief at 2, Florida Power & Light, Docket No. 160021-EI (Fla. Pub. Serv. Comm'n filed Sept. 19, 2016). "FPL's performance compares extremely well on all principal measures against other electric utilities both within Florida and elsewhere in the Southeast U.S." *Id.* at 58.

6.4.1.5.3 Franchise competition

Comparison competition can lead to franchise competition—competition for the right to be the franchise monopoly. Whereas head-to-head retail competition is competition *in* the market, franchise competition is competition *for* the market.[190] A realistic threat of losing one's government-protected monopoly will pressure a utility to control costs and improve service.[191] Indeed, competition for a natural monopoly market "can be just as beneficial to consumers as competition within an ordinary market"[192]—"even though that competition be an elimination bout."[193]

Franchise competition can take at least three forms: an investor-owned utility replacing another; a municipality taking over an investor-owned utility; and an investor-owned utility taking over a municipal utility.[194] Active franchise competition is rare—not because it lacks economic benefit but because states lack clear legal procedures.[195] If franchise competition becomes legally and practically feasible, each utility's neighbor—with its reputation, assets, experience and regional knowledge—will pose a constant competitive threat that disciplines its neighbor's performance.[196] A horizontal merger of adjacent companies removes that competitive threat permanently.

* * *

---

[190] *See generally* Harvey L. Reiter, *Competition Between Public and Private Distributors in a Restructured Power Industry*, 19 ENERGY L.J. 333 (1998).

[191] *See, e.g.*, Town of Massena v. Niagara Mohawk Power Corp., No. 79-CV-163, 1980 U.S. Dist. LEXIS 9382, at *28 (N.D.N.Y. Sept. 8, 1980) (finding that "it is this very potential [for franchise competition] that provides an incentive for [utilities] to control costs and improve their performance in the areas that they serve").

[192] 3 PHILLIP E. AREEDA & HERBERT HOVENKAMP, ANTITRUST LAW 658b3 (3d ed. 2008); *accord* HERBERT HOVENKAMP, FEDERAL ANTITRUST POLICY: THE LAW OF COMPETITION AND ITS PRACTICE 34 (4th ed. 2011) (in natural monopoly markets, competitive threats can cause the incumbent firm to lower its costs).

[193] Hecht v. Pro-Football, Inc., 570 F.2d 982, 991 (D.C. Cir. 1977) (quoting Union Leader Corp. v. Newspapers of New England, Inc., 284 F.2d 582, 584 n.4 (1st Cir. 1960). *See also* Reiter, *supra* note 190, at 343 (describing the benefits of allowing "public and private ownership structures to be pitted against one another").

[194] FRANKENA & OWEN, *supra* note 120, at 120.

[195] *See* SCOTT HEMPLING, *Competition for the Monopoly: Why So Rare?*, *in* PRESIDE OR LEAD? THE ATTRIBUTES AND ACTIONS OF EFFECTIVE REGULATORS 211 (2013), http://www.scotthemplinglaw.com/essays/competition-for-monopoly. We will discuss solutions in Part IV.

[196] *See* Borough of Ellwood City v. Pa. Power Co., 462 F. Supp. 1343, 1346 (W.D. Pa. 1979) ("If plaintiffs [municipalities] were to become unable to serve their customers profitably, Penn Power [the investor-owned utility serving that area] would logically be in the best position to assume plaintiffs' present service.").

Despite dozens of adjacent-utility mergers, regulators have not considered their effects on head-to-head competition, yardstick competition or franchise competition. We will explore the reasons for these omissions in Part III.

6.4.2 Vertical Mergers: Controlling Key Inputs

6.4.2.1 Definitions, benefits and risks

A vertical merger joins an upstream company with a downstream company— two companies whose products provide different links in the same chain of production: McDonald's buys a cattle ranch, a paper company buys a forest company. Electricity examples include a generating company merging with a transmission or distribution company in the same geographic market; a coal-fired generating company merging with a coal mining company; a gas producer merging with a gas pipeline or gas distribution company; a long dis-tance telephone company merging with a local exchange company that owns the "last mile." Unlike a horizontal merger, a vertical merger does not by itself eliminate a competitor; it combines two companies selling different products rather than two companies selling the same product.[197]

Supporters of vertical mergers identify four types of benefits:

1. By coordinating product design, production processes and sales strategies, a vertically merged company can improve quality and lower cost.
2. If the merger combines complementary products (products that go together, so that a decrease in the price of one increases demand for the other), the merged entity will want to lower the price for its downstream product to increase demand for its upstream product. That action benefits both down-stream customers and upstream suppliers.
3. By avoiding the profit markups previously charged by the upstream sup-plier, the merged entity can lower the price of the downstream product, thereby making more sales. (Netted against this benefit is the profit forgone by the upstream supplier.)
4. One-stop shopping saves customers time and money.[198]

But vertical mergers also can damage competition: in downstream markets, by foreclosing competitors' access to inputs; in upstream markets, by foreclosing competitors' access to customers; and in both upstream and downstream markets, by enabling the merged company to collude with competitors and

---

[197] Order No. 642, *supra* note 5, at 71,003 n.85.
[198] Guidelines on Assessment of Non-horizontal Mergers, *supra* note 32, at 7 ¶ 14, 15–16 ¶¶ 55–58.

manipulate inter-affiliate prices.[199] Testing for these adverse effects involves the standard analysis used for horizontal mergers:[200] (1) define the relevant upstream and downstream products sold by the merging firms; (2) define the relevant geographic markets in which the firms sell these products; (3) evaluate the merger's effects on each relevant market's competitiveness, using HHI numbers and competitive effects analysis;[201] and (4) identify any mitigating factors, like ease of entry and merger efficiencies.[202] After describing each of these potential harms, this subsection describes four situations in which a vertical merger raises no competitive concerns.

6.4.2.2 Damaging the downstream market: input foreclosure

Input foreclosure damages downstream competition by raising downstream competitors' input costs, degrading the quality of inputs sold to them or blocking their access to inputs entirely. With its competitors weakened or eliminated, the merged company's downstream affiliate can raise its prices.[203] Here are five examples.

1. Generation and transmission: Consider a vertically merged company that owns generation and transmission, and engages in wholesale and retail sales, all in the same geographic market. Assume the company owns the only transmission system available to its generation competitors. The merged company can foreclose their access to transmission, directly or indirectly, by raising the transmission price or by manipulating its availability—such as by taking a facility offline for maintenance, declaring it unavailable when it actually is available (while suppressing availability data) or dispatching its own generation to cause transmission shortages in locations needed by its competitors.[204]

---

[199] Order No. 642, *supra* note 5, at 71,003, text accompanying nn.85–86 (citing *San Diego Gas & Electric-Southern California Gas*, 79 F.E.R.C. ¶ 61,372, at p. 62,560 (1997)).

[200] As described in Chapter 6.4.1.2.

[201] As explained in Chapters 6.4.1.2 and 6.4.1.4.

[202] Order No. 642, *supra* note 5, at 71,003, text accompanying n.82.

[203] *Id.* at 71,003–71,004, text accompanying nn.87–88. *See also* Guidelines on Assessment of Non-horizontal Mergers, *supra* note 32, at 10 ¶ 31, 11 ¶ 33 (explaining that consumers are harmed if the upstream affiliate restricts its sale of inputs to downstream competitors, causing them to exit the market or raise their prices).

[204] *See, e.g., Ohio Edison-Pennsylvania Power Merger*, 81 F.E.R.C. ¶ 61,110, at p. 61,401 (1997) (expressing concern "that Applicants could plan and operate their transmission system in such a way as to potentially exercise the substantial generation market power indicated by the relatively high levels of merger-induced market concentration"); *PSColorado-Southwestern Public Service Merger II*, 78 F.E.R.C. ¶ 61,267, at p. 62,141, text accompanying nn.17–18 (1997) (requiring that the merged entity's transmission planning and selection process "minimize the possibility that the proposed interconnection could be situated, operated and controlled in such a way as to adversely

2. Gas and electricity: Southern California Gas (SoCalGas) held a monopoly franchise for retail natural gas sales. It also owned gas pipelines, along with some gas-fired electric generators that sold their output at wholesale. San Diego Gas & Electric held a monopoly franchise for retail gas and electricity sales, and also owned a wholesale electric power marketer. The upstream product was gas sales; the downstream product was electricity produced from gas-fired generators. SoCalGas delivered gas to SDG&E's gas-fired generators and to 96 percent of southern California's nonaffiliated electricity generators. Among those nonaffiliated generators were entities that competed with SDG&E downstream to make wholesale electricity sales. These generators had few gas supply alternatives to SoCalGas; moreover, due to electricity transmission constraints into Southern California, wholesale buyers of electricity had few alternatives to those generators. Third-party entry into the upstream gas market was unlikely because SoCalGas, as the franchised monopoly utility, controlled the region's gas distribution and storage infrastructure.

If SoCalGas and SDG&E merged (through their holding companies, Pacific Enterprises and Enova, respectively), the merged company could commit a host of anticompetitive acts. It could

1. use competitive market information gained from the competing generators (such as their gas consumption and service requirements) to advantage SDG&E;
2. offer transportation discounts to SDG&E but not to competing generators;
3. withhold or deny the generators' access to pipeline capacity;
4. by manipulating storage injection schedules, effectively withhold pipeline capacity from competing generators at strategic times, thereby creating electricity shortages that would allow SDG&E to raise its wholesale electricity prices;
5. force competing generators to take their gas at inconvenient delivery points or to buy extra firm pipeline capacity, by claiming operational constraints on SoCalGas's system; or

---

affect competition"); *American Electric Power-Central & South West Merger*, 90 F.E.R.C. ¶ 61,242, at p. 61,785 (2000) (explaining that market power can be exercised not merely by denying transmission access outright, but by "strategic manipulation of transmission or generation"—such as by dispatching merged company-owned generation in a manner that reduces available transmission needed by others or by failing to disclose accurate data on transmission availability); *Duke Energy-Progress Energy Merger I*, 136 F.E.R.C. ¶ 61,245 at P 160 (2011) (explaining that "by denying rival firms access to inputs or by raising their input costs, a firm created by the transaction could impede entry of new competitors or inhibit existing competitors' ability to undercut an attempted price increase in the downstream wholesale electricity market").

6. apply SoCalGas's intrastate gas tariffs discriminatorily, favoring SDG&E and disfavoring its electric generation competitors.[205]

Based on these facts, FERC conditioned its merger approval on the Applicants' agreeing to take five actions:[206]

1. comply with the Commission's Code of Conduct, prohibiting discrimination against non-affiliates;
2. maintain all affiliate relationships at arm's-length;
3. heed all affiliate requirements imposed by the California Commission on the in-state gas pipeline company;
4. for SoCalGas, use a web-based reservation and information system that makes all interactions transparent; and
5. adopt "firewalls" between the monopoly and competitive businesses—including separating transportation employees from marketing employees—so as to prevent SoCalGas's power marketing affiliates from receiving any confidential market information that SoCalGas receives as a gas transporter, unless SoCalGas shares that information comparably with unaffiliated power marketers.[206]

3. Coal, gas and electricity: Dominion Resources's retail electric utility in Virginia owned coal-fired and gas-fired generators. Dominion also owned oil and gas subsidiaries. Consolidated Natural Gas (CNG) had retail gas utilities in Virginia and adjacent states, as well as a regional natural gas pipeline system selling gas to generating facilities in eastern states. Their merger, FERC found, would concentrate both the upstream delivered gas markets and the downstream electricity sales markets. Worse, CNG would have competitively sensitive information about its gas customers—electric generating companies that were rivals of Dominion. The merged company could share that information with CNG's upstream and downstream affiliates, who would use the information to raise costs and deny service to their generation rivals. As a condition of approval, FERC required the merged company to accept its Standards of Conduct, and to adopt two other nondiscriminatory practices: "open tap" (offering nondiscriminatory interconnection to its pipeline); and "open season" (allocating available pipeline capacity on a nondiscriminatory basis).[207]

---

[205] *San Diego Gas & Electric-Southern California Gas*, 79 F.E.R.C. ¶ 61,372, at pp. 62,563–64 (1997). We will discuss codes of conduct and arm's-length dealing in Chapter 6.5.4.

[206] *Id.*

[207] *Dominion Resources-Consolidated Natural Gas Merger*, 89 F.E.R.C. ¶ 61,162, at pp. 61,477–78 & n.23 (1999).

4. Wireless spectrum: Spectrum is "the range of radio frequencies within which wireless communications providers may operate."[208] Wireless service is the downstream product, spectrum is the upstream product. By joining two spectrum-owning providers of wireless mobile service, the AT&T-Cingular merger raised concerns about whether the merged company could deny scarce spectrum to its wireless competitors.[209] And recall the proposed merger of AT&T and Deutsche Telekom. Approval would leave the top two wireless providers, post-merger AT&T and Verizon Wireless, with 75 percent of U.S. mobile wireless customers, while controlling spectrum in "many already concentrated retail mobile wireless markets."[210]

5. Immature downstream markets: By denying its competitors essential inputs, a vertically merged company can gain a first-mover advantage in an immature downstream market. Three hypotheticals:

1. The downstream utility can tie meters (a potentially competitive product) to its physical distribution service (a monopoly product) by telling customers: "If you want any electricity delivered over my distribution lines you have to buy my meters."
2. The utility can tie customer information (an input to potentially competitive products) to its distribution interconnection service (a monopoly product) by telling meter providers: "If you want to connect your meter to my distribution lines you must let me have exclusive access to your customer data." Meanwhile the utility can gain a first-mover advantage when designing and marketing other products that use the data. The meter provider is stuck selling bare meters, unable to market competitively a bundle that combines its meters with other consumer products.
3. The utility can gain preferential access to its competitors' technological advances by telling marketers of new products: "If you want access to our customers' data you must let me own your technology."

These hypotheticals point to two of electricity's current challenges: introducing ways for customers to reduce their dependence on their traditional utility, and ways for non-utility companies to provide distribution-level services. While the physical distribution system itself may remain a natural

---

[208] Cincinnati Bell Telephone Corp. v. FCC, 69 F.3d 752, 756 n.1 (6th Cir. 1995).

[209] AT&T Wireless-Cingular Merger, 19 FCC Rcd. 21,522, 21,552 ¶ 58, 21,525 ¶ 4 (explaining that the transaction was "the first large license-transfer proceeding since the removal of [the] spectrum aggregation limit, which the Commission had employed to encourage new entry and prevent undue concentration of limited resources in the developing mobile telephony sector").

[210] AT&T-Deutsche Telekom Merger, 26 FCC Rcd. 16,184, 16,208–209 ¶ 42 (2011).

monopoly, substitutes are emerging: advanced metering to help reduce usage, storage to pair with solar and wind generation, electric vehicle charging stations, and the distinct services associated with the term "smart grid."[211] The incumbent utility owner of the monopoly distribution system has incentive and opportunity to block competitive entry, then provide those services itself. Consider three of smart grid's "bottleneck facilities":

Last mile: The "last mile" of infrastructure, and the associated data, are essential for competition but not economically duplicable by competitors:

> End-to-end communication requires initially developing the missing communications link between consumers' premises and the rest of the energy network (the "last mile") by deploying an Advanced Metering Infrastructure (AMI), along with smart meters. ... The last-mile infrastructure cannot be substituted or replicated within a reasonable time and cost frame. Moreover, together with the meter data, the infrastructure provides an essential input allowing efficient downstream markets, i.e. complementary services, products, and applications, to emerge.

Meter data: Non-duplicable bottlenecks can consist not only of tangible assets like poles and wires, but also "intangible" assets like "intellectual property rights, such as proprietary standards, protocols, or interfaces," and smart meter data—"[t]he data retrieved from smart meters can also be regarded as essential inputs for authorized actors. The data aids them in improving grid management and monitoring, streamlining business processes, and enabling innovative energy efficiency measures and value-added services." These conditions create the recipe for actions by incumbent utilities to block competitors; these utilities could

> deter entry by raising rivals' costs through practices such as exclusive dealing, refusals to deal, tying, or defining of proprietary protocols and standards to artificially increase rivals' transactions and consumers' switching costs. ...
> ... They could also define incompatible data formats or interfaces for each distribution area, or they could intentionally delay data access and provision.

---

[211] Two German scholars have defined smart grid as "a communications layer's virtual overlay on the existing power grid. This overlay allows all actors and components within the electricity value chain to exchange information, thereby facilitating supply and demand's coordination. This overlay closes the communication gap between consumers' premises and the rest of the network, but requires the deployment of an [advanced metering] infrastructure." KRANZ & PICOT, *supra* note 47, at 1 (citation omitted).

Interoperability: New entrants need to connect to and communicate with the distribution system's components:

> Data's seamless exchange requires open and non-proprietary standards and communication protocols that allow each component and actor within the smart grid to communicate end-to-end. ... [P]rotocols and standards can resemble essential inputs. ... Open systems benefit modular innovation, the number of potential market entrants, and market dynamics. ... [Incumbent utilities] may use protocols and standards as "strategic weapons" to build closed systems in which they safeguard interface information.[212]

6.4.2.3 Damaging the upstream market: customer foreclosure

A vertical merger can damage competition in the upstream (input) market if the merged company (1) has market power in the downstream market and (2) refuses to buy inputs from non-affiliates.[213] The merged company's downstream operation could also get price quotes and other sensitive competitive information from unaffiliated upstream suppliers, then provide that information to its upstream affiliate, giving it an unearned competitive advantage in sales to downstream customers.[214]

Another way to harm upstream competitors is to keep downstream customers from reaching them. A vertically merged utility can design the planning, construction, access, cost and cost allocation of transmission facilities to favor its own generation (the upstream input) over other options. RTOs can constrain this tendency by carrying out those steps independently of the transmission owners. But many RTO decisions on location, design and timing of transmission are influenced by voting within various advisory committees. A merger can increase the merged company's voting power within those committees, and therefore its influence over regional transmission decisions.[215]

---

[212] *Id.* at ii, 4, 13, 17, 21–22.

[213] Order No. 642, *supra* note 5, at 71,004 n.87.

[214] *Id.* at 71,004 n.90.

[215] Early in the era of regional transmission organizations, voting power drew FERC's attention. The Commission rejected initial governance proposals from the New England and New York independent system operators because "the vertically integrated utility members of the ISO would have too much voting power in the various advisory committees that provide advice and recommendations to the non-stakeholder Boards." *Regional Transmission Organizations*, Order No. 2000, F.E.R.C. Stats. & Regs. ¶ 31,089 (1999), 65 Fed. Reg. 810, 89 F.E.R.C. ¶ 61,285, slip op. at 26 (1999), *order on reh'g*, Order No. 2000-A, F.E.R.C. Stats. & Regs. ¶ 31,092, 65 Fed. Reg. 12,088 (2000), *aff'd sub nom.* Pub. Util. Dist. No. 1 v. FERC, 272 F.3d 607 (D.C. Cir. 2001). The Commission declared that it "cannot remain agnostic about the ownership of voting interests in an RTO by individual market participants, their affiliates or classes of market participants." *Id.* at 214–15.

6.4.2.4 Facilitating collusion in upstream and downstream markets

Anticompetitive collusion occurs when companies exercise market power together, by either formal agreement or informal coordination. A vertical merger can facilitate collusion by (1) making it easier for competitors to reach agreement on raising prices or restricting supply, or at least (2) reducing their incentive to compete vigorously. Two examples:

1. Shopping for inputs, the downstream affiliate gets price quotes from unaffiliated upstream suppliers. It then provides that information to its upstream affiliate. When the upstream suppliers all have the same information, they can more easily coordinate to raise prices or restrict supply.
2. The upstream transmission owner gets from downstream generation customers competitively sensitive information on generation unit scheduling, technological improvements and marketing strategies. Sharing that information with its generation affiliate and with other downstream customers would assist their efforts to collude.[216]

6.4.2.5 Evading regulation by manipulating inter-affiliate prices

Unmerged, a downstream utility buys its inputs from non-affiliates. To induce utility prudence and protect the customers from imprudence, the utility's regulators (FERC for wholesale sellers, state commissions for retail sellers) compare the invoiced price to market prices, disallowing any excess purchase

---

In the PJM RTO, the rule at the highest-level committees is one vote per holding company, specified by industry sector. So a merger of two utility holding companies would actually lessen that one company's influence. But in lower-level committees—these committees shape the proposals that rise to the upper levels—each affiliate has a separate vote. *See* PJM Stakeholder Affairs Dep't, PJM Manual 34: PJM Stakeholder Process 54 (2019) (stating that for Standing Committees, Senior Task Forces and Subcommittees that report to the Senior Standing Committees, "[a]ny Member, be they a Voting Member or an affiliate Member, may vote"). So a merger of two utility holding companies, each with multiple utility affiliates, could increase those companies' influence. *See also* Christina Simeone, Kleinman Ctr. for Energy Policy, PJM Governance: Can Reforms Improve Outcomes? 37 (2017). Simeone explains that the PJM RTO's senior committees, while relatively balanced between buyer and seller interests, usually confine themselves to rejecting or endorsing what comes from the lower-level committees, which are dominated by seller interests. That domination occurs because on the lower-level committees, vertically integrated companies and their generation affiliates all have voting rights. Simeone concludes that the sum of (a) proposal initiation at the seller-dominated lower level, plus (b) the ability of vertically integrated companies and their generation affiliates to cumulate their votes, plus (c) insufficiently active representation of and participation by new market entrants in the supply-side voting sectors, yields (d) RTO decision-making disproportionately influenced by incumbents.

[216] Order No. 642, *supra* note 5, at 71,004 & n.90.

costs from rates. That risk of disallowance causes the downstream utility to minimize its purchase costs. But after a vertical merger, the downstream utility will buy those inputs from its affiliate. That inter-affiliate transaction creates opportunity for abuse: the merged company can increase its earnings by regulatory evasion: inflating the input price while obscuring that act from regulators—by, for example, attributing the high input price to overheads and other misallocated costs.[217] In vertical merger cases, FERC has recognized this risk, but addressed it only in the wholesale context. FERC will not address abuse of the retail customer, "unless a state lacks adequate authority to consider such matters and requests us to do so."[218] State commissions tend to rely on their existing rules on inter-affiliate relations.[219]

6.4.2.6 Five exceptions from concern

A vertical merger will not raise competition concerns in any of these five situations:

1. If the upstream firm sells no input to the downstream market, the merged company will have no incentive to foreclose suppliers or customers.
2. If the upstream firm sells only a small percentage of the inputs purchased by downstream firms, the merged company will be unable to influence price or quantity in the input market. Suppose most of the downstream utilities sell from coal-fired plants. A vertical merger of a gas supplier with a downstream gas-fired utility will not damage competition among the downstream utilities.[220]
3. If the downstream retail customers have multiple purchase options, the upstream gas supplier cannot overcharge its downstream affiliate without that downstream affiliate losing retail sales.
4. If the downstream firm uses all its capacity to serve its obligatory franchise customers, it will have no ability to take customers from its competitors.

---

[217] For more detail on inter-affiliate abuse, see Chapters 3.2.3.3 and 6.5.5.

[218] Order No. 642, *supra* note 5, at 71,005, text accompanying n.94.

[219] *See, e.g.*, Exelon-PHI Merger, Case No. 9361, Order No. 86990, slip op. at 47, text accompanying n.221 (Md. Pub. Serv. Comm'n May 15, 2015) ("We condition this transaction on the commitment by Exelon to cause Pepco, Delmarva, and other Exelon affiliates to comply with the Maryland statutes and regulations applicable to Delmarva and Pepco regarding affiliate transactions.").

[220] *See id. See also* Order No. 642, *supra* note 5, at 71,005, text accompanying n.95 (explaining that no analysis is required "when the upstream merging firm supplies one energy source, but almost all of the energy in the downstream market is produced from generating capacity which uses a different energy source") (citing *Duke Power-PanEnergy Merger*, 79 F.E.R.C. ¶ 61,236, at p. 62,039 (1997)).

5. If the upstream company's input is economically duplicable by others, the merged company will have no market power with which to manipulate price or supply.

6.4.3   Mergers and Innovation: Bidirectional Effects

Innovators differentiate. Differentiating one's product supports higher prices, attracts customers and sustains their loyalty. Competitive companies therefore compete not only on cost, price, output and quality, but on innovation.

Innovating includes creating new products and improving existing products. Innovating also can produce technological breakthroughs that reduce entry barriers. The electric industry needs innovators. It needs companies to develop microgrids and reduce cybersecurity risks. It needs companies that can integrate electric vehicles, storage and renewable sources with conventional generation, transmission and distribution; companies that can help consumers reduce consumption without reducing comfort. So when assessing how a merger affects competition, regulators should look not only at cost, price, output and quality, but also at innovation. Doing so requires four sequential steps:

1. Identify consumers' unmet needs.
2. Determine whether that market's sellers are failing to innovate to address those needs.
3. Describe the market structures and seller conduct that will produce the performance that addresses those needs.
4. Determine whether the proposed merger will move the market structure and seller conduct in the desired direction.

Mergers can affect innovation positively or negatively. This subsection explains why; then offers ways for merger regulators to anticipate and address those effects.

6.4.3.1   Positive and negative effects
In terms of stimulating or discouraging innovation, mergers can affect competitive and non-competitive markets differently.

Competitive markets: A firm facing strong competition in the market for its current products needs to differentiate by developing new products. Competition induces innovation. A merger that reduces the competitors could weaken this pressure. But also possible is the opposite: if competition lowers profit margins, it leaves less money for researching and developing, experimenting and failing. So a merger that reduces competition could raise the merged company's profit margins, allowing it to take more risks.

Monopoly markets: "[T]he best of all monopoly profits is a quiet life."[221] No rivals means no pressure to innovate.[222] Quiet life aside, a monopolist might view innovating as "cannibalizing its existing business"[223]—reducing demand for its legacy products. Utilities have hesitated to innovate on energy efficiency and solar panels because success would reduce their sales of conventionally generated electricity.[224] Again, the opposite could be true: a monopolist threatened by technological or political forces might innovate to gain first-mover advantages and discourage potential entrants.[225]

The preceding two paragraphs described some of competition's effects on innovation. What about innovation's effects on competition? Innovation increases competition when it creates substitutes for traditional products or reduces barriers to entry. Advanced meters, microgrids and storage facilities help new entrants by giving customers alternatives to the traditional utility service. That's innovation's pro-competitive effect. As for anticompetitive effect, recall Microsoft's designing Windows and Internet Explorer to block entry by competing web browsers.[226]

All these effects, positive and negative, can change over time. A merger might reduce competition for a product initially; but if the merged company's

---

[221] John R. Hicks, *Annual Survey of Economic Theory: The Theory of Monopoly*, 3 ECONOMETRICA 1, 8 (1935).

[222] Michael L. Katz & Howard A. Shelanski, *Mergers and Innovation*, 74 ANTITRUST L.J. 1, 18 (2007). *See also* United States v. Auto. Mfrs. Ass'n, 307 F. Supp. 617, 618 (C.D. Cal. 1969) (finding that carmakers conspired "to eliminate competition in the research, development, manufacture and installation of motor vehicle air pollution control equipment"), *aff'd in part, appeal dismissed in part*, 397 U.S. 248 (1970).

[223] Katz & Shelanski, *supra* note 222, at 18.

[224] That hesitance has lightened where regulators addressed cannibalizing, at least as it affected profit, by decoupling utilities' earnings from their sales. For case studies on state commissions' use of decoupling, see REGULATORY ASSISTANCE PROJECT, REVENUE REGULATION AND DECOUPLING: A GUIDE TO THEORY AND APPLICATION (2016), https://www.raponline.org/knowledge-center/revenue-regulation-and-decoupling-a-guide-to-theory-and-application/.

[225] For more detail on competition's effects on innovation, see John Kwoka, *The Effects of Mergers on Innovation: Economic Framework and Empirical Evidence*, *in* PAUL NIHOUL & PIETER VAN CLEYNENBREUGEL, THE ROLES OF INNOVATION IN COMPETITION LAW ANALYSIS 13 (2018). Kwoka describes the differing perspectives of two economics giants—Joseph Schumpeter (who argued that competition is not conducive to technological progress) and Kenneth Arrow (who argued that compared to a company facing competition, a monopolist has less incentive to innovate because its gain would be smaller). Kwoka also explains the methodological difficulties in evaluating mergers' effects on innovations, and describes the conflicting data on the merger-innovation effect in the pharmaceutical industry.

[226] United States v. Microsoft Corp., 253 F.3d 34 (D.C. Cir. 2001), *cert. denied*, 534 U.S. 952 (2001), is discussed in Chapter 6.3.2.3.

actions threaten competitors, they might innovate to create substitutes, making the merger less harmful. Or the opposite: competitors of the merged company might respond to its dominance by innovating initially, only to give up and compete elsewhere, leaving the merged company to enjoy its "quiet life."

6.4.3.2 Traditional merger analysis is static; innovation analysis is dynamic

The typical merger analysis is static: How will the merger affect the price and output of current products? Innovation analysis should be dynamic: How will the merger affect research, development and innovation for future products?[227]

A merger having no competition-reducing effect statically could undermine competition dynamically. Consider a merger of two utilities, each serving a different, remote geographic market. A static analysis would raise no competition concerns, because the companies don't compete with each other. But a dynamic analysis might discover that their merger would allow them to combine and scale up their R&D activities, then aim those activities at creating entry barriers. Dynamic analysis can reveal problems missed by static analysis. And again, the opposite is possible. Static analysis might predict adverse effects—two companies combining horizontally or vertically in the same market to weaken competition; but dynamic analysis might predict that competitors would respond with innovations that break down entry barriers. Put another way: if innovation produces different future products, then HHI calculations based on current products will mis-predict post-merger market shares.[228]

Regulators typically analyze mergers statically. FERC applies the HHI and other tests to existing assets and traditional products; primarily generation and transmission. If those tests detect danger, FERC will require partial divestiture (physical or contractual), rate caps, new transmission construction or special tariff provisions that assist non-incumbents. FERC does not look at a merger's

---

[227] Katz & Shelanski, *supra* note 222, at 11 ("By 'static' we mean it takes a short-term perspective focused on products and markets as they exist at the time of (or within a limited time frame after) a proposed merger and predicts the likely, short-run impact on prices and outputs of those goods as the level of competition changes with the merger."). Dynamic analysis, in contrast, is not constrained by the current array of products and markets. The authors' static-dynamic distinction aligns well with economists' distinction between static efficiency and dynamic efficiency. *See, e.g.*, STIGLITZ & WALSH, *supra* note 7, at A9, A3 (defining static efficiency as "the efficiency of the economy with given technology"; and dynamic efficiency as "an economy that appropriately balances short-run concerns (static efficiency) with long-run concerns (focusing on encouraging R&D)").

[228] Katz & Shelanski call this effect the "innovation impact" effect. *Supra* note 222, at 12–13.

effects on innovation. Merger applicants' strategies for storage, smart grid, renewable energy, energy conservation and demand management receive no FERC attention.[229] And in the dozens of merger orders by state commissions reviewed for this book, no discussion of innovation appears.

In contrast, the FCC has addressed the merger-innovation relationship from several perspectives. The FCC found that the NBC Universal-Comcast merger would assist the two companies' innovation efforts by "reduc[ing] some of the barriers and friction that exist when unaffiliated content providers and distributors negotiate to reach agreements" (though the benefits, the FCC acknowledged, were "hard to specify in advance"). On the negative side, the combined company "will have the incentive and ability to ... thwart the development of" online video distributors—companies that can, through innovation, "provide and promote more programming choices, viewing flexibility, technological innovation and lower prices."[230]

6.4.3.3 Regulatory solutions

The merger-innovation relationship will vary with the facts. Tradeoffs are likely, since at least in theory competition and concentration can each affect innovation positively and negatively. Merger-specific analysis should address at least these four questions:

1. What innovations do we want to induce? Utility-scale solar, storage, electric vehicles and their charging stations, remote control of thermostats, houses that stay cool without air conditioning or what? Unless regulators know their goals, "innovation" becomes a slogan used by applicants to sell their transaction. Do we need a large company with a large market share, protected from competition so it can take innovation risks? Or will a government-protected

---

[229] A Lexis search—"merg! w/50 innovat!"—produced zero examples of FERC addressing a merger's effects on innovation. Indeed, the only cases produced by that search quoted the same boilerplate from FERC's *1996 Merger Policy Statement*, where the Commission applied the term "innovative" not to new products and operational measures, but to various forms of mergers and acquisitions.

[230] NBC Universal-Comcast Merger, 26 FCC Rcd. 4238, 4268–69 ¶ 78, 4333 ¶ 231 (2011). The FCC has expressed similar concerns in other merger cases, including SBC-Ameritech (1999), GTE-Bell Atlantic (2000), AT&T Wireless-Cingular Wireless (2004) and AT&T-BellSouth (2007). *See also* Kwoka, *supra* note 225, at 32 ("Overall, the careful economic studies in the literature as well as other relevant evidence do not support the proposition that industry consolidation results in more R&D or greater R&D efficiency. In fact, there is evidence in the best of these studies that suggests that these mergers may adversely affect R&D or R&D productivity."). For a critical study of the FCC's merger policies, particularly its treatment of the NBCU-Comcast transaction, see SUSAN CRAWFORD, CAPTIVE AUDIENCE: THE TELECOM INDUSTRY AND MONOPOLY POWER IN THE NEW GILDED AGE (2013).

utility avoid innovating, for fear of lowering entry barriers and giving custom-ers choices? Would the desired innovations emerge more readily from markets with numerous, diverse, smaller competitors—markets where nimbleness is more valuable than size?

2. How will the post-merger market structure affect innovation? Will the merger's concentrating effect increase or decrease the players' incentives and abilities to innovate? Will the merger improve R&D coordination among the players?[231]

3. How will innovation affect market structure? Will innovation make concentrated market shares less important than static analysis says they are?

4. Is the incumbent already innovating? The electric industry needs breakthroughs—in energy efficiency, cybersecurity, pipeline leak detection and broadband deployment, among other areas. If a utility fails to innovate, is the regulator prepared to replace it with a company that will? Hawai´i, Maine, Oregon and Vermont did just that, appointing franchised providers of energy efficiency services.[232] And if the utility already is innovating, do these inno-vations give the customers more choices or do they increase the incumbent's advantages over prospective competitors?

These questions all point to the same place: merger policy, merger decisions and post-merger oversight all require attention to how markets affect innova-tion, how mergers affect markets and therefore how mergers affect innovation. But all else being equal, the better path to stimulating industry innovation is to preserve industry diversity.[233]

---

[231]   Katz & Shelanski call this innovation effect the "innovation incentives" effect. *Supra* note 222, at 12–13.

[232]   *See What We Do*, EFFICIENCY VERMONT, https://www.efficiencyvermont.com/about/what-we-do (last visited Jan. 1, 2020) (describing Efficiency Vermont's respon-sibility to provide technical assistance and financial incentives to help Vermont house-holds and businesses reduce their energy costs with energy-efficient equipment and lighting, and energy-efficient approaches to construction and renovation); *About*, HAWAII ENERGY, https://hawaiienergy.com/about (last visited Jan. 1, 2020) (describ-ing Hawaii Energy's ratepayer-funded conservation and efficiency programs); *About Us*, ENERGY TRUST OF OREGON, http://energytrust.org/about (last visited Jan. 1, 2020) (describing Energy Trust of Oregon's responsibility to invest in cost-effective energy efficiency and assist with the above-market costs of renewable energy); *About Efficiency Maine*, EFFICIENCY MAINE, http://www.efficiencymaine.com/about (last visited Jan. 1, 2020) (describing Efficiency Maine's technical assistance, cost-sharing, training and education programs to reduce the use of electricity and heating fuels through energy-efficiency improvements and the use of cost-effective alternative energy).

[233]   *See* Carstensen & Lande, *supra* note 98, at 812–813 ("Generally, stimulus for innovation comes from preserving a wide range of private efforts to innovate. It is extremely difficult to determine *a priori* which innovation will be successful and which

6.4.4 FERC's Blind Spots: Performance, Harm, Retail Competition, Compliance

Whereas each state commission addresses only the electricity mergers involving its in-state utilities, FERC has addressed all the transactions. This large body of decisions reveals a pattern of policy errors and omissions. This sub-section addresses five. FERC (a) under-appreciates how mergers affect performance, (b) defines competition incorrectly, (c) never addresses the cumulative effects of its dozens of merger approvals, (d) ignores mergers' effects on retail competition almost completely, and (e) allows mergers to consummate before their participants have satisfied the Commission's requirements.

6.4.4.1 Performance: undefined

FERC has stated, "as customer protection is increasingly dependent upon vibrant competition, it is critically important that mergers be evaluated on the basis of their effect on market structure and performance."[234] The Commission has paid plenty of attention to market structure—requiring HHI calculations, transmission access and regional transmission planning. But it has never fully defined desirable industry performance—not in terms of seller diversity, product quality, costs, prices or innovation. Without a picture of performance, FERC cannot credibly determine how a merger affects performance. And without defining desirable performance, the Commission cannot define—and has not defined—the type of conduct that produces that performance.

6.4.4.2 Competition: existing defects accepted

FERC says a merger must cause no harm to pre-merger competition. But its decisions disregard defects in that competition. FERC doesn't ask whether the transaction will perpetuate those defects, enable the merged company to benefit from them or preclude competitive improvements. What matters is only that the merger doesn't make things worse.[235] But what if these pre-existing market

---

will prove a failure. Thus, it is vital to continue to have many options being explored and developed at the same time. The more centralized decision-making about innovation the greater is the probability that the paths pursued will be limited and focused on those some bureaucracy has selected as promising.") (footnote omitted).

[234] *1996 Merger Policy Statement, supra* note 124, at 68,599.

[235] *See, e.g., Potomac Electric Power-Conectiv Merger*, 96 F.E.R.C. ¶ 61,323 (2001). The Commission there dismissed wholesale customers' competition concerns for failing to explain how the merger made an existing problem worse:

While Delmarva may be a load pocket in which Conectiv has a large market presence, interveners have not demonstrated how their concerns regarding Conectiv's potential ability to exercise market power in this area are related to the Merger. Given that the proposed Merger will result in only a minor increase

defects—defects that allow the target utility to succeed for reasons other than merits—are precisely what makes the target valuable to the acquirer? If acquirers pay higher gains to targets serving in defective markets, then prospective targets will seek to create and preserve those defects—a result both contrary to the public interest and directly attributable to the Commission's policy of approving mergers without correcting those defects.

The Commission's disregard for competitive defects in the merger context contrasts sharply with its long-running efforts to improve competition in the wholesale sales context. In Order No. 888, FERC imposed nondiscriminatory transmission tariffs on all jurisdictional transmission owners. The reason, FERC said, was because § 211 (added by the Energy Policy Act of 1992 (hereafter EPAct 1992) to provide a complaint-only path for comparable transmission service) failed sufficiently to improve status quo competition.[236] Four years later, FERC found that the Order No. 888 tariffs were not sufficient to ensure effective competition.[237] So FERC not only created a path for transmission owners to form regional transmission organizations, it required all subsequent merger applicants to join RTOs. In Order No. 890, FERC found that even with Order No. 888 tariffs, and even with regional transmission organizations, "opportunities for undue discrimination continue to exist."[238] So it ordered more improvements. Then in Order No. 1000, the Commission again

---

in Conectiv's total capacity, and because the PEPCO capacity is economically viable for only a small number of hours each year, there is little difference in Applicants' ability, pre- and post-Merger, to profitably limit output and raise market prices.

Id. at 62,235.

[236] Order No. 888, *supra* note 127, at 21,547, text accompanying nn.66–67 (finding that "section 211 alone is not enough to eliminate undue discrimination"; it is an "inadequate procedural substitute for readily available service under a filed non-discriminatory open access tariff").

[237] Order No. 2000, *Regional Transmission Organizations, supra* note 215 (finding that the "nature of the emerging markets and the remaining impediments to full competition that became apparent in the nearly four years since the issuance of Order Nos. 888 and 889 ... have made clear that the Commission must take further action if we are to achieve the fully competitive power markets envisioned by those orders"). *See also* Wabash Valley Power Ass'n v. FERC, 268 F.3d 1105, 1108-09 (D.C. Cir. 2001) (describing how FERC issued Order Nos. 888, 889 and 2000 to improve wholesale competition).

[238] Order No. 890, *Preventing Undue Discrimination and Preference in Transmission Service*, F.E.R.C. Stats. & Regs. ¶ 31,241, 72 Fed. Reg. 12,266, 12,271 ¶ 26 (2007) [hereinafter Order No. 890], *order on reh'g and clarification*, Order No. 890-A, F.E.R.C. Stats. & Regs. ¶ 31,261, 73 Fed. Reg. 2984, *order on reh'g and clarification*, Order No. 890-B, 123 F.E.R.C. ¶ 61,299, 73 Fed. Reg. 39,092 (2008), *order on reh'g and clarification*, Order No. 890-C, 126 F.E.R.C. ¶ 61,228, 74 Fed. Reg. 12,540, *order on clarification*, Order No. 890-D, 129 F.E.R.C. ¶ 61,126, 74 Fed. Reg. 61,511 (2009).

found that wholesale competition needed improvement. So it required transmission owners to create regional planning processes not just in RTO regions,
but everywhere.[239] In Order Nos. 719 and 745, FERC found that even with all
the preceding improvements, RTO-organized energy markets still were insufficiently competitive. Only if RTOs allowed demand aggregators both to sell
into those markets and to receive the same compensation wholesale generators
received, would competition be sufficient to make rates just and reasonable.[240]
FERC has initiated similar improvements with a major order on storage.[241] On
wholesale sales, FERC presses for continuous improvement. On mergers, the
status quo is sufficient. It is as if two FERC policies, one on mergers and one
on wholesale sales, are being run out of two separate agencies.

6.4.4.3 Cumulative effects and incipiency: ignored

FERC ignores mergers' cumulative effects. Recall that with PUHCA 1935's
repeal, utilities can merge remotely.[242] Remote companies sell in different
markets, so they avoid FERC's market power screen[243] and cause FERC no
concern. But if each merger stimulates another, eventually concentrating
control within the same market, treating them as isolated events is illogical.
This problem gives FERC no pause; it insists it need not assess a merger "not
only on its own specific terms but [also] as a harbinger of change." FERC has
acknowledged that "as markets evolve, product market and geographic market

---

[239] Order No. 1000, *supra* note 68, at PP 30–31, 42 (finding that the reforms adopted
in Order No. 890 "provide an inadequate foundation for public utility transmission providers to address the challenges they are currently facing or will face in the near future";
"additional reforms … are necessary … to address remaining deficiencies in transmission planning and cost allocation processes so that the transmission grid can better
support [competitive] wholesale power markets"; the new requirements will "enhance
the ability of the transmission grid to support wholesale power markets").

[240] Order No. 719, *Wholesale Competition in Regions with Organized Electric
Markets*, F.E.R.C. Stats. & Regs. ¶ 31,281, 73 Fed. Reg. 64,100 (2008), *order on
reh'g*, Order No. 719-A, F.E.R.C. Stats. & Regs. ¶ 31,292, 74 Fed. Reg. 37,776, *order
on reh'g*, Order No. 719-B, 129 F.E.R.C. ¶ 61,252 (2009); Order No. 745, *Demand
Response Compensation in Organized Wholesale Energy Markets*, 134 F.E.R.C. ¶
61,187, 76 Fed. Reg. 16,658, *order on reh'g*, Order No. 745-A, 137 F.E.R.C. ¶ 61,148
(2011), *vacated*, Elec. Power Supply Ass'n v. FERC, 753 F.3d 216 (D.C. Cir. 2014),
rev'd, FERC v. Elec. Power Supply Ass'n, 136 S. Ct. 760 (2016).

[241] Order No. 841, *Electric Storage Participation in Markets Operated by Regional
Transmission Organizations and Independent System Operators*, F.E.R.C. Stats. &
Regs. ¶ 31,398, 83 Fed. Reg. 9580, 9582 (2018) (finding that existing market rules
create barriers to entry by storage, "thereby reducing competition and failing to ensure
just and reasonable rates").

[242] As explained in Chapters 4.2.2 and 8.2.

[243] FERC's screen for horizontal market power was described in Chapter 6.4.1.2.

definitions can change," but it won't "speculate on what general trends might emerge; rather, [it] will evaluate the effect of [a particular] merger on competition based on the record in [that] case."[244]

What a difference thirty years make. What FERC in 2005 called speculation, its predecessor in 1976 saw as real cause for concern. Addressing a merger of two electric utilities in Maine, the Federal Power Commission (FPC) cited as a "guideline" the Clayton Act's concern with "incipiency." That Act, said the FPC,

> looks not merely to the present effect of a merger but to impact upon future competition between many small entities by "arresting a trend toward concentration in its incipiency before that trend developed to the point that a market was left in the grip of a few big companies." …
>
> Thus, where concentration is gaining momentum in a market, we must be alert to carry out Congress' intent to protect competition against ever increasing concentration through mergers.[245]

Given the "national trend toward concentration," the FPC considered incipiency.[246]

The "national trend toward concentration" in electricity today is far stronger than it was in 1976. Given the Commission's obligation to apply antitrust principles,[247] its merger decision-making must reflect the Clayton Act's concern with incipiency. Processing mergers in isolation ignores incipiency. Perhaps in 1985, when Toledo Edison and Cleveland Electric Illuminating merged, one might not have predicted that nearly eighty mergers would follow; or

---

[244] *Duke Energy-Cinergy Merger*, 113 F.E.R.C. ¶ 61,297 at P 78 (2005) (paraphrasing arguments of American Public Power Association and National Rural Electric Cooperative Association; holding that the Commission "cannot deny or condition a proposed merger based on speculation about general trends that may or may not occur in the future").

[245] *Central Maine Power-Rangeley Power Merger*, 55 F.P.C. 2477 (1976) (quoting United States v. Von's Grocery Co., 384 U.S. 270, 277 (1966) (interpreting Clayton Act § 7, 15 U.S.C. § 18)).

[246] The Commission did say mergers could further the public interest by addressing "optimal scale generating facilities, the scarcity of EHV transmission for long range transmission of electric power and the existence of exclusive franchise areas." *Id.*

[247] *See* Gulf States Utils. Co. v. FPC, 411 U.S. 747, 759 (1973) (interpreting the "public interest" under FPA section 204 to require the Commission to consider "the fundamental national economic policy expressed in the antitrust laws"). *But see* Northeast Utils. Serv. Co. v. FERC, 993 F.2d 937, 947 (1st Cir. 1993) ("Although the Commission must include antitrust considerations in its public interest calculus under the FPA, it is not bound to use antitrust principles when they may be inconsistent with the Commission's regulatory goals.") (citing Otter Tail Power Co. v. United States, 410 U.S. 366 (1973)).

that Toledo Edison and Cleveland Electric would become minor members of a multi-company, multi-state holding company system.[248] But by 2005, when FERC expressly rejected cumulative analysis, it had approved over forty-five transactions. So there was ample basis, evidentiary and logical, for considering the problem of concentration and complication. It did not require much speculation to predict that if Companies A and B merge, so will Companies C and D, and so on. By 2005 it was also reasonable to expect that the remaining pure-play utilities would worry that remaining stand-alone would disadvantage them. And it was reasonable to expect that CEOs of potential targets, on seeing large control premia paid to other utilities' shareholders, would feel pressure to seek similar gains for their shareholders. Facts and logic say that individual merger decisions have cumulative effects. Whether those cumulative effects are positive or negative can be debated. But it is not speculation to say they exist.

Instead of ignoring cumulative effects, FERC should preserve what scholars Carstensen and Lande call "resilient redundancy." Current antitrust enforcement, they argue, "assumes that if N significant competitors are necessary for competition, N - 1 competitors could well be anticompetitive, but blocking an N + 1 merger would not confer any gains" to competition. And because the antitrust agencies assume that mergers usually improve efficiency and innovation, they allow the merger that reduces N + 1 companies to N. Resilient redundancy does the opposite: it preserves in the market at least N + 1 companies, for three reasons:

First, the relationship between concentration and competition, and between concentration and innovation, is uncertain. Underestimating the minimum necessary number of firms needed for competition and for innovation is likely to result in harm to consumer welfare. Second, one or more of the N firms frequently can wither or implode as a result of normal competition, or from an unexpected shock to the market, often surprisingly quickly. This leaves only N - 1 or N - 2 remaining significant competitors. Finally, when enforcers challenge a merger that would have resulted in N competitors, they often allow the merger subject to complex remedies. But if the remedy fails, as they often do, the market will have too few competitors by the enforcers' own estimate. Taken together these scenarios often leave markets with too few firms.[249]

Resilient redundancy is not inefficient redundancy, any more than buying health insurance while eating well and exercising daily is inefficient redun-

---

[248] The holding company FirstEnergy now comprises ten utilities—Ohio Edison, The Illuminating Company, Toledo Edison, Met-Ed, Penelec, Penn Power, West Penn Power, Jersey Central Power & Light, Monongahela Power and Potomac Edison.

[249] Carstensen & Lande, *supra* note 98, at 781.

dancy.[250] Resilient redundancy insures against the risk of ending up with N - 1 competitors. That risk exists because N "is always an unknown number. The best anyone can ever conclude is that it is very likely to lie within a range of values. Moreover, both N and the number of significant competitive firms in a market can change over time, often quickly."[251]

The argument against preserving N + 1 is that the N + 1 merger will bring efficiencies. But as Chapter 4.4 explained, electric utilities' efficiency arguments are usually only arguments; they come with few guarantees about future savings and no data on prior mergers' savings.[252]

6.4.4.4   Retail competition: ignored

The Federal Power Act assigns to the Commission "consumer protection responsibility."[253] Section 203 requires mergers to be "consistent with the public interest." Because "consumers" are ultimate consumers, and because section 203 makes no distinction between wholesale and retail customers, the public interest necessarily includes both customer categories. FERC has acknowledged its duty to address each merger's effects on retail competition.[254] But it has declined to carry out that duty, unless a state commission both (a) lacks state statutory authority to consider a merger's retail competition effects, and (b) asks FERC for help. So in the following plausible scenarios, FERC would do nothing:

1. A state commission has state statutory authority to address a merger's effects on retail competition but never addresses the subject—because of lack of expertise, resources or curiosity; or because the utility has pressured the commission to approve the proposal regardless of its retail competition effects.

---

[250]   *Id.* at 786–89 (citing Thomas J. Horton, *Efficiencies and Antitrust Reconsidered: An Evolutionary Perspective*, 60 ANTITRUST BULL. 168, 174–78 (2015)).

[251]   Carstensen & Lande, *supra* note 98, at 787. *See also* Peter C. Carstensen, *The* Philadelphia National Bank *Presumption: Merger Analysis in an Unpredictable World*, 80 ANTITRUST L.J. 219, 220 (2015) ("Markets are dynamic and the future is notoriously unpredictable. How such mergers might specifically adversely affect competition over a period of years can be answered as well by use of a dartboard as by high-priced economic experts.").

[252]   For examples of studies demonstrating the paucity of evidence on merger efficiencies, see Carstensen & Lande, *supra* note 98, at 801–805, 809, 815–22 (concluding that "most studies have found that mergers do not on average increase net corporate efficiency").

[253]   *New York Independent System Operator, Inc.*, 135 F.E.R.C. ¶ 61,170 at P 15 (2011).

[254]   *1996 Merger Policy Statement*, *supra* note 124, at 68, 604–605.

2. The state commission lacks state statutory authority but does not understand or appreciate the potential for adverse effects (either due to lack of
   expertise, resources or curiosity), so never asks FERC to help.
3. The state commission lacks state statutory authority, the state commission
   understands the adverse effects, but because the merging utilities have
   offered a temporary rate freeze or short-term rate credit at retail, the state
   commission decides that getting the rate credit for current ratepayers is
   more important than preserving retail competition for future ratepayers.
4. The state commission has state statutory authority, but dismisses concerns
   as "speculative" without investigating the facts.

The "speculation" argument deserves special attention. In approving the
merger of Louisville Gas & Electric and Kentucky Utilities, the Kentucky
Commission dismissed retail competition concerns as "highly conjectural and
theoretical"; it held that the absence of authorized retail competition "makes
implausible any attempt to prove market power and obviates the need, at
this time, to consider this issue."[255] Contrast the Maryland Commission: in
approving the proposed (later withdrawn) Pepco-BG&E merger, it said that
though "the retail competition picture is too undefined to weigh the impact of
the merger on it now," retail competition "is sufficiently possible to cause us to
take steps adequate to assure that the merger does not disadvantage the public
interest should retail competition materialize." But the Maryland Commission
then took no real steps, merely promising to "retain [its] full jurisdiction to
mitigate" the merger's later effects on any future retail competition.[256] In legal
and practical effect the Maryland and Kentucky decisions were identical: both
commissions approved a merger that would affect future retail competition
while taking no action to protect that competition. Indeed, eighteen years later,
after Maryland had authorized retail competition, its Commission approved
the merger of Pepco and BG&E—companies whose affiliates would be the
two most likely retail competitors—without ever mentioning retail competition. Common to all three decisions? FERC inaction.

The Federal Power Act does not allow FERC to delegate its duties to state
commissions. On retail competition FERC commits a double error: it delegates

---

[255] Louisville Gas & Electric-Kentucky Utilities Merger, 1997 Ky. PUC LEXIS
274, at *12.

[256] Baltimore Gas & Electric-Pepco Merger, 1997 Md. PSC LEXIS 205, at *32.
In the Maryland situation, the FERC-state handoff failed. FERC had found that retail
competition concerns "merit[ed] consideration" because in any new retail electricity
market the merged company would control "100 percent of the market for firm energy
and between 80–88 percent of the market for non-firm energy." *Baltimore Gas &
Electric-Pepco Merger*, 79 F.E.R.C. ¶ 61,027, at p. 61,115 (1997). FERC deferred the
issue to the Maryland Commission—which did nothing.

without authority, and it delegates without ensuring that its delegatee acts. There is no handoff to the states; there is only a dropped baton.[257]

6.4.4.5 Consummation before compliance

In several mergers FERC found problems but allowed consummation before they were fixed. Public Service of Colorado and Southwestern Public Service accompanied their 1996 merger proposal with a "centerpiece": a new transmission line allowing trade between the Western and Eastern Interconnections.[258] The Commission approved the merger but left the applicants with "unilateral discretion to abandon the effort to complete the line if for economic or various other reasons they choose to do so." For FERC, it was enough that the applicants agreed "to timely and in good faith pursue the processes necessary to build the line." If the line never got built, or got delayed, FERC did say it would "consider appropriate remedial steps if necessary to mitigate market power" resulting from the merger.[259] But the new transmission line was needed not only to prevent market power but also to allow efficient trades—trades that

---

[257]   The situation therefore differs from FERC's logical and permissible reliance on a state commission's finding of retail cost imprudence as a basis for eliminating the utility's rebuttable presumption of wholesale cost prudence. *See Southern California Edison Co.*, 8 F.E.R.C. ¶ 61,198, at p. 61,680 (1979) (shifting burden of going forward to the utility on prudence of nuclear construction costs, due to state commission's finding of imprudence; utility had offered FERC only "vague generalizations about the problems inherent in all building projects"), *aff'd sub nom.* Anaheim v. FERC, 669 F.2d 799 (D.C. Cir. 1981).

[258]   The U.S. electricity network comprises three main Interconnections: the Eastern Interconnection, the Western Interconnection and the Electric Reliability Council of Texas. The three Interconnections "operate largely independently from each other with limited transfers of power between them." *See The U.S. Electric System is Made up of Interconnections and Balancing Authorities*, U.S. Energy Info. Admin. (July 20, 2016), https://www.eia.gov/todayinenergy/detail.php?id=27152. One of my Georgetown Law students cited this fact in class, out of the blue. Surprised and impressed by his knowledge of this obscure fact, I asked him how he knew. The emailed response:

> I believe that I learned it while playing the game *Fallout: New Vegas*, which is set in a dystopian future where a nuclear war in the 1950s led to freakish mutations and societal breakdown. The main plot of the game is a struggle between a new Californian democracy and an autocracy based on ancient Rome, specifically over which side will control the Hoover Dam, electricity for the region, and the fate of civilization. I believe that somewhere in the 80-hour long game, there was a pre-war map of the US power grid, or the three segment regions are mentioned in some of the dialogue. However, I wasn't able to find the exact reference, so don't quote me on it!

[259]   *PSColorado-Southwestern Public Service Merger II*, 78 F.E.R.C. ¶ 61,267, at pp. 62,141, 62,138 n.6 (1997).

would produce economic benefit to offset the consolidation's costs. Allowing consummation before compliance exposed the public to those costs without ensuring the benefits.[260]

Similarly, FERC allowed UtiliCorp, St. Joseph Light & Power and Empire District to merge without determining whether integrating the companies' generation operations would cause transmission congestion—congestion that could "hamper competitors' ability to reach certain customers."[261] FERC conditioned its approval on the Applicants submitting a competition analysis after the merger but six months before integrating their operations, with the submission to include remedies for any adverse competitive effects. Again—merge first, assess damage later.

* * *

The Federal Power Act's "history … indicates an overriding policy of maintaining competition to the maximum extent possible consistent with the public interest."[262] In addressing mergers, FERC doesn't insist on competition "to the maximum extent possible consistent with the public interest," because FERC has not defined the public interest. The Commission has failed to define the public's interest in performance. It has defined harm too narrowly, ignored incipiency and cumulative effects, and rarely assessed a merger's effects on the retail markets that comprise the most electricity sales.

6.4.5 Current Conflict: Distribution Franchise Consolidation vs. Distributed Energy Competition

In electricity mergers, competition analysis has historically focused on bulk power—power produced by large generators, and the transmission services that bring the output to loads. While the inputs might differ—generating capacity, transmission capacity, firm wholesale energy, non-firm wholesale energy, retail bundled electricity, ancillary services—the ultimate retail product has been the same: electric current needed to run industrial equipment and residential refrigerators.

Retail electricity product markets are now diversifying. New companies offer thermostat controls, two-way smart meters, electricity prices based on hourly production costs, energy efficiency services and renewable energy

---

[260] The line did get built. It's called the Holcomb-Finney to Lamar 345 kV line. There is a 200 MW high-voltage direct current tie at Lamar, Colorado.

[261] *UtiliCorp United-St. Joseph Light & Power Merger*, 92 F.E.R.C. ¶ 61,067, at p. 61,232 (2000).

[262] Otter Tail Power Co. v. United States, 410 U.S. 366, 374 (1973).

packages. Solar panels, storage and neighborhood-level microgrids allow residential consumers, neighborhoods and industrial parks to self-supply. Aggregators of demand response pay consumers to use less, then sell that non-usage into organized energy markets.

These developments are causing regulators to rethink market structure at the distribution level. They hope to democratize demand, by allowing consumers to custom-design their own services; and to diversify supply, by attracting non-utility providers of these new products. Some states commissions are starting by identifying new monopoly roles. An airport needs an air traffic controller to schedule plane departures and arrivals. Electric distribution counterparts include the "distribution system platform provider" discussed in New York and the "smart grid coordinator" discussed in Maine.[263] The market structure question involves not only whether to create this new monopoly role but also who should fill it—that is, whether the coordinator should be the incumbent distribution monopoly, or instead a new entity selected competitively. A distinct market structure question is whether to allow the monopoly service provider to also sell the new competitive services; and under what conditions to prevent the provider from exploiting vertical market power, excluding competitors and benefiting from unearned advantages.[264]

---

[263] *See, e.g.*, Order Adopting Regulatory Policy Framework and Implementation Plan, Case 14-M-0101 (NY Pub. Serv. Comm'n Feb, 26, 2015) (describing distribution system platform provider); ME. STAT. tit. 35-A, § 3143(1)(B), (5) (repealed 2019) (defining "smart grid coordinator" to mean an "entity ... that manages access to smart grid functions and associated infrastructure, technology and applications within the service territory of a transmission and distribution utility").

[264] Consider Florida Power & Light's SolarNow program. Customers could voluntarily contribute $9.00 monthly to a solar investment fund. FPL would use the funds to build, own and operate utility-scale solar facilities, while FPL's parent would contribute $200,000 yearly to nonprofit organizations chosen by the program participants. No non-FPL companies had an opportunity to build the funded facilities. This three-year pilot, begun in 2015, enabled FPL to use its retail monopoly status to gain an unearned advantage in the market for solar development. FPL used its customer list, monthly bill (which every customer has to open), website (which allowed customers to track the program's progress) and internal staff—all resources previously funded by its captive electricity customers—to design, promote and carry out the program. (FPL would absorb some of the prospective marketing and administrative costs.) None of these resources were available to FPL's solar competitors. The Florida Commission's four-page approval order said nothing about the effects on solar competition. Petition for Approval of Voluntary Solar Partnership Pilot Program and Tariff, 2014 Fla. PUC LEXIS 349. By 2017, the program had over 50,000 FPL participants—all of whom could have been customers of non-FPL solar companies if those companies had had access to FPL's non-replicable, ratepayer-funded resources. Rebuttal Testimony of Matthew Valle at 5, Petition for Approval of FPL SolarTogether Program and Tariff, Docket No. 20190061-EI (Fla. Pub. Serv. Comm'n filed Sept. 23, 2019).

How do these facts interact with merger policy? An incumbent utility will likely want the new monopoly role for itself; it will also want a chance to provide the new competitive services, directly or through an affiliate.[265] That

---

A new FPL program continues this unearned advantage. As approved by the Florida Commission, SolarTogether allows customers to volunteer to fund 1490 MW of new solar capacity. The utility would build, operate and own the capacity itself, rather than allow non-utility companies to compete for the opportunity. Customers would receive a credit on their bills for a portion of the system savings created by the new capacity. Like the Pilot Program order, the Commission's SolarTogether order said nothing about the program's effects on competition. Petition for Approval of SolarTogether Program and Tariff, by Florida Power & Light Co., Docket No. 20190061-EI, Order No. PSC-2020-0084-S-EI (Fla. Pub. Serv. Comm'n Mar. 20, 2020), http://www.floridapsc .com/library/filings/2020/01555-2020/01555-2020.pdf.

[265] Consider these developments: **Georgia Power** is partnering with Georgia Tech to integrate with the utility's main grid a microgrid capable of accommodating micro-turbines, solar panels and electric vehicle chargers. *Georgia Tests Cost-Effectiveness and Benefits of Microgrids*, SMART ENERGY INT'L (Mar. 14, 2019), https://www.smart -energy.com/industry-sectors/business-finance-regulation/georgia-tech-tests-cost -effectiveness-benefits-microgrids/. Constellation (a subsidiary of **Exelon**, which owns six utilities) is partnering with Schneider Electric to bring distributed energy resources to a U.S. Marine Corps Logistics Base in Albany, Georgia. The resources include "an 8.5 MW biomass-fueled, steam-to-electricity (STE) generator, high-efficiency trans-formers, lighting and boiler upgrades, … system controls for a landfill gas electric-ity generator and centralized monitoring and operation of electricity generation and distribution." *Schneider Electric to Help Enable Energy Resiliency at USMC Base*, POWERGRID INT'L (Mar. 14, 2017), https://www.elp.com/articles/2017/03/schneider -electric-to-help-enable-energy-resiliency-at-usmc-base.html#gref.

Also: **Alabama Power**, a subsidiary of Southern Company, plans to develop a Smart Neighborhood with "62 single-family homes and a nearby community-scale microgrid, consisting of solar panels, battery energy storage and a natural gas generator." *Alabama Power's Smart Neighborhood*, T&D WORLD (Jan. 4, 2019), https://www.tdworld.com/ microgrids/alabama-power-s-smart-neighborhood. **Southern California Edison** has installed its "Circuit of the Future," a utility distribution circuit powered by smart grid technology, including a "digital systems controller that functions like the circuit's brain to identify, analyze and isolate circuit problems." *Southern California Edison Unveils Smart Neighborhood Electricity Circuit*, T&D WORLD (Oct. 24, 2007), https://www .tdworld.com/smarter-grid/southern-california-edison-unveils-smart-neighborhood -electricity-circuit.

And more: **Consolidated Edison** is partnering with NRG Energy to develop mobile storage batteries that can be deployed to stressed parts of the grid during periods of increased demand. *How ConEd's Mobile Battery REV Demo Could Build a New Storage Business Model*, UTIL. DIVE (Mar. 7, 2017), https://www.utilitydive .com/news/how-coneds-mobile-battery-rev-demo-could-build-a-new-storage-business -mode/437364/. **Exelon** is partnering with the Norwegian firm Nel Hydrogen to inte-grate a hydrogen production, storage and utilization facility into its existing nuclear facilities. *Exelon Is Exploring Nuclear Power Plant Hydrogen Production*, POWER (Aug. 29, 2019), https://www.powermag.com/exelon-is-exploring-nuclear-power

utility's acquirer will pay an acquisition premium based on the expected future earnings from those two roles. If the state instead hands the new monopoly functions to some other company, or prohibits the incumbent from providing the new competitive services—either action conflicting with the acquirer's earnings expectations—the acquirer will have overpaid for the utility. The acquirer will naturally resist these measures; and commissions might hesitate to adopt them to avoid causing the acquirer financial stress. This tension—between the potential for competition and diversity in distributed energy services, and mergers that consolidate distribution franchises—has received no attention in regulators' merger decisions. Some commissions have even given the merged company a first-mover advantage in distribution services, by treating as a merger benefit the applicants' offer to invest in that space.

To keep their market structure options open, state commissions' merger policies should explicitly deny any intent to grant the post-merger entity a right to (a) become the provider of any new monopoly platform services, or to (b) compete in any of the new distributed services markets. This pre-merger clarity

---

-plant-hydrogen-production/. **Southern Company**'s subsidiary PowerSecure, Inc. is partnering with Compass Energy Platform, LLC to help "cities and energy companies build more sustainable and resilient energy solutions" through "distributed generation, energy storage and renewables, energy efficiency and utility infrastructure." *PowerSecure Becomes Microgrid Implementation Provider for New Innovative Energy Joint Venture Compass Energy Platform LLC*, PR NEWSWIRE (May 17, 2019), https://www.prnewswire.com/news-releases/powersecure-becomes-microgrid -implementation-provider-for-new-innovative-energy-joint-venture-compass-energy -platform-llc-300852476.html. PowerSecure is also working with Bloom Energy to offer 50 MW of distributed fuel cells to long-term customers. *Southern's PowerSecure Contracts with Bloom for Fuel Cell + Storage Solution*, UTIL. DIVE (Oct. 26, 2016), https://www.utilitydive.com/news/southerns-powersecure-contracts-with-bloom-for -fuel-cell-storage-solutio/429091/.

And still more: **Commonwealth Edison** has committed to incorporating more distributed energy resources into its Illinois infrastructure. *It's All About the Value of the Network: ComEd Gears Up for a Distributed Energy Boom*, GREENTECH MEDIA (July 1, 2016), https://www.greentechmedia.com/articles/read/comed-gears-up-for-a -distributed-energy-boom#gs.1zddpv. **Oncor** (a Texas retail utility), S&C Electric Company and Schneider Electric have produced an advanced "grid-tier system [that] consists of four inter-connected microgrids and nine different distributed generation resources: two solar PV arrays, a microturbine, two energy storage units, and four generators." *Oncor, S&C and Schneider Electric Complete a Unique Four-Part Microgrid*, GREENTECH MEDIA (Apr. 7, 2015), https://www.greentechmedia.com/articles/read/ oncor-sc-and-schneider-electric-complete-their-innovative-four-part-microgr#gs .1zd9pa. **Potomac Electric Power** is planning to build two advanced microgrids to "serve 19 facilities with 13.6 MW of solar and natural gas-fired generation and 1.8 MW of battery energy storage." *Maryland Utility Proposes $44.2M Pilot for Public Purpose Microgrids*, MICROGRID KNOWLEDGE (Oct. 3, 2017), https://microgridknowledge.com/ public-purpose-microgrids-pepco/.

will warn the acquirer not to offer a premium expecting to maintain, extend or exploit the target's monopoly position. Absent this two-part condition, the merging entities could infer that the future will be like the past: that the merged entity will continue to control poles and wires, provide the platform services and be allowed to compete (likely through an affiliate) in the markets whose essential infrastructure the incumbent utility controls. (That inference will be shared by prospective entrants, who then will be less likely to enter these markets—leaving customers dependent on the incumbent.) With that inference in place, suppose then that the commission, sometime post-merger, announces a competition for one or more distribution roles. The merged company's stock value would drop, because the prospect of competition will have contradicted the stock markets' pre-merger expectation of continued monopoly. That value loss would support no legal claim, because the utility's shareholders made their bets voluntarily. Nor is the value loss the economy's loss, because it will be matched by the value gain to whoever wins the competition. But given the service territory's dependence on the incumbent, commissions will tend to protect the utility rather than press forward with competition. Establishing pre-merger conditions avoids post-merger awkwardness.

6.4.6 Arguments against Competition Concerns: How Persuasive?

While merger applicants provide the technical analyses required by FERC's rules, they also use arguments less rooted in facts. Consider four examples:

Plenty of competitors: Opponents of the Exelon-PHI merger argued that Exelon's competitive retail electric affiliates would get unearned advantages from Exelon's monopoly utility subsidiaries. Exelon's witness responded that the retail market had many suppliers.[266] But the number of suppliers, by itself, does not describe a market's competitiveness. One needs more information: on those suppliers' market shares and viability, on the market's entry barriers, on customers' propensity to change suppliers; and on the competitive affiliates' advantages gained from name recognition, service territory knowledge and existing customer relationships.

Promises to obey the rules: Responding to concerns about anticompetitive inter-affiliate abuse, the Exelon-PHI applicants promised to heed their commissions' inter-affiliate rules, along with the companies' internal standards and procedures. But promises to obey don't produce obedience unless regulatory monitoring is effective and penalties large. In 1996, FERC's Order No. 888 required transmission owners to submit Commission-crafted, 100-page

---

[266] Supplemental Direct Testimony of Julie R. Solomon at 14–15, Exelon-PHI Merger, Formal Case No. 1119 (D.C. Pub. Serv. Comm'n filed Feb. 4, 2015).

tariffs. A decade later, FERC acknowledged in Order No. 890 that those tariffs, and the Commission's mammoth efforts to enforce them, had not prevented transmission owners from practicing undue discrimination.[267]

Competitive affiliates independent of the monopoly affiliates: One Exelon witness insisted that Exelon's acquisition of PHI would not damage generation competition because Exelon's competitive generation affiliates would operate separately from its monopoly utility affiliates.[268] This statement is contradicted by common sense—and by the U.S. Supreme Court: a holding company's affiliates and parent "have a complete unity of interest," like a "multiple team of horses drawing a vehicle under the control of a single driver."[269] The witness's statement also contradicted the acquisition's asserted purpose—to spread Exelon's "best practices" and its "culture" throughout its subsidiaries. The affiliates cannot be competitive rivals, keeping secrets from each other, if their holding company master is compelling them to cooperate.

Competition concerns are "speculative": Merger applicants often say that competitive concerns are speculative. But common sense says, and cases hold, that regulators must not ignore the risk of harm until the harm occurs. In anti-trust law, action is justified by a company's "mere ability" to exercise market power; by an "appreciable danger" of price increases; by a "probabilit[y], not [a] certaint[y,]" of harm.[270]

---

[267] Order No. 890, *supra* note 238, at 12,267. And if rules and procedures were sufficient, Constellation, the holding company for BG&E (now owned by Exelon), would not have "agreed to pay a $135 million civil penalty," along with "$110 million in disgorgement," to settle a FERC investigation into its trading practices. Exelon Corp., Annual Report (Form 10-K) at 398 (Feb. 22, 2013) (relating to "certain of Constellation's power trading activities in and around the ISO-NY from September 2007 through December 2008").

[268] Supplemental Direct Testimony of Julie R. Solomon, *supra* note 266, at 5–6.

[269] Copperweld Corp. vs. Independent Tube Corp., 467 U.S. 752, 771 (1984).

[270] Exelon-Constellation Energy Group Merger, 2012 Md. PSC LEXIS 12, at *66–67 ("[M]ere ability to exercise market power would … constitute a harm both to [Baltimore Gas & Electric's] customers and the public interest that would be wholly incompatible with [Maryland Code] § 6-105."); AT&T-Deutsche Telekom Merger, 26 FCC Rcd. 16,184, 16,196 ¶ 16 (2011) (stating that regulatory action is justified by "appreciable danger" of merger-induced price increases; in passing the antitrust laws, "Congress used the words 'may be substantially to lessen competition' [] to indicate that its concern was with probabilities, not certainties") (quoting United States v. H&R Block, Inc., 833 F. Supp. 2d 36 (D.D.C. 2011); and then quoting FTC v. H.J. Heinz Co., 246 F.3d 708, 713 (D.C. Cir. 2001)).

6.5   REGULATORY ACTIONS TO PROTECT COMPETITION ON THE MERITS

We have explained that when a merged entity operates in both a monopoly market and a potentially competitive market, it can exercise market power, act anticompetitively or exploit unearned advantages, all to beat or deter non-utility competitors. If a merger otherwise deserves approval, regulators address these concerns with three overlapping devices: separating the company's monopoly activities from its competitive activities, mandating nondiscriminatory access to bottleneck facilities and establishing arm's-length rules for inter-affiliate pricing. After summarizing the legal standards that support these regulatory actions, we discuss solutions that apply uniquely to horizontal mergers, then those that apply uniquely to vertical mergers, followed by solutions that apply to all mergers.

Rules provide little help without enforcement measures, like financial and structural penalties. Because enforcement of competition rules often takes the same form as enforcement of rules against customer harm, we will address that subject at the end of Chapter 7 on customer harm, specifically Chapter 7.4.8.

To emphasize: this section on regulator actions applies only to mergers that otherwise deserve approval. Mergers that embody a conflict between the applicants' interest and the public interest cannot be fixed by regulatory action.

6.5.1   General Legal Standards

On a commission's authority to assess a merger's competitive effects, statutes vary. The Supreme Court has declared that the Federal Power Act's "public interest" standard requires FERC to act consistently with antitrust law—"the Magna Carta of free enterprise."[271] Some state commissions address competitive concerns under their statutes' general public interest standard. Other state commissions apply statutes explicitly requiring a competition analysis. Consider:

1. The Pennsylvania Commission must consider whether the combination "is likely to result in anticompetitive or discriminatory conduct, including the

---

[271] Gulf States Utils. Co. v. FPC, 411 U.S. 747, 759 (1973) (requiring the Commission to "consider matters relating to both the broad purposes of the Act and the fundamental national economic policy expressed in the antitrust laws"). *See also* United States v. Topco Assocs., 405 U.S. 596, 610 (1972) ("Antitrust laws in general, and the Sherman Act in particular, are the Magna Carta of free enterprise. They are as important to the preservation of economic freedom and our free-enterprise system as the Bill of Rights is to the protection of our fundamental personal freedoms.").

unlawful exercise of market power, which will prevent retail electricity customers in this Commonwealth from obtaining the benefits of a properly functioning and workable competitive retail electricity market."[272]

2. The New Jersey Board of Public Utilities must "monitor proposed acquisitions of electric generating facilities by electric power suppliers as it deems necessary, in order to ascertain whether an electric power supplier has or is proposed to have control over electric generating facilities of sufficient number or strategic location to charge non-competitive prices to retail customers in this State." The Board can deny, suspend or revoke a supplier's license if the supplier "has or may acquire such control."[273]

3. The California Commission must find that the proposed merger cannot "adversely affect competition." Before making its decision, the Commission must get from the Attorney General an advisory opinion on whether the merger will adversely affect competition and whether mitigation measures could prevent that effect.[274]

6.5.2   Actions Aimed at Horizontal Market Power

To address horizontal mergers, regulators have two categories of remedies: structural and conduct.

Structural remedies aim to bring merger-caused concentration below the HHI trigger point. These remedies increase the number of sellers that can physically and economically compete for the merged company's customers. FERC has described two main approaches: increase the size of the market, and reduce concentration within the existing market. To increase the size of the market, FERC might require that the merger applicants either expand transmission capacity; or transfer control of their transmission capacity to an independent entity.[275] To reduce concentration within the existing market, regulators use generation divestiture—either actual or virtual.

---

[272]   66 PA. CONS. STAT. § 2811(e)(1).

[273]   N.J. STAT. ANN. § 48:3-78f.

[274]   CAL. PUB. UTIL. CODE § 854(b)(3).

[275]   *See* Order No. 642, *supra* note 5, at 71,001, text accompanying n.73 ("[Regional transmission organizations] can mitigate market power, eliminate rate pancaking and better manage grid congestion, thereby enlarging geographic markets."); *UtiliCorp United-St. Joseph Light & Power Merger*, 92 F.E.R.C. ¶ 61,067 (2000) (relying on applicants' commitment to join an RTO as a condition of merger approval). States also have conditioned merger approvals on the applicants' agreeing to join an RTO. *See, e.g.*, Union Electric-Central Illinois Public Service Merger, 1997 Mo. PSC LEXIS 1, at *23–24 (requiring merging companies to participate in a regional "independent system operator," so as to eliminate "pancaked" transmission rates that made market access costly for competitors of the merging companies).

Actual divestiture is the permanent sale of assets. Regulators like actual divestiture because it "most immediately eliminate[s] the competitive problems created by the merger ... and [entails] the least amount of risk."[276] It does so by "preserv[ing] an independent profit-maximizing entity whose behavior should replicate the competition otherwise extinguished by the transaction."[277] Actual divestiture comes with five cautions:

1. The divested capacity must be the type of capacity that caused the HHI screen failure. Because "generation" involves different products, such as long-term capacity, short-term capacity, interruptible energy and ancillary services, FERC performs a distinct HHI analysis for each product. If the market power arises from control of gas-fired peaking capacity during peak periods, for example, the divested capacity must be peaking capacity, not baseload capacity.
2. Divesting an ownership share of a generating asset does not necessarily remove the owner's market power if the merged company retains operational control of the asset. In the AEP-CSW merger, the applicants proposed to divest a 50 percent share in specified plants, but would still control the plants' operations. FERC said no: "By retaining operational control of the generating facilities, Applicants will have the ability to withhold capacity from the market and thus affect electricity prices." FERC required the merging applicants to transfer to a third party both ownership and control of all the HHI-violating capacity.[278]
3. The divested capacity must go to purchasers that will not themselves gain market power from the purchase.[279]

---

[276] Catherine Fazio, *Merger Remedies: The Greater Use by the DOJ and FTC of an Expanding Toolkit*, in RECENT DEVELOPMENTS IN ANTITRUST LAW 51 (2013), 2013 WL 3773855, at *3 (alteration in original) (quoting RICHARD FEINSTEIN, FED. TRADE COMM'N, NEGOTIATING MERGER REMEDIES 5 (2012)). FERC conditioned its approval of the Wisconsin Electric-Northern States Power merger on the applicants agreeing to divest enough generation to avoid violating an HHI test. *See Northern States Power-Wisconsin Electric Power Merger*, 79 F.E.R.C. ¶ 61,158, at pp. 61,699–700 (1997) (stating that divestiture would "mitigate increases in [the merged entity's] post-merger market power as measured by increases in the HHIs in the relevant market"). Following FERC's order, the merger applicants withdrew the transaction.

[277] KWOKA, *supra* note 6, at 137.

[278] *American Electric Power-Central & South West Merger*, 90 F.E.R.C. ¶ 61,242, at p. 61,792 (2000).

[279] *Northern States Power-Wisconsin Electric Power Merger*, 79 F.E.R.C. ¶ 61,158, at 61,700 (emphasizing that a divestiture plan's appropriateness depends on "the type and operating costs of capacity divested and the present market role of the entities which would acquire the generation assets"); *American Electric Power-Central & South West Merger*, 90 F.E.R.C. ¶ 61,242, at 61,792 (accepting applicants' commit-

4. Divestiture might take time, especially where FERC has restricted the universe of purchasers to entities that will not themselves gain market power from the acquisition. Because allowing the merger to consummate before divestiture creates market power risks, FERC has required the merged entity to accept interim restrictions, like price caps.[280]
5. Divest what—specific assets or a full line of business? Divestiture will more likely achieve its remedial purpose—replicating the competition otherwise diminished by the merger—if the divested assets stay in the market, operated by the chosen buyer. After studying all its divestiture orders from 1990 to 1994—thirty-five orders involving fifty specific divestitures—the Federal Trade Commission found that the assets were more likely to stay in the market if what was divested was an entire line of business rather than just the assets—likely because a divested line of business would include experienced management, supplier relationships and customers.[281]

With *virtual divestiture* (also called contractual divestiture), the merged company retains legal ownership of the capacity, but rents the HHI-triggering amount to unrelated third parties. The rental lasts long enough to allow the market to de-concentrate, such as through new generation entry or market-expanding transmission construction.[282] Other examples of virtual divestiture include requiring the merged entity to (1) make its HHI-triggering capacity and energy available to non-affiliates through a competitive bidding

---

ment that "the divested generating capacity [will] not be sold in a way that would cause changes in market concentration to exceed acceptable thresholds").

[280] *See, e.g.*, Order No. 642, *supra* note 5, at 71,000 (describing the use of price caps, imposed for time periods and geographic areas in which the merger company has market power); *Consolidated Edison-Orange and Rockland Utilities Merger*, 86 F.E.R.C. ¶ 61,064 (1999) (allowing merger to consummate prior to divestiture, provided merged company bids energy into the New York Independent System Operator's day-ahead and real-time markets); *American Electric Power-Central & South West Merger*, 90 F.E.R.C. ¶ 61,242 (allowing two-year delay of divestiture of specific units due to merged entity's native load obligation, subject to "interim measures" including making interim sales to third parties of capacity that triggered HHI concern).

[281] Kwoka, *supra* note 6, at 128–29.

[282] *See Duke Energy-Progress Energy Merger I*, 136 F.E.R.C. ¶ 61,245 at P 117 n.277 (2011) (defining virtual divestiture). The FCC also has required virtual divestiture. Addressing the market for wholesale "special access services," the FCC found that the AT&T-BellSouth merger would "reduce from two to one the number of competitors with direct connections to a handful of buildings where other competitive entry is unlikely." For a remedy, AT&T agreed to give third-party competitors ten-year leases in the fiber capacity linked to these buildings. AT&T-BellSouth Merger, 22 FCC Rcd. 5662, 5664 ¶ 2 (2007).

process;[283] or to (2) sell the capacity into an RTO-administered market—where generation dispatch is determined by objective rules rather than subjective strategies.[284] As with actual divestiture, virtual divestiture works only if it actually reduces concentration. If the merged company retains control of the virtually divested capacity, it can still "withhold such output (or output from similar capacity) to drive up electricity prices."[285] And FERC has rejected a merger applicant's proposed rental to a buyer that was already in the market.[286]

Turning from structural to *conduct measures*: these solutions aim at two ways sellers exercise market power: raising prices above competitive levels, and withholding product from the market. FERC has allowed the merged company to retain its assets (despite the concentration caused by the merger), if the company either (a) caps its prices at competitive levels or (b) bids the resource into an organized market at a price low enough to ensure its selection. One problem with conduct remedies: they don't "alter the firm's incentives to engage in the harmful practices in question—those are inherent in the merger—and so the conduct remedy must succeed in preventing the firm from acting in its own interests."[287]

6.5.3 Actions Aimed at Vertical Market Power

By controlling upstream inputs needed by their downstream competitors, utilities can exercise vertical market power. They can use their legitimate control of monopoly transmission or distribution facilities to impair competition in the competitive markets for wholesale generation or retail sales. Regulators have three standard responses, as follows.

---

[283] *See, e.g., Ameren-Dynegy Merger,* 108 F.E.R.C. ¶ 61,094 at P 61 (2004); *American Electric Power-Central & South West Merger,* 90 F.E.R.C. ¶ 61,242; *Ameren Services-Central Illinois Light Merger,* 101 F.E.R.C. ¶ 61,202 at P 41 (2002) (same concept but with the price established by a market value index).

[284] *See, e.g., Consolidated Edison-Orange and Rockland Utilities Merger,* 86 F.E.R.C. ¶ 61,064 at 61,246. *See also* PECO Energy-Public Service Electric & Gas Merger, 2006 Pa. PUC LEXIS 33, at *59 (approving stipulated condition that divested the merged company of 6600 MW of generation, "through the outright sale of 4,000 MW of fossil generation and virtual divestiture of 2,600 MW of nuclear generation"—the latter consisting of selling firm energy 24/7 to third parties).

[285] *Allegheny Energy-DQE Merger,* 84 F.E.R.C. ¶ 61,223, at p. 62,070 (1998).

[286] *Duke Energy-Progress Energy Merger II,* 137 F.E.R.C. ¶ 61,210 at PP 68–72 (2011), *reh'g denied,* 149 F.E.R.C. ¶ 61,078 (2014). The companies eventually satisfied the Commission and won approval of their merger. *See also Allegheny Energy-DQE Merger,* 84 F.E.R.C. ¶ 61,223, at 62,070–71 (finding that due to restrictions in the request for proposals, there was no guarantee that the output specified in the virtual divestiture proposal would actually be sold).

[287] KWOKA, *supra* note 6, at 137.

6.5.3.1   Nondiscriminatory transmission or distribution tariff

In the early 1990s, FERC began requiring transmission tariffs as a condition of merger approval.[288] This merger condition became redundant in 1996, when FERC Order Nos. 888 and 889 required all transmission-owning, investor-owned utilities, merged or unmerged, to have tariffs providing nondiscriminatory transmission service. As competitors seek to enter the distributed energy resources space, state regulators will need to design distribution-level counterparts to these transmission measures.

6.5.3.2   Independent oversight of transmission availability

A merged company can exercise vertical market power by misinforming competitors that transmission capacity is unavailable, then using that same capacity for its own transactions. To prevent this conduct, FERC in the pre-RTO era required merging companies to have an independent entity calculate and post data on available transmission capacity (ATC). The merged company would provide the independent entity information on generation dispatch, transmission constraints and generation re-dispatch actions taken to relieve constraints. The independent entity would analyze the data, then submit both the analysis and the data to FERC.[289] This independent review process would discourage the anticompetitive conduct.

6.5.3.3   Membership in regional transmission organization

Even after submitting a nondiscriminatory tariff, the merged company can plan and operate its transmission system in ways that give its own generators favorable access to its transmission capacity. To prevent those practices, FERC conditions most of its merger approvals on the applicants joining an independent regional transmission organization. The RTO not only provides transmission service; it also plans and operates the regional transmission system, conducting all these activities independently of market participants. And if the merger involves utilities outside an RTO region, FERC will require them to turn transmission control over to an independent system operator.

---

[288] *El Paso Electric-Central & South West Merger*, 68 F.E.R.C. ¶ 61,181, at pp. 61,891, 61,914, text accompanying n.125 (1994) (finding that given the trend toward utility consolidation, FERC's goal of effective competition in bulk power markets and the statutory prohibition against undue discrimination justified the condition of comparable transmission service) (citing *American Elec. Power Serv. Corp.*, 67 F.E.R.C. ¶ 61,168 (1994) (establishing comparability standard).

[289] *American Electric Power-Central & South West Merger*, 90 F.E.R.C. ¶ 61,242, at p. 61,790–91 (2000).

6.5.3.4 Other conduct remedies

An upstream supplier can exercise market power by gathering competitively sensitive information from potential customers in the downstream market, then sharing that information with its downstream affiliate. Common solutions include:

1. erecting firewalls between the merged company's upstream and downstream segments, to prevent information flow between them;
2. requiring the merged company to grant its competitors access to its bottleneck facilities—not just physical ones, but also intangible ones like data, interoperability protocols and intellectual property not economically replicable by the competitors; and
3. prohibiting the merged company from retaliating against customers who buy from competitors.[290]

6.5.4 Actions Aimed at Corporate Structure: Separating Monopoly Activities From Competitive Activities

Horizontal and vertical market power are two species of a single, larger problem: when a corporate family conducts both monopoly and competitive businesses, or owns both monopoly and competitive assets, it has incentive and opportunity to use the monopoly assets to exercise market power or gain unearned advantage in the competitive markets. To prevent this conduct, regulators choose from three categories of solutions: unbundling, limits on non-utility investments and divestiture.

Utilities sometimes argue that regulators need not restrict conduct because they can punish misconduct—by disallowing costs, imputing revenues, lowering the authorized return on equity or imposing penalties.[291] But these financial measures can leave the utility less able to meet its service obligations, pay back its debts and pay dividends to shareholders; as a result, regulators are less likely to use them. Knowing of regulators' hesitance to impose financial consequences, holding company executives are more likely to take risks they shouldn't. Thus restrictions on conduct: it is more logical and less risky to reduce temptation than to penalize companies for acting on temptation.[292]

---

[290] *See, e.g.*, Fazio, *supra* note 276, at *4.

[291] *See* Tutorial § 4.1. *See also* HEMPLING, *supra* note 102, chs. 6.A, 6.B, 6.C.

[292] The next three subsections—on unbundling, limits on competitive investments and divestiture of competitive activities—are drawn in part from Hempling, *Regulating Public Utility Performance*, *supra* note 102, with permission of the publisher, American Bar Association.

6.5.4.1 Unbundling: divisional and corporate

In the corporate structure context, unbundling means placing the monopoly and competitive activities in separate parts of the corporate family. Those parts can be divisions within the same corporation (divisional unbundling), or affiliated corporations (corporate unbundling).

6.5.4.1.1 *Divisional unbundling*

In divisional unbundling, often called "functional unbundling," a single corporation carries out monopoly and competitive businesses, in separate divisions using separate employees. FERC Order Nos. 888 and 889 allow a single utility corporation to provide both competitive wholesale generation and monopoly transmission service. To prevent anticompetitive conduct—such as inter-divisional sharing of information denied to competitors—FERC requires the company and its employees to comply with a Code of Conduct.[293]

6.5.4.1.2 *Corporate unbundling*

Sometimes referred to as "affiliate unbundling," "structural separation" or "structural safeguards," corporate unbundling requires a holding company to place its monopoly and competitive services in separate corporate affiliates. In the 1980s, FERC sought to make wholesale gas markets more competitive by requiring gas pipelines to provide nondiscriminatory transportation service (a utility service) unbundled from gas supply sales (a competitive service). With those services unbundled, independent marketing companies and local distribution companies could buy the transportation service from the monopoly pipeline while buying gas from unaffiliated competitive suppliers. Corporate families wishing to pursue both businesses—monopoly gas transportation and competitive wholesale gas sales—had to carry the latter business out through corporately separate "marketing affiliates." Similarly, states that authorized

---

[293] Discussed in Chapter 6.5.4.1.3 below. In the telecommunications industry, where incumbent companies provided both local wireline service (historically a state-protected monopoly) and long-distance service (emerging in the 1980s as a potentially competitive service), functional unbundling took the form of "non-structural safeguards." *See* Amendment of Section 64.702 of the Commission's Rules and Regulations (*Computer III*), 104 F.C.C.2d 958 (1986), *on recon.*, 2 FCC Rcd. 3035 (1987), *on further recon.*, 3 FCC Rcd. 1135 (1988), *on second further recon.*, 4 FCC Rcd. 5927 (1989), *vacated in part sub nom.* California v. FCC, 905 F.2d 1217 (9th Cir. 1990), *cert. denied*, 514 U.S. 1050 (1995) (vacating Report & Order and Order on Reconsideration). Like FERC's Code of Conduct, these safeguards restrict employee behavior rather than build structural walls. The primary *Computer III* non-structural safeguards included requirements for "comparably efficient interconnection" and "open network architecture." *See* PETER W. HUBER, MICHAEL K. KELLOGG & JOHN THORNE, FEDERAL TELECOMMUNICATIONS LAW § 12.5.2 (2d ed. 1999).

competition in retail gas or electricity sales have allowed their monopoly utilities to provide competitive retail service, but only through retail marketing affiliates corporately separate from the affiliate that provides the monopoly distribution service.[294]

Corporate separation differs from divisional separation because separate corporations, even when affiliated, have separate financial statements, separate debt financing and separate accounting. These features help the regulator detect cross-subsidies and favoritism, because any dealings must be backed by a contract and an invoice. Regulators can audit those documents, comparing their prices to competitive market prices. (Divisions, in contrast, simply share resources—bathrooms, lunch rooms, employees, overhead costs—making favoritism in access and pricing harder to detect). Corporate separation also allows each entity's managers and employees to focus on, and be rewarded or penalized based on, their own entity's business purpose and performance. Applying that logic, the California Commission required that, "[w]ith the exception of the fully-compensated sharing of a small number of corporate officers," the utility must have a "utility management team dedicated solely to utility activities." This solution prevented utility management from becoming "preoccupied with nonutility activities to the detriment of utility activities."[295]

Once competition has become effective, should regulators relax these structural limits? Doing so would be like removing seatbelts once traffic deaths

---

[294] Rhode Island requires separate affiliates for the competitive and non-competitive functions, unless the commission has granted a "public interest" exception. R.I. GEN. LAWS § 39-1-27(a). New Jersey requires Board approval for any mixing of competitive and non-competitive services within the same corporate family, with or without separate affiliates. The Board must ensure that (a) tariffs for the competitive services do not "adversely impact the ability of the electric public utility to offer its non-competitive services to customers in a safe, adequate and proper manner"; and that (b) those tariff prices are not lower than the fully allocated cost of the competitive service. N.J. STAT. ANN. § 48:3-55a. Fully allocated cost, sometimes called "fully distributed cost," refers to rates designed to recover all costs of production, both variable and fixed. *See* Associated Gas Distribs. v. FERC, 824 F.2d 981, 1007 (D.C. Cir. 1987) (defining fully allocated cost as a rate such that "if the pipeline carries projected volume at the specified unit price, it should exactly recover all costs allocable to the relevant service for the period") (citing 18 C.F.R. § 284.7(c)(3)).

Section 272 of the Communications Act, 47 U.S.C. § 272, added in 1996, prohibits a Bell operating company from engaging in certain manufacturing activities, and from providing certain long distance and information services, except through a separate affiliate that "operate[s] independently" of the utility affiliate. Most of section 272's structural separation requirements are subject to sunset. *See* 47 U.S.C. § 272(f)(1)–(2). That sunsetting does not remove the FCC authority under other provisions of the Act "to prescribe safeguards consistent with the public interest, convenience, and necessity." *See* 47 U.S.C. § 272(f)(3).

[295] Southern California Edison Co., 1988 Cal. PUC LEXIS 2, at *12.

have dropped. In the 1980s, the FCC relieved the Bell Operating Companies (BOC) of having to place their monopoly communications services in corporate affiliates separate from their unregulated competitive services. (This distinction was known as POTS vs. PANS—"plain old telephone service" vs. "pretty amazing new stuff.") The Commission reasoned that the enhanced service market had become "extremely competitive." The Ninth Circuit Court of Appeals struck the decision as arbitrary and capricious:

> Because competition in the unregulated enhanced services market does nothing to decrease the BOCs' monopoly power in the basic services market, we fail to see how it can diminish the BOCs' ability to shift costs to their regulated services without detection in ratemaking proceedings. If anything, increased competition in the enhanced services market simply increases the BOCs' incentive to shift costs so they can engage in predatory price-cutting as a means of maintaining or increasing their share of the market for enhanced services.[296]

6.5.4.1.3   Codes of conduct

Because separation does not remove temptation, commissions that require divisional or corporate separation add codes of conduct. These codes aim to make the monopoly-competitive relationship an arm's-length relationship.[297]

FERC's Order No. 717 applies to providers of pipeline transportation services and providers of electricity transmission (both called "transmission providers"), if they conduct "transmission transactions with an affiliate that engages in marketing functions." Order No. 717 established three main requirements:

1. The "transmission function employees must function independently from [the] marketing function employees, except as permitted in this part or otherwise permitted by Commission order."
2. A "transmission provider and its employees, contractors, consultants and agents are prohibited from disclosing, or using a conduit to disclose, non-public transmission function information to the transmission provider's marketing function employees."
3. The transmission provider must "provide equal access to non-public transmission function information disclosed to marketing function employees

---

[296]   California v. FCC, 905 F.2d 1217, 1234 (9th Cir. 1990) (emphases omitted).

[297]   Order No. 642, *supra* note 5, at 71,009 & n.105 (citing *San Diego Gas & Electric-Southern California Gas Merger*, 79 F.E.R.C. ¶ 61,372, at p. 62,565 (1997)) (explaining the need to condition merger approvals on codes of conduct, including restrictions on affiliate transactions).

to all its transmission customers, affiliated and non-affiliated, except as permitted in this part or otherwise permitted by Commission order."[298]

States also have adopted codes. Ohio's retail electric competition statute prohibits an electric utility from engaging in both competitive and noncompetitive services, directly or through an affiliate, without a Commission-approved "corporate separation plan." The plan must create a level of corporate separation sufficient to prevent "unfair competitive advantage" and "the abuse of market power." There can be no "undue preference or advantage to any affiliate, division, or part of its own business" in the provision of "utility resources," including but not limited to "trucks, tools, office equipment, office space, supplies, customer and marketing information, advertising, billing and mailing systems, personnel and training."[299]

6.5.4.1.4 Management prerogative: Does it block structural limits?

When a commission requires separation of the non-utility business, has it exceeded its statutory authority to regulate the utility business? Public Service Company of New Mexico (PNM) wanted to offer its customers optional services: transient voltage surge suppression, appliance maintenance and repair, energy information services and power quality solutions. The utility would offer these services through an unincorporated division, subject to Commission-approved tariffs. The Commission rejected the proposal, citing the risks of cross-subsidies, utility liability for performance errors and unfair trade practices. If PNM reapplied through an unregulated corporate subsidiary, the Commission would reconsider. The utility appealed, arguing that the Commission had gone beyond regulating the utility; it was now trying to run the whole company—a violation of the management prerogative doctrine.[300] The New Mexico Supreme Court upheld the Commission. By requiring a separate subsidiary, the Commission was not exercising jurisdiction over non-utility activities; rather, it was carrying out its duty "to ensure that PNM [did] not engage in activities that could harm PNM's ability to set just and

---

[298] Order No. 717, *Standards of Conduct for Transmission Providers*, F.E.R.C. STATS. & REGS. ¶ 31,280, 73 Fed. Reg. 63,796 (2008); 18 C.F.R. § 358.2(b)-(d). FERC has defined "affiliate" to include a "division of the specified entity that operates as a functional unit." 18 C.F.R. § 358.3(a)(1).

[299] OHIO REV. CODE ANN. § 4928.17.

[300] Also called "management prerogative," "invasion of management" or, more colloquially, "regulators don't run companies," this doctrine limits the regulator's discretion to direct a utility's business activities.

reasonable rates."[301] Other cases reiterate the point: to protect utility customers, commissions can restrict a utility's non-utility activities.[302]

6.5.4.2   Limits on non-utility investments

Separate from structural separation are limits. Regulators and legislators can limit a utility system's non-utility investments, in terms of dollars, type of businesses or both. Limits reduce the incentive and opportunity to behave anticompetitively. They also reduce the risk that failures of the non-utility businesses will harm the utility business.[303]

6.5.4.2.1   *Dollar and percentage limits*

For limits on non-utility investments based on total dollars or percentages, consider these examples:

1. The California Commission prohibited a utility holding company from investing more than 15 percent of its total capital assets in non-utility subsidiaries, without notifying the Commission.[304]

---

[301] PNM Elec. Servs. v. N.M. Pub. Util. Comm'n, 961 P.2d 147, 149–51 (N.M. 1998).

[302] *See, e.g.*, Strawberry Prop. Owners Ass'n, v. Conlin-Strawberry Water Co., 1997 Cal. PUC LEXIS 954, at *1, *12–15 (ordering water company to "immediately replace" its manager after the company "suffer[ed] pump failures, water supply deficiency, lack of system alarms, inaccurate monthly water quality reporting, questionable daily monitoring, and non-use of an automated control system"); West Virginia-American Water Co., 2011 W. Va. PUC LEXIS 2425, at *7–8 (citing W. Va. Code § 24-3-7) (ordering water company not to carry out planned layoffs pending commission investigation into the layoffs' effect on water quality); General Tel. Co. v. Pub. Utils. Comm'n, 670 P.2d 349, 355–56 (Cal. 1983) (upholding commission order that utility use competitive bidding to replace outdated central office switching equipment, rather than purchase from affiliate). *But see* Mountain States Tel. & Tel. Co. v. Pub. Serv. Comm'n, 745 P.2d 563, 571 (Wyo. 1987) (holding that the commission lacked power to order utility to use competitive bidding for a phone directory contract, which management had awarded to a sister company).

[303] *See, e.g.*, Southern California Edison Co., 1990 Cal. PUC LEXIS 847, at *38 (establishing limits because "new unregulated ventures should not impair the utility's ability to raise capital, its bond rating, etc. ... and [because they help] ... avoid[] ... any subsidization by the regulated entity (and thus its ratepayers) of the unregulated business"). *See generally* Judy Sheldrew, Note, *Shutting the Barn Door Before the Horse is Stolen: How and Why State Public Utility Commissions Should Regulate Transactions Between a Public Utility and Its Affiliates*, 4 Nev. L.J. 164, 167 (2003).

[304] San Diego Gas & Elec. Co., 1986 Cal. PUC LEXIS 198, *69–70.

2. The Arizona Corporation Commission limited a utility's investment in non-utility businesses to $25 million.[305]
3. Wisconsin law limits the "sum of the assets of all non-utility affiliates" to roughly 25 percent of the holding company system's utility assets.[306]
4. Maine law authorizes competition for retail electricity sales. It also allows the incumbent utility's affiliate to compete in the utility's monopoly service territory, provided the affiliate's sales don't exceed 33 percent of the total kilowatt-hours sold.[307]

6.5.4.2.2 Type-of-business limits

Wisconsin's statute allows a utility holding company affiliate to make unrestricted investments in certain energy-related businesses, but limits investments in other non-utility businesses. The list of permissible investments includes assets used for

1. "Producing, generating, transmitting, delivering, selling or furnishing gas, oil, electricity or steam energy";
2. "Providing an energy management, conservation or efficiency product or service or a demand-side management product or service";
3. "Providing an energy customer service, including metering or billing";
4. "Recovering or producing energy from waste materials";
5. "Processing waste materials";
6. "Manufacturing, distributing or selling products for filtration, pumping water or other fluids, processing or heating water, handling fluids or other related activities";
7. "Providing a telecommunications service"; and
8. "Providing an environmental engineering service."[308]

The now-repealed Public Utility Holding Company Act (PUHCA) 1935 limited most utility holding company systems to a single "integrated

---

[305] Tucson Elec. Power Co., 167 P.U.R.4th 221, 221–22 (Ariz. Corp. Comm'n 1996).

[306] WIS. STAT. § 196.795(6m)(b)(1)(a). *See also* WICOR, Inc., 1987 Wisc. PUC LEXIS 53, at *22 (describing investment cap as "reduc[ing] the pressure for funds from the utility" and "reducing the degree of financial risk from possible nonutility losses"). The Seventh Circuit upheld this portion of the Wisconsin statute against Commerce Clause challenge. Alliant Energy Corp. v. Bie, 330 F.3d 904, 919 (7th Cir. 2003). The author was a witness for the Wisconsin Attorney General in the U.S. District Court case leading to this Seventh Circuit decision.

[307] ME. STAT. tit. 35-A, § 3205(2)(B).

[308] WIS. STAT. § 196.795(6m)(a)(2).

public-utility system."[309] This restriction confined non-utility affiliates to activities that benefited the utility's performance. So-called "exempt" holding companies (mostly intrastate companies) could own non-utility businesses, but only if the ownership was not "detrimental to the public interest or the interest of investors or consumers."[310] The non-exempt holding companies (called "registered" holding companies, and consisting mainly of multi-state systems) faced a stricter limit: they could own, in addition to integrated public utilities, only "such other businesses as are reasonably incidental, or economically necessary or appropriate to the operations of [the holding company's] integrated public–utility system."[311] If a utility owned coal-burning generating units, its holding company could own a coal mine to service those units; but it could not own hotels and restaurants to house and feed the coal miners.

6.5.4.3 Divestiture of all competitive activities
The ultimate monopoly-competitive separation is divestiture—selling off either the monopoly or the competitive business to an unaffiliated company. Among the states introducing retail electricity competition, some induced or required their utilities to divest their generation assets. Competitive generators then could enter the market unworried about a generation-owning incumbent utility using its control of transmission and distribution facilities to discriminate against them.

6.5.4.4 Periodic competition for the right to provide the monopoly service
An incumbent utility is less likely to act anticompetitively if doing so risks having its franchise revoked in favor of a more deserving company. That risk is low today, because states have no habit of subjecting franchises to periodic competition. But they should keep that option open, by making clear that a merger approval creates or implies no right in the merged company (a) to

---

[309] PUHCA 1935 defined an electricity "integrated public-utility system" as a system consisting of one or more units of generating plants and/or transmission lines and/or distributing facilities, whose utility assets, whether owned by one or more electric utility companies, are physically interconnected or capable of physical interconnection and which under normal conditions may be economically operated as a single interconnected and coordinated system confined in its operations to a single area or region, in one or more states, not so large as to impair (considering the state of the art and the area or region affected) the advantages of localized management, efficient operation, and the effectiveness of regulation. ...

PUHCA 1935 § 2(a)(29)(A), 15 U.S.C. § 79b(a)(29)(A) (repealed 2005).

[310] *Id.* § 3(a).

[311] *Id.* § 11(b)(1).

continue providing the current monopoly services, or (b) to provide any new monopoly services. No one should acquire control of a utility franchise thinking they are entitled to keep it forever.

To make credible the possibility that utility misbehavior will result in franchise revocation, state commissions will need the statutory authority and expertise to take these four steps:

Determine the franchise's term of years: The term needs to be long enough to prevent distorted decision-making (e.g., putting off capital expenditures to keep rates low); and short enough to make utility management responsive to customers' needs.

Determine the competitive procedure and ranking criteria: Commissions need to establish pre-qualification standards, so they can screen contestants objectively for experience, skill and financial strength. Then come the subjectivities: Does each contestant have a corporate culture that places public service first—one that accepts regulation's mission and role? Is there a business plan that identifies the products and services customers need and the most cost-effective means to design and deliver them? (Commissions will need to provide all prospective contestants with essential data about the service territory and customer base; otherwise the incumbent will have an unearned advantage in the franchise competition.)

Establish, in advance, post-selection regulatory policies: Commissions need to describe the expectations, rewards and penalties that will likely apply during the franchise term. Only that way can prospective contestants project their risks and their earnings. While policymakers can't pour cement around their policies—change is inevitable—they should promise that reasonable costs incurred to accommodate changes will be recoverable from customers.

Establish legal path and appropriate price for asset transfer: State statutes will need to create a litigation-free process for transferring the incumbent utility's assets to its successor. At what price? Since these assets' value is connected to serving the service territory's customers, and since the incumbent will be losing the privilege of serving those customers, the assets have no value in the incumbent's hands. In the new franchisee's hands, their value is the net present value of the stream of earnings available from selling electricity at rates set by the commission. That net present value should not depart much from the assets' book cost, since in cost-based ratemaking book cost is the basis for the rates that produce the stream of earnings. By establishing the transfer price in advance, and basing it on book cost, the commission would prevent a bidding war based on price—the central policy flaw described in Chapter 4.1. With the purchase price fixed by the Commission, contestants can design their bids to serve the public rather than to please incumbent shareholders.

6.5.5   Inter-affiliate Pricing: Enforcing the Arm's-length Principle to Prevent Cross-subsidization

[O]ne must wonder whether Consumers [Power Company] has once again negotiated with itself and lost.[312]

By making its monopoly utility subsidiary overpay or undercharge its competitive affiliates, a holding company can both increase its earnings and give those competitive affiliates an unearned advantage. These inter-affiliate transactions have two dimensions: parties and products. The parties are the utility and a non-utility affiliate; in any transaction either party can be seller or buyer. The products can be utility products or non-utility products. Combining these two dimensions yields four transaction categories. For each category, this subsection provides an illustration, identifies the risks and describes the common regulatory solution. Then it describes three types of affiliate transactions that have special solutions: asset uses, employee transfers and financial transactions.[313]

---

[312]   Midland Cogeneration Venture Ltd., 1989 Mich. PUC LEXIS 176, at *48.

[313]   In 2005, Congress added to Section 203 of the Federal Power Act a requirement that the transaction "not result in cross-subsidization of a non-utility associate company or the pledge or encumbrance of utility assets for the benefit of an associate company, unless the Commission determines that the cross-subsidization, pledge, or encumbrance will be consistent with the public interest." Federal Power Act § 203(a)(4), 16 U.S.C. § 824b(a)(4). To implement this provision, FERC issued rules in Order No. 669, *Transactions Subject to FPA Section 203*, F.E.R.C. STATS. & REGS. ¶ 31,200, 71 Fed. Reg. 1348, *order on reh'g*, Order No. 669-A, F.E.R.C. STATS. & REGS. ¶ 31,214, 71 Fed. Reg. 28,422, *order on reh'g*, Order No. 669-B, F.E.R.C. STATS. & REGS. ¶ 31,225, 71 Fed. Reg. 42,579 (2006).

One problem: FERC's merger decisions have never defined "cross-subsidization." Given the political content of the term, and even its multiple uses by experts, I share here what I was taught by economists years ago. Suppose the holding company wants to use its monopoly transmission service to subsidize its competitive generation service. It will force purchasers of the transmission service to pay a price exceeding the standalone (fully allocated) book cost of the transmission service, then use the excess revenues to lower the price of generation below its incremental cost. That is the technically correct definition of cross-subsidy—charging the captive customer a price above the fully allocated cost, then charging the competitive customer a price below the incremental cost. But many people, including even experts, use the term cross-subsidy when referring to an allocation of sunk costs disproportionate to load responsibility. In the political realm, "cross-subsidy" is the term used when Person X pays, unhappily, for something that benefits Person Y. As former U.S. Senate Finance Chairman Russell Long has been quoted as saying: "Don't tax him, don't tax me; tax that fellow behind the tree."

More detail: Incremental cost is the "added cost to the producer of a small amount of incremental output." 2 KAHN, *supra* note 29, at 66. "Fully allocated cost," sometimes called "fully distributed cost," refers to rates designed to recover all costs of production,

6.5.5.1 Four scenarios

6.5.5.1.1 Sale by the utility to the non-utility affiliate, of utility services
An affiliate can lower its competitive product prices by using resources paid for by the utility's captive ratepayers. Southern California Edison's competitive affiliates openly attributed their success in part to having "a financially strong and highly reputable parent ... [and] easy access to Edison's management employees and their expertise." The affiliates had no need to "maintain[] expensive staffs of experts, office space, and associated support functions."[314]

Illustration—wholesale electricity: A utility's affiliated wholesale marketer receives FERC permission to sell electricity at market-based rates. The utility, using generating capacity paid for by its captive retail customers, sells surplus electricity to the affiliated wholesale marketer at a price equal to the utility's incremental cost of 2 cents/kWh. Assume that the utility's fully allocated cost is 5 cents/kWh. Now assume that the wholesale market price is 11 cents/kWh. By paying 2 cents and charging 11 cents, the wholesale affiliate can make a large profit. Or it can discount, all the way down to 2 cents, to kill its competitors.

Risks: This low inter-affiliate price of 2 cents causes two harms. First, paying only incremental cost gives the marketing affiliate an unearned advantage in wholesale markets, because non-utility competitors have to bear their own fully allocated cost to produce comparable power. Second, by allowing the wholesale marketing affiliate to keep the entire difference between the utility's 2 cent incremental cost and the 11 cent market price, the inter-affiliate transaction deprives the utility's customers of benefits that match their historic burdens. They paid rates to support the full cost of the infrastructure whose higher market value now allows the competitive affiliate to increase its profit without bearing risk.

Solution: For this utility's sales to its affiliate, most commissions would apply a higher-of-cost-or-market rule. They would require a sales price of 11 cents; alternatively, when setting the utility's rates they would impute to the utility sales revenue of 11 cents times the volume sold to the competitive affiliate. This approach puts the affiliate on the same cost plane as its competitors, while compensating the utility's customers for their historic burdens.[315]

---

both variable and fixed, including a profit on investment. *See* Associated Gas Distribs. v. FERC, 824 F.2d 981, 1007 (D.C. Cir. 1987).

[314] Southern California Edison Co., 1988 Cal. PUC LEXIS 2, at *20.

[315] *See, e.g.,* Tucson Elec. Power Co., 1995 WL 627726 (Ariz. Corp. Comm'n 1995) (applying higher-of-market-or-cost pricing standard to affiliate transactions); San Diego Gas & Elec. Co., 1995 Cal. PUC LEXIS 931 (same); Pacific Bell, 1992 Cal. PUC LEXIS 676 (same); *PSColorado-Southwestern Public Service Merger I,* 75

This rule also aligns with the prudence standard, since a prudent utility with surplus would have minimized its customers' cost by selling the surplus at the highest possible price—11 cents—then using the revenue to reduce its revenue requirement.

Some utilities defend the incremental cost price (the 2 cents in the illustration) on grounds of economic efficiency: pricing at incremental cost does not produce overconsumption of the service, they say, because the price is not below "cost." But incremental pricing still undermines effective competition because it gives the competitive affiliate an unearned advantage—access to a price below the fully allocated cost that its unaffiliated competitors have to bear.

Even setting the inter-affiliate price at fully allocated book cost (5 cents in the above example) undermines effective competition. Fully allocated book cost, like incremental cost, does prevent cross subsidies—in the narrow sense that because the price covers incremental costs, the utility's captive customers do not see an increase in cost (which would occur if electricity costing 2 cents to produce was sold to the affiliate at 1.5 cents). Fully allocated book cost also can eliminate some of the affiliate's competitive advantage; at least it can't lower its price all the way down to 2 cents. But an unearned advantage remains. The proper sales price is the higher of cost or market—11 cents.

Utilities have made two other arguments against higher-of-cost-or-market. First, they say that inter-affiliate pricing at fully allocated cost is common in unregulated industries. But in those industries, inter-affiliate pricing plays a different role. Unregulated businesses use inter-affiliate pricing to allocate costs; they allocate costs to assess the productivity and internal profitability of different business activities. That assessment requires a home for every cost; cost allocation determines those homes. So cost allocation doesn't set the prices for the competitive market; the market sets the prices. But in the regulated context, cost allocation does set prices, because the allocated cost enters the revenue requirement that forms the basis for regulated rates. The second utility argument against the higher-of-market-or-book rule is this: the combined company can afford to grant this favor to the competitive affiliate because the combined company has economies of scale and scope; adjusting the inter-affiliate price upwards denies the competitive affiliate the benefits of those economies of scale and scope. But those economies don't come from performance merit; they come from the state's decision to grant the utility an

---

F.E.R.C. ¶ 61,325, at p. 62,046 n.23 (1996) (requiring that sales of non-power goods and services by a utility to its affiliates be priced at the higher of the utility's cost or the electricity's market value); *Duke/Louis Dreyfus L.L.C.*, 73 F.E.R.C. ¶ 61,309, at pp. 61,868–69 (1995) (discussing FERC's inter-affiliate transaction rules), *order on reh'g*, 75 F.E.R.C. ¶ 61,325 (1996).

exclusive service territory whose size makes the economies of scale and scope possible.

Conclusion on sale by utility to non-utility affiliate of utility service: Pricing a sale from the utility to the competitive affiliate at market value achieves all objectives: it reflects and induces economic efficiency, avoids cross-subsidy, promotes effective competition and minimizes the revenue requirement imposed on utility customers.

6.5.5.1.2 Sale by the utility to the non-utility affiliate, of non-utility services

Illustration—office rental: The utility's competitive affiliate is a real estate development company. It rents space in the utility's headquarters building. Suppose the utility's incremental cost for space (i.e., the cost of heating it and cleaning it daily) is $5/sq. foot. Suppose the space's fully allocated cost (mortgage, taxes, annual repairs, along with the incremental cost) is $24/sq. foot. Finally, assume the market rents in comparable buildings nearby are $35/ sq. foot.

Risk: The risks repeat the first example. Renting at $5 would avoid a utility loss but would cover incremental cost only, defraying no fixed costs. Renting at $24 would cover all costs, sunk and incremental, but make no profit for the ratepayers, whose rates cover, and have historically covered, the headquarters' full cost. Renting at $35 would align the utility's revenue with its responsibilities (maximizing revenue for the ratepayer)—while placing the competitive affiliate on the same cost plane as its non-utility competitors—all of whom have to pay market rents.

Solution: As with the first example, by charging its affiliate the market price of $35, the utility satisfies its duty to minimize its customers' costs; it does so by maximizing its revenue. If the utility could charge a non-affiliate $35, it must charge the same to its affiliate. Any lower price gives the affiliate an unearned advantage over its real estate competitors, who have to pay $35/sq. foot.[316]

Another illustration—customer information: The non-utility competitive affiliate installs home alarms in the utility's service territory. It needs data on prospective customers: names, addresses, consumption levels (as a proxy for home size) and payment history. A non-affiliate would have to spend many hours and dollars to gather just the names and addresses; it would have no access to data on consumption and payment history. If the utility gave away this data to its competitive affiliate, charging only the incremental cost

---

[316] *Cf.* WIS. STAT. § 196.795(5)(dr) ("No public utility affiliate may provide any nonutility product or service in a manner or at a price that unfairly discriminates against any competing provider of the product or service.").

of organizing and transmitting it, the competitive affiliate would have an unearned advantage. Meanwhile the utility's ratepayers would receive none of the data's market value, though they paid in rates for the utility's original cost to create it.

The Texas Commission had the right solution. In approving the merger of Southwestern Public Service (SPS) and New Centuries, the Commission required that if SPS

> shares any information with its affiliates regarding customer energy service needs, such information shall be available to all other competitors and such affiliates shall pay market prices for such information so that they do not receive a competitive advantage. If SPS shares any other information related to strategic planning or retail markets with its affiliates, such information shall be shared equally with all other competitive resource bidders.[317]

And another illustration—fiber optic cable: To install its transmission and distribution lines, a utility buys rights-of-way, recovering the costs from its ratepayers. Five years later, the utility's telecommunications affiliate wants to string fiber optic cable on the rights-of-way. What price should the utility charge its affiliate: incremental cost (zero); book cost (the utility's original cost of purchasing the rights-of-way); or the now higher fair market value? The standard solution is fair market value: since the ratepayers have borne the burden, they receive the reward. The fair market value price also denies the affiliate an unfair advantage over its competitors.

6.5.5.1.3   Sale by the non-utility affiliate to the utility, of utility services

Illustration—sale of wholesale power: The utility has a "merchant" generation affiliate—a company with no franchise obligation to serve, so no guaranteed customer base and no guaranteed revenues. This affiliate owns a generating unit, from which it sells electricity to the affiliated monopoly utility, which resells the electricity to its captive customers. Suppose the non-utility affiliate's incremental cost is 2 cents/kWh, its fully allocated cost

---

[317] Southwestern Public Service-PSColorado Merger, 1997 Tex. PUC LEXIS 4, at *16–17. Concern about customer data privacy is outside the scope of this discussion of mergers' effects on competition, but worth the reader's pursuit. For a discussion of the tradeoffs between profit and privacy in the regulated utility context, see *Fair Information Practice Principles*, FED. TRADE COMM'N, https://web.archive.org/web/20090331134113/http://www.ftc.gov/reports/privacy3/fairinfo.shtm (archived Sept. 10, 2013); SHERRY LICHTENBERG, NAT'L REGULATORY RESEARCH INST., SMART GRID DATA: MUST THERE BE CONFLICT BETWEEN ENERGY MANAGEMENT AND CONSUMER PRIVACY? (2010), https://pubs.naruc.org/pub/FA86CF1A-E9F2-69CA-E93F-1B5E56D116B9.

(which includes a reasonable profit on the investment) is 5 cents/kWh, and the wholesale market price is 11 cents.

Risk: The non-utility affiliate wants to charge the utility 11 cents, to maximize earnings for the holding company's shareholders. But the utility could have built the generating unit itself, then charged its customers only 5 cents. Buying from its affiliate rather than building the unit itself, the utility fails to minimize its customers' costs.

Solution: When the non-utility affiliate sells to the utility, regulators typically require a price of "lower of cost or market." They reason that if the non-utility can build and operate a unit at a cost below market (in this example, 5 cents), so can a prudent utility. Without this rule, the holding company system could move activities from the utility to the affiliate—using corporate structure to increase shareholder return at customer expense.[318] So the proper inter-affiliate price is the lower of book cost or market—5 cents. This price places the utility customer, and the utility, in the same position they would have been in had the utility made the investment.

On these merchant affiliate sales to retail monopoly utilities, FERC has raised a different concern: if the merchant affiliate has preferred access to its affiliated utility's resources, wholesale competitors will not likely enter the market—leaving the merchant affiliate free to raise its prices above competitive levels. To prevent that weakening of market forces, FERC created the *Edgar Electric* requirement. If the merchant wholesale affiliate wants to charge a market price for a sale to an affiliated utility with captive customers, the wholesale affiliate must show one of three things:

1. that it won the sale in direct head-to-head competition with competing unaffiliated suppliers, through either a formal solicitation or an informal negotiation process—thereby demonstrating that market forces disciplined the merchant affiliate's prices;
2. evidence that the proposed price resembles prices that nonaffiliated buyers were willing to pay for similar services from the merchant affiliate; or
3. benchmark evidence, showing that proposed price, terms and conditions resembled those for sales made by non-affiliated sellers in that market.[319]

---

[318] *Cf.* WIS. STAT. § 196.795(5)(dm) ("No public utility affiliate may provide utility service to any consumer of such public utility service or to any nonutility affiliate with which the public utility affiliate is in a holding company system except on the same terms or conditions that it provides such utility service to consumers in the same class.").

[319] *Edgar Elec. Energy Co.*, 55 F.E.R.C. ¶ 61,382 (1991). The Commission later added that "these [three] examples were not an all-inclusive list; the individual facts of a case could bring forth other examples not expressed in *Edgar* to show that a transac-

And if the seller relies on a formal solicitation (option #1 above), the solicitation must have four features:

1. Transparency: The competitive solicitation process should be open and fair.
2. Definition: The product or products sought through the competitive solicitation should be precisely defined.
3. Evaluation: Evaluation criteria should be standardized and applied equally to all bids and bidders.
4. Oversight: An independent third party should design the solicitation, administer bidding and evaluate bids prior to the company's selection.[320]

While *Edgar Electric* applied this requirement to sales by affiliates at market-based rates, the Commission later applied the requirement to all affiliate wholesale sales, whether cost-based or market-based.[321]

6.5.5.1.4 Sale by the non-utility affiliate to the utility, of non-utility services

Illustration: The utility has an affiliated real estate development company. That company owns a building from which it rents space to the utility. The real estate company's incremental cost for the space is $5, and the fully allocated cost is $24/sq. foot. Market rents in that area are $35/sq. foot.

Risk: To maximize earnings, the real estate affiliate will want to charge the utility $35.

Solution: Applying the lower-of-cost-or-market rule, most regulators will set (or impute) rent at $24. If the utility pre-existed the real estate affiliate, the utility could have built its own building at a cost of $24; a rent of $35 siphons funds from utility customers to the shareholders. But the appropriateness of this solution depends on the facts. If the utility was new to town, and if all its options were $35, paying that price to its affiliate does no harm. The better solution, though, is for the utility to host a competitive bidding process, run by an independent party, to ensure that the final price is a competitive market price.[322]

---

tion is without affiliate abuse." *Ameren Energy Generating Co.*, 108 F.E.R.C. ¶ 61,081 at P 12 n.14 (2004).

[320] *Id.* at P 70.

[321] *Id.* at P 69; *Southern California Edison Co.*, 109 F.E.R.C. ¶ 61,086 (2004) (requiring application of *Edgar Electric* to cost-based affiliates sales because cost-based rates could exceed market-based rates). FERC now applies these *Edgar* requirements not only to affiliate-to-utility power sales but also to affiliate-to-utility asset transfers. *Ameren Energy Generating Co.*, *supra* note 319.

[322] *But see* Mountain States Tel. & Tel. Co. v. Pub. Serv. Comm'n, 745 P.2d 563, 571 (Wyo. 1987) (holding that Wyoming Commission lacked power to order utility to use competitive bidding for a phone directory contract).

* * *

Subject to the same principles but involving special complexity are three other types of inter-affiliate transactions: financial transactions, employee transfers and transfers of intangibles, each discussed next.

6.5.5.2 Financial transactions

Inter-affiliate financial transactions include direct money transfers (e.g., dividend payments, equity investments or loans); and indirect financial support (e.g., guarantees of indebtedness, or pledging of one affiliate's assets to support another affiliate's debt). In any of these transactions, the holding company could make the utility giver or taker. Four examples:

1. The holding company injects equity into, or loans money to, the utility.
2. The utility makes dividend payments to its holding company owner.
3. The utility loans money to a non-utility affiliate.
4. The utility guarantees the debt of a non-utility affiliate, or pledges the utility's assets as security for that affiliate's debt.

A utility should bear no financial costs or risks associated with non-utility affiliates. Applying that principle, along with the higher-of-cost-or-market and lower-of-cost-or-market rules described in the previous subsection, yields these straightforward results:

1. If the holding company or non-utility affiliate lends money to the utility, the interest rate should be the lower of the lender's actual cost or the market interest rate.
2. A utility's dividend payments to its holding company owner should leave the utility (a) with a debt-equity ratio sufficient to maintain good credit ratings, and (b) with enough retained earnings to finance (along with debt) its capital expenditures cost-effectively.
3. Under no circumstances should the utility make loans to, or guarantee the debt of, an affiliate, unless the affiliate is supplying the utility with a necessary input like fuel.[323] Otherwise the utility's ratepayers bear non-utility risks, while the utility's competitive affiliate gets an unearned advantage.

---

[323] *See, e.g.*, Wis. Stat. § 196.795(5)(c) ("No public utility affiliate may lend money to any holding company which is not a public utility or to any nonutility affiliate with which it is in the holding company system."); *id.* § 196.795(5)(d) ("No public utility affiliate may guarantee the obligations of any nonutility affiliate with which it is in a holding company system.").

Special problem—cash management programs: Utility holding companies use these programs to make short-term cash available to their subsidiaries. The programs take several forms:

1. Some programs "concentrate and transfer funds from multiple accounts into a single bank account in the parent company's name."
2. Some programs use "a single summary account with interest earned or charged on the net cash balance position[, where there] is no movement of funds between accounts of the entities participating in the pool" (a practice known as a cash pooling or money pooling).
3. The program can be a "zero balance account, [which] empties or fills the balances in an affiliated company's account at a bank into or out of a parent's account each day."[324]

Investigating these programs in the early 2000s, FERC discovered that gas and electric companies under its jurisdiction had about $16 billion in cash management accounts in 2002, increasing to $25 billion in 2003—"an enormous, mostly unregulated, pool of money ... that may [have] detrimentally affect[ed] regulated rates."[325] The Commission also found over $1 billion in fund transfers "between regulated pipeline affiliates and non-regulated parents whose financial conditions were precarious."[326] The programs had no written agreements and faced only "minimal" regulatory scrutiny. Based on these facts, FERC saw a "potential for degradation of the financial solvency of regulated entities if non-regulated parent companies declare[d] bankruptcy and default[ed] on the accounts payable, advances or borrowings owed to their regulated subsidiaries."[327] To reduce this risk, FERC now requires all cash management agreements to be in writing. Utilities must keep records of all deposits and borrowings. They also must prepare documents describing the duties of program participants and administrators, the methods for calculating interest, the methods for allocating interest income and expenses among affiliates, and any restrictions on participants' deposits or borrowings.[328]

---

[324] Order No. 634, *Regulation of Cash Management Practices*, F.E.R.C. Stats. & Regs. ¶ 31,145, 68 Fed. Reg. 40,500, 40,500 (2003) [hereinafter Order No. 634].

[325] Order No. 634-A, *Regulation of Cash Management Practices*, F.E.R.C. Stats. & Regs. ¶ 31,152, 68 Fed. Reg. 61,993, 61,996 (2003) [hereinafter Order No. 634-A].

[326] Order No. 634, *supra* note 324, at 40,501.

[327] Notice of Proposed Rulemaking, *Regulation of Cash Management Practices*, 67 Fed. Reg. 51,150, 51,151 ¶ 9 (2002).

[328] Order No. 634, *supra* note 324; Order No. 634-A, *supra* note 325.

6.5.5.3 Employee transfers

Utility employees have high value—years of experience, and knowledge ranging from generating unit heat rates to neighborhood-level consumption patterns. A utility holding company has incentive and opportunity to spread that value to its non-utility affiliates. But doing so diverts employees from their utility tasks, fails to compensate ratepayers for the dollars they paid to create that value and gives the non-utility affiliates an unearned advantage over competitors that have no captive ratepayers to fund their learning curves.

The California Commission addressed this problem by

1. prohibiting the utility and any non-utility affiliate from employing the same individual simultaneously;
2. prohibiting an employee who moves to an affiliate from returning to the utility for one year, unless the affiliate goes out of business; and if the employee does return to the utility, prohibiting her from moving back to the affiliate for two years;
3. when a utility employee transfers to an affiliate, requiring that the affiliate pay the utility 25 percent of the employee's base compensation unless the affiliate can prove the appropriateness of a lower percentage (with a 15 percent minimum); and
4. prohibiting temporary, intermittent or rotating assignments between the utility and its affiliates.[329]

Wisconsin's holding company statute takes a different tack. It allows a non-utility affiliate to use a utility employee under three conditions: (a) the arrangement is in writing and approved by the Commission; (b) the affiliate pays the utility the employee's fair market value; and (c) the Commission finds that the arrangement has no anticompetitive effect on any competitor of the non-utility affiliate. The Commission may reject the arrangement if it finds that (a) "the potential burden of administering" the contract exceeds the "potential benefits to the [utility's] customers"; or (b) the affiliated utility "has not minimized the use of such employees" by non-utility affiliates.[330]

6.5.5.4 Transfers of intangibles: the royalty solution

Inter-affiliate pricing rules work best when applied to products and services that are tangible and quantifiable—like power, land, office space and employees. What about the intangibles and the non-quantifiables? A non-utility affiliate benefits from the utility's name recognition, goodwill and implicit

---

[329] Standards of Conduct Governing Relationships Between Utilities and Their Affiliates, 1997 Cal. PUC LEXIS 1139.

[330] WIS. STAT. § 196.795(5)(r).

financial backing—benefits made possible by decades of involuntary ratepayer support, none of it available to unaffiliated competitors. To address this source of unearned advantage, the New York Commission imputed to the utility's retail revenue requirement a royalty payment made by the non-utility affiliate to the utility:

> Because ratepayers have funded the salaries, training, advertising, and other activities that generate good will, they are entitled to rate recognition of revenues received by the utility in exchange for the use of that asset by an affiliate or otherwise. Where the asset is used and no revenues are received in exchange, an imputation may well be warranted. ...
>
> ... A utility in an arms-length transaction could be expected to receive revenues for allowing the use of its employees or goodwill, and our statutory obligation to set just and reasonable rates permits us to impute such revenues ... where they are not in fact received.[331]

For legal support, the Commission cited the seminal case of *Hope Natural Gas*,[332] which held that the statutory just and reasonable standard, and the Due Process Clause (applying the Fifth Amendment's Takings Clause to the states), require no particular rate method. The Commission also held that the imputed royalty payment was not an unconstitutional taking without just compensation, because shareholders have no reasonable investment-backed expectation of keeping for themselves the full value of an affiliate's relationship with a regulated utility.[333]

6.5.6   Timing of Merger Conditions

This Chapter 6.5 has provided regulatory solutions to horizontal and vertical market power, to the simultaneous presence of monopoly and competitive activities in the same corporate structure, and to the risks from inter-affiliate transactions between utility and non-utility affiliates. There remains a question of timing: When should commissions impose these protections? Conditions that mitigate market power must be in place at and during the time any affiliate within the holding company system has market power. This principle has three implications.

---

[331] Rochester Telephone Corp., 1993 N.Y. PUC LEXIS 13, *44–45.

[332] FPC v. Hope Nat. Gas Co., 320 U.S. 591 (1944).

[333] *Rochester Telephone Corp.*, 1993 N.Y. PUC LEXIS 13, at *44. *See also* Germantown Tel. Co., 1996 N.Y. PUC LEXIS 23, at *6 (reserving for ratepayers an imputed royalty because the utility's reputation will benefit the unregulated affiliate and because the affiliation puts ratepayers at risk of the "diversion of managerial attention and regulated resources").

First, the merging companies should have the protections in place before they merge. To address market power concerns, Duke Energy and Progress Energy proposed a virtual divestiture,[334] along with an independent entity to monitor their post-merger conduct. FERC required the merging companies to commit that the independent entity be approved by the Commission, that it would run a public, transparent electronic platform and that all terms of the monitoring arrangement be in place prior to consummation.[335]

Second, the regulator should retain the power to add or modify conditions if the original ones become ineffective. When Enron sought to acquire Portland General Electric (PGE), intervenors objected that Enron could exercise vertical market power by withholding or over-pricing gas sales to PGE's gas-fired wholesale generating competitors. FERC did not impose vertical market power conditions, but did reserve the power to address any misbehavior.[336]

Third, not all market concentration is permanent. New transmission can dilute a merged company's market share by expanding the market's geographic boundaries. When it does, a merger condition of virtual divestiture can terminate. But if boundary expansion is unlikely, the appropriate divestiture is not virtual and temporary, but actual and permanent. When future facts are unclear, therefore, regulators do not commit to a date for removing remedies. In the Duke-Progress Energy merger, applicants proposed their virtual divestiture remedy for eight years, a period they argued was "more than ample" for new entrants to site and build gas-fired or renewable generators. Finding the "more than ample" claim unsupported, FERC rejected the eight-year limit and left the end date open.[337]

---

[334] A concept described in Chapter 6.5.2 above.

[335] *Duke Energy-Progress Energy Merger II*, 137 F.E.R.C. ¶ 61,210 at P 90 (2011) (explaining that the Commission "is not pre-disposed towards accepting post-merger updates or imposing filing requirements designed to ensure the adequacy and completeness of Applicants' commitments"; for the Commission to find a transaction "consistent with the public interest," it must evaluate whether the monitoring arrangement "will ensure adequate oversight of the mitigation proposal"), *reh'g denied*, 149 F.E.R.C. ¶ 61,078 (2014). *But see* Puget Sound Power & Light-Washington Natural Gas Merger, 1997 Wash. UTC LEXIS 6, at *59 (approving merger despite uncertainty about effects on future retail competition, and requiring merged company to establish, with input from Staff and others, "a program to monitor competitive impacts of the merger for all services, not just distribution").

[336] *Enron-Portland General Merger*, 78 F.E.R.C. ¶ 61,179, at pp. 61,733–34 (1997) (citing FERC's authority under section 203(b) to, "from time to time for good cause shown[,] make such orders supplemental to any order made under [that] section as it may find necessary or appropriate," and further noting opportunities for complainants to seek revocation of Enron's permission to charge market-based rates).

[337] 137 F.E.R.C. ¶ 61,210 at 16.

* * *

"Competition" has two meanings. It is a type of market structure, with variations ranging from pure competition to hard monopoly. Competition is also a process involving seller conduct—a process in which rivals vie for customers' favor, differentiating themselves by price, quality and other factors. What works best for buyers, sellers and the general economy is effective competition. Effective competition is competition on the merits. Under effective competition, there is no market power, no anticompetitive conduct and no unearned advantages.

Mergers affect both market structure and seller conduct. Horizontal mergers reduce the number of competitors; vertical mergers can give the merged company control of inputs needed by their competitors. Protecting competition on the merits means screening mergers for market power, while establishing conditions that prevent anticompetitive conduct and eliminate unearned advantages.

Art Buchwald's column, reprinted from Justice Douglas's concurrence in *United States v. Pabst Brewing Co.*, 384 U.S. 546, 593–94 (1966)

By this time every company west of the Mississippi will have merged into one giant corporation known as Samson Securities. Every company east of the Mississippi will have merged under an umbrella corporation known as the Delilah Company.

It is inevitable that one day the chairman of the board of Samson and the president of Delilah would meet and discuss merging their two companies.

"If we could get together," the president of Delilah said, "we would be able to finance your projects and you would be able to finance ours."

"Exactly what I was thinking," the chairman of Samson said.

"That's a great idea and it certainly will make everyone's life less complicated."

The men shook on it and then they sought out approval from the Anti-Trust Division of the Justice Department.

At first the head of the Anti-Trust Division indicated that he might have reservations about allowing the only two companies left in the United States to merge.

"Our department will take a close look at this proposed merger. It is our job to further competition in private business and industry, and if we allow Samson and Delilah to merge we may be doing the consumer a disservice."

The chairman of Samson protested vigorously that merging with Delilah would not stifle competition, but would help it.

"The public will be the true beneficiary of this merger. The larger we are, the more services we can perform, and the lower prices we can charge."

The president of Delilah backed him up.

"In the Communist system the people don't have a choice. They must buy from the state. In our capitalistic society the people can buy from either the Samson Company or the Delilah Company."

"But if you merge," someone pointed out, "there will be only one company left in the United States."

"Exactly," said the president of Delilah. "Thank God for the free enterprise system."

7. Hierarchical conflict harms customers

Chapter 6 explained how mergers can harm competition. Harming competition harms customers. Mergers can also harm customers in other ways. Three sources of harm are merger cost overcharges, acquisition debt risk and non-utility business risk. Before addressing these three problems, this chapter describes their common source: the inherent conflict between the parent company's business goals and the subsidiary utility's service obligations.

7.1 PARENT-UTILITY CONFLICT: BUSINESS DIFFERENCES, HIERARCHICAL CONTROL

Most mergers make the target utility a subsidiary of a multi-business parent. The resulting parent-utility relationship involves multiple conflicts, arising from four sources: differences in objectives, hierarchical control, pressure for "growth," and market power.[1] A common regulatory response, requiring independent directors, does not remove these problems because regulators misunderstand what independence means.

7.1.1 Holding Company and Utility Subsidiary: Differing Objectives

A utility's corporate board must fulfill two main legal duties: its fiduciary duty to maximize value for its holding company shareholder, and its utility law duty to provide reliable service to its customers at just and reasonable rates. These two duties present no inherent conflict, because any company's fiduciary duty to its shareholders is always constrained by other laws: child labor law, hazardous waste law, tax law, minimum wage law—and utility law.

While a utility board has no inherent conflict, its holding company does. Unlike its utility subsidiaries, the holding company has no statutory obligation

---

[1]   *See, e.g.*, Order Instituting Rulemaking Concerning Relationship Between California Energy Utilities and Their Holding Companies and Non-Regulated Affiliates, 2006 Cal. PUC LEXIS 241, at *4–5 ("[C]ircumstances which create conflicts for the utilities between serving their customers or helping their holding companies and other affiliates are becoming more widespread."); Alliant Energy Co. v. Bie, 330 F.3d 904, 917 (7th Cir. 2003) ("The more products a firm is responsible for, the easier it is for the firm to misreport the allocation of its costs.").

to utility customers. Nor has it any statutory obligation to provide the utility with equity and debt at reasonable cost. With the 2005 repeal of the Public Utility Holding Company Act of 1935 (PUHCA),[2] the holding company parent—with rare exceptions—is not subject to any utility-type regulation, federal or state. Free of statutory obligations, its goals can conflict with the utility's obligations. Consider two examples.

1. The utility's need for equity: As the utility's sole shareholder, the parent is the utility's sole source of equity. But while the utility has a legal obligation to serve, the holding company has no legal obligation to invest. Most state statutes give the state commission authority over the utility only, not the holding company; moreover, state and FERC merger approval orders rarely impose on the parent any obligation to support all the utility's needs financially.[3] So the parent always has a choice: put money in the utility or put it elsewhere. The parent will make the choice that maximizes system-wide profit. The utility's cost-effectiveness will compete with other holding company goals.

2. The destination of the utility's profits: By selling service at commission-set rates, a prudent utility earns a reasonable profit. That profit's destination is determined by the parent, which can order the utility to:

- keep the profit within the utility as retained earnings, ready to finance utility capital expenditures that earn more profit;
- send dividends to the parent, so that parent can invest them in other businesses, use them to retire debt or pay them out to the ultimate shareholders—leaving the utility dependent on the parent for future equity; or
- use the profit to provide financial support to other holding company affiliates—leaving the utility vulnerable to those affiliates' losses, and dependent on the parent for more equity.

The holding company will choose among these options based on its strategic goals, not on the utility customers' needs. That is the source of the conflict.[4]

---

[2]   Public Utility Holding Company Act of 1935, Pub. L. No. 74-333, 49 Stat. 803, *repealed by* the Energy Policy Act of 2005, Pub. L. No. 109-58, § 1263, 119 Stat. 594, 974.

[3]   A common merger condition requires the utility to maintain a specified equity-debt ratio. Besides applying only to the utility and not also to its holding company or to the consolidated system, this condition has the limited aim of maintaining the utility's credit rating merely at investment grade. Nor does it guarantee the utility sufficient capital from the holding company to minimize the utility's total cost or to enable the utility to fund infrastructure cost-effectively.

[4]   *See, e.g.,* Order Instituting Rulemaking Concerning Relationship Between California Energy Utilities and Their Holding Companies and Non-Regulated Affiliates,

Caution: No utility holding company is indifferent to its utility subsidiary's health. Letting a utility's finances weaken and its operational capabilities decline can trigger regulatory penalties. Still, the holding company aims to maximize the value of its portfolio, not the cost-effectiveness of any one member. And capital, like any economic resource, is scarce. So the risk of conflict exists—between the utility's service obligation to its customers, and the holding company's portfolio obligation to its shareholders. As the D.C. Commission found: Pepco, after its acquisition by Exelon, "will face competition for shareholder capital from a larger number of regulated affiliates as well as a number of unregulated affiliates who may need resources to stem losses."[5]

7.1.2   Hierarchical Control: Subordinating Utility Needs to Holding Company Aims

To carry out the obligation to serve, utility management defines its customers' needs, identifies the capital and operational resources necessary to satisfy those needs, raises the capital and organizes the resources, then directs the activities that satisfy the needs. When making these decisions, utility management is accountable to a utility board. In a pure-play utility corporation, the utility's management is accountable to a single board. That board is accountable in turn to the thousands of shareholders who own millions of utility shares. But when that utility is acquired by a holding company, its management becomes accountable to a different board. The utility subsidiary will still have its own board, but that board's members will be chosen by, and be accountable to, the holding company's board.

When the two boards have different priorities, the holding company's board necessarily prevails, because 100 percent control is complete control. Exelon limited the Pepco Board's spending authority in multiple ways, while reserving its power to change that spending authority at any time.[6] Holding

---

2006 Cal. PUC LEXIS 241, at *4–5, *7 (finding that with PUHCA 1935's repeal in 2005, entry of utility holding companies into competitive businesses, and the close ties between competitive and monopoly affiliates, both "call[] into question the ability or willingness of the utility holding companies to fulfill their obligations to make the utility's capital requirements a first priority").

[5]   Exelon-PHI Merger, 2015 D.C. PUC LEXIS 203, at *173–74 ¶ 142.

[6]   *See* Nonunanimous Full Settlement Agreement and Stipulation ¶ 103 & tbl.5, *attached as* Exhibit A to Motion of Joint Applicants to Reopen the Record in Formal Case No. 1119, Exelon-PHI Merger, Formal Case No. 1119 (D.C. Pub. Serv. Comm'n filed Oct. 6, 2015) [hereinafter Exelon-PHI Settlement Agreement]. *See also* Exelon's Response to GRID2.0 Data Requests at DR 1-70, Exelon-PHI Merger, Formal Case No. 1119 (D.C. Pub. Serv. Comm'n filed Nov. 3, 2014) [hereinafter Responses to GRID 2.0 Data Requests for Formal Case No. 1119] ("It is therefore Mr. O'Brien's

company executives like to describe the holding company-utility relationship as one of "review," "collaboration" and mutual "input."[7] But control is control. As Exelon made clear, the utility subsidiary's executives and board have only a voice:

> The preparation of budgets for Exelon and its subsidiaries is a collaborative process between Exelon management and management of each subsidiary. The resulting subsidiary budgets are submitted to the subsidiary boards of directors, and the consolidated budget for Exelon is submitted to the Exelon Board of Directors for approval. Under the Delegations of Authority for Exelon and its subsidiaries, the Board of Directors of Exelon Corporation has final approval authority over the consolidated budget for Exelon and its subsidiaries.[8]

"Preparation" might be "collaborative" but the "final approval" will be hierarchical. And "collaborative" cannot mean "each participant has equal say," when one of the collaborators has the final say.

A standalone utility faces no hierarchical control. Its own board, advised by management and unconstrained by a holding company's conflicting objectives, calls the shots.

7.1.3 Pressure for "Growth": Adding to Parent-Utility Conflict

Utility law directs utilities to provide value to their customers. A holding company aims to provide value to its shareholders. One way to add value, holding companies say, is to get "growth." A utility focuses on its existing customers; the holding company looks for new customers. The reality of scarce resources puts those two objectives in tension.

Exelon's proposal to acquire PHI made that tension explicit. Content to serve their existing customers, PHI's three utilities were not looking for more. But Exelon was:

> Management continually evaluates growth opportunities aligned with Exelon's existing businesses in electric and gas distribution, electric transmission, generation,

---

understanding that permission of a regulatory authority is not required for change in the PHI or Pepco delegations of authority.").

[7]   *See, e.g.*, Direct Testimony of Denis P. O'Brien at 4–12, Exelon-PHI Merger, Formal Case No. 1119 (D.C. Pub. Serv. Comm'n filed June 18, 2014) (describing the parent-utility relationship as one of "review," "collaboration" and "mutual input").

[8]   Applicants' Responses to Office of the People's Counsel Data Requests at DR 6-3, Exelon-PHI Merger, Formal Case No. 1119 (D.C. Pub. Serv. Comm'n filed Nov. 3, 2014).

customer supply of electric and natural gas products and services, and natural gas exploration and production activities, leveraging Exelon's expertise in those areas.[9]

Indeed, financial analysts viewed Exelon's prior acquisition of Constellation (the holding company for Baltimore Gas & Electric) not as an operational expansion to benefit BGE's ratepayers, but as a strategic move to benefit Exelon's shareholders:

> With nuclear generation accounting for nearly 140 terawatt hours (TWh) of the company's 150 TWh total generation in 2010, Exelon is the most exposed of its peers to a decline in natural gas prices, which would drive down its margins. ... In our opinion, acquisition of retail power operations is consistent with Exelon's strategy because these operations offer a natural hedge against natural gas exposure.[10]

Exelon's effort to balance a risky portfolio with a monopoly acquisition was, according to one prominent outside analyst, part of a larger plan to add even more risk:

> Moody's believes that the combined entity [i.e., Exelon and Constellation] will still be exposed to earnings and cash flow volatility due to a large unregulated business platform whose financial performance is influenced by market determined commodity pricing levels. ... [W]e believe that it will be very challenging for [Exelon] to easily transform the company's business mix into one that is materially more balanced across regulated operations given the sheer size of the existing unregulated footprint. Moreover, given the competitive position that this merger reinforces, we believe that management, along with the board, *will be more inclined in the future to pursue acquisitions of additional unregulated properties* as a natural extension of an existing strategy, particularly given the more streamlined and less challenging regulatory approval requirements that tend to accompany unregulated acquisitions.[11]

As Chapter 7.4 will explain, adding risk increases the opportunity for shareholder returns, but it also increases the possibility of customer harm.

---

[9]   Exelon Corp., Annual Report (Form 10-K) at 88 (Feb. 14, 2014).
[10]   STANDARD & POOR'S, RESEARCH UPDATE: RATINGS ARE AFFIRMED ON EXELON COMPANIES ON NEWS IT WILL MERGE WITH CONSTELLATION; CONSTELLATION IS ON CW POSITIVE 3–4 (2011), *attached as* Exhibit KLA-1 to Direct Testimony of Karie L. Anderson, Exelon-Constellation Energy Group Merger, Case No. 9271 (Md. Pub. Serv. Comm'n filed May 25, 2011).
[11]   *Id.* (emphasis added).

7.1.4   Substance Conflicts: Generation, Transmission, Renewable Energy, Distributed Energy

Differing objectives, hierarchical control, tension over scarce capital and pressure for growth: they all lead to direct conflicts over substance. Exelon's acquisition of PHI illustrated three types.

Generation owner vs. generation customer: Rating agencies praised the "strategic benefits of linking a company that is long on generation resources [Exelon] with a company that is long on customer load [PHI's three utilities]."[12] But those "strategic benefits" become customer risks. The PHI utilities—Pepco, Delmarva Power & Light and Atlantic City Electric—owned no bulk generation, whereas Exelon then controlled 44,563 mW of generation.[13] As a generation investor, Exelon had bet billions on high generation prices.[14] But as buyers of electric power for its non-shopping customers,[15] PHI's utilities would want low generation prices.[16] Without a merger, and with its three utilities owning no generation, PHI would want to limit its utilities' power purchase costs—by investing in transmission, storage, demand resources, energy efficiency and distributed generation. But these very actions would dampen demand for generation, thereby lowering prices for Exelon's generation and lowering profits for its shareholders. With Exelon controlling PHI, that useful tension between buyer and seller, that dampening effect, would diminish. Exelon's priorities would take control.

---

[12]   *Id.*

[13]   Exelon Corp., *supra* note 9, at 9.

[14]   As Exelon acknowledged in discovery:

Exelon, as well as other power generators and independent analysts, believe[s] that power prices are in the process of recovering (or moving upward) as natural gas prices move up, demand increases and coal-fired power plants exit the market. However, such factors are not always believed to be reflected adequately in the future price of power. If such events do occur, Exelon Generation would see its profitability increase as it could sell its power at a higher price. In other words, *it would realize upside to its currently projected profitability.*

Applicants' Response to D.C. Government Data Requests at DR 1-10, Exelon-PHI Merger, Formal Case No. 1119 (D.C. Pub. Serv. Comm'n filed Nov. 3, 2014) (emphasis added) (referring to analysts' Apr. 30, 2014 presentation, Slide 11 of which was entitled "Transition Economics are Attractive").

[15]   Each of Pepco, Delmarva and Atlantic City Electric served in states—D.C., Maryland, Virginia, Delaware and New Jersey—that had authorized retail competition. Each utility served as the "default" provider for customers who choose not to buy electricity from non-utility competitive companies.

[16]   *See* Pepco Holdings, Inc., Annual Report (Form 10-K) at 5 (Feb. 27, 2014) ("PHI's business objective is to be a top-performing, regulated power delivery company that delivers safe and reliable electric and natural gas service to its customers.").

Indeed, for the fifteen years before Exelon proposed acquiring PHI, the D.C. Commission wanted its retail utilities to have no profit interest in generation sales. Prior to 1999, Pepco was vertically integrated—it owned the generation that served its customers. But when in 1999 D.C. legislation authorized competition in retail electricity, the Commission welcomed Pepco's proposal to sell off its generation. With Pepco no longer owning generation, the Commission said, the utility will have

> less motivation ... to act as an inhibitor to the development of a competitive generation market in the District. ... [T]he prospect that District ratepayers will reap the benefits of a competitive [retail] marketplace [is] greatly enhanced.[17]

But in approving Exelon's acquisition, the Commission reversed that policy. It allowed Pepco to be controlled by an entity that would have precisely that "motivation ... to act as an inhibitor to the development of a competitive generation market." About this 180-degree turn, the Commission said nothing.

When a generation-owning holding company controls a generation-dependent utility, conflict arises in three more areas: transmission access, renewable energy and distributed energy resources.

Transmission access: A generation-dependent utility wants transmission paths that reach the lowest-cost power sources. Its generation-owning holding company has the opposite interest: keeping generation prices high requires limiting transmission access and raising transmission costs. With FERC Order No. 1000,[18] this implicit conflict became explicit. Aiming to lower transmission costs by injecting competition into historically monopolistic transmission markets, FERC removed from incumbent transmission owners' tariffs their "right of first refusal" (ROFR) to build new regional transmission facilities. The ROFR had allowed incumbent transmission owners to keep those investment opportunities for themselves. In submissions to FERC and to the reviewing court, Exelon's three utility subsidiaries (along with many other utilities) opposed deleting the ROFRs—an opposition contrary to their customers' interests in reducing the transmission cost. And when PJM, the regional transmission organization, submitted to FERC the required tariff revi-

---

[17]   In the Matter of the Investigation into Electric Service Market Competition and Regulatory Practices, 1999 D.C. PUC LEXIS 56, at *33 (Commission summarizing Pepco's position).

[18]   Order No. 1000, *Transmission Planning and Cost Allocation by Transmission Owning and Operating Public Utilities*, F.E.R.C. STATS. & REGS. ¶ 31,323, 136 F.E.R.C. ¶ 61,051 at P 7 (2011), *order on reh'g*, Order No. 1000-A, 139 F.E.R.C. ¶ 61,132, *order on reh'g and clarification*, Order No. 1000-B, 141 F.E.R.C. ¶ 61,044 (2012), *aff'd sub nom.* S.C. Pub. Serv. Auth. v. FERC, 762 F.3d 41 (D.C. Cir. 2014).

sions that removed the ROFRs, Exelon's utility subsidiaries objected again. Exelon's SEC filings explained why:

> FERC's order could enable third parties to seek to build certain regional transmission projects that had previously been reserved for the PJM Transmission Owners, *potentially reducing ComEd's, PECO's and BGE's financial return* on new investments in energy transmission facilities.[19]

Renewable energy and distributed energy resources: The D.C. Commission is seeking to bring more renewable energy and distributed energy into its resource mix.[20] But Exelon, as an owner of nuclear and fossil generation, has viewed wind and solar as a threat to its profitability:

> The rate of expansion of subsidized low-carbon generation such as wind and solar energy in the markets in which [Exelon] Generation's output is sold can negatively impact wholesale power prices, and in turn, Generation's results of operations.
> [N]ational regulation or legislation addressing climate change through an RPS [renewable portfolio standard] could also increase the pace of development of wind energy facilities in the Midwest, which could put downward pressure on wholesale market prices for electricity from [Exelon] Generation's Midwest nuclear assets. ...
> The Registrants are potentially exposed to emerging technologies that may over time affect or transform the energy industry, including technologies related to energy generation, distribution and consumption. ... Such technologies could also result in further declines in commodity prices or demand for delivered energy.[21]

Some of Exelon's subsidiaries do invest in renewable energy, but those actions don't remove the conflict. These renewable investments are not acts of charity; they exist either because a state required them, or because Exelon acted to diversify its generation portfolio to minimize its risks. Exelon remains a conventional generation company, heavy on nuclear and fossil generation. Its acquisition of PHI's utilities, all generation-dependent, increased the chance of conflict.

---

[19] Exelon Corp., *supra* note 9, at 96 (emphasis added).
[20] The D.C. Commission has created a docket, originally called Modernizing the Energy Delivery System for Increased Sustainability (MEDSIS) initiative, to explore and assess non-wires alternatives to traditional distribution investments. The Commission's initiating Order tasked a working group to compile recommendations on rate design, customer impact, microgrids and pilot projects. *See* SMART ELEC. POWER ALL., FINAL REPORT v1.0 OF THE MEDSIS STAKEHOLDER WORKING GROUPS (2019), https://dcpsc.org/PSCDC/media/PDFFiles/Final-Report.pdf.
[21] Exelon Corp., *supra* note 9, at 85, 52 and 44 respectively.

7.1.5   Independent Directors: Not Independent of the Holding Company

Responding to concerns over parent-utility conflict, merger applicants often agree to place independent directors on the utility's board.[22] This action does not remove parent-utility conflict. A utility board's independent directors are independent of the utility's management; they are not independent of the utility's parent.[23] Indeed, independent directors are independent of management so that their sole allegiance will be to the parent. Independent directors are not independent like a regulatory commission's members are independent. A commission's members are independent of the utility so they can serve the public interest. The utility's directors are independent of the utility's management so they can serve the holding company's interests. If the independent director sees a conflict between the holding company's and the utility customers' interests, the holding company prevails.

If a utility board member were truly independent of the holding company, she could veto any holding company instruction that conflicted with the utility's obligation to its customers. Precedent exists in the "golden share" granted to the special purpose entity sometimes positioned between the utility and the holding company.[24] If the holding company enters bankruptcy and orders the utility to join it, the holder of that golden share has the power to veto the holding company's order. But no holding company has ever proposed, and no commission has ever required, a golden share that empowered a utility board member to veto a holding company order that conflicted with the utility's obligation to its customers.

Vermont designed a distinct approach. For over fifty years, the state's transmission system had been owned and controlled by Vermont Electric Power Company (VELCO), a for-profit corporation owned by most of Vermont's utilities. The proposed merger of Central Vermont Public Service and Green Mountain Power would give the merged company control over 78 percent of VELCO's transmission system—allowing it to "exercise sole control over

---

[22]   In the Exelon-Constellation merger, for example, the applicants accepted the Maryland Commission's requirement that at least one-third, and no fewer than two, of the members of BG&E's Board be independent directors. Exelon-Constellation Energy Group Merger, 2012 Md. PSC LEXIS 12, at *9.

[23]   "[T]he concern is independence of management." NYSE LISTED COMPANY MANUAL § 303A.02(a)(ii) cmt. (2013), http://wallstreet.cch.com/LCMTools/PlatformViewer.asp?selectednode=chp%5F1%5F4%5F3%5F3&manual=%2Flcm%2Fsections%2Flcm%2Dsections%2F.

[24]   Exelon-PHI Settlement Agreement, *supra* note 6, ¶¶ 72–74 (Exelon committing to create a special purpose entity that holds a golden share empowering its holder to veto voluntary entry into bankruptcy by PHI).

Vermont's transmission system—an undesirable outcome that would radically alter the existing balance of power in the management and operation of Vermont's power grid." The Vermont Public Service Board approved a negotiated governance solution with these main features:

- The merging companies would transfer to VLITE, a new public benefit, nonprofit corporation, an amount of stock sufficient to reduce their VELCO ownership from 78 percent to 40 percent.
- VLITE would be governed by a board of directors drawn from representatives of the energy, utility and public interest sectors.
- VLITE would nominate three independent directors, selected by the Vermont Department of Public Service, to serve on VELCO's 13-member board of directors. VLITE will have the power to establish criteria for voting on the basis of its VELCO shares.
- The merged company would have no power to unilaterally remove VELCO as the manager of Vermont's transmission system.
- VLITE would invest the dividends from its VELCO stock in a manner consistent with Vermont energy policy.[25]

Vermont's solution, complicated on the surface, was simple at the center. Needing independent directors, Vermont made the directors independent—independent of all economic interests which might conflict with the public interest. No other regulatory commission has done so.

7.2 MERGER OVERCHARGE RISKS

Commissions consider—or should consider—a merger's benefits and costs at two stages. At the approval stage, the benefit-cost ratio signals whether the transaction uses the merging companies' resources efficiently. At the rate-setting stage, commissions determine whether, when and how to reflect the merger's costs and benefits in rates. Having discussed the approval stage in Chapters 4.2, 4.3 and 4.4, we address aspects of the rate-setting stage now.

To make rates just and reasonable, commissions must prevent merger overcharges. This section identifies three types, then evaluates actions regulators can take to prevent them.

---

[25] Central Vermont Public Service-Gaz Metro Merger, 2012 Vt. PUC LEXIS 279, at *276–80.

7.2.1   Utility Devices for Overcharging

Merging companies have three ways to recover merger costs without appearing to. They can (a) use regulatory lag to keep rates above actual costs; (b) use double-leveraging to charge ratepayers for equity-level returns on equity financed with lower-cost debt; and (b) recover the acquisition premium implicitly.

7.2.1.1   Regulatory lag: a path to excess returns

7.2.1.1.1   Who gets the merger savings—ratepayers or shareholders?
If a merger reduces costs, who gets the savings? Conventional ratemaking sets rates based on reasonable costs.[26] For a newly merged company, applying that principle requires re-setting rates based on post-merger costs. All merger savings (net of costs to achieve them) then would go the customers. If rates instead stay at their pre-merger level, the merger savings would go to the shareholders, until the commission sets new rates to reflect the post-merger cost levels. Those are the two poles—all savings to the customers, or all savings to the shareholders for some period of time.

Between those two poles, the commission could allocate the savings between shareholders and customers. But allocating savings with precision is impossible, for at least two reasons. First, distinguishing cost reductions uniquely due to the merger from cost reductions achievable without the merger requires guesswork. Merged or unmerged, all companies change their practices and their costs over time. Second, even for savings uniquely due to the merger, it is hard to synchronize rate reductions with cost reductions. Not all savings occur at identifiable points in time (e.g., while a cost-lowering amendment to a gas purchase contract has a definite start date, a productivity gain from new software doesn't); moreover, rate changes require complex legal procedures whose schedules don't mesh with cost changes. Both problems caused the Kanas Commission to reject the merging utilities' proposal for tracking cost reductions and rate reductions:

> The basis of the proposed [tracking] system is the determination of the costs that would have been incurred on a stand-alone basis had KPL and KGE remained stand-alone entities. This would effectively require the Commission to make a finding regarding the cost of service and revenue requirement levels for utility companies that ceased to exist. The Commission would be in a position of taking into account any and all events, technological, economic, natural phenomena or oth-

---

[26]   Plus, of course, a fair return on prudent, used-and-useful investment. *See* Tutorial § 4.1.

erwise, in determining revenue requirement levels for nonexistent companies. The Commission refuses to head down the path in which it will be required to engage in guesswork regarding nonexistent companies to determine savings from the merger. Nor can the Commission ignore the subjectivity inherent in Applicants' proposal for identifying savings events. The expense and time needed to track, quantify and audit the thousands of savings events that Applicants anticipate they will identify would represent a substantial cost which would diminish the benefits of the merger.[27]

So commissions face a challenge. They must allocate merger savings somehow, because not acting affirmatively cedes the decision to the merged entity, as discussed next.

7.2.1.1.2 Who decides—commission or company?
Once a commission establishes a utility's rates, the utility must charge only those rates—even if the utility's costs, sales or cost of equity deviate from the projections underlying the rates. Informed of deviations, the commission can change the rates, but prospectively only. These two legal constraints—the utility may charge only the approved rates, and the commission can change rates only prospectively—come from the filed rate doctrine and its offspring, the prohibition against retroactive ratemaking.[28] Given these constraints, if the utility's costs drop before a commission lowers the rates (a situation known as regulatory lag), the utility keeps the difference.

Turning to post-merger ratemaking: The sooner the merged company introduces cost reductions and the later it applies for new rates, the longer the lag and the more savings it keeps. By exercising control over both decisions, the merged company effectively displaces the commission as the allocator of savings between shareholders and ratepayers. Some commissions even cede their ratemaking power to the merged entity explicitly, by committing not to open a rate case for a specified post-merger period. Information asymmetry makes the actual savings allocation opaque, because the cost-reduction actions and cost data lie within the merging companies. Unless the commission eavesdrops on the actions and audits the data, it will never know how many savings dollars the companies kept. The merged company will know that number—and the merging companies likely based their acquisition price on it.

---

[27] Kansas City Power & Light-Kansas Gas & Electric Merger, Consolidated Docket Nos. 172,745-u, 174,155-D, slip op. at 73 (Kan. Corp. Comm'n Nov. 18, 1991).

[28] *See* SCOTT HEMPLING, REGULATING PUBLIC UTILITY PERFORMANCE: THE LAW OF MARKET STRUCTURE, PRICING AND JURISDICTION, chs. 9 (filed rate doctrine) and 10 (prohibition against retroactive ratemaking) (American Bar Association 2013). A commission can avoid the prohibition against retroactivity if it gives advance notice that it might change the previously established rate levels, provided the change is retroactive only to the date of the notice.

This last point deserves emphasis. Chapter 5.3.2 explained that the acquirer's willingness to pay a control premium depends in part on its expectation that the acquired target will earn a return exceeding the commission-authorized return. So if the commission insists on allocating more savings to customers than the merger applicants projected when setting their acquisition price, they will argue that the commission is rattling the bond markets, causing the share price to drop or otherwise threatening a transaction that financial markets expect to occur on the terms negotiated by the applicants.[29] These statements say nothing about the merits of the commission's allocation; they aim instead to have the acquirer's projections control the ratemaking outcome. Yet some commissions have adjusted proposed allocations, in favor of customers.[30]

Allocating some merger savings to the merging companies has a valid basis. In competitive markets, if a merged company can reduce its costs while charging market prices for its products, the company keeps the merger savings. Merging utilities deserve a comparable opportunity. And regulatory lag—letting utilities keep, between rate cases, the cost savings they create—is a common means of encouraging and rewarding utility efficiency. The point here is different: allocating merger savings via regulatory lag, where the merging companies control both the cost data and rate case timing, is allocating in the dark.

Regulatory practice outside of mergers offers a solution. When a commission suspects that a utility's existing rates exceed reasonable cost (including profit), it can declare the rates "interim subject to refund" as of the declaration date.[31] The commission also can direct the merged company to present its

---

[29] *See, e.g.,* Louisville Gas & Electric-Kentucky Utilities Merger, 1997 Ky. PUC LEXIS 274, at *18 (summarizing applicants' argument that increasing the customer share of savings based on the company's current earnings "would require them to terminate the merger because it is a *fully priced* transaction and any *reduction in their earnings* would result in an *unacceptable loss of shareholder value*" (emphasis added)).

[30] *Id.* at *21 (finding that in merger's non-fuel merger savings in Year 6 would increase significantly; requiring the companies to present a sharing plan in Year 5). *See also* Central Illinois Public Service-Union Electric Merger, 1997 Ill. PUC LEXIS 546, at *76 (requiring the merged company to submit a new rate case within six months of merger consummation, because "the one-year time frame proposed by CIPS would result in an unreasonable delay in the [retail] ratepayers' receipt of an appropriate share of merger-related savings"). Reviewing that transaction, FERC found that the proposed "shared savings plan" for wholesale customers would make the merger risk-free to the shareholders because ratepayers would bear all merger costs in the merger's early years, whereas "many of the merger benefits are more speculative in nature and will not be realized, if at all, until much later." FERC ultimately approved the merger with different sharing conditions. *Union Electric-Central Illinois Public Service Merger*, 77 F.E.R.C. ¶ 61,026, at text accompanying n.21 (1996).

[31] *See* HEMPLING, *supra* note 28, at 330–31.

savings plans for approval, then execute them as of specific dates. These two actions enable the commission to gather the facts on merger savings, set rates that reflect those savings, then adjust the rates as new information arrives—all without violating the prohibition against retroactivity. That way, the savings allocation is decided by the commission, not by the merged company.

7.2.1.2 Double-leveraging: another path to excess returns

Chapter 5.3.2.1 explained double-leveraging. The acquirer finances its acquisition with a mix of debt and equity. Debt costs less than equity because the lender has a contractual right to interest on and repayment of principal; equity investors, in contrast, receive no promises from their company. Conventional ratemaking reflects that cost difference by establishing separate costs of capital for debt and equity. Acquirers see the debt-equity difference as an opportunity for gain. If they can use debt to buy the target's equity, but persuade the commission to authorize an equity-level return on that target's equity (including the portion purchased with lower-cost debt), the target's value to the acquirer rises. This extra value comes not from operational improvement but from financing technique. It causes the acquirer to pay a premium, which becomes gain to the target shareholders.

Ratepayers argue that this practice—charging ratepayers an equity-level return on equity purchased with lower-cost debt—violates ratemaking's central principle: that rates must reflect "lowest feasible cost."[32] The portion of the target's equity purchased with debt, they say, should be compensated at the cost of debt, not the cost of equity. Acquirers disagree. Since the holding company holds the debt, they say, the holding company bears the risks associated with that debt. Ratepayers should not get the benefit of debt financing when they avoid the debt's risk.

But ratepayers do bear risk. By increasing its debt, the holding company decreases its ability to raise equity for the utility. (The holding company, recall, is the utility's sole source of equity.) And because a debt-burdened holding company will need access to acquired utility's earnings to help pay off the holding company's debt, lenders will view the utility as less able to pay off its own debts, and so demand a higher interest rate on prospective utility debt.[33]

---

[32] Potomac Elec. Power Co. v. Pub. Serv. Comm'n, 661 A.2d 131, 137 (D.C. 1995). *See also* State v. Okla. Gas & Elec. Co., 536 P.2d 887, 891 (Okla. 1975) (requiring Commission to set "lowest reasonable rates consistent with the interests of the public and the utilities").

[33] *See* Direct Testimony of Adam Gatewood at 41, Great Plains Energy-Westar Energy Merger I, Docket No. 16-KCPE-593-ACQ (Kan. Corp. Comm'n filed Dec. 16, 2016) (explaining that credit rating agencies recognize that a weakness in either parent or subsidiary will reduce the creditworthiness of the other, especially when the

And debt burdens, whether at the holding company or utility level, can distract management from its core responsibility—providing a utility service reliably and cost-effectively. The real inconsistency, the argument goes, is with the merger applicants: they want to deny ratepayers the benefit of acquisition debt, while telling lenders that ratepayers' very presence ensures repayment of that debt. As the Kansas Commission explained, double-leveraging causes ratepayers to "subsidiz[e] the acquisition premium;" by doing so, "GPE is using the ratepayers as its bank."[34]

But merger applicants argue back. When a commission applies an equity-level return to a utility's total book equity, applicants say, it doesn't care whether individual shareholders bought their stock with debt— so why treat a corporate acquirer any differently? Here's why: an individual's ordinary purchase and sale of a utility's individual shares differs fundamentally from the bulk purchase and sale of all the utility's shares. The individual stock sales occur in a competitive stock market. Each share is a commodity—indistinguishable from any other share. Because an objective market sets the price, no individual shareholder can extract a price exceeding the market price. But an entire company is not a commodity. It is a differentiable product—indeed, a monopoly product, so its shareholders when acting together have market power. They use that market power to extract the control premium—the excess of purchase price over market value. And as Chapter 1.2.2 explained, the sale is a sale of more than a company; it is a sale of control of a franchise—a government-protected right to provide a monopoly service.

The Kansas Commission didn't bite. With the premium exceeding the applicants' savings claims by $600 million, the Commission found the applicants' commitment not to seek premium recovery not "credible": "[I]t appears ... the Joint Applicants ... still plan to recover the acquisition premium indirectly from ratepayers."[35]

7.2.2   Regulatory Actions to Prevent Overcharges

To prevent overcharges—rates exceeding reasonable cost and profit— commissions need to allocate cost savings between shareholders and ratepayers so that post-merger rates align with post-merger costs. This subsection describes the traditional techniques, then explains why commissions need to discipline those techniques with clear principles and procedures. We

companies have the same directors setting each company's dividend and capitalization policies).

[34]   Great Plains Energy-Westar Energy Merger I, 2017 Kan. PUC LEXIS 1142, at *39–40 ¶ 44.

[35]   *Id.* at *39 ¶ 40.

then address a distinct challenge: allocating costs and benefits not between shareholders and ratepayers, but between the ratepayers of the two merging companies.

7.2.2.1 Aligning rates with costs post-merger: traditional techniques
We have described two sources of merger-related overcharge: controlling regulatory lag, and earning equity-level returns on equity purchased with debt. To prevent or limit these overcharges, regulators have five common techniques. Here is a summary with commentary.

7.2.2.1.1 Freezing pre-merger rates
A rate freeze keeps post-merger rates at pre-merger levels, for some period of time. Its effects depend on the facts. If rates would have increased without the merger, a rate freeze benefits the customers to the extent of the avoided increase.[36] But without a full rate case to establish what the increase would have been, a commission cannot know the benefit's size. What if rates would not have risen without a merger; and instead, the merger reduces costs below the level underlying pre-merger rates? Then a rate freeze lets the shareholders earn a return exceeding the authorized return. Again without a full rate case, the commission cannot measure the over-earnings.

To eliminate this dual uncertainty, to know whom a rate freeze benefits, a commission can hold a general rate case contemporaneously with the merger proceeding. By establishing the target's actual costs just prior to the merger, this technique provides an accurate cost base from which to deduct merger savings. The Maryland Commission used this approach in the proposed (later withdrawn) merger between Baltimore Gas & Electric and Potomac Electric Power. The rate case showed that the companies' pre-merger rates already exceeded reasonable costs. So the Commission both lowered the merging companies' rates and required a post-merger rate freeze. It also required a rate reduction reflecting a portion of the merger-produced savings.[37] In another freeze variation, the Idaho Commission, like the Maryland Commission, first found that the target utility's pre-merger rates already exceeded its costs. The Idaho Commission then imposed a cap on the utility's rate of return, effectively sharing merger savings between shareholders and ratepayers.[38]

---

[36] *See, e.g.,* Puget Sound Power & Light-Washington Natural Gas Merger, 1997 Wash. UTC LEXIS 6, at *30 (finding that given utility's past history of rate increases, a five-year period of rate stability will benefit consumers).

[37] Baltimore Gas & Electric-Pepco Merger, 1997 Md. PSC LEXIS 205.

[38] Washington Water Power-Sierra Pacific Power Merger, 1995 Ida. PUC LEXIS 89. The applicants withdraw this transaction.

7.2.2.1.2 Rate credits

Some commissions require rate credits in the merger's first year.[39] This method guarantees ratepayers some share of merger cost savings. What share, no one knows unless the commission holds a contemporaneous rate case to determine the merged company's actual cost structure.

In the Exelon-Constellation merger, the Maryland Commission combined direct ratepayer cost savings with public policy expenditures. The merged company had to:

- fund a one-time, $100 per customer credit, amounting to $112 million; and
- invest 50 percent of its projected "synergy savings" ($43.5 million), along with another $70 million, into a Customer Investment Fund. The Commission would spend the fund on energy assistance, energy efficiency and weatherization for low-income customers; zero- and low-interest financing for customer efficiency and conservation projects; and other programs to remove "barriers to adoption of technologies and behaviors related to energy use in homes and small businesses."

These amounts were only a down payment on merger savings. Exelon also had to track the savings so the Commission could allocate them prospectively in the next rate case.[40]

7.2.2.1.3 Trackers

Without a contemporaneous rate case to establish the target's pre-merger cost basis, rate freezes and rate credits allocate merger cost savings in the dark. To get more clarity while avoiding a full rate case, some commissions establish trackers. A tracker first screens out savings that would or should have occurred without the merger.[41] Then it identifies merger-induced cost reductions as they occur, allocating those reductions between shareholders and ratepayers via

---

[39] *See* Kansas City Power & Light-Kansas Gas & Electric Merger, Consolidated Docket Nos. 172,745-u, 174,155-D (Kan. Corp. Comm'n Nov. 18, 1991) (ordering rate refunds of $32 million in three installments); Wisconsin Electric-Northern States Power Merger, 1996 Mich. PSC LEXIS 94 (conditioning approval on immediate rate decrease, to last four years) (merger later withdrawn); Southwest Public Service Co., Case No. 2678, 1997 WL 78696 (N.M. Pub. Util. Comm'n Jan. 28, 1997) (requiring $1.2 million annual credit to ratepayers through fuel adjustment clause, to prevent utility from keeping merger savings by delaying the filing of a new rate case).

[40] Exelon-Constellation Energy Group Merger, 2012 Md. PSC LEXIS 12, at *164–65, *169.

[41] *Cf.* Kansas Power & Light-Kansas Gas & Electric Merger, 1991 Mo. PSC LEXIS 44 (finding applicants' proposed tracking mechanism inadequate because it did not exclude all non-merger savings from the pool of savings to be shared).

a sharing formula.[42] Trackers usually operate for only a few years, because beyond that point it becomes hard to know whether a particular cost reduction would or should have occurred without the merger.

7.2.2.1.4 Hybrids

Merger negotiations have produced hybrids that mix rate credits and trackers with later rate cases to verify the outcomes. Consider this Vermont stipulation, requiring that

- over the first three years, customers receive a credit totaling $15.5 million against current rates, while the merged company keeps any remaining savings from operations and maintenance (O&M) costs;
- for years 4–8, shareholders and customers share operations and maintenance cost savings 50-50;
- for year 9 and thereafter, customers receive all operations and maintenance savings, through rate-setting on a traditional cost-of-service basis; and
- customers receive all non-O&M cost savings.

The parties expected that over 10 years, customers would receive $144 million (including the $15.5 million in the first three years), out of projected O&M savings of $226 million.[43]

7.2.2.1.5 Most-favored-nation clauses

Multistate mergers can produce different outcomes in different states, because parties bargain differently and because commissions tend to defer to the bargains reached. This fact has led some state commissions to make merger applicants match the most favorable terms reached in other states.[44]

---

[42] *See, e.g.*, Green Mountain Power-New England Energy Merger, 2007 Vt. PUC LEXIS 74, at *29–30 (accepting Green Mountain Power's proposal to track by FERC account, for seven years, "actual savings resulting from the proposed merger and compare them to estimated savings; such savings shall reflect a flat 2.5 percent inflation rate for ease of tracking"); *Southwest Public Service Co.*, 1997 WL 78696 (requiring tracking mechanism to compare operations and maintenance expense post-merger to the expense expected without the merger).

[43] Central Vermont Public Service-Gaz Metro Merger, 2012 Vt. PUC LEXIS 279, at *90–92 (Findings 194–198).

[44] *See, e.g.*, Duke Energy-Union Light, Heat & Power Merger, 2005 Ky. PUC LEXIS 1005, at *23–24 (requiring reconsideration of shareholder-customer sharing ratio after all the other states complete their proceedings).

7.2.2.2 Missing: principles and procedures

We have described five techniques commissions use to allocate merger savings between shareholders and ratepayers: freezes, credits, trackers, hybrids and most favored nation clauses. All five have the same two suboptimalities: the lack of current cost information leaves the actual allocation unknown; and whatever allocation does occur is disconnected from any stated regulatory principle. Parties and commissions might describe the outcome as "fair"; but no one defines fairness or explains why it is fair for a government-protected company to earn returns above the authorized return (the necessary result of allowing the merged company to keep any of the savings). When the commission lacks both cost information and allocation principles, while the merging companies control both the cost information and the decisions on when to produce savings, the resulting allocation—whether implicit or explicit—will likely favor the merging companies. The principle and procedure discussed next provide a more objective, factual basis for the allocation decision.

7.2.2.2.1 Principle: allocate merger savings based on relative contribution

Chapter 5.5 recommended allocating the control premium based on share-holders' and ratepayers' relative contributions to the value underlying the premium. The same principle works here: shareholders' and ratepayers' share of merger savings should reflect their relative contribution to those savings.

Consider economies of scale and best practices—two commonly cited sources of merger savings. Economies of scale, as Chapters 5.3.2.3 and 6.1.2 explained, reflect a product's inherent cost function. A cost function relates per-unit cost to quantity of sales. For an electric utility, the quantity of sales depends on the size of the population within the government-granted franchise territory, along with the general economic conditions and regulatory policies that affect demand and consumption levels within that territory. Because economies of scale owe nothing to shareholder risk-taking or utility decision-making, the shareholders have no logical claim to those savings. They exist only because government policy makes customers captive. Those facts support allocating all economies of scale savings to customers. As for best practices, unless the merging companies' practices are patented, they are likely ones conventionally used by prudent utilities—practices integral to a utility's obligation to serve. Since prudent practices are what ratepayers pay for, again the associated savings should go fully to them.

If the evidence on benefit-entitlement is absent or inconclusive, the commission can apply a default presumption of 50-50—a rebuttable presumption that shareholders and ratepayers contributed to the savings equally.

This principle for allocating merger savings—benefits to the benefit-producers, except where benefit production is part of the obligation to serve—has several advantages. First, it can discipline the control premium: no longer will the acquirer base the premium on an expectation of earning excess returns through withholding merger savings from customers. Second, it will cause prospective acquirers to predict savings (and their causes) with more precision, and even to seek advance commission rulings on who will receive which savings—again disciplining the premium by aligning the acquisition price with post-merger rate treatment. Third, and a result of the first two benefits: the competition among acquirers will focus more on performance, because the control premium—which target shareholders seek to maximize—will be recoverable only to the extent of unique benefits not achievable without a merger. Mergers will emerge from a competition where the main criterion is merger savings rather than acquisition price.

7.2.2.2.2 Procedure: combine merger case with rate case

Cost-based rates should reflect a company's cost structure. If a merger changes the cost structure, the commission should change the rates. The appropriate rate procedure depends on the facts.

If the pre-merger rates already reflect pre-merger costs: Rates set within the 12-month period preceding the merger will likely reflect actual cost, so they will provide an accurate basis for merger-related adjustments. The merger approval order should require the utility to file new rate tariffs in, say, 90 days. Those new tariffs would adjust the pre-merger rates to reflect merger costs and merger cost reductions in two categories: (1) those the commission approved or ordered in the merger case, based on solid evidence; and (2) those the applicants are now ready to present, having had 90 days to start the merger integration process. The first category of costs and cost reductions would enter rates automatically. The second category would be litigated in this first post-merger rate case. For this second category, the commission would either (a) decide their fate and reflect the results in the new rates; or (b) use a tracker so that rates change as actual costs change.

If the pre-merger rates don't reflect pre-merger costs: Rates that were set more than 12 months before the merger will not likely reflect actual costs, so will not provide an accurate basis for merger-caused adjustments. The commission then has two main choices.

a. Combine merger case with rate case. Setting rates simultaneously with approving the merger makes clear the financial consequences for all parties upfront. In 1997, it had been several years since the Maryland Commission had reviewed either of Pepco's or BG&E's rates. The applicants' proposed rate freeze would extend this unexamined period for another 2.5 years. The Commission didn't take the bait. Insisting that "[w]e need to evaluate all reasonable methods of providing customers with a fair share of merger savings," it held a full rate case alongside the merger case.[45]

b. Combine merger approval with a directive to file a full rate case within 90 days. This rate filing would reflect the commission's decisions about the acquisition premium, intercompany and interjurisdictional allocations of costs and benefits, treatment of transaction and transition costs, and any required or projected cost reductions. The directive would also make the pre-merger rates "interim subject to refund." Doing so gives the commission time to set the new rates, then allows it to make the new rates effective back to the date of the merger approval order without violating the prohibition against retroactivity.

Most states have used none of these options. Instead they adopt one of the five non-rate case measures—freeze, credit, tracker, hybrid or most favored nation clause—then wait to open a new rate case until excess earnings appear,[46] or until the merged company or intervenors ask.

7.2.2.3 Allocating costs and benefits between the merging companies

Two merging utilities will have two different cost structures: different types and vintages of generating capacity, different load shapes, different fuel contracts, different equity-debt ratios, different costs of equity and debt capital. Different cost structures mean different rate levels.

Merging these two companies poses an immediate problem: if the commission melds their pre-merger rate structures into a single average rate structure, the lower-cost company's rates will rise. If the two companies serve in different states, that prospect dooms the transaction because no commission will approve a merger that raises rates. Even where the merging companies serve in the same state, their commission will not likely risk the political fallout of raising the lower-cost company's rates. On the other hand, maintaining separate rate structures conflicts with creating a unified post-merger entity.

The common approach? Let sleeping dogs lie, at least for a while.[47] Commissions can also phase in average rates over a time period long

---

[45] Baltimore Gas & Electric-Pepco Merger, 1997 Md. PSC LEXIS 205, at *36.

[46] *See, e.g.*, NSTAR-Northeast Utilities Merger, 2012 Mass. PUC LEXIS 84, at *8 (holding that "even with approval of the Proposed Merger, if at any time the Department has any reason to believe that the earnings of NSTAR Electric, NSTAR Gas, or WMECo are excessive or if we have concerns about their prices or quality of service, we will investigate the propriety of rates" under existing ratemaking authority); Northeast Utilities-NSTAR Merger, 2012 Conn. PUC LEXIS 47, at *65 (committing to hold a future proceeding that "would involve a determination of the appropriateness of the merger-related costs expended in order to achieve the merger related savings").

[47] *See, e.g.*, Pacific Power & Light-Utah Power & Light Merger, 1988 Mont. PUC LEXIS 20 (holding that lack of clarity over interjurisdictional cost allocations was not sufficient grounds for rejecting the merger, since commission will decide post-merger

enough to soften opposition. Or they can allocate the merger cost reductions non-proportionally to the higher cost company, as a way to reduce rate differentials over time.

Differing capital structures present a distinct challenge. Because acquisition debt increases the consolidated entity's debt-equity ratio, the acquired utility will be subject to new financial risks, possibly increasing its future debt and equity costs. Even without acquisition debt, merging two different capital structures changes the debt-equity ratio for the whole. The less debt-leveraged utility becomes part of a more debt-leveraged company; the less equity-heavy utility becomes part of a more equity-heavy company.[48] Whether these changes affect either company's cost of capital will depend on the size of the change, the amount of any acquisition debt and each utility's pre-merger financial condition.

7.3   ACQUISITION DEBT RISKS

To buy a target with cash, the acquirer needs cash. That cash can come from four sources: the acquirer's retained earnings, new debt incurred by the acquirer, new equity issued by the acquirer, and proceeds from selling the acquirer's or target's assets.[49] Using debt is attractive because it costs less than equity while keeping the acquirer's retained earnings and assets intact.

---

allocation methodology later); PacifiCorp, 95 P.U.R.4th 96 (Or. Pub. Util. Comm'n July 15, 1988) (finding no reason to delay merger due to absence of interjurisdictional allocation method, because companies agreed to absorb costs not fully allocated); Utah Power & Light Co., Docket No. 9266, 90 P.U.R.4th 482 (Wyo. Pub. Serv. Comm'n Feb. 24, 1988) (deferring interjurisdictional allocation issues); Kansas City Power & Light-Kansas Gas & Electric Merger, Consolidated Docket Nos. 172,745-u, 174,155-D (Kan. Corp. Comm'n Nov. 18, 1991) (deferring intercompany allocation of merger savings and acquisition premium to a post-merger rate case); Kansas Power & Light-Kansas Gas & Electric Merger, 1991 Mo. PSC LEXIS 44 (requiring merging companies to prepare an interjurisdictional cost allocation study within five years of merger); *Cincinnati Gas & Electric-PSI Energy Merger*, 64 F.E.R.C. ¶ 61,237 (1993) (directing applicants to allocate costs and benefits among jurisdictions using general principles to be filed in a later rate proceeding).

[48]   *See, e.g.*, Southern California Edison-San Diego Gas & Electric Merger, 1991 Cal. PUC LEXIS 253, at *218 (expecting that parties will pressure the Commission "to recognize the merged company's less leveraged real capital structure, even though doing so would raise the merged company's revenue requirement").

[49]   Here's an example. In Exelon's acquisition of PHI, the total out-of-pocket acquisition cost was $7.3 billion: $6.826 billion for the cash purchase price, and $0.514 billion for transaction costs. The sources of financing for the $7.3 billion were $3.5 billion in new debt, $1.841 billion in new equity, $1.0 billion in mandatory convertible debt and $1.0 billion from the sale of certain Exelon generating assets. Exelon would also assume $6.197 billion in PHI's consolidated outstanding debt. *See* Direct

And as we will see, using acquisition debt also reduces the acquirer's need to issue new equity shares, an action that can dilute the value of existing shares. But when acquisition debt enters the merged company's capital structure, the acquired utility faces new risks. This section describes five. Individually and together, these risks illustrate the conflicts between debt-leveraged consolidations and the public interest in cost-effective utility service.

7.3.1   Acquisition Lenders Want the Acquirer to Control the Target Utility's Financial Resources

An acquirer plans to pay $1.2 billion in cash for a target whose current stock market value is $1 billion. The acquirer's shareholders will receive something (a $1 billion company) worth less than they paid ($1.2 billion). Assume the acquirer raises some of the $1.2 billion by issuing new equity shares. Doing so will dilute the value of existing equity shares. To reduce that dilution—and to persuade its existing shareholders to approve the transaction despite the dilution—the acquirer will weight the acquisition financing toward debt and away from new equity. But to make that new debt low-cost, the acquirer must make the debt low-risk. How does a utility's acquirer persuade its lender that its large acquisition loan will be low-risk? By getting control of the acquired utility's cash flow—the cash flow from captive customers. That control will help convince lenders that the borrower will repay the debt.

NextEra faced this situation when seeking to pay a premium for the Texas utility Oncor. To reduce dilution of its existing shareholders' equity, NextEra needed to finance the acquisition in large part with debt. But the large acquisition debt would be costly. It would also reduce NextEra's bond ratings, making it harder to finance future acquisitions. How might NextEra use Oncor's captive customers to gain favorable terms from NextEra's lenders, so as to reduce the equity dilution that might spark opposition from NextEra's shareholders? The answer was "credit linkage": consolidating Oncor's strong financial metrics (strong because it had captive customers) with NextEra's already debt-heavy metrics. If NextEra could control Oncor's cash flow, bond rating agencies would view NextEra's financial condition as enhanced by Oncor's financial strength.[50]

Testimony of John W. Wilson at 8, Exelon-PHI Merger, Formal Case No. 1119 (D.C. Pub. Serv. Comm'n filed Nov. 3, 2014) (citing discovery submissions).

[50]   *See* Direct Testimony of Staff Witness Randall Vickroy at 27, Oncor Electric Delivery-NextEra Energy Merger, PUC Docket No. 46238 (Tex. Pub. Util. Comm'n filed Jan. 18, 2017) (explaining that NextEra's credit linkage to Oncor would "offset the increased financial leverage associated with the transaction's financing plan, allowing NextEra Energy [the acquirer] to maintain its current credit rating level").

How then would NextEra get control over the utility's cash? NextEra proposed to control appointments to Oncor's Board (except for three "disinterested directors"), and to eliminate the Oncor minority shareholders' veto rights over Oncor's dividend and budget decisions. Those two changes would allow NextEra to control Oncor's cash flow: its spending, investments and dividend payments. All this was confirmed by Standard and Poor's:

> NextEra will be in a position to exercise effective control over Oncor's resources and cash flows with no additional meaningful insulation imposed elsewhere; this would strengthen its business risk profile to offset the weakened financial profile that results from the proposed [acquisition debt] funding, and leave ratings at the current level.[51]

The Texas Commission saw things differently. It wanted Oncor's Board to retain "control over Oncor's decisions on capital expenditures and operating expenses." It saw Oncor's independence from NextEra's financial needs as "a critical part of the ring fence protecting Oncor." But NextEra had made clear that Oncor's independence "would be unacceptable," so the Commission had no choice: it rejected the transaction.[52]

By rejecting the NextEra-Oncor transaction, the Texas Commission made the problem go away. But the tensions it addressed will exist whenever an acquirer pays a premium: to avoid equity dilution the acquirer needs to borrow money; but the lenders will want assurance that the acquirer can control the utility's cash. To please its shareholders the acquirer must have access to the ratepayers. That is one risk from acquisition debt.

7.3.2 Acquisition Debt Creates Financial Risk for the Target Utility

The acquirer's acquisition debt puts financial pressure on the acquired utility, in at least five ways.

---

[51] *Id.* at 28 (quoting NextEra Energy's Response to Texas Industrial Energy Consumers' Request for Information 1-4, Attachment 3 at 118, STANDARD & POOR'S RESEARCH UPDATE (Aug. 2, 2016)).

[52] Oncor Electric Delivery-NextEra Energy Merger, 2017 Tex. PUC LEXIS 1310, at *19. The Commission soon after approved Oncor's acquisition by Sempra (the holding company for San Diego Gas & Electric). The Texas Commission's rejection of NextEra's acquisition was one of only six merger rejections, out of nearly eighty transactions, in the last thirty-five years. A discussion of those six rejections, explaining why they stand out from the many approvals, appears in Chapter 11.2.

Decrease in utility's access to equity: When Northeast Utilities proposed acquiring the bankrupt Public Service of New Hampshire, Connecticut regulators found that NU's high debt and PSNH's weak earnings would put

> additional, though indirect, financial stress on [Connecticut Light & Power, an NU subsidiary] and may hinder its access to the financial markets and distort its cost of debt and/or equity. Since CL&P is dependent on NU for infusions of equity, a merger that leaves NU financially weak and saturates the market with NU common equity jeopardizes CL&P's access to equity.[53]

And GPE's high acquisition debt caused the Kansas Commission to label the original GPE-Westar transaction "too risky." Moody's had downgraded GPE's long-term bond ratings, warning that the transaction would "result in consolidated financial metrics [that] reflect levels that are typically associated with a speculative grade financial profile. ..." The Commission concluded:

> [E]ven if all of GPE's [financial] projections are accurate, its ability to maintain an investment grade credit rating is tenuous. If its projections are overly optimistic or a negative event such as an increase in interest rates occurs, GPE's ability to service its debt could be in jeopardy.[54]

And GPE's troubles would make it less able to put equity into Westar's two utilities.

Increase in utility finance costs: The acquirer attracts acquisition lenders by projecting the merged entity's earnings. If actual earnings lag those projections, future lenders will view the acquirer as riskier—leading to lower bond ratings and higher interest costs on future debt. Then money put by the acquirer into the utility will come at a higher cost, causing the utility to seek higher rates.[55] Indeed, an acquisitive holding company's interest rates can rise

---

[53]   Northeast Utilities-Public Service of New Hampshire Merger, 1992 Conn. PUC LEXIS 23, at *40–41.

[54]   Great Plains Energy-Westar Energy Merger I, 2017 Kan. PUC LEXIS 1142, at *26–34 ¶ 30–36. *But see* Puget Sound Energy-Macquarie Merger, 2008 Wash. UTC LEXIS 1023 (approving Australian company's acquisition of local utility; though 20 percent of the acquisition cost would be financed with debt, (a) the resulting leverage would be less than prior transactions approved by the Commission, (b) the new acquisition debt would be held at the holding company level rather than at the utility level, (c) commission-imposed conditions would protect ratepayers from bearing the risks attributable to the debt, and (d) in the near future the utility will have to incur new debt anyway). One Commissioner dissented.

[55]   *See, e.g.*, Southern California Edison-San Diego Gas & Electric Merger, 1991 Cal. PUC LEXIS 253, at *218 ("To some extent ... the merged company's financial condition depends on future Commission willingness to have ratepayers absorb increased costs resulting from the merged company's capital structure."); Great Plains

merely because rating agencies expect the company to make debt-leveraged acquisitions. As Fitch stated, in assessing Exelon's proposed acquisition of PHI: "Even without the completion of this merger, ratings may also be lowered in recognition of [Exelon's] willingness to pursue a leveraged acquisition."[56]

Reduced debt access for the utility subsidiaries: While a 100-percent-owned utility depends on its parent for equity, it can borrow externally in its own name. But the utility's lenders will worry that a debt-burdened holding company will be unable to provide the utility equity. Less equity means the utility can make fewer infrastructure investments—the investments that produce the earnings that give lenders the confidence to lend.

Reduced value for existing bondholders: The utility's pre-merger debt carries interest rates reflecting the utility's pre-merger risks. Post-merger, buyers of the bonds associated with that debt will pay less than they would have pre-merger, because they will be buying an income stream (the existing bonds' repayment obligation) made less certain by the acquisition.

Higher cost of holding company equity: By taking on acquisition debt, the holding company lowers the probability that its earnings will satisfy prospective equity investors' expectations. As the Missouri Commission explained: "Although a company's credit rating applies most directly to its access [to] and cost of debt, companies with a lower credit quality also find fewer equity investors willing to risk their investment dollars on their stock."[57] Equity investors will require a higher return—making it more expensive for the holding company to finance the utility.

7.3.3 If the Acquirer Defaults, its Creditors Can Become the Target Utility's Owners

Because an acquiring holding company is not a utility company, it does not have the revenue certainty that lenders prefer. Lenders will insist on collateral—like the acquired utility's stock. If the utility's stock is collateral for the acquisition loan, then on default the acquirer's creditors can become the

---

Energy-Kansas City Power & Light Merger, 2008 Mo. PSC LEXIS 693, at *244 (finding that "debt and equity investors demand a higher cost or return on their investment dollars to compensate them for the higher credit risk. This increased cost of capital can translate directly into higher costs for customers.").

[56] Direct Testimony of John W. Wilson at 16, Exelon-PHI Merger, Formal Case No. 1119 (D.C. Pub. Serv. Comm'n filed Nov. 3, 2014) (quoting D.C. Government's Data Request 1-9, Attachment A, 20) (confidential data removed).

[57] Great Plains Energy-Kansas City Power & Light Merger, 2008 Mo. PSC LEXIS 693, at *244.

utility's owners.[58] The creditors then could remain owners, or they could sell the company to the highest bidder and get out. Neither result—a utility run by creditors lacking experience in utility operations, or run by a company selected based on its ability to pay off the acquisition debt—serves the public interest.[59] As one commentator described the utility-stock-as-collateral problem:

> In keeping with the spirit of speculation that led to the 1929 stock market crash, these kinds of holding companies had frequently pledged as collateral their owner-ship interests in public utilities (regulated businesses with guaranteed but unspec-tacular profit margins) for loans that could in turn be invested in more flamboyant ventures possessing greater potential for outsized, speculative gains. When the stock market crash took down the speculative ventures, the holding companies defaulted on these loans and the lenders foreclosed on the underlying collateral, the nation's supposedly "boring" public utility companies themselves. Thus, an unexpected artifact of the stock market crash was the indirect financial chaos it spawned even in safe sectors of the economy, including industries providing such bedrock services as fresh water and electric power.[60]

Creditor takeover should not happen automatically. Any commission order approving a debt-financed acquisition should make clear that a default-triggered acquisition will require commission approval. Otherwise, the commission's decision about the original acquirer's appropriateness would become meaning-less should that acquirer be replaced by creditors.

The path just described assumed the parties resolved the default outside of bankruptcy. But default can also lead to bankruptcy. Remember that the acquisition debtor is not a traditional utility—a company whose stable revenue makes bankruptcy rare. The acquisition debtor is a holding company—an investment vehicle that likely holds less stable, non-utility companies like merchant generation companies—a type of company for which bankruptcy is

---

[58]   *See, e.g.*, Tom Hals, *NRG Energy's GenOn Unit Files for Bankruptcy*, Reuters (June 14, 2017), https://www.reuters.com/article/us-nrg-energy-genon-bankruptcy -idUSKBN1952G7 (describing how GenOn's creditors became its owners).

[59]   *See* Atlantic Tele-Network Co. v. Pub. Serv. Comm'n, 841 F.2d 70, 72–73 (3d Cir. 1988) (upholding Virgin Islands commission's conditions attached to the acquisi-tion of telephone company stock, where the commission found (in the court's words) that "since the [utility] stock is pledged as security for the [acquisition] debt, default would result in a chaotic situation for the utility"; and further holding, based on Virgin Islands statute, that "we do not believe the Virgin Islands legislature intended that the PSC would have to wait until disaster struck before taking remedial action").

[60]   Donald T. Hornstein, *Adaptation and Resiliency in Legal Systems: Resiliency, Adaptation, and the Upsides of Ex Post Lawmaking*, 89 N.C. L. Rev. 1549, 1562 n.67 (2011).

not rare.[61] If the combination of acquisition debt and other failing investments leaves the holding company unable to meet its obligations, it could enter, or its creditors could push it into, bankruptcy.

Then what? The bankruptcy trustee will carry out its legal duty—to maximize the bankruptcy estate's value so the creditors can recover what they can.[62] A major value will be the holding company's stock in the acquired utilities. So the trustee will auction those utilities off to the highest bidder. Recall Oncor: a healthy Texas utility whose private equity, highly leveraged owner went bankrupt; Oncor was sold to the highest bidder.[63] Nothing in bankruptcy law requires the trustee to select the most cost-effective utility operator. What the trustee must maximize is dollars, not performance.

But an alert commission can make performance the priority, if it acts affirmatively. It can add to its acquisition approval a condition stating that it will approve a post-default or post-bankruptcy owner only if that candidate, among all possible candidates, best meets the commission's criteria for performance. With that condition in place, the bankruptcy court's choice of acquirer will need to satisfy the commission's priorities.

This commission action is available because bankruptcy law does not preempt a commission's state law authority over ownership transfers.[64] That was the Texas experience. Oncor was owned 80 percent by Energy Future Holdings Corp (EFHC). Due to its high acquisition debt and its merchant generation troubles, EFHC went bankrupt. The bankruptcy court approved Oncor's acquisition by NextEra. The Texas Commission then rejected NextEra's

---

[61] Examples are subsidiaries of holding companies FirstEnergy, Exelon, Calpine and NRG. *See, e.g., Some of FirstEnergy's Power-Generation Businesses File for Bankruptcy*, WALL ST. J. (Apr. 1. 2018), https://www.wsj.com/articles/some-of -firstenergys-power-generation-businesses-file-for-bankruptcy-1522621469 ("A fleet of FirstEnergy Corp. power-generation businesses filed for chapter 11 bankruptcy ..."); *Troubled Calpine Files Bankruptcy*, N.Y. TIMES (Dec. 21, 2005), https://www.nytimes .com/2005/12/21/business/troubled-calpine-files-bankruptcy.html; Editorial, *Exelon Generation Texas Power Files Chapter 11 Bankruptcy*, POWER ENGINEERING (Nov. 7, 2017), https://www.power-eng.com/articles/2017/11/exelon-generation-texas-power -files-chapter-11-bankruptcy.html; Hals, *supra* note 58.

[62] *See* Commodity Futures Trading Comm'n v. Weintraub, 471 U.S. 343, 352 (1985) (holding that trustee has "the duty to maximize the value of the estate").

[63] *See Sempra Bests Berkshire with $9.45 Billion Offer for Oncor*, BLOOMBERG (Aug. 21, 2017), https://www.bloomberg.com/news/articles/2017-08-21/sempra-bests -berkshire-s-bid-for-oncor-with-9-45-billion-offer.

[64] The absence of preemption arises from Bankruptcy Code section 362(b)(4), which exempts from bankruptcy law's automatic stay "the commencement or continuation of an action or proceeding by a governmental unit ... to enforce such governmental unit's or organization's police and regulatory power." 11 U.S.C. § 362(b)(4). An explanation of this provision and the applicable case law appears in Appendix A.2.

acquisition application. No one suggested that the bankruptcy court's prior approval of NextEra bound the Texas Commission. EFHC's creditors had to return to bankruptcy court to repeat the process, producing a new winning bidder, Sempra (the holding company for San Diego Gas & Electric). Sempra then had to get the Texas Commission's permission to acquire Oncor. Again, no one suggested the bankruptcy court's approval of Sempra prevented the Texas Commission from finding otherwise, or from adding conditions to any the bankruptcy court had imposed.[65]

While the Texas Commission faced no federal preemption, its method—waiting for and reacting to what emerges from the bankruptcy court—limited its options, because the bankruptcy process emphasizes price over performance. Commissions instead should state in their merger policy that bankruptcy outcomes must satisfy the commission's specific performance criteria. Seeing this policy upfront, prospective acquisition lenders will know that if default occurs, their wish for the highest payback will take a back seat to the commission's performance priorities. And if then no lenders want to finance the acquisition, we will know that the transaction's purpose was not performance.

7.3.4   Acquisition Debt Limits Commissions' Ability to Extract Performance and Attract New Performers

An acquirer incurs acquisition debt because it expects post-acquisition earnings. If regulators, post-acquisition, act to reduce the expected earnings, they might weaken the holding company. Because a weakened holding company cannot provide capital support to the utility, regulators will hesitate to take such actions. By approving debt-financed acquisitions, then, regulators limit their future options. This problem arises in two main areas: cost discipline and competitive discipline.

Cost discipline: Chapter 5.3 explained that the acquirer pays a premium because it expects post-acquisition returns to exceed both its acquirer's required returns (its hurdle rate) and the commission's authorized returns. Suppose the commission approves a debt-financed acquisition. Suppose a year later the commission determines that the acquired utility's authorized return exceeds its required return. Lowering the authorized return to reflect the required return will push the utility's earnings below the projections that supported the acquisition debt. The utility, holding company, rating agencies, lenders and stockholders will all pressure the commission to reconsider—to

---

[65]   The Texas Commission approved the transaction (and all terms of a settlement among the parties) in *Oncor Electric Delivery-Sempra Energy Merger*, 2018 Tex. PUC LEXIS 592.

set the authorized return based not on proper capital market theory but on the holding company's private needs, needs that arose from its acquisition debt rather its utility service obligations. The concern applies not only when a commission adjusts the authorized return; it applies to any form of regulatory discipline, including disallowing imprudent costs and allocating to sharehold-ers the risk of investments that are prudent but turn out to be not used and useful.[66] The more debt in the utility's holding company family, the greater the post-acquisition pressure on the commission to refrain from imposing fiscal and operational discipline.

Competitive discipline: Chapter 1.2.2.3 explained another reason for acquisi-tion debt: the acquirer expects the utility to increase its earnings by rate-basing future infrastructure projects. What if the regulator decides that the utility must outsource those future projects competitively, thereby reducing the utility's own rate-basing opportunities? This action, like the cost-disciplining actions just discussed, will lower the utility's earnings below the acquirer's expec-tations. That lowering will put pressure on regulators to scrap competitive bidding and award all capital projects to the utility. Approving debt-financed acquisitions reduces regulators' flexibility.

7.3.5 Solutions: Five Regulatory Signals, Sent in Advance

"[H]igh acquisition premiums ... intensify the inherent conflict between shareholders and ratepayers."[67] To reduce the conflict, reduce the acquisition debt by limiting what acquirers pay. Commissions can do so by announcing a five-part policy.

1. Prohibit excessive acquisition prices: Commissions can establish a stand-ard for the acquisition price. Section 10(b) of PUHCA 1935 prohibited holding company acquisitions of utilities if the acquisition cost was "not reasonable or does not bear a fair relation to the sums invested in or the earning capacity of the utility assets to be acquired or the utility assets underlying the securities to be acquired."[68] Commissions can adopt a similar standard, backing it with metrics based on earnings expectations that preserve regulatory flexibility to discipline future performance.

---

[66] *See, e.g., New England Power Co.*, 8 F.E.R.C. ¶ 61,054 (1979), *aff'd sub nom.* NEPCO Mun. Rate Comm. v. FERC, 668 F.2d 1327 (D.C. Cir. 1981) (upholding FERC's decision to disallow rate-basing of prudent unamortized expenditures on can-celled (i.e., not used-and-useful) plant, while allowing their recovery over five years; treatment was a reasonable balance of policy objectives).

[67] Direct Testimony of Adam Gatewood at 6, Great Plains Energy-Westar Energy Merger I, Docket No. 16-KCPE-593-ACQ (Kan. Corp. Comm'n filed Dec. 16, 2016).

[68] PUHCA of 1935 § 10(b)(2)–(3), 15 U.S.C. § 79j(b)(2)–(3) (repealed 2005).

2. Limit recovery of the acquisition premium: The limit can be a complete prohibition, or a cap based on the prudence standard; specifically, that the benefit-cost ratio, calculated to include the premium in the cost variable, must equal or exceed the next most beneficial investment of those funds.[69]

3. Adjust the target utility's revenue requirement to reflect the true cost of capital: Commissions should make clear that if the acquirer buys the target's equity with debt, the utility's authorized return on rate base will reflect the cost of that debt; the equity financed with debt will not earn an equity-level return. Commissions also should establish authorized returns on equity reflecting the low risk of a conservatively financed, pure-play utility rather than a utility affiliated with a higher-risk, more leveraged holding company system.[70] And commissions should make clear that they will adjust the authorized return on equity to reflect the true cost of equity.

4. Establish ring-fencing requirements: As described in Chapters 7.4.8.2 and 7.4.8.3 below, ring-fencing prevents the holding company and its affiliates from extracting excess dividends from the utility, or using the utility's assets as security to support non-utility debt—two actions that encourage lenders to over-lend and acquirers to over-borrow.

5. Dampen expectations of automatic future rate-basing opportunities: Prior to any acquisition, the commission should make clear that an acquisition approval includes no implicit promise that future capital expenditure opportunities will necessarily go to the incumbent utility.

Together, these five measures will discipline prospective acquirers' earnings expectations and therefore their offer prices, bringing them closer to levels reflecting the discipline of a competitive market. Competition among acquirers will more likely be based on who can create the most customer benefits rather than who can finance the highest price. Bond-rating agencies will evaluate acquisition debt in light of the commission's limits on future utility earnings, signaling their support or concern accordingly. It is better to have the rating agencies warn acquirers away from debt-heavy transactions than

---

[69]   As explained in Chapter 4.3.3.
[70]   As the Connecticut regulators stated:
       [I]t may no longer be appropriate to use the NU holding company as a proxy for CL&P for the purposes of determining the cost of equity for ratemaking purposes. Not only might the degree of leveraging differ between the two entities, but the market perception of business risk might differ as well. ... It is not appropriate for CL&P ratepayers to incur capital costs that reflect the additional leveraging and business risk associated with NU's acquisition of the PSNH system.
Northeast Utilities-Public Service of New Hampshire Merger, 1992 Conn. PUC LEXIS 23, at *42.

to allow those transactions to occur and then have the rating agencies warn regulators against imposing appropriate cost discipline.

No commission has announced these policies ahead of a merger, though some variants appear in merger settlements approved by a commission—but only in a form acceptable to merger applicants that designed their transactions without these constraints. FERC in fact has no standards for acquisition financing—not in its 1996 Merger Policy Statement, not in its Order Nos. 642, 667 and 669, and not in its many merger opinions. Indeed, many FERC merger decisions fail even to describe a proposed merger's financing, let alone assess the financing's consistency with the public interest.

7.4   NON-UTILITY BUSINESS RISKS

> In a laboratory setting, it might be possible to take a utility apart and analyze it so as to insulate ratepayers from all of the potential costs and risks of [investing in non-utility businesses]. Then we could begin to discuss whether the utility can be expected to prudently diversify its activities so as to take advantage of opportunities to minimize its costs. In the real world, ratepayers are unavoidably involved.[71]

Non-utility businesses bring risks to the utility and its customers. This sub-section first identifies the types of business risks; then describes five adverse effects: contagion, weakened utility finances, quality-of-service slippage, reduced accountability to regulators and loss of regulatory control over future acquisitions. Merger applicants tell regulators these risks are speculative but tell shareholders the risks are material. Given that materiality, the section closes with recommendations for rules that limit the risks and contain their effects.

7.4.1   Types of Business Risk

With PUHCA 1935's repeal, a utility's holding company owner can buy, or be bought by, non-utility businesses of any type or size, located anywhere. These businesses involve risks different from and greater than those associated with providing a monopoly utility service. Pure-play utilities, protected from competition and legally assured of just and reasonable rates, have a record of stable earnings and growth. Holding company systems with large non-utility businesses change that model:

> In the past, utility managers failed their investors when they bet the company on a technology they did not understand (nuclear power), when they entered businesses

---

[71]   Pacific Power & Light Co., 1985 Wash. UTC LEXIS 45, at *36–37.

far afield from their experience (diversification), and when they plunged into seemingly related businesses without adjusting their finances to the new risk levels (merchant generation, power marketing, and foreign investment).[72]

Non-utility business risks are sufficiently large to trigger the holding company's disclosure obligations under federal securities law. Consider these four examples, drawn from Exelon's submission to the Securities and Exchange Commission when it was seeking to acquire the non-generation-owning PHI:

- *Operational risk:* For reasons within and outside the company's control, older generation could suffer operational failure, requiring new expenditures that could adversely affect operations, financial condition or cash flow.
- *Climate change risk:* Exelon owned over 12,000 MW of fossil generation plants. The "possible physical risks of climate change," and "mandatory programs to reduce GHG emissions," could adversely affect operations and finance.
- *Economic risk from low-cost shale:* The development of low-cost shale gas sources could lower the value of Exelon's embedded generation investment.
- *Nuclear-specific risk:* Exelon's nuclear generation fleet "is subject to liability, property damage and other risks associated with major incidents at any of its nuclear stations." Exelon says it "has reduced its financial exposure to these risks through insurance and other industry risk-sharing provisions." By how much, Exelon didn't say—except to say that on nuclear waste it is at risk for "losses [that] could have a material adverse effect on Exelon's and Generation's [Exelon's generation affiliate] financial condition and results of operations."[73]

Then there is the nuclear waste. Exelon's nuclear-owning subsidiary is legally responsible for its disposal, but the nation remains undecided on a permanent burial place.[74] Exelon has bet that someday, somehow, somewhere, someone will take care of its nuclear waste, without unanticipated cost to Exelon.

---

[72] Leonard S. Hyman, *Investing in the "Plain Vanilla" Utility*, 24 ENERGY L.J. 1, 10 (2003). *See also* Markian M.W. Melnyk & William S. Lamb, *PUHCA's Gone: What Is Next for Holding Companies?*, 27 ENERGY L.J. 1, 10 (2006) (finding that utilities' non-utility investments in the 1980s were "not particularly successful").

[73] Exelon Corp., *supra* note 9, at 50, 33, 44, 14, respectively.

[74] *See* OFFICE OF PUB. AFFAIRS, U.S. NUCLEAR REGULATORY COMM'N, BACKGROUNDER: RADIOACTIVE WASTE 2 (2019), https://www.nrc.gov/docs/ML0501/ML050110277.pdf ("At this time there are no facilities for permanent disposal of high-level waste."); *Key Issues: Disposal of High Level Nuclear Waste*, U.S. GOV'T

Foreign holding companies, which now own at least twenty U.S. utilities,[75] represent a distinct set of risks. Foreign laws on taxes, financial disclosure, service quality, and competitive conduct affect those companies' financial results in ways unfamiliar to U.S. regulators and investors. Also unfamiliar are (a) how foreign corporate executives evaluate new business risks and finance new acquisitions, (b) how foreign utility regulators set standards and compensate for performance, and (c) how foreign political sectors intervene in business and regulatory decision-making. Irritation in the political and trade relationships between the U.S. and foreign governments can also affect the foreign affiliates' business prospects. Currency differences and changing exchange rates make the inter-affiliate prices hard to determine. Remote records and foreign language add to regulators' difficulties in finding facts. These distinct foreign risks have not drawn much regulatory attention.[76] Indeed, FERC granted a German acquirer a waiver from having to produce information on foreign energy interests: "We find that it is not necessary for E.ON to provide information at this time about its subsidiaries and affiliates that are not doing business in the United States or are transacting with other subsidiaries and affiliates within the United States."[77] The waiver was unaccompanied by explanation.

7.4.2   Contagion

Holding companies have corporate boundaries between their utility and non-utility affiliates, but risks seep through. For pure-play utilities, bond rating agencies base ratings on predictable factors like debt-equity ratios, operational performance and regulatory treatment. But for utility members of complex holding companies, the rating agencies' "presumption is typically that the

---

ACCOUNTABILITY   OFFICE,   https://www.gao.gov/key_issues/disposal_of_highlevel _nuclear_waste/issue_summary (last visited Jan. 15, 2020) ("The amount of waste is expected to increase to about 140,000 metric tons over the next several decades. However, there is still no disposal site in the United States. After spending decades and billions of dollars to research potential sites for a permanent disposal site, ... the future prospects for permanent disposal remain unclear.").

[75]   *See* Table 3.3.

[76]   One significant exception: Chapter 11.2 will describe how the Province of Ontario's interference in the management of its utility holding company, Hydro One, led Washington State's commission to reject Hydro One's acquisition of Avista, one of the state's utilities.

[77]   *E.ON-Powergen Merger*, 97 F.E.R.C. ¶ 61,049, at p. 61,285 (2001) (authorizing acquisition, granting waiver of information requirements in Part 33.2(c)(2)).

utility subsidiaries will be affected by the nonutility businesses of a holding company"—unless there are "insulating factors."[78] Consider these examples:

- *Oncor:* This Texas utility was owned by a debt-heavy, bankrupt parent. Moody's found that the parent's debt pressured Oncor's credit ratings: "Uncertainties surrounding the bankruptcy process include the high level of parent company debt that sits on top of Oncor and constrains Oncor's rating at this time." Freeing Oncor from its parent, Moody's said, would "[resolve] ... family contagion risk and [reduce] ... parent holding company debt, both credit positives."[79]
- *Entergy:* In the early 1990s, Entergy (formerly Middle South) was the holding company owner of four utilities, each housed in a separate corporation. Entergy proposed to acquire a fifth utility, Gulf States, then in mid-litigation over the prudence of its River Bend nuclear investment. FERC found that "the potential for an adverse judgment [in the prudence litigation] may affect [acquirer] Entergy Corporation's risk in capital markets and, thus, its cost of capital. The cost of capital for the parent, in turn, will affect all of the subsidiaries."[80]
- *Pinnacle West:* In the 1980s, Pinnacle West, the holding company owner of the utility Arizona Public Service, bought Merabank, a savings and loan company. When Merabank failed, Pinnacle West proposed filing for bankruptcy as a way to avoid having to provide the bank with more capital. That impending bankruptcy caused rating agencies to downgrade APS's bonds to near-junk bond status, raising its borrowing costs.[81]

---

[78]   *See* Melnyk & Lamb, *supra* note 72, at 23.

[79]   Direct Testimony of John Reed at 35, Oncor Electric Delivery-NextEra Energy Merger, PUC Docket No. 46238 (Tex. Pub. Util. Comm'n filed October 31, 2016) (quoting MOODY'S INVESTORS SERVICE, ONCOR ELECTRIC DELIVERY COMPANY LLC: EXPLORING THE LIMITS OF PARENT COMPANY LEVERAGE, AGAIN 1, 4 (2015)).

[80]   *Entergy-Gulf States Merger*, 62 F.E.R.C. ¶ 61,073, at p. 61,371 n.75 (1993) (hearing order).

[81]   The Arizona Commission described the Pinnacle West situation in an order addressing Tucson Electric's affiliates' business failures. *See* Tucson Elec. Power Co., 1997 Ariz. PUC LEXIS 2, at *25–26. In 1990–91, the author represented the Arizona Corporation Commission in its complaint seeking to have the Securities and Exchange Commission revoke Pinnacle West's exemption under the now-repealed Public Utility Holding Company Act of 1935. The Arizona Commission argued that the exemption, which allowed Pinnacle West to own non-utility businesses, had become, in the language of PUHCA section 3(a), "detrimental to the public interest and the interest of investors and consumers." 15 U.S.C. § 79c(a) (repealed 2005). The SEC ignored the complaint.

For additional examples of contagion—non-utility business risk affecting the utility—see *Exelon-PHI Merger*, 2015 D.C. PUC LEXIS 203, at *174 ¶ 142 (finding

7.4.3 Weakened Utility Finances

A holding company's non-utility risks affect its decisions on the utility's finances, in two directions: taking money out and putting money in.

Taking money out: A utility's captive customers provide predictable cash, monthly. The holding company can use that cash, and the assets that produce it, to help its higher-risk affiliates. It can compel the utility to (a) pay dividends to the holding company in amounts necessary to finance the non-utility affiliates, (b) lend money directly to those affiliates, or (c) pledge the utility's assets as collateral for third-party loans to the affiliates. The Wisconsin Commission spelled out the problem:

> The combination of [the utility holding company] WICOR's dividend policy and its business objectives, which include acquisition as a major goal, puts pressure on Wisconsin Gas Company to provide an ample flow of cash to WICOR. Thus, the needs of WICOR could inappropriately become the "driver" in determining the amount of the Wisconsin Gas dividend.

Prior dividend payouts had not harmed the utility, the Commission found. But by continuing to extract dividends while ignoring the utility's needs, the holding company risked "an increase in the long-term overall cost of capital for the utility due to a reduction in its current credit standing." Extracting dividends "could benefit WICOR's shareholders, but at the expense of Wisconsin Gas Company ratepayers."[82]

---

that Pepco "will be exposed to additional financial risks from the Proposed Merger due to Exelon's unregulated businesses"); *id.* ¶ 259 (finding that that "ratepayers could be impacted if the cost of capital available to Pepco ... is higher because of Exelon's ownership of non-jurisdictional business operations in general and nuclear operations in particular"); Southern California Edison-San Diego Gas & Electric Merger, 1991 Cal. PUC LEXIS 253 (expressing concern about the proposed merger's mixing of utility and non-utility businesses); Oncor Electric Delivery-NextEra Energy Merger, 2017 Tex. PUC LEXIS 807, at text accompanying nn.8 & 14 (finding that "the expansive and diversified structure of NextEra Energy and its affiliates would subject Oncor to new and potentially substantial risks," including, but not limited to, "potential changes in renewable demand resulting from changes in climate or tax policy, commodity risks, retail electric provider risks, as well as power and nuclear generation risks, ... [which] in conjunction with the high amount of leverage at NextEra Energy, increase the likelihood that unforeseen events could jeopardize Oncor's financial stability").

[82] WICOR, Inc., 1987 Wisc. PUC LEXIS 53, at *19–20. *See also* Ariz. Corp. Comm'n v. State *ex rel.* Woods, 830 P.2d 807, 818 (Ariz. 1992) (en banc) ("The Commission must certainly be given the power to prevent a public utility corporation from engaging in transactions that will so adversely affect its financial position that the ratepayers will have to make good the losses ... .").

Putting money in: The utility business is capital-intensive. A utility continuously adds, repairs, upgrades and modernizes its capital equipment. Large generating plants and transmission lines cost billions and take years to build. Under traditional cost-based ratemaking, rates do not start recovering these construction costs from customers until the assets begin commercial operation.[83] So the utility needs to finance plant construction with equity and long-term debt. A utility's holding company is the utility's sole source of new equity. But when the holding company puts scarce dollars into non-utility businesses it has less equity for its utilities.

7.4.4   Quality of Service Slippage

A holding company's business risks affect not only its finances but also its utilities' operations, in two ways.

Business complexity distracts management: Whether succeeding or failing, non-utility businesses distract management. Successes cause management to take more risks to produce more success; failures force management to invest time in saving or selling the troubled businesses. El Paso Electric Company had a real estate subsidiary that ran hotels and developed other opportunities. It lost $195 million—in the Texas Commission's words, a "complete failure." Utility management's efforts to finance, save, then sell off these operations consumed "a significant amount of time, energy, and resources," diverting attention from utility operations.[84]

Non-utility financial pressures cause cost-cutting: If the holding company diverts utility funds to help the non-utility businesses, the utility's operations and infrastructure can suffer. The Kansas Commission found that to repay its acquisition debt, GPE would take from the to-be-acquired Westar utilities the savings from post-acquisition utility operations. Doing so would cause the utilities to cut "vegetation management activities, and defer maintenance and system improvements"—all actions that would endanger public safety.[85]

---

[83]   Some state legislatures and commissions have authorized recovery of plant investment, or at least a return on the investment, prior to the construction's completion. For examples, see SCOTT HEMPLING & SCOTT H. STRAUSS, NAT'L REGULATORY RESEARCH INST., PRE-APPROVAL COMMITMENTS: WHEN AND UNDER WHAT CONDITIONS SHOULD REGULATORS COMMIT RATEPAYER DOLLARS TO UTILITY-PROPOSED CAPITAL PROJECTS? (2008), http://www.nrri.org/documents/317330/f3ce2129-7fdf-419f-948d-00f3694dc087.

[84]   El Paso Elec. Co., 1990 Tex. PUC LEXIS 188, at *18.

[85]   Great Plains Energy-Westar Energy Merger I, 2017 Kan. PUC LEXIS 1142, at *79 ¶ 88. *But see* Southern California Edison-San Diego Gas & Electric Merger, 1991 Cal. PUC LEXIS 253 (quality of service under merger will neither improve nor deteriorate); Kansas Power & Light-Kansas Gas & Electric Merger, 1991 Mo. PSC LEXIS

7.4.5   Reduced Regulatory Accountability

Some holding companies acquire utilities to diversify regulatory risk.[86] Diversifying regulatory risk means, literally, making the holding company's financial health less dependent on the decisions of any single state's commission. Exelon's acquisition of Pepco shrank Pepco's financial importance to its holding company by a factor of five[87]—a factor that will grow as Exelon makes more acquisitions.

Diversifying risk sounds sensible, from the shareholders' perspective. From the customers' perspective there is a catch. The less the holding company depends on a commission, the less attention it need pay to that commission. A commission's tools are limited. It cannot force a utility to perform. It cannot create or fix a utility's culture. It cannot replace the company's executives or its board.[88] A commission can try to change behavior through financial rewards and penalties, but these tools are imprecise: they cause executives to chase after specific dollars (such as for energy efficiency, transmission construction, fuel purchases or generation performance) rather than improve performance as a whole; and when the inducements disappear the desires diminish. Worse, financial penalties can be counterproductive if they weaken the utility's ability to improve. And as each utility's earnings shrink in relation to the holding company's total earnings, so diminishes the influence that any of these measures will have on holding company decisions.

44, at *15 (no showing that merger would "interfere with KPL's capacity to render safe and adequate service to its Missouri ratepayers").

[86]   *See, e.g.*, Exelon Corp., Registration Statement (Form S-4) at 64 (June 27, 2011) (describing diversification of regulatory risks as a benefit from acquiring BG&E).

[87]   Prior to the Exelon acquisition, Pepco's contribution to PHI's revenues was 43 percent; after the transaction, its contribution to Exelon's revenues would be 8.2 percent. *See* Exelon Corp., *supra* note 9, at 74; Pepco Holdings, Inc., *supra* note 16, at 5 (together showing that Exelon's 2013 operating revenue was $24.9 billion, PHI's 2013 operating revenue was $4.67 billion and Pepco's operating revenue was $2.03 billion). An alternative view: prior to their acquisition by Exelon, PHI's three utilities earned 95 percent of PHI's operating revenues. *Id.* (showing that in 2013, "power delivery" accounted for $4.472 billion while total holding company operating revenue was $4.675 billion; thus "power delivery"—traditional electric service—accounted for 95 percent of PHI's operating revenue).

[88]   *Cf.* Cal. Sys. Operator Corp. v. FERC, 372 F.2d 395, 401 (D.C. Cir. 2004) (holding that FERC's authority over "practice[s] ... affecting ... rate[s]," under Federal Power Act section 206, did not include the authority to order a utility to replace its board).

7.4.6   Loss of Regulatory Control over Future Acquisitions

The typical utility merger is a merger of holding companies. The post-acquisition entity is not a single combined utility company; it is a corporate family controlled by a holding company. This section (7.4) has explained how a holding company with non-utility businesses subjects its utilities to the risks of contagion, financial weakening, quality-of-service slippage and reduced accountability. When a state commission receives an acquisition application, it can identify these risks, then take action to address them.[89]

Then what? Once the holding company completes a utility acquisition subject to a state commission's jurisdiction, it can buy businesses that are not subject to the commission's jurisdiction. So the commission's approval has two components, one explicit and one implicit. Explicitly, the commission approves its utility's affiliation with what the original application described—the business mix controlled by the holding company today. But implicitly, the commission has approved its utility's affiliation with every business the holding company acquires in the future. The reason: most state commissions have jurisdiction over only the utility, not the holding company; and most states when they approve a holding company's acquisition of their utility say nothing about the holding company's future acquisitions of other companies. So even the simplest transaction—a utility's executives placing a shell holding company above the utility, a transaction easily winning state commission approval because no non-utility risk exists at that time—can transform a pure-play utility into a subsidiary of a conglomerate. That simple shell holding company can then make unlimited acquisitions and investments outside the state commission's jurisdiction. By a holding company's own admission, the associated risks are material:

> [Exelon's acquisition] initiatives may involve significant risks and uncertainties, including distraction of management from current operations, inadequate return on capital, and unidentified issues not discovered in the diligence performed prior to launching an initiative or entering a market. As these markets mature, there may be new market entrants or expansion by established competitors that increase competition for customers and resources.[90]

That holding companies and their non-utility acquisitions fall outside most state commissions' jurisdiction caused less concern prior to 2005, because PUHCA 1935 imposed prohibitions and limits on holding companies and their

---

[89]   We will discuss options for risk-reducing actions shortly, in Chapter 7.4.8.
[90]   Exelon Corp., *supra* note 9, at 63.

acquisitions. But with few exceptions, states did not react to the Act's 2005 repeal by upgrading their own jurisdiction.

Holding company risk-taking can also increase the acquisition premium. The greater the holding company's non-utility risks, the more it will value the utility target as a hedge, so the higher the premium it will offer. The higher the acquirer's premium, the more attractive will the acquirer be to the utility target. All else being equal, then, a utility target will prefer an acquirer with high risks over an acquirer with low risks—precisely the opposite of what a commission should approve. And a holding company can have so many high-risk businesses that buying even a multi-billion-dollar utility monopoly fails to lower overall risk sufficiently. That's how Moody's assessed Exelon's proposed purchase of PHI. Despite "the strategic benefits of linking a company that is long on generation resources with a company that is long on customer load,"

> the combined entity will still be exposed to earnings and cash flow volatility due to a large unregulated business platform whose financial performance is influenced by market determined commodity pricing levels. ... [W]e believe that it will be very challenging for [Exelon] to easily transform the company's business mix into one that is materially more balanced across regulated operations given the sheer size of the existing unregulated footprint.[91]

7.4.7   The "Speculation" Defense

Merger applicants, and some commissions, dismiss business-risk concerns as speculative. Though the type, timing and level of harm is uncertain, identifying risks is not speculating—not given these two facts: (1) the post-acquisition company can acquire non-utility businesses of any type at any time, without any commission's permission or even knowledge, so the risks will emerge only after the fact; and (2) the acquired businesses will likely have objectives that conflict with the local utility's service obligations. To dismiss those two facts is to assume that when a utility's sole shareholder is free to engage in unlimited, unrelated business activities, the utility and its customers will never face harm. That is the real speculation.

Only in utility regulation is the term "speculate" considered pejorative. John Snow speculated that London's 1854 cholera epidemic might be related to

---

[91] MOODY'S INVESTORS SERVICE, MOODY'S REVIEWS EXELON AND EXELON GENERATION FOR POSSIBLE DOWNGRADE; AFFIRMS CONSTELLATION, OUTLOOK POSITIVE 1 (2011), *attached as* Exhibit KLA-3 to Direct Testimony of Karie L. Anderson, Exelon-Constellation Energy Group Merger, Case No. 9271 (Md. Pub. Serv. Comm'n filed May 25, 2011).

a water pump—and was right.[92] Astronomers speculated about black holes—and then discovered them. Nikola Tesla and Thomas Edison speculated about ways to move electric current over long distances—and found solutions.[93] The likelihood of having a car accident is very small, yet people who wear seatbelts are not accused of speculating. If speculating means guessing without evidentiary or logical basis, regulators should not speculate. But regulators should extrapolate—identify possible outcomes, assign probabilities, and weigh harms and benefits. The harms described in this chapter are the logical, predictable results of this fact: in a monopoly market context, private motivations deviate from the public interest. Combine that fact with uncertainty, and one must extrapolate. Extrapolating is not speculating.

7.4.8   Regulatory Solutions

Reducing risk requires constraints—on utilities, their holding companies and their affiliates. Absent statutory constraints, the solution is merger conditions. Those conditions should include ring-fencing, which seeks to protect the utility from non-utility business risks. But instead of requiring protections against risks, it is better to eliminate or reduce those risks, through six other measures. This subsection assesses each of these tools, then closes by discussing enforcement options and their difficulties.

Commissions should establish these requirements well ahead of any merger. That way, merger negotiators will arrive at a purchase price that reflects earnings expectations disciplined by the commission's policies. Otherwise, the merging parties will negotiate a price based on higher earnings expectations—expectations unconstrained by the commission's guardrails—then pressure the commission to remove those guardrails or risk killing the transaction.

7.4.8.1 Merger rules: indirect authority over holding companies
This chapter has described the utility's risks: exposure to excess leveraging from debt-sourced equity, holding company extraction of utility funds, bond downgrades, reduced access to equity, holding company control of utility budgets, service quality slippage and the prospect of ownership change if the holding company defaults. Those risks can come from actions at any corporate level—holding company, non-utility subsidiary, utility subsidiary. To protect

---

[92] This drama is beautifully retold by Edward Tufte in his Visual Explanations 27–37 (1997). See a photograph of London's John Snow Pub, located at the site of the deadly pump, at https://www.edwardtufte.com/bboard/q-and-a-fetch-msg?msg_id=0002Je.

[93] For a fine fictional account, see Graham Moore, The Last Days of Night (2017).

the utility and its customers, commissions need authority to limit and review corporate actions, and to intervene at trouble points, wherever in the holding company they occur.

But nearly all commissions lack the necessary authority over the holding company and its non-utility affiliates. As previously explained, that authority gap was not a problem before 2005, because PUHCA 1935 required SEC permission for corporate activities at all levels—the top holding company, sub-holding companies and all affiliates, whether utility or non-utility.[94] The SEC then was obligated to block any holding company securities issuance that tripped any of these six wires:

- "the security is not reasonably adapted to the security structure of the declarant and other companies in the same holding-company system";
- "the security is not reasonably adapted to the earning power of the declarant";
- "financing by the issue and sale of the particular security is not necessary or appropriate to the economical and efficient operation of a business in which the applicant lawfully is engaged or has an interest";
- "the fees, commissions, or other remuneration, to whomsoever paid, directly or indirectly, in connection with the issue, sale, or distribution of the security are not reasonable";
- "in the case of a security that is a guaranty of, or assumption of liability on, a security of another company, the circumstances are such as to constitute the making of such guaranty or the assumption of such liability an improper risk for the declarant"; or
- "the terms and conditions of the issue or sale of the security are detrimental to the public interest or the interest of investors or consumers."[95]

Congress mandated these tests because holding companies had been issuing securities based on "fictitious or unsound asset values having no fair relation to the sums invested in or the earning capacity of the properties and upon the basis of paper profits from intercompany transactions, or in anticipation of excessive revenues from subsidiary public-utility companies."[96]

With PUHCA 1935's repeal, review of holding company financings needs to come from the state commissions and FERC. But neither state utility finance

---

[94] This authority applied to what practitioners call the "registered" holding companies—mostly multi-state entities. The SEC also had authority to subject non-registered holding companies (known as "exempt" companies—mostly single-state companies) to these reviews if necessary to prevent detriment to the public interest.

[95] PUHCA of 1935 § 7(d), 15 U.S.C. § 79g(d) (repealed 2005).

[96] *Id.* § 1(b)(1).

statutes, nor the Federal Power Act, authorize regulators to check and reject financings by utility holding companies or their non-utility subsidiaries.[97] The result? Once a holding company has acquired a utility, no state or federal law allows a regulator to block the holding company from issuing securities that create risks to its utilities.

Regulators do have authority over securities issuances by utilities. FERC's authority comes from Federal Power Act section 204.[98] For utilities seeking to issue securities to finance non-utility businesses, FERC has established four requirements:

- If the utility's to-be-issued debt is secured by utility assets, the debt's proceeds must go to utility purposes only.
- If the utility secures its debt with its assets, then divests those assets to a third party or spins them off to shareholders, the debt must depart along with the assets. The utility may not dump the assets but keep the debt.

---

[97] The prominent exception is Wisconsin's statute, providing that "[n]o holding company system may be operated in any way which materially impairs the credit, ability to acquire capital on reasonable terms or ability to provide safe, reasonable, reliable and adequate utility service of any public utility affiliate in the holding company system." Wis. Stat. § 196.795(5)(g). Upholding this statute, the U.S. Court of Appeals for the Seventh Circuit held that states may regulate actions at the holding company level without violating the U.S. Constitution's Commerce Clause, provided the regulation treats interstate and intrastate actions comparably and does not pose an excessive burden on interstate commerce relative to the putative in-state benefits. *Alliant Energy Corp. v. Bie*, 330 F.3d 904, 916-17 (7th Cir. 2003). The author was an expert witness for the State of Wisconsin in the U.S. District proceeding reviewed by the Seventh Circuit. The *Alliant* decision cited, among other cases, *Baltimore Gas & Elec. Co v. Heintz*, 760 F.2d 1408, 1424–25 (4th Cir. 1985), which upheld against Commerce Clause attack a Maryland statute prohibiting non-utilities from acquiring more than 10 percent of a Maryland utility. The *Heintz* Court reasoned that "a necessary adjunct to ensuring the protection of consumers is the authority to regulate the corporate structure of public utilities," given the possibility that holding companies will engage in "deceptive financing practices, non-disclosure of important corporate accounts and the manipulation of various 'service charges'"—all to the consumers' detriment.

[98] Section 204 requires FERC approval whenever a public utility proposes to "issue any security, or assume any obligation or liability as guarantor, endorser, surety, or otherwise in respect of any security of another person." The issuance must be

> or some lawful object, within the corporate purposes of the applicant and compatible with the public interest, which is necessary or appropriate for or consistent with the proper performance by the applicant of service as a public utility and which will not impair its ability to perform that service, and ... is reasonably necessary or appropriate for such purposes.

Federal Power Act § 204(a), 16 U.S.C. § 824c(a). These provisions "ensure the financial viability of public utilities obligated to serve consumers of electricity." *FirstLight MA Hydro LLC*, 167 F.E.R.C. ¶ 61,008 at P 10 (2019).

- If the utility divests or spins off assets financed with unsecured debt, the associated unsecured debt must follow the assets.[99]
- If the utility has used the proceeds from unsecured debt for non-utility purposes, then divests or spins off the non-utility business, the debt must follow the non-utility business.[100]

But these requirements don't apply when the issuer is the holding company. And they don't apply to most utilities, because under Federal Power Act section 204 FERC's authority over utility security issuances exists only when a state lacks that authority.[101]

Like the Federal Power Act, state statutes address financings—but only by utilities. These statutes do have useful features. Typically, they:

- identify the types of securities issuances triggering review;[102]
- specify permissible uses of the proceeds;[103]
- establish criteria for commission approval;[104] and

---

[99] *Westar Energy, Inc.*, 102 F.E.R.C. ¶ 61,186 at PP 20–22 (2003); *Westar Energy, Inc.*, 104 F.E.R.C. ¶ 61,018 at PP 5–6 (2003). In this proceeding, the author represented the Kansas Corporation Commission. In a separate FERC proceeding, the Kansas Commission (represented by the author) had argued that FERC misinterpreted Federal Power Act section 204, which requires utility issuances to be "necessary or appropriate for or consistent with the proper performance by the applicant of service as a public utility," because raising funds for an unrelated nonutility business is not "necessary" for the proper performance of public utility service. FERC disagreed.

[100] *UtiliCorp United Inc.*, 99 F.E.R.C. ¶ 61,293, at p. 62,243 (2002) (finding that given UtiliCorp's favorable interest coverage ratio, the issuance would not "impair the utility's ability to perform as a public utility"). In this proceeding, the author represented the Kansas Commission.

[101] *See* FPA § 204(f) ("The provisions of this section shall not extend to a public utility organized and operating in a State under the laws of which its security issues are regulated by a State commission.").

[102] An Arizona statute requires Commission approval of any utility issuance of stocks and stock certificates, bonds, notes and other evidence of indebtedness having terms of more than one year. Ariz. Rev. Stat. § 40-301.

[103] An Illinois statute requires that the "money, property or labor to be procured or paid for by such [security] issue [must be] reasonably required for the purpose or purposes specified in the [regulatory approval] order." 220 Ill. Comp. Stat. 5 / 6-102(a).

[104] A Minnesota statute requires that the amount of debt or equity issued must "bear a reasonable proportion ... to the value of the property, due consideration being given to the nature of the business of the public utility, its credit and prospects, [and] the possibility that the value of the property may change from time to time." The Commission also must consider the issuance's effect on the "management and operation" of the public utility. Minn. Stat. § 216B.49. *See also* Md. Code Ann., Pub. Util. § 6-101 (securities issuance must be "consistent with the public convenience and necessity"); Ariz. Rev. Stat. § 40-301 (securities issuance must be "compatible ... with sound

- authorize or require commissions to set conditions and limits on the size and use of the financing's proceeds.[105]

But again, these features apply only when the issuer is a utility, not its holding company or a non-utility affiliate.

Lacking statutory authority to regulate the holding company directly, commissions can use merger conditions to regulate the holding company and its non-utility affiliates indirectly. We turn now to the merger conditions regulators use.

7.4.8.2 "Ring-fencing": necessary but not sufficient

Ring-fencing aims to reduce contagion—a utility's exposure to and harm from its holding company's business risks. Typical ring-fencing measures do the following:

- prohibit the holding company from extracting excess funds from the utility.
- prohibit the utility from charging ratepayers for any debt costs or equity costs attributable to the holding company's business risks.
- prevent the holding company from forcing the utility to join the holding company in bankruptcy. One such measure is a "special purpose entity" (SPE), placed between the holding company and the utility. The SPE is controlled by an independent director whose affirmative vote is required for the utility to enter bankruptcy.[106]
- prohibit the utility from financially supporting, or bearing any risk associated with, affiliated non-utility businesses—such as by loaning money to, guaranteeing loans of, pledging its assets to support the debt of or otherwise supporting the debt of, any holding company affiliate.[107]

Any early version of ring-fencing appeared in a stipulation attached to the Oregon Commission's order approving MidAmerican's acquisition of

---

financial practices"); Ohio Rev. Code Ann. § 4905.40 (commission must consider the issuance's effect on "the present and prospective revenue requirements of the utility").

[105] *See, e.g.*, Ariz. Rev. Stat. § 40-302 (authorizing the commission to condition issuances "as it deems reasonable and necessary").

[106] In Figure 3.2, depicting Exelon's corporate structure, notice the SPE between Exelon Energy Delivery Company (the holding company for all the utility companies) and PHI (the holding company for Pepco, Delmarva Power & Light and Atlantic City Electric).

[107] For an extensive discussion of ring-fencing—its history, purposes and alternative measures—see *Hawaiian Electric-NextEra Energy Merger*, Docket No. 2015-0022, Order No. 33795, at sec. VIII.A.6 (Haw. Pub. Util. Comm'n July 15, 2016).

PacifiCorp in 2006. (MidAmerican was a holding company owning several other utilities.) The stipulation included these elements:

- *Separate financing:* PacifiCorp (the acquired utility) must maintain its own debt and preferred stock, as well as its own ratings for its long-term debt and preferred stock.
- *Dividend limits:* Without Commission approval, PacifiCorp may not pay to its holding company owner any dividends that would reduce the utility's equity ratio below Commission-specified levels. Nor may the utility pay any dividends if its debt ratings fall below specified levels.
- *Limits on holding company leveraging:* The holding company's capital structure must maintain specified percentages of equity for five years.
- *No utility support of non-utility businesses:* Without Commission approval, PacifiCorp and its subsidiaries may not loan or transfer funds to, or assume liabilities on behalf of, or pledge assets as security for, any of the merged company's subsidiaries.
- *Insulation from debt costs:* PacifiCorp may not seek in rate cases a cost of capital higher than what the cost would have been absent the acquisition. And if PacifiCorp refinances its debt within a year of the acquisition, its rates cannot rise due to the refinancing. Also, if a rating agency downgrades PacifiCorp's senior long-term debt and attributes the downgrade to the acquisition, the Commission will not allow in rates any cost increase associated with the downgrade.
- *Information access:* Both the utility and the holding company must provide the Commission all credit rating agency reports relating to MidAmerican and PacifiCorp, and any information about non-utility affiliates that might affect the utility.
- *Bankruptcy avoidance:* The holding company must provide the Commission a "non-consolidation opinion" demonstrating that these ring-fencing provisions are sufficient to prevent the utility from being pulled into the holding company's bankruptcy.[108]

And in conditioning its approval of Exelon's acquisition of Constellation (Constellation was the holding company for Baltimore Gas & Electric), the

---

[108] MidAmerican Energy-PacifiCorp Merger, 2006 Ore. PUC LEXIS 113, at *64. *See also* Iberdrola-Energy East Merger, 2008 N.Y. PUC LEXIS 448, at *23–24 (requiring each New York utility subsidiary of Iberdrola, a Spanish holding company, to register with major bond rating agencies and maintain at least investment grade ratings, as a condition of allowing the utility subsidiaries to pay dividends to the holding company).

298 *Regulating mergers and acquisitions of U.S. electric utilities*

Maryland Commission adopted much of the Oregon model, with these additions among others:

- BGE can make no dividend payments to its holding company for two years. After that period it must notify the Commission 30 days before paying any new dividend (and provide calculations showing that BGE's equity ratio will not fall below 48 percent).
- Exelon may not seek a change in the acquisition approval order's financial conditions for three years, and then only if there is a material change in circumstances.
- For any reorganization that does not trigger Commission jurisdiction, Exelon must give the Commission 90 days' notice. That notice must include an opinion from bankruptcy counsel either (a) stating that the change will not diminish the existing protections' effectiveness, or (b) specifying the new steps necessary to maintain that effectiveness (in which case Exelon must commit to taking those steps).[109]

Ring-fencing is like a seatbelt. A seatbelt reduces the probability of harm; it does not address the sources of harm—bad driving, unsafe roads, dangerous car design. Similarly, ring-fencing does not address the causes of harm. It does not limit the amount, type, location, financing or timing of the holding company's non-utility investments. As a result, ring-fencing leaves utilities vulnerable in the following five ways.

Loss of utility's access to equity capital: Ring-fencing does not eliminate the risk that non-utility business losses will leave the holding company unable to supply the utility with sufficient equity capital. (Recall that the holding company is the utility's sole source of equity.) Ring-fencing prevents the holding company from draining capital from the utility; it doesn't make the holding company put sufficient capital into the utility.

---

[109] Exelon-Constellation Energy Group Merger, 2012 Md. PSC LEXIS 12. *See also* Aquila-Black Hills Merger, 2007 Iowa PUC LEXIS 341, at *9–14 (approving the acquisition by Black Hills, a multistate utility, of Aquila's natural gas assets in Iowa; expressing concern about Black Hills' already "low investment-grade rating" and including conditions (a) barring any financial support by Black Hills's Iowa utility for Aquila's non-utility businesses, (b) barring loans from the non-utility businesses to the utilities, (c) requiring regulatory approval for any utility dividend payments that would put Black Hills's standalone equity level below 40 percent of total long-term capitalization, (d) requiring that sales from the utility to the affiliates be at the higher of cost or market price, and (e) requiring the utilities to hold their public service assets in their own names).

For a more advanced form of ring-fencing, see Appendix A.3. This Appendix excerpts ¶¶ 61–107 of the D.C. Commission's March 2016 Order approving the Exelon-PHI transaction.

Utility's cost of debt: The higher the holding company's investment risks, the less certain its ability to financially support the utility, the more risk the utility's lenders bear, the higher interest rates they charge. Ring-fencing does nothing to prevent this result, because it does nothing to limit the holding company's risk-taking. Exelon admitted as much:

> Despite [Exelon's proposed] ring-fencing measures, the credit ratings of [Exelon's utilities] ComEd, PECO or BGE could remain linked, to some degree, to the credit ratings of Exelon. Consequently, a reduction in the credit rating of Exelon could result in a reduction of the credit rating of ComEd, PECO or BGE, or all three. A reduction in the credit rating of ComEd, PECO or BGE could have a material adverse effect on ComEd, PECO or BGE, respectively.[110]

Merger applicants typically commit not to raise utility rates to reflect holding-company-caused increases in the utility's cost of debt. But if due to financial troubles the utility needs the rate increase to continue serving, the commitment has no real value.

Utility default: While ring-fencing typically prevents the holding company from forcing the utility into bankruptcy, it doesn't prevent the utility from entering bankruptcy on its own. If, for example, the holding company is in bankruptcy, the bankruptcy court could limit the holding company's capital flows, leaving the utility without sufficient financial support. The utility then could default on its debts and enter bankruptcy. Because ring-fencing does not address the sources of risk, it leaves this problem unsolved. The commission could require that someone—either an SPE or an independent director on the utility's board—hold a "golden share"—a share having the power to veto any utility decision to enter bankruptcy voluntarily. But if the utility's own failures require bankruptcy, nothing prevents a golden-share holder from voting for it. Indeed, Exelon admitted that the SPE structure "is not intended to" do any of the following: "protect a PHI utility from increases in the cost of capital experienced by the holding company"; "protect a PHI utility from increases in debt cost when lenders worry that insufficient equity will be available to the utility from the holding company because of the holding company's business risks"; or "protect a PHI utility against competition for capital within the holding company family."[111]

Disruption to central services: Most holding companies have a central service affiliate that provides support services to all affiliates, including the utility. Under this arrangement, the utility does not retain its own attorneys,

---

[110] Exelon Corp., *supra* note 9, at 46.
[111] Responses to GRID 2.0 Data Requests for Formal Case No. 1119, *supra* note 6, at DR 1-114.

accountants, fuel purchasers, human resources experts or other input providers; the utility buys these services from the service affiliate. The holding company's cash flow problems, caused by non-utility business failures, could disrupt those services. Ring-fencing does not address this problem.

Holding company control: Chapter 7.1 described how the parent's business objectives conflict with the utility's service obligations—and how that conflict combines with hierarchical control to put the utility at risk. Ring-fencing leaves this problem unaddressed. It does not prevent the holding company from (a) imposing spending limits on the utility, (b) placing allies on the utility's board, (c) choosing the top utility executives, and (d) dictating the utility's investment decisions and rate case strategies.

* * *

Ring-fencing has obvious value, but the phrase overstates its effects. "Ring" implies that the protections encircle the utility fully; "fence" implies that the protections have no holes. Neither implication is accurate.

7.4.8.3 Patching ring-fencing's holes: six measures
To patch ring-fencing's holes—to keep the utility undistracted and unaffected by the holding company's unrelated activities—regulators have available six measures. They can limit the holding company's business risks, separate the non-utility activities from the utility activities, prohibit the holding company from interfering with utility management, prohibit the utility from supporting the non-utility businesses, establish service metrics and prevent the opportunistic sale of the utility.

7.4.8.3.1 Limit the holding company's business risks
To shield a utility from its holding company's risks fully requires divesting all non-utility businesses. Less effective are limits and reviews. The commission could:

* limit the corporate family's business activities to some percentage of the utility's assets—a percentage low enough to prevent unrelated business failure from harming the utility or its customers;
* prohibit specified activities or transactions as inherently risky, such as nuclear power construction or operation, commodities trading or banking;
* require commission approval for any business activity defined by the commission as potentially harmful;
* require that no non-utility businesses be owned by the utility;
* require commission access to all books and records of all affiliated interests, to the extent relevant to the utility's health;

- require an annual affiliated interest report, to include an organization chart, a description of each affiliate, financial statements of each affiliate, and a record of all inter-affiliate transactions and their compliance with the commission's affiliate pricing rules; or
- require the holding company to notify the commission prior to (a) any acquisition of a business resulting in a specified percentage relationship to the utility's or the holding company's capitalization, or (b) any material change in control of the utility or any of its direct or indirect owners.[112]

A commission also could create a set of tiered reviews, based on the type of transaction:

- *Minor or routine:* No commission review necessary.
- *Possibly risky:* The holding company must provide details; if the commission takes no action for 60 days, the transaction can proceed.
- *Definitely risky with risks potentially mitigatable:* Affirmative commission approval required.
- *Inherently dangerous, due to type of business, size of financing or other factors:* Prohibited without review.

Exelon's CEO complained that conditions like these would "cripple [Exelon's] ability to adapt to a continually changing marketplace and to make decisions that are in the best interests of all of Exelon's stakeholders."[113] This comment exemplified the parent-utility conflict that commissions must remove. A holding company's "marketplace" is not the commission's concern; the utility's performance is. And when utility performance matters, the only relevant "stakeholders" are the customers of the utility service, and the investors whose investments are necessary to provide that service. A holding company's aspirations for "marketplace" success are irrelevant.

---

[112] For examples of these limits, see *MidAmerican Energy-PacifiCorp Merger*, 2006 Ore. PUC LEXIS 113, at *23–27; and Baltimore Gas & Electric-Pepco Merger, 1997 Md. PSC LEXIS 205, at *134–36 (conditioning the later-withdrawn BGE-Pepco merger on the merged company's agreeing to report unregulated utility activities as they take place, and to develop a cost allocation methodology to prevent discrimination in favor of non-utility operations). *See also* Wis. Stat. § 196.795(5)(g) (providing that "[n]o holding company system may be operated in any way which materially impairs the credit, ability to acquire capital on reasonable terms or ability to provide safe, reasonable, reliable and adequate utility service of any public utility affiliate in the holding company system").

[113] Rebuttal Testimony of Christopher M. Crane at 22, Exelon-Constellation Energy Group Merger, Case No. 9271 (Md. Pub. Serv. Comm'n filed Oct. 12, 2011).

7.4.8.3.2   Separate the utility business from its non-utility affiliates
Addressing market power and unearned advantage, Chapter 6.5.4 described
the three main ways to separate the utility business from the non-utility businesses: divisional unbundling, corporate unbundling and divestiture. The same
options can address the consumer risks discussed in this chapter. Corporate
separation, for example, produces separate accounting, financing and financial
statements. With inter-corporate dealings backed by contracts and invoices,
commission auditors can look for cross-subsidies and favoritism, such as
inter-affiliate prices that deviate from arm's-length dealings. Separation—not
just of finances but of management—also allows each entity to focus solely on
its distinct business purpose.[114]

7.4.8.3.3   Prohibit the holding company from interfering with utility
*   management*
To reduce parent-utility conflict, a commission should prohibit parent-utility
interference. It can require that (a) utility management create its own budget
without holding company limits, and that (b) the holding company provide
the utility with all funds necessary to carry out the utility-created budget. The
holding company could modify the utility's budget, above some minimum
amount, only with commission approval. And if the commission orders
a utility expenditure that exceeds the utility's budget, adjusting the utility's
rates appropriately, the holding company could not block the expenditure—
although it could protest and appeal the order.

No commission has limited a holding company's control in these ways. The
Oregon Commission did require PacifiCorp's holding company acquirer to

> ensure that senior [utility] management personnel located in Oregon continue to
> have authority to make decisions on behalf of PacifiCorp pertaining to (1) local
> Oregon retail customer service issues related to tariff interpretation, line extensions,
> service additions, DSM [Demand-Side Management] program implementation and
> (2) customer service matters related to adequate investment in and maintenance of
> the Oregon sub-transmission and distribution network and outage response.[115]

---

[114] *See, e.g.*, Southern California Edison Co., 1988 Cal. PUC LEXIS 2, at *12
(holding that "[w]ith the exception of the fully-compensated sharing of a small number
of corporate officers," the utility must have a "utility management team dedicated
solely to utility activities," so as to prevent utility management from becoming "preoccupied with nonutility activities to the detriment of utility activities"); BNG, Inc., 1996
Md. PSC LEXIS 41, at *12–22 (requiring financial separation of natural gas brokering
services from regulated activities, and administrative separation of employees from the
regulated and unregulated operations).
[115] MidAmerican Energy-PacifiCorp Merger, 2006 Ore. PUC LEXIS 74, at *89.

But no limit applied to the holding company's control of the utility's major capital expenditures, its rate case strategies or its board membership.

7.4.8.3.4 *Prohibit the utility from providing financial support to non-utility businesses*

To prevent a holding company from using its utility's financial strength to support non-utility activities, a commission should take these measures:

- require the holding company to supply the utility with sufficient equity;
- prohibit the utility from paying, and the holding company from extracting, excess dividends;[116]
- prohibit the utility from incurring any debt other than that necessary to finance its own operations and capital expenditures; and
- prohibit the utility from pledging or encumbering any of its assets or revenues to support any business activities other than its own franchise obligations.[117]

7.4.8.3.5 *Establish service quality metrics*

To cover acquisition debt and business risks, a holding company will be tempted to extract excess funds from the utility. To protect the utility's operations, some commissions have accompanied merger approvals with service quality metrics, reliability spending requirements, monitoring procedures and penalties. Consider the following examples.

Baselines and penalties: The Washington State Commission adopted a Customer Service Guarantee and Service Quality Index (SQI). The SQI established performance baselines for customer satisfaction, service reliability, safety and business office performance. Substandard performance could trigger up to $7.5 million in penalties.[118] The Oregon Commission required merger applicants to (1) propose service quality standards for industrial

---

[116] *See, e.g.*, Oncor Electric Delivery-NextEra Energy Merger, 2017 Tex. PUC LEXIS 807, at *15 (finding that the Oncor Board's "ability ... to make an independent decision about when it is appropriate to pay dividends and when it is necessary to retain funds for operations, without undue interference from a parent company, is an essential part of the ring fence").

[117] *See, e.g.*, Melnyk & Lamb, *supra* note 72, at 23 n.86. The article describes how Enron's gas pipeline subsidiaries, Northern Natural Gas Company and Transwestern Pipeline Company, pledged their pipeline assets as collateral for loans of $450 million and $550 million. The loan proceeds went to Enron. When Enron declared bankruptcy, both pipelines were left with the debt. FERC found that the two pipeline companies imprudently increased their credit risk and their cost of capital. *Investigation of Certain Financial Data*, 100 F.E.R.C. ¶ 61,143 at P 16 (2002).

[118] Puget Sound Power & Light-Washington Natural Gas Merger, 1997 Wash. UTC LEXIS 6, at *61–62.

customers, focusing on high-tech companies; (2) make best efforts to achieve specified transmission infrastructure improvements; and (3) commit to continue, for a specified period, then-existing customer service guarantees and performance standards.[119]

Spending requirements: In its order approving Exelon's acquisition of Constellation, the Maryland Commission accepted the applicants' commitment to (a) "maintain [utility subsidiary] BGE's capital and O&M expenses for 2012 and 2013 at or above 95 percent of its projected needs"; and (b) provide comparisons of projected and actual capital and operations and maintenance (O&M) spending for the first two years after the merger. The Commission also required post-acquisition BGE to comply with the Commission's recently updated service quality standards.[120]

Monitoring: Concern about cost-cutting has led some states to create special monitoring procedures. The Idaho Commission accepted the merging companies' commitment to submit post-merger outage reports and customer complaint data.[121]

7.4.8.3.6   *Prevent opportunistic sale of the utility*

Chapter 4.1 explained that an acquisition serves the public interest only if it emerges from a competition based on performance rather than price. Whoever wins that competition should understand that its future acquirers will face the same situation: a competition based on performance rather than price. Commissions can ensure this understanding by embedding it in the merger approval conditions: specifically, by stating that should the acquirer later seek to sell the utility, it must use competitive procedures designed by the commission to produce the most cost-effective acquirer. Assisted by this clarity, each acquirer will avoid paying an excessive premium when it buys, because it will not be receiving an excessive premium when it sells.

7.4.8.4   Enforcement: financial and structural sanctions

As with speeding and jaywalking, merger rules and conditions are only as good as their enforcement. Enforcement requires consequences. Consequences fall

---

[119]   *MidAmerican Energy-PacifiCorp Merger*, 2006 Ore. PUC LEXIS 74.
[120]   Exelon-Constellation Energy Group Merger, 2012 Md. PSC LEXIS 12, at *156–58.
[121]   Washington Water Power-Sierra Pacific Power Merger, 1995 Ida. PUC LEXIS 89 (withdrawn). *See also* Baltimore Gas & Electric-Pepco Merger, 1997 Md. PSC LEXIS 205, at *143 (commission will "monitor carefully customer observations concerning the quality of service").

into two categories: financial and structural.[122] Financial sanctions penalize misbehavior; structural sanctions change the corporate characteristics that breed misbehavior.

Financial sanctions have a direct cost feature and a deterrent feature. The direct cost feature should make the wrongdoer compensate victims for the costs it causes: excess customer charges, reduced service quality and competitors' lost profits. The deterrent feature should make the wrongdoer lose more than it gained.[123] Structural changes limit the holding company's ability to invest in non-utility businesses. Stronger medicine is to return to simpler times, by disaffiliating the utility from its holding company.

Financial and structural sanctions can work together. When the California Commission authorized utilities to create affiliates to compete for retail customers in the utilities' service territory, it warned against giving those affiliates competitive advantages:

> [U]tilities and their affiliates should not perceive potential penalties as simply a cost of doing business. To this end, we may consider such penalties as not allowing a utility affiliate to switch any new customers to it for a specified period of time, or we may consider penalties for severe or recurring violations such as revocation of an affiliate's registration.[124]

Comments on financial and structural measures follow.

7.4.8.4.1 Financial penalties on shareholders

Shareholder penalties include fines, cost disallowances from the revenue requirement and reductions in the authorized return on equity. These measures all share two practical problems.

First, the larger the abuse, the greater the penalty; but the greater the penalty, the more likely it is to weaken the company, so the less likely it is that the

---

[122] A third category is criminal. Frank J. Boehm, a vice president and director of Union Electric, was convicted of lying to an SEC hearing officer during a proceeding under the Public Utility Holding Company Act of 1935. The SEC found that the utility "had engaged for a long time in the practice of collecting a fund of money in cash, or a slush fund, by means of rebates from attorneys and supply companies and by means of padded expense accounts, and that the fund was used for various political purposes." The conviction was upheld in Boehm v. United States, 123 F.2d 791 (8th Cir. 1941).

[123] For a detailed discussion of FERC's penalty system, see Conrad Bolston, *Improving FERC's Penalty Guidelines: A Comparative Analysis* (2012) (originally published at electricitypolicy.com) (on file with the author).

[124] Standards of Conduct Governing Relationships Between Utilities and Their Affiliates, 1997 Cal. PUC LEXIS 1139, at *161.

regulator will impose it.[125] Absent an alternative company ready, willing and able to replace the incumbent, the public interest in having a viable supplier competes with the public interest in holding the erring company accountable. This moral dilemma exists in every too-big-to-fail setting. The too-big-to-fail premise deserves skepticism, however. Acquirers regularly compete to buy a utility franchise at a premium. They would be even more willing to buy one at a discount—a likely result if the commission were revoking the incumbent's franchise due to misbehavior.[126]

Second, penalizing shareholders for violations committed by executives and employees lacks logic and effectiveness. Regulators should focus on penalizing the individual violators, discussed next.

7.4.8.4.2 *Financial penalties on specific individuals*

Absent personal penalties, executives have a "perverse incentive": if a venture succeeds, they get bonuses; if it fails, shareholders take the loss. And so "major players are encouraged to take outsize risks because they can earn princely amounts from their actions. At the same time, they know that they rarely have to ... face ... costly consequences from taking dangerous actions."[127] The same problem afflicts utility regulation. If undetected violations produce bonuses for executives, while detected violations produce penalties on shareholders, violations will occur. Regulators can fix this problem only by penalizing individual violators. One solution is to require executives to put part of their compensation into a "performance pool." Penalties for violations—anyone's violations—get paid first from the pool, and then from shareholder profits.[128] (Shareholders still should have skin in the game, so that they elect the right board members who then hire the right executives.)

---

[125] *See, e.g., Exelon-Constellation Energy Group Merger*, 2012 Md. PSC LEXIS 12, at text accompanying nn.319–20 (stating that in some situations fines "would not be sufficient to bring a public service company into compliance and may even be counterproductive").

[126] In addressing Pacific Gas & Electric's responsibility for the San Bruno gas line explosion, the California Commission found that under section 2107 of the California Public Utility Code, the statutorily permissible fine could be anywhere from $9 billion to $254 billion. But the statute also required the Commission to consider the penalty's financial effects on the utility. The Commission concluded that the penalty "must be significantly decreased from that potential level in consideration of PG&E's financial resources." The Commission dropped the penalty to $1.6 billion. Pacific Gas & Elec. Co., 2015 Cal. P.U.C. LEXIS 230, at *124–26, *147.

[127] *See* Gretchen Morgenson, *Ways to Put the Boss's Skin in the Game*, N.Y. Times (Mar. 21, 2015), http://www.nytimes.com/2015/03/22/business/economy/ways-to-put-the-bosss-skin-in-the-game.html.

[128] *Id.*

Commissions also should require the holding company to create, prior to merger approval, internal training programs, independent auditing procedures, and consequences for violators sufficient to detect and prevent all violations. Equally important, the holding company should demonstrate that no employee, executive or board member has any financial or career incentive to violate the rules.

Of course, the best way to prevent conflicting incentives for executives and employees is to eliminate conflicts within the corporate family. That point brings us full circle. This chapter started with the problem's source: parent-utility conflict. The most direct paths to ending that conflict are disaffiliation and franchise revocation, discussed next.

7.4.8.4.3 Disaffiliation and franchise revocation

We have explained that when state commissions lack statutory authority to regulate a holding company directly, they can do so indirectly through merger conditions. What if the acquiring holding company accepts the conditions, completes the acquisition, then violates the conditions—arguing that the commission lacks statutory authority to enforce them? Challenges could also come from entities aligned with the holding company—bondholders, shareholders or contractors—who are not bound by the conditions. What if the court agrees that the conditions are unenforceable? The commission then has two related choices: order disaffiliation of the utility company from the holding company; or revoke the utility's franchise.

Disaffiliation: Because the utility's stock is wholly owned by the holding company, the utility cannot disaffiliate on its own. The holding company needs to act—by selling the utility to a third party or by spinning it off to the holding company's ultimate shareholders. Here is a draft merger condition that reserves the commission's authority to order those actions:

> By consummating this transaction, the acquirer accepts the commission's authority to order the acquirer to spin off the acquired utility to the acquirer's ultimate shareholders or to sell the utility to a third party approved by the commission, under procedures to be determined by the commission. The Commission may issue this order if it (a) finds that the holding company, any affiliate, or any employee of either has violated any commission rule or condition; or (b) determines that the utility's continuing affiliation with the holding company conflicts with the public interest. This condition does not diminish any authority the commission has under current law.

What events could trigger disaffiliation? Here is a non-exhaustive list:

- The holding company has blocked utility actions required or approved by the commission.

- The holding company has declined to provide equity capital to the utility in amounts and types the commission deems necessary.
- The utility's cost of equity or debt exceeds what it would have been absent its affiliation with the holding company.
- The magnitude or types of holding company business activities have reached a level that creates unmitigable risk for the utility.
- A rating agency has downgraded, or has indicated the serious possibility of downgrading, the utility's debt due to its affiliation with the holding company.
- The utility is a party to an inter-affiliate transaction that violates the commission's rules.
- The holding company or an affiliate resists reasonable requests, by the commission or others, for information about holding company or affiliate business activities that could affect the utility.
- The holding company has interfered in the utility's decision-making in a way that could adversely affect the utility's operations or raise its costs.
- The holding company or utility has failed to honor commitments it made to win merger approval.

If one or more of these events occurred, the commission first would decide whether disaffiliation would solve the problem without causing other problems, like loss of economies of scale. Then, if disaffiliation is the right result, the commission would establish a process for choosing the utility's new owners.

Franchise revocation: If the holding company resists disaffiliating, the commission can revoke the utility's franchise. Revoking the utility's franchise would eliminate the utility's value to the holding company. At that point a rational holding company, wanting at least to get back the utility's book value, would more likely comply with the commission's order to sell or spin off the utility or its business to a commission-appointed franchisee.

Placing the disaffiliation and revocation options within the merger conditions creates accountability. To win merger approval, applicants must offer benefits and commit to complying with the commission's requirements. Making the value of their transaction depend on both elements disciplines the benefit claims and induces compliance. And the disaffiliation and revocation conditions create symmetry. If the transaction doesn't work out for the holding company it can depart—by selling the utility to a third party or spinning it off to its shareholders. If the transaction doesn't work out for the commission, it will have its own exit.

Both disaffiliation and revocation became conditions on the 2012 merger of the Exelon Corporation (then the owner of Commonwealth Edison and Philadelphia Electric) and Constellation Energy Group (then the owner of Baltimore Gas & Electric). The Maryland Commission explained that imposing fines for violations would, in some situations, "not be sufficient to bring a public service company into compliance and may even be counterproductive."[129] So the merger approval conditions included settlement language authorizing the Commission to order BG&E's "severance" from Exelon if the Commission finds one of four facts:

> (i) a nuclear accident at an Exelon facility that results in a material disruption of operations and material financial loss to Exelon that is not covered by insurance or indemnity, or the permanent closure of a material number of Exelon nuclear plants as a result of such accident, (ii) a bankruptcy filing by Exelon or a subsidiary, subject to certain additional conditions, (iii) the rating for Exelon's senior unsecured debt is downgraded to a rating that indicates "substantial risk" by two of three major credit rating agencies for a period of more than six months, or (iv) Exelon and/or BGE have committed a pattern of material violations of lawful Commission orders or regulations, and after notice and an opportunity to cure, have continued to commit those violations.[130]

In adopting this language, the Commission distinguished among (a) its pre-existing franchising authority, (b) its divestiture authority, and (c) the authority reserved to it by the settlement language. The Commission held, preliminarily, that its "implied and incidental powers needed or proper to carry out its functions" already included the authority to revoke a franchise. But the Commission saw "no necessity, and certainly no expediency, in threatening to revoke the exercise of a franchise to indirectly accomplish the end of getting a holding company to divest a utility ... Instead, under extreme circumstances, the Commission would have the authority to require the divestiture of BGE directly." The Commission then explained that the settlement did not, and could not, restrict its pre-existing authority to order divestiture; on the contrary, the settlement meant only that if any of the four listed circumstances arose, the holding company had waived any right to contest the divestiture. Under other circumstances, the Commission could order divestiture with its existing authority, but the Applicants would be free to challenge the order.[131]

Disaffiliation and revocation conditions have two weaknesses—one legal, the other practical. First, as already discussed, disaffiliation or revocation

---

[129] *Exelon-Constellation Energy Group Merger*, 2012 Md. PSC LEXIS 12, at *147. In this proceeding, the author was a witness for the State of Maryland and the Maryland Energy Administration. He proposed a divestiture condition in his rebuttal testimony.

[130] *Id.* at *139–40.

[131] *Id.* at *144, *147 & n.314 (citing MD. CODE ANN., PUB. UTIL. §§ 2-112(b)(2), 5-201; and then citing Highfield Water Co. v. Public Service Commission, 416 A.2d 1357 (Md. App. 1980)) (explaining the Commission's power to revoke, "in extreme cases," a utility's right to exercise its franchise).

conditions accepted by the merging companies could be challenged, by them or others, as unauthorized by statute. Second, at the time of merger approval, the commission cannot know whether at the time of disaffiliation or revocation an appropriate entity will be available to replace the non-compliant incumbent. Both these uncertainties should give a commission pause. For if the commission lacks the legal and practical means to undo the affiliation it has approved, it should avoid that affiliation to begin with—unless the transaction's long-term benefits outweigh its long-term risks.

7.4.8.4.4 Enforcement resources

Corporate complexity stretches regulatory resources. Commissions need to track new affiliate investments and assess their risks, monitor dividend payments, audit inter-affiliate transactions, and sort out the effects of holding company investments on the utility's costs of debt and equity. Commission resources sufficient to regulate a pure-play utility are not sufficient to protect a utility subsidiary of a multi-state, multi-industry holding company.[132] When commissions impose merger conditions, they need to address their capacity to enforce those conditions.

But no state commission has conditioned its merger approval on the merged company committing to compensate the commission for the necessary resource costs. No state commission has rejected a merger due to the insufficiency of its resources. Except California. Its merger statute required the Commission to consider whether the merger preserves its capacity "to effectively regulate and audit public utility operations in the state."[133] In assessing the Southern California Edison-San Diego Gas & Electric merger, a transaction that would mix utility and non-utility businesses, the Commission cited Southern California Edison's past inter-affiliate abuses, then declared:

> The discovery of these abuses is also an example of how our regulatory system can uncover and remedy such unlawful activities. But expanded markets and service areas will increase our staff's responsibilities and tax our resources to uncover future self-dealing, especially in light of Edison's intransigence in obeying the information access requirements set forth in the holding company decision.[134]

Based on this factor and others, the Commission rejected the merger.

---

[132] The 1935 Congress saw the problem: holding companies' "activities extending over many States are not susceptible of effective control by any State and make difficult, if not impossible, effective State regulation of public-utility companies." PUHCA of 1935 § 1(a), 15 U.S.C. § 79a(a) (repealed 2005).

[133] Cal. Pub. Util. Code § 854(c)(7).

[134] Southern California Edison-San Diego Gas & Electric Merger, 1991 Cal. PUC LEXIS 253, at *165–66, *170–71.

* * *

Holding companies are hierarchical and conflicted: hierarchical because the parent controls the subsidiaries, conflicted because the non-utility subsidiaries' profit goals do not align with the utility subsidiaries' service obligations. The holding company's desire for earnings growth puts pressure on the utility's finances; while its desire to maintain the utility's dominant market position puts pressure on regulators' efforts to introduce competition. These conflicts bring multiple risks: excess acquisition debt, rate increases to pay for merger costs, non-utility business failure, and regulatory hesitance to introduce financial and competitive discipline if those measures could weaken the debt-bearing holding company.

One set of solutions calls for merger conditions that seek to protect utility customers from these conflicts. But the more effective solution is to prevent the couplings that cause these conflicts.

PART III

Regulatory lapses: visionlessness, reactivity, deference

Despite the concentration and complication they cause, nearly all electricity mergers proposed have been approved. How does it happen? How do private strategies to monetize a public franchise win approval so consistently, so often? How do merger promoters—whose transactions waste resources, divert value from customers, weaken competition and impose risks on customers—persuade so many regulators so readily?

Chapter 8 offers one answer: regulators' unreadiness. If a commission defines a positive, public interest vision, prospective merger partners will compete to suit that vision. But few commissions have a positive vision. Statutes require mergers to satisfy the public interest, but commissions don't define the public interest. Instead of establishing expectations for industry performance, then prescribing the merger features required to produce that performance, most commissions have only checklists: subjects to discuss rather than standards to satisfy.

Into this vacuum enter the merger applicants. Their strategy? Frame their transaction as simple, positive and inevitable. As Chapter 9 explains, they offer short-term benefits that distract from the transaction's essence: selling a public franchise for private gain.

How do regulators respond? Most commissions accept the applicants' frame, along with the short-term benefits. Chapter 10 explains that commissions also treat each proposed transaction as the only option available. Commissions don't require their utility to choose a suitor based on maximum customer benefits; they accept the transaction before them as long as it offers minor benefits. Regulators fail to play their strong hand.

Why don't regulators play their strong hand? One explanation is a passion gap. Investors want maximum gain, commissions want no harm. That one difference explains why each merger allocates benefits between shareholders and customers so lopsidedly. Another explanation: regulators are human. The pathbreaking work of behavioral economists like Daniel Kahneman, Amos Tversky and Richard Thaler has revealed our susceptibility to systematic mental errors: our subjective instincts exert power over objective analysis. Chapter 11 describes how twelve of these common mental errors affect and afflict commission's merger decisions.

8. Regulators' unreadiness: checklists instead of visions

A utility's economic performance depends on multiple factors. Among them: (a) the level of competition it faces; (b) the standards its regulators establish; (c) the vigor with which those standards are enforced; and (d) the conflicts within its holding company's structure. To align the utility's performance with the public interest, a commission's merger policy should establish expectations for each factor.

Most commissions have no such policy. As Professor Carstensen has observed:

> [A]gencies have ... largely reacted to proposals initiated by the firms in the [regulated] industries and generally permitted almost all combinations. The unfortunate result is that planning has not occurred, market structures have become more concentrated than necessary for efficiency and long-run competition may be undermined.[1]

Before 2005 this gap had less importance, because the Public Utility Holding Company Act (PUHCA) of 1935 limited utilities and their holding company owners to structures and activities that would produce economical and efficient service for consumers, and reasonable returns for investors. But after the 2005 Congress removed those limits, most commissions did nothing to replace them. Commissions today have only checklists—topics for merger applicants to address rather than standards they must satisfy.

---

[1]   Peter C. Carstensen, *Reflections on Mergers and Competition in Formerly Regulated Industries*, in COMPETITION POLICY AND MERGER ANALYSIS IN DEREGULATED AND NEWLY COMPETITIVE INDUSTRIES 225, 235 (Peter C. Carstensen & Susan Beth Farmer eds., 2008). *See also* DAVID APTER, INTRODUCTION TO POLITICAL ANALYSIS 5 (1977) ("If politics has as its object the survival of human society through the meshing of individual and collective intelligence, it is equally true that those who govern are never quite up to the task.").

8.1 THE PUBLIC INTEREST: A STANDARD IN SEARCH OF A POLICY

Utility statutes require each merger to satisfy the "public interest."[2] The public interest is broader than the interests of shareholders and ratepayers,[3] but is bounded by the statute's purpose.[4] What is a merger statute's purpose?

The purpose of a utility regulatory statute is to produce performance comparable to what effective competition would produce.[5] A merger transaction, therefore, should have terms and conditions, and should produce outcomes, reflecting the pressures of effective competition. To satisfy that standard, the transaction must be economically efficient, and must align the legitimate interests of shareholders and customers.

---

[2]   *See, e.g.*, Federal Power Act § 203(a), 16 U.S.C. § 824b(a); MD. CODE ANN., PUB. UTIL. § 6-105(g); CAL. PUB. UTIL. CODE § 854.

[3]   *See, e.g.*, PacifiCorp-Utah Power & Light Merger, 1987 Ida. PUC LEXIS 376, at *4–6 (explaining that Idaho's merger statute requires a public interest finding separate from findings on rates and service); Jim Chen, *The Echoes of Forgotten Footfalls: Telecommunications Mergers at the Dawn of the Digital Millennium*, 43 HOUS. L. REV. 1311, 1325 (2007) (citing appellate decisions describing the Communications Act of 1934's public interest standard as "supple" and "as concrete as the complicated factors for judgment in such a field of delegated authority permit"; though not so broad as "to be interpreted as setting up a standard so indefinite as to confer an unlimited power"). *See generally* ERIC FILIPINK, HARRISON INST. FOR PUB. LAW, SERVING THE "PUBLIC INTEREST": TRADITIONAL VS. EXPANSIVE UTILITY REGULATION (2009), https://pubs .naruc.org/pub/FA864C03-DC7D-B239-9E29-4D68D1807BE4 (describing expanding regulatory roles).

[4]   NAACP v. FPC, 425 U.S. 662, 669 (1976) (holding that "the use of the words 'public interest' in a regulatory statute is not a broad license to promote the general public welfare. Rather, the words take meaning from the purposes of the regulatory legislation."). The Court upheld the FPC's decision that it had no statutory power to issue a rule prohibiting racial discrimination by utilities. The Federal Power Act's purpose was to promote the economic performance of the electricity and gas industries, not to address racial discrimination. For the author's take on how regulators can, consistent with *NAACP*, consider racial diversity when regulating utility performance, see Scott Hempling. *Promoting Diversity and Prohibiting Discrimination: Is There a Regulatory Obligation to Society?*, http://www.scotthemplinglaw.com/essays/promoting-diversity.

[5]   Delmarva Power & Light Co. v. Pub. Serv. Comm'n, 803 A.2d 460 (Md. 2002) (holding that a commission "takes the place of competition and furnishes the regulation which competition cannot give") (quoting OSCAR L. POND, A TREATISE ON THE LAW OF PUBLIC UTILITIES § 901 (3d ed. 1925)). *See also* 2 ALFRED E. KAHN, THE ECONOMICS OF REGULATION: PRINCIPLES AND INSTITUTIONS 112 (MIT Press 1988) (1970) (stressing the "importance of making regulation more intelligent and more effective in those circumstances in which competition is simply infeasible"). For an explanation of effective competition, see Chapters 6.1 and 6.2.

Economic efficiency: Economic efficiency means the biggest bang for the buck, no waste, no economic opportunity foregone.[6] For investors, economic efficiency means the highest possible return for a given level of risk; for consumers it means the lowest price for a given quality of product; for business managers it means the highest possible output for a given level of input. To be economically efficient, a transaction must allocate benefits to the benefit-creators, and allocate costs to the cost-causers and benefit-recipients.

Alignment of legitimate shareholder and customer interests: An economically efficient transaction advances both legitimate shareholder and consumer interests, with no conflict between the two. That is how effective competition works: in a market with many sellers and buyers, low entry barriers, with no competitor acting anticompetitively or operating with unearned advantages, the most cost-effective sellers have the most satisfied customers.

To produce economic efficiency, and to align the interests of the utility's shareholders and customers, a merger policy needs to

- identify the mix and quality of services that utility customers need and want;
- shape investors', executives' and workers' incentives so that the merged company produces that mix and quality cost-effectively;
- describe the types of companies best able to provide those services at the required quality; and
- discourage any business activities, corporate structures and financial arrangements that conflict with or distract from the utility's mission.

With these criteria in place, the commission can establish:

- guidelines and screens that attract the right couplings and discourage the wrong ones;
- conditions that induce the post-acquisition company to perform as required and prevent it from acting harmfully; and
- clear consequences for the merged company should it fail to perform as required.

If commissions don't define the public interest, they will receive merger proposals that pursue private interests. If commissions don't describe the services, quality, corporate structures and market structures that the public interest requires, they will receive merger proposals reflecting the services, quality and structures that the merging companies desire. Imagine a town without zoning

---

[6]   *See* PAUL KRUGMAN & ROBIN WELLS, MICROECONOMICS 29 (4th ed. 2015) (explaining that "an economy is efficient if there are no missed opportunities—there is no way to make some people better off without making other people worse off").

policies—without established preferences for housing locations, commercial locations, parks or traffic patterns. The town zoning board will react to each developer's self-interested proposal without a public interest context. A dozen developments later, how well will the town work? To guide mergers toward public interest results, regulators must make the first move. They must have a public interest definition and they must have a merger policy.

8.2   THE 70-YEAR POLICY: PUHCA'S INTEGRATED PUBLIC-UTILITY SYSTEM

Until 2006, the nation had a merger policy, one based on an explicit public interest vision. PUHCA 1935 required that each electricity holding company:

* be confined to a single "integrated public-utility system";
* face limits (and in some cases prohibitions) on non-utility business investments;
* issue debt and equity securities only as necessary to serve the utility business; and
* make acquisitions of utilities only if they caused those utilities to operate more economically.[7]

This policy envisioned an industry in which utilities with state-granted monopolies would have a singular purpose: to serve customers cost-effectively. All utilities would be structured uncomplicatedly, financed conservatively; they would be local, and accountable to regulators. There would be no conflict among the interests of investors, consumers and the public. Every merger or acquisition would be motivated by, and would carry out, that public interest vision.

8.3   PUHCA REPEAL, REGULATORY SILENCE

Until 2005, utility regulators had little need to create their own merger policies, because PUHCA 1935 provided one. They knew that if the SEC enforced the Act, any proposed merger would "serve the public interest by tending towards the economical and efficient development of an integrated public-utility sys-

---

[7]   For a reminder of PUHCA 1935's details, see Chapter 4.2.2.

tem."[8] With that standard in place, no merger could cause their local utility to become:

* an affiliate of remote, non-integrated utility businesses;
* exposed to the risks of non-utility businesses;
* exposed to financial pressures arising from debts incurred by the holding company or other affiliates; or
* a victim of abusive inter-affiliate transactions.[9]

With the Act's 2005 repeal, the national vision embodied in the "integrated public-utility system" principle disappeared. Gone were the prohibitions against acquiring remote, non-integrating utilities. Gone were the limits on mixing utility and non-utility businesses. Gone were the prohibitions against issuing risky securities and entering abusive inter-affiliate transactions. FERC and state commissions do review utility mergers, but their reviews share no common vision for the types of companies those reviews should produce. Congress repealed one vision but did not replace it with another.

Neither did anyone else. Because the federal repeal statute expressed no preemptive intent, it left states and FERC with this question: What merger policies will best distinguish efficient transactions from inefficient ones, benefit-producing couplings from harm-causing ones? Advocates for repeal argued that states would fill the resulting policy gap,[10] but no state did. No state reacted to repeal by creating its own policy vision, then revising its statutes and rules to carry out that vision. States continued to approve mergers after 2005 just as they had before 2005.[11] None of these post-2005 transactions were guided or disciplined by a state-articulated vision for business activities, corpo-

---

[8]   Public Utility Holding Company Act 1935 §10(c)(2), 15 U.S.C. § 79j(c)(2) (repealed 2005).
[9]   Whether the SEC did actually enforce PUHCA 1935 in its final two decades was a matter of debate. For a critique of the SEC's pre-repeal enforcement, see Scott Hempling, *Corporate Restructuring and Consumer Risk: Is the SEC Enforcing the Public Utility Holding Company Act?*, ELECTRICITY J., July 1988. For two appellate decisions reversing the SEC's applications of the Act, see *Wisconsin's Environmental Decade, Inc. v. SEC*, 882 F.2d 523 (D.C. Cir. 1989); and *National Rural Electric Cooperative Ass'n v. SEC*, 276 F.3d 609 (D.C. Cir. 2002). In both cases, the author was appellate counsel for petitioners.
[10]   *See, e.g.*, CONG. RESEARCH SERV., RL33739, THE REPEAL OF THE PUBLIC UTILITY HOLDING COMPANY ACT OF 1935 AND ITS IMPACT ON ELECTRIC AND GAS UTILITIES (2006), https://www.everycrsreport.com/reports/RL33739.html (stating that repeal supporters argued that "enhanced federal and state laws and regulations since the enactment of PUHCA provide for adequate customer protection").
[11]   *See* Table 3.1 in this book (showing no major difference in the pace of acquisitions before and after 2005).

rate and governance structure, financial structure or market structure. Though not preempted, states acted as if they were. The Maryland Commission acted as if it were helpless:

> It is not obvious to us that tying our regulated utility companies to this business model [subordinating Baltimore Gas & Electric (BGE) to Exelon's holding company structure, which was heavily weighted toward higher-risk, non-utility businesses] will be good in the long run for ratepayers or regulated utilities. Having watched major financial institutions become "too big to fail," we wonder too if further consolidation in the electricity sector could expose BGE to a wider range of unregulated business risks or bury BGE deeper down Exelon's priority list if the company grows still bigger in the future. But these general reservations do not afford us a basis to deny approval to a transaction that otherwise passes muster under § 6-105. By repealing the Public Utility Holding Company Act and passing Maryland's electric restructuring laws, the United States Congress and the Maryland General Assembly created the legal and policy backdrop for transactions and companies like these, and it is not our role to thwart or second-guess those judgments here.[12]

FERC behaved similarly. The 2005 repeal statute did grant FERC some authority to review acquisitions that previously lay outside its jurisdiction; and it clarified federal and state access to utilities' and holding companies' books and records.[13] But in none of FERC's merger issuances, before or after 2005—not in its 1996 Policy Statement, its Order Nos. 642, 667 and 669 or its eighty-plus approval orders—is there any effort to define the public interest. Nowhere does FERC require that a utility merger reflect the discipline of

---

[12]   Exelon-Constellation Merger, 2012 Md. PSC LEXIS 12, at *6. The Commission's reference to a "legal and policy backdrop" had, and has, no supporting authority. The repeal of PUHCA 1935 authorized transactions like Exelon's, but it left states entirely free to reject them. The state legislature's enactment of retail competition legislation nowhere diminished the commission's discretion and duty to judge the quality of proposed mergers. In this Maryland Commission proceeding, the author was an expert witness for the state of Maryland and the Maryland Energy Administration.

[13]   Section 1264(a) and (b) of the Energy Policy Act of 2005, Pub. L. No. 109-58, 119 Stat. 594, requires holding companies and their associate and affiliate companies to provide FERC with the information the Commission deems necessary "for the protection of customers with respect to jurisdictional rates." Section 1264(c) authorizes FERC to examine the books and records of any member of a holding company system if "necessary or appropriate for the protection of utility customers with respect to jurisdictional rates." Section 1266 exempts from this federal records provision any holding company that has that status merely because it owns a PURPA qualifying facility, a "foreign utility company," or an "exempt wholesale generator." Section 1275(b) directs FERC, on request of a state commission or a holding company system, to "review and authorize" the allocation of costs of goods and services provided by a holding company's service affiliate to its utility subsidiaries. Section 1267 preserves the Commission's authority, in setting rates, to disallow costs arising from inter-affiliate transactions.

effective competition. Nowhere does FERC say what features of corporate structure, governance structure and finance structure will ensure cost-effective industry performance. Nowhere do FERC's merger issuances even define desirable industry performance. FERC's 1996 Policy Statement does state a purpose: to make mergers "consistent with the competitive goals" of the Energy Policy Act of 1992.[14] But that stated purpose is general and aspirational; it contains no performance metrics by which anyone can hold FERC accountable.

The Commission has made some adjustments. On drawing geographic boundaries for purposes of testing market power, it has substituted the Appendix A "delivered price test" for the discredited "hub-and-spoke" method, and made other improvements.[15] But FERC has revealed no vision for performance.

8.4   CHECKLISTS WITHOUT STANDARDS

Regulatory statutes cite the public interest but don't define the phrase. That job falls to each commission. But commissions don't define the phrase either. Instead of establishing visions—enforceable expectations for types of services, business mixes, inter-corporate relationships and financial structure—states create lists. But these lists provide only subjects, not expectations. Consider the three following examples.

The District of Columbia Commission looks at these subjects:

1. ratepayers, shareholders, the financial health of the utilities standing alone and as merged, and the economy of the District;
2. utility management and administrative operations;
3. public safety and the safety and reliability of services;
4. risks associated with all of the Joint Applicants' affiliated non-jurisdictional business operations, including nuclear operations;
5. the Commission's ability to regulate the new utility effectively;
6. competition in the local retail, and wholesale markets that impacts the District and District ratepayers; and

---

[14] Order No. 592, *Inquiry Concerning the Commission's Merger Policy Under the Federal Power Act; Policy Statement*, F.E.R.C. STATS. & REGS. ¶ 31,044, 61 Fed. Reg. 68,595, 68,596 (1996), *reconsideration denied*, Order No. 592-A, 79 F.E.R.C. ¶ 61,321, 62 Fed. Reg. 33,341 (1997).

[15] The "hub-and-spoke" method is discussed in FERC's Merger Policy Statement, *id.*, at Part III.B.2.b. For recent improvements on the reporting and measurement of market power in the context of market-based pricing, see Order No. 860, *Data Collection for Analytics and Surveillance and Market-Based Rate Purposes*, 168 F.E.R.C. ¶ 61,039 (2019).

7. conservation of natural resources and preservation of environmental quality.[16]

The Louisiana Commission asks

1. whether the transfer is in the public interest;
2. whether the purchaser is ready, willing and able to continue providing safe, reliable and adequate service to the utility's ratepayers;
3. whether the transfer will maintain or improve the financial condition of the resulting public utility or common carrier ratepayers;
4. whether the proposed transfer will maintain or improve the quality of service to public utility or common carrier ratepayers;
5. whether the transfer will provide net benefits to ratepayers in both the short term and the long term and provide a rate making method that will ensure, to the fullest extent possible, that ratepayers will receive the forecasted short- and long-term benefit;
6. whether the transfer will adversely affect competition;
7. whether the transfer will maintain or improve the quality of management of the resulting public utility or common carrier doing business in the state;
8. whether the transfer will be fair and reasonable to the affected public utility or common carrier employees;
9. whether the transfer would be fair and reasonable to the majority of all affected public utility or common carrier shareholders;
10. whether the transfer will be beneficial on an overall basis to state and local economies and to the communities in the area served by the public utility or common carrier;
11. whether the transfer will preserve the jurisdiction of the Commission and the ability of the Commission to effectively regulate and audit public utility's or common carrier's operations in the state;
12. whether conditions are necessary to prevent adverse consequences which may result from the transfer;
13. the history of compliance or noncompliance of the proposed acquiring entity or principals or affiliates have had with regulatory authorities in this State or other jurisdictions;
14. whether the acquiring entity, persons or corporations have the financial ability to operate the public utility or common carrier system and maintain or upgrade the quality of the physical system;

---

[16] Exelon-PHI Merger, 2015 D.C. PUC LEXIS 203, at *5 (quoting Exelon-PHI Merger, Formal Case No. 1119, Order No. 17597 (D.C. Pub. Serv. Comm'n Aug. 22, 2014)).

15. whether any repairs and/or improvements are required and the ability of acquiring entity to make those repairs and/or improvements;
16. the ability of the acquiring entity to obtain all necessary health, safety and other permits;
17. the manner of financing the transfer and any impact that may have on encumbering the assets of the entity and the potential impact on rates; and
18. whether there are any conditions which should be attached to the proposed acquisitions.[17]

And the California statute requires its Commission to address whether the merger will

1. maintain or improve the financial condition of the resulting public utility doing business in the state;
2. maintain or improve the quality of service to public utility ratepayers in the state;
3. maintain or improve the quality of management of the resulting public utility doing business in the state;
4. be fair and reasonable to affected public utility employees, including both union and nonunion employees;
5. be fair and reasonable to the majority of all affected public utility shareholders;
6. be beneficial on an overall basis to state and local economies, and to the communities in the area served by the resulting public utility;
7. preserve the jurisdiction of the commission and the capacity of the commission to effectively regulate and audit public utility operations in the state; and
8. provide mitigation measures to prevent significant adverse consequences which may result.[18]

A list is not a policy. It states no standards. A standard is "a level of quality or attainment";[19] "something set up and established by authority as a rule for

---

[17] Commission Approval Required of Sales, Leases, Mergers Consolidations, Stock transfers, and All Other Changes of Ownership or Control of Public Utilities Subject to Commission Jurisdiction, 1994 La. PUC LEXIS 222 (customarily referred to as the "General Order").

[18] CAL. PUB. UTIL. CODE § 854 (c)(1)–(8).

[19] *Standard*, LEXICO/OXFORD FREE DICTIONARY, https://www.google.com/search ?q=standard+definition&sourceid=ie7&rls=com.microsoft:en-US:IE-Address&ie=& oe=&rlz=&gws_rd=ssl (last visited Jan. 8, 2020).

the measure of … value, or quality";[20] "something established by authority, custom, or general consent as a model or example."[21] A car repair shop has a checklist—brakes, steering, transmission, emissions, air conditioning. But the shop uses that list to apply standards—the manufacturer's standards for performance, the legal standards for safety, the competitive market's standards for efficiency and cleanliness. The repair shop uses its checklist to assess whether your car meets those standards. But the checklist is not itself a standard. Without standards, commissions' checklists won't, and don't, cause merger strategists to align their transaction with a commission vision. Checking the boxes on a checklist says only that the regulator has looked at the issue; it does not tell us whether the transaction has satisfied a standard.

There are two exceptions. The Wisconsin merger statute limits the size and type of non-utility investments permitted in a utility's holding company system.[22] The Montana Commission has a "Statement of Factors" containing general standards for the merger applicants' financial strength and capability; energy supply; infrastructure; demonstrable Montana focus; utility focus; customer focus; energy utility management experience; and effective functioning in the Montana constitutional, statutory and regulatory framework.[23] But both examples, while better than silence, fail to affirmatively describe and require the performance and performers that customers deserve.

* * *

Some may argue that by establishing preferences upfront, a commission loses flexibility later. The reality is the opposite. Once the merging entities agree on transaction terms—merger partner, merger price, merger financing—and once the acquirer incurs acquisition debt based on expected revenue necessary to pay off that debt— the transaction terms become brittle. Intervenors that propose, and commissions that impose, unexpected standards on already-negotiated terms get labeled as deal-breakers. Stating requirements ahead, in contrast, aligns investor expectations with public interest visions, increasing the chance that what gets proposed deserves to be approved.

This chapter has described commissions' unreadiness—an absence of public interest vision, and an absence of policy standards designed to attract only those transactions that satisfy that vision. Chapter 9 will describe how

---

[20] *Standard*, MERRIAM-WEBSTER DICTIONARY, https://www.merriam-webster.com/dictionary/standard (last updated Jan. 8, 2020).

[21] *Id.*

[22] As described in Chapters 5.4.4, 6.5.5.3, 7.4.8 and 12.2.3.

[23] Statement of Factors for Evaluating Proposals to Acquire NorthWestern Energy, Docket No. N2004.10.166 (Mont. Pub. Serv. Comm'n Oct. 18, 2004) (on file with the author).

merger promoters use commissions' unreadiness to frame the issues in a way that favors their transactions. Chapter 10 then will show how regulators react—largely by accepting the applicants' frame rather than exercising leadership. Chapter 11 offers two possible explanations for regulators' habits: a passion gap, and systematic mental errors of the types discovered by behavioral economists.

These outcomes are not inevitable. Part IV will present multiple ways for utility merger regulators to become merger policy leaders.

9. Promoters' strategy: frame mergers as simple, positive, inevitable

When commissions have only checklists instead of purposes, merger applicants can check the boxes while pursuing their own purposes. To make their box-checking persuasive they use six strategies: (a) frame their transaction as simple and positive; (b) argue that mergers are inevitable and corporately necessary; (c) offer benefits that distract from the merger's real purposes; (d) downplay negatives; (e) frame opponents as anti-benefit and anti-business; and (f) maintain deadline pressure. This chapter explains each strategy.

9.1 FRAME THE TRANSACTION AS SIMPLE AND POSITIVE

Chapter 8 described the policy void. Statutorily directed to make mergers serve the "public interest," commissions do not define the phrase. They lack a vision of the company types—business mix, corporate structure and financial structure—that can best produce the performance customers need. Because they lack that vision, they also lack the screens and standards necessary to attract optimal transactions and discourage suboptimal ones.

Merger applicants fill that void with a narrative. They describe their transaction as the right fit—natural, normal and public-spirited. They emphasize simplicity and compatibility; they de-emphasize complexity and conflict. They talk of what the transaction brings, not what it removes.

This narrative becomes the frame. A frame fills the regulator's eye-space. Like a painting's frame, the applicants' frame creates a boundary—on what facts to consider, what questions to ask. Facts and questions within the frame are relevant, facts and questions outside the frame are irrelevant. Framing marginalizes what the frame excludes. So when intervenors say what is missing— the private gain from the public franchise, the parent-utility conflicts, the rating agencies' warnings, the constraints on future commission decisions—they're accused of speculating about irrelevancies.[1]

---

[1] *See* David Brooks, *Description is Prescription*, N.Y. Times, Nov. 25, 2010 ("Description is prescription. If you can get people to see the world as you do, you have unwittingly framed every subsequent choice."). *See also* Robert H. Frank, *The Impact*

This framing strategy applies to substance, context and law. On *substance*, the applicants treat the mechanics as mundane—this entity is buying that entity's shares at this price, with that financing. They cast their objectives in generic, business-school-speak—expanding scale, sharing best practices, positioning for the future, unlocking value, serving the customer. But their substance frame excludes necessary substance: reliable data on economies of scale; tangible commitments to back up the generic aspirations; explanations for why the target company doesn't already use best practices. The frame also omits explanations of why the target chose its acquirer based on price instead of performance; why the target is keeping a gain unrelated to any value the target created; why the acquirer paid a control premium; how it will recover that premium—likely by earning returns exceeding the real cost of equity.[2] On *context*, merger applicants present their transaction as part of an innocuous merger trend regularly approved by other commissions. But they omit relevant context—that no commission's merger selection process is disciplined by effective competition; that targets regularly put price ahead of performance; that the concentration-and-complication trend brings real risks, to customers current and future. Finally on *law*, applicants frame the statutory public interest standard as requiring only no harm, whereas the correct standard—the standard consistent with regulation's very purpose—is positive outcomes comparable to what effective competition would produce.[3]

To see how applicants' frames focus on the favorable and exclude the unfavorable, consider the comparison between applicants' frames and accurate frames shown in Table 9.1.

Some frames don't just omit facts; they make up facts. Westar's CEO Mark Ruelle insisted: "This merger is the best means of containing rising costs."[4] PHI's CEO Joseph Rigby said Exelon's offer of benefits was in the shareholders' and customers' "best interests."[5] "Best" means best. Used truthfully, the term requires a comparison to all feasible options, focusing on performance. But as both companies' proxy statements reveal, Mr. Ruelle and Mr. Rigby

---

of the Irrelevant on Decision-Making, N.Y. Times, May 29, 2010 (stating that framing a discussion appropriately is "an ethically significant act") (quoting psychology professors Daniel Kahneman and Amos Tversky).

  [2]   As explained in Chapter 5.3.2.
  [3]   As explained in Chapter 4.2.
  [4]   Rebuttal Testimony of Mark A. Ruelle at 46, Great Plains Energy-Westar Energy Merger I, Docket No. 16-KCPE-593-ACQ (Kan. Corp. Comm'n filed Jan. 4, 2017).
  [5]   Direct Testimony of Joseph M. Rigby at 3, Exelon-PHI Merger, Formal Case No. 1119 (D.C. Pub. Serv. Comm'n filed June 18, 2014).

Table 9.1   Applicants' framing strategies

Applicants' frames	Accurate frames
1. The transaction's purpose is to exploit economies of scale and spread best practices.	1. The target CEO's purpose was to solve his "flat sales" problem by selling franchise control for gain. The acquirer's purpose was to buy a new platform from which to acquire more companies.
2. Your local utility will have the financial backing of a major infrastructure company.	2. The acquirer sought to balance its high-risk investments with a competition-free utility that provides the government-assisted, low-risk cash flow that comes from captive customers.
3. Your local utility will continue to be run by local management.	3. The acquiring holding company will have, and will exercise, hierarchical control over the target utility's board, budget, finances and rate proposals.
4. This transaction will keep rates reasonable.	4. The acquirer paid a premium above market, expecting to recover it by keeping rates high enough to earn returns exceeding both the commission-authorized return and the real cost of equity.
5. The transaction is in the customers' best interests.	5. This transaction converts a pure play utility into a subsidiary of a conglomerate. Over time, this change in corporate character will change the mix of shareholders from conservative, buy-and-hold types to more aggressive, risk-taking types.

each looked for the highest price, not the best performer.[6] "Best" is puffery, not fact.

Psychologists have proven that framing works. Chapter 11 will explain how.

9.2   ARGUE INDUSTRY INEVITABILITY AND CORPORATE NECESSITY

Besides framing the transaction as simple and positive, merger applicants describe it as inevitable and necessary. Appearing frequently are four arguments.

1. Our transaction continues a natural industry evolution arising from objective economic forces. Edison Electric Institute, the association of investor-owned utilities, insisted that mergers deserve FERC's deference

---

[6]   *See* Chapter 1.2.1 (quoting from proxy statements).

because they "represent the natural evolution of the markets."[7] A prominent utility-side witness testified that utility mergers were "commonplace."[8]

"Natural evolution" is inaccurate. When the target owes its existence to government protection from competition, the coupling is not natural—not in the sense of objective economic efficiency. In a monopoly context, absent strong franchise competition, locational competition, border competition, inter-fuel competition or large-scale self-supply—each of which would pressure the incumbent competitively—a utility faces little of the accountability that sellers subject to effective competition face. As for "evolution," the term implies organic, logical, public-benefitting change from some past condition to a better future. But those who talk of evolution describe neither a past nor a future. The past—until the mid-1980s—was an industry hosting hundreds of government-protected monopolies, mostly local and pure-play, each part of a PUHCA-mandated single integrated public-utility system. The present and future are the products of those companies' consolidating and complicating themselves, a trend that accelerates as the previously merged merge again.[9] With transactions motivated not by customer benefits but by target gain-seeking and acquirer territory-seeking, the "evolution" may be "natural" from the strategic perspectives of the transactions' planners; but it is not natural from the perspective of regulation's purpose—which is to produce performance comparable to competition.

2. We need to merge because everyone else is merging. Said Westar's CEO, "[O]ther utilities across the nation continue to combine to become more efficient to help offset rising costs coupled with flat sales … It would not be in Kansas' best interest to be left behind."[10]

This sentiment has two problems. First, despite nearly eighty transactions over thirty-five years, no one—least of all merger applicants—has produced an objective study proving that electricity mergers have actually made companies "more efficient" or "offset rising costs." Second, the concern about flat sales is really a concern about the target's flat share price. A merger of two companies with flat sales produces a larger company with flat sales. It doesn't increase

---

[7]   *See* Order No. 642, *Revised Filing Requirements Under Part 33 of the Commission's Regulations*, F.E.R.C. Stats. & Regs. ¶ 31,111, 65 Fed. Reg. 70,984, 71,012 pt. IX.C (2000) (FERC attributing the view to EEI), *order on reh'g*, Order No. 642-A, 94 F.E.R.C. ¶ 61,289, 66 Fed. Reg. 16,121 (2001).

[8]   Direct Testimony of John J. Reed at 8, AltaGas-Washington Gas Light Merger, Case No. 9449 (Md. Pub. Serv. Comm'n filed Apr. 24, 2017) (asserting that from 1995 to 2016, the number of independent, investor-owned electric utility holding companies declined by 52 percent).

[9]   See Table 3.4 in this book.

[10]   Rebuttal Testimony of Mark A. Ruelle, *supra* note 4, at 38–39.

total sales. If a merger can produce efficiencies, those efficiencies are useful regardless of flat sales. And if mergers create efficiencies, utilities—legally obligated to minimize costs—should pursue them regardless of their flat sales. Westar's CEO mentioned flat sales because they lead to flat share value—and dissatisfied shareholders. By selling all shares for a gain—which is what he proposed—they would become satisfied shareholders. But that sale and gain have nothing to do with creating efficiencies. In the original GPE-Westar proposal, efficiencies were beside the point.

3. Bigger is better. The NextEra-Hawaiian Electric applicants argued that "[m]any small and medium-sized utility companies … are finding that mergers … allow them to increase their size and financial strength." Larger size, they argued, enables scale and scope; operating efficiencies; diversification of business, operating and weather risks; access to capital markets; and better project management.[11]

Despite nearly eighty transactions over three decades, merger applicants have presented no objective study to support the generic idea that bigger is better. In the electric industry, even small is big. A single-city utility, Madison Gas & Electric, is a $1.3 billion company.[12] It has no financial problems; no serious complaints about its operating costs. Certainly there is some sweet spot—some range of company sizes within which performance will be most cost-effective. But at some size, economies of scale diminish, exhaust and then turn negative. What those points are for electric utilities generally, and for specific merger applicants, no merger witness has ever said. No one has offered even non-systematic evidence comparing, for example, operating and financial metrics for a small company like Madison Gas & Electric with a large company like Pacific Gas & Electric. Small utilities do not tell commissions that their size makes it difficult to find lenders. The municipal bond market works well for large and small cities; and the utility bond market works well for large and small utilities—as long as they charge the right rates, manage their budgets and pay off their loans on time. The bigger-is-better argument is mere advertising—possibly true, possibly false, but in no way resembling substantial evidence.

From this absence of evidence, one might infer that applicants seek relative size, not absolute size; that "bigger is better" means get bigger to gain advantage over smaller companies, or to avoid losing advantage to larger companies. But relative size is a pecuniary benefit to a particular company; it is not

---

[11]   Applicants' Response to CA-IR-95, Hawaiian Electric-NextEra Merger, Docket No. 2015-0022 (Haw. Pub. Util. Comm'n 2015) (citing MOODY'S INVESTORS SERVICE, A RATING AGENCY PERSPECTIVE ON THE UTILITY INDUSTRY 24 (2012)).

[12]   Measured by total capitalization. MGE Energy, Inc., Annual Report (Form 10-K) at 56 (Feb. 22, 2019).

necessarily a benefit to the industry or its customers—unless bigger-than-big necessarily means lower cost, a point no one has proved.

This tension, between (a) merger applicants' drive for relative size and (b) the public's interest in improved industry performance, has an analogy in the animal kingdom. Economist Robert Frank compares the gazelle to the bull elk. An individual gazelle's advantage relative to its peers advances the gazelle community as a whole: the fastest gazelles outrun their predators; as the slower gazelles get eaten, their inferior DNA departs the species. As the faster gazelles procreate, the species gets speedier. And so on. Contrast the bull elk. In the battle for females, the winners have the largest antlers. So procreation produces elk with larger antlers. But "[l]arge antlers compromise mobility in densely wooded areas, ... making bulls more likely to be killed and eaten by wolves." For bull elk, the pursuit of relative advantage among individuals makes life miserable for bulls as a group.[13]

If utilities are gazelles, then each company's drive for size will improve both its own performance and its industry's. But if utilities are bull elks, mergers aimed at relative superiority can hurt the whole industry—by making each entity more remote, less consumer-responsive, less accountable—and more prone to error because its too-big-to-fail status protects it from penalties proportional to its shortcomings. Absent objective information on efficiencies, and absent state and national policies that guide mergers toward industry-wide efficiency, merger approvals based on bigger-is-better have no evidentiary support.

4. This transaction was blessed by the rating agencies and our financial advisors. A rating agency's purpose does not coincide with a commission's public interest duties, so its blessing does not promise a public interest outcome. Rating agencies test whether the merged company can repay its lenders, not whether it can perform well for customers. And these agencies base their optimism on what they know about the merger applicants today—their current debt, current activities and current plans. Positive projections last only as long as positive facts last. Ratings issued at merger time make no promises about the merged company's financial condition in future times—when additional acquisitions can add riskier activities, and additional acquisition debt can weaken the merged company's balance sheet.

As for the applicants' financial advisors, they provide "fairness opinions"; they opine on whether the transaction's terms are fair to each company's

---

[13]   Robert H. Frank, The Darwin Economy: Liberty, Competition, and the Common Good 21 (2012).

shareholders.[14] A fairness opinion says nothing about customer benefits or operational performance, or about whether the target selected the acquirer most likely to provide the most customer benefits.

9.3   MAKE OFFERS TO DISTRACT AND PERSUADE

To win support from regulators, applicants make promises. Some promises, like solemnly stated commitments to comply with statutes and rules, are literally and legally illusory.[15] Others are facially unconstitutional: commission-approved promises to favor in-state contractors over out-of-state contractors discriminate against interstate commerce.[16] While some promises come from the utility's pocket (such as Exelon's offer of a $100 check to every BG&E customer), others are activities whose costs are borne by ratepayers (such as promises to upgrade transmission facilities—also illusory if the upgrade merely carries out the utility's obligation to serve). Some offers, like commitments to install, and control the data from, new "smart meters," even become profit opportunities and first-mover advantages for the utility.

---

[14]   *See, e.g.*, Great Plains Energy Inc., Amendment No. 1 to Registration Statement (Form S-4/A) at 72 (Aug. 17, 2016) (stating that "Goldman Sachs' [GPE's advisor] opinion addresses only the fairness from a financial point of view, as of the date of the opinion," of the price paid for the target's stock).

[15]   A promise is illusory if one party gives no "consideration," i.e., nothing of value, to the other party. A party's offer to do something he is already obligated to do is not consideration. *See* Berger v. Burkoff, 92 A.2d 376, 379 (Md. 1952) ("The general rule is that a promise to do, or actually doing that which a party to a contract is already under legal obligation to do, is not a valid consideration to support the promise of the other party ... .").

[16]   A private entity can discriminate against out-of-state businesses; but under the Dormant Commerce Clause a state law or state regulatory agency cannot. *See, e.g.*, Wyoming v. Oklahoma, 502 U.S. 437, 454 (1992) ("It is long established that ... the Commerce Clause ... directly limits the power of the States to discriminate against interstate commerce."); New England Power Co. v. New Hampshire, 455 U.S. 331, 338 (1982) (finding a state commission's prohibition of a local utility's out-of-state sales impermissible under the Commerce Clause, which "preclude[s] a state from mandating that its residents be given a preferred right of access, over out-of-state consumers"). When a utility's discriminatory contract preference becomes a commission-mandated merger condition, it is a regulatory action, thus unconstitutional. Only if the state is a market actor, rather than a market regulator, is such discrimination permitted. *See* New Energy Co. of Indiana v. Limbaugh, 486 U.S. 269, 277 (1988) (finding that where the state acts not in its "distinctive governmental capacity, ... [but] in the more general capacity of a market participant," the dormant Commerce Clause does not apply; there the state's "business methods, including those that favor its residents, are of no greater constitutional concern than those of a private business").

When merger applicants make offers, intervenors start negotiating—over the offers' timing and sufficiency, and the allocation of the associated benefits. These negotiations distract attention from the transaction itself. This section describes the main types of offers, the distractions they cause and the strings applicants attach.

9.3.1   Savings Attributable to the Merger

For true merger savings—cost reductions not achievable without a merger[17]—applicants frequently offer a precise dollar amount, like Exelon's offer of $100 to each PHI customer.[18] Putting money with mouth gains credibility. But because merger applicants know and control the actual cost savings data, they have both incentive and opportunity to promise less than they can produce, then keep the difference. As a prominent utility-side witness openly acknowledged:

> Announced merger synergies and savings expectations should be high enough to win investor support but low enough to keep substantial benefits out of regulatory gain-sharing.[19]

Applicants also promise categories of savings—like those from economies of scale and best practices—while committing to no specific actions or outcomes.

Commissions want to see savings relative to the target utility's status quo costs. But as Chapters 11.3.3.5 and 11.3.3.6 will explain, the status quo too readily becomes a psychological anchor that causes mental error. The difference between a level of benefits that just exceeds the status quo (and therefore satisfies the commission), and the level that would come from the best performer, is opportunity cost. Basing the savings comparison on the status quo ignores opportunity cost—a class mental error.

9.3.2   Offers Redundant of the Utility's Obligations

Some merger offers merely carry out the target utility's existing obligations. Examples include investing in energy efficiency, coordinating capacity and

---

[17]   Chapter 4.4 addressed the distinction between savings achievable with and without a merger.

[18]   *See* Rebuttal Testimony of Christopher M. Crane at 23, Exelon-PHI Merger, Case No. 9361 (Md. Pub. Serv. Comm'n filed Jan. 7, 2015).

[19]   William Kemp, Presentation to the International Association for Energy Economics, Economies of Scale and Scope in Electric Utility Mergers (Oct. 10, 2011), http://www.usaee.org/usaee2011/submissions/Presentations/Kemp_MA%20Economics_10-10-2011.pdf.

energy supplies with neighbors, improving reliability, joining a regional trans-mission organization and completing specified transmission projects. Though each of these actions would or should occur without the merger, applicants list them as benefits from the merger. Some involve fixing suboptimalities in the target's current performance. Exelon offered to improve Pepco's record on distribution-level outages—a record that made newspaper headlines,[20] elicited a letter from the Governor,[21] and prompted a separate investigation by the Maryland Commission.[22] The Commission's order approving Exelon's acqui-sition treated Exelon's reliability offer as a benefit from the merger. But proper outage management was a Pepco obligation without a merger.

With these types of offers, customers receive no more than what they already pay for—no more than what they would have received had their commission enforced the target utility's obligation to serve. Meanwhile the target gets the acquisition premium and the acquirer gets control of a monopoly franchise. Adding to the imbalance is this oddity: the more suboptimal the pre-merger target's performance and the less effective the commission's pre-merger regulation of that performance, the more beneficial the merger appears to the commission and the more readily the commission approves it.

9.3.3 Offers Unrelated to the Merger

Applicants often propose benefits not dependent on the merger: new head-quarters buildings (a merger that reduces redundancy does not need a new building); charitable contributions (standard practice without mergers—and never anonymous, so they strengthen the incumbent's government-assisted name recognition); the hiring of and contracting with minorities, women

---

[20] *See, e.g., Pepco's Power Outages Infuriate Washingtonians*, WASHINGTON EXAMINER (July 27, 2010), https://www.washingtonexaminer.com/pepcos-power-outages-infuriate-washingtonians ("Fuming residents, business owners and politi-cians alike lashed out at Pepco Monday, blaming the power company for another slug-gish response indicative of failures that can't be attributed to poor weather."); Opinion, *A Different Storm Brews*, BALT. SUN (Sept. 2, 2010), https://www.baltimoresun.com/opinion/bs-xpm-2010-09-02-bs-ed-pepco-outages-20100902-story.html ("Reliability, not rates, is what has many of Pepco's 778,000 residential customers seething.").

[21] Letter from Martin O'Malley, Governor, State of Md., to Joseph Rigby, Chairman, Pepco Holdings Inc. (Jan. 29, 2011), https://maryland-politics.blogspot.com/2011/01/governors-letter-to-pepco.html?m=0.

[22] Investigation into the Reliability and Quality of the Electric Distribution Service of Potomac Electric Power Company, 2011 Md. PSC LEXIS 37, at *3–4 (imposing $1 million fine for utility's poor outage performance, including "inconsistent and some-times contradictory tree trimming practices [over a decade]" and "failure to conduct periodic inspections of sub-transmission and distribution lines or to direct after-storm inspections or patrols").

and veterans (worthy of attention without a merger—hardly something to be withheld pre-merger so as to attribute the benefits to the merger); special programs for low-income customers (same); and hiking trails.[23] Another common example: the two-year freeze on worker layoffs. Layoffs are either appropriate or inappropriate, depending on how policymakers balance the value of utility workers' employment security with the value of cost reduction. A thoughtful policy on employment stability is necessary to attract and retain the best workers. But making employment decisions is management's continuing job; it has nothing to do with any given merger.

Merger strategists often aim these offers at specific constituencies. Doing so creates two problems. First, constituency-specific satisfaction is not among a commission's statutory responsibilities. Commissions have no statutory authority over downtown building construction, charitable contributions or hiking trails; so they have no statutory authority to care about constituents who want those things. Yet commissions count them as relevant to the merger authority they do have. Commissions with legal authority over only utility performance become extra-legal benefit extractors and benefit distributors, making political decisions about community values outside their legal domain.

Second, by encouraging merger applicants to use these benefits to win intervenor support, commissions lend their government imprimatur to monopoly discrimination. Merger applicants offer benefits to constituents based on their relative presence and influence rather than on their relative need. In legislative bargaining, that discrimination is unseemly but lawful; in utility regulation it is unseemly and unlawful. Constituents who did not know enough about the merger process to lobby the applicants for benefits, or who lacked the presence and influence deemed useful by the applicants, get nothing—as do non-settling intervenors who opposed the transaction on its legal merits. Consider: Exelon and PHI promised to allocate "$3.5 million for expansion of renewable generation in the District, $3.5 million to support the District's energy efficiency efforts, and $10.05 million to support the District's Green Building Fund."[24] It takes nothing away from renewable energy's merits to recognize that these dollars come at the expense of more broad-based causes, such as reducing the bills of all customers, or funding the additional commission staff necessary to monitor the post-merger holding company system, or hiring bilingual customer complaint specialists capable of speaking the many languages present

---

[23] The Exelon-PHI applicants offered, and the Maryland Commission accepted, all these items. *See* Exelon-PHI Merger, Case No. 9631, Order No. 86990, slip op. app. A (Md. Pub. Serv. Comm'n May 15, 2015).

[24] Motion of Joint Applicants to Reopen the Record in Formal Case No. 1119 at 4, Exelon-PHI Merger, Formal Case No. 1119 (D.C. Pub. Serv. Comm'n filed Oct. 6, 2015).

in any metropolitan area. Giving out benefits to renewable energy advocates and trail-hikers while ignoring these other needs is discrimination, plain and simple. And even if renewable energy investment were a proper merger topic, the correct way to shape it is through generic policymaking, as part of an integrated resource plan, crafted for practicality and cost effectiveness to benefit all citizens. Using renewable energy policy investment to sweeten a merger proposal is arbitrary.

Consider also Exelon's offer to "provide $6.75 million for energy efficiency programs developed or designated by the District in consultation with the National Consumer Law Center [NCLC] and National Housing Trust [NHT]."[25] Outside the merger context, Exelon can invite NCLC and NHT into its boardroom to influence corporate decisions. But Exelon here was proposing to grant these two organizations preferred influence over a government decision—a practice not only discriminatory but inconsistent with participatory democracy. Discrimination and favored access—these are the results of commissions allowing—and encouraging—merger applicants to make offers unrelated to the merger.

Using benefits unrelated to the merger, applicants have even discriminated among states based on relative regulatory muscle. Northeast Utilities (now EverSource) was the holding company for electric utilities serving in Connecticut, Massachusetts and New Hampshire. NSTAR was the holding company for electric and gas utilities serving in Massachusetts. Their 2012 merger took place at the holding company level, making NSTAR a first-tier, wholly owned subsidiary of Northeast Utilities. Connecticut's statute gave its regulatory agency jurisdiction over mergers at the holding company level, while New Hampshire's statute gave its Commission jurisdiction only over mergers at the utility level. Connecticut's customers got a one-time, $25 million rate credit; a distribution service rate freeze until December 1, 2014; a $15 million plan for "energy efficiency and related initiatives" (with the cost not recoverable from the customers); and a utility commitment to develop "micro grid infrastructure." New Hampshire's customers got nothing.[26]

---

[25]   *Id.*, Exhibit A at 5 (Non-unanimous Full Settlement Agreement and Stipulation).
[26]   *See* Northeast Utilities-NSTAR Merger, 2012 Conn. PUC LEXIS 47, at *3 (citing CONN. GEN. STAT. § 16-47(b), providing that without regulatory approval, "[n]o … electric, electric distribution … company, or holding company, … shall, … directly or indirectly, … exercise or attempt to exercise authority or control over any … electric … company engaged in the business of supplying service within this state"); Northeast Utilities-NSTAR Merger, 2011 N.H. PUC LEXIS 15, at *13–15 (citing N.H. REV. STAT. ANN. § 374:30, as granting Commission authority over only direct transfers of the franchise (in the NU-NSTAR transaction, the franchise stayed with the New Hampshire utility); and citing *id.* § 374:33, granting jurisdiction if a public utility or

9.3.4 Offers that Enhance the Applicants' Profitability and Market Position

Merger applicants frequently offer to invest in renewable energy, smart grids, storage, energy efficiency, demand response or microgrids. Each action could well align with commission priorities, customer needs and public sentiment. So merger applicants frame these offers as a favor to the community. But the favor works in the other direction, because each action gives the applicants two things: (1) a first-mover advantage over competitors who might perform more cost-effectively; and (2) a profit boost if the merged company can rate-base the investment. Public policy initiatives like these should come not from opportunistic applicant bargaining but from commission-guided resource planning, planning that determines three things: the appropriate mix of services, the mix of competitive and monopoly market structures that will induce suppliers to efficiently provide those services and the providers that will perform the services most cost-effectively.

9.3.5 Distraction Achieved

Merger applicants' many offers, from $100 refunds to hiking trails to microgrids, divert regulatory attention from their transaction's essence—the sale of a public franchise for private gain. The offers become the frame. Within that frame, intervenors and commissioners bargain over details, focusing narrowly on improving the status quo and matching other jurisdictions' outcomes rather than gaining for customers the benefits that couplings designed for performance would produce.[27] Outside the frame are the larger issues: (a) the lopsidedness of the outcome—where the selling shareholders receive the multi-hundred-million-dollar control premium, the acquirer gets a government-protected earnings stream, while the customers get only minor

---

public utility holding company acquired more than 10 percent of an in-state utility (here, the acquiree was NSTAR, a Massachusetts entity)).

[27] Some commissions require of merger applicants a "most favored nation clause," guaranteeing not a particular level of benefit but a benefit at least as large as the most favored state. *See, e.g.,* AltaGas-Washington Gas Light Merger, Case No. 9449, Order No. 88631, slip op. at 47 (Md. Pub. Serv. Comm'n April 4, 2018) (referring to such clauses as "common in multi-jurisdictional mergers"); *id.* at 17 (paraphrasing Commission Staff's concern that the applicants' proposed most favored nation clause did not "bring Maryland into parity with the District of Columbia, which should be the driving consideration for the provision").

Chapter 11.3.3.7 will explain that when regulators compare the applicants' offers to the status quo, or to offers made in other states, they make a common mental error: using the wrong reference point.

benefits, some illusory; (b) the absence of competition to discipline the choice of merger partners and merger terms; and (c) the absence of regulatory standards that substitute for competition's discipline. What should be central becomes marginal, even extraneous.

9.3.6   Applicant Expectations Accompanying the Offers

Accompanying the applicants' explicit offers are usually implicit expectations —expectations of specific regulatory action and inaction in four major areas.

Rate treatment: The acquirer expects the target's post-merger rates to produce a return on equity at least equal to the acquirer's hurdle rate, taking into account all merger costs—transaction cost, transition cost and acquisition cost. Applicants typically promise not to recover those costs explicitly, but they expect to do so implicitly—by persuading commissions to allow post-acquisition rates exceeding the actual cost of service. As Chapter 5.3.2 explained, rates can exceed the cost of service if the commission (a) allows the utility to charge pre-merger rates while incurring lower post-merger costs; or (b) applies an equity-level return to the target utility's entire equity, including the portion financed with lower-cost debt.

Governance control: The acquirer is buying the target utility for its stable cash flow. The acquirer's lenders base their loan terms, and the rating agencies base their ratings, on the acquirer having control of that cash flow. So the acquirer will establish governance rules giving it control over rate increases, capital investments, dividend payments, board of director membership and executive hiring. Commissions regularly allow this result.[28]

Future rate base opportunities: The acquirer bases its price offer in part on its projections of the utility's earnings. Those projections likely assume that the commission will make all future rate base opportunities available to the target utility, rather than allow third parties to compete for those opportunities on the merits.

Future corporate acquisitions: The applicants' frame depicts the post-acquisition entity as it will look on consummation day—two companies previously separate, now coupled. But the commission's approval of one acquisition does not necessarily diminish the acquirer's appetite for more. No acquirer tells the commission "This is our last acquisition." The post-acquisition entity described by the applicants is not an end point; it is a new starting point. Merger proposals never seek explicit permission to make

---

[28]   The prominent exception was the Texas Commission, which rejected NextEra's proposal to acquire Oncor precisely because NextEra wanted to control the utility's dividends and its board. For specifics, see Chapter 11.2.

unlimited future acquisitions; raising the issue would expose the issue. But the applicants expect that the commission's approval of the current acquisition will leave them free to make future acquisitions, without review. Because the applicants' expectation remains implicit, and because their frame depicts only the post-acquisition entity, commissions do not realize that in approving the coupling they see, they are allowing every future acquisition the acquirer decides to make. No commission has imposed, or even considered, a condition on an acquisition allowing it to review and limit future acquisitions.[29]

* * *

Applicants frame their offers of benefits as acts of generosity. They can do so because commissions do not require benefits equal to what effective competition would provide. No commission says "Your offers must replicate what a competitive market would produce"; or even "Your offers must be sufficiently large so that the transaction's benefits flow equally to acquirer, target, and customers." If the commission has no requirements, if the checklist is an empty vessel, then applicants can fill the vessel as they like, frame their offers as generosity, and then make minor additions so that everyone can claim to have improved the transaction. Distraction from the transaction's core purposes is achieved.

9.4   DOWNPLAY NEGATIVES

A fourth applicant strategy is to downplay the negatives, in four distinct ways.

Focus regulators' attention on the short term: Merger applicants present themselves in their current state—their current corporate structure, management, operations, financial statements, debt-equity ratios, bond ratings and non-utility business holdings. But the present does not depict the future—not when the acquirer has unlimited discretion to acquire other businesses. The holding company's risk picture will change as the holding company changes. Applicant witnesses don't testify about, and regulators don't ask about, future acquisition plans.

---

[29]   In his merger testimony in Maryland, District of Columbia, Connecticut and Louisiana, the author proposed that the acquirer submit future acquisitions or business ventures, above a minimal level, to the commission for advance review. In each case the merger applicants opposed the condition. No commission has expressly addressed it.

Cite the rating agencies' comfort: Merger applicants cite rating agency comfort as evidence of low risks. As one Exelon witness testified (responding to the author's testimony on risk):

> If the investment community believed it likely that Exelon management intended to invest in the type of highly risky ventures that Hempling envisions, Exelon would have weaker credit ratings and wider spreads than it actually has. [Instead] investors are confident that Exelon management's future acquisitions will be prudent and that management will continue to attempt to enhance shareholder value by making relatively conservative investments such as the PHI acquisition under consideration here.[30]

The argument incorrectly equates bondholder interests with customer interests. Bondholders take risks in return for interest income. Their risk-reward gamble serves their private interests; it doesn't represent the public interest. And if bondholders don't like how the risks play out, they can sell their bonds, take their losses and invest elsewhere, leaving the risks to others. The target utility's customers cannot go elsewhere. They are captive to the holding company's risks.

Assert that no previous merger has gone sour: Merger applicants can say, accurately, that no previous merger has gone sour. Focusing on the short-term, and assuming a no-harm standard,[31] this position is plausible. Despite the variety of transactions (domestic and international; adjacent and remote; cash buyouts and stock-for-stock; vertical, horizontal and conglomerate), acquisition failures are rare. Indeed, the two prominent examples of failed acquirers—the private equity consortium of KKR, Goldman Sachs and others that acquired the Texas utility Oncor;[32] and Enron, which acquired Puget Sound Energy[33]—are often cited as examples of how ring-fencing protected the target utilities from their acquirers' financial failure.[34]

But the short-term and no-harm perspectives are not the statutory perspectives. The statutory public interest is a long-term interest—the interest in

---

[30]   Rebuttal Testimony of Ellen Lapson at 18, Exelon-PHI Merger, Case No. 9361 (Md. Pub. Serv. Comm'n filed Jan. 7, 2015).

[31]   Described and critiqued in Chapter 4.2.

[32]   Described in Chapter 11.2.

[33]   Enron-Portland General Electric Merger, 1997 Ore. PUC LEXIS 15 (imposing twenty-two conditions relating to service quality, pricing of inter-affiliate transactions, allocation of merger costs, financial separation and other matters), *reh'g denied*, 1997 Ore. PUC LEXIS 236.

[34]   *See* Markian M.W. Melnyk & William S. Lamb, *PUHCA's Gone: What Is Next for Holding Companies?*, 27 ENERGY L.J. 1, 20 (2006) (describing as advantages of the holding company form "its ability to provide strong structural separation," including protection of utilities from non-utility debts and other financial risks).

making a regulated industry perform like a competitive industry. Effective competition does not merely prevent harm; it produces continuous improvement. Allowing mergers that cause no harm precludes transactions that would produce benefits. If the correct question is "Do these transactions produce competitive performance?" then the response "Nothing has gone wrong—yet" is a non sequitur.

Argue that eliminating all risk is not practical: This argument fails to distinguish two types of risk. Customers appropriately bear risk when the risk arises from a consumer benefit—like the risk associated with building a new power plant to satisfy customer load. But subjecting a utility's customers to risks from activities aimed at improving the holding company's profitability creates a mismatch of risk and reward.

9.5 LABEL OPPOSITION AS ANTI-BUSINESS AND ANTI-BENEFIT

By likening their transaction to dozens of previous ones—part of a "natural evolution"—applicants can cast opponents as progress-blockers. By making the transaction about benefits, they can position opponents as threatening those benefits—the $100 refund, the new headquarters building, the renewable energy investments, the charitable contributions, the two years' job security. These tangibles trump abstractions like control premium, double-leveraging and future acquisition risk, even though the benefits are short-term and small while the risks are long-term and large.

9.6 MAINTAIN DEADLINE PRESSURE

To keep regulators and intervenors focused on the transaction as framed, merger applicants have used three tactics.

Pour the concrete, early and unilaterally: Before targets look for acquirers, and before acquirers look for targets, merging companies don't check in with their commissions or their customers. Before signing merger agreements, they don't ask the public questions like these:

- What services do customers need and want?
- What type of company can best serve those needs and wants?
- What corporate couplings, transaction financing, and post-acquisition structures and actions, will best serve the public?
- How should we, the merging companies, be held accountable for the benefits we project and the costs we estimate?

Instead of approaching their commission and their customers for ideas, merger applicants design the details themselves. They decide which businesses and assets to combine, which company will pay how much to whom and in what form, which executives will retire and which ones will stay, who will sit on which boards and whose interests they will serve, which lenders will lend which amounts to which companies, who will file for rate increases when, and which companies will offer which benefits to which constituencies. They mix the cement and pour it into their mold. After the cement hardens, they present the package as fixed—and brittle. Months of complex negotiations have produced a balance so delicate, they say, that any material change in either party's financial outcome will kill the deal and sacrifice the benefits.

Most times this strategy works; commissions avoid adding conditions that applicants won't accept. Two exceptions involved Maryland and Kansas. In conditionally approving the 1997 BG&E-Pepco merger, the Maryland Commission required the first year's base rates to reflect 75 percent of the applicant-estimated merger savings. But because the applicants needed to retain 100 percent of the savings for three years to help pay for the acquisition premium,[35] they withdrew the transaction. The poured-concrete strategy also failed in the initial GPE-Westar acquisition, as the Kansas Commission explained:

> [T]he transaction was presented to the Commission as a take it or leave it proposal. Repeatedly, the Joint Applicants advised the Commission that any significant safeguards that would protect consumers, such as maintaining a separate, independent Westar Board of Directors, would halt the transaction. Therefore, the proposed transaction could not be salvaged and the Commission is left with no choice but to reject the proposed transaction.[36]

Create do-or-die deadlines: The typical merger agreement allows either party to withdraw if the transaction has not received all regulatory approvals by a stated deadline.[37] Because the applicants control both that deadline and

---

[35] Baltimore Gas & Electric-Pepco Merger, 1997 Md. PSC LEXIS 205, at *55–60 pt. IV.D.

[36] Great Plains Energy-Westar Merger I, 2017 Kan. PUC LEXIS 1142, at *4–5 ¶ 5. Other transactions that died because commissions required concessions the applicants would not accept include the Northern States Power-Wisconsin Electric Power transaction of 1997; and the Exelon-Public Service Electric & Gas transaction of 2006. Chapter 11.2 will describe transactions that state commissions directly rejected. FERC has never directly rejected a major electric utility merger.

[37] *See, e.g., Tucson Electric Power-San Diego Gas & Electric Merger,* 44 F.E.R.C. ¶ 61,441, at p. 62,387 n.1 (1988) (describing applicants' agreement that if "the required regulatory approvals [have] not been received by [a stated deadline], either [party could] terminate its obligations ... without penalty").

the date they submit their application, they can limit the commission's and intervenors' time to react.[38] This time-constraining strategy exacerbates the chronic resource asymmetry between applicants and commission and between applicants and intervenors.[39] The applicants' filing starts the tight procedural clock, but they have done all their case preparation ahead—submitting their application only when their team is ready.[40] The resource differential plays out in multiple ways. The applicants have multiple cross-examiners who divide up the opposing witnesses, easing the per-person workload and raising the quality; while commissions and intervenors make do with thinner staffs. The applicants can rent and staff a nearby boiler room that prepares mid-hearing pleadings during the day, whereas intervenors can do this work only at night. These differentials make a difference in the quantity and quality of information coming to the tribunal.

Deadlines do have a legitimate commercial purpose. Merging parties nego-tiate their agreement based on predictions of stock prices, interest rates and other financial factors. The longer the wait between agreement and closing,

---

[38]   Illustrating this time squeeze was the Electricité de France-Constellation trans-action. In its proceeding, the Maryland Commission creates two phases: the first to determine its jurisdiction over the transaction; the second to determine the transaction's merits. The companies filed their application in June 2009. For Phase I, the Commission "established a schedule for discovery, testimony, and hearings designed specifically to complete this Phase by the original Transaction closing date of September 17, 2009." Given that tight deadline, the Commission presided over

> an intensive litigation process that has demanded extreme effort and endurance from everyone[, a process that] … has required us, and everyone, to begin and finish in a little over four months a case that normally would consume the full six-to-seven-and-half months the statute allows. To accomplish this, we trun-cated every deadline, expedited every procedure, filled in every empty time slot, and expected the lawyers and parties to come as early or stay as late as it took to get the work done.

In the Matter of the Current and Future Financial Condition of Baltimore Gas & Electric Co., 2009 Md. PSC LEXIS 59, at *12–13 (citing MD. CODE ANN., PUB. UTIL. § 6-105(g)(6)).

[39]   For the author's thoughts on the resource differential, see these essays: *Regulatory Resources: Does the Differential Make a Difference? (Parts I and II)*, SCOTT HEMPLING LAW (Sept. 2008), http://www.scotthemplinglaw.com/regresources1, http://www.scotthemplinglaw.com/regresources2; and *Regulatory Expense: Is Asymmetry Inevitable?*, SCOTT HEMPLING LAW (Feb. 2015), http://www.scotthemplinglaw.com/essays/regulatory-expense.

[40]   Rough analogy: Imagine a cross-country race where one team designs the course, then spends months practicing on it. Only when its runners are ready does that team reveal the location and set the race date, leaving its competitors scrambling to prepare. I said the analogy was rough. As a 9th grade runner, I knew my home course better than my competitors, so in home meets, I had an advantage.

the more likely the actuals vary from the predictions. But if a transaction's true purpose is efficiencies and innovations, those benefits don't depend on market timing. In pressuring a commission to constrict its schedule, merger applicants place their private interest in expedition ahead of the public's need for methodical analysis. In doing so they reveal their main motivation: investor benefit, not customer benefit.

Oppose merger policymaking in a merger proceeding: Merger applicants want policy predictability. If a commission has expressed no merger vision before the proceeding, applicants discourage the commission from creating one during the proceeding. As one utility witness put it, a commission should not "us[e] a merger to legislate or otherwise adopt new regulatory or other public policies."[41]

But in administrative regulation, making or revising policy in an adjudicated proceeding is neither uncommon nor unlawful.[42] And making new policy in a merger case does not involve reversing promises on prior utility investments—a regulatory practice that would trigger legitimate legal attacks as arbitrary and capricious under regulatory statutes, and possibly confiscatory under the Fifth Amendment's Takings Clause.[43] In the merger context, shareholders do bet dollars on the regulatory outcome. But those bets are private bets involving dollars spent on stock rather than dollars spent on utility infrastructure; stock bets fall outside a regulatory commission's statutory concern. Still—predictability is better, for customers and investors, so commissions should have policies in place before a merger is filed. But there is no legal bar to a commission making policy within a merger proceeding. And if no policy exists, then giving a multi-billion dollar transaction a pass compounds the problem.

* * *

In seeking commission approvals, merger applicants (a) frame their transaction as simple and positive, (b) argue industry inevitability and corporate necessity, (c) make offers of benefits to distract and persuade, (d) downplay negatives, (e) label opponents as anti-business and anti-benefit, and (f) maintain deadline

---

[41] Rebuttal Testimony of Susan Tierney at 9, Exelon-Constellation Energy Group Merger, Case No. 9271 (Md. Pub. Serv. Comm'n filed Oct. 12, 2011).

[42] *See generally* SEC v. Chenery Corp., 332 U.S. 194 (1947).

[43] *See* Duquesne Light Co. v. Barasch, 488 U.S. 299 (1989) (warning that "a State's decision to arbitrarily switch back and forth between [rate-setting] methodologies in a way which required investors to bear the risk of bad investments at some times while denying them the benefit of good investments at others would raise serious constitutional questions").

pressure. These six strategies need not succeed, but nearly always they do—because regulators allow them to. The next chapter explains how and why.

10. How do regulators respond? By ceding leadership, underestimating negatives and accepting minor positives

Commissions have checklists instead of visions. They don't define the public interest, so they neither describe nor prescribe the types of acquirers or merger partners best able to satisfy the public interest. See Chapter 8. Merger applicants fill that void by framing their transactions as simple, positive, normal and inevitable; by making minor benefit offers that persuade and distract; by treating intervenor concerns dismissively; by labeling opponents anti-benefit and anti-business; and by maintaining deadline pressure. See Chapter 9.

How do regulators respond? Too often they cede leadership to the applicants—adopting their frame, underestimating negatives and using reactive procedures.[1] Recognizing they cannot approve billions in applicant gain without getting customers something, regulators pose as legislators, horse-trading on benefits that fall outside their subject matter jurisdiction.

10.1 CEDING LEADERSHIP TO APPLICANTS

A regulatory merger proceeding involves two separate struggles: between the applicants and the opponents, over who gets what; and between the applicant and the commission, over who leads the proceeding. Most commissions let the applicants lead. The applicants' goals become the proceeding's focus, their deadlines determine the procedural schedule. Commissions describe the transaction the way applicants do—a simple transfer of ownership—rather than call the transaction what it is—a sale of public franchise for private gain. Some commissions even advocate for the transaction: by helping the applicants fix its flaws or by ordering parties to talk settlement so the transaction

---

[1] As exemplified by this candid comment by the Maryland Public Service Commission: "[W]e have ... sought, wherever possible, to preserve the structure of the Proposal's proffered conditions, even where, in some instances, we find that the law requires us to modify them." FirstEnergy-Allegheny Energy Merger, 2011 Md. PSC LEXIS 5, at text near n.72.

can proceed. Most commissions leave unplayed their strong hand—their legal authority to require of any merged company the level of performance that competition would produce.

10.1.1   Accepting the Applicants' Frame

Merger applicants insist that their purpose is customer benefit. When commissions accept that frame rather than recognize the transaction's real purposes— gain for the target and market position for the acquirer—they commit five distinct errors.

Making incorrect comparisons: Commissions should ask: Does the transaction satisfy our public interest vision for performance? Instead they ask: Does the transaction not harm, and maybe improve on, the status quo? By focusing on what applicants proposed—modest improvement on the status quo—rather than what they should have proposed—the performance that effective competition would have required—commissions limit their range of motion. They act only within the area bounded by the applicants' proposal rather than the area defined by what customers deserve. This reactive posture departs from everyday behavior. Prudent home buyers don't look at the types of houses their broker wants to sell; they tell the broker the type of houses they want to buy. They compare a candidate house not to their status quo quarters but to their ideal.

Adopting unproven premises: Applicants describe their transaction as a public-spirited joining of assets to achieve financial strength, scale economies and best practices; necessary because bigger is better. Regulators rarely demand proof of these premises. Seeking to acquire three gas utilities in New England, the Spanish holding company Iberdrola described its financial resources as among "the largest in the world"—resources that would "strengthen[] the financial stability and resources accessible to" the three acquired utilities, giving them more "access to both U.S. and global financial markets." The Connecticut regulatory agency copied these assertions into its approval order as bases for its approval,[2] without asking whether the to-be-acquired gas companies actually needed more access to financial markets.

Giving weight to non-committal aspirations: Merger applicants talk aspirationally. Great Plains Energy (GPE) and Westar said their merger would "create a leading utility." It would have "the operational expertise, scale and financial resources to meet the region's future energy needs"; and "a strong commitment to high-quality customer service, innovative energy efficiency

---

[2]   Iberdrola-Energy East Merger, 2007 Conn. PUC LEXIS 316, at *18, *20.

programs, environmental stewardship, reliability and safety." They stated their "belief that the merger should over time generate cost savings and operating efficiencies through consolidation and integration of certain functions."[3] Beliefs and aspirations, formulaic and factless—these things don't count as commitments, so they should not count as evidence supporting the transaction. (In fact, Westar admitted that neither its Board nor its executives had considered any (a) "studies of economies of scale in the generation, transmission, distribution or marketing of electric service"; or (b) "studies of whether prior electric utility mergers and acquisitions actually achieved the savings their supporting witnesses said would result."[4]) Contrast merging companies' linguistic looseness in the applications with the rigorous math they use to test each other's financial statements, or the legal rigor they inject into their hundred-page merger agreements. No target CEO would sell franchise control for mere aspirations of a premium. No merger lawyer would base a multi-billion dollar merger agreement on good faith. Yet the bases for merger approval orders are usually that soft.[5]

Allocating regulatory attention disproportionately to applicant purposes rather than public interest purposes: Suppose one day a commission's staff submitted a proposal to break up the local vertically integrated utility into four independent companies—generation, transmission, physical distribution and retail sales. No commission would devote a six-month proceeding to the proposal, with the proceeding's boundaries, issues and questions all based on the staff's preferences. Yet whenever that local utility and its prospective acquirer propose the opposite—to combine the local utility's generation, transmission, distribution and retail sales with all the acquirer's assets—the commission gives the idea full procedural attention. Why the difference? Suppose, alternatively, the commission staff proposed a competition to select the best company to control the incumbent utility's franchise. Again, no commission would likely take up the question. But when a utility hosts its own competition for the franchise, and chooses a winner based on price rather than performance,

---

[3]   Great Plains Energy Inc., Amendment No. 1 to Registration Statement (Form S-4/A) at 78–79 (Aug. 17, 2016).

[4]   Response to KCC Staff Interrogatory 210, Great Plains Energy-Westar Merger I, Docket No. 16-KCPE-593-ACQ (Kan. Corp. Comm'n filed Oct. 21, 2016).

[5]   Though not in the GPE-Westar transaction. The Kansas Commission did say that "based on [the two companies'] geographies a merger makes sense," but then rejected the initial proposal because "the purchase price is simply too high." Great Plains Energy-Westar Energy Merger I, 2017 Kan. PUC LEXIS 1142, at *4 ¶ 5. In fact, in a subsequent order approving a revised transaction that lacked a control premium, the Commission found no disagreement that the transaction would produce "significant quantifiable benefits." Great Plains Energy-Westar Energy Merger II, 2018 Kan. PUC LEXIS 899, at *38, *41.

the proposal gets the commission's full six-month attention. Again, why the difference?

Missing the transaction's essence—franchise control and parent-utility conflict: No merger application says: "The acquirer wants to buy control of a government-protected franchise; the target wants to sell that control for the highest possible price." No merger application says: "This transaction brings a formerly pure-play utility into a holding company system with multiple risks and conflicts." Those sentences accurately describe most mergers, but no commission order says so. Most orders describe the transaction the way the applicants do: the stock exchange mechanics, the purchase price, the financing, the customer-oriented purpose, the accompanying benefit offers. Missing the transaction's essence means asking no questions about that essence—questions about whether and how the applicants' motivations conflict with or diverge from the public's interest in performance, and about how that conflict or divergence will affect the local utility. Accepting the applicants' frame means missing facts about the public interest frame.[6]

10.1.2   Advocating for the Transaction

By focusing solely on the applicants' transaction, commissions risk advocating for the transaction. Here are two ways:

Using conditioning authority to "fix" the transaction: Merger statutes allow commissions to accompany their approvals with conditions.[7] The applicants then have a choice: accept the conditions or withdraw the proposal. Using its conditioning authority, FERC has induced merger applicants to grant transmission access, join regional transmission organizations and divest strategic assets

---

[6]   The habit of accepting the applicants' frame risks slipping into a state known as "regulatory capture." Properly understood, regulatory capture occurs not when regulated utilities pressure commissions, but when commissions don't have, don't express and don't press for their own visions—and so allow themselves, willingly or inadvertently, to make the regulated entity's priorities their priorities. *See* Scott Hempling, *Regulatory Capture: Sources and Solutions*, 1 EMORY CORP. GOVERNANCE & ACCOUNTABILITY REV. 23 (2014), http://law.emory.edu/ecgar/content/volume-1/issue-1/essays/regulatory-capture.html.

[7]   *See, e.g.*, Federal Power Act § 203(b), 16 U.S.C. § 824b(b) (authorizing conditions as the Commission "finds necessary or appropriate to secure the maintenance of adequate service and the coordination in the public interest of facilities subject to the jurisdiction of the Commission"); MD. CODE ANN., PUB. UTIL. § 6-105(f)(3)(ii) (allowing conditions to ensure "the applicant's satisfactory performance or adherence to specific requirements").

to prevent merger-produced market power.[8] States have attached financial and structural conditions to reduce the risks of non-utility affiliate failures.[9]

Commissions may attach conditions only to make the transaction lawful;[10] not to fix problems that pre-dated the transaction or that fall outside the commission's jurisdiction.[11] When commissions combine these statutory constraints with a no-harm standard (instead of a best performance standard—see Chapter 4.2), the conditioning power can become a means of saving suboptimal transactions rather than inducing market actors to find optimal ones.

Directing parties to talk settlement: A commission's generic procedural schedule lists all the standard steps: discovery requests and responses, pre-filed direct and rebuttal testimony, evidentiary hearing, settlement discussions, briefs, decision. In a merger proceeding, all those steps make sense—except the settlement discussions. Settlement discussions can make sense in rate cases. Parties disagree over dollars; absent some fundamental difference over assumptions, reasonable people taking reasonable positions can find common ground. But requiring settlement discussions in a merger proceeding sends an

---

[8]   As explained in Chapter 6.5.2.

[9]   As explained in Chapter 7.4.8.

[10]   *See Northeast Utilities-Public Service of New Hampshire Merger*, 50 F.E.R.C. ¶ 61,266, at p. 61,842 (1990) (explaining that the Commission may "impose conditions" only to the extent needed to make a proposed merger "consistent with the public interest"); *Utah Power & Light-PacifiCorp Merger*, 45 F.E.R.C. ¶ 61,095, at p. 61,289–90 (1988) (justifying conditions as "the minimum necessary" to reduce likely anticompetitive effects).

[11]   AT&T-Bellsouth Merger, 22 FCC Rcd. 5662, 5674–75 ¶ 22 (2007) (FCC may impose conditions "only to remedy harms that arise from the transaction ... and that are related to the Commission's [statutory] responsibilities"). Consider *Duke Energy-Progress Energy Merger I*, 136 F.E.R.C. ¶ 61,245 at PP 59, 147 (2011). Pre-merger, the North Carolina Commission had (a) prohibited Duke, the in-state utility, from treating the wholesale customer's retail load comparably to the utility's own retail native load; and (b) allocated, for retail rate purposes, certain of Duke's wholesale power costs at incremental rather than system average costs. In the FERC proceeding on the Duke-Florida Progress merger, a wholesale customer sought from FERC conditions protecting against these policies, because North Carolina's requirements meant that Duke treated its retail customers better than its wholesale customers. FERC rejected the request, because the state policies pre-dated the merger, and therefore did not arise from it. *See also Boston Edison-Cambridge Electric Light Merger*, 117 F.E.R.C. ¶ 61,083 at P 34 (2006) (rejecting the wholesale customer's concerns about the state commission's allocation of transmission cost because "there [did] not appear to be a direct connection" to the merger); AT&T Wireless-Cingular Merger, 19 FCC Rcd. 21,522, 21,546 ¶ 43 (2004) (declining to "impose conditions to remedy pre-existing harms or harms that are unrelated to the transaction").

illogical signal.[12] In a merger proceeding the central question is this: "Does this transaction satisfy the public interest?" Settlement discussions can't answer that threshold question. So any settlement discussion would necessarily occur under the assumption that the transaction does satisfy, or can be made to satisfy, the public interest; the only remaining question being the conditions. But an assumption that the transaction satisfies the public interest ignores the principle that a transaction chosen by the target based on price rather than performance undermines the public interest. A command to talk settlement misses this point completely.

Similar to encouraging settlements is accompanying a rejection with an invitation. The Kansas Commission rejected GPE's proposed cash acquisition of Westar because the price and the premium were too high. One month later, the Commission's Order on Reconsideration encouraged the two companies to "revise the Transaction to address the Commission's concerns related to purchase price, capital structure and other issues."[13] A few months later, the two companies proposed a stock-for-stock exchange without a premium. With the revised purchase price lower (zero) and the revised benefits higher, the Commission voted yes.[14]

10.1.3   Leaving the Commission's Strong Hand Unplayed

With veto power over the transaction, the commission has a strong hand. When allocating the transaction's value between shareholders and ratepayers, how well do commissions play that hand? Consider three approaches.

The first approach focuses on the control premium—the value placed by the acquirer on gaining control. Chapter 5 explained that ratepayers deserve the control premium to the extent they contributed to its value. The second approach focuses on the economic benefits attributable to the merger. If the Commission wants the transaction, it must grant the acquirer an amount of benefits that will keep the acquirer in the transaction—likely, the amount that makes the acquirer's benefit-cost ratio just exceed its hurdle rate. All remaining benefits should go to the ratepayers. That result replicates competition, because where the target's product is subject to competition, each prospective

---

[12]   *See, e.g.*, Exelon-PHI Merger, Order 17654, 2014 D.C. PUC LEXIS 315, at *93 attachment A (Revised Procedural Schedule). This procedural schedule directed the parties to talk settlement and give the Commission a report on the talks, four times: before intervenors filed their direct testimony; after intervenors filed their direct testimony; after all parties filed their rebuttal testimony; and after the evidentiary hearing.

[13]   Order on Reconsideration, Great Plains Energy-Westar Energy Merger I, 2017 Kan. PUC LEXIS 1382, at *6 ¶ 9.

[14]   Great Plains Energy-Westar Energy Merger II, 2018 Kan. PUC LEXIS 899.

acquirer would bid up the offered benefits to the point where the acquisition becomes less attractive than alternative investments.

The problem with both approaches: they require information commissions don't have. Merger applicants know their operating costs, their financing sources, their hurdle rates and their tolerance for risk. They know what they can give up before walking. Because commissions lack that information, they cannot assess applicants' threats to walk. Information asymmetry makes the commission's strong hand a weak hand.

Solving this problem requires a third approach: a franchise competition run by the commission rather than by the target. In the typical utility merger, the target utility selects an acquirer based on price; the two companies then submit their transaction to the commission. Because the commission doesn't know the acquirer's hurdle rate, the psychological anchor for the value-allocation decision becomes the applicants' self-interested proposal.[15] If instead the commission requires a competition based on customer benefits, the competing proposals will reflect the prospective acquirers' hurdle rates, because each will bid their offered benefits up to that point—or risk losing.

No commission uses any of these three approaches. Instead of playing their strong hand—using their veto and their statutory public interest obligation to allocate benefits the way competition would—commissions seek only to avoid harm, and maybe improve on the status quo. Instead of affirmatively causing contestants to compete for the customers' favor, commissions let the target utility cause contestants to compete for its shareholders' favor. That is how commissions cede leadership.

10.2 CEMENTING THE APPLICANTS' FRAME WITH REACTIVE PROCEDURES

The purpose of procedure is to help commissions make the best decisions. The typical merger procedures do not achieve this purpose. Without a public interest definition, without a vision for the optimal outcome, with anchoring based on applicant strategy rather than commission leadership, commissions organize each proceeding to process the applicants' proposal rather than to carry out optimal merger policy. This mismatch, between necessary purpose and typical procedure, appears in each of seven procedural steps, presented sequentially here.

---

[15] We will define and discuss anchoring, and other psychological tendencies relevant to commissions' merger decision-making, in Chapter 11.3.

10.2.1   The Merger Application: Generic and Self-serving

Because commissions have checklists instead of standards, merger applicants fill in the blanks with generic language. Their merger applications and pre-filed testimony describe business objectives (market positioning, access to capital, diversification); customer benefits (economies of scale, best practices, rate refunds); and community benefits (charitable contributions, economic development). These generic objectives and benefits often come with adjectives unaccompanied by facts; assertions that the transaction is "the best" lack comparative data proving the claim true. Merger applications say nothing of the transaction's real purposes and origins: the target seeking highest price, the acquirer seeking control of a monopoly franchise, the auction process dominated by price. Because commissions don't define the public interest, they don't require applicants to explain how their transactions satisfy the public interest. The public interest becomes a label that applicants place on their application, rather than a standard they satisfy with their transaction.

10.2.2   Interventions: Positions Instead of Perspectives

Under typical commission procedures, intervenors seeking party status need only describe their self-interest, then explain how that self-interest is relevant to the merger statute. They have no obligation to explain how pursuing their private interest advances the public interest—an unsurprising result where the commission hasn't defined the public interest. Only rarely does an intervenor use its intervention request to compare the merger application to the public interest, to expose facts missing from the application, to identify questions the commission should ask or to reframe the proceeding's purpose from "This merger, yes or no?" to "What type of company should control the franchise?"

So at this opening stage, the commission's mental space is filled with the applicants' promotional material and the intervenors' self-interested reactions. The proceeding has become a fight between opposing interests rather than an effort to advance the public interest. The proceeding has become an adjudication among positions rather than exploration of perspectives.

10.2.3   Hearing Order: a Failure to Reframe

Having received the merger application, the applicants' direct testimony and the requests to intervene, the commission publishes a hearing order. A hearing order establishes the issues and the schedule. If the commission had a merger policy, the hearing order would list questions that test the proposed transaction against that policy—questions like these:

- Why did the target decide to seek an acquirer? Why did the target select this acquirer over others?
- Which claimed benefits are real and which are aspirational?
- What are the direct costs and the opportunity costs?
- Given these clear definitions of benefits and costs, what is the predicted benefit-cost ratio?
- What are the risks that actual benefits and costs will vary from the predicted? Who bears those risks?
- What utility resources are being diverted, from which activities, to make one company out of two?
- What are better uses for those resources?
- What transactions are precluded by this one?
- What markets will be made less competitive, or will not be made more competitive—and at whose expense?
- What acquisitions will follow this one?
- Does the commission have the resources to induce the merged company to perform well, and to protect customers from harm?
- Will the merged company's acquisition debt constrain future commission decisions?

But the commission without a policy has only this question: "Should we approve the merger, yes or no; and if yes, with what conditions?" The hearing order might list subsidiary questions, but those questions usually ask only about the transaction as presented: the specifics of the financing, the precise wording of the ring-fencing, the layoffs of workers, the time periods for the benefits. The rare intervenor who recommends "Let's first establish a merger policy before deciding this merger" is ignored, or told "That is not this case."[16]

10.2.4 Intervenors' Pre-filed Testimony: Three Purposes

Responding to the applicants' pre-filed direct testimony, intervenors submit theirs. Intervenor testimony tends to fall into three main categories, each treated differently by the commission.

---

[16] The author has frequently urged commission clients to create a merger policy. He usually gets one of two responses: "We have no merger pending, so we don't care about it"; or, "We have a merger pending, so we can't talk about it." That doesn't leave a lot of alternatives.

Intervenor who opposes the merger on fundamental grounds—such as wrong coupling, wrong motivations, market power that can't be fixed, too much debt, too much holding company control: These intervenors direct their opposition at the merger applicants, calling them out for prioritizing profit over the public interest. But the applicants are only doing what comes naturally: the acquirer seeking the most profitable franchises, the target seeking the highest price. These goals are not unlawful, so the critiques lack legal relevance. The problem is not pursuing profit; the problem is pursuing profit in the absence of competition, undisciplined by regulatory standards that replicate competition. Neither the absence of competition nor the lack of regulatory discipline is the applicants' fault; that fault lies with the regulators. Merger opponents criticize the applicants for what comes naturally when they should be educating the commission about what is necessary legally.

Intervenors who don't oppose the merger fundamentally but see negatives needing remedies: These intervenors aim to improve the transaction; by, for example, making acquisition debt non-recourse to the utility, shielding the utility from non-utility business risks, protecting customers from excess merger costs or getting customers more benefits. These intervenors accept the applicants' frame. They don't address the applicants' motivations, and they don't question the commission's passive role.

Intervenors who are indifferent to the transaction and its risks, but see an opportunity to gain non-merger benefits. These intervenors seek benefits that the applicants have no obligation to provide, like low-income assistance, renewable energy expansion and job protections. They know, or learn, that if they keep their requests modest, ask for nothing that diminishes the applicants' market position or profitability, and agree to support the transaction, the applicants will likely accommodate these requests.

How do commissions treat these three intervenor types? The first category—intervenors who critique the transaction on fundamental grounds—gets little commission attention, because real commission attention would require fashioning a policy for all mergers instead of processing the pending application for a single merger. The third category—intervenors who use the merger to get non-merger benefits—does receive commission attention but should not. Commissions should exclude interventions and testimony that treat a merger proceeding like a bazaar, a place to trade support for goods unrelated to the transaction. The second category is crucial to making the merger safe; but by itself does not address whether the proposed merger is the right merger. Yet this second category is where commissions put most of their attention. Commissions do not ask about the motivations behind a transaction or the alternatives precluded by it; they treat the transaction as a legitimate "ask" and do what they can to make it work.

10.2.5 Applicants' Rebuttal: Keep the Focus on the Frame

Applicants then file testimony rebutting the intervenor testimony. To keep the commission focused on the applicants' frame, they respond differently to each intervenor type. Responding to the fundamental opponents, applicants argue that the concerns are speculative, that the transaction resembles the dozens that won prior approvals, that pleas for general merger policies don't belong in a merger-specific proceeding and that the public interest standard requires only a non-harmful transaction rather than the best transaction. The intervenors attempting to improve the transaction get different treatment: applicants will work with them offline to adjust language and add provisions, as long as the changes don't materially reduce the acquirer's and target's gains. As for the intervenors seeking unrelated benefits, the applicants' doors remain open throughout the proceeding, usually finding ways to keep those benefits modest but also to give those intervenors reason to support the transaction or withdraw from the case.

10.2.6 Evidentiary Hearing: a Sequence of Narrow Questions

In merger hearings, the applicants' witnesses appear first, one at a time. The sequence usually starts with the CEOs, who tell their story while the commissioners' attention is at maximum. The CEOs tend to have none of the technical information that matters, so their responses to cross-examination resembles their pre-filed testimony: generalities, aspirations and self-praise. They act as spokespeople, not expert witnesses. Though the hearing consists mainly of opponents cross-examining the witnesses (because the witnesses have pre-filed their direct testimony), the cross is bounded by the transaction. Cross-examination can narrow or undermine the applicants' arguments for their transaction, but it cannot easily advance a vision different from the transaction as proposed. So for the sitting commissioners, the applicants' frame remains prominent.

Then come the applicants' more technical witnesses—the chief financial offer, the operations specialists, the external financial analysts. Their technical testimony—about sources of acquisition funds, reactions of the financial markets, descriptions of internal reorganizations—stays within, and therefore cements, the applicants' framing.

Sometime in the second or third week the opposing witnesses appear, ready to describe the transaction's flaws, alternatives to the merger, and proposals for merger policies that are cost-effective and pro-competitive. By then, though, commissioner attention has diminished—not intentionally, but inevitably. Somehow a witness appearing on Day 9 seems less important than one appearing on Day 1, like a newspaper story's ninth paragraph seems less important than its first paragraph—especially if the Day 9 witness is arguing for something—like the elements of a coherent merger policy—that seem remote from the current proposal.

Other elements of the evidentiary hearing embed the applicants' frame. Because the witness sequence is organized by party rather than by issue, the treatment of any particular issue—say, acquisition debt or acquisition premium—will be scattered across disparate days and hundreds of non-sequential transcript pages. Because the opposing witnesses' appearances are separated by days or weeks, the commissioners have no chance to provoke debate—leaving them less informed about the transaction's defects and cementing the applicants' frame.

10.2.7   The Final Order: Positions Instead of Policy

These procedural practices—generic applications, benefit-seeking interventions, hearing orders that fail to reframe, applicant rebuttals that dismiss policy issues, and evidentiary hearings that cement the applicants' frame—combine to box commissions in. Once the applicants have negotiated their transaction and submitted their application, and once the intervenors have reacted to that result—no one guided by the commission's public interest vision or invited to presented their own vision—the commission has only two choices: reject or approve. A variation on each choice gives four options: (a) reject with prejudice; (b) reject without prejudice, inviting the applicants to return with an improved proposal; (c) accept, conditioned on tangible performance benefits, some unrelated benefits and protections against customer harm; and (d) approve as proposed, without conditions. Nearly every merger order falls into one of those categories. No merger order actually describes a merger policy.[17]

The orders themselves are dominated by the parties' positions. They read more like a summary of a tennis match than an assessment of whether the transaction satisfies the commission's merger policy. These orders describe the merger clinically rather than strategically—who is buying what, not why the buyer is buying and why the seller is selling. No merger opinion starts by saying what the transaction really is; no merger opinion starts with a sentence like this one: "Target shareholders propose to sell control of a government-granted franchise for an unearned control premium of 25 percent, while the acquirer

---

[17]   The prominent exception is the Hawaii Commission's order rejecting the proposed acquisition of Hawaiian Electric by NextEra. The Order's Appendix details criteria that should apply to future proposed acquisitions. NextEra-Hawaiian Electric Merger, Docket No. 2015-0022, Order No. 33795, slip op. app. A (Haw. Pub. Util. Comm'n July 15, 2016). For a discussion of that order and its Appendix, see Chapter 11.2.

seeks to buy a government-protected revenue flow to balance its higher-risk portfolio." The signal sent is this: the commission will assess the merger based on the parties' positions rather than on the commission's policy.

10.3 UNDERESTIMATING THE NEGATIVES

Accepting the applicants' frame—that the transaction is simple, inevitable and good—means downplaying—sometimes not even mentioning—the negatives. Most commonly missed or underestimated are five: private-public utility conflict; constraints on future regulatory decisions; effects of future holding company decisions; future regulatory costs; and the cumulative effects of multiple state approvals.

10.3.1 Private-Public Conflict

Whether a merger occurs in a regulated monopoly market or a competitive market, its signatories have a private interest purpose: to buy and sell a business that generates earnings. Regulated monopoly markets and competitive markets also have a public interest purpose: to provide consumers the services they want, at a price reflecting the services' value.

In an effectively competitive market, these private and public interests align. With many sellers vying for many customers, merger strategists will choose the coupling that maximizes cost-effectiveness and product differentiation—two features most likely to gain and retain customers. A merger based on those features is pro-competitive and pro-consumer, because it pressures competitors to raise their performance too. But in a monopoly market, the private and public interests do not align. Absent regulatory action, four private-public conflicts are unavoidable.

Value diversion: As Chapter 5 explained, the target utility shareholders sell franchise control for a premium. By keeping the entire premium for themselves, the target shareholders take value away from those who created that value. When target CEOs say they are "unlocking value," they are actually diverting public value to private actors.

Weakened competition: If the transaction gives the merged company market power or unearned advantage, it weakens competitive forces. Couplings that seem to increase static efficiency by lowering current costs can reduce dynamic efficiency by disadvantaging existing sellers and discouraging new entrants. And if the merged company can sustain prices above competitive levels, the merger causes a loss in static efficiency—deadweight loss.[18]

Economic waste: The target chose its acquirer based on highest price, not best performance. For competitive market mergers those two criteria can coincide, but in monopoly market mergers they will not. A merger based on price precludes one based on performance. The result is opportunity cost— economic waste.[19]

Information asymmetry: "[Merger] efficiencies are difficult to verify and quantify, in part because much of the information relating to efficiencies is uniquely in the possession of the merging firms."[20] In a competitive market, prices emerge from objective forces—the intersection of the market's demand and supply curves, which in turn reflect the preferences of numerous buyers and the cost structures of numerous sellers. In a regulated monopoly market, prices are set by the commission based on cost information provided by the seller. A merger changes the merging companies' cost structures. So a commission's knowledge of the pre-merger utility's cost structure will be insufficient to set prices accurately. The merging companies control information on post-merger cost changes, because they control the cost changes. This knowledge advantage enables the merged entity to win rates that exceed its actual costs plus profit—at least until the regulator discovers more facts and adjusts the rates.

To a merger's designers these four factors are central; in commission merger decisions they are marginal. Regulatory decisions have no section entitled "Private-Public Conflicts"—a section describing the conflicts at the transaction's core. Because commissions don't identify and explain these conflicts, they don't structure their decision-making to remove them. Opinion-writing style leans the other way—citing the applicants' aspirations for market advantage without explaining how their advantage can cause others' disadvantage. Contrast other regulatory policies. Commissions routinely recognize that utilities have a capital expenditure bias—an inherent conflict between

---

[18]   Deadweight loss is "the difference between what producers gain and (the monetary value of) what consumers lose, when output is restricted under imperfect competition." JOSEPH E. STIGLITZ & CARL E. WALSH, ECONOMICS, at A2 (3d ed. 2002). *See also* N. GREGORY MANKIW, PRINCIPLES OF ECONOMICS 163 (3d ed. 2004) ("When a [market distortion, such as the exercise of market power,] raises the price to buyers … it gives buyers an incentive to buy less … than they otherwise would. As buyers and sellers respond to these incentives, the size of the market shrinks below its optimum. Thus, because [the exercise of market power] distort[s] incentives, [it] cause[s] markets to allocate resources inefficiently," leading to a deadweight societal loss.).

[19]   As explained in Chapter 4.1.

[20]   DEP'T OF JUSTICE & FED. TRADE COMM'N, HORIZONTAL MERGER GUIDELINES §10 (2010).

profit-seeking shareholders and cost-minimizing ratepayers. And in their forty-year efforts to bring competition to wholesale and retail markets in electricity, gas and telecommunications, commissions explicitly acknowledged that incumbent utilities have incentive and opportunity to use their control of bottleneck facilities—transmission and distribution in gas and electricity, the "last mile" and central office equipment in telecommunications—to exclude competitors and then raise prices to customers.[21] In those two examples—ratemaking and competition—commissions' open acknowledgement of private-public conflict has led to policy decisions that reduce the conflict. In merger regulation, that acknowledgment, and the resulting decisional care, are missing.

10.3.2 Constraints on Future Regulatory Decisions

Chapter 7.3 explained how high acquisition debt can constrain a commission's future decisions. Bond rating agencies base their ratings in part on "constructive regulation."[22] For rating agencies, regulation is constructive when it allows a utility's earnings to meet the agencies' expectations. Those expectations of constructive regulation have a basis in market structure and in ratemaking.

Market structure: The market structure expectation is straightforward: that the target utility will maintain its franchise monopoly. If so, then all new infrastructure investments required for the service territory, and the associated rate base earnings, will go to that utility.[23] This expectation constrains the commission, because if later it offered those infrastructure investment opportunities to more efficient competitors, the merged company—supported by the rating agencies—will argue that the reduced earnings will leave it unable to pay off its acquisition debt. Worries about weakening the post-merger company

---

[21] As explained in Chapter 6.4.2.

[22] *See, e.g.,* Great Plains Energy, Project Wizard: Moody's Investors Service Presentation 15, 18 (Apr. 27, 2016), *attached as* Response to Staff Data Request 024, Great Plains Energy-Westar Energy Merger I, Docket No. 16-KCPE-593-ACQ (D.C. Pub. Serv. Comm'n Apr. 19, 2017) (describing the Kansas Commission as practicing "constructive regulation"); Direct Testimony of Cameron Bready at 24, Entergy Mississippi-Transmission Company Mississippi Merger, Docket No. 2012-UA-358 (Miss. Pub. Serv. Comm'n filed Oct. 5, 2012) (citing Standard & Poor's statement that the International Transmission Company has a "positive outlook" due to improved cash flow attributable in part to FERC's "constructive regulation").

[23] Among GPE's reasons for acquiring Westar was "[i]ncreased access to attractive rate-based growth opportunities"—one feature among the transaction's "compelling strategic rationales." GREAT PLAINS ENERGY INC., INVESTOR PRESENTATION 6 (2016) (filed pursuant to Rule 425 under the Securities Act of 1933 and Rule 14a-12 under the Securities Exchange Act of 1934).

can discourage a commission from doing its job: getting customers the most cost-effective service from the most cost-effective providers.

The problem arises not only with rate-basing opportunities but with the monopoly franchise itself. Historically, consumers bought a uniform electricity product—electric service—from a single supplier—the local franchised monopoly. But new technologies are creating opportunities for diverse suppliers, including customer self-supply. New companies are offering thermostat controls, time-of-use pricing and renewable energy packages. Consumers are installing solar panels. Cities are creating microgrids, and organizing community-level companies to provide solar and wind. Aggregators of demand response are offering to pay consumers to use less—creating load-shifting behaviors that can displace higher-cost distribution, transmission and generation facilities. Each of these initiatives will reduce the local utility's cash flow, making it harder for the acquirer to pay off its acquisition debt. But no commission has considered this problem before approving acquisitions financed with debt.

Ratemaking: When a utility earns a return exceeding its required return—the level required to attract investment—we have economic waste. Customers pay more than necessary, leaving them with less disposable income to purchase more valuable goods. The utility earns more than its performance warrants, creating a false sense of entitlement that conflicts with competition's pressure to excel. To avoid these results, commissions must calibrate authorized returns to required returns, then monitor actual returns to keep them aligned with the authorized returns. But as Chapter 5.3 explained, acquirers pay premia because they expect post-acquisition earnings to exceed both their required return and their authorized return. If regulators later propose to set the merged company's return correctly, they will face pressure from the financial community— pressure to set the authorized return based not on proper capital market theory but on the merged company's financial condition, as that condition is affected by the premium paid by the acquirer. The circularity should be obvious.

In sum: by approving a transaction financed with acquisition debt, commissions guarantee future conflict between (a) providing the merged company the market conditions and regulatory policies that enable it to pay off its debt, and (b) providing competitors and customers the market conditions and regulatory policies that carry out the commission's duty to make the electric service cost-effective. Commission merger approvals do not address these concerns.

10.3.3   Status Quo vs. Future

"[P]eople are generally attentive even to small costs and benefits that are certain to affect them immediately, but they tend to give short shrift to even large costs and benefits that either are uncertain or occur with significant delay."[24] How does this tendency affect commission merger decisions? Do regulators over-value the short-term rate freezes and small-time charitable contributions, but under-value the long-term effects of concentration and complication?

Merger applicants present the post-acquisition company as it will exist on consummation day: the same two pre-merger companies, locally managed, with overhead costs lowered and best practices implemented. But a merged company is not static. It will have motivations, plans and strategies, all unconstrained by the repealed Public Utility Holding Company Act 1935 or by any substitute regulatory vision. Those motivations, plans and strategies will cause the merged company to change its form, add new affiliates, and merge with other companies, more than once.[25] Yet merger approval orders focus not on what the merged company might become but on the picture the applicants present. No commission requires the applicants to discuss their future activities—their plans for cross-country acquisitions, their future acquisition debt or their future non-utility investments. Commissions focus on the short-term rate freeze, the new headquarters building, the promise to invest next year in renewables projects. They focus on the present.

As do the applicants. Imagine a merger application containing these three statements and questions:

- "The acquirer has based its offer price on an expectation that the Commission will continue to protect the target utility from competition. We therefore expect that every investment opportunity in generation, transmission, distribution and retail sales service will continue to be exclusively ours, even if other companies could make these investments more cost-effectively. Does the Commission intend to honor this expectation?"
- "Our holding company activities fall outside the commission's jurisdiction. After the acquisition, we intend to make any acquisition of any company, in any business line in any part of the world, whenever it serves our interests, using any type of financing available, without asking the Commission's permission—and without telling the Commission. Does the Commission intend by its merger approval to authorize this behavior?"
- "Our holding company will be the target utility's sole shareholder. So we will have the power to remove any utility executive and any utility board member at any time, for any reason not prohibited by employment law or contract law. Before taking these actions we will not ask or even inform

---

[24]   ROBERT H. FRANK, THE DARWIN ECONOMY: LIBERTY, COMPETITION, AND THE COMMON GOOD 23 (2012).

[25]   Recall from Figures 3.1 and 3.2, and the introduction to Chapter 3, how Baltimore Gas & Electric used to look like Madison Gas & Electric.

the Commission. Does the Commission intend its merger approval to grant us this discretion?"

Asking these questions out loud would put the Commission in a tough position. If the Commission answered "yes" it would admit to denying customers the benefits of competitive outsourcing, placing them at risk of future business failures and turning control of the local utility over to an acquisition-oriented holding company over which the Commission has no jurisdiction. If the Commission answered "no," it would be doing the right things—reserving its authority to grant infrastructure opportunities to the most meritorious, avoiding unnecessary business risks and keeping control local. But it would also likely cause the applicants to withdraw the transaction. The financial community would label the Commission "inhospitable"; the benefit-seeking intervenors would call the Commission insensitive. So the applicants don't ask these questions and the commissions ignore them—as obvious as they are.

10.3.4   Regulatory Costs

A commission's job is to set standards, assess performance and assign consequences. Corporate complexity—multiple service territories, conflicting objectives, financial engineering, business risk—all make the job harder. Suppose the post-acquisition utility's cost of capital rises. Is the reason outside the utility's control, like general market conditions? Within the utility's control, like management errors and risks? Or was the cost caused by risks or failures elsewhere in the post-acquisition corporate family? Analytical methods to answer these questions lack precision and reliability. Now suppose a utility cannot access, at reasonable cost, sufficient capital to complete necessary infrastructure projects. Similar questions arise: Is the reason general capital market shortages, poor utility management or holding company decisions to divert utility dollars to other investments? As corporate complexity grows, the regulatory tasks of identifying a problem's source, fixing the problem and assigning accountability become more time-consuming, more resource-intensive and less certain to succeed.

With rare exceptions, merger approvals do not address regulatory preparedness.[26] Some commissions impose filing fees on applicants, but those fees cover only the cost of the merger proceeding, not the cost of post-acquisition

---

[26]   One exception: The California Commission found that the expanded "geographic scope and extent of potential self-dealing" in inter-affiliate relations, and the expanded scope of unregulated activities, "[would] increase [its] staff's responsibilities and tax the resources required to ensure that ratepayers [were] protected in the post-merger environment. ... [I]t [would] be increasingly difficult to ensure that inappropriate costs

regulation. No commission requires merging companies to supplement commission budgets to pay for the post-acquisition workload their transactions add.

10.3.5 Tragedy of the Commons: the Cumulative Effects of Individual State Approvals

When commissions approve mergers based on in-state benefits, they overlook multi-state costs. For the cumulative effect of dozens of states approving mergers separately is a concentrated, complicated industry—one whose suboptimal performance causes opportunity costs for all consumers. State commissions have created a merger version of Garret Hardin's famous tragedy of the commons:

> Picture a pasture open to all. ... As a rational being, each herdsman seeks to maximize his gain. Explicitly or implicitly, more or less consciously, he asks, "What is the utility to *me* of adding one more animal to my herd?" ... [T]he rational herdsman concludes that the only sensible course for him to pursue is to add another animal to his herd. And another; and another. ... But this is the conclusion reached by each and every rational herdsman sharing a commons. Therein is the tragedy. Each man is locked into a system that compels him to increase his herd without limit—in a world that is limited. Ruin is the destination toward which all men rush, each pursuing his own best interest in a society that believes in the freedom of the commons. Freedom in a commons brings ruin to all.[27]

Like Hardin's herdsmen, each state acts rationally, perceiving the value of its internal gains as exceeding its share of the cumulative losses. But the calculation is wrong. The commons—for Hardin, the pasture; for commissions, long-term market performance—is damaged. Looking inwards harms all.

The problem is worsened by our tendency to underestimate the sum of small harms:

> Some research in social psychology suggests that our brains are not well adapted to protect ourselves from gradually encroaching harms. We evolved to be wary of saber-toothed tigers and blizzards, but not of climate change—and maybe that's also why we in the news media tend to cover weather but not climate.[28]

[were] not passed on to ratepayers." Southern California Edison-San Diego Gas & Electric Merger, 1991 Cal. PUC LEXIS 253, at *170–171, *262.

[27] Garret Hardin, *The Tragedy of the Commons*, SCIENCE (Dec. 13, 1968), http://www.garretthardinsociety.org/articles/art_tragedy_of_the_commons.html.

[28] Nicholas Kristof, *Our Beaker is Starting to Boil*, N.Y. TIMES (July 17, 2017), https://www.nytimes.com/2010/07/18/opinion/18kristof.html.

A concentrated, complicated electric industry does not threaten the human race like climate change does. But our proven tendency to pay more attention to large immediate stimuli than to modest but accumulating damage helps explain regulators' tendency to value the immediate gains over the long-term losses.

Some commissions miss even the medium-term losses. Some applicants say their merger will "position us competitively" (the "us" referring to the applicants). So its commission, associating the state's interest with the applicants' interest, says yes. But "position us" relative to what? If the merger strengthens the applicants' market position, it necessarily weakens some other utility's position. So there is no necessary net gain. Worse, that other utility, arguing that "everyone else is doing it," will itself want to merge so it too can be "positioned competitively." That second merger erases the first merger's advantage. The first state now is not only no better off; it is worse off because there is less competition—fewer places for its utility to buy wholesale power, fewer utilities for the commission to use as benchmarks in assessing its own utility's performance. In effectively competitive markets, this type of maneuvering can make customers better off—if it's aimed at efficiencies. But where the utility has a government-protected monopoly in the home market, "competitive positioning" implies a government-assisted advantage in some other market, to the detriment of all customers who buy from that market. It's Robert Frank's bull elk problem again—pressure for individual advantage undermining the welfare of the whole.[29]

Some state commissions don't merely ignore national interests; they actively oppose them. Consider these three examples of commissions approv-

---

[29]   We discussed Professor Frank's comparison of the gazelle to the bull elk in Chapter 9.2. For an airline example, see this comment from the legendary Alfred Kahn, its pithiness matched by its insightfulness:

[E]ven apart from the direct suppression of horizontal competition that has resulted from some of these mergers, I don't see how anyone can avoid being worried about the cumulative process of competition by preemption that they have entailed. It is not merely—probably not even primarily—the ability to offer better service that motivates the linking of route systems; rather, it is the ability to control traffic. Once the Department of Transportation swallowed the elephant of United's acquisition of the trans-Pacific assets of Pan American (thereby reducing from three to two the number of U.S. competitors in this closed market, and dismissing the Antitrust Division's proposed divestitures that would have created a third viable competitor), it would have been difficult for the Department to strain at the gnat of Northwest's attempt to acquire Republic in order to gain additional feed to support its operations competing with United. Delta's reluctant acquisition of Western was evidently similarly compelled by the need to assure itself feed to support its transcontinental operations in competition with the vaster route systems of United, American and Texas Air.

ing a merger in their states, while urging FERC away from addressing the merger's adverse effects on other states:

- The Kentucky Commission found that the proposed merger of Louisville Gas & Electric and Kentucky Utilities would involve FERC inquiries into the merged entity's market power. The Kentucky Commission's approval order required the merging utilities to use "reasonable best efforts" to avoid federal conditions requiring them to (a) participate in a regional transmission organization, (b) divest operating assets, or (c) forgo benefits from using their generating facilities to serve their in-state loads.[30]
- Similarly, in the Duke-Progress Energy merger, the North Carolina Commission's Public Staff urged FERC not to condition its approval on the merged company joining a regional transmission organization—a condition FERC has imposed on other mergers to increase market trading for the benefit of all consumers.[31]
- Addressing Exelon's acquisition of Constellation (the holding company for Baltimore Gas & Electric), FERC required the merged company to divest certain generating units. To avoid market concentration, the Commission said that the merger companies could not sell the units to major market participants, including certain holding companies that serve captive customers in Virginia. The Virginia Commission objected because it hoped its utilities could buy some of the divested capacity.[32]

10.4   ACCEPTING MINOR POSITIVES

Merger applicants offer, and intervenors accept, items unrelated to mergers—downtown headquarters construction, charitable contributions, renewable energy investments, hiking trails.[33] Commissions that request and accept these things are not regulating industry performance; they are acting as political decision-makers. This practice causes five problems.

Alfred E. Kahn, *Deregulatory Schizophrenia*, 75 Calif. L. Rev. 1059, 1064 (1987). For this author's memoriam to Dr. Kahn, see *Alfred Kahn (1917–2010)*, http://www.scotthemplinglaw.com/essays/alfred-kahn.

[30]   PPL-E.ON Merger, 2010 Ky. PUC LEXIS 1147, at *75.

[31]   *Duke Energy-Progress Energy Merger II*, 137 F.E.R.C. ¶ 61,210 at P 29 (2011) (describing Public Staff's opposition to requiring the merged company to join an RTO because, in FERC's paraphrasing, "neither Duke Energy Carolinas' nor Progress Energy Carolinas' retail customers would benefit"), *reh'g denied*, 149 F.E.R.C. ¶ 61,078 (2014).

[32]   *Exelon-Constellation Energy Group Merger*, 138 F.E.R.C. ¶ 61,167 at PP 88, 107 (2012).

[33]   As Chapter 4.4.2.3 explained.

10.4.1 Extra-legal Actions Blur Regulatory-Legislative Boundaries

In a merger proceeding, a commission has no legal power to make policy unrelated to the merger[34]—including extracting benefits unrelated to the merger. Doing so makes the commission a legislative decision-maker without electoral accountability. Legislatures make subjective, political decisions to satisfy constituents; regulators use objectivity and expertise to improve industry performance. By blurring the legislature-regulator boundary, commissions weaken both bodies. The commission-approved benefits reveal legislative failures to act; the commission becomes a place to politick for extras rather than a forum to get the right answers.

10.4.2 Political Decisions are Influenced by a Utility Monopoly

By definition, conditions unrelated to a merger are not necessary to the merger's lawfulness, so the applicants have a legal right to resist them. This legal reality has this practical result: unrelated conditions will include only what the utility accepts. A commission obligated to produce merger outcomes replicating competitive outcomes instead produces non-merger policies reflecting a utility monopoly's preferences.

10.4.3 Unrelated Offers Distract Intervenors and Commissioners from the Merger's Merits

By encouraging settlements with unrelated conditions, a commission invites applicants to create merger support unrelated to the merger's merits.[35] Intervenors with no expertise in mergers don't see target shareholders selling a public franchise for private gain; nor do they see the commission ceding local control to an acquisitive holding company. Intervenors instead see a chance to trade their support for a basket of benefits uniquely valuable to them.[36] The

---

[34] Recall, for example, that when a wholesale customer asked FERC to address, in a merger case, the discrimination arising from North Carolina's differential treatment of retail load and wholesale load, the Commission declined because the problem pre-existed, and therefore was unrelated to, the merger. *See Duke Energy-Progress Energy Merger I*, 136 F.E.R.C. ¶ 61,245 (2011).

[35] A significant exception was Washington State's rejection of Hydro One's acquisition of Avista. The Commission rejected it despite unanimous support from the intervenors, each of whom received something from the applicants. Hydro One-Avista Merger, 2018 Wash. UTC LEXIS 272. For detail, see Chapter 11.2.

[36] *See, e.g.*, the D.C. Commission's order approving the Exelon-PHI merger, quoting the National Consumer Law Center and National Housing Trust's comments that "[s]hould the merger collapse," the losses would include the "loss of sizeable

proceeding's focus—the testimonial submissions, the commissioners' questions, the negotiating sessions—all veer away from expertise and objectivity, and toward intervenor satisfaction. The very point of regulation—industry performance—becomes secondary. If commissions ceased this practice, opponents of the merger would be real opponents, focusing their expertise on the merits to help the commission make the decision best for the community. There would be fewer mergers producing no true merger benefits, leaving space for mergers that do.

10.4.4 Discrimination: Litigating Parties get Favors Unavailable to Others

Allowing non-merger benefits means tolerating discrimination. The merger applicants accept conditions sought by intervenors but ignore the needs of non-intervenors. Microgrid intervenors get microgrids, renewable energy intervenors get renewable energy and low-income housing intervenors get aid for low-income housing. But unless they intervene, the blind don't get the bills in Braille, Ethiopian immigrants don't get customer service reps who speak Amharic, paraplegics don't get ramps at bill-paying locations and school orchestra leaders don't get free cellos. A utility merger proceeding becomes a way to help the better-connected. The best predictor of commission-approved merger benefits is which entities intervened, not what the community needs.

10.4.5 Granting the Utility Non-franchise Roles Denies those Roles to More Efficient Competitors

Some non-merger-related conditions give the utility roles outside its current franchise obligations—roles like installing microgrids, building renewable energy infrastructure and carrying out energy efficiency programs. This practice—sought by intervenors, accepted by the merging companies and approved by the commission—eliminates competition for roles that should be subjected to competition. Worse, it gives the incumbent an unearned, first-mover advantage in these new product markets. No commission has recognized the problem.

* * *

---

funding that would defer future rate increases[,] ... the loss of funding for much-needed energy efficiency investments in affordable housing[,] ... [and the] develop[ment of] an Arrearage Management Program." Exelon-PHI Merger, 2016 D.C. PUC LEXIS 32, at *36 ¶ 25. None of these public-spirited items had any connection to the merger transaction.

Merger applicants have persuasive strategies, and they work. Rather than reject the oversimplifications and the offers of unrelated benefits, commissions usually accept the applicants' frame, often even advocating for the transaction while failing to play their strong statutory hand—the hand that allows only those mergers that serve the public interest. Regulatory proceedings place the applicants' goals at the center; ideas for attracting performance-motivated couplings at the perimeter. Instead of searching for the best merger partners, commissions seek minor benefits, often to fill policy gaps left by legislative bodies. Why do commissions cede leadership so readily and so frequently? Chapter 11 will provide two main reasons: passion gaps and systematic mental errors.

11. Explanations: passion gaps and mental shortcuts

Commissions lack a vision for the types of couplings that best serve customers. Merger applicants fill that gap by framing their future as simple, inevitable and better than the status quo. Regulators respond by accepting the applicants' frame, underestimating negatives and using reactive procedures. Commissions approve the applicants' strategies, applying a no-harm standard and requiring only minor benefits, mostly unrelated to the merger. The merger's real value—control of a government-protected franchise—goes to the merging companies, even though that value was created largely by government action and customer captivity.

The question is why. Why do nearly all utility commissions, with their professional staffs, formal adjudicative procedures, relative independence from political pressure and broad legal authority, approve merger strategies so clearly rooted in private interests? This chapter offers two possible explanations. The first explanation is a passion gap: applicants want their merger more than regulators want an economically efficient merger policy. Six state commissions did reject merger proposals, but each based that rejection on the proposal's unique, serious deficiencies rather than on any affirmative commission merger policy. The second explanation comes from the field of behavioral economics: when faced with complex decisions, regulators make the same systematic errors most people make. This chapter will discuss twelve.

11.1 PASSION GAPS LEAD TO DEFERENCE

Why do commissions have issue checklists instead of industry visions? Why do they accept the applicants' frame? Why do they "struggle"?[1] Common to the many merger approvals is this fact: merger promoters and their regulators differ in desire.

---

[1] Exelon-Constellation Energy Group Merger, 2012 Md. PSC LEXIS 12, at *62–63, text accompanying nn.143–46 ("[W]e have struggled at the threshold with whether this Merger is good for Maryland, good for BGE, or good for its ratepayers. It certainly is good for [Exelon's and Constellation's] shareholders ... .") (order approving merger).

Merger applicants want these transactions badly enough to spend millions—to find counterparties, negotiate terms and grind through multiple regulatory fora. The acquirers want them badly enough to incur large acquisition debt; the targets want them badly enough to give up their autonomy. Both parties have a singular focus: increase shareholder value—the acquirer by growing market share, buying strategic assets and leveraging monopoly positions; the target by selling franchise control for gain. To maximize shareholder value, merging parties act affirmatively.

Merger regulators don't act affirmatively; they act defensively. Lacking a vision for public interest performance, they don't pursue the companies capable of producing that performance. They sit back and wait, for proposals with purposes other than performance. Then, instead of applying to those proposals objective standards for performance, they accept the applicants' subjective aspirations for performance—mere mantras about economies of scale and best practices.

This differential—in purposefulness, posture and desire—leads to deference. Commissions credit the applicants' stated purposes—strengthening the companies, improving service—and ignore the real purposes— the acquirer gaining control of an expansion-ready revenue stream, the target auctioning off franchise control for the highest price—even though those real purposes are clear in the proxy statements and fairness opinions. These deferential commissions see the merger as a free-market transaction to accommodate rather than a monopoly-market action to discipline; a simple exchange of cash for stock rather than the sale of a public privilege for private gain.

This difference in desire—merger applicants wanting the benefit-cost ratio maximized, regulators wanting it not lower than 1.0—produces a difference in outcome. When promoters maximize while regulators satisfice, shareholders benefit disproportionately. But why? Why does deference come so naturally? Why does it happen so predictably? Consider four contributors.

1. No crisis: No merger has caused a crisis. That statement includes even the bankruptcies of Enron and the Texas holding company Energy Future Holdings. Neither of their acquired utility subsidiaries—Portland General Electric and Oncor, respectively—were directly harmed by their parents' bankruptcies. Without crises, commissions face no obvious reason to say no. So they say yes. But the absence of crisis does not justify indifference to outcomes, any more than a child not failing in school justifies accepting his C average. That utilities—even utility subsidiaries of bankrupt holding companies—don't fail should cause no surprise. Every utility runs a business free from competition, assured by statute and the Constitution of rates sufficient to earn a reasonable return on used-and-useful investment under prudent operations. Fuel clauses, trackers, surcharges and infrastructure pre-approvals shift major cost risks from shareholders to customers.[2] So there have been no crises. But regulation's real purpose is maximizing performance, not avoiding crises.

2. Comfort in numbers: Commissions defer to avoid being labeled deal-killers and outliers. Though legally insulated from politics, regulators work in a political world. In that world, simple defeats complex, positive defeats negative. An electric utility stands among the state's largest employers, a foundation of the state's economy. When it proposes to "grow," or to merge with a company promising "growth," rejecting the request risks being seen as anti-business, as impeding market forces. When merger applicants frame the issue as "Merger yes or no," saying yes is positive; saying no is negative. Yes brings tangible benefits in the near term; no requires abstract explanations about the long term. Asking the correct question—"Is this merger the most cost-effective way to get customers the service improvements they need?"—involves more complexity than this question: "Are we going to allow our utility to grow?" And who wants to be an outlier? It is hard enough to say no instead of yes; it is even harder when for thirty years nearly every other commission has said yes.

3. Inexperience: Most commissioners have five-year terms. Most stay for only one term; many don't stay for the full term. In any given state in any five-year period, a commissioner will see only one merger. Contrast rate cases. They occur nearly continuously—each of a state's multiple utilities seeking a rate increase every few years. So through education and repetition, a commissioner will learn rate case basics: capital expenditures, operating costs, fuel costs, taxes, debt-equity ratios, return on equity, rate design. Regulators receive no comparable exposure to utility mergers—their essence as a sale of franchise control, their contribution to industry consolidation, the complexity and conflicts they bring. Lacking knowledge specific to mergers, commissioners focus on what they understand—the side offers: the $100 credits, the temporary rate freezes, the promised improvements in outage performance, the spending on renewable energy.

4. Everyone's doing it: Merger applicants describe their transactions as no different from prior ones—so raising new questions would "change the rules mid-game."[3] So the deferential commission limits itself to answering

---

[2] *See generally* Scott Hempling & Scott H. Strauss, Nat'l Regulatory Research Inst., Pre-Approval Commitments: When And Under What Conditions Should Regulators Commit Ratepayer Dollars to Utility-Proposed Capital Projects? (2008); Scott Hempling, Riders, Trackers, Surcharges, Pre-Approvals and Decoupling: How Do They Affect the Cost of Equity? (2012).

[3] *See, e.g.*, Transcript of Evidentiary Hearing at 3535–36, Exelon-PHI Merger, Formal Case No. 1119 (D.C. Pub. Serv. Comm'n Apr. 22, 2015). There D.C. Commissioner Fort questioned the author on "[w]hy [it] would be fair for us to substi-

the applicants' question—"Should we approve the transaction?"—rather than asking the public interest question—"What market structure, corporate structure and company type will produce the best performance?" By asking the wrong question, commissions fail to compare the pending proposal to alternatives—a mental practice key to maintaining alertness and avoiding bias.[4]

This tendency to defer can become so strong as to overcome a commission's own common-sense inclinations. Consider this admission by the Maryland Commission, in deferring to Exelon's acquisition of Baltimore Gas & Electric (BEG) and its holding company Constellation Energy Group (CEG):

> [W]e have struggled at the threshold with whether this Merger is good for Maryland, good for BGE, or good for its ratepayers. It certainly is good for CEG's shareholders—they will be paid a substantial premium over the value of their shares at the time the deal was announced. Exelon's shareholders will receive CEG and all of its businesses and assets, as well as the opportunities that come with them. Although they are paying a premium for CEG's stock, they are paying less than 40 cents on the dollar of CEG's peak price from early 2008. The Applicants' bankers ($118.5 million), lawyers ($15 million), accountants ($2 million) and consultants ($2 million) will be paid generously and in full at closing. CEG's senior executives will collect change-of-control payments totaling $21 million after closing, and both companies will pay confidential "retention payments" of a similar magnitude to certain current employees of both companies.[5]

---

tute a new set of rules in the middle of the proceeding to be used for this particular joint applicant." *See also* Rebuttal Testimony of Susan F. Tierney, Ph.D. at 5, Exelon-PHI Merger, Formal Case No. 1119 (D.C. Pub. Serv. Comm'n filed Dec. 17, 2014) (arguing that intervenors who raise new issues are "attempt[ing] to transform this adjudicatory proceeding into what would, in effect, become a rulemaking docket on policy issues having to do with the future direction of the electric industry and character of electric services").

[4]   See Chapter 11.3.3.4 for a discussion of the mental bias that occurs when viewing an isolated item rather than a making a comparison.

[5]   Exelon-Constellation Energy Group Merger, 2012 Md. PSC LEXIS 12, at *62–63, text accompanying nn.143–46. In that proceeding, the author was an expert witness for the State of Maryland and the Maryland Energy Administration.

At the Federal Energy Regulatory Commission, deference has become so ingrained that billion-dollar transactions are approved at the office director level, with no official Commissioner involvement. Even two separate proposals, by two very different companies, to acquire the same Texas electric monopoly (from a bankrupt owner whose excessively leveraged acquisition ten years ago was also approved by FERC) were approved by office directors. *See Oncor Electric Delivery-NextEra Energy Merger*, 158 F.E.R.C. ¶ 62,005 (2017) (office director approving NextEra's request to buy Oncor); *Oncor Electric Delivery-Sempra Energy Merger*, 161 F.E.R.C. ¶ 62,187 (2017) (office director several months later approving Sempra's request to buy the very same Oncor). Ten years earlier, the debt-leveraged acquisition of Oncor by the now-bankrupt owner was approved by the full Commission, without any analysis of the acquisition financ-

Deference can make sense if a utility's interest and the public interest are aligned. If the regulator has established affirmative performance standards, and the utility's earnings depend on meeting those standards, the interests are aligned. The regulator then has some reason to accept the utility's choices. But commissions have not established affirmative merger standards. Their deference frees utilities to choose their own standards—the acquirer seeking to add territory or balance a risky portfolio, the target seeking to maximize gain. Deference leaves the public interest behind.[6]

11.2   CONTRAST: SIX COMMISSIONS THAT SAID NO

Of the nearly eighty mergers since the mid-1980s, only six met permanent rejection by a state commission.[7] What factors made these six commissions depart from the deferential supermajority? This subsection summarizes the cases and offers possible explanations.

11.2.1   California (1991): Southern California Edison, San Diego Gas & Electric[8]

This proposal appeared early in our thirty-year period, well before mergers became routine. It would have reduced the number of California's

---

ing. On that financing, FERC's decision had only a summary of the applicants' description. *Oncor Electric Delivery-TXU Portfolio Management Merger*, 120 F.E.R.C. ¶ 61,215 at P 18, text accompanying nn.20–21 (2007). *See also Iberdrola-UIL Holding Merger*, 151 F.E.R.C. ¶ 62,148 (2015) (office director approving Spanish holding company's acquisition of United Illuminating). In none of these transactions does FERC consider the harms from remote management, diseconomies of scale, management distraction or financing risk. Deference is complete.

⁶   One cannot talk of regulatory deference on mergers without citing the regulatory legend Peter Bradford. Analogizing to boxing, he described a hierarchy of regulatory decisiveness: Rocky, Rope-a-Hope and Canvasback. *Gorillas in the Mist: Electric Utility Mergers in Light of State Restructuring Goals*, 18 Nat'l Regulatory Research Inst. Q. Bull. 1 (1997).

⁷   Some mergers were self-withdrawn after regulatory conditions made them unattractive to one or both parties. Those mergers included Baltimore Gas & Electric-Potomac Electric (1997); Northern States Power-Wisconsin Electric Power (1997); and Exelon-Public Service Electric & Gas (2005). Then there were transactions initially rejected by a commission, where the rejection order explicitly or implicitly invited the applicants to return with a revised application which the commission then approved. Those transactions included Iberdrola-United Illuminating (2015); Exelon-PHI Holdings (2016); Macquarie-Central Louisiana Electric (2016); and Great Plains Energy-Westar (2017).

⁸   Southern California Edison-San Diego Gas & Electric Merger, 1991 Cal. PUC LEXIS 253.

investor-owned electric utilities from three to two. It also preceded FERC's transmission access rules, rules that made wholesale generation competition more likely.[9] These facts, plus a well-organized, professional advocacy community and a deep internal professional staff, led the California Commission to examine rigorously issues that later commissions have treated less seriously. Not helping the applicants' case was Southern California Edison's (SCE's) history of anticompetitive practices and regulatory disobedience. So the Commission had concerns about competition, the benefit-cost relationship and holding company abuse.

Four adverse effects on competition: First, by combining San Diego Gas & Electric's (SDG&E's) and SCE's transmission facilities, the merged company would have "transmission dominance" in five separate transmission markets. It then could continue SCE's longstanding practice of blocking municipal power systems' efforts to buy their wholesale power needs from lower-cost sources instead of from SCE. SCE had already engaged in anticompetitive price squeezing, a practice that the merger would make easier. Second, the merger would eliminate SDG&E's growing competitive influence as a disrupter, including its contribution to across-the-fence rivalry.[10] Third, the transaction would give the merged company buyer market power over multiple non-firm and short-term bulk power markets—markets in which SCE had already exercised buyer market power. Fourth, the merged company could exercise vertical market power by using its control of SDG&E's distribution facilities to give SCE's unregulated generation an unearned advantage. The Commission saw no feasible means of reducing these anticompetitive effects.

Flawed benefit-cost analysis: The applicants described long-term benefits, but the Commission found them to be overstated or unverifiable. The companies had (1) disregarded possible diseconomies associated with the merger-expanded labor force; (2) attributed to the merger administrative efficiencies that could occur without the merger; (3) inflated the savings from resource deferrals; (4) failed to consider the possibility of future higher payments for power purchased from third parties; (5) ignored the possibility of future cost-of-capital increases; (6) downplayed the costs of merger-caused environmental impacts; and (7) proposed no credible way to attribute post-merger cost reductions to the merger, leaving the Commission unable to allocate those savings to customers. In short, assumptions and projections substituted for analysis and accountability. Projection detail stopped

---

[9]   The proposal preceded FERC Order No. 888 (mandatory transmission access) by five years and FERC Order No. 2000 (voluntary regional transmission organizations) by nine. *See* Tutorial § 2.3.

[10]   Price-squeeze and across-the-fence rivalry were explained in Chapters 6.3.2.2 and 6.4.1.5, respectively.

at 2000, too early to satisfy the statute's requirement of long-term benefits. And the applicants guaranteed rate reductions only through 1994, "implicit[ly] recogniz[ing] that [their] forecast of benefits becomes less reliable in later years."[11]

Holding company abuse: The holding company's complexity posed a distinct problem:

> [I]f Edison's past violations of the regulatory compacts set forth in our holding company decision are any indication of what will transpire in the future, it will be increasingly difficult to ensure that inappropriate costs are not passed on to ratepayers. ... Edison has attempted to use [its holding company form] to shield its activities rather than open the Commission's access to expeditious and thorough review.[12]

11.2.2   Arizona (2005): Tucson Electric, UniSource, KKR, J.P. Morgan, Wachovia[13]

UniSource Energy was the holding company for Tucson Electric Power, two other in-state gas and electric utilities, and some non-utility affiliates. In a leveraged, going-private transaction, a partnership proposed to buy out UniSource's shareholders for a 30 percent cash premium. The private partnership comprised investment funds affiliated with Kohlberg Kravis Roberts & Co. L.P. (KKR), J.P. Morgan Partners and Wachovia Capital Partners. These entities described themselves, in the Commission's words, as "patient, long-term investors who do not plan on managing the day-to-day operations of UniSource." Instead of taking dividends now, they would get their gain by selling the company later.[14]

Viewed by the Commission as a "case of first impression," the transaction triggered memories of past problems. In the 1980s, Tucson Electric's "mismanagement and self-serving deals by its former management," its inter-affiliate transactions at inflated prices, along with the souring of its non-utility ventures in car leasing, real estate, security investments, hotels and motels, had brought the utility close to bankruptcy. The company avoided that outcome only through "ratepayer sacrifice"—rates based on hypothetical equity levels for a company whose only capital was debt.[15] The Commission now expected the applicants to offset that prior ratepayer sacrifice with tangible benefits.

---

[11]   *Southern California Edison-San Diego Gas & Electric Merger*, 1991 Cal. PUC LEXIS 253, at *34.

[12]   *Id.* at *170–71.

[13]   UniSource Energy-Saguaro Acquisition Merger, 2005 Ariz. PUC LEXIS 1.

[14]   *Id.* at *19–20.

[15]   *Id.* at *63.

But the applicants offered no real benefits. Their commitments to spend sufficiently on operations and maintenance added nothing to Tucson Electric's obligation to serve. Their claim of "better access to capital markets" went nowhere: it lacked numbers, downplayed the markets' likely concern about post-acquisition debt levels and ignored how the utility's debt/equity ratio had been improving on its own. The applicants' other claim—that any other acquirer would move the utility's headquarters and reduce charitable contributions—made no sense because any other acquisition would require Commission approval.[16]

Then there was the debt. The post-acquisition partnership would have more debt than before, likely below investment grade. The utility would face pressure to pay the dividends necessary to cover its owners' debt service. And if the partnership failed financially and entered bankruptcy, control of the utility would pass to the creditors, while the bankruptcy court might undo any Commission-designed structural protections.[17]

The Commission's largest concern was governance. Given Tucson Electric's history of non-utility business failure, the Commission wanted full access to affiliate information. But Tucson's post-acquisition status—a limited partnership—would make essential information unavailable. Most of the corporate decision-making power would sit with two individuals, one of whom had no utility experience. His oral intent to defer to the utility CEO's decisions was neither binding nor credible: "We do not believe that this structure, with so much power in the limited partners who do not believe the Commission has oversight over them, and who have expressed the belief they can prevent the disclosure of relevant financial information to the Commission, is in the public interest."[18] As the Commission summed things up,

> The risks of increased leverage, and the detriments of the partnership structure with a concentration of power in a general partner inexperienced in the public utility sector, and uncertainties concerning Commission oversight over the new entities, outweigh the claimed benefits.[19]

---

[16]   *Id.* at *66–67.
[17]   *Id.* at *75–76.
[18]   *Id.* at *73.
[19]   *Id.* at *63–64.

11.2.3 Montana (2007): NorthWestern Corp., Babcock & Brown Infrastructure[20]

In 2007, the Australian holding company Babcock & Brown Infrastructure Ltd. (BBIL) proposed to acquire NorthWestern Energy, Montana's major electric utility. NorthWestern's 2003–04 bankruptcy, caused by its affiliate's unsuccessful bets on merchant generation, made the Commission wary of complicated corporate structures. The "overriding issue," therefore, was whether the acquisition "poses a threat to NorthWestern's financial health and, therefore, harm or risk of harm to Montana customers."[21] The Commission described three major concerns.

The $700 million acquisition premium: "No prudent business owner would make such a sizeable investment unless it could recover its costs. ... Ratepayers ... will foot the bill."[22]

Milking the utility: BBIL would force the utility to pay dividends in amounts exceeding its earnings, leaving the utility without enough cash to operate adequately. Then there was the high acquisition debt, along with BBIL's practice of keeping its operating subsidiaries excessively debt-leveraged.[23] This combination of dividend extraction and excess debt "presents the likelihood that NorthWestern's capital structure will deteriorate and become unacceptably leveraged."[24]

Parent-utility conflict: Once NorthWestern dividended all its retained earnings to BBIL, the utility would be completely dependent on its holding company for equity. But BBIL had many subsidiaries, all with competing needs. The Commission saw no enforceable guarantee that NorthWestern would get what it needed.[25]

Applicants' post-hearing promises did not move the Commission: "BBIL said all the right things ... But for the most part, those statements of good intentions were not supported with substantive and binding commitments ..."[26]

---

20 NorthWestern-Babcock & Brown Merger, 2007 Mont. PUC LEXIS 54.
21 *Id.* at *93 ¶ 143.
22 *Id.* at *93–94 ¶¶ 145, 147.
23 *Id.* at *100–101 ¶ 155.
24 *Id.* at *101–102 ¶ 156.
25 *Id.* at *96–97 ¶ 149.
26 *Id.* at *110 ¶ 170.

11.2.4   Hawai'i (2016): NextEra, Hawaiian Electric[27]

NextEra owns Florida Power & Light, wholesale generating companies and other entities. It proposed acquiring Hawaiian Electric Industries, a holding company that owns Hawai'i's three investor-owned utilities and a local bank. The transaction ran into trouble from the beginning.

Unanimous state government opposition: All three Hawai'i government agency intervenors—the Office of State Planning, the Office of Consumer Advocacy, and the Department of Business, Economic Development and Tourism—opposed the transaction. In crediting these entities' positions, the Commission distinguishing their public interest mandate from the "specialized interests" represented by non-governmental intervenors.[28]

Benefits—"inadequate and uncertain": NextEra claimed its better credit would lower the utilities' interest costs, but the Commission found the claim neither sufficiently documented nor supported by guaranteed rate reductions. Other claimed benefits were only aspirational; or illusory because they added nothing to the utilities' existing legal obligations. NextEra offered a four-year, $60 million rate benefit, but could withdraw the offer if the company suffered undefined "financial stress." Claims of non-rate benefits—estimated by NextEra in the hundreds of millions—were disputed, unproven or not clearly attributable to the acquisition.[29]

Restrictions on commission authority: In return for these unclear benefits, NextEra wanted the Commission to commit not to change existing cost trackers that allowed Hawaiian Electric to recover specified expenses outside of general rate cases.[30]

Uncertain commitment to clean energy goals: Central to Hawai'i is a clean energy future. NextEra had provided insufficient information and commitments about how it would achieve that future. "The Commission is left to speculate whether this was simply an oversight, or, possibly, indicative of a predisposition for utility-scale solutions."[31]

Risks from non-utility businesses: The state's utilities would shrink in importance. They accounted for over 90 percent of their holding company's current value; post-merger they would be only three of literally hundreds of NextEra subsidiaries. The transaction would "fundamentally transform the

---

[27]   NextEra-Hawaiian Electric Merger, Docket No. 2015-0022, Order No. 33795 (Haw. Pub. Util. Comm'n July 15, 2016).

[28]   *Id.*, slip op. at 4. The author was a witness for the Office of State Planning, reporting directly to the Governor.

[29]   *Id.* at 7.

[30]   *Id.* at 23.

[31]   *Id.* at 11.

corporate nature of the [Hawaii Electric] companies," with a "corresponding increase" in financial risk.[32] Normal ratemaking could protect the state's customers from NextEra's nuclear plant costs and its "uneconomic business activities"; but ratemaking, the Commission said, would not protect against the risks of a NextEra bankruptcy. The proposed ring-fencing measures were insufficient.[33]

Competition: The Commission wanted "robust competition" in energy services. But:

> The entity responsible for designing, conducting, and evaluating competitive solici-tations [for generation, transmission and distribution resources] would transfer from an entity that currently [had] no meaningful commercial interests in the services procured through a solicitation (beyond possibly owning the assets as a regulated utility) to an entity that [had] an extensive network of non-regulated subsidiaries and affiliates with significant commercial interests in the supply of services.[34]

NextEra would control the state's distribution and transmission monopoly services while having a commercial interest in supplying generation services. Despite this conflict, NextEra had made no commitment to separate its com-petitive activities from its monopoly activities. So whether the acquisition would undermine the Commission's pro-competition goals depended on "future speculation about [NextEra's] conduct" of competitive bidding. Even with a Commission-appointed independent observer, the utility—controlled by the conflicted NextEra—would be making the final resource decisions.[35]

Corporate governance: Ultimate control of the state's utilities would lie with NextEra's CEO. Governance documents were neither complete nor unambiguous, especially in terms of who, at what corporate entity, would control the state's utilities.[36] Unclear were the "roles, functions, and limita-tions" of the corporate entities layered above the state's utilities, "as well as the compositions of their boards of directors and their respective duties and responsibilities." Local management could mostly make only recommenda-tions, not decisions. Since the state's utilities would be only a small part of a complex holding company system, the Commission would have no way to prevent conflict between NextEra's corporate-wide objectives and the state's unique needs.[37]

---

[32] *Id.* at 158.
[33] *Id.* at 8.
[34] *Id.* at 245.
[35] *Id.* at 243.
[36] *Id.* at 152.
[37] *Id.* at 12, 158.

11.2.5   Texas (2017): NextEra, Oncor[38]

NextEra proposed to buy the Texas utility Oncor from its bankrupt holding company, Energy Future Holdings Corporation (EFHC). It took the Commission only 22 pages (compared to the Hawaii Commission's 265) to explain its four reasons for rejection.

Excess debt: NextEra would finance over 80 percent of the purchase price with debt. The bankrupt EFHC's debt would move to a NextEra affiliate. That total debt would leave NextEra with a "limited tolerance for financial risk"—leading to a higher probability of a bond downgrade. Oncor would face pressure to generate earnings to service NextEra's debt and raise its credit rating. The utility would also have to compete with NextEra's many other subsidiaries for equity capital.[39]

Non-utility business risk: NextEra's unregulated businesses, especially its merchant generation and nuclear plant operations, exposed Oncor to risks. Pre-acquisition Oncor didn't face those specific risks because its holding company had spun off its unregulated generation. Other risks NextEra would bring included, without limitation, "potential changes in renewable demand resulting from changes in climate or tax policy, commodity risks, [and] retail electric provider risks." NextEra's combination of new risks and high debt would "increase the likelihood that unforeseen events could jeopardize Oncor's financial stability."[40]

Weakened ring-fencing: Given its high acquisition debt, NextEra would need what rating agencies call "linkage"—linkage between the debt-heavy NextEra and the low-risk Oncor. Linkage meant giving NextEra control over Oncor's dividend decisions, so that NextEra's lenders would have more confidence of being repaid. NextEra would convert Oncor's existing board (which had a majority of independent directors) into a NextEra-controlled board (where all but three members would be NextEra appointees). But the Oncor Board's current independence, the Commission found, had been "critical in protecting Oncor" from EFHC's bankruptcy. Losing that independence meant NextEra could extract Oncor's earnings not only to pay off NextEra's debt, both current and future, but to bail out NextEra's non-utility businesses.[41]

Insufficient benefits: NextEra's promised benefits approached zero: $3.2 million a year for four years, arising only from interest rate savings rather than operations. The other offered benefits were either not quantified (such as

---

[38]   Oncor Electric Delivery-NextEra Energy Merger, 2017 Tex. PUC LEXIS 1310.
[39]   *Id.* at *10.
[40]   *Id.* at *10–11.
[41]   *Id.* at *19–20.

benefits from Florida Power & Light-Oncor collaboration); or were achievable without the transaction and therefore not properly attributable to the transaction.[42]

11.2.6 Washington State (2019): Hydro One, Avista[43]

Hydro One, the government-owned utility serving in Ontario, sought to acquire Avista (formerly Washington Water Power). The Commission rejected the transaction for two main reasons.

Political interference: While application was pending in Washington State, Ontario's political players were interfering with Hydro One's utility operations in Canada. They (1) ousted Hydro One's entire board and CEO; and (2) during Ontario's elections, made campaign promises of large rate reductions without considering the effects on safety, reliability and finance. The result, according to the Commission: "significant losses of shareholder value at both corporations, downgrades to Hydro One's credit ratings, [and] downgrades by equity analysts." The Commission wanted no such interference with Avista. Another result: continuing uncertainty about whether Hydro One's new board and CEO, "whose identity remains unknown," would share the Washington Commission's values.[44]

Benefit lopsidedness: The Commission found that Avista's shareholders would receive value that was six to twelve times what ratepayers would get.[45]

* * *

What factors distinguished these six rejected transactions from the near eighty approvals? Each of the six presented concerns comparable to those that arose in the dozens of approved transactions: debt, non-utility risk, control of the local utility by distant executives, uncertain benefits. But each also had something out of the ordinary, something that clashed with the routine. Consider:

• Southern California Edison's past was littered with anticompetitive practices, rule violations and resistance to regulatory oversight. The merged entity would have gained horizontal and vertical market power at the very

---

[42] *Id.* at *12–14.
[43] Hydro One-Avista Merger, 2018 Wash. UTC LEXIS 272.
[44] *Id.* at *20, *75.
[45] *Id.* at *98 (noting that ratepayers' prospective rate credits and other financial benefits, estimated at \$73.7 million, were not "particularly generous when compared against the \$450 million to \$900 million stream of revenue" which stood to flow to shareholders).

beginning of the wholesale competition era. The merger would also have eliminated SDG&E as a disrupter and benchmarker.

- Arizona and Montana had just experienced near failures of their utilities' holding companies. That history made the commissions suspicious of anything out of the ordinary. A leveraged private equity buyout (Arizona) and a foreign holding company insisting on draining the utility's equity (Montana) both qualified as out of the ordinary.

- Hawai'i did not want control of its local, isolated utilities transferred to a distant CEO who failed to appear at the hearing, and whose holding company—heavy on coal and nuclear—had offered no plans on how to advance the state's clean energy goals. The Commission also worried about the conflict between NextEra's desire to own the state's new renewable facilities while its 100 percent-controlled utility ran the competitions that would select the renewable providers.

- Texas was dealing with a bankrupt holding company already. The Commission did not want an acquirer so debt-heavy that it needed to control the utility's dividends. With the applicants' benefit offer nearly worthless, the Commission saw only negatives.

- The Hydro One-Avista transaction reeked of political interference—a problem occupying nearly the entire Commission order.

With their antennae alerted, these six commissions replaced deference with skepticism. They

- took nothing for granted, in contrast to commissions that credit mere aspirations;
- specified the conflicts between the applicants' interests and the public interest;
- dismissed as illusory all boilerplate offers to merely obey the law; and
- reversed the typical evidentiary burden on risk: instead of accepting the applicants' view that concerns about debt repayment risk and non-utility business risks were "speculative," these commissions deemed the risks real while treating assurances of no harm as speculative.

Despite these strengths, the six orders share three omissions. First, each order said what the commission did not want; none said what the commission did want. Second, none described the transaction's essence—private interests seeking to monetize a public privilege, undisciplined by competitive forces. Third, none insisted on a true competition for the privilege of serving electricity customers. Montana's separately issued Statement of Factors,[46] and Appendix A to the Hawaii Commission's order rejecting NextEra, attempt to describe a merger policy; but neither of these admirable efforts takes the two steps just stated. So these six states remain with the other forty-four, and FERC, in lacking a utility merger policy that aligns shareholders' legitimate interests in growing value with the public's interest in improving industry performance. We will lay down the steps toward such a policy in Part IV.

The contrast between these six rejections and the dozens of approvals, between skepticism and deference, will occupy the next section. There we will summarize discoveries made by psychologists and behavioral economists about two modes of thinking—the instinctive mode and the analytical mode. What stimulates the analytical mode are unusual facts—facts that raise alarms, pushing the brain outside its habit of accepting the world the way it is. In the six rejections, unusual facts—bad facts—caused commissions to focus on the package rather than the packaging; and then to substitute skepticism for deference. In the many merger approvals, those stimuli, and the regulatory alertness that results, were missing.

11.3   MENTAL SHORTCUTS LEAD TO SYSTEMATIC ERRORS: BEHAVIORAL ECONOMISTS' DISCOVERIES

The proxy statements tell the truth: the target wants the highest price, the acquirer wants a government-protected monopoly. Performance for the customer isn't the real story; it's the story applicants use to sell the transaction to the regulators. Merger applicants say their transaction is the "best," but then oppose standards requiring the transaction to be the best.

Why do these tactics work? Why do regulators accept the story over the facts? Possible answers lie in the developing fields of decision-making psychology and behavioral economics. Psychologist Daniel Kahneman won the Nobel Prize in Economics for his work (with Amos Tversky) on common mental errors. His masterpiece for the lay reader, *Thinking, Fast and Slow*, describes their discoveries. Richard Thaler won the same prize for pioneering

---

[46]   The Montana Commission's Statement of Factors established general standards for any future merger applicants: financial strength and capability; energy supply; infrastructure; demonstrable Montana focus; utility focus; customer focus; energy utility management experience; and effective functioning in the Montana constitutional, statutory and regulatory framework. Statement of Factors for Evaluating Proposals to Acquire NorthWestern Energy, Docket No. N2004.10.166 (Mont. Pub. Serv. Comm'n Oct. 18, 2004).

the field of behavioral economics. His *Misbehaving* is another masterpiece. Both books are required reading for regulatory practitioners.[47]

This section applies their insights to the merger decision-making process. It starts by explaining two modes of thinking—what Kahneman calls System 1 (the instinctive, automatic system) and System 2 (the analytical, effortful system). It then argues that merger applicants aim at regulators' mental processes. If the applicants can keep a regulator's System 1 in control, unaffected by System 2, their simple story takes hold, unaffected by complex facts. The chapter then describes twelve systematic errors that System 1 can cause regulators to make when deciding merger cases.

A note on humility: My goal here is not to draw conclusions. The sophistication underlying Nobel-Prize-winning work is beyond this book's scope and this author's capacity. Still, the insights provided by these pioneers deserve our attention. Whether these insights help explain the policy errors this book identifies, readers will decide. I hope that my effort to connect policy decisions with behavioral tendencies will stimulate more research and produce more insights—all toward the goal of improving merger decision-making.

11.3.1   Two Modes of Thinking: System 1 vs. System 2, Automatic vs. Effortful

Kahneman describes two "modes of thinking." System 1 is the "automatic system." It "operates automatically and quickly, with little or no effort and no sense of voluntary control." Most of the time, System 1 acts "without your conscious awareness of its activities." We use System 1 to "orient to the source of a sudden sound"; or to complete the phrase "bread and ..."; or "2 + 2 = ?" System 1 "provides the impressions that often turn into your beliefs." System 1 also is "the source of the impulses that often become your choices and your actions"; the "source of your rapid and often precise intuitive judgments."[48]

System 2 is the "effortful system." It "allocates attention to the effortful mental activities that demand it, including complex computations." It is illustrated by the mental effort it takes to multiply 17 x 24. System 2's operations "are often associated with the subjective experience of agency, choice, and concentration."[49]

---

[47]   DANIEL KAHNEMAN, THINKING, FAST AND SLOW (2011); RICHARD H. THALER, MISBEHAVING: THE MAKING OF BEHAVIORAL ECONOMICS (2015). For a third, less technical book about how all three—Kahneman, Tversky and Thaler—made their discoveries, working together and apart, see MICHAEL LEWIS, THE UNDOING PROJECT: A FRIENDSHIP THAT CHANGED OUR MINDS (2017).

[48]   KAHNEMAN, *supra* note 47, at 20–21, 58.

[49]   *Id.* at 20–21.

System 1 has power over System 2. System 1 "continuously generates … impressions, intuitions, intentions, and feelings." When System 2 adopts System 1's suggestions, "impressions and intuitions turn into beliefs, and impulses turn into voluntary actions." This susceptibility of System 2 to System 1's influence causes a problem for decision-makers, because System 1 is ignorant of logic and statistics. Operating automatically, it is "radically insensitive to both the quality and the quantity of the information that gives rise to impressions and intuitions." As a result, it is "the origin of many of the systematic errors in your intuitions." And because System 1 operates auto-matically, it "cannot be turned off." So "errors of intuitive thought are often difficult to prevent." In short: if System 2 fails to detect the errors in System 1's suggestions, we get biased decision-making.[50]

System 1 has an offspring—"What you see is all there is" (WYSIATI). It is our tendency to ignore the possibility that critical evidence is missing; to treat the information we have "as if it were all there is to know." From that incomplete information we "build the best possible story, . . … and if it is a good story, [we] believe it." The less information we have, the more easily we can build that story and believe it. Kahneman writes: "[W]e pay more attention to the content of messages than to information about their reliability, and as a result end up with a view of the world around us that is simpler and more coherent than the data justify."[51] Because System 1 operates on instinct, it does not supply missing facts. It constructs "the best possible story" from the available facts, regardless of their quality. And by "suppress[ing] doubt and ambiguity," System 1 favors first impressions. So if System 2 is not activated, WYSIATI "operates as a machine for jumping to conclusions."[52]

Kahneman hypothesizes a non-profit organization's search committee. It describes a CEO candidate as "intelligent and strong." Based on those words, the board concludes she will make a good leader. But what if she was also corrupt and cruel? The board's error—a common one—is to fit the facts they have into their impression of a good leader. The board should have asked: "What characteristics make a good leader, and what facts do I need to gather before I form an opinion?"[53]

---

[50] *Id.* at 22–25, 58, 86.
[51] *Id.* at 85, 118, 201.
[52] *Id.* at 85–88.
[53] *Id.* at 85–86.

11.3.2　Applicants' Strategy: Keep Regulators' System 1 in Control

Kahneman describes a dial. The dial measures cognitive effort, ranging from easy to strained. Under conditions of cognitive ease, System 1 dominates. As more mental effort becomes necessary, System 2 takes over. (Remember 2 + 2 vs. 17 x 24.) Merger applicants want to keep the dial in the easy zone. So they craft their application using three contributors to cognitive ease: repeated experience, clear display and primed ideas.[54]

- *Repeated experience:* They describe how the proposed merger resembles those that came before; how this latest transaction is normal and routine.
- *Clear display:* They present simple themes: consensual transaction, straightforward terms, shareholder support, "synergies," economies of scale, best practices. Who could be against these things?
- *Primed ideas:* The primed ideas will include the tangible benefits—the rate refunds, charitable contributions, the promise to avoid layoffs.

Generic language, simple ideas, positive tone. Having received an impression of the transaction as simple and normal, a regulator can readily say to himself: "The same reliable company that keeps our lights on wants to bring us benefits, wants to thrive and grow just like other utilities do. 2 + 2 = 4. We should approve this merger because we've approved other mergers and because everyone else approves mergers." The cognitive dial is turned to "low."[55]

How does System 2 respond? Does it take control, by actively questioning what System 1 has delivered? Or do System 1's "impressions and intuitions turn into [System 2's] beliefs"?[56] Early merger proposals—PacifiCorp-UP&L (1988), Northeast Utilities-Public Service of New Hampshire (1991), Kansas Gas & Electric-Kansas Power & Light (1991)—raised new and complex questions—about regional market power, federal-state relationships and acquisition debt. They drew major intervenor opposition, triggered much trade press coverage and involved complex proceedings in multiple fora. System 2 was in place, leading to long, detailed proceedings and long, detailed commission decisions. But thirty years later, mergers tread familiar paths. System 1 is ascendant. Two factors—each attributable to regulators' practices—explain why.

---

[54]　*Id.* at 59–60.

[55]　*See* Daniel Kahneman, *supra* note 47 ("The successful execution of a plan is specific and easy to imagine … [T]he alternative of failure is diffuse, because there are innumerable ways for things to go wrong.").

[56]　*Id.* at 22–25.

The first factor was Chapter 8's theme: commissions lack an affirmative vision for the industry. Having that vision would cause regulators to ask questions: Why doesn't proposed transaction ABC have qualities XYZ? Why are target shareholders getting gain they didn't earn? Why did the target CEO seek the highest price rather than the best performer? The contrast between proposal and vision activates System 2. No vision, no contrast, no questions—System 1 dominates.

The second factor is adjudicative procedure. Before submitting their application formally, merging entities usually visit the commissioners informally. They bring PowerPoints designed to create cognitive ease.[57] Once they file their formal application—usually accompanied by a media and ad campaign also constructed for cognitive ease—weeks go by before opposing intervenors file their testimony. During those weeks, the commissioners' System-1-generated impressions deepen their influence.

When the intervenor testimony does arrive, it splits in multiple ways— some supporting the transaction unconditionally, others resigned to its likely approval but seeking minor adjustments, a very few opposing it fully because of its inherent conflicts with the public interest, still others seeking benefits in return for their non-opposition. With so many disparate voices—most of them fitting themselves within the applicants' frame—the merger applicants' position remains the clearest, easiest-to-grasp position. It continues to dominate.

Then comes the evidentiary hearing. Commissioners, hearing examiners and commission staff ask few questions; those they do ask usually take the transaction as a given, focusing mostly on the applicants' offers. No one asks the target, "Why didn't you seek the best performer?" or "What is missing from your current performance that makes this transaction necessary?" When administrative law judges hear the case, institutional habit confines them to the transaction as presented; they see their job as building a record rather than advising on policy. System 2 is not activated, no one questions the applicants' frame. System 1 dominates.

---

[57] *See* EDWARD TUFTE, THE COGNITIVE STYLE OF POWERPOINT: PITCHING OUT CORRUPTS WITHIN (2006). No rational reader of this 32-page masterpiece will ever again torture their audience with PowerPoint bullets—or tolerate presenters who do. Complex diagrams, yes; bullets no. The front cover has a 1956 photograph of a thousand Soviet soldiers lined up before a statue of Stalin. From the soldiers emit comic-like bubbles:
> *"For re-education campaigns, nothing is better than the AutoContent Wizard!"*
> *"[Next slide, please]"*
> *"Comrade, why are we having this meeting? The rate of information transfer is asymptotically approaching **zero**!"*
> *"There's **no** bullet list like Stalin's bullet list!"*
> *"But why read aloud **every** slide?"*

* * *

Merger applicants construct a simple story: the transaction will reduce overhead costs, enable volume discounts, spread best practices, improve access to capital, preserve local management and continue charitable contributions. Everyone else is merging. No harm, $100 refunds for all. The regulators' System 1 adopts the coherent story. What you see is all there is. But that simple story omits these facts:

- The target company selected the acquirer because it offered the highest acquisition price, not because it offered the best performance. Indeed, the target insisted on a contractual right to sell to any acquirer that offered a higher price.
- The target shareholders are receiving a premium, though they did little to create its value. Because they are cashing out, they have no interest in the merged company's future health or quality of service.
- The premium reflects the acquirer's expectation of increasing the target utility's earnings above the commission-authorized level.
- The applicants' claims about overhead cost savings are only estimates, made on limited information after the merging parties reached agreement on the transaction. So the studies were not the basis for the transaction; they were done to create the story.
- The acquirer, its board and its CEO will have legal power to dictate the acquired utility's decisions—spending, rate increases, capital structure, board membership, executive leadership, everything.
- The acquirer has no limit on, and makes no promises about, its future acquisitions and business risks. It is free to acquire any company, in any industry anywhere in the world, without the commission's approval.

This information might come out in discovery, but only if intervenors have freed themselves from the applicants' frame, activated their own System 2, found the omitted facts—and from those facts constructed the full story. Even if they take these steps, that full story becomes the intervenors' story—more complicated, harder to make coherent (because complexity is not easily made coherent), created by "opponents" and therefore biased—and arriving on the commissioners' desks weeks after the applicants' simpler story has taken hold. Unless fully examined by System 2, System 1 will control.

And System 1 can cause systematic errors. Twelve types, each relevant to merger strategy, are discussed next.

11.3.3 System 1's Power: Twelve Systematic Errors

11.3.3.1 Framing is everything

The cognitive scientist George Lakoff describes frames as "mental structures that shape the way we see the world."[58] A merger proceeding's frame influences which problems receive regulators' attention. Merger applicants frame their private interest quest as a public interest benefit. The acquirer's goals are market position, market extension and monopoly revenues to balance non-utility business risks; the target's goal is gain from sale. Their frame presents "synergies" and customer benefits. Unless regulators have an alert System 2, that frame enters the commissioners' consciousness through System 1. It becomes the way they see the case—a simple, logical corporate coupling with nothing but tangible public benefit.

By excluding inconvenient facts, the frame diverts regulators' attention from their duties. Some kind of corporate restructuring might make sense, because most utilities' corporate structures, physical holdings and service territory boundaries were determined decades ago, uninfluenced by today's technologies and trading opportunities. Whether today's technologies and opportunities favor smaller companies (by allowing the efficient separation of presently integrated functions) or larger companies (by allowing the integration of non-adjacent assets and unrelated activities) is a question deserving regulators' attention. But it falls outside the applicants' frame.

Framing happens so often we accept it as normal. Commissions don't reject merger applications for incompleteness, because their merger application rules don't require completeness. Framing doesn't depend on deception or dishonesty; it lies within the boundaries of advocacy that commissions view as acceptable. And because the frame has substantive elements that make intuitive sense (synergies and best practices sound like good things), regulators find the frame favorable. But those substantive elements are not the only substance that matters. What you see is not all there is.

11.3.3.2 Availability

"The more easily people can call some scenario to mind—the more *available* it is to them—the more probable they find it to be."[59] What is available to the

---

[58] George Lakoff, Don't Think of an Elephant! Know Your Values and Frame the Debate, at xi (2004). Frames are part of our "cognitive unconscious"— "structures in our brains that we cannot consciously access, but we know by their consequences." *Id.* at xii.

[59] Lewis, *supra* note 47, at 190 (referring to Kahneman & Tversky's *Availability: A Heuristic for Judging Frequency and Probability*, 5 Cognitive Psychol. 207 (1973)).

regulator? At least three things: the applicants' simple story, the knowledge of recent merger approvals and the absence of any trouble arising from those approvals. What is not available—in the sense of mental immediacy—are the internal strategies motivating the merging companies, and the facts revealing the transaction's essence. And so the regulator judges the transaction based on the easily available story rather than the more complicated, less available facts. Yes, those facts can become available later through intervenor discovery; but that later availability lacks the influence of the immediate availability that causes regulators to accept the applicants' frame.

11.3.3.3 Representativeness

Related to availability is representativeness. "When people make judgments, ... they compare whatever they are judging to some model in their minds."[60] Regulators use representativeness when they ask themselves this question: "Does this merger look like prior mergers—none of which caused a problem?" If the answer is yes, regulators tend not to ask the more complex questions: "What products and services do our customers need? What types of companies will provide those products and services most cost-effectively? Does this proposed merger meet that criterion? Will our approval preclude better performers from offering their services? Is this the best we can do?"

11.3.3.4 Isolated option vs. comparison

When presented with an isolated option instead of a comparison, System 1 responds, likely unaffected by System 2. A comparison, in contrast, "involves a more careful and effortful assessment, which calls for System 2."[61] Experimenters described a crime victim who lost an arm to a gunshot wound. They asked participants how much compensation he should get. One group had to consider two scenarios simultaneously:

1. The man was shot when shopping at his regular store.
2. His regular store was closed for a funeral, so he shopped at a different store, where he was shot.

This group concluded that location was irrelevant; in both situations the compensation should be the same. But when the experimenters used two other groups, giving each group only one of the two scenarios, the group exposed

---

[60] *Id.* at 183 (referring to Kahneman & Tversky's *Subjective Probability: A Judgment of Representativeness*, 3 Cognitive Psychol. 430 (1972)).

[61] Kahneman, *supra* note 47, at 355.

to the second scenario offered more compensation. Emotion—"if only he had shopped at his regular store"—influenced the outcome.[62]

In merger cases, commissions receive only one transaction to consider, rather than multiple transactions to compare. System 1 operates, unaffected by System 2. If instead commissions held competitions for the best acquirers, or instructed the target utility to do so (the competition being based on consumer benefits rather than highest share price), System 2 would take over, forcing more careful, analytical, non-instinctive thinking. Ironically, target companies do conduct competitions. When they compare price bids from various acquirers they trigger an army of System 2s—investment bankers, negotiating teams, fairness opinion analysts and rating agency comments. The target companies would agree with Kahneman: "[R]ationality is generally served by broader and more comprehensive frames, and joint evaluation is obviously broader than single evaluation."[63] But commissions don't follow this simple principle. By processing a single transaction in isolation from others, they overvalue the merger before them and undervalue the ones not sought. And they undervalue—probably valuing at zero—the reality that by approving Merger ABC they lose forever Mergers DEF and GHI.

11.3.3.5 Evaluation vs. prediction

Merger analysis should be an exercise in prediction: Over its lifetime, will this coupling provide the best possible service compared to alternative utility actions? Is the likely lifetime benefit-cost ratio better than all feasible alternative uses of investor and customer resources? But people tend not to predict. We substitute our evaluation of the present for a prediction of the future.

Kahneman worked with military trainers assigned to select candidates for officers' school. He asked the trainers to predict the candidates' future grades in the school. They based their predictions on the candidates' grades on the selection exam. They did not address the uncertainties inherent in their predictions, such as obvious differences between what the application exam tested and what the school curriculum would test. Nor did they address the possibility that a high grade on that single application exam could be a random occurrence rather than an accurate representation of skills. (If the grade were a random occurrence, the candidate would then revert to the mean—making the prediction useless.[64])

---

[62] *Id.* at 353–54 (referring to Dale T. Miller & Cathy McFarland, *Counterfactual Thinking and Victim Compensation: A Test of Norm Theory*, 12 PERSONALITY & SOC. PSYCHOL. BULL. 513 (1986)).

[63] *Id.* at 360–61.

[64] Reverting to the mean is a statistical phenomenon with a simple explanation. Any performer has, over the long run, an average performance level—a long run mean. Any

In merger cases, commissions tend to focus on the applicants' current characteristics and performance. Instead they should be predicting the merged company's future characteristics and performance. Commissions do consider projections of operational savings. But they base those considerations on company presentations created to sell the transaction. And these projections are good for only a few years, since beyond that period no one can accurately project how the target would have performed without a merger. Commissions don't attempt to predict other factors affecting the merged company's performance—like its skill at managing major construction projects, or its ability to weather economic disruptions like interest rate increases, labor shortages, economic downturns or storms. Commissions don't attempt to predict—in fact they don't ask about—the acquirer's future acquisitions or future business ventures, including how the merged company will manage the resulting risks. Instead, commissions do what Kahneman's military trainers did: they substitute an evaluation of the status quo for a prediction of the future.

11.3.3.6 Anchoring and adjustment

The anchoring effect is "one of the most reliable and robust results of experimental psychology."[65] A utility proposes a $75 million rate increase. The consumer advocate persuades the commission to accept $40 million. "We saved customers $35 million," he declares. The $75 million request was the anchor; the anchor influenced the perception of success. It also diverted attention from the relevant issue. The anchored question was: "Has the company justified a $75 million increase?" The relevant question is: "What should it cost to supply this service territory?"

Why do anchors influence our thinking? As Kahneman explains, "people who are asked difficult questions clutch at straws, and the anchor is a plausible straw."[66] If one must estimate a value, but is first exposed to some other value, that other value influences the estimate.

Anchoring raises two concerns. First, the anchor might be irrelevant to the problem. In a famous example, experimenters rigged a wheel of fortune so that it always stopped on 10 or 65. They told two separate groups of students to watch the wheel spin, write down the resulting number, then guess the percentage of African nations in the United Nations. For the group whose wheel stopped at 10, the average answer was 25 percent; for the group whose

---

single test grade will vary from that level. So an above-average grade is likely to be followed by a below-average grade, and vice versa.

[65]   KAHNEMAN, *supra* note 47, at 119.

[66]   *Id.* at 125.

wheel stopped at 65, the average answer was 45 percent. The irrelevant anchor influenced the guess.[67]

The second concern has direct application to merger regulation: those who recognize an anchor's powers have an advantage over those who don't. They can use that advantage to cause their counterpart to act against self-interest. When negotiating for a house, or for a good in a bazaar, the offer price—stated by the person who knows the real value—affects the final price.[68] What about mergers? Merger applicants offer benefits. As profit-maximizers and cost-minimizers, they will offer no more than necessary to get the regulators' approval. Their offer is the anchor. They can increase the anchor's influence by showing how it resembles—or slightly exceeds—what prior commissions have accepted; or by warning that demands for more benefits will kill the transaction. Intervenors and commissions will try to adjust the anchor upwards, but not by much for fear of looking unreasonable. "The adjustment [to an anchor] typically ends prematurely, because people stop when they are no longer certain that they should move farther."[69]

On merger benefits, commissions should cause applicants to offer the amount that, if just exceeded, would make the acquirer drop the transaction because its benefit-cost ratio dropped below its hurdle rate. But that number never becomes the anchor—because the applicants don't reveal it and because the commission and intervenors have no way to discover it. So the applicants can use their superior knowledge to establish an anchor that serves their strategy.

Why do applicants have this superior position? Because each commission cedes the selection of acquirers to the target rather than conduct the competition itself. A competition run by the commission would induce each competing acquirer to offer the correct amount of benefits—the amount which, if just exceeded, would cause its benefit-cost ratio to fall below its hurdle rate. And because the competition would cause the commission to examine alternatives rather than react to an isolated option, it would be using System 2,[70] uninflu-

---

[67]   *Id.* at 119 (referring to an experiment published in a seminal paper with Tversky, *Judgment under Uncertainty: Heuristics and Biases*, 185 SCIENCE 1124 (1974)). Another demonstration from that paper: when one group of students had to guess at the solution to 8x7x6x5x4x3x2x1 while another group had to guess at 1x2x3x4x5x6x7x8, the first group's average answer was always higher. *Id.* app. A at 427.

[68]   *Id.* at 126.

[69]   *Id.* at 120. Kahneman gives two everyday examples. People don't reduce speed sufficiently when they exit the highway for city streets; and teenagers told by parents to turn their music down don't adjust enough. *Id.* at 121 (referring to examples from Robyn LeBoeuf & Eldar Shafir, *The Long and Short of It: Physical Anchoring Effects*, 19 J. BEHAV. DECISION MAKING 393 (2006)).

[70]   As discussed in "Isolated option vs. comparison" in Chapter 11.3.3.4 above.

enced by any anchor. But when the commission's standard is no-harm, or at best give-us-what-you-give-the-other-states, the anchor comes from the applicants.

An anchor's influence—a product of System 1—is magnified when you assume that the anchor's source has specialized knowledge that you should trust. If a forester asks us "How much does the height of a redwood vary from 1200 feet?" we assume the answer is somewhere near 1200 feet. Experimenters asked the same question of two different groups, with one group given an anchor of 1200 feet and the other of 180 feet. The average answers were 844 and 282, respectively.[71] So when merger applicants offer a particular level of benefits, and warn that demands for more will kill the transaction, commissions and intervenors will tend to accept the anchor—especially if their merger experience is low,[72] and especially if they trust the applicants for unrelated reasons (like, their ability to operate giant machines that keep our lights on).

11.3.3.7 Reference point

A reference point is a metric by which you judge whether an outcome makes you better or worse off. Most people's reference point is the status quo. Two other common reference points are the outcome you expect, and the one to which you feel entitled.[73] In a utility merger, each applicant has its own reference point. The acquirer's reference point will likely be its hurdle rate; or perhaps the benefit-cost ratio achieved by its prior transactions or similar transactions. The target's reference point will likely be the acquisition premium received by targets in similar transactions. Being profit maximizers, neither acquirer nor target would be satisfied with merely improving its status quo.

But the regulator's reference point will likely be the status quo. Applicants frame their transaction in terms of "savings"—by definition, improvements on

---

[71] KAHNEMAN, *supra* note 47, at 123–24 (referring to Karen E. Jacowitz & Daniel Kahneman, *Measures of Anchoring in Estimation Tasks*, 21 PERSONALITY & SOC. PSYCHOL. BULL. 1161 (1995)). The less relevant the anchor, the scarier the result. In one experiment, experienced German judges had to decide a shoplifter's sentence. But before the sentencing, the experimenter had the judges throw dice, secretly weighted to produce a three and a nine. Then they were asked whether the sentence, in months, should be more or less than the number produced by the dice. The judges who rolled a nine averaged eight months; the judges who rolled a three averaged five months. *Id.* at 125–26 (citing Birte Englich et al., *Playing Dice with Criminal Sentences: The Influence of Irrelevant Anchors on Experts' Judicial Decision Making*, 32 PERSONALITY & SOC. PSYCHOL. BULL. 188 (2006)).

[72] While the total number of electricity mergers is high, the number for any state is low. And given the short average term for a commissioner, it is likely that most commissioners on a case will be seeing a merger for the first time.

[73] KAHNEMAN, *supra* note 47, at 282.

the status quo. They offer a refund against status quo rates. They offer charitable contributions that match or exceed status quo levels. When status quo is the reference point, commissions will view the transaction favorably if it merely improves on the status quo. So if the applicants can design the transaction to satisfy their own, profit-maximizing reference points, while offering commissions only small improvements on the status quo, they can keep most of the transaction's gains for themselves and still win approval.

A commission whose reference point is the status quo makes two errors. First, if the status quo is a target utility failing to use all prudent practices, then the commission would be treating the acquirer's elimination of imprudence—replacing roman numerals with computers—as a merger benefit. Second, status quo improvements improve only static efficiency—they reduce the cost of operating existing assets. A reference point based not on the status quo but on what competitive pressures would bring would include improvements in dynamic efficiency—the new technologies, asset combinations and operational solutions that emerge when competitors vie for market share. So the regulator's proper reference point is not the status quo; it is the outcome customers would experience if their supplier were subject to effective competition.

This difference in reference points—the merging parties maximizing gain, the regulator improving on the status quo—has a predictable result: most of the transaction's gains go to the applicants.

11.3.3.8 Vividness bias

Experimenters invited students to choose between drawing a marble from one of two bowls. Drawing a red marble would win a prize. Bowl A had 10 marbles, one of which was red. Bowl B had 100 marbles, eight of which were red. About 30–40 percent of students chose Bowl B. The larger number of bright red marbles caused them to blow a simple probability problem. Says Kahneman: "If your attention is drawn to the winning marbles, you do not assess the number of nonwinning marbles with the same care. Vivid imagery contributes to denominator neglect ..."[74]

Merger applicants know that vivid, tangible offers distract from abstract probabilities. In the regulator's benefit-cost ratio, tangible offers are the numerator, the risks and costs are the denominator. The immediate $100 rate refund, the headquarters building, the promise of no layoffs for two years—these benefits are vivid. They occupy more mental space than the merged entity's future business risks. Vividness causes denominator neglect;

---

[74] *Id.* at 328–29 (referring to Dale T. Miller et al., *When a Coincidence Is Suspicious: The Role of Mental Simulation*, 57 J. PERSONALITY & SOC. PSYCHOL. 581 (1989)).

regulators under-appreciate and underestimate the probability of future harm. The tangible promise of no layoffs in the first two years distracts from the likelihood that a merger promising immediate cost reductions will lead to layoffs later. Vividness prevails over probabilities.

11.3.3.9 Optimism bias

"The successful execution of a plan is specific and easy to imagine ... [T]he alternative of failure is diffuse, because there are innumerable ways for things to go wrong." Because the brain prefers simplicity, people tend to over-weigh the probability of success and under-weigh the probability of failure. The tendency is especially strong if the negative outcome is rare. "[I]n 2007 no banker had personally experienced a devastating financial crisis. ... When it comes to rare events, our mind is not designed to get things quite right."[75]

Merger applicants focus commissions' attention on the positive plan—the refunds, the cost savings, the charitable contributions. The plan's execution is easy to imagine. The negatives are more complicated, their likelihoods unknown. Will the acquisition debt cause a bond rating downgrade at the holding company? How will that downgrade affect the utility? How will the acquirer recover the control premium? Will the acquirer buy more companies—where, and at what risk level? With the utilities' funds? When will layoffs occur? How will the commission pay for the staff to watch over things? Positives are simple, negatives are complicated. Commission decisions always describe the positives; they rarely assign probabilities to the negatives—or they dismiss the negatives as speculative.

11.3.3.10 Halo effect

You're a fundraiser for a charitable organization. At a party you meet John, whom you find amicable. You like John, so you put him on your list of possible donors. But amicability is not generosity; you've viewed the relationship as "simpler and more coherent than the real thing." That's the halo effect—when making a decision, your positive emotions about a person become trust in his competence, trustworthiness or other features important to the decision.[76] A major investor visits Ford Motor's new car show. Impressed, he buys $10 million in Ford stock. If a company makes good cars, it's a good bet. Wrong. In buying a company's stock, the relevant question is: "Is the stock currently underpriced?" The investor's emotions distracted from the relevant facts.[77]

---

[75]   *Id.* at 325–26, 332–33.
[76]   *Id.* at 82.
[77]   *Id.* at 12.

Electricity is awesome, literally: flip a switch, 500 miles away a puff of smoke appears, your house lights up. Does our awe of the utility's technology, and our gratitude for its comforts, cause us to view the utility's strategic goals uncritically? Wrote the Kansas Commission: "Both KCP&L and Westar have a long history of providing sufficient and efficient service in Kansas and the Commission agrees that based on their geographies a merger makes sense."[78] Notice how the conjunction "and" connects two completely unrelated points. The utilities' "long history" of keeping the lights on has nothing—literally nothing—to do with whether the merger of two monopolies will create long-term consumer benefits. A merger's merits depend not on history but on the future—which executives will control which decisions, what additional acquisitions the merged company will make, how the acquirer will pay off its acquisition debt, what effects the combination will have on future competition; and especially, whether this transaction precludes better ones. The Commission's reference to "geographies" epitomizes superficiality and imprecision. We don't know if the Commission is referring to adjacency, terrains, size, customer mix or what. And "makes sense" how—economically, physically, financially? If each company has already exhausted economies of scale, then a merger "based on their geographies" does not necessarily "make sense." And if these adjacent companies are competitors or potential competitors for wholesale or retail sales, then the merger hurts consumers by reducing competition.

The Kansas example illustrates both System 1 and System 2. The above-quoted passage reflects System 1: the Kansas regulators relied on positive history and geographic adjacency to favor, instinctively, a merger of potential competitors. But the original transaction's high control premium and high acquisition debt triggered System 2, so the Commission rejected that version of the transaction. The two companies then returned with a stock-for-stock exchange—no control premium, no acquisition debt. The Commission quickly accepted the transaction—without addressing the loss of competition between formidable competitors or the merged company's possible future acquisitions. System 1 was back on top.

11.3.3.11 Confirmation bias and desirability bias
People have impressions and beliefs. They tend to search for and favor information that supports those impressions and beliefs, while downplaying, ignor-

---

[78] Great Plains Energy-Westar Energy Merger I, 2017 Kan. PUC LEXIS 1142, at *4 ¶ 5. The Commission did say, in the next sentence, "But not this merger," because the price was too high and the acquisition debt too large. When the companies recast their merger as a stock-for-stock exchange with no premium, the Commission approved it.

ing or disfavoring information that does not.[79] This confirmation bias comes from System 1, which "favors uncritical acceptance of suggestions." System 2 does our doubting and unbelieving, but is "sometimes busy, and often lazy."[80] Desirability bias differs from confirmation bias. Whereas confirmation bias confirms the impressions or beliefs one already has, desirability bias emphasizes and credits information that supports what one wants to believe.[81]

Before the official merger application hits their desks, the commissioners and staff have likely heard the following, perhaps from applicants in pre-filing meetings: (1) dozens of utility mergers have already occurred nationally; (2) mergers have been approved by their predecessors at this commission; (3) mergers have been approved by neighboring commissions; and (4) these mergers have produced tangible benefits and no ill effects. These facts can create and support an early impression and belief that utility mergers are routine and harmless. They can cause commissioners, on later reading the application and watching the witnesses at hearing, to pay more attention to facts that support their impressions and beliefs. That's the confirmation bias. And if commissioners also *want* to believe that mergers are harm-free, public-interest-motivated and competitively-disciplined—and that what is good for the companies is good for the public—that's desirability bias at work.

Biases toward beliefs and desires can cause regulators to de-emphasize facts that conflict with those beliefs and desires. Facts like these: that the target selected the acquirer solely based on price; that the target's goal is to increase share value rather than to improve customer service; that the acquirer wants to fill a monopoly earnings slot in its high-risk portfolio; that "synergies" are but post-hoc rationalizations for a transaction arranged for other purposes; that the acquirer intends to recover the control premium from the ratepayers, somehow. Both biases are deepened by regulatory procedures. As Chapter 10.2 explained, the evidentiary hearing starts with the commissioners' System 1 absorbing the applicants' simple story. The intervenors' response comes months later, its complexity straining System 2, leaving it less able to counteract the biases that come from System 1.

11.3.3.12 Loss aversion, endowment effect

For nearly all commissions, the central merger standard is the no-harm standard. Merger regulators seek to avoid harm rather than maximize benefits. This Kansas Commission statement exemplifies the posture: "The threshold ques-

---

[79]   THALER, *supra* note 47, at 172.

[80]   KAHNEMAN, *supra* note 47, at 81.

[81]   Ben Tappin et al., *You're Not Going to Change Your Mind*, N.Y. TIMES (May 27, 2017), https://www.nytimes.com/2017/05/27/opinion/sunday/youre-not-going-to -change-your-mind.html.

tion facing the Commission is how much financial risk can be accepted before the proposed transaction does not serve the public interest."[82] As Chapter 11.2 showed, each of the six commission rejections emphasized the presence of negatives.

This error, while analytical, has roots in the psychological. We are more inclined to avoid losses than to seek gains—"losses hurt about twice as much as gains make you feel good." Psychologists call this tendency the "endowment effect"—"people value[] things that ... [are] already part of their endowment more highly than things ... that ... [are] available but not yet owned."[83] Loss aversion has additional power if one lacks a positive goal. Chapter 8 explained that regulators lack a vision—a set of performance goals against which to rate a proposed merger. So they focus on what they might lose, not on what they might gain. I do not suggest that harm-avoidance is an improper policy; this book's four chapters in Part II addressed harm. The error is not in making harm avoidance a goal, but in making it the dominant goal.

* * *

The behavioral economists have described numerous mental habits—rules of thumb, shortcuts, biases—that affect everyone's decisions. Regulators are not immune. Understanding the problems leads to solutions. Through specific actions—establishing visions, creating filing requirements that cause the right comparisons, organizing evidentiary hearings around issues rather than parties and drafting merger opinions that point the industry in the most productive directions—regulators can ensure that analysis prevails over instinct. These solutions are the subject of Part IV.

---

[82] *Great Plains Energy-Westar Energy Merger I*, 2017 Kan. PUC LEXIS 1142, at *81–82 ¶ 92 (rejecting Great Plains Energy's acquisition of Westar as "too risky"). For the full critique of the no-harm standard, see Chapter 4.2.

[83] THALER, *supra* note 47, at 18, 34.

PART IV

Solutions: regulatory posture, practices and infrastructure

Chapter 11 described how mental habits cause systematic errors. If those habits can affect judges when sentencing shoplifters, they can affect regulators when assessing mergers. I don't suggest that regulators have become robots programmed by merger applicants, all System 1 and no System 2, all instinct and no analysis. But field studies conducted by the most credentialed academics have proven and re-proven two facts: System 1 and System 2 are embedded in the human brain, and System 1 exerts power over System 2. Science has alerted us: regulators need practices and procedures that put System 2 in control.

Evaluating mergers requires objectivity and skepticism—conscious doubt about the applicants' claims. But "[c]onscious doubt is not in the repertoire of System 1; it requires maintaining incompatible interpretations in mind at the same time, which demands mental effort. Uncertainty and doubt are the domain of System 2."[1] So we need to design practices and procedures that activate the "enhanced monitoring and effortful activity of System 2."[2] To achieve that purpose, Chapter 12 proposes five sequential actions:

1. **Establish screens**—for company activities, corporate and governance structure, financial structure and for the transaction's effect on market structure.
2. **Establish conditions**—on transaction terms and on post-merger actions.
3. **Create filing requirements**—ones that cause comparisons between the proposed merger and the commission's vision.
4. **Organize evidentiary hearings** around issues, not parties.

---

[1] DANIEL KAHNEMAN, THINKING, FAST AND SLOW 80 (2011).
[2] *Id.* at 28.

5. **Issue merger opinions that guide the future**—by distinguishing suboptimal transactions from optimal ones.

Each of these five actions aims to turn a commission's cognitive dial to "high."

To do all these things, and do them well, we need two additional steps, proposed in Chapter 13. Regulators should strengthen their resources to match merger complexity. They should also conduct a multi-jurisdictional study of these past three decades, asking these questions: Which ones lived up to their claims? Which ones caused harm or precluded better alternatives? Which ones spurred competition, and which ones reduced competition? With that knowledge, and with this book's other recommendations, commissions can create and apply merger policies that produce the operational efficiencies and competitive pressures that customers deserve.

12. Regulatory posture and practice: less instinct, more analysis; less reactivity, more preparation

Chapter 11.3.1 explained that System 1 is instinctive, System 2 is analytical and System 1 has power over System 2. To make private-interest mergers serve public-interest goals, regulators need to replace deference with action. They need to shift from passenger to driver; they need to activate System 2. They need to create screens, conditions and filing requirements. They need to re-cast their evidentiary hearings from party-centric to issue-centric. Their merger opinions need to center less on parties' desires and more on regulatory principles. This chapter explains these points.

12.1 ESTABLISH SCREENS FOR COMPANY TYPES

12.1.1 Categories of Concern

Electric service is no longer a commodity, electric current traveling over wires. It is now a category, comprising distinct services customers can combine themselves. We still have the traditional trio of generation, transmission and distribution. But generation now comes in different colors—conventional and renewable; home-scale, neighborhood-scale and utility-scale; monopoly-provided and competitively-provided; investor-owned, cooperatively-owned and municipally-owned. We have new services and the assets that make them possible: automated, two-way customer meters; pricing plans that track the utility's actual hourly costs; neighborhood-level service provided by microgrids; electric vehicle charging stations; energy efficiency services; demand response aggregation.

An electric utility merger affects all these options because common to them all is an electric utility. To preserve these options—to cause the best to rise to the top—commissions must avoid mergers that cause conflict, between the utility's service obligations and its holding company's strategic objectives. Whether a merged company will have conflict depends on four factors: (a) its mix of business activities; (b) the corporate and governance structures that stimulate and guide those activities; (c) the internal financial relationships that support or limit those activities; and (d) the external market structures that either discipline or accommodate the merged company's conduct. These are the ingredients of performance.[1]

Business activities: The post-merger holding company system should have at all levels, from the holding company's CEO to the utility's substation repair team, a single focus: performing for the utility's customers. No affiliate, executive or employee should bear pressures or face incentives that distract from or conflict with that focus. A standalone utility—pure-play, unaffiliated with any unrelated business—has that focus, so it experiences no inter-business conflict.[2] The risk of conflict rises as the merged company's business activities expand. Geographic expansion (acquiring utilities in other locations) can benefit customers if there are economies of scale; but expansion for expansion's sake distracts from performance. Type-of-business expansion (acquiring companies that sell other services) is also a double-edged sword: non-utility affiliates can support a utility (as might a subsidiary specializing in land acquisition or fuel purchasing); or distract it (like affiliates investing in nuclear power or commodities trading). Commissions should allow these expansions only if justified by customer's benefits. Otherwise expansion conflicts with performance.

Corporate and governance structure: A utility's shares can be owned (a) directly by ultimate shareholders (e.g., individuals, mutual funds and pension funds); (b) by a holding company (which might own other businesses, utility-related or not utility-related, geographically nearby or remote) whose own shareholders are the ultimate shareholders; or (c) by a holding company that is owned in turn by another holding company. Alternatively, the utility could itself be the top-level holding company, owning one or more other companies. Within a holding company's structure, subsidiaries can engage in inter-affiliate transactions (such as loans, guarantees of indebtedness, and sales and purchases of goods and services).[3] These ownership and affiliate relationships affect (a) who controls or influences the utility's decisions, and (b) what purposes that control or influence serves. These relationships need to support the utility's performance, not undermine it.

---

[1]   As a leading industrial organization text explains: "[T]he most severe stumbling block in evaluating industrial performance is likely to be securing agreement on what is considered good or bad attributes of performance. Conflicting value judgments concerning performance attributes and their weights undoubtedly underlie many disputes as to the proper public policy toward monopolistic business enterprises." FREDERIC M. SCHERER & DAVID R. ROSS, INDUSTRIAL MARKET STRUCTURE AND ECONOMIC PERFORMANCE 55 (3d. ed. 1990) (crediting Adam Smith).

[2]   For the numerous types of parent-utility conflict see Chapter 7.

[3]   As discussed in Chapter 6.5.5.

Financial structure: A holding company's financial structure involves (1) the mix of equity and debt, and (2) the sources of that equity and debt. Along with governance structure, financial structure influences which business activities have priority when capital is scarce. To avoid internal conflicts, the merged entity should not have so much debt that the holding company can't finance the utility's needs; or worse, diverts the utility's cash to serve non-utility needs. The problem is not debt per se; capital-intensive businesses like utilities always have debt. The problem is debt unrelated to the utility business—acquisition debt and non-utility debt. Nor should the holding company incur non-utility risks that increase the utility's cost of debt or equity.

Market structure: For a given service in a given geographic area, market structure refers to the number and types of entities selling or buying that service, their shares of the total transactions, the assets they control and the ease with which sellers can enter and exit the market. A horizontal merger reduces the number of players; a vertical merger changes who controls key inputs. Either type can make a market structure more or less competitive, thereby affecting the parameters of performance: efficiency, cost, quality, customer responsiveness and innovation. Commissions need to envision, and guide transactions toward, the market structures most likely to cause sellers to produce the desired performance. Only by envisioning the right market structures can a commission assess whether a proposed transaction affects progress toward those market structures.

12.1.2   Selection Criteria Instead of Static Checklists

Having established general principles for company types, commissions can transform their merger checklists—today, a static list of subjects without accountable standards—into a list of must-haves, must-not-haves and discretionary haves. Consider the following examples.

12.1.2.1 Must-haves

- Specific experience providing the desired services with excellence.
- Financial capability to execute the purchase and finance future utility investments.
- An executive compensation system that aligns pay with operational performance and that gives executives no reason to pursue shareholder interests that conflict with customer interests.
- An internal disciplinary system that makes company wrongdoers fully accountable for their wrongdoing.
- Productive labor relations, including third-party audit procedures that ensure all employees' fair pay, health and safety.

- A record of respect for the regulatory process, including its key features: candor, transparency and reliance on facts, logic and law instead of less rational forms of persuasion.
- Diversity at all levels of the company, reflecting the diversity of the service territory's population.
- For non-U.S. holding companies, a home-country legal infrastructure (including accounting rules, regulatory practices and corporate transparency) that is compatible with U.S. law and accessible to U.S. regulators.

12.1.2.2 Must-not-haves

- A record of law-breaking or rule-breaking.
- A record of poor performance in other franchises.
- A record of anticompetitive practices, or of opposition to competition where competition can improve performance—such as competition that allows qualified, cost-effective companies to compete for roles currently performed by the applicant.
- Control of facilities that would give the merged company horizontal or vertical market power in any market, or contribute to a concentration trend that could reasonably lead to market power, unless regulators can remove that market power fully.
- Control by a holding company system that is overly complex, overly leveraged or overly invested in businesses whose risks or strategies undermine or conflict with a utility's obligation to serve.
- Asymmetrical compensation plans—ones that reward risk-taking executives for the upsides but make shareholders, creditors and customers bear the downsides.

12.1.2.3 Discretionary haves
The must-haves screen in the positive transactions; the must-not-haves screen out the negative ones. Commissions can assess the surviving merger candidates by applying discretionary criteria like these:

- A culture of experimentation and innovation.
- Cost-effective use of subcontractors.
- Willingness to forgo additional acquisitions, of specified magnitudes and types, without commission permission aimed at preserving economies and preventing distractions.
- Active, educated board members who are not over-compensated relative to their value.

- Compensation systems for executives and employees that reward good work appropriately, including a non-excessive ratio of CEO compensation to line-worker compensation.
- Type of ownership (e.g., government-owned vs. investor-owned, private equity vs. publicly traded, mutual funds vs. hedge funds).

* * *

Corporate Structure Event	Regulatory Action		
	Prohibition?	Reviews, Limits and Conditions?	Permission w/o Review?
1. Utility merger with another utility			
a. operationally integrated			
b. not operationally integrated			
2. Utility acquisition of non-utility			
a. for utility purpose			
b. not for utility purpose			
3. Non-utility acquisition of utility			
a. acquirer has operational relationship to utility			
b. acquirer has no operational relationship to utility			
4. Inter-affiliate transactions			
a. goods and services: sale to utility			
b. goods and services: sale by utility to non-utility			
c. financing: loan or guarantee to utility			
d. financing: loan or guarantee from utility to non-utility			
5. Issuance of debt or equity			
a. at the holding company level, for utility purposes			
b. at the holding company level, for non-utility purposes			
c. at the utility level, for utility purposes			
d. at the utility level, for non-utility purposes			
e. at the non-utility level, for utility purposes			
f. at the non-utility level, for non-utility purposes			
6. Divestiture or spin-off			
a. of utility assets serving your state			
b. of utility assets serving other states			
c. of non-utility assets or businesses			
7. Use of utility assets for non-utility business			
a. utility assets in your state			
b. utility assets in other states			

Figure 12.1   Corporate restructuring by public utilities: how should regulators prepare and respond?

Figure 12.1 provides a matrix that can guide the screening. The left-hand column lists the main categories of corporate structure events affecting utilities, their holding companies and their affiliates: mergers and acquisitions, affiliate transactions, issuances of debt or equity, divestiture or spin-off of assets, and the use of utility assets for non-utility businesses. Within each category are the ways in which a utility or its holding company owner could use the utility's state-protected status to advance its business objectives. For each such action (there are 21), the policymaker has three choices: prohibit the action entirely, permit it without any review or conditioning, or subject it to review and possible conditioning. A full regulatory policy will make one of those three decisions for each of the 21 actions. Within the middle regulatory option, review and conditioning, there are many variations. That middle option is where regulation does its work.

* * *

Should commissions give weightings to the criteria? Doing so avoids arbitrariness. When we shop for a new car, we're thinking about looks, speed, safety, fuel economy, maintenance needs, reputation, comfort. Our brain is assigning weights whether we know it or not and whether we like it or not:

> Whenever you form a global evaluation of a complex object ... you assign weights to its characteristics. ... [S]ome characteristics influence your assessment more than others do. The weighting occurs whether or not you are aware of it; it is an operation of System 1.[4]

If we don't assign weights explicitly the brain will do it anyway—just not according to our needs. No applicant will be the best at everything. Also, some criteria involve mutual tradeoffs. Under those circumstances, assigning weights explicitly helps align the commission's decisions with its goals.

12.2 ESTABLISH CONDITIONS—ON THE TRANSACTIONS AND ON POST-MERGER ACTIONS

Screens help select the transaction; conditions establish and enforce the selected entity's obligations. By setting conditions before acquirers and targets start their searches, commissions can guide transactions toward public-spirited results. These conditions can address transaction terms as well as the merged company's operations. After describing these two categories, we address federal constitutional limits on state-level conditions.

12.2.1 Conditions on Transaction Terms

12.2.1.1 Control premium: limited to the level that properly compensates target shareholders

Effective utility regulation should produce performance comparable to effective competition. Applying that principle to mergers, regulation should produce transactions that provide customers the best benefit-to-cost ratio. That

---

[4] DANIEL KAHNEMAN, THINKING, FAST AND SLOW 310 (2011).

ratio should count only those benefits that satisfy three criteria: unachievable without the transaction, supported by evidence, and committed to by the applicants.[5]

A target utility that puts its customers first will seek whatever coupling brings its customers the best benefit-cost ratio, provided the transaction leaves the utility no worse off. But most utility targets do the precise opposite: they choose the acquirer that offers the target shareholders the highest price, provided it leaves customers no worse off (though as Part II's four chapters detailed, most transactions expose customers to four types of harm). Outside mergers, commissions regularly reject utility behavior that puts shareholders ahead of customers. A utility cannot favor high-priced fuel from its affiliate over low-priced fuel from a non-affiliate; nor can it build high-cost generation for its rate base when it can buy lower-cost power from a third party. But in the merger context, commissions routinely discard that principle; they allow the target utility to choose the highest-paying acquirer regardless of whether it is the most customer-benefitting one. Customers lose twice: the highest-price transaction displaces the most cost-effective one; and the high premium paid to the target shareholders reduces whatever benefits the acquirer could give the customers.

To prevent targets from choosing price over performance, commissions need a two-part solution: (a) require the target utility to choose the acquirer offering the most customer benefits, and (b) limit the control premium received by target shareholders (assuming the acquirer offers one) to the value those shareholders truly created—through shareholder risk-taking and management excellence. Any additional premium offered by acquirers should go to customers because, as Chapter 5.5 explained, it is their government-enforced captivity that provides the stable earnings that support the premium. Limiting the control premium in this way recognizes, as Chapter 5.4 explained, that franchise control is not the target utility's asset to sell for gain; it is a privilege, granted by government, to serve the customers at minimum cost and reasonable profit.

12.2.1.2 Transaction financing: conservative and customer-focused

Commissions need to "safeguard[] the public against unsound financial practices which make impossible the proper and most economic performance of public utility functions."[6] Mergers affect a utility's financial position.

---

    [5]   All as explained in Chapter 4.4.

    [6]   *Pacific Power & Light Co.*, 27 F.P.C. 623, 626–27 (1962) (quoting S. Comm. on Interstate Commerce, S. Rep. No. 74-621, at 50 (1935)). *See also Citizens Energy Corp.*, 35 F.E.R.C. ¶ 61,198 (1986) (describing the purpose of Federal Power Act section 204 as "ensur[ing] the financial viability of public utilities obligated to serve

Concerns arise in two contexts: acquisition debt, and other changes in financial circumstances.

Acquisition debt: In a cash buyout, the acquirer pays cash to buy the target company's stock. If to pay that cash the acquirer incurs new debt, the merged company will have more debt than had the two unmerged companies. This extra debt creates a risk: that to pay it down, the acquirer will demand dividends from the utility, leaving it less able to fund its operations and infrastructure, and less able to pay down its own debts. These facts can discourage lenders from lending to the utility, or raise the cost of loans they do make.[7]

Other changes in financial circumstances: In a stock-for-stock exchange, there is no acquisition debt because no money changes hands. But the transaction still affects capital structure, in two ways. First, because the merging families will have different capital structures (a near certainty), the merged company's consolidated capital structure will differ from its two predecessors'; so each utility subsidiary will face new financial circumstances. Second, most stock-for-stock exchanges still involve a control premium; usually the target shareholders receive stock worth more than the stock they give up.[8] This implicit premium, paid by the acquirer, dilutes the value of the acquirer's existing shares. The acquirer's shareholders presumably expect their situation to improve; otherwise they would have voted against the transaction. But if this

---

consumers of electricity"); Wis. Stat. § 196.795(5)(g) ("No holding company system may be operated in any way which materially impairs the credit, ability to acquire capital on reasonable terms or ability to provide safe, reasonable, reliable and adequate utility service of any public utility affiliate in the holding company system.").

[7] *See, e.g.*, Great Plains Energy-Kansas City Power & Light Merger, 2008 Mo. PSC LEXIS 693, at *244 ("Although a company's credit rating applies most directly to its access and cost of debt, companies with a lower credit quality also find fewer equity investors willing to risk their investment dollars on their stock. In both instances, debt and equity investors demand a higher cost or return on their investment dollars to compensate them for the higher credit risk. This increased cost of capital can translate directly into higher costs for customers."). *But see* Puget Sound Energy-Macquarie Merger, 2008 Wash. UTC LEXIS 1023. There the Washington State Commission approved an Australian company's acquisition of the local utility. The Commission held that although 20 percent of the acquisition cost would be financed through debt, ratepayers faced no harm for four reasons: (a) the resulting leverage would be less than prior transactions approved by the Commission; (b) the new acquisition debt would be held at the holding company level rather than at the utility level; (c) conditions will protect customers from bearing the risks attributable to the debt; and (d) in the near future the utility will have to incur new debt anyway. One Commissioner dissented.

[8] A prominent exception was the 2018 merger arranged by Great Plains Energy and Westar, after the Kansas Commission in 2017 rejected their first proposal. The first involved a control premium financed in part by acquisition debt; the second was a stock-for-stock exchange with no premium and no debt.

dilution makes future investors less confident in the merged company's value, future financing will become less accessible or more expensive.

Solutions: Commissions need merger requirements that limit acquisition debt and equity dilution to prudent levels; specifically, no more than necessary to complete a transaction that has the best possible benefit-cost ratio for consumers. An example of a standard was section 10(b) of the repealed Public Utility Holding Company Act 1935, requiring that acquisition-related securities (1) bear a "fair relation to the sums invested in or the earning capacity of" the property acquired, and (2) not "unduly complicate the capital structure of the holding-company system."[9] Also, the merged company's consolidated capital structure should produce no pressure on the utility subsidiaries to pay dividends exceeding ordinary levels, or render the holding company unable to support the utility subsidiaries' capital needs at reasonable cost.[10]

This type of financial oversight does not duplicate SEC review of securities issuances. Utility regulation focuses on how financing decisions affect the cost and quality of utility service; the purpose is to protect the utility customer from imprudent transactions. SEC regulation focuses on the accuracy and timing of disclosures about securities; the purpose is to protect the shareholder from inaccurate information about a business's value.

12.2.2   Conditions on the Merged Entity's Actions

Besides the regulatory conditions on the transaction's terms, commissions should establish conditions on the merged entity's actions. The five categories described here aim to maximize positives and minimize negatives. Establishing them in advance disciplines the purchase price, while discouraging companies whose post-acquisition strategies conflict with the commission's priorities. These conditions echo the technical solutions to harms as presented in Part II's four chapters.

Post-consummation rates: Under conventional just-and-reasonable rate-making, rates must reflect the projected cost of service. The post-merger rates therefore should reflect all merger savings as they occur, net of the cost to achieve them. Costs incurred to produce savings over a multi-year period should be amortized over that period. Equity purchased with debt should earn a return reflecting the cost of that debt. To align rates with costs, the commission will need either to set new rates before merger consummation, or declare

---

    [9]   Public Utility Holding Company Act of 1935 § 10(b), 15 U.S.C. § 79j(b) (repealed 2005).

    [10]   *See, e.g.*, CAL. PUB. UTIL. CODE § 854(c)(1) (requiring the Commission to consider whether the merger will "[m]aintain or improve the financial condition of the resulting public utility").

rates "interim subject to refund" as of the date of merger consummation, then start a rate case to determine the actual cost of service for the acquired utility's first year.

Corporate structure and governance: The utility's budgets must be controlled by its professional management, free of holding company constraints. To verify the holding company's non-interference, the commission should (a) require the utility to submit its proposed budgets to the commission and to the holding company simultaneously, and (b) require the holding company's executives to submit sworn affirmations of non-interference. The holding company also must provide to the utility whatever financing the utility needs to carry out the activities budgeted.[11] For a separate level of protection, the commission should require the holding company's board to have at least one independent director with the special power and obligation to veto any holding company decision that conflicts with the utility's interests.

Financial protections: To protect the acquired utility from the holding company's other businesses, the utility must have the most advanced form of ring-fencing.[12] Necessary elements include limiting holding company's borrowings to avoid impairing the utility's own access to debt and equity capital, and prohibiting the holding company from financing its non-utility businesses with excess dividends extracted from the utility. Some statutes already empower commissions to require those protections—by (1) identify-

---

[11] *See, e.g.*, this condition imposed by the Oregon Commission on the MidAmerican-PacifiCorp merger:

> PacifiCorp and MEHC [MidAmerican Energy Holding Company] will ensure that senior management personnel located in Oregon continue to have authority to make decisions on behalf of PacifiCorp pertaining to (1) local Oregon retail customer service issues related to tariff interpretation, line extensions, service additions, DSM [Demand-Side Management] program implementation and (2) customer service matters related to adequate investment in and maintenance of the Oregon sub-transmission and distribution network and outage response. Such decisions will be subject to normal and prompt corporate approval procedures, senior executive approval and board approval, as appropriate.

MidAmerican Energy-PacifiCorp Merger, 2006 Ore. PUC LEXIS 74, at *89.

[12] Chapter 7.4.8.2 described ring-fencing and assessed its strengths and weaknesses. For an advanced version available as of the time of this book's publication, see Appendix A.3, which excerpts ¶¶ 61–107 of the D.C. Commission's March 2016 Order approving the Exelon-PHI transaction.

ing the types of securities issuances triggering commission review;[13] and (2) specifying permissible uses of the proceeds.[14]

Future acquisitions and expansions into other markets: The holding company's future acquisitions must comply with limits set by the commission.[15]

Inter-affiliate transactions: The holding company system must comply with all inter-affiliate transaction rules.[16]

12.2.3   Constitutional Limits on State-level Conditions

The Constitution's Commerce Clause grants Congress the power "to regulate commerce with foreign nations, and among the several states, and with the Indian tribes."[17] Courts have applied the Clause to limit state regulatory actions that affect interstate commerce. These court-imposed limits take two forms:

*   *Discrimination against interstate commerce—prohibited:* When regulating business activity, states may not practice "economic protectionism—that is, regulatory measures designed to benefit in-state economic interests by burdening out-of-state competitors."[18]
*   *Burdens on interstate commerce—permitted, subject to limits:* All economic regulation affects commerce. If a regulation treats in-state actors and out-of-state actors similarly, the burden is not discriminatory. But the burden must not be "clearly excessive in relation to the putative local benefits."[19]

Those two statements only scratch the surface of the law; a longer summary is beyond this book's scope.[20] But a challenge to three provisions in Wisconsin's

---

[13]   *See, e.g.*, ARIZ. REV. STAT. § 40-301 (requiring advance commission approval of any utility issuance of stocks and stock certificates, bonds, notes and other evidence of indebtedness with terms of more than one year).

[14]   *See, e.g.*, 220 ILL. COMP. STAT. 5 / 6-102(a) (requiring that the "money, property or labor to be procured or paid for by such issue [be] reasonably required for the purpose or purposes specified in the order"); MD. CODE ANN., PUB. UTIL. § 6-101 (requiring securities issuance to be "consistent with the public convenience and necessity").

[15]   A detailed discussion of those limits and their justification appears in Chapter 7.4.8.3.

[16]   Those rules and their justification were detailed in Chapter 6.5.5.

[17]   U.S. CONST. art I, § 8, cl. 3.

[18]   Wyoming v. Oklahoma, 502 U.S. 437, 454 (1992).

[19]   Pike v. Bruce Church, Inc., 397 U.S. 137, 142 (1970).

[20]   For an overview, see SCOTT HEMPLING, REGULATING PUBLIC UTILITY PERFORMANCE: THE LAW OF MARKET STRUCTURE, PRICING AND JURISDICTION, ch. 12.B.1 (American Bar Association 2013) and the many sources cited there.

holding company statute provides one appellate court's insights on how the Commerce Clause applies to utility mergers.[21]

State ban on out-of-state utility companies—upheld as non-discriminatory: Only a company incorporated in Wisconsin may hold a license to "own operate, manage or control" assets used for utility service in Wisconsin.[22] Utilities serving in Wisconsin challenged this provision as discriminating against interstate commerce. The Seventh Circuit disagreed: "The provision of public utilities that are generated, distributed, and consumed in Wisconsin is an inherently local and intrastate business." Applying the Commerce Clause's balancing test announced in *Pike v. Bruce Church*,[23] the Court assumed "that a local incorporation requirement has a minimal burden on *inter*state commerce and serves a legitimate and important state interest in regulating *intra*state commerce."[24]

State ban on out-of-state holding companies—invalidated as discriminatory: Another provision required that a holding company owning a Wisconsin public utility be incorporated under Wisconsin law.[25] Invalidating this provision, the court saw a "fundamental distinction" between the business activities of a public utility and those of a holding company: "The provision of public utilities within Wisconsin is intrastate commerce. An investment opportunity in a Wisconsin utility is, on the other hand, an article of interstate commerce." Put another way, the business of a utility holding company is to own stock in a utility: "If ownership of a Wisconsin utility company must lie with a Wisconsin Corporation, a potential article of interstate commerce, i.e., the investment in the utility, is stopped at the border." And if every State adopted Wisconsin's rule, "there would be no interstate investment in public utilities at all. No holding company parent could own public utility companies in more than one State." A state can prohibit all holding companies, but once it allows them it cannot prohibit their interstate ownership. Prior courts had applied the same rule to garbage: "States may choose not to zone land for dumping, but once the land is opened up for trash it must be opened up for all refuse, no matter where it originates."[26]

---

[21] *See* Alliant Energy Co. v. Bie, 330 F.3d 904 (7th Cir. 2003). The author was an expert witness for the State of Wisconsin in the litigation before the U.S. District Court that led to the Seventh Circuit opinion.

[22] WIS. STAT. § 196.53.

[23] 397 U.S. 137 (1970).

[24] *Alliant Energy*, 330 F.3d at 915 (citing Eli Lilly & Co. v. Sav-On-Drugs, Inc., 366 U.S. 276, 279 (1961); Union Brokerage Co. v. Jensen, 322 U.S. 202, 211 (1944)).

[25] WIS. STAT. § 196.795(5)(L).

[26] *Alliant Energy*, 330 F.3d at 912, 914 (footnote omitted) (citing Lewis v. BT Inv. Managers, Inc., 447 U.S. 27 (1980) (holding that Florida statute prohibiting out-of-state banks, trusts and bank holding companies from providing investment advisory services

State regulation of holding company structure and finance—upheld as not excessively burdensome: Wisconsin utilities challenged three provisions regulating the holding company's financial transactions and business activities:

- Section 196.795(3) required Commission review before a person could acquire 10 percent or more of a utility holding company's outstanding stock.
- Section 196.795(6m)(b) limited the amount that a utility holding company could invest in non-utility businesses.
- Sections 196.795(5)(a) and (7)(a), 201.01(2) and 201.03(1) authorized the commission to regulate a utility's securities issuances.[27]

The Court upheld all three. Unlike the in-state incorporation requirement for holding companies, none of these provisions discriminated against out-of-state activities. The holding company acquisition provision applied to acquirers wherever located or incorporated; the asset cap applied to assets wherever located; and the securities regulation provisions applied whether the securities entered interstate commerce or remained in Wisconsin. The three provisions did affect interstate commerce, but extraterritorial effect does not automatically invalidate a facially neutral statute. To determine the constitutionality of non-discriminatory burdens, courts balance the interstate commerce effects against the in-state benefits. While Wisconsin's provisions had "no small impact" on interstate commerce, the regulation of public utilities was "one of the most important of the functions traditionally associated with the police power of the States." The more complicated the corporate structure, the stronger the justification for state regulation:

> This [state] interest is served well by the structural provisions because they help to prevent such abuses as cross-subsidization and deceptive reporting of cost allocation. ... The more products a firm is responsible for, the easier it is for the firm to misreport the allocation of its costs. This danger can be tempered by limiting the public utility holding company's involvement with and ownership of businesses and assets unrelated to providing the public utility [service].[28]

---

within the state violated Commerce Clause); Or. Waste Systems, Inc. v. Dep't of Envtl. Quality, 511 U.S. 93 (1994); and City of Philadelphia v. New Jersey, 437 U.S. 617 (1978)).

  [27] Wis. Stat. §§ 196.795(3), (6m)(b), (5)(a), (7)(a); 201.01(2), 201.03(1).

  [28] *Alliant Energy*, 330 F.3d at 916–17 (quoting Ark. Elec. Coop. Corp. v. Ark. Pub. Serv. Comm'n, 461 U.S. 375, 377 (1983)) (citing S. Union Co. v. Mo. Pub. Serv. Comm'n, 289 F.3d 503, 507–508 (8th Cir. 2002) (upholding against Commerce Clause challenge Missouri's requirement that the state commission approve a utility's purchase of another utility; the court reasoned that "[a] public utility's investments in other com-

12.3 CREATE FILING REQUIREMENTS THAT FORCE COMPARISONS BETWEEN THE PROPOSED MERGER AND THE COMMISSION'S VISION

12.3.1 Purpose: Get the Full Story Upfront

Recall from Chapter 11.3.1: System 1 is instinctive, System 2 is effortful. Knowing the dangers of their System 1, regulators should create procedures that trigger their System 2. Filing requirements should extract, upfront, the full transaction story in all its complexity: Why is the acquirer buying control? Why is the target selling control? How did the parties arrive at the acquisition price? If the acquirer gets control, what actions will it take, internally and externally? What changes will it make in governance, operations, capital expenditures and financing? What are the probabilities of what types of harm? What is the off-ramp if there is harm? Is this coupling the best way to provide the services customers need and want?

By lacking filing requirements that force out the full story, commissions free the applicants to tell their story. Their story is a simple one, designed for System 1: the merger is a natural step in a natural industry evolution; the transaction was smoothly negotiated, at arm's-length, between two companies motivated to help consumers. It will bring customers economies of scale, best practices and a $100 refund for all customers; charitable contributions for the community; no immediate layoffs of the workers. This story feeds System 1, embeds positive impressions, leaves System 2 dormant. Over the next several months, maybe the rest of the story trickles out, the key facts scattered over data responses, intervenors' answering testimony and transcript pages. The full story never forms a full picture in the regulator's mind.

The filing requirements proposed here avoid this suboptimal result because they produce the full complexity upfront. The answers to these detailed questions should come in the form of pre-filed testimony, submitted by the executives directly responsible for the matters addressed by the questions— rather than in the form of scattered discovery responses written by lawyers and back-room strategists.

One more reason to require the detail upfront: intervenors need the full story before the statutory clock starts running. Before filing their application, applicants will have gathered all the information they need. When they file, the statutory clock starts. Understanding the transaction then takes intervenors many weeks of discovery, limiting the time they have to prepare their testimony. If

---

panies can affect its regulated rate of return, if investment losses are allocated to the regulated business")).

instead the application contains the full story, the scarce resource of time is allocated more fairly. An added benefit: intervenors will need less discovery time, allowing the commission to complete the case sooner.

Commissions should supplement these requirements with guidelines that discipline the pre-filed testimony. No applicant witness should make claims she cannot document and support; there should be no puffery, self-praise, non-substantive adjectives or other non-factual phrasings aimed at swaying emotions; no aspirations not backed by commitments. Intervenors' testimony should not include requests for benefits unrelated to the merger, because unrelated benefits have no relevance to the commission's statute-constrained assessment.

These filing requirements also require the applicants to disclose all material risks to their utilities' customers. This disclosure obligation, and the legal consequences for misstatements or omissions, should resemble what companies and executives face when discussing investor risks in official securities filings.[29] Without this obligation to disclose, merger applicants will not likely provide information that undermines their interests.[30]

12.3.2   Filing Requirements: Ten Categories

While these filing requirements seem extensive, they seek nothing more than the information that typically emerges in merger proceedings. But they extract the information upfront, so that the commission understands the full transaction from the beginning. Not every question will be relevant to every transaction. Some will require reshaping to fit a specific transaction. Submitters should accompany written answers with all relevant internal documents.

12.3.2.1 Transaction purposes and goals
i.   Identity, in order of importance, all the reasons (a) why the acquirer wants to acquire control of or merge with the target; and (b) why the target wants

---

[29]   *See* 17 C.F.R. § 229.105 (requiring securities registrant to discuss "the most significant factors that make an investment in the registrant or offering speculative or risky"); 17 C.F.R. § 229.303 (requiring registrant to discuss "events or uncertainties that will result in or that are reasonably likely to result in the registrant's liquidity increasing or decreasing in any material way"). For any material deficiency, the registrant must "indicate the course of action that the registrant has taken or proposes to take to remedy the deficiency." *Id.*

[30]   JOHN E. KWOKA, JR. & LAWRENCE J. WHITE, AM. ANTITRUST INST., PUBLIC COMMENT: AAI CRITICIZES SURFACE TRANSPORTATION BOARD'S RAILROAD MERGER GUIDELINES (2000) (arguing that a regulatory methodology which allows merging parties "to offer information and remedies that are against their own interest" is "fundamentally flawed and will not result in the protection of consumers [or] competition").

to sell control (or merge). Include all reasons discussed with the board, advisors, rating agencies, shareholders, bondholders and others.

ii. To what extent is the target's decision to sell influenced by current interest rates?

iii. To what extent is this transaction a reaction to other mergers? Which ones? What features of these other transactions influenced the decision to do this transaction?

iv. Is the dominant purpose of this transaction to improve service for the customer? If the answer is yes, what is the evidence to support the answer?

v.   Five and ten years from now: By what criteria will you judge this transaction a success or failure? By what criteria should the commission judge this transaction a success or failure?

12.3.2.2 Transaction form and terms

i.   Provide the full narrative of the negotiation process. At a minimum, include all details stated in any proxy statement filed with the Securities and Exchange Commission. For each stage of the negotiation process, provide the documents that the participants in the negotiations, including the corporate boards, reviewed.

ii. [For a cash buyout] Why did you fashion this transaction as a cash buyout rather than a stock-for-stock exchange?

iii. [For a stock-for-stock merger with a cash component] What were the reasons for the specific mix of cash and stock?

iv. Describe all criteria and calculations each party used to determine that the final price was acceptable.

v.   In determining the acquisition price, what facts did each party assume about the target utility's exclusive franchise? The answer should consider, but not be confined to, these questions: (a) For what number of years did each party assume that the target utility would retain its franchise? (b) For each of those years, what level of earnings did each party assume the utility would have? (c) What future rate-basing opportunities did each party assume the utility would have? (d) What penetration into the utility's exclusive service territory, from direct retail competition or distributed energy resources, did each party assume?

vi. What objections will the merged company have if, within five years of consummation, the commission or the legislature decides that (a) one or more activities then performed by the target utility should be performed by one or more entities chosen competitively (where the target utility can compete for the role); or (b) the exclusive franchise itself should be offered to others on a competitive basis (again, where the target utility can compete for the role)?

vii. Assume the commission intends to include in any transaction approval
a condition stating that if the merged company violates a merger condition,
commission rule or state statute, the commission will start a proceeding to
determinate appropriate consequences, including possible transfer of the
utility's franchise to a more deserving provider. (a) State your acceptance
of this condition; or (b) state that if the commission requires this condition
the applicants will withdraw their application. (c) Provide the language
for the most consumer-protective divestiture-disaffiliation condition that
would not cause the applicants to withdraw the transaction.

12.3.2.3 Transaction costs and transition costs

i.   Describe all transaction costs: explain who paid what to whom, for what
services.
ii. Describe all transition costs, at the full level of detail presently available,
by category and by year. For each category of expenditure, explain the
purpose, and identify the individuals and the associated executives responsible for achieving that purpose.

12.3.2.4 Capital structure

i.   Provide all rating agency reports relating to the transaction.[31]
ii. Provide all rating agency reports, for both merging companies and their
affiliates, for the prior five years.
iii. Describe the current capital structure of each of the merging systems, and
of each utility within each merging system.
iv. Describe the capital structure of the post-merger consolidated system, and
of each utility in that system.

12.3.2.5 Acquisition cost

i.   What is the total cost to the acquirer for control (not counting transaction
cost and transition cost)? Describe each component: cash, stock and taking
on the target's debt.
ii. Describe all types, sources and terms of the acquisition financing for this
transaction.
iii. What percentage of the purchase cost is attributable to the value the
acquirer sees in controlling the target utility's exclusive franchise?

---

[31]   Intervenors routinely request this type of information in discovery. After weeks
of opposition, debate and negotiation, sometimes involving motions to compel and
commissioner-level decisions, the applicants usually produce the documents. There is
no reason to repeat this time-wasting dance, merger after merger. Commissions should
require the information with the application.

iv. What is the acquirer's expected return on the full acquisition cost? What are the specific net revenue flows that the acquirer projects will produce that expected return?

v. The target utility's retail rates earn an authorized return on only book cost. The acquirer's acquisition cost exceeds that book cost. Given those facts, how will the acquirer make up the difference between what the utility can earn on book cost and what the acquirer expects to earn on its full acquisition cost? To what extent is the acquirer relying on the following factors to recover its acquisition costs: (a) regulatory lag, (b) earning an equity-level return on target equity financed with debt, and (c) other factors?

12.3.2.6 Risks of harm

i. For each affiliate having a book value exceeding [some minimum level defined by the commission], describe (a) the business activities; and (b) the material risks, including but not limited to all material risks you have disclosed to stockholders.

ii. For each listed risk, describe the specific events that would convert the risk into harm to the utility or its customers. State the probability that each event would occur, and the range of harms it would cause. For each risk, describe the actions you are committing to take to reduce the risk and to reduce the probability and severity of harm.[32]

12.3.2.7 Benefits

i. Of the benefits applicants are offering: (a) Which would be achievable without the merger? (b) Provide all reasons why the target is not achieving those benefits now. (c) Explain why you are offering as benefits from the merger, benefits that are achievable without the merger.

ii. (a) Precisely what operational practices or other changes are you intending to bring or make, when and for what reasons? (b) At the target company, who is responsible for those areas now? (c) Why is the target not carrying out those practices or changes now? (d) If the Commission today ordered the target company to carry out the changes now, without a merger, would the changes occur? If not, why not?

iii. To produce the claimed benefits, what specific actions will the merged company take, on what specific schedule? Provide a month-by-month and

---

[32] *Comment:* This question prevents merger applicants' common attack that concerns about harm are speculative. All predictions involve uncertainty. If an asserted harm is an impossibility, i.e., has a probability of zero, then the applicants should say so and the commission should ignore the assertion of harm. But every harm with a probability above minimal is real. Requiring information on probability and severity moves the commission from System 1 (passively dismissing) to System 2 (calculating and planning).

year-by-year plan. Identify the specific individuals who will be responsible for these actions, along with the compensation and career consequences if they produce or fail to produce the claimed benefits.

iv. At what point in the process of considering and fashioning this transaction did you study cost savings and management improvements? Who performed the studies? Identify all instructions or guidance provided to the individuals responsible for performing the studies.

v. Re prior mergers to which either applicant was a party: (a) List, and provide references for, all claims and commitments that you made about benefits. (b) Which individuals made or supported each claim? (c) For each claim, which individuals were responsible for producing the results? (d) For each claim, what were the results?

12.3.2.8 Corporate structure and governance

i. Provide an annotated diagram of (a) the pre-acquisition corporate structures associated with each company, and (b) the merged entity's corporate structure.

ii. Describe fully the board of directors of the holding company and of the target utility. The description should include, but not be limited to, leadership, structure, committees, biographies, compensation and terms. Which directors are independent? Precisely what does "independent" mean?

iii. Within the holding company structure, who will have what powers over which utility decisions? Identify all decisions affecting the utility that will be under the ultimate control of one or more individuals outside the utility.

iv. Who will make decisions about dividend payments from the utility? Based on what considerations?

v. Who will make decisions about injecting equity into the utility? Based on what considerations?

vi. Indicate your commitment to this proposition: if the holding company ever has insufficient financial resources to cover the needs of the to-be-acquired utility as well as the holding company's other affiliates, the utility's needs will have priority.

vii. Describe all existing inter-affiliate contractual relationships, in terms of goods and services, pricing and other terms.

viii. For each of the merging companies, describe all existing internal rules on compliance with regulations, and internal consequences for non-compliance.

ix. Describe existing ring-fencing measures.

x. Describe fully all utility assets and employees used for non-utility purposes, including the reasons for and terms of the use.

xi. Describe fully all non-utility assets and employees used for utility purposes, including the reasons for and terms of the use.

12.3.2.9 Competitive advantages
i. Identify each market (identifying product dimension and geographic dimension) in which any affiliate of the merged entity will be selling services in competition with others.
ii. For each market identified, explain what competitive advantages the affiliate will have due to its affiliation with the target utility.

12.3.2.10 Merger history
i. Identify all mergers and acquisitions in the last ten years to which each merging entity was a party.
ii. For each listed merger, provide all evidence showing that the transaction made consumers better off compared to what would have happened had there been no merger. In answering this question, take into account the possibility that the merging companies would have improved their performance without the merger.

12.4   ORGANIZE EVIDENTIARY HEARINGS AROUND ISSUES RATHER THAN PARTIES

12.4.1   The Objective Staff Report

On receiving a merger application, commission staff should prepare a public, objective analysis—not a for-or-against position paper, but rather a full analysis of the transaction's benefits, costs and risks. This analysis would also list unanswered questions (fewer than normal, due to the expanded information produced by the new filing requirements). The commission then would require the parties to address those questions in their testimony.

This step has several benefits:

* It triggers System 2, causing the commission to adopt an alert, objective, active role.
* It creates an objective, complex, public-interest frame, to replace the applicants' subjective, over-simplifying, self-serving frame. It puts the focus on merger policy rather than merger strategy.
* It teaches the transaction to intervenors who are unfamiliar with merger issues.
* It saves everyone time and money by reducing the number of duplicative discovery requests coming from multiple intervenors.

One problem: This step will consume at least a month of the statutory time period, leaving less time for the other steps. The obvious solution is for the legislature to extend the statutory period. Or the applicants could submit their application informally to the staff first. Then once the staff has completed its analysis, the application and the staff analysis can be made public simultaneously. This step reduces to near-zero the risk that anyone's System 1 will be lulled into accepting a one-sided story.

12.4.2   The Evidentiary Hearing[33]

In adjudicative proceedings, including merger proceedings, commissions typically organize the evidentiary hearings around parties. The parties' lawyers cross-examine witnesses on their pre-filed testimonies: party by party, witness by witness. After all the parties' questioning, the commissioners will ask a few questions, though extensive commissioner questioning is infrequent.

This approach elevates parties over issues. And because the applicants' witnesses always appear first, they have a new opportunity (after their application and pre-filed testimony) to get their simplified frame into the commissioners' System 1. Detailed discussion of a specific issue—say, acquisition debt—will be scattered over disparate witnesses on disparate days. Few people can remember on Day 5 what an opposing witness said about the subject on Day 1. Opposing witnesses never confront each other; and those witnesses whose opponents fear cross-examining them usually go unquestioned by opponents or the tribunal—party strategy precluding tribunal curiosity. An attorney's fear of an opposing witness has nothing to do with the tribunal's duty to learn from experts and probe their thinking.

The better approach: organize evidentiary hearings around issues rather than parties. The commission can divide the hearing days into issue segments, sequenced logically: transaction formation, transaction execution, post-consummation corporate structure and governance, harms, benefits. For each issue segment, all parties' witnesses who address that issue would appear on a panel simultaneously ("hot-tubbing," the Australian regulators call it). Instead of watching opposing parties poke at each other's private strategies, the tribunal would question the experts on issues affecting the public interest. Once the tribunal completes its questioning, the opposing parties' lawyers would get their chance—taking much less time than normal because the tribunal had asked the necessary questions. A variation on the panel approach is to have opposing witnesses testify in pairs, back to back.[34] Either of these approaches increases the proceeding's value-per-minute ratio, because (1) the

---

[33]   This subsection is adapted, with permission, from my article *Litigation Adversaries and Public Interest Partners: Practice Principles for New Regulatory Lawyers*, 36 ENERGY L.J. 1 (2015), http://www.felj.org/sites/default/files/docs/elj361/14-1-Hempling-Final-4.27.pdf.

[34]   RICHARD A. POSNER, REFLECTIONS ON JUDGING 311 (2013) (discussing juries' difficulties dealing with complex issues).

witnesses debate their positions with each other, forcing them to sharpen their reasoning; (2) the full discussion of each issue will occur on the same day and on the same transcript pages; and (3) the questions will more likely reflect the commission's public interest priorities rather than the parties' strategic goals.

The Hawaii Commission used the panel approach in a diverse set of proceedings—on renewable portfolio standards, energy efficiency programs, competitive bidding, distributed generation, feed-in-tariffs, decoupling, renewable energy surcharges and other initiatives aimed at reducing the state's dependence on fossil fuels. Carlito Caliboso, the Commission's Chair during that period, has praised the format for helping to expose differences earlier, with more clarity, than the more typical format. Because that exposure occurred not through adversarial cross-examination but through Commission-led questioning, it was easier to test solutions and discover commonalities.[35]

Daniel Kahneman also recommends a *pre-mortem*. Applied to merger proceedings it would go like this: after closing the record but before completing its deliberations, the commission gathers a small group of staff who are knowledgeable about mergers, have reviewed the transaction, but are not involved in the decision. The commission asks them to imagine that a year after consummation, the transaction is a disaster; then write a brief history of the disaster. This practice, Kahneman says, overcomes groupthink and "unleashes the imagination of knowledgeable individuals in a much-needed direction."[36]

12.4.3 Applicant Opportunities to Amend

To reduce intervenor opposition, merger applicants often revise their proposals mid-proceeding, adding customer benefits and accepting risk-reducing conditions. Commissions allow these revisions. Some commissions even invite the practice: they issue a post-hearing order rejecting the application but identifying the "adds" that would gain the transaction's approval. Tolerating revisions, rather than holding applicants to their original proposals, has at least two adverse effects.

First, it creates in applicants an incentive to hold back benefits from their original application, because if no intervenor is sufficiently prepared or resourced to demand benefits, the applicants won't have to provide them. If prospective acquirers were competing based on benefits, not knowing what their competitors will be offering, and having only one shot, each competitor

---

[35] Email correspondence between Carlito Caliboso and author (Oct. 2014) (on file with author). The author participated in these proceedings as the Commission's moderator.

[36] KAHNEMAN, *supra* note 4, at 265 (crediting Gary Klein).

would offer the maximum benefit it could afford—the amount just above which their expected return would drop below their hurdle rate. To replicate that result in the monopoly context, the commission needs to hold the applicant to its original proposal. That way, the applicant worried about rejection will make that maximum benefit offer, instead of holding back in hopes of giving less.

Second, the improvements offered in the revised proposal would likely be ones the applicants had already researched and designed before submitting the original application. But the intervenors and commission will have to squeeze their review of the revised proposal into the deadline-constrained, heavy-workloaded adjudicative process. To examine the revised proposal, intervenors often have to call back their out-of-town experts, at additional cost to already constrained budgets. Because the statutory clock is ticking, the time available for discovery into these amendments is limited, worsening the existing asymmetry of resources between applicants and intervenors.

Prohibiting applicant-initiated revisions prevents this gamesmanship. It does not preclude the commission itself from requiring revisions. And it signals to future merger aspirants that transactions must meet the competitive standard.[37]

12.5   ISSUE MERGER OPINIONS THAT DISTINGUISH THE SUBOPTIMAL FROM THE OPTIMAL

Most merger opinions are organized around, and give most of their space to, private interests. The opinions describe what the applicants ask for, what the intervenors criticize, what the intervenors want and which benefits the applicants offer to which intervenors. This format reflects the decisional reality: a commission reacting to a private interest proposal rather than leading a public interest effort. Merger opinions would more likely guide future transactions toward the public interest if they were organized around the public interest: by (1) first describing the commission's vision for goods and services, market structure, corporate structure and governance structure; the must-have

---

[37] *Cf.* Thomas L. Greaney, *Hospital Mergers, in* Competition Policy and Merger Analysis in Deregulated and Newly Competitive Industries 126, 141 (Peter C. Carstensen & Susan Beth Farmer eds., 2008) (criticizing settlements reached by state attorneys general in hospital mergers for "accepting price concessions as well as commitments to offer specified amounts of charity care or other community benefits in return for permitting the merger to go forward"—thereby "substitut[ing] a crude form of rate regulation for competition"); Steven C. Salop, *Merger Settlement and Enforcement Policy for Optimal Deterrence and Maximum Welfare*, 81 Fordham L. Rev. 2647, 2662 (2013) (reasoning that "[a]gency settlement policy must treat deterrence [of anticompetitive transactions] as a central goal").

and must-not-have criteria; and the elements of a cost-effective transaction; and then (2) showing how the proposal fares against those elements. A merger rejection organized this way will save commission resources by deterring future transactions that don't meet its standards. And a commission will be more likely to organize its merger opinions around public-interest standards if it has established those standards to begin with.

* * *

Merger policy can improve if commissions adjust their posture and their practices. They can establish screens—must-have and must-not-haves—that cause merging parties to pursue the commission's priorities. They can establish conditions, on the transaction terms and on the merged entity's actions, that make those priorities binding. They can create filing requirements that elicit the facts that matter, rather than the stories applicants want to tell. They can organize adjudicative proceedings around their priorities, rather than around the parties and their private goals. Each of these steps puts System 2 in control. They bring to merger decision-making the active, analytical, muscular mindset that these complex transactions require.

13. Regulatory infrastructure: strengthen regulatory resources, clarify statutory powers, assess prior mergers' effects

Parts I and II of this book described merger transactions—their structures, their promoters' motivations, and their risk of harm. Throughout those first seven chapters we presented solutions to the policy problems presented. Part III identified problems in regulatory decision-making—unreadiness, reactivity and the passion gap—along with twelve mental biases that cause errors, in humans' everyday life and in regulators' merger decision-making.

This Part III has turned to regulatory institutions. Chapter 12 focused on regulatory posture and practice—offering solutions to the problems of unreadiness, reactivity, passion differential and mental bias. Chapter 13 now looks at regulatory infrastructure. Commission resources are overmatched, their statutory powers insufficiently clear. And though nearly eighty mergers have happened, no one has objectively studied their effects. Addressing each of these gaps will help prepare regulators to create and carry out policies that align private merger strategies with the public interest.

13.1   STRENGTHEN REGULATORY RESOURCES

Mergers demand every type of regulatory expertise: financial analysis of merged company capital structure, engineering analysis of power supply integration, economic analysis of the projected rate paths, competition analysis of the post-merger market structure, accounting analysis of the pre- and post-merger cost structures, managerial analysis of post-merger operations, corporate analysis of the post-merger governance structure, legal analysis of the commitments and their enforceability. Commissions must apply that expertise to the post-merger complexity—multiple service territories, business risks, financing sources, and profit centers. Corporate complexity makes regulatory oversight—the prevention, detection and correction of activities that conflict with the public interest—more time-consuming, more resource-intensive and less certain to succeed.

Regulation's open secret: utilities have more regulatory resources than commissions do. At evidentiary hearings, the typical utility has a separate witness for each of five to ten major issue areas, each witness supported by a boiler room of reviewers and number crunchers. Behind each utility executive is a bench of up-and-comers, groomed by the company to take over when their superiors retire. Legal representation is usually handled by outside counsel with decades of experience, themselves backed by a platoon of researchers and pleading-drafters. Contrast commissions: most commissioners enter office with no utility regulatory experience; few stay longer than five years. Commission staffing practices lag behind the industry's complexity: staff sizes, job classifications, and salary structures reflect a prior era when regulatory life centered around rate cases and financial audits, rather than climate change, environmental mandates, renewable energy requirements, terrorism protection, new forms of financing and hedging, and the corporate complexity resulting from three decades of mergers. Then there's demographics. Staff veterans hired in the 1970s and 1980s, in the eras of Middle East oil boycotts and nuclear cost overruns, are retiring and taking their expertise with them, because state commissions can't afford the developmental benches that utilities have.

The causes of this resource differential, and its effects on regulatory quality, are beyond this book's scope.[1] But to make merger policy effective, we must diminish the differential. The smart solution: state statutes should authorize commissions to establish fees on regulated companies, sufficient to evaluate merger applications but also to monitor post-merger conduct and performance.

13.2 CLARIFY STATUTORY POWERS: CAN COMMISSIONS ORDER MERGERS?

Chapter 4 explained that an acquisition emerging from non-competitive conditions, with the target utility seeking the highest price rather than the best performer, wastes economic resources. It deprives customers of the performance they deserve. Yet commissions approve these transactions routinely, as if the proposed merger were the only available merger. Can commissions break this habit? Can they require or induce mergers that help customers,

---

[1] For a partial explanation and some solutions, see Scott Hempling, *Regulatory Resources: Does the Differential Make a Difference? (Parts I and II)* (Sept. 2008), http://www.scotthemplinglaw.com/regresources1, http://www.scotthemplinglaw.com/regresources2; and Scott Hempling, *"Regulatory Capture": Sources and Solutions*, 1 EMORY CORP. GOVERNANCE & ACCOUNTABILITY REV. 23 (2014), http://law.emory.edu/ecgar/content/volume-1/issue-1/essays/regulatory-capture.html.

rather than accept mergers sought by investors?[2] This section describes three possible paths. These three paths have two prerequisites. The first prerequisite is a commission-established policy, as described in Chapters 8.1 and 12, that describes the services customers need, the company types suitable for satisfying those needs and the market structures most likely to attract those companies. (These three paths apply only to state commission orders. Any merger ordered or induced by a state would still likely require approval by the FERC.) The second prerequisite is statutory authority.

13.2.1   Path 1: Commission Orders Two In-State Utilities to Merge

If two utilities serve solely in one state, that state's commission could order them to merge. (Given the large number of multi-state mergers, this option will be infrequent.) Possible reasons: economies of scale, financial strengthening, a desire to equalize rate structures across the state, a wish to reduce the number of rate cases, or a view that one company's culture could improve service at the other utility. Weighed against those possible benefits would be these negatives: the loss of head-to-head competition in wholesale or retail sales, the loss of across-the fence rivalry,[3] and the loss of industry diversity.

13.2.2   Path 2: Commission Sets Rates for Two In-State Utilities as if They Had Merged

What if two in-state utilities could lower their costs by merging—but one or both resists? Can the commission penalize the resistor by lowering its rates?

In a 1984 order, the Maine Commission tried. Previously it had declared imprudent 47.3 percent of Maine Public Service Company's (MPS's) invest-

---

[2]   As one competition scholar has written:

Given their industry expertise and assuming a commitment to developing workably competitive markets, the [regulatory] agencies would be far better positioned than conventional antitrust enforcers to identify the classes of combinations that would assist the transition [to competition]. ... However, in actuality, the agencies have not engaged in this kind of transition management, but instead, have largely reacted to proposals initiated by the firms in the industries and generally permitted almost all combinations. The unfortunate result is that planning has not occurred, market structures have become more concentrated than necessary for efficiency and long-run competition may be undermined.

Peter C. Carstensen, *Reflections on Mergers and Competition in Formerly Regulated Industries, in* COMPETITION POLICY AND MERGER ANALYSIS IN DEREGULATED AND NEWLY COMPETITIVE INDUSTRIES 225, 235 (Peter C. Carstensen & Susan Beth Farmer eds., 2008).

[3]   For discussion of those types of competition, see Chapter 6.4.1.5.

ment in the Seabrook nuclear plant. Wanting MPS to stay solvent while the company sought buyers for its Seabrook share, the Commission set rates higher than cost-of-service principles would normally dictate—allowing MPS to recover its prudent Seabrook portion over 56 months rather than the more typical 360 months. The Commission also started an inquiry into whether customers would benefit from MPS merging with one or more other Maine utilities, or otherwise reorganizing.

Meanwhile in an unrelated case, Central Maine Power (CMP) had committed to the Commission to pursue an acquisition of MPS. Examining that possibility, the Commission found that a CMP-MPS merger would reduce MPS's retail rates by 9.2 percent. Based on that finding, the Commission warned MPS that if its management didn't pursue that merger, the Commission would "give serious consideration" to reducing its rates:

> Action by management that rejects a cheaper source of power—whether a generation source, a purchase, a cost-saving measure or a change in corporate form—is presumptively unreasonable and/or imprudent.
> It is not up to Maine Public Service's management to determine whether a particular merger offer is in the best interests of the offeror or the offeror's other customers any more than MPS would make such a determination regarding an offer from a power or equipment supplier. If a proposed transaction is likely to provide the best alternative for MPS's customers (especially as in this case where the shareholders are also benefitted), MPS management has an obligation to pursue it. A failure to fulfill this duty may be the basis for an adjustment to rates commensurate with the economic loss to ratepayers.[4]

When Maine Public Service challenged the Commission's order, the state's highest court reversed:

> When considered in context, the decision constitutes an order requiring MPS to pursue a specific merger with a party who is under an order to pursue the acquisition of MPS. ...
> Once having characterized the decision as an order to pursue a merger, the merits present little difficulty. The Commission does not contend that it has such authority. ... [T]he Commission may not use its rate setting authority to attach conditions to the rates it sets, if it could not have attached those conditions in reliance on statutory authority distinct from its rate setting authority.[5]

---

[4] Maine Pub. Serv. Co. v. Pub. Utils. Comm'n, 524 A.2d 1222, 1225 (Me. 1987) (emphases omitted) (quoting Commission decision in *Maine Public Service Co.*, 75 P.U.R.4th 295 (Me. Pub. Utils. Comm'n May 15, 1986)).

[5] *Id.* at 1225–26 (citing New England Tel. & Tel. Co. v. Pub. Utils. Comm'n, 362 A.2d 741, 754 (Me. 1976)).

The Court reasoned that because the Commission had no statutory authority to order a merger, it could not hold a utility financially responsible for not pursuing a merger.

The Court's reasoning lacks logic. A commission can condition a rate increase on the utility's agreeing to take specific prudent actions (such as retiring a poorly functioning generating unit). And if the utility fails to take those prudent actions, the commission can set rates as if it did. That the commission might lack the authority to order prudent actions does not remove its obligation to set rates that reflect those prudent actions.[6] A utility that imprudently hired High-Cost Contractor H instead of Low-Cost Contractor L faces a disallowance for the cost difference, regardless of whether the commission had authority to tell the utility whom to hire.

13.2.3   Path 3: Commission Orders a Competition to Find the Best Coupling

The prior two paths involved utilities in the same state. What if a commission wants its utility to seek an acquirer from out of state? The commission would identify shortcomings in the utility's current performance, describe the types of acquirers that could improve the performance, and prescribe any must-haves and must-not-haves on the transaction terms (as detailed in Chapter 12.1.2). The commission would also establish whatever post-merger rate treatment and service expectations prospective acquirers would need to know about. With this guidance in place, the commission could comfortably leave the search and initial selection to the local utility, subject to the commission's approval.

If the utility resisted the acquisition idea, the commission could conduct the acquisition competition itself, directly or through an independent entity. Governments regularly use competitive bidding to buy services. There is no reason not to use competitive bidding for utility franchises. Comparison-through-competition, with the commission doing the comparing based on its specific goals, would make the merger market work for the

---

[6]   *See, e.g.,* Rochester Gas & Elec. Corp. v. Pub. Serv. Comm'n, 754 F.2d 99, 101-06 (2d Cir. 1985) (upholding a commission decision imputing the value of unsold surplus capacity to a utility's annual revenue requirements; even though the commission could not directly compel wholesale sales, it could "take into account activities it cannot regulate [i.e., wholesale sales] in setting rates for activities that it may regulate [i.e., retail sales]"). For additional discussion of this imputation solution to utility inaction, see Scott Hempling, Regulating Public Utility Performance: The Law of Market Structure, Pricing and Jurisdiction 243–46 (American Bar Association 2013).

customers—unlike the present practice of prospective acquirers competing to please the target utility's shareholders rather than its customers.

An obvious question arises: assuming the commission has the statutory authority to compel the acquisition (see the paragraphs that follow), does the commission's action violate the Constitution by taking private property—the utility's or its shareholders'—without just compensation? The Takings Clause protects legitimate, investment-based expectations.[7] A utility's shareholders have no legitimate expectation that an exclusive franchise, once granted, can never be revoked or revised. But they will have legitimate expectations about the procedures, conditions and compensation accompanying revocation. Those expectations will depend on the circumstances surrounding the state's original grant, as well as subsequent regulatory actions. To play it safe, legislatures should expressly revise franchises, or direct commissions to revise them, to reflect the possibility of the commission requiring an acquisition of the incumbent, based on public interest findings and accompanied by appropriate shareholder compensation.

* * *

To avoid unnecessary litigation, state legislatures should grant their commissions the explicit statutory authority to pursue the three merger paths just discussed. But even under existing statutory language state commissions have three arguments.

First, if the commission can grant and revoke a franchise, it can condition the franchise on the utility taking all prudent actions to operate it cost-effectively. Whether the required action is building a power plant, buying power from third parties, investing in energy efficiency or finding the best merger partner, the commission's authority should be the same. The purpose of utility regulation is to align utility actions with the public interest—to induce the right actions and penalize the wrong actions. There is no logical reason for a merger exception. Second, to deny a commission this merger-inducing power is to treat service territory control asymmetrically: change in control would be permitted only when the utility wants it; not when the public interest requires it. Third, where the commission has the authority to determine a utility's service territory boundaries, it has the authority to change those boundaries. Ordering two

---

[7] *See* Penn Cent. Transp. Co. v. New York City, 438 U.S. 104, 124 (1978) (holding that in Takings Clause cases, courts must consider the "economic impact of the regulation on the claimant and, particularly, the extent to which the regulation has interfered with distinct investment-backed expectations"). Chapter 5.4 discussed the application of the Takings Clause to regulatory treatment of the control premium.

in-state utilities to merge is an order to change the boundaries. A utility cannot negate a commission's boundary-changing authority by refusing to merge.

13.3   ORGANIZE A MULTI-JURISDICTIONAL EVALUATION OF PRIOR MERGERS' EFFECTS

No state has studied the long-term effects of the mergers it has approved. Neither has FERC. In none of its nearly eighty approval orders over these three decades, and in none of its five policy issuances,[8] has FERC assessed the industry's consolidation and complication.[9] No one knows if the nation is better off.[10]

The regulatory profession has a rich history of professional conversation on diverse issues—return on equity, rate design, renewable energy penetration, electric vehicles, fuel diversity, integrated resource planning, nuclear safety and cybersecurity. But not merger policy. The last serious, public study of utility mergers was over eighty years ago, when the Federal Trade Commission produced its massive report on concentration and complication, leading to the enactment of Public Utility Holding Company Act of 1935.[11] No similar commitment to study these subjects exists today.

---

[8]   In 1996, 2000, 2005, 2006 and 2007.

[9]   *See* Mark J. Niefer, *Explaining the Divide Between DOJ and FERC on Electric Power Merger Policy*, 33 ENERGY L.J. 505, 534 (2012) ("Although there have been some retrospective studies of the effect of mergers on consumers, there are [few], if any, explicitly addressing the net effect of electric power mergers on consumers."). The problem is not limited to electricity mergers:

> What has remained largely unchanged throughout these decades ... has been the relative dearth of detailed evaluations of the effects of mergers and of the effectiveness of merger policy. ... [O]ur understanding of mergers is based on fragmentary evidence, and we know even less about the effectiveness of policy. [This absence of understanding] has left observers with wide latitude to argue for more stringent or less stringent policy based on weak evidence and strong beliefs.

JOHN KWOKA, MERGERS, MERGER CONTROL, AND REMEDIES: A RETROSPECTIVE ANALYSIS OF U.S. POLICY, at ix–x (2015).

[10]   *Compare, e.g.*, Markian M.W. Melnyk & William S. Lamb, *PUHCA's Gone: What Is Next for Holding Companies?*, 27 ENERGY L.J. 1, 2 (2006) (asserting that PUHCA repeal "is a positive change that should lead to a more vibrant and resilient industry and better service at a lower cost"), *with* Niefer, *supra* note 9, at 532 (urging that FERC gain a "deeper understanding of the connection between market structure, firm behavior, and competitive effects").

[11]   *See* Public Utility Holding Company Act of 1935 §1 (b), 15 U.S.C. § 79a(b) (repealed 2005) (citing "reports of the Federal Trade Commission made pursuant to S. Res. 83 (Seventieth Congress, first session), the reports of the Committee on Interstate and Foreign Commerce [Committee on Energy and Commerce], House of

To fill this knowledge gap, commissions should create a multi-jurisdictional task force to open a multi-disciplinary inquiry. The task force would have a five-part mission: (a) define the types of performance that consumers need; (b) describe the types of utility conduct that will produce that performance; (c) identify the types of corporate structures and market structures likely to produce the desired conduct; (d) assess whether the last three decades of merger approvals have produced the performance that customers need; and (e) create alternative merger policies that replicate the competitive discipline necessary to produce the envisioned structure, conduct and performance. The key metrics? "[P]roduct price, quality, choice, costs and technological progressiveness, all of which directly affect consumer welfare."[12] The task force would organize technical conferences aimed at collecting real data and insights; it would emphasize experts' perspectives over advocates' positions. Among the specific research questions:

- What conclusions can we draw about prior mergers' effects on structure, conduct and performance? This question can address both a single individual merger's effect on the merging companies, as well as the trend's cumulative effects on the industry, regionally and nationally.
- What have been the effects on capital and operating expenditures, and on reliability? Do these transactions truly exploit economies of scale, scope, integration and diversity? Or have those economies already been exhausted at the non-merged firm size? Does the answer depend on region, company size, asset mix or other factors?
- Is there any factual basis to "bigger is better"? Better in what ways, and for whom? What information and insights can we gather about economies of scale and scope for each aspect of the business, from distribution system planning to major capital expenditure financing?
- What are the consequences, short-term and long-term, of financing acquisitions of equity with debt? Does the increased leveraging in the industry have a danger point, in terms of the risk of financial failure or decline in investor confidence?
- At what point in the merger trend is the next merger one merger too many, either because of how it affects existing and future competition or because the small number of large remaining entities makes each one "too big to fail"? How might we adjust current merger policy so we do not reach that point? Should merging companies be required to create a counterpart to

---

Representatives, made pursuant to H. Res. 59 (Seventy-second Congress, first session) and H. J. Res. 572 (Seventy-second Congress, second session)").

[12]   Kwoka, *supra* note 9, at 1.

the "living will" currently required of systemic banks by the Dodd-Frank legislation?[13]

- To what extent do mergers give the merged entities competitive advantages that are unearned; that is, not attributable to their merits?
- To what extent does each target's focus on highest purchase price rather than best performer discourage prospective acquirers who cannot compete on merger price but could bring the industry more efficiencies and innovation than could more traditional acquirers?
- How might regulators update traditional competition analysis, which focuses on generation market shares and transmission control, so that we consider other products, like transmission construction, demand response, retail sales, storage and distributed generation?
- What are the precise regulatory standards and metrics that will replicate the discipline of effective competition, so that the dominant motive behind each merger is serving customers more efficiently—rather than maintaining or growing current market presence (for the acquirer) or maximizing gain (for the target's shareholders)?[14]
- What revisions to merger statutes are necessary to clarify that the "public interest" requires outcomes consistent with what effective competition would produce?
- Merger statutes usually require commission action within a specified period after the application arrives. But complexity, discovery disputes and resource constraints cause time squeezes that make deliberation difficult. Since some kind of time requirement is necessary, what solutions would satisfy the competing values of procedural efficiency and investigative sufficiency? Would a better approach be for the commission to establish the deadline once it received the application and assessed its complexity in light of its resources?

Announcing a comprehensive inquiry could trigger a rush of merger applications seeking approval before the standards change. Rushed applications are even less likely than prior ones to align with this book's public interest rec-

---

[13] *See* Dodd-Frank Wall Street Reform and Consumer Protection Act § 165(d), 12 U.S.C. § 5365(d) (requiring certain bank holding companies and nonbank financial companies to have "resolution plans"). *See also Living Wills (or Resolution Plans)*, Fed. Reserve Bank, https://www.federalreserve.gov/supervisionreg/resolution-plans .htm (last updated Dec. 17, 2019).

[14] For additional study questions relating to wholesale competition, see Niefer, *supra* note 9, at 532–33 (recommending that the FERC or Department of Justice study their merger review procedures).

ommendations. Under these circumstances, it is worth considering a statutory pause in approvals until we understand these transactions better.

* * *

Active merger regulation requires a solid regulatory infrastructure. State legislatures should clarify commission powers to (a) order mergers where feasible and performance-enhancing, (b) set rates reflecting the cost savings from prudent mergers when companies imprudently fail to merge, and (c) order utilities to use public interest criteria when inviting and choosing acquisition proposals. Commissions, facing retirements of their 1970s- and 80s-era veterans, need to rebuild their staffs with the financial, engineering, economic and corporate governance expertise necessary to develop the policies that attract the right transactions and discourage the wrong ones. Finally, after nearly eighty mergers involving almost all fifty states, regulators should join in a multi-jurisdictional, multi-disciplinary study that asks the question we should have addressed before this three-decade trend started, the question that has motivated this book: What market structures, corporate structures and business combinations will bring us an electric industry that serves the public most cost-effectively?

The U.S. electric industry: a tutorial

This Tutorial introduces industry newcomers to electricity's physical functions, market structures, power transactions, pricing, and company types. It also covers merger terminology, forms of merger transactions and merger jurisdiction at the national and state levels. This Tutorial does not substitute for a full education on any of the included topics.

1. **Physical functions: How is electricity produced and delivered?**
2. **Market structures: monopoly markets and competitive markets**
   - 2.1 Markets and market structures
   - 2.2 Converting monopoly structures into competitive structures
   - 2.3 Electricity market structures
3. **Transactions: Who sells what to whom?**
4. **Pricing: What do customers pay?**
   - 4.1 Cost-based rates
     - 4.1.1 Rate-setting arithmetic
     - 4.1.2 Rate-setting procedure
   - 4.2 Market-based rates
5. **Company types: ownership forms and corporate forms**
6. **Merger basics: terminology and transaction forms**
   - 6.1 General terminology
   - 6.2 Transaction types—by type of value exchanged
   - 6.3 Transaction types—by market structure effects
   - 6.4 Private equity buyouts
7. **Merger jurisdiction: Which commissions regulate which transactions, based on what standards?**
   - 7.1 Jurisdiction in general
   - 7.2 Jurisdiction over mergers
     - 7.2.1 State statutory triggers
       - 7.2.1.1 Transactional level
       - 7.2.1.2 Acquirer or target
       - 7.2.1.3 Control or influence
       - 7.2.1.4 General commission authority
     - 7.2.2 Federal statutory triggers

1. PHYSICAL FUNCTIONS: HOW IS ELECTRICITY PRODUCED AND DELIVERED?

Producing and delivering electricity involves assets and activities in these major categories:

- *Generating units* convert energy—from fossil, nuclear, renewable, hydro-electric or other sources—into electric current.
- *Transmission facilities*—wires and towers—form a network of circuits that carry the electric current over long distances, from the generating units to distribution substations located near load centers.
- *Distribution facilities*—wires and poles—form local networks that deliver the electric current to individual customers.
- *Substations and transformers:* Between generation units and transmission networks, and between transmission networks and distribution networks, are substations and transformers. They transform the electric current's voltage up (from the generator to the transmission network) and down (from the transmission network to the distribution network, and from the distribution network to individual homes and businesses) so that it can travel reliably and safely.
- *Retail aggregation and sales* involves forecasting customers' total needs (called "load" or "demand"), then developing or acquiring sufficient generation, transmission and distribution resources to meet those needs reliably. Retail aggregation and sales also involves managing the retailer-customer relationship: installing, reading and maintaining meters; billing customers; and processing payments.

2. MARKET STRUCTURES: MONOPOLY MARKETS AND COMPETITIVE MARKETS

2.1 Markets and Market Structures

A market is a place where, or a medium by which, sellers and buyers exchange goods or services for value. Every market has a product dimension—the product which a customer seeks; and a geographic dimension—the area within which a customer shops for that product. Examples of markets are vegetarian lunches in downtown Baltimore, and firm wholesale electric energy in New England. A market can also have a time element, when time is essential to the consumer: restaurants serving Sunday brunch, intra-city rail service after extra-inning baseball, gas pipeline transportation on winter weekdays.

With its product and geographic dimensions defined, every market has a structure. That structure consists of these elements: (a) the identities, locations, sizes and market shares of its sellers and buyers; (b) the differentiation among the products that sellers sell; (c) the extent to which any buyer or seller controls assets or inputs essential for entry into that market; and (d) the ease of entry into and exit from the market.

Market structures range in their competitiveness. The main points on that range, in descending order of competitiveness, are pure competition (sometimes called perfect competition), effective competition (sometimes called workable competition), monopolistic competition, oligopolistic competition, monopoly-in-fact (with or without realistic threats of entry) and legal monopoly (where the law prohibits competition, such as when a state grants an exclusive franchise, or when the U.S. Patent Office grants a patent).

For more detail on markets and market structures, see Chapters 6.1, 6.2 and 6.3.

2.2   Converting Monopoly Structures into Competitive Structures

In regulated industries, conscientious policymakers—legislatures and regulatory commissions—design and shape market structures to improve industry performance. They aim for "the best possible mix of inevitably imperfect regulation and inevitably imperfect competition."[1] Applying that principle to historically monopolistic industries like electricity, policymakers take six steps.

1. Determine which services should be provided by a monopoly and which should be provided by a competitive market: Policymakers start by identifying which services are natural monopoly services. A service is a natural monopoly service if its cost function (the relationship of production cost to quantity produced) declines over the market's entire demand. Customers' costs are minimized if a natural monopoly service is provided by a monopoly company. Today, most observers view the following electricity services as natural monopoly services:

- Transmission
- Distribution
- Control area operation[2]

---

[1]   1 ALFRED KAHN, THE ECONOMICS OF REGULATION: PRINCIPLES AND INSTITUTIONS, at xxxvii (MIT Press 1970, 1988).

[2]   Just as each airport has a single air traffic controller, each electricity service territory has a single balancing authority (formerly called a control area operator). Why? A stable electricity network must have, at every point in time, equal amounts of loads and resources—consumption and production. To ensure that equality within a given territory, a balancing authority schedules, controls and monitors the injection of electric current into, and the export of electric current from, the transmission and distribution networks that serve that territory.

Meanwhile, most observers view the following services as not having natural monopoly characteristics:

- Generating capacity
- Electric current
- Metering and billing
- Storage
- Demand aggregation
- Microgrid service
- Electric vehicle charging
- Energy efficiency
- Energy auditing

Because these services lack natural monopoly characteristics, policymakers in many U.S. states have allowed non-utility entities to offer them as competitive services.

2. Unbundle competitive services from monopoly services: To unbundle services is to make them available for sale separately. In electricity, the utility monopoly historically provided all the electricity services. Unbundling means allowing customers to buy the monopoly service from the utility but the competitive services from someone else. Unbundling involves three steps:

- **Product unbundling:** This step separates the services legally, so that customers gain the right to buy the competitive services from non-utility companies while buying the monopoly service from the traditional utility.
- **Cost unbundling:** This step uses accounting techniques to separate monopoly costs from competitive costs. Doing so ensures that the price charged by the utility for the monopoly service does not recover any costs associated with the utility's competitive services.
- **Corporate or functional separation:** This step modifies the utility's corporate organization, separating its monopoly functions from its competitive functions. Doing so reduces its ability to gain an unearned competitive advantage by using its monopoly employees and resources to provide its competitive services.[3]

3. Determine which company or companies should provide which monopoly services: Most states give the monopoly services role automatically to the incumbent utility. But it is also possible to host a competition for the right to provide monopoly services.

---

[3] For detail on unbundling, see Chapter 6.5.4.

4. Determine the licensing requirements for providers of competitive services: In medicine, law and other professions, states protect customers from poor performance by establishing licensing requirements. In electricity competition, licensing ensures that sellers have the necessary experience and resources.

5. Address entry barriers that might allow the incumbent utility to exclude, or gain unearned advantage over, new competitors: For electricity, the most prominent examples are transmission and distribution facilities. Usually owned by the incumbent utility, these facilities are essential to competition but not economically duplicable by the utility's competitors. So if the utility denies its competitors access to these facilities there can be no electricity competition. Other possible entry barriers include the incumbent's long-term contracts with large customers (preventing new entrants from competing for these customers until the contracts end); and customer inertia—a customer's tendency to stay with the incumbent utility even when more favorable options emerge.[4]

6. Address the incumbent utility's unrecovered costs: In the pre-competition era, the incumbent utility made capital expenditures to carry out its franchise obligation to serve. The utility typically recovers these costs from its customers over a thirty- or forty-year period. When the policymaker introduces competition—which normally happens midway through that period—the competitive market prices might be lower than the prices the utility needs to charge to recover the still-unrecovered costs. Because these past costs were legitimate customer-service costs, policymakers design ways for the customers to pay them off.

2.3   Electricity Market Structures

The U.S. electric industry has had, and has today, a range of market structures.

Until the 1980s: Most retail and wholesale customers of investor-owned utilities bought their electricity from a local utility monopoly. The utility was vertically integrated: it owned the generation, transmission and distribution facilities necessary to produce electricity and deliver it to its customers. The typical utility had seven key features:

- **Exclusive franchise:** The utility had an exclusive franchise, granted by state law, to provide electricity to retail customers within a defined geographic area.

---

[4]   For more detail on entry barriers, see Chapter 6.3.3.

- **Obligation to serve:** The utility had an obligation to serve—including an obligation to plan to serve, all retail customers within that area, without undue discrimination.
- **Consent to regulation:** By agreeing to provide electric service, the utility consented to all reasonable forms of regulation.
- **Quality of service:** The utility had to comply with quality of service standards established by state law or regulation.
- **Eminent domain:** Most utilities received from the state the power of eminent domain—the legal power to take private property (paying the property owner just compensation), when that property is necessary to carry out their obligation to serve.
- **Limits on negligence liability:** In most states the utility was insulated from lawsuits for ordinary negligence, but not gross negligence.
- **Just and reasonable rates:** The utility had a statutory right to charge rates, set by the regulator, that are just and reasonable and not unduly discriminatory. By statute and constitutional law, these rates had to provide shareholders a reasonable opportunity to earn a fair return on capital expenditures that were prudently incurred and used and useful to the customers.[5]

Many of these utilities also had wholesale customers, such as municipal government utilities and rural cooperatives. These wholesale customers would buy "bulk power" (generation and transmission) from the utilities, then handle physical distribution and customer relations themselves.

Until the 1980s, most of these utilities were known as "pure plays." They served only a single geographic area, and engaged only in the business of selling electricity at retail and wholesale. This relative simplicity derived from the Public Utility Holding Company Act of 1935 (PUHCA 1935). That Act confined each electric utility system to a single "integrated public-utility system." It also prohibited or limited a utility's investment in non-utility businesses, and prevented holding companies from owning or acquiring separate utilities that could not be operated efficiently together. The Act's 2005 repeal made possible many of the mergers and acquisitions addressed in this book.[6]

Beginning in the 1980s: State and national policymakers gradually introduced competition at various industry levels: wholesale electricity sales, retail sales and certain services that support the transmission network (known as

---

[5]   The first six features are detailed in Scott Hempling, Regulating Public Utility Performance: The Law of Market Structure, Pricing and Jurisdiction (American Bar Association 2013) at Chapter 2; the seventh feature is discussed there in Chapter 6.

[6]   For more detail on PUHCA 1935, see Chapters 4.2.2 and 8.2.

ancillary services). More recently, policymakers have introduced competition in demand aggregation, energy efficiency, transmission construction, storage, electric vehicle charging stations, and solar and wind energy production. A brief history follows.[7]

1978: Responding to the second Arab oil embargo of the 1970s, Congress sought to (a) reduce the demand for fossil fuels, and (b) overcome utilities' traditional "reluctan[ce] to purchase power from, and to sell power to, ... nontraditional facilities."[8] The result was the Public Utility Regulatory Policies Act of 1978 (PURPA).[9] PURPA modified the pre-existing vertically integrated, monopoly market structure by introducing wholesale sellers. Investors could form and acquire specialized generators, called "qualifying facilities" (QFs). To become a qualifying facility, a generator had to be either a "cogenerator" or a "small power producer."[10] PURPA granted each QF the right to compel its "host utility" (the utility in whose service territory the QF was located) to buy the QF's capacity and energy, at a price equal to the utility's "avoided cost"—the incremental cost the utility would have incurred, but for the QF, to procure the capacity and energy necessary to serve its load.[11] A QF was exempt from PUHCA 1935's integrated public-utility system requirement.[12]

1992: With the Energy Policy of 1992 (EPAct 1992), Congress aimed to inject competition into wholesale generation markets. One provision amended PUHCA 1935 to allow investors to create and acquire "exempt wholesale generators" (EWGs), without having to satisfy PUHCA 1935's integrated public-utility system test. This change allowed any type of company to enter wholesale generating markets anywhere, thus increasing the number and types of potential wholesale generation competitors. (Unlike a QF, an EWG could use any type of fuel; also unlike a QF, an EWG had no right to compel a pur-

---

[7] The following summary is excerpted from Chapter 3.A.1 of HEMPLING, *supra* note 5. American Bar Association, the copyright owner, requires this notice: "Reprinted with permission. All rights reserved. This information or any portion thereof may not be copied or disseminated in any form or by any means or stored in an electronic database or retrieval system without the express written consent of the American Bar Association." For a fine history of the industry, see CRAIG R. ROACH, SIMPLY ELECTRIFYING: THE TECHNOLOGY THAT TRANSFORMED THE WORLD, FROM BENJAMIN FRANKLIN TO ELON MUSK (2017).

[8] FERC v. Mississippi, 456 U.S. 742, 750 (1982).

[9] Public Utility Regulatory Policies Act of 1978, Pub. L. No. 95-617, 92 Stat. 3117.

[10] The terms "cogenerator" and "small power producer" are defined in 16 U.S.C. § 796(18)(A) and 18 C.F.R. § 292.203. A "cogenerator" uses fossil fuels efficiently by producing both heat and electricity; a "small power producer" produces specified types of renewable energy within specified size limits.

[11] 18 C.F.R. § 292.101(b)(6).

[12] 18 C.F.R. § 292.602(b).

chase by a retail utility.) Another EPAct 1992 provision authorized FERC, on complaint (but not on its own motion), to order transmission-owning utilities to provide transmission service to others on FERC-set terms. FERC later found that this 1992 transmission authority did little to encourage wholesale competition: few prospective customers filed complaints, and the complaint process was unwieldy.[13] This weakness in FERC's 1992 transmission authority led, in 1996, to Order No. 888.

1996: Recognizing that generation competitors need access to incumbents' monopoly transmission networks, FERC issued its landmark Order Nos. 888 and 889. Order No. 888 required each investor-owned, transmission-owning utility to sign and submit FERC-drafted tariffs committing the utility to provide transmission service to eligible customers. The tariffs must offer transmission customers access "on the same or comparable basis, and under the same or comparable terms and conditions, as the transmission provider's uses of its system." Eligible customers include (a) buyers and sellers of wholesale power, and (b) buyers and sellers of retail power within states that have authorized retail competition.[14] Order No. 889 required each utility to place its transmission functions and its generation functions in physically separate divisions, so that the generation functions could not receive favorable transmission treatment denied to non-utility generating companies.[15]

1996–2000: Nearly half the states investigated whether to introduce competition for retail electricity service into historically exclusive service territories. A subset of these states enacted statutes or issued rules to do so. States allowing retail electricity competition in some form today include California, Connecticut, Delaware, District of Columbia, Illinois, Maine, Maryland,

---

[13] *See* Order No. 888, *Promoting Wholesale Competition Through Open Access Non-discriminatory Transmission Services by Public Utilities; Recovery of Stranded Costs by Public Utilities and Transmitting Utilities*, F.E.R.C. STATS. & REGS. ¶ 31,036, 61 Fed. Reg. 21,540, text accompanying n.67 (1996) ("[T]he ability to spend time and resources litigating the rates, terms and conditions of transmission access is not equivalent to an enforceable voluntary offer to provide comparable service under known rates, terms and conditions.") (quoting *Hermiston Generating Co.*, 69 F.E.R.C. ¶ 61,035 (1994)), *order on reh'g*, Order No. 888-A, 78 F.E.R.C. ¶ 61,220, *order on reh'g*, Order No. 888-B, 81 F.E.R.C. ¶ 61,248 (1997), *order on reh'g*, Order No. 888-C, 82 F.E.R.C. ¶ 61,046 (1998), *aff'd in relevant part sub nom.* Transmission Access Policy Study Grp. v. FERC, 225 F.3d 667 (D.C. Cir. 2000), *aff'd sub nom.* New York v. FERC, 535 U.S. 1 (2002).

[14] Order No. 888, *supra* note 13, at text accompanying nn.72, 194, 284 & 289–290.

[15] Order No. 889, *Open Access Same-Time Information System (formerly Real-Time Information Networks) and Standards of Conduct*, 75 F.E.R.C. ¶ 61,078 (1996), *order on reh'g*, Order No. 889-A, 78 F.E.R.C. ¶ 61,221, *order on reh'g*, Order No. 889-B, 81 F.E.R.C. ¶ 61,253 (1997).

Massachusetts, Michigan, New Hampshire, New Jersey, New York, Ohio, Oregon, Pennsylvania, Rhode Island, Texas and Virginia.[16]

1999: FERC issued Order No. 2000, encouraging (but not requiring) transmission-owning utilities to form and join regional transmission organizations (RTOs).[17] An RTO receives from its member utilities the contractual authority and obligation to plan and control the utilities' transmission systems. That control makes the RTO the legal provider—a "public utility" under the Federal Power Act—of the transmission service over a large, multi-utility, multi-state region (except in the cases of California, New York and Texas, where the RTO operates only within the state). The RTO's transmission service must comply with Order No. 888. RTOs today provide transmission services in all parts of the U.S. except the Southwest, the non-California West and the Southeast. Besides planning and providing transmission services, most RTOs administer organized markets for electric energy; some also administer organized markets for capacity.

2005: Among the many provisions of the Energy Policy Act of 2005 was its repeal of the Public Utility Holding Company Act of 1935. With the integrated public-utility system test no longer in place, any type of entity, U.S. or non-U.S., can acquire any type of utility asset, perform any type of electric service function and compete in any location through any type of corporate form. Most post-PUHCA acquisitions are subject to certain reviews by FERC under section 203 of the Federal Power Act and under a vestige of PUHCA 1935 called the Public Utility Holding Company Act of 2005.

2008–2009: FERC required RTOs to allow providers of demand response to bid their products into the RTOs' organized energy markets, and to compensate them comparably to bidders of generation.[18] FERC has since expanded the

---

[16] *See* 21st Century Power P'ship, Nat'l Renewable Energy Lab, An Introduction to Retail Electricity Choice in the United States (2017), https://www.nrel.gov/docs/fy18osti/68993.pdf.

[17] Order No. 2000, *Regional Transmission Organizations*, F.E.R.C. Stats. & Regs. ¶ 31,089, 65 Fed. Reg. 809 (1999), *order on reh'g*, Order No. 2000-A, 90 F.E.R.C. ¶ 61,201 (2000), *aff'd sub nom.* Pub. Util. Dist. No. 1 v. FERC, 272 F.3d 607 (D.C. Cir. 2001).

[18] FERC defines demand response as "[c]hanges in electric usage by demand-side resources from their normal consumption patterns in response to changes in the price of electricity over time, or to incentive payments designed to induce lower electricity use at times of high wholesale market prices or when system reliability is jeopardized." *Reports on Demand Response & Advanced Metering*, Fed. Energy Regulatory Comm'n, https://www.ferc.gov/industries/electric/indus-act/demand-response/dem-res-adv-metering.asp (last updated Dec. 11, 2019). *See* Order No. 719, *Wholesale Competition in Regions with Organized Electric Markets*, 125 F.E.R.C. ¶ 61,071 (2008), *aff'd in part and modified in part on reh'g,* Order No. 719-A, 128 F.E.R.C. ¶ 61,059, *reh'g d denied,* Order No. 719-B, 129 F.E.R.C. ¶ 61,252 (2009); Order No.

types of services that providers can bid into RTO markets to include certain ancillary services, energy efficiency[19] and storage.[20]

2011: In Order No. 1000, FERC required each public utility transmission provider—inside and outside RTOs—to participate in a regional transmission planning process that produces a nondiscriminatory regional transmission plan. The planning process must consider all feasible "non-transmission alternatives" to conventional transmission facilities. Utility transmission providers also had to delete tariff provisions giving them a right of first refusal (ROFR) to build and own transmission facilities that serve a regional purpose. Eliminating the ROFR would allow non-incumbent developers to compete head-to-head with incumbent utilities in providing regional transmission solutions, except where states banned that competition.[21]

Today: States are introducing ways for non-traditional resources to substitute for conventional distribution facilities. These resources include storage, demand response, home-based solar energy, utility-scale solar and microgrids.[22]

These four decades of change, from 1978 to today, mean that within any state the following market structures could exist:

- **Retail electricity:** In all states, the franchised utility still provides the physical distribution service on a monopoly basis. In about eighteen states, retail marketers compete to sell retail electricity. In the remaining states, the franchised utility provides both the physical distribution service and the electricity itself on a monopoly basis. Some of those franchised utilities own the generation they use to serve their customers; other utilities buy the necessary generation service at wholesale.

- **Distributed energy resources:** In a limited but growing number of states, providers of distributed energy resources (local wind and solar, storage, demand aggregation, microgrids) compete to provide substitutes for new

---

745, *Demand Response Compensation in Organized Wholesale Energy Markets*, 134 F.E.R.C. ¶ 61,187, 76 Fed. Reg. 16,658, *order on reh'g*, Order No. 745-A, 137 F.E.R.C. ¶ 61,148 (2011), *vacated*, Elec. Power Supply Ass'n v. FERC, 753 F.3d 216 (D.C. Cir. 2014), *overruled by* 136 S. Ct. 760 (2016).

[19] *Advanced Energy Economy*, 161 F.E.R.C. ¶ 61,245 (2017), *order on reh'g*, 163 F.E.R.C. ¶ 61,030 (2018).

[20] Order No. 841, *Electric Storage Participation in Regions with Organized Wholesale Electric Markets*, 162 F.E.R.C. ¶ 61,127 (2018).

[21] *See* Order No. 1000, *Transmission Planning and Cost Allocation by Transmission Owning and Operating Public Utilities*, 136 F.E.R.C. ¶ 61,051 at PP 256–57, 76 Fed. Reg. 49,842 (2011), *order on reh'g*, Order No. 1000-A, 139 F.E.R.C. ¶ 61,132, *order on reh'g and clarification*, Order No. 1000-B, 141 F.E.R.C. ¶ 61,044 (2012). Order No. 1000 was upheld in *South Carolina Public Service Authority v. FERC*, 762 F.3d 41 (D.C. Cir. 2014).

[22] For more detail see Chapter 6.4.5.

distribution facilities that the incumbent franchised utility would otherwise build.

- **Transmission:** In the RTO regions, the RTO plans and operates the multi-utility, multi-state transmission system, providing transmission service to all who need it: wholesale generators, franchised utilities and retail marketers. In the non-RTO regions, transmission remains owned and operated mostly by traditional franchised utilities, although there are some examples of transmission-only companies (known as Transcos).

- **Wholesale generation:** In the RTO regions, owners of generation (including retail utilities and wholesale generation companies) sell their electric energy, and in some RTOs capacity also, into RTO-administered organized markets. Retail utilities and competitive marketers (together, called load-serving entities (LSEs)) buy their needs from those markets, reselling the electricity to their retail customers. Outside of RTO regions, wholesale transactions occur through bilateral contracts—transaction-specific arrangements between a single buyer and a single seller.

3.   TRANSACTIONS: WHO SELLS WHAT TO WHOM?

Sales of electricity occur at retail (to consumers) and at wholesale (to resellers).

Retail transactions: Retail residential customers buy firm electric service— the service available all 8760 hours of the year. Large industrial and commercial customers also buy firm electric service. If a large customer owns its own generating unit, it might also buy interruptible service, for periods when the seller's price is lower than the customer's variable cost of operating its unit. Under a typical interruptible contract, neither buyer nor seller has an obligation to buy or sell any particular amount. Interruptible electric service costs less than firm electric service because the seller has no obligation to maintain the capacity to produce it.

Wholesale transactions: To understand wholesale markets it is necessary first to understand capacity and energy. Capacity is the capability to produce electric current. Energy is the electric current. The cost of capacity is the cost of the generation infrastructure—the generating unit, associated equipment and the land under it. The cost of energy is the variable cost of operating the infrastructure to produce energy. The largest variable cost is the cost of fuel— the coal, gas, uranium or other energy source. Other variable costs include the employees necessary to put the fuel into the unit and control its operations.

Capacity and energy are twinned with two other concepts: load and consumption, respectively.

- **Load** refers to instantaneous demand—the demand for power at a given point in time. To avoid blackouts, there must be enough generating capacity to serve load on a hot August afternoon. Load is measured in kilowatts or megawatts.
- **Consumption** refers to the amount of energy consumed over a period of time. It is measured in kilowatthours or megawatthours. In a month, a typical home might consume 600–1000 kWh.

Wholesale sellers can be owners of generation; or they can be wholesale marketers that have purchased contractual rights to generation owned by others. Wholesale buyers are the load-serving entities—entities that have an obligation to serve retail customers; they buy wholesale power to meet their obligations. This LSE category includes traditional retail utilities; and, in retail competition states, independent retail marketers. Traditional utilities have a franchise obligation to serve, while retail marketers have a contractual obligation to serve.

Load-serving entities often buy capacity and energy separately. Since load-serving entities provide firm retail electricity—electricity available at all times—they must buy capacity—the right to call for energy at any time during the period covered by their obligation. Having contracted to buy enough capacity to meet their loads, wholesale buyers then buy energy to service the consumption needs of that customer load. They could buy the energy from the owner of the capacity they've purchased, or from others—such as through an RTO-organized energy market.

In wholesale markets, transmission providers sell transmission service separately from generating capacity and energy. In each RTO region, the transmission service provider is the RTO; in the non-RTO region, the transmission service providers are the owners of transmission facilities—incumbent utilities and Transcos. The buyers of transmission service are the load-serving entities: they need transmission service to move to their customers the electric current that they generate themselves or buy at wholesale.

4. PRICING: WHAT DO CUSTOMERS PAY?

In the electric industry, retail customers of state-franchised monopolies pay cost-based rates—rates set by state commissions based on the utility's costs. Wholesale customers in non-competitive markets also pay cost-based rates, set by FERC. Most wholesale customers, however, buy in competitive markets at rates set by market forces. These two pricing regimes—cost-based rates and market rates—are discussed here.[23]

4.1   Cost-based Rates

4.1.1   Rate-setting arithmetic

When a utility provides a monopoly service, its rates are set by a government regulator. Otherwise the utility would (a) overcharge, because its customers have no alternative suppliers; and (b) discriminate, because a monopoly can increase its earnings by varying its prices based on each customer's ability and willingness to pay. For these monopoly companies, regulators set prices sufficient to allow the utility a reasonable opportunity to (a) recover its prudent expenses and (b) earn a fair return on its prudent capital expenditures.[24] That standard performs two essential functions: it prevents the utility from abusing its customers; while keeping a prudently performing utility financially able to operate and to attract debt and equity financing at reasonable cost.

Regulatory commissions base rates on cost evidence submitted by the utility and other parties. The ratemaking process has three main steps:

Step 1: Establish the annual revenue requirement. The annual revenue requirement (ARR) is a projection of the total annual expenditures the utility needs to make to provide obligatory service for a specified upcoming year. Those annual expenditures fall into two main categories: expenses and cost of capital. Expenses include operations and maintenance costs, labor, fuel, taxes

---

[23]   A more detailed description of electricity pricing appears in HEMPLING, *supra* note 5, at Chapters 6 (cost-based rates) and 7 (market-based rates) and in the sources cited there.

[24]   In setting rates, regulators are bound by the statutory requirement that rates be "just and reasonable"; as well as by the Takings Clause and Due Process Clause in the Fifth and Fourteenth Amendments of the U.S. Constitution, respectively. The constitutional provisions prohibit the government from taking private property (such as the utility's investment in infrastructure) for public use (such as public utility service) without providing the utility just compensation. The standard constitutional analysis is this: when the utility incurs capital expenditures to carry out its obligation to serve, those expenditures represent a government "taking" of shareholder property. The government satisfies the "just compensation" requirement by setting rates sufficient to allow the utility a reasonable opportunity to earn a fair return on its prudent, used-and-useful investment. The most frequently cited sources for these propositions are Justice Brandeis's concurrence in *Missouri ex rel. Southwestern Bell Telephone Co. v. Public Service Commission*, 262 U.S. 276, 290 (1923); and the Supreme Court's majority decisions in *Bluefield Water Works & Improvement Co. v. Public Service Commission of West Virginia*, 262 U.S. 679 (1923); and *FPC v. Hope Natural Gas*, 320 U.S. 591, 602, 605 (1944).

and depreciation. Cost of capital consists of (a) interest payments to lenders and (b) return on equity (ROE) to shareholders. Here is the equation:

$$ARR = (O\&M + fuel + labor + taxes + depr) + [(interest\ rate \times debt) + (ROE \times equity)]$$

Or, more concisely:

$$ARR = expenses + return\ on\ rate\ base$$

where "rate base" is the original cost of all capital assets less accumulated depreciation (otherwise called net book value) and "return" is the weighted average of (a) the interest rates on all outstanding debt and (b) the commission-authorized return on equity, with those two terms weighted according to the role that debt and equity each plays in the utility's capital structure.

Step 2: Allocate costs among customer classes. A customer class is a group whose members have roughly homogeneous load patterns. Examples of distinct customer groups are residential, commercial, industrial and street lighting. The regulator allocates to each group an appropriate share of the revenue requirement's variable costs and fixed costs. *Variable costs* are costs that vary with the amount of electricity consumed—e.g., fuel costs. *Fixed costs* are costs that remain constant regardless of the amount of electricity consumed—e.g., the costs of distribution lines, transmission lines, generating units, substations, trucks, buildings and equipment. Fixed costs can then be subdivided into (i) costs directly attributable to particular customer groups or services (e.g., substations serving particular large customers), and (ii) common costs incurred for multiple purposes (e.g., shareholder relations, headquarters building, CEO's desk and salary).

To achieve economic efficiency and fairness, regulators *allocate costs to the cost-causers.* For variable costs, the process is straightforward: since these costs vary by the amount of kWh (energy) produced, regulators place these costs in the per-kWh rate. Fixed costs require more thought. Utilities build infrastructure to meet "peak demand": the simultaneous demand on a hot summer afternoon. Many commissions allocate fixed costs to the classes in proportion to each class's contribution to peak demand.

Step 3: Design rates. Once the regulator has set the revenue requirement, then allocated to each customer class its appropriate share of that revenue requirement, it is time to design the actual rates that individual customers within each class pay. (Within a class, all customers pay the same rates.) The goal is to cause the sum of all customers' rate payments to produce total revenues equal to the revenue requirement. So whereas cost allocation determines how many dollars to collect from each class, rate design determines how to collect each class's allocated share from the individual customers within that class.

Most customer classes pay both a fixed charge and a variable charge. The fixed charge (which varies by customer group) collects some portion of the fixed costs attributable to that group. It is calculated by dividing the fixed costs allocated to a group by the number of members in that group. The variable charge collects the variable costs allocated to the class, plus the portion of the class's fixed costs that were not included in the calculation of the fixed charge. The regulator calculates the variable charge by dividing those costs (the variable costs and the remaining fixed costs) by that class's projected volume of sales (kWh), to get a rate ($/kWh).

4.1.2   Rate-setting procedure

Ratemaking is prospective only: Once a commission sets the utility's rates, the rates are fixed until the commission sets new rates. This principle means that: (a) if the rates produce profits higher than what the commission authorized (because, for example, expenditures were lower than projected, or sales were higher than projected), the utility does not refund the excess to customers; and, conversely, (b) if the rates produce profits lower than authorized, the customers do not have to make up the difference. Bygones are bygones. The solution to overearnings or under-earnings is to change rates prospectively.

Because the utility need not refund profits exceeding the authorized level, it has an incentive to save on costs—and also to persuade the commission to set rates based on costs that are higher than the real costs. Every dollar the utility saves in a year, relative to the cost level used to set rates for that year, increases its profits in that year.

Exception for special costs: Because ratemaking is prospective only, and because rates are based in part on projected costs and projected sales,[25] the annual results will always vary from the projections. Those variances can cause financial uncertainty for the utility and its customers. To reduce that uncertainty, most commissions allow some costs to be fully recovered through some version of a "true-up" clause. The most prominent of these devices is the fuel adjustment clause, used by most utilities since the 1970s because fuel costs are unpredictable. The approved revenue requirement will reflect a projected fuel cost; then actual deviations from that base, above or below, are refunded or charged to customers monthly. More recently, some commissions

---

[25]   Only in part, because much of a utility's revenue requirement consists of costs that are known and unchangeable. Examples are its pre-existing capital expenditures (which must be recovered through a known annual depreciation expense), its existing fuel contracts and the interest rates on existing debt.

have added special adjustments by which customers pay for the actual costs of renewable energy infrastructure, storm restoration and pollution control expenditures.

A commission's rate decision does not require the utility to take any particular operational action: Suppose that when applying for rate increase, the utility projects that employee salaries will rise 10 percent. Suppose that the commission approves this projection as reasonable, and so includes that cost in the annual revenue requirement used to set the utility's rates. If the utility keeps the salary increase to 8 percent, the utility keeps the difference. Neither the company's projection, nor the Commission's decision, created any obligation to raise salaries by 10 percent. The same goes for any other expenditure, except in the unusual situation where the commission specifically mandates an expenditure.

4.2 Market-based Rates

The Federal Power Act requires wholesale electricity prices to be "just and reasonable." Applying this standard, FERC allows wholesale sellers to set their own rates, without any regulatory review of their costs, if the seller proves that it does not have "market power"—the ability to "profitably ... maintain prices above competitive levels for a significant period of time."[26] FERC and reviewing courts have held that "where neither buyer nor seller has significant market power, it is rational to assume that the terms of their voluntary exchange are reasonable, and specifically to infer that price is close to marginal cost, such that the seller makes only a normal return on its investment."[27] The industry calls these rates "market-based rates," to distinguish them from the "cost-based rates" just discussed.

---

[26] DEP'T OF JUSTICE & FED. TRADE COMM'N, HORIZONTAL MERGER GUIDELINES § 0.1 (1992, rev. 1997). The most recent Horizontal Merger Guidelines provide a broader definition: market power exists where a firm can "raise price, reduce output, diminish innovation, or otherwise harm customers" given "diminished competitive constraints or incentives." DEP'T OF JUSTICE & FED. TRADE COMM'N, HORIZONTAL MERGER GUIDELINES § 1 (2010) (revising 1997 guidelines). FERC defines seller "market power" similarly, as the ability to "significantly influence price in the market by withholding service and excluding competitors for a significant period of time." *Citizens Power & Light Corp.*, 48 F.E.R.C. ¶ 61,210, at p. 61,777 (1989). For a more detailed discussion of market power, see Chapters 6.3.1, 6.3.2, 6.4.1 and 6.4.2.

[27] Tejas Power Corp. v. FERC, 908 F.2d 998, 1004 (D.C. Cir. 1990). *See also* California *ex rel.* Lockyer v. FERC, 383 F.3d 1006 (9th Cir. 2004) (agreeing with *Tejas*).

5.   COMPANY TYPES: OWNERSHIP FORMS AND CORPORATE FORMS

In the U.S., utility ownership falls into three major categories. *Investor-owned utilities* serve the majority of U.S. customers. *Government-owned utilities* include those owned by the national government (e.g., Tennessee Valley Authority); state government (e.g., the South Carolina Public Service Authority, also known as Santee Cooper); or municipal government (e.g., Los Angeles, Tallahassee, and many small cities and towns). *Cooperative ownership* exists in rural areas, where "generation and transmission" cooperatives are owned by "distribution cooperatives," which in turn are owned by their members. This book focuses on mergers involving investor-owned utilities.

Investor-owned utilities use different corporate forms. Most are part of a holding company system—a pyramided structure consisting of a holding company and its subsidiaries. The top holding company's owners are the ultimate retail shareholders, such as mutual funds, pension funds, hedge funds and individuals. This holding company owns multiple subsidiaries, some of which can themselves be holding company owners of other subsidiaries. Each family member is an affiliate of each other family member, whether the relationship is parent-child, sibling-sibling, aunt-nephew or great grandparent-child. This book uses the terms "subsidiary" and "affiliate" generically. Regulatory statutes will define these terms more precisely, and not always consistently across jurisdictions. In most utility corporate families, the holding company owns 100 percent of each of its subsidiaries, but statutes often define a subsidiary as a company owned more than, say, 10 percent by another company. Ownership percentages aside, a subsidiary is a company owned by another company; affiliates are companies that have a common direct or indirect owner.

In most cases, a utility's holding company owner has stock that is publicly traded. A small number of utilities are owned by private equity, i.e., companies or partnerships whose stock is not publicly traded.

6.   MERGER BASICS: TERMINOLOGY AND TRANSACTION FORMS

Understanding a merger or acquisition starts by asking five questions:

- The merging entities: What are their true purposes?
- The transaction's terms: (a) Are the parties exchanging cash for stock, or stock for stock? (b) What is the control premium, if any? (c) If the exchange is cash for stock, what are the cash sources—retained earnings, new debt, new stock or proceeds from the sale of assets?

- In terms of the businesses being combined, what is the transaction type—horizontal, vertical, horizontal-and-vertical, convergence, product extension or conglomerate?[28]
- Will the post-merger company's stock be traded publicly or privately?
- After the transaction, who will control or influence the utility's decisions?

These questions allow the analyst to identify the policy issues that emerge—in particular, whether and how the merging parties' aims and plans coincide with or conflict with the public interest.

6.1   General Terminology

Practitioners use the terms "merger," "acquisition," "consolidation," "combination" and "change in control" interchangeably. Common to these terms is this fact: the transaction referred to causes two utilities, previously not owned and controlled in common, to be owned and controlled in common. Like practitioners, this book also uses the terms interchangeably, distinguishing by type when relevant. When referring to the transacting parties, practitioners use these terms:

- *Utility* is shorthand for the company that has an exclusive retail franchise granted by state law.
- *Acquirer* is the entity that is buying the utility.
- *Target* is the utility that is being acquired.
- *Applicants* are the entities that are asking regulators to approve their transaction—the acquirer and target, or the two merging companies.

In nearly all the transactions discussed in this book, the acquisition of the target's stock involves 100 percent of the target's stock; while a merger involves one company's shareholders exchanging 100 percent of their stock for stock in the merged company.

6.2   Transaction Types—by Type of Value Exchanged

Two companies can combine using one of three main transactional forms. Each form can produce similar outcomes. That is, in each form the target corporation remains or disappears; while the target's shareholders either remain as stockholders in the acquirer, or take cash and depart.

Merger: Target's assets and liabilities pass to Acquirer; Target disappears. A merger can be either cash-for-stock or stock-for-stock. In a cash-for-stock

---

[28]   These terms are defined and illustrated in this Tutorial at § 6.3.

merger, Acquirer pays cash to Target's shareholders, who depart. In a stock-for-stock merger (also known as a "pooling of interests"), Acquirer issues new Acquirer stock to Target's shareholders in return for their Target shares. At closing, Target's stock is retired. Acquirer remains, its stock now owned by the original shareholders of both Acquirer and Target.[29]

Purchase of shares: Acquirer buys Target's shares, so Target retains its identity as a distinct corporation, becoming a subsidiary of the acquirer. Whether the purchase is done with cash or stock determines the universe of post-acquisition shareholders. If Acquirer pays with cash, Target's shareholders depart with their money; their Target shares are retired. If Acquirer pays for Target's stock with its own shares, then Target's shareholders join Acquirer's shareholders as Acquirer's owners.

Purchase of assets: Acquirer buys some or all of the Target's assets. Acquirer either absorbs the assets into its own corporation, or places them in a new or an existing subsidiary. If the Acquirer pays for the assets with stock, Target's shareholders join Acquirer's shareholders as shareholders of Acquirer; their target stock is retired. If Acquirer buys the assets with cash (and assuming Acquirer is purchasing all of Target's assets), Target's shareholders depart with their money, their target stock is retired and Acquirer's shareholders become owners of a larger company.[30]

* * *

For each of these three transaction types, the form is independent of the type of value exchanged. That is, under merger, purchase of shares, or purchase of assets, the value provided to target shareholders can be cash or stock. The form of value exchanged does affect the target shareholders' incentives. In a cash buyout, the target shareholders have no stake in the post-acquisition company's health; their priority is to maximize the purchase price. In a stock-for-stock exchange, the target shareholders' desire to maximize their own value received will be tempered by their stake in the merged company's long-term health.

---

[29] *See, e.g.*, Qwest-CenturyLink Merger, 2010 Iowa PUC LEXIS 387 (describing stock-for-stock exchange in which Qwest shareholders would receive 0.1664 shares of CenturyLink stock for each Qwest share, and CenturyLink would assume $12 billion in Qwest debt); Northeast Utilities-NSTAR Merger, 2012 Conn. PUC LEXIS 47 (describing stock-for-stock exchange with no new debt).

[30] *See, e.g.*, Aquila-Black Hills Merger, 2007 Iowa PUC LEXIS 341 (approving Black Hills's acquisition of Aquila's natural gas assets in Iowa as part of a larger acquisition of all of Aquila's gas assets in Kansas, Nebraska and Colorado, and its electric assets in Colorado). For a more detailed explanation of merger forms, see JEFFREY D. BAUMAN & RUSSELL B. STEVENSON, JR., CORPORATIONS LAW & POLICY 578–82 (8th ed. 2013); THERESE H. MAYNARD, MERGERS & ACQUISITIONS 47–53 (4th ed. 2017).

6.3   Transaction Types—by Market Structure Effects

Whether and how a merger changes market structure depends on its category. There are six:

A *horizontal merger* joins companies that compete with each other. They compete with each other if they sell the same or similar services to customers in the same geographic area. Common example: a merger of two electric companies owning generation in the same region (each having transmission access to the same customers).[31]

A *vertical merger* joins companies in the same chain of production, where one company makes or sells an input used by the other company.[32] Examples: an owner of coal-fired generating plants merges with a coal mining company; an owner of generating plants merges with an owner of transmission serving the same geographic market; a gas producer or gas distributor merges with a nearby pipeline; a telecommunications company that controls the local exchange network merges with a long distance company (where customers prefer to buy local distance and local service in a bundle).

A merger can be both *horizontal and vertical*. Consider a merger of adjacent, vertically integrated electric utilities. Wisconsin Electric Power and Northern States Power each was a potential wholesale seller of generation in the same geographic market (horizontal); each owned transmission that would be available to the other company's generation (vertical).

A *convergence merger* joins companies whose products have some complementary relationship—such as where the purchase of one product leads to the purchase of the other, or where the sale of two products together lowers costs or increases customer convenience. An electric utility merging with a gas utility could sell a combined "energy product" to homeowners and businesses. A physical distribution company merging with an energy conservation company could sell a "reduce your energy bills" product.

A *market extension merger* joins two companies that sell the same product in different geographic markets (such as a utility in New Jersey merging with a utility in California). Some analysts include in this market extension cate-

---

[31]   *See* AT&T-Bellsouth Merger, 22 FCC Rcd. 5662, 5675 ¶ 23 n.82 (2007) (defining a horizontal merger as one that occurs "when the merging firms sell products that are in the same relevant markets and are therefore viewed as reasonable substitutes by purchasers of the products") (citing News Corp.-Hughes Electronics Merger, 19 FCC Rcd. 473, 485 ¶ 18 (2004)).

[32]   *See id.* at 5675 ¶ 23 n.83 (describing a vertical merger as one in which "one of the merging firms sells products in an upstream input market while the other merging firm sells products [i.e., products that require the input] in a downstream output market") (citing *News Corp.-Hughes Electronics Merger*, 19 FCC Rcd. 473 at 508 ¶ 71)).

gory mergers of companies that sell different but complementary products in the same geographic market (such as an electric utility buying a home alarm installation company serving the same area). The first example represents geographic extension; the second example represents product extension.

A *conglomerate merger* joins companies selling unrelated products. The concept

> ranges from the pure conglomerate, in which there are no discernible economic relationships between the businesses of the acquiring and the acquired firm, through a variety of what may be called mixed conglomerates ... Mixed conglomerate[acquisitions] include acquisition of a ... company manufacturing a different product which is nevertheless related to a product or products of the acquiring firm because it can be produced with much the same facilities, sold through the same distribution channels, or made a part of the same research and development efforts.[33]

* * *

Not every corporate transaction fits neatly into one of these six categories. If each of the merging companies is itself engaged in multiple business activities, their combination could be all of the above: horizontal, vertical, horizontal-and-vertical, convergence, market extension and conglomerate.

6.4   Private Equity Buyouts

The stock of most utilities (or their holding companies) is publicly traded. The same goes for most acquirers of utilities. But in a few utility acquisitions, the acquirers have "taken the company private"; meaning that after the acquisition neither the utility nor its corporate owner was a publicly traded company. In these private equity transactions,

> the acquiring "firm" is a group of investors. These investors are known as the equity partners. The group includes the general partner (who has responsibility for managing the investment, i.e., determining how the acquired firm will be operated), plus other partners (called limited partners) who contribute capital, but are otherwise passive owners. The "business" of private equity firms is investing, and is different from the business of, for example, manufacturing or transportation, or operating a public utility.[34]

---

[33]   Gen. Foods Corp. v. FTC, 386 F.2d 936, 944 (3d Cir. 1967) (quoting Donald F. Turner, *Conglomerate Mergers and Section 7 of the Clayton Act*, 78 HARV. L. REV. 1313, 1315 (1965)).

[34]   STEPHEN G. HILL, NAT'L REGULATORY RESEARCH INST., PRIVATE EQUITY BUYOUTS OF PUBLIC UTILITIES: PREPARATION FOR REGULATORS 9 (2007), https://pubs .naruc.org/pub/FA86433D-A820-85E7-B1C7-D3038BF5155E.

Examples include the 2007 acquisition of the Texas retail utility TXU Energy (now called Oncor) by Kohlberg, Kravis, Roberts & Co., TPG Capital and Goldman Sachs Capital Partners; and the 2016 acquisition of Central Louisiana Electric by a private partnership led by Macquarie, an Australian holding company.

Most of this book's subjects apply to both company types—publicly traded and private equity. A private equity buyout then raises at least four unique issues:

Heavy debt financing: Private equity buyers finance their acquisitions largely with debt. As a result, the acquired utility will be joining a family more indebted than the utility was, with the lenders having more influence over utility decisions:

> Today's private equity buyouts use a financing method introduced in the 1980s— the leveraged buyout (LBO). In an LBO, a large proportion of the monies necessary to complete the transaction (i.e., purchase the target company's outstanding stock) is provided by debt capital (leverage). ... The debt capital that is used to buy the target firm is ... is secured by the income stream of the acquired firm. This acquisition debt ... can be made to reside on either the target company balance sheet or that of the parent/acquiring company, but, in either event, [the debt] becomes the responsibility of the merged company.[35]

Short investor time horizon: Private equity acquirers intend to resell the company in five-to-ten years, at a gain, to an acquirer that will probably, like the first acquirer, finance its purchase with debt.

Limited utility experience: The private equity owners might be experienced utility acquirers but they will not necessarily be experienced utility operators. The managers they hire might reflect the owners' goal of preparing the utility for short-term resale, rather than the public interest goal of improving the utility's long-term performance. On the other hand, new owners and new management might create a more responsive, streamlined service culture.

Public disclosure: If the going-private transaction retires or eliminates the target's publicly-traded securities, the post-merger entity will not be subject to the same Securities and Exchange Commission (SEC) financial disclosure rules as publicly-traded companies. The SEC's rules and enforcement apparatus aim to ensure that companies report their financial condition timely and accurately, disclose all insider trading and explain fully all material risks. While utility commissions can impose on private equity their own financial reporting requirements, they will lack the SEC's expertise and enforcement infrastructure. A counterargument is that non-publicly traded companies are

---

[35] *Id.* at 9.

subject to less pressure to set and meet the short-term profit goals normally expected of publicly-traded companies.

7   MERGER JURISDICTION: WHICH COMMISSIONS REGULATE WHICH TRANSACTIONS, BASED ON WHAT STANDARDS?

7.1   Jurisdiction in General

Regulatory jurisdiction is the power to regulate. All regulators regulate verbs—the actions of actors. In the electric industry, the most frequently regulated actions include:

*   Selling electric capacity and energy at wholesale
*   Selling electric service at retail
*   Selling transmission service
*   Selling distribution service
*   Issuing debt or equity
*   Siting infrastructure
*   Merging with or acquiring utilities or utility assets

For the electric utility industry, the Federal Power Act allocates regulatory power over these actions between the states and FERC. State legislatures, in turn, enact statutes that delegate regulatory powers to state commissions. The combination of these legislative and regulatory decisions has produced the jurisdictional results displayed in Table T.1, placed at the end of this Tutorial. The first column describes the industry action that triggers regulation. The second column identifies the type of actor—usually a public utility but occasionally another entity or simply a "person." The third column identifies the subject matter, such as rates, reliability or need. The final four columns identify who has jurisdiction: FERC exclusively, states exclusively; concurrent jurisdiction; or in one case, "other."

7.2   Jurisdiction Over Mergers

Most electric utility mergers trigger the jurisdiction of FERC, and of the state commissions with jurisdiction over the to-be-acquired utility. Statutes differ over which transaction types require regulatory approval, and over the standards regulators must or may apply. This section describes and illustrates the most common transactional triggers and standards. It also addresses how federal and state regulatory laws interact in the merger-and-acquisition space.

7.2.1 State statutory triggers

7.2.1.1 Transactional level

Some state statutes require regulatory approval only of transactions to which the in-state utility is a direct party. In those states, a transaction whose signatories are holding companies rather than utilities avoids regulatory review, even though the entity controlling the utility will change. Ameritech Corporation owned the telephone utility serving in Indiana. Its holding company-level merger with SBC Communications did not trigger the Indiana merger statute, because that statute applied only when a utility sold its system. The holding company owned the utility but was not itself a utility.[36]

Other states' statutes require the commission to review any transaction that changes who controls the utility, whether the change occurs at the utility level or the holding company level. To signal this jurisdictional breadth, the statute will often couple the verb "merge or acquire" with a broadening phrase like "directly or indirectly" or "by whatever means accomplished."[37]

7.2.1.2 Acquirer or target

Under most state statutes, the commission has jurisdiction over the transaction only if its utility is the target. When the in-state entity (or its holding company) is instead the acquirer, of a utility or any other business, that utility's state

---

[36] Indiana Bell Tel. Co. v. Indiana Util. Regulatory Comm'n, 715 N.E.2d 351 (Ind. 1999) (applying IND. CODE § 8-1-2-83(a), providing that "no public utility ... shall sell, assign, transfer, lease or encumber its franchise, works, or system ... without approval of the commission"). *See also* U.S. West-Qwest Merger, 2000 Neb. PUC LEXIS 97, at *5 (holding that the transaction would "occur upstream from the level of the wholly owned subsidiary of U.S. West Communications, Inc., the entity that holds the certificate to operate" in Nebraska).

[37] *See, e.g.*, the Illinois Public Utilities Act, which provides that

"reorganization" means any transaction which, *regardless of the means by which it is accomplished*, results in a change in the ownership of a majority of the voting capital stock of an Illinois public utility; or the ownership or control of any entity which owns or controls a majority of the voting capital stock of a public utility; or by which 2 public utilities merge, or by which a public utility acquires substantially all of the assets of another public utility.

220 ILL. COMP. STAT. 5 / 7-204 (emphasis added). When two independent utilities, Central Illinois Public Service Company and Union Electric, applied to become corporate subsidiaries of the holding company Ameren, the Illinois Commission had jurisdiction under a statute requiring approval before a public utility "*by any means, direct or indirect*, can merge or consolidate its franchises, licenses, permits, plants, equipment, business or other property with that of any other public utility." Central Illinois Public Service-Union Electric Merger, 1997 Ill. PUC LEXIS 546, at *31 (emphasis added) (interpreting the Illinois Public Utilities Act sec. 7-102(d), 220 ILL. COMP. STAT. 5 / 7-102(D)).

commission usually has no authority to review the transaction (unless, of course, the target is also an in-state entity). The result: once a utility becomes a subsidiary of a holding company, that holding company can acquire any other business anywhere; the utility's regulator will have no say. The 2012 merger of Duke and Florida Progress combined utilities with customers in North Carolina, South Carolina, Florida, Indiana, Kentucky and Ohio. The Florida Commission had no say.[38]

7.2.1.3   Control or influence

While for most state merger statutes, the jurisdictional trigger is the acquisition of formal ownership, some focus on control or influence. In Ohio, no person may "acquire control" of a utility or a utility holding company without commission permission. The statute defines "control" broadly to mean "the possession of the power to direct the management and policies of [an Ohio utility or its holding company] through the ownership of voting securities, by contract, or otherwise." Anyone with 20 percent of the corporation's voting power is deemed to have control.[39]

Applying a similar statute, the Maryland Commission exercised jurisdiction when Electricité de France International, SA (EDF) sought to buy a 49.99 percent interest in Constellation Energy Nuclear Group (CENG). CENG was a subsidiary owned by Constellation Energy Group (CEG), which in turn owned the Maryland utility Baltimore Gas & Electric (BGE). Transaction documents gave EDF the rights to (a) place a director on the CEG Board, and (b) buy specified amounts of CEG stock and bonds. The Commission held that EDF would have the power to exercise substantial influence over BG&E, based on these factors:

- "BGE's ability to maintain an appropriate, and investment-grade, debt to equity ratio depend[ed] heavily on decisions regarding the flow of dividends and capital between BGE and CEG."
- EDF's ownership stake in CENG would allow it to "control the flow of dividends" from CENG to CEG.

---

[38]   *Duke Energy-Progress Energy Merger I*, 136 F.E.R.C. ¶ 61,245 at P 175 & n.388 (2011) (citing Applicants' summary of state commission authority over the transaction).

[39]   OHIO REV. CODE ANN. § 4905.402(A)(1), (B). *See also* VT. STAT. ANN. tit. 30, § 107 (subjecting to Commission review any acquisition of a "controlling interest"; and defining "controlling interest" to mean 10 percent or more of a company's voting securities "or such other interest as the Public Utility Commission determines … to constitute the means to direct or cause the direction of the management or policies of a company").

- That control, in turn, "could affect substantially the decisions CEG and BGE make as to the financing and financial structure of the utility."
- EDF's power to nominate a director to CEG's Board increased that influence, "especially as CEG's nuclear joint ventures compete[d] with BGE for scarce capital resources."

EDF's executives insisted they had no intent to influence BGE, but the Commission found intent irrelevant. Statutorily, what mattered was "the power" to influence.[40]

7.2.1.4   General commission authority

Lacking explicit statutory authority over mergers, a commission might find jurisdiction in its general enabling authority. The Australian holding company Babcock & Brown Infrastructure sought to acquire NorthWestern Energy, a utility doing business in Montana, South Dakota and Nebraska. The Montana Commission based its jurisdiction on three factors:

- The "unique status of public utilities ... as entities affected with a public interest" meant that they "may not sell assets or transfer control of them without the approval of the Commission."
- The Commission said it had statutory authority over "acts or practices ... that affect utility service," and authority to "substitute[] ... other ... practices ... or acts. ... The sale and transfer of a utility or of utility assets is obviously an act or practice of a utility company."
- The Commission also inferred jurisdiction over the acquisition from its express authority to approve issuances of securities.[41]

And when National Grid (a United Kingdom holding company) proposed to acquire KeySpan (both holding companies owning utilities in Massachusetts and elsewhere), the Massachusetts Department of Telecommunications and Energy reviewed the transaction under its "general supervisory powers."[42]

---

[40]   Baltimore Gas & Electric Co., 2009 Md. PSC LEXIS 39, at *2, *46 (applying MD. CODE ANN., PUB. UTIL. § 6-105(e)(1)).

[41]   NorthWestern Energy-Babcock & Brown Merger, 2007 Mont. PUC LEXIS 54, at *15–26 (quoting MONT. CODE ANN. § 69-3-330(3)) (citing Munn v. Illinois, 94 U.S. 113 (1877)).

[42]   In 2008, the state legislature amended the statute to authorize review of holding company-level mergers. This history is explained in National Grid-KeySpan Merger, 2010 Mass. PUC LEXIS 28, at *2 n.2.

7.2.2   Federal statutory triggers

Prior to its 2005 repeal, PUHCA 1935 defined triggering transactions in multiple ways. These triggers allowed the SEC to limit a holding company's corporate complexity, debt-heaviness and business mix so as to align those features with the interests of investors, consumers and the public interest. When Congress repealed PUHCA 1935, it expanded, and made more specific, FERC's Federal Power Act authority to address changes in the control of utilities. Under FPA section 203,[43] FERC must review transactions where:

1. a public utility disposes of "facilities subject to the jurisdiction of the Commission, or any part thereof of a value in excess of $10,000,000";[44]
2. a public utility "merge[s] or consolidate[s], directly or indirectly, its facilities subject to the jurisdiction of the Commission, or any part thereof, with the facilities of any other person, or any part thereof, that are subject to the jurisdiction of the Commission and have a value in excess of $10,000,000, by any means whatsoever";[45]
3. a public utility acquires stock in or securities of any other public utility in excess of $10 million;[46] or
4. a public utility acquires an existing generation facility, if the facility has a value in excess of $10 million and is "used for interstate wholesale sales and over which the Commission has jurisdiction for ratemaking purposes."[47]

Congress also added a provision requiring FERC to review certain combinations occurring at the holding company level.[48]

---

[43]   Federal Power Act of 1935 § 203, 16 U.S.C. § 824b.

[44]   FPA § 203(a)(1)(A).

[45]   FPA § 203(a)(1)(B). The reference to "facilities" in sections 203(a)(1)(A) and 203(a)(1)(B) requires some explanation. The phrase includes transmission facilities but not "local distribution" or "generation" facilities. *See* FPA § 201(b)(1) (defining facilities over which the Commission has jurisdiction). The phrase also includes "paper" facilities such as contracts, rate schedules, and books and records relating to jurisdictional transactions (e.g., wholesale sales of electric energy and sales of transmission service). *See* Hartford Elec. Light Co. v. FPC, 131 F.2d 953, 961 (2d Cir. 1942); *Enova-Pacific Merger*, 79 F.E.R.C. ¶ 61,107 (1997) (concluding that "facilities" under section 203 includes contracts of power marketers).

[46]   FPA § 203(a)(1)(C).

[47]   FPA § 203(a)(1)(D).

[48]   FPA § 203(a)(2), which to the author borders on the incomprehensible, states:
No holding company in a holding company system that includes a transmitting utility or an electric utility shall purchase, acquire, or take any security with a value in excess of $10,000,000 of, or, by any means whatsoever, directly or indirectly, merge or consolidate with, a transmitting utility, an electric utility company, or a holding company in a holding company system that includes

The Federal Power Act's merger provisions do not preempt state law. Even if FERC has approved a merger, a state commission can reject it. Electricity merger applicants must get their ticket punched by each agency with statutory jurisdiction, federal and state.

What if a state commission, as part of its merger review, reviews matters ostensibly within FERC's exclusive jurisdiction? When Southern California Edison and San Diego Gas & Electric proposed to merge, the California Commission examined the merger's effects on transmission access and wholesale competition. The applicants argued that the state commission was preempted from reviewing those matters because FERC had exclusive jurisdiction over them. The California Commission disagreed: "[C]ompetition is a relevant factor in weighing the public interest," and the public interest is the central concern of the state's merger statute.[49] The California Commission was not exercising authority over transmission or wholesale sales; it was considering the merger's effects on those markets. The Commission's position has not been tested in federal court.

---

a transmitting utility, or an electric utility company, with a value in excess of $10,000,000 without first having secured an order of the Commission authorizing it to do so.

[49] Southern California Edison-San Diego Gas & Electric Merger, 1991 Cal. PUC LEXIS 253, at *2, *39, *42–43 (quoting N. Cal. Power Agency v. Pub. Util. Comm'n, 486 P.2d 1218 (Cal. 1971)) (citing Cal. Pub. Util. Code § 854(c)).

Table T.1 Economic regulatory jurisdiction in the U.S. electric industry

Action	Actor	Legal Subject	Jurisdiction			
			FERC exclusive[a]	State Exclusive	Concurrent FERC and State	Other
Electric Energy and Capacity						
Sell retail electricity	Public utility	Rates		FPA 201		
Sell wholesale electricity	Public utility	Rates	FPA 201			
Purchase wholesale electricity	Public utility	Rates		FPA 201[b]		
Set regional capacity requirement	RTO	Rates, reliability	FPA 201			
Allocate regional capacity obligation to LSEs	RTO	Rates, reliability	FPA 201			
Own, use or operate "bulk power system"	Owner, user or operator of the bulk power system	Reliability			FPA 215[c]	
Set reliability standards	ERO	Reliability	FPA 215			
Site and construct generation facilities	Public utility	Need, rates		FPA 201		
Construct and operate nuclear power plants	Person	Safety				NRC
Demand Response						
Sell DR into wholesale organized market	Anyone	Rates	FPA 201			
Sell DR to retail utilities	Retail customer	Rates		FPA 201		
Purchase DR from retail customers	Public utility	Rates		FPA 201		
Purchase DR from wholesale organized markets	LSE	Rates			FPA 201[d]	
"Transmit" retail electricity, bundled[e]	Public utility	Rates		FPA 201		

| Action | Actor | Legal Subject | Jurisdiction | | | |
			FERC exclusive[a]	State Exclusive	Concurrent FERC and State	Other
Transmit retail electricity, unbundled[b]	Public utility	Rates	FPA 201, Order 888, *New York v. FERC*			
Transmit wholesale electricity, bundled	Public utility	Rates	FPA 201			
Transmit wholesale electricity, unbundled	Public utility	Rates	FPA 201			
"Local" distribution of retail electricity[f]	Public utility	Rates		FPA 201		
"Non-local" distribution of wholesale electricity[f]	Public utility	Rates	FPA 201			
Site transmission facilities[g]	Person	Transmission need, siting				FPA 216
Other						
Merge with utility; acquire utility or utility assets	Public utility, person	Corporate structure			FPA 203, PUHCA 2005	DoJ, FTC (antitrust)
Issue equity or debt[h]	Public utility	Finance				FPA 204

Source: This table, created by the author while Executive Director of the National Regulatory Research Institute, first appeared in Nat'l Regulatory Research Inst., Effective Regulation: Guidance for Public-Interest Decisionmakers (2009). The author has since expanded it. It is used here with permission.

Notes:

[a] Section 201 restricts FERC's authority to transactions in interstate commerce. Court, FPC and FERC cases have found that due to the interconnectedness of the electricity network, all electricity transactions are in interstate commerce, regardless of their contractual origin or destination, with the exception of transactions wholly within Alaska, Hawai'i and Texas. See *Florida Power & Light Co. v. Federal Power Commission,* 404 U.S. 453 (1972).

[b] Except in the unusual situation where FERC's approval of a capacity allocation to retail utilities is viewed by the courts as FERC "ordering" the utility to purchase the allocated capacity. See *Mississippi Power & Light v. State of Mississippi ex rel. Moore,* 487 U.S. 354 (1988).

c Federal Power Act Section 215(i)(3) preserves from preemption state regulation of reliability-related actions, unless the state regulation is "inconsistent with" federal standards. Section 215 does not apply to Alaska or Hawai'i. See Section 215(k).

d FERC sets the compensation but states can determine the prudence of the utility's purchase. *Cf. Kentucky West Virginia Gas Co. v. Pennsylvania Public Utilities Comm'n*, 837 F.2d 600 (3d Cir. 1988); *Pike County Light & Power v. Pennsylvania PUC*, 465 A.2d 735, 737–38 (Pa. Commw. Ct. 1983).

e Transmission service is "unbundled" when the customer buys transmission service from the transmission provider while buying generation service from someone else. When transmission service is unbundled, the rates, terms and conditions are exclusively FERC-jurisdictional. *New York v. FERC*, 505 U.S. 144 (2002) (upholding FERC's ruling in Order No. 888). In a traditional sale of retail electricity, transmission remains bundled with the generation service; thus the state retains jurisdiction over the associated transmission cost. In two other situations, FERC has determined that transmission service is unbundled: (a) where the state has authorized retail customers to shop for power among competing retail sellers (FERC Order No. 888); and (b) where the retail utility has joined a regional transmission organization, because in that situation the utility is buying unbundled transmission service from the RTO (FERC Order No. 2000).

f Section 201(b) denies FERC jurisdiction over "local" distribution. FERC has found that the transportation of wholesale power over a distribution system is non-"local" distribution. This situation arises when a generator is connected to a distribution system, and its wholesale customer is not the distribution owner.

g Before 2005, states had exclusive jurisdiction over transmission facility siting. Concerned that one state might block projects necessary to serve other states, Congress in 2005 added Section 216. This section empowers FERC to grant an applicant a preemptive siting permit for transmission projects located in DOE-designated "national interest electric transmission corridors." FERC obtains this power only if the state has "withheld" siting approval for more than 12 months or attaches conditions making the project uneconomic or unable to reduce congestion; or if there is no state agency with authority to grant siting permission. FERC also must make certain public interest findings. The Fourth Circuit has held that a state that denies approval has not "withheld" approval. If FERC does get jurisdiction, three contiguous states may form a compact to oust FERC. Section 216 does not apply to Alaska or Hawai'i.

h Federal Power Act Section 204 provides that FERC has jurisdiction over a utility's securities issuances only if the state does not.

Appendix A.1 List of companies referenced

This list comprises every company listed in the book, whether a utility, a utility holding company, or some other company. Omitted from the names are suffixes like Company or Incorporated.

Allegheny Energy
Alliant Energy
AltaGas
Ameren
Ameren Energy Generating
Ameren Services
American Electric Power
American Power & Light
American Telephone & Telegraph
AmerUS Services
AOL
Aquila
Arizona Public Service
AT&T Wireless
Atlantic City Electric
Avista
Babcock and Brown Infrastructure
Baltimore Gas & Electric
Bellsouth
Berkshire Hathaway
Boise Water
Boston Edison
Boston Gas
California Energy Utilities
California Pacific Electric
California System Operator Corp.
Carolina Power & Light
Central & South West
Central and South West

Central Illinois Public Service
Central Louisiana Electric
Central Maine Power
Central Vermont Public Service
Centurytel
Cincinnati Gas & Electric
Citizens Utilities
Cleveland Electric Illuminating
Comcast
Commonwealth Edison
Conectiv
Connecticut Light & Power
Consolidated Edison
Consolidated Natural Gas
Constellation Energy
Dayton Power & Light Co.
Delmarva Power & Light
Deutsche Telekom AG
Dominion Resources
Duke Energy
Duquesne Light
East Tennessee Natural Gas
El Paso Electric
El Paso Natural Gas
Electric Public Utilities
Electricité de France
Empire District
Energy Future Holdings
Energy Services
Enron
Entergy
Eversource
Exelon
FirstEnergy
Florida Power
Florida Power & Light
Florida Progress
Goldman Sachs
Great Plains Energy
Green Mountain Power
GTE
Gulf States Utilities

Hawaiian Electric Industries
Hope Natural Gas
Hydro One
Iberdrola
Iowa Power
Iowa Public Service
ITC Holdings
J.P. Morgan Partners
Jersey Central Power & Light
Kansas City Power & Light
Kansas Gas & Electric
Kansas Power & Light
Kentucky Utilities
Kinder Morgan
Kohlberg, Kravis Roberts
Locust Ridge Gas
Louisiana Gas & Electric
Louisville Gas & Electric
Macquarie
Madison Gas & Electric
Maine Public Service
Metropolitan Edison
Microsoft
MidAmerican Energy Holdings
Midland Cogeneration Venture Ltd Partnership
Midwest Power Systems
Midwestern Gas Transmission
Monongahela Power
Mountain States Telephone & Telegraph
N.Y. State Electric & Gas
N.Y. Telephone
N.Y. Water Service
National Grid
NBC Universal
Nevada Power
New England Electric System
New England Power
New Orleans Gas-Light
New Orleans Water Works
NextEra
Niagara Mohawk Power
North American

Northeast Utilities
Northern New England Energy
Northern States Power
Northwest Central Pipeline
NorthWestern Energy
NSTAR Electric
NSTAR Gas
Nynex
Ohio Edison
Oklahoma Gas & Electric
Oncor Electricity Delivery
Otter Tail Power
Pacific Gas & Electric
Pacific Power & Light
PacifiCorp
PanEnergy
Penelec
Penn Power
Pennsylvania Power
Pepco Holdings
Philadelphia Electric
Pinnacle West
PNM Electric Services
Portland General Exchange
Potomac Electric Power
PPL
Progress Energy
PSI Energy
Public Service Commission of Missouri
Public Service Company of New Mexico
Public Service Electric and Gas
Public Service of Colorado
Public Service of Indiana
Public Service of New Hampshire
Puget Holdings
Puget Sound Energy
Qwest Communications International
San Diego Gas & Electric
SBC Communications
SCEcorp
Scottish Power
Sempra

Sierra Pacific Resources
Southern California Edison
Southern California Gas
Southwestern Bell Telephone
Southwestern Public Service
St. Joseph Light & Power
Sunshine Cellular
Tampa Electric
Time Warner
T-Mobile
Toledo Edison
Tucson Electric Power
U.S. West
U.S. West Communications
UGI Utilities
Union Electric
UniSource Energy
United Illuminating
Utah Power & Light
UtiliCorp United
Vanguard Cellular System
Vermont Electric Power
Wachovia Capital Partners
Washington Gas Light
Washington Gas Light Holdings
Washington Water Power
West Penn Power
Westar
Western Massachusetts Electric
Western Resources
Wisconsin Electric Power

Appendix A.2 Does federal bankruptcy law preempt a state commission's franchising authority?[1]

When a state-regulated utility enters bankruptcy, what happens to the state commission's normal franchising authority? Does federal bankruptcy law preempt the state's utility commission or legislature from (a) conditioning the utility's franchise; (b) revoking and transferring the franchise to a new company; or (c) approving, rejecting or conditioning a bankruptcy-court-approved acquisition of the bankrupt utility? The answer, in all three situations, appears to be no.

A debtor's filing of a bankruptcy petition triggers an "automatic stay."[2] The stay blocks any litigation against the debtor to enforce or collect on financial claims that pre-dated the petition. The automatic stay does not apply, however, to "the commencement or continuation of an action or proceeding by a governmental unit ... to enforce such governmental unit's or organization's police and regulatory power."[3]

Applying this language, courts have distinguished between two governmental purposes: pecuniary and public policy. If the government is acting to protect its pecuniary interest in the debtor's property, the stay still applies. But if the government is acting on matters of policy—public safety or welfare—the stay does not apply. In this public policy context, the stay does not apply even if the regulatory action affects the debtor economically.[4]

The pecuniary-policy distinction arose in Pacific Gas & Electric's (PG&E) 2001 bankruptcy case. Before PG&E filed its bankruptcy petition, the California Public Utilities Commission had required the utility to transfer negative bal-

---

[1] This Appendix's first four paragraphs are adapted from *Motion to Amend June 18, 2019 Assigned Commissioner and Administrative Law Judge's Ruling to Align it with the Scope*, filed with the California Public Utilities Commission in *Investigation 15-08-019* (July 1, 2019). The Motion was filed by the California Public Advocate's Office, to which the author was an advisor.

[2] Bankruptcy Code, 11 U.S.C. § 362.

[3] *Id.* § 362(b)(4).

[4] *See generally* NLRB v. Continental Hagen Corp., 932 F.2d 828, 833 (9th Cir. 1991).

ances to a Transition Cost Balancing Account. After filing for bankruptcy, PG&E argued that the Commission's effort to enforce that decision violated the stay. The bankruptcy court disagreed, holding that the Commission's primary purpose was public policy. The result might affect PG&E's finances negatively and its customers positively, the court reasoned, but ratemaking is public policymaking. PG&E also argued that the Commission's decision adjudicated private rights (a sign of pecuniary purpose, which cannot avoid the stay), by favoring consumers at PG&E's expense. The court disagreed again: the Commission's action was "more legislative in character"; indeed, regulating utilities "is one of the most important of the functions traditionally associated with the police power of the states."[5]

When a bankruptcy court approves an acquirer's bid for a debtor utility, does that approval preempt the utility's state commission from rejecting the acquisition? The answer appears to be no. The Texas retail utility Oncor was owned 80 percent by Energy Future Holdings Corp (EFHC). EFHC entered bankruptcy due to its own heavy debt and its merchant generation affiliates' failures. The federal bankruptcy court approved Oncor's acquisition by NextEra (the holding company for Florida Power & Light). But the Texas Commission rejected NextEra because NextEra wanted control of Oncor's cash flow so as to pay off NextEra's high acquisition debt. The court then approved a bid from Sempra (the holding company for San Diego Gas & Electric). Sempra, like NextEra, had to get the Texas Commission's approval, which the Commission granted, subject to conditions. Both times, no one argued preemption.[6]

---

[5] *Pac. Gas & Elec. Co. v. Lynch (In re Pac. Gas & Elec. Co.)*, 263 B.R. 306, 318–20 (Bankr. N.D. Cal. 2001) (citing Ark. Elec. Coop. Corp. v. Ark. Pub. Serv. Comm'n, 461 U.S. 375, 377 (1983)).

[6] On NextEra, see *Oncor Electric Delivery-NextEra Energy Merger*, Docket No. 46238 (Tex. Pub. Util. Comm'n Apr. 13, 2017). On Sempra, see *Sempra Energy-Oncor Electric Delivery Merger*, Docket No. 47675 (Tex. Pub. Util. Comm'n Mar. 8, 2018). *See also* Chapter 11.2 in this book's main text. While the Texas experiences shows that bankruptcy litigants behave as if the state commission is not preempted from rejecting a bankruptcy-approved acquirer, the courts have not explicitly decided that question. The Ninth Circuit, applying 11 U.S.C. § 1142(a), has held that a court-approved bankruptcy reorganization plan preempts state regulation "relating to financial condition." Pacific Gas & Elec. Co. v. California *ex rel.* Cal. Dep't of Toxic Substances Control, 350 F.3d 932, 937, 948 (9th Cir. 2003). While the appeal was pending, the bankruptcy judge terminated debtor's exclusivity. The Commission then filed its own competing plan, leading to confirmation. No court has decided whether Commission regulation of corporate ownership structure is regulation "relating to financial condition."

Appendix A.3 Ring-fencing provisions approved by the D.C. Public Service Commission[1]

61.   Pepco will maintain its separate existence as a separate corporate subsidiary and its separate franchises, obligations and privileges.

62.   Pepco will not incur or assume any debt, including the provision of guarantees or collateral support, related to this Merger or any future Exelon acquisition.

63.   Pepco shall maintain separate debt so that Pepco will not be responsible for the debts of affiliate companies and preferred stock, if any, and Pepco shall maintain its own corporate and debt credit rating, as well as ratings for long-term debt and preferred stock.

64.   Exelon has established the SPE, a limited liability company, as a special purpose entity for the purpose of holding 100% of the equity interest in PHI.

65.   The SPE will be a direct subsidiary of EEDC.

66.   EEDC will transfer 100% of the equity interest in PHI to the SPE as an absolute conveyance with the intention of removing PHI and its utility subsidiaries from the bankruptcy estate of Exelon and EEDC.

67.   The SPE will have no employees and no operational functions other than those related to holding the equity interests in PHI.

68.   The SPE shall maintain adequate capital in light of its contemplated business purpose, transactions and liabilities; provided, however, the foregoing shall not require the owners to make any additional capital contributions.

69.   The SPE will have four directors appointed by EEDC. One of the four SPE directors will be an independent director, who will be an employee of an administration company in the business of protecting SPEs, and must meet the other independence criteria set forth in the SPE governing documents. One other director will be appointed from among the officers or employees of PHI

[1]   Excerpted from Exelon-PHI Merger, Formal Case No. 1119, Order No. 18148, Attachment B at ¶¶ 61–105 (D.C. Pub. Serv. Comm'n Mar. 23, 2016).

or a PHI subsidiary. The other two SPE directors may be officers or employees of Exelon or its affiliates, including PHI and its subsidiaries.

70.   The SPE will issue a non-economic interest in the SPE (a "Golden Share") to an administration company in the business of protecting SPEs and separate from the administration company retained to provide the person to serve as the independent director for the SPE. The holder of the SPE's Golden Share will have a voting right on matters specified in the SPE governing documents, as described below.

71.   A voluntary petition for bankruptcy by the SPE will require the affirmative consent of the holder of the Golden Share and the unanimous vote of the SPE board of directors (including the independent director). A voluntary petition for bankruptcy by PHI will require the affirmative consent of the holder of the Golden Share, the unanimous vote of the SPE board of directors (including the independent director), and the unanimous vote of the PHI board of directors. A voluntary petition for bankruptcy for any of PHI's subsidiaries will require the unanimous vote of the PHI board of directors (including its independent directors) and the unanimous vote of the board of directors of the relevant PHI subsidiary.

72.   The SPE will maintain arms-length relationships with each of its affiliates and observe all necessary, appropriate and customary company formalities in its dealings with its affiliates. PHI and PHI's subsidiaries will maintain arms-length relationships with Exelon and its affiliates, including the SPE.

73.   PHI's CEO and other senior officers who directly report to the CEO will hold no positions with Exelon or Exelon affiliates other than PHI and PHI's subsidiaries.

74.   At all times, the SPE will hold itself out as an entity separate from its affiliates, will conduct business in its own name through its duly authorized directors and officers and comply with all organizational formalities to maintain its separate existence and shall use commercially reasonable efforts to correct any known misunderstanding regarding its separate identity. PHI and its subsidiaries will hold themselves out as separate entities from Exelon and the SPE, conduct business in their own names (provided that PHI and each of PHI's utility subsidiaries may identify itself as an affiliate of Exelon on a basis consistent with other Exelon utility subsidiaries).

75.   The SPE shall maintain its own separate books, records, bank accounts and financial statements reflecting its separate assets and liabilities. PHI and each of PHI's subsidiaries will maintain separate books, accounts and financial statements reflecting its separate assets and liabilities.

76.   The SPE shall comply with Generally Accepted Accounting Principles in all material respects (subject, in the case of unaudited financial statements, to the absence of footnotes and to normal year-end audit adjustments) in all

financial statements and reports required of it and issue such financial statements and reports separately from any financial statements or reports prepared for its affiliates; provided that such financial statements or reports may be consolidated with those of its affiliates if the separate existence of the SPE and its assets and liabilities are clearly noted therein.

77.   The SPE shall account for and manage all of its liabilities separately from any other entity, and pay its own liabilities only out of its own funds.

78.   The SPE shall neither guarantee nor become obligated for the debts of any other entity nor hold out its credit or assets as being available to satisfy the obligations of any other entity.

79.   Each PHI utility will maintain separate debt and preferred stock, if any, so that none will be responsible for the debts or preferred stock of affiliated companies, and each will maintain its own corporate and debt credit rating as well as ratings for long-term debt and preferred stock, if any. PHI and its subsidiaries will use reasonable efforts to maintain separate credit ratings for their publicly traded securities. PHI will not issue additional long-term debt securities. In particular, PHI shall not rollover or otherwise refinance its currently outstanding long-term debt by issuing new long-term debt. PHI and its utility subsidiaries will use reasonable efforts and prudence to preserve investment grade credit ratings.

80.   PHI will not assume liability for the debts of Exelon, the SPE, or any other affiliate of Exelon other than a PHI subsidiary. The PHI subsidiaries will not assume liability for the debts of Exelon, PHI, the SPE, the other PHI subsidiaries, or any other affiliate of Exelon. The SPE shall not acquire, assume or guarantee obligations of any affiliate. PHI will not guarantee the debt or credit instruments of Exelon, the SPE or any other Exelon affiliate other than a PHI subsidiary. The PHI utilities will not guarantee the debt or credit instruments of Exelon, PHI or any other Exelon affiliate including the SPE.

81.   The SPE shall not pledge its assets for the benefit of any other entity or make loans to, or purchase or hold any indebtedness of, any other entity. The PHI utilities will not pledge or use as collateral, or grant a mortgage or other lien on any asset or cash flow, or otherwise pledge such assets or cash flow as security for repayment of the principal or interest of any loan or credit instrument of, or otherwise for the benefit of, Exelon, PHI or any other Exelon affiliate including the SPE.

82.   Pepco will not include in any of its debt or credit agreements cross-default provisions between Pepco securities and the securities of Exelon or any other Exelon affiliate. Pepco will not include in its debt or credit agreements any financial covenants or rating-agency triggers related to Exelon or any other Exelon affiliate.

83.   The SPE will not commingle its funds or other assets with the funds or other assets of any other entity and shall not maintain any funds or other

assets in such a manner that it will be costly or difficult to segregate, ascertain or identify its individual funds or other assets from those of its owners or any other person.

84.   PHI and its subsidiaries will maintain in its own name all assets and other interests in property used or useful in their respective business and will not transfer its ownership interest in any such property to Exelon or an Exelon affiliate (other than a PHI subsidiary) without requisite approval of the Commission and any approval required under the Federal Power Act; provided that the foregoing shall not limit the ability of PHI to transfer to Exelon or Exelon affiliates any business or operations of PHI or PHI subsidiaries that are not regulated by state or local utility regulatory authorities.

85.   The SPE shall ensure that its funds will not be transferred to its owners or affiliates except with the consent and authority of the SPE board of directors.

86.   The SPE shall ensure that title to all real and personal property acquired by it is acquired, held and conveyed in its name.

87.   No entities other than PHI and its subsidiaries, including the PHI utilities and PHISCo, will participate in the PHI utilities' money pool. The PHI utilities will not participate in any money pool operated by Exelon, and there will be no commingling of the PHI money pool funds with Exelon. Any deposits into or loans through the PHI money pool by PHI utilities shall be on terms no less favorable than the depositor or lender could obtain through a short-term investment of similar funds with independent parties. Any borrowings from the PHI money pool by a PHI utility shall be on terms no less favorable and cost effective than the PHI utility could obtain through short-term borrowings from (including sales of commercial paper to) independent parties. Exelon will give notice to the Commission within seven (7) days in the event that any participant in the PHI money pool is rated below investment grade by any of the three major credit rating agencies. The documents and instruments creating the PHI money pool (and any modification thereof) will be subject to approval by the Commission.

88.   Immediately following the Merger close, PHISCo will remain as a subsidiary of PHI and will continue to perform functions and to maintain related assets currently involved in providing services exclusively to the PHI utilities. Other functions that are currently provided by PHISCo, including those that are provided to PHI utilities and to other current PHI subsidiaries, will be transferred to EBSC or another Exelon affiliate in a phased transition over a period of time following the Merger closing. To address concerns that there would be two service companies under the proposed Merger, Exelon will file a plan within six (6) months after the Merger's close for Commission approval to integrate PHISCo within EBSC and other entities. The plan to integrate PHISCo with EBSC shall not include any net transfer of PHISCo

employees located in the District of Columbia pre-Merger to any location outside of the District, subject to the provisions of Paragraph 19.

89.   PHI subsidiaries, other than PHISCo and the PHI utilities, that are currently engaged in operations that are not regulated by a state or local utility regulatory authority will be transferred to Exelon or an Exelon affiliate; provided that: (a) PHI may retain ownership of Conectiv LLC ("Conectiv") as a holding company for ACE and Delmarva Power; (b) Conectiv may transfer its 50% ownership interest in Millennium Account Services LLC to PHI; and (c) Conectiv or subsidiaries of Conectiv may retain ownership of real estate and other assets that are used in whole or in part in the business of the PHI utilities. PHI may elect to hold the stock of Delmarva and ACE directly, and cease the use of Conectiv as a holding company.

90.   The SPE will maintain a separate name from and will not use the trademarks, service marks or other intellectual property of Exelon, PHI, or PHI's subsidiaries. PHI and its utility subsidiaries will each maintain a separate name from and will not use the trademarks, service marks or other similar intellectual property of Exelon or its other affiliates, except that PHI and each of PHI's utility subsidiaries may identify itself as an affiliate of Exelon on a basis consistent with other Exelon utility subsidiaries.

91.   Any amendment to the organizational documents of the SPE that would remove or alter the voting or other ring-fencing requirements described above will require the unanimous vote of the board of directors of the SPE, including the independent director, and the affirmative consent of the holder of the Golden Share.

92.   Within 180 days following completion of the Merger, Exelon will obtain a legal opinion in customary form and substance and reasonably satisfactory to the Commission, to the effect that, as a result of the ring-fencing measures it has implemented for PHI and its subsidiaries, a bankruptcy court would not consolidate the assets and liabilities of the SPE with those of Exelon or EEDC, in the event of an Exelon or EEDC bankruptcy, or the assets and liabilities of PHI or its subsidiaries with those of either the SPE, Exelon or EEDC, in the event of a bankruptcy of the SPE, Exelon or EEDC. In the event that such opinion cannot be obtained, Exelon will promptly implement such measures as are required to obtain such opinion.

93.   Pepco shall maintain a rolling 12-month average annual equity ratio of at least 48%. Pepco will not pay dividends to its parent company if, immediately after the dividend payment, its common equity level would fall below 48%, as equity levels are calculated under the ratemaking precedents of the Commission.

94.   Pepco shall not make any distribution to its parent if Pepco's corporate issuer or senior unsecured credit rating, or its equivalent, is rated by any of the three major credit rating agencies below investment grade.

95.   Pepco shall file with the Commission, within five (5) business days after the payment of a dividend, the calculations that it used to determine the equity level at the time the board of directors considered payment of the dividend and the calculations to demonstrate that the common equity ratio immediately after the dividend payment did not fall below 48%, as equity levels are calculated under the ratemaking precedents of the Commission.

96.   Pepco will file with the Commission an annual compliance report with respect to the ring-fencing and other requirements.

97.   At the time of Merger close and every year thereafter, Pepco shall provide the Commission with a certificate from an officer of Exelon certifying that: (a) Exelon shall maintain the requisite legal separateness in the corporate reorganization structure; (b) the organization structure serves important business purposes for Exelon; and (c) Exelon acknowledges that subsequent creditors of PHI and Pepco may rely upon the separateness of PHI and Pepco and would be significantly harmed in the event separateness is not maintained and a substantive consolidation of PHI or Pepco with Exelon were to occur.

98.   Exelon shall not, without prior Commission approval, alter the corporate character of EEDC to become a functioning corporate entity providing common support services for PHI utilities.

99.   Exelon shall not engage in an internal corporate reorganization relating to the SPE, PHI or Pepco, or EEDC for which Commission approval is not required without ninety (90) days prior written notification to the Commission. Such notification shall include: (a) an opinion of reputable bankruptcy counsel that the reorganization does not materially impact the effectiveness of PHI's existing ring-fencing; or (b) a letter from reputable bankruptcy counsel describing what changes to the ring-fencing would be required to ensure PHI is at least as effectively ring-fenced following the reorganization and a letter from Exelon committing to obtain a new non-consolidation option following the reorganization and to take any further steps necessary to obtain such an opinion. Exelon will not object if the Commission elects to open an investigation into the matter if the Commission deems it appropriate. Notwithstanding the above language in this paragraph, the Joint Applicants shall not materially alter the ring-fencing plan described in these Terms and Conditions without first obtaining approval in a written order from the Commission.

100.   None of the cost of establishing, operating or modifying the SPE will be borne by Pepco or its distribution customers. The cost of obtaining the opinion of legal counsel referred to above (or any future opinion) will not be borne by Pepco or its distribution customers.

101.   …

102.   Exelon shall conduct an analysis of its operational and financial risk to determine the adequacy of existing ring fencing measures. Exelon shall file

this analysis with the Commission no later than the end of the third quarter in 2017.

103.   The Joint Applicants agree to implement the ring-fencing and corporate governance measures set out in Paragraphs 51–55 and 63–102 within 180 days after Merger closing for the purpose of providing protections to customers. Not earlier than five (5) years after the closing of the Merger, the Joint Applicants shall have the right to review these ring-fencing provisions and to make a filing with the Commission requesting authority to modify or terminate those provisions. Notwithstanding such right, Joint Applicants agree not to proceed with any such modification or termination without first obtaining Commission approval in a written order. In addition, the Joint Applicants recognize that the Commission at any time may initiate its own review or investigation regarding ring-fencing measures (or upon petition by any party) and order modifications that it deems to be appropriate, in the public interest and the best interest of Pepco customers.

104.   After the Merger, PHI will not initiate or invest in new non-utility operations without first obtaining Commission approval in a written order.

105.   Notwithstanding any other powers that the Commission currently possesses under existing, applicable law, the Joint Applicants agree that the Commission may, after investigation and a hearing, order Exelon to divest its interest in Pepco on terms adequate to protect the interests of utility investors (including Exelon investors) and consumers and the public, if the Commission finds that: (a) one or more of the divestiture conditions described below has occurred, (b) that as a consequence Pepco has failed to meet its obligations as a public utility, and (c) that divestiture is necessary to allow Pepco to meet its obligations and to protect the interests of its customers in a financially healthy utility and in the continued receipt of reasonably adequate utility service at just and reasonable rates. Any divestiture order made pursuant to this commitment shall be applicable to Pepco only to the extent consistent with the application of the criteria in the preceding clauses (a)–(c) and shall be limited to the assets and operations of Pepco in the District of Columbia. The divestiture conditions covered by this commitment are: (i) a nuclear accident or incident at an Exelon nuclear power facility involving the release or threatened release of radioactive isotopes, resulting in (x) a material disruption of operations at such facility and material loss to Exelon that is not covered by insurance or indemnity or (y) the permanent closure of a material number of Exelon nuclear plants as a result of such accident or incident; (ii) a bankruptcy filing by Exelon or any of its subsidiaries constituting 10% or more of Exelon's consolidated assets at the end of its most recent fiscal quarter, or 10% or more of Exelon's consolidated net income for the twelve (12) months ended at the close of its most recent fiscal quarter; (iii) the rating for Exelon's senior unsecured long-term public debt securities, without third-party credit enhancement, are downgraded to

a rating that indicates "substantial risks" (i.e., below B3 by Moody's or B- by S&P or Fitch) by at least two of the three major credit rating agencies, and such condition continues for more than six (6) months; or (iv) Exelon and/or PHI have committed a pattern of material violations of lawful Commission orders or regulations, or applicable provisions of the D.C. Code and, despite notice and opportunity to cure such violations, have continued to commit the violations.

References

BOOKS

Allen, William T., et al., *Commentaries and Cases on the Law of Business Organizations* (Aspen 2009).

Apter, David, *Introduction to Political Analysis* (Winthrop 1977).

Areeda, Phillip E. & Hovenkamp, Herbert, *Antitrust Law* (Wolters Kluwer 2008).

Areeda, Phillip E., et al., *Antitrust Analysis* (Aspen 2004).

Bauman, Jeffrey D. & Stevenson, Russell B., Jr., *Corporations Law & Policy* (Thomson/West 2013).

Baumol, William J., Panzar, John C. & Willig, Robert D., *Contestable Markets and the Theory of Industry Structure* (Harcourt Brace Jovanovich 1982).

Bonbright, James C. & Means, Gardiner C., *The Holding Company: Its Public Significance and Its Regulation* (McGraw Hill 1932; 1969 ed.).

Brudney, Victor & Bratton, William W., *Brudney and Chirelstein's Cases and Materials on Corporate Finance* (West Academic 1993).

Carstensen, Peter C., *Competition Policy and the Control of Buyer Power* (Edward Elgar 2017).

Crane, Daniel A., *The Institutional Structure of Antitrust Enforcement* (Oxford University Press 2011).

Crawford, Susan, *Captive Audience: The Telecom Industry and Monopoly Power in the New Gilded Age* (Yale University Press 2013).

Dos Passos, John, *The Prospect Before Us* (Greenwood Press 1950).

Frank, Robert H., *The Darwin Economy: Liberty, Competition, and the Common Good* (Princeton University Press 2012).

Frankena, Mark W. & Owen, Bruce M., *Electric Utility Mergers: Principles of Antitrust Analysis* (Praeger Publishers 1994).

Gladwell, Malcom, *Outliers: The Story of Success* (Little, Brown and Company 2008).

Gwartney, James D., et al., *Economics: Private & Public Choice* (Cengage Learning 2002).

Hempling, Scott, *Regulating Public Utility Performance: The Law of Market Structure, Pricing and Jurisdiction* (American Bar Association 2013).

Herrera Anchustegui, Ignacio, *Buyer Power in EU Competition Law* (Concurrences 2017).

Hovenkamp, Herbert, *Federal Antitrust Policy: The Law of Competition and Its Practice* (West Group 2011).

Hovenkamp, Herbert, *The Antitrust Enterprise* (First Harvard University Press 2005).

Huber, Peter W., Kellogg, Michael K. & Thorne, John, *Federal Telecommunications Law* (Wolters Kluwer 1999).

Hyman, Leonard S., *America's Electric Utilities: Past, Present and Future* (Public Utilities Reports 1994).

Kahn, Alfred, *The Economics of Regulation: Principles and Institutions* (MIT Press 1988) (1970).

Kahneman, Daniel, *Thinking, Fast and Slow* (Farrar, Strauss and Giroux 2011).

Krugman, Paul & Wells, Robin, *Microeconomics* (Macmillan 2015).

Kwoka, John, *Mergers, Merger Control, and Remedies: A Retrospective Analysis of U.S. Policy* (The MIT Press 2015).

Lakoff, George, *Don't Think of an Elephant! Know Your Values and Frame the Debate* (Chelsea Green Publishing 2004).

Lewis, Michael, *The Undoing Project: A Friendship That Changed Our Minds* (Penguin Books 2017).

Libby, Robert, et al., *Financial Accounting* (McGraw Hill 2009).

Mankiw, N. Gregory, *Principles of Economics* (Cengage Learning 2004).

Maynard, Therese H., *Mergers & Acquisitions* (Aspen 2017).

McConnell, Campbell R. & Brue, Stanley L., *Economics: Principles, Problems, and Policies* (McGraw Hill/Irwin 17th ed. 2008).

Moore, Graham, *The Last Days of Night* (Random House 2017).

Morgan, Thomas D., *Cases and Materials on Modern Antitrust Law and Its Origins* (West Academic Publishing 2009).

Morris, Joseph M., et al., *Mergers and Acquisitions: Business Strategies for Accountants* (John Wiley & Sons 2000).

Parkin, Michael, *Economics* (Pearson Education 2012).

Pond, Oscar L., *A Treatise on the Law of Public Utilities* (Bobbs-Merrill 1925).

Posner, Richard A., *Reflections on Judging* (Harvard University Press 2013).

Ravenscraft, David J. & Scherer, F.M., *Mergers, Sell-Offs, and Economic Efficiency* (Brookings Institution 1987).

Roach, Craig R., *Simply Electrifying: The Technology that Transformed the World, from Benjamin Franklin to Elon Musk* (BenBella Books 2017).

Ross, Stephen A., et al., *Corporate Finance* (McGraw Hill 2016).

Samuelson, Paul A. & Nordhaus, William D., *Economics* (McGray Hill 2010).

Scherer, Frederic M. & Ross, David, *Industrial Market Structure and Economic Performance* (Houghton Mifflin 1990).

Shenefield, John & Stelzer, Irwin, *The Antitrust Laws: A Primer* (The AEI Press 2001).

Stiglitz, Joseph E., *The Price of Inequality* (Penguin Books 2012).

Stiglitz, Joseph E. & Walsh, Carl E., *Economics* (W.W. Norton 2002).

Taylor, John B. & Weerapana, Akila, *Principles of Economics* (Cengage Learning 2010).

Thaler, Richard H., *Misbehaving: The Making of Behavioral Economics* (W.W. Norton 2015).

Tufte, Edward, *The Cognitive Style of PowerPoint: Pitching Out Corrupts Within* (Graphics Press 2006).

Tufte, Edward, *Visual Explanations* (Graphics Press 1997).

Viscusi, W. Kip, Harrington, Joseph E. & Vernon, John M., *Economics of Regulation and Antitrust* (The MIT Press 2005).

SCHOLARLY ARTICLES AND BOOK CHAPTERS

Andrade, Gregor, et al., *New Evidence and Perspectives on Mergers*, 15 J. Econ. Persp. 107 (2001).

Azagury, Jack, et al., *The Race to Consolidate*, Pub. Util. Fortnightly (Sept. 2012).

Baker, Jonathan, *Comcast/NBCU: The FCC Provides a Roadmap for Vertical Merger Analysis*, 25 Antitrust 36 (2011).

Bolston, Conrad, *Improving FERC's Penalty Guidelines: A Comparative Analysis*, Electricitypolicy.com (2012).

Bradford, Peter, *Gorillas in the Mist: Electric Utility Mergers in Light of State Restructuring Goals*, 18 Nat'l Regulatory Research Inst. Q. Bull. 1 (1997).

Breyer, Stephen G., *Antitrust, Deregulation, and the Newly Liberated Marketplace*, 75 Calif. L. Rev. 1005 (1987).

Burr, Michael T., *Squeezing Synergies*, Pub. Util. Fortnightly, Oct. 2004.

Bush, Darren & Mayne, Carrie, *In (Reluctant) Defense of Enron: Why Bad Regulation Is to Blame for California's Power Woes (or Why Antitrust Law Fails to Protect Against Market Power When the Market Rules Encourage Its Use)*, 83 Or. L. Rev. 207 (2007).

Carlton, Dennis W. & Picker, Randal C., "Antitrust and Regulation," in *Economic Regulation and its Reform: What Have We Learned?* 25 (Nancy L. Rose ed., 2014).

Carstensen, Peter C., *Antitrust Law and the Paradigm of Industrial Organization*, 16 U.C. Davis L. Rev. 487 (1983).

Carstensen, Peter C., "Reflections on Mergers and Competition in Formerly Regulated Industries," in *Competition Policy and Merger Analysis in Deregulated and Newly Competitive Industries* 225 (Peter C. Carstensen & Susan Beth Farmer eds., 2008).

Carstensen, Peter C., *The* Philadelphia National Bank *Presumption: Merger Analysis in an Unpredictable World*, 80 Antitrust L.J. 219 (2015).

Carstensen, Peter C. & Lande, Robert H., *The Merger Incipiency Doctrine and the Importance of "Redundant" Competitors*, 2018 Wis. L. Rev. 781 (2018).

Chen, Jim, *The Echoes of Forgotten Footfalls: Telecommunications Mergers at the Dawn of the Digital Millennium*, 43 Hous. L. Rev. 1311 (2007).

Chen, Jim, *The Magnificent Seven: American Telephony's Deregulatory Shootout*, 50 Hastings L.J. 1503 (1999).

Cowie, Michael G. & Denis, Paul T., *The Fall of Structural Evidence in FTC and DOJ Merger Review*, Antitrust Source (Feb. 2013).

Craig, J. Dean & Savage, Scott J., *Market Restructuring, Competition and the Efficiency of Electricity Generation: Plant-level Evidence from the United States 1996 to 2006*, 34 Energy J. 1 (2013).

Cramton, Peter, *The Efficiency of the FCC Spectrum Auctions*, 41 J.L. & Econ. 727 (1998).

Crane, Daniel A., *Rethinking Merger Efficiencies*, 110 Mich. L. Rev. 347 (2011).

Crocioni, Pietro, *Leveraging of Market Power in Emerging Markets: A Review of Cases, Literature, and a Suggested Framework*, 4 J. Competition L. & Econ. 449 (2008).

Cudahy, Richard, *The FERC's Policy on Electric Mergers: A Bit of Perspective*, 18 Energy L.J. 113 (1997).

Cudahy, Richard D. & Henderson, William D., *From Insull to Enron: Corporate (Re) Regulation After the Rise and Fall of Two Energy Icons*, 26 Energy L.J. 35 (2005).

Englich, Birte, et al., *Playing Dice with Criminal Sentences: The Influence of Irrelevant Anchors on Experts' Judicial Decision Making*, 32 Personality & Soc. Psychol. Bull. 188 (2006).

Estreicher, Samuel & Revesz, Richard L., *Nonacquiescence by Federal Administrative Agencies*, 98 Yale L.J. 679 (1989).

Fazio, Catherine, "Merger Remedies: The Greater Use by the DOJ and FTC of an Expanding Toolkit," in *Recent Developments in Antitrust Law* 51 (Thomson Reuters Westlaw 2013).

Fleischer, Arthur, Jr. & Sussman, Alexander R., "Directors' Fiduciary Duties in Takeovers and Mergers" (31st Annual Securities Regulation Institute 2004).

Frattaroli, Sarita, *Dodging the Bullet Again: Microsoft III's Reformulation of the Foremost Technological Tying Doctrine*, 90 B.U. L. Rev. 1909 (2010).

Furman, Jason & Orszag, Peter, "A Firm-Level Perspective on the Role of Rents in the Rise in Inequality," in *Toward a Just Society: Joseph Stiglitz & Twenty-First Century Economics* 19 (Martin Guzman ed., 2018).

Gaynor, Daniel E., *Technological Tying* (FTC Bureau of Econ., Working Paper No. 284, 2006).

Greaney, Thomas L., "Hospital Mergers," in *Competition Policy and Merger Analysis in Deregulated and Newly Competitive Industries* 126 (Peter C. Carstensen & Susan Beth Farmer eds., 2008).

Hardin, Garrett, *The Tragedy of the Commons*, Science (Dec. 13, 1968).

Hartman, Raymond S., *The Efficiency Effects of Utility Mergers: Lessons from Statistical Cost Analysis*, 17 Energy L.J. 425 (1996).

Hempling, Scott, "Competition for the Monopoly: Why So Rare?," in *Preside or Lead? The Attributes and Actions of Effective Regulators* 211 (2013).

Hempling, Scott, *Corporate Restructuring and Consumer Risk: Is the SEC Enforcing the Public Utility Holding Company Act?*, Electricity J., July 1988.

Hempling, Scott, *Inconsistent with the Public Interest: FERC's Three Decades of Deference to Electricity Consolidation*, 39 Energy L.J. 233 (2018).

Hempling, Scott, *Litigation Adversaries and Public Interest Partners: Practice Principles for New Regulatory Lawyers*, 36 Energy L.J. 1 (2015).

Hempling, Scott, "Regulatory Resources: Does the Differential Make a Difference?" (Parts I and II), in *Preside or Lead? The Attributes and Actions of Effective Regulators* (2013).

Hempling, Scott, "Alfred Kahn (1917–2010)," in *Preside or Lead? The Attributes and Actions of Effective Regulators* (2013).

Hempling, Scott, "Commissions Are Not Courts; Regulators Are Not Judges," in *Preside or Lead? The Attributes and Actions of Effective Regulators* (2013).

Hempling, Scott, *Regulatory Capture: Sources and Solutions*, 1 Emory Corp. Governance & Accountability Rev. 23 (2014).

Hempling, Scott, *Riders, Trackers, Surcharges, Pre-Approvals and Decoupling: How Do They Affect the Cost of Equity?* Electricitypolicy.com (March 2012).

Hicks, John R., *Annual Survey of Economic Theory: The Theory of Monopoly*, 3 Econometrica 1 (1935).

Hornstein, Donald T., *Adaptation and Resiliency in Legal Systems: Resiliency, Adaptation, and the Upsides of Ex Post Lawmaking*, 89 N.C. L. Rev. 1549 (2011).

Horton, Thomas J., *Efficiencies and Antitrust Reconsidered: An Evolutionary Perspective*, 60 Antitrust Bull. 168 (2015).

Hyman, Leonard S., *Investing in the "Plain Vanilla" Utility*, 24 Energy L.J. 1 (2003).

Jacowitz, Karen E. & Kahneman, Daniel, *Measures of Anchoring in Estimation Tasks*, 21 Personality & Soc. Psychol. Bull. 1161 (1995).

Kahn, Alfred E., *Deregulatory Schizophrenia*, 75 Calif. L. Rev. 1059 (1987).

Kahneman, Daniel & Tversky, Amos, *Availability: A Heuristic for Judging Frequency and Probability*, 5 Cognitive Psychol. 207 (1973).

Kahneman, Daniel & Tversky, Amos, *Subjective Probability: A Judgment of Representativeness*, 3 Cognitive Psychol. 430 (1972).

Katz, Michael L. & Shelanski, Howard A., *Merger Analysis and the Treatment of Uncertainty: Should We Expect Better?*, 74 Antitrust L.J. 537 (2007).

Katz, Michael L. & Shelanski, Howard A., *Mergers and Innovation*, 74 Antitrust L.J. 1 (2007).

Krattenmaker, Thomas G. & Salop, Steven C., *Anticompetitive Exclusion: Raising Rivals' Costs to Achieve Power over Price*, 96 Yale L.J. 209 (1986).

Kwoka, John, *The Changing Nature of Efficiencies in Mergers and Merger Analysis*, Antitrust Bull., Sept. 2015.

Kwoka, John, "The Effects of Mergers on Innovation: Economic Framework and Empirical Evidence," in Nihoul, Paul & Van Cleynenbreugel, Pieter, *The Roles of Innovation in Competition Law Analysis* 13 (2018).

Kwoka, John & Shumilkina, Evgenia, *The Price Effect of Eliminating Potential Competition: Evidence from an Airline Merger*, 58 J. Indus. Econ. 767 (2010).

Lamb, William S. & Didriksen, Michael, *Electric and Gas Utility Mergers and Acquisitions: Trends in Deal Terms, Contract Provisions, and Regulatory Matters*, 38 Energy L.J. 133 (2017).

LeBoeuf, Robyn & Shafir, Eldar, *The Long and Short of It: Physical Anchoring Effects*, 19 J. Behav. Decision Making 393 (2006).

Lipsky, Abbott B., Jr. & Sidak, J. Gregory, *Essential Facilities*, 51 Stan. L. Rev. 1187 (1999).

Littlechild, Stephen C., "The Nature of Competition and the Regulatory Process," in *"Effective Competition" in Telecommunications, Rail and Energy Markets* (Intereconomics Forum ed., 2011).

Mahinka, Stephen Paul & Gebhard, Theodore A., *Deregulation and Industry Restructuring: Antitrust Issues in Electric Utility Mergers and Alliances*, 12 Antitrust 38 (1998).

Mahinka, Stephen Paul & Gebhard, Theodore A., *Preclosing Cooperation in Energy Mergers: Antitrust Issues and Practical Concerns*, 13 Electricity J. 68 (2000).

Melnyk, Markian M.W. & Lamb, William S., *PUHCA's Gone: What Is Next for Holding Companies?*, 27 Energy L.J. 1 (2006).

Miller, Dale T. & McFarland, Cathy, *Counterfactual Thinking and Victim Compensation: A Test of Norm Theory*, 12 Personality & Soc. Psychol. Bull. 513 (1986).

Miller, Dale T., et al., *When a Coincidence Is Suspicious: The Role of Mental Simulation*, 57 J. Personality & Soc. Psychol. 581 (1989).

Moot, John S., *Electric Utility Mergers: Uncertainty Looms over Regulatory Approvals at FERC*, 12 Energy L.J. 1 (1991).

Mueller, D., *Mergers and Market Share*, 67 Rev. Econ. & Stat. 259 (1985).

Nelson, Caleb, *Statutory Interpretation and Decision Theory*, 74 U. Chi. L. Rev. 329 (2007).

Niefer, Mark J., *Explaining the Divide Between DOJ and FERC on Electric Power Merger Policy*, 33 Energy L J. 505 (2012).

Philadelphia National Bank *at 50: An Interview with Judge Richard Posner*, 80 Antitrust L.J. 205 (2015).

Pierce, Richard J., "Mergers in the Electric Power Industry," in *Competition Policy and Merger Analysis in Deregulated and Newly Competitive Industries* 8 (Peter C. Carstensen & Susan Beth Farmer eds., 2008).

Pindyck, Robert S., *Sunk Costs and Real Options in Antitrust Analysis*, 1 Issues Comp. L. & Pol'y 619 (2008).

Pitofsky, Robert, *Efficiency Considerations and Merger Enforcement: Comparison of U.S. and EU Approaches*, 30 Fordham Int'l L.J. 1413 (2007).

Pitofsky, Robert, et al., *The Essential Facilities Doctrine Under United States Antitrust Law*, 70 Antitrust L.J. 443 (2002).

Posner, Richard A., *Natural Monopoly and Its Regulation*, 21 Stan. L. Rev. 548 (1969).

Ravenscraft, D. & Scherer, F.M., *The Profitability of Mergers*, 7 Int'l J. Indus. Org. 101 (1989).

Reiter, Harvey L., *Competition Between Public and Private Distributors in a Restructured Power Industry*, 19 Energy L.J. 333 (1998).

Reiter, Harvey L., *Implications of Mergers and Acquisitions in Gas and Electric Markets: The Role of Yardstick Competition in Merger Analysis*, Nat'l Regulatory Research Inst. Q. Bull., Summer 1999.

Salop, Steven C., *Merger Settlement and Enforcement Policy for Optimal Deterrence and Maximum Welfare*, 81 Fordham L. Rev. 2647 (2013).

Schuck, Peter H., *Mass Torts: An Institutional Evolutionist Perspective*, 80 Cornell L. Rev. 941 (1995).

Sheffi, Yossi & Lynn, Barry C., *Systemic Supply Chain Risk*, The Bridge (Fall 2014).

Sheldrew, Judy, *Shutting the Barn Door Before the Horse is Stolen: How and Why State Public Utility Commissions Should Regulate Transactions Between a Public Utility and Its Affiliates*, 4 Nev. L.J. 164 (2003).

Stout, Lynn A., *Are Takeover Premiums Really Premiums? Market Price, Fair Value, and Corporate Law*, 99 Yale L.J. 1235 (1990).

Turner, Donald F., *Conglomerate Mergers and Section 7 of the Clayton Act*, 78 Harv. L. Rev. 1313 (1965).

Tversky, Amos & Kahneman, Daniel, *Judgment under Uncertainty: Heuristics and Biases*, 185 Science 1124 (1974).

Werden, Gregory J., *Essays on Consumer Welfare and Competition Policy* (2009).

Werden, Gregory J., *The Law and Economics of the Essential Facility Doctrine*, 32 St. Louis U. L.J. 433 (1987).

GENERAL AND TRADE PRESS ARTICLES

Alabama Power's Smart Neighborhood, T&D World (Jan. 4, 2019).

Bottom Line on Ten Big Mergers, The, Fortune, May 1982.

BTU Convergence Spawning Gas Market Opportunities in North America, Oil & Gas J. (June 29, 1998).

Convergence on a Small Scale: Ohio Coop Buys IOU Gas Co., Electricity Daily (May 28, 1998).

CP&L Wants in on Gas Service, Electricity Daily (Apr. 3, 1998).

Description is Prescription, N.Y. Times, Nov. 25, 2010.

Different Storm Brews, A, Balt. Sun (Sept. 2, 2010).

DQE Leaving Electricity, Plans to Invest in Water & Sewer Companies, Pitt. Post-Gazette (Nov. 25, 1998).

EEI Reports on Electric Industry Key Trends, Foster Nat. Gas Report, Jan. 14, 1999.

Exelon Generation Texas Power Files Chapter 11 Bankruptcy, Power Engineering (Nov. 7, 2017).

Exelon Is Exploring Nuclear Power Plant Hydrogen Production, Power (Aug. 29, 2019).

Exelon Puts Texas Plants Totaling 3,500 MW into Bankruptcy, Am. Pub. Power Ass'n (Nov. 7, 2017).

Exelon, PSEG Have Highest Business Risk Among 34 Utilities in Moody's Report, Util. Dive (Nov. 8, 2018).

Exelon to Buy PSEG for $12 Billion, Wall St. J. (Dec. 21, 2014).

FERC Clears Exelon-PSEG Merger, Nat. Gas Intelligence (July 5, 2005).

Georgia Tests Cost-Effectiveness and Benefits of Microgrids, Smart Energy Int'l (Mar. 14, 2019).

How ConEd's Mobile Battery REV Demo Could Build a New Storage Business Model, Util. Dive (Mar. 7, 2017).

Impact of the Irrelevant on Decision-Making, The, N.Y. Times, May 29, 2010.

It's All About the Value of the Network: ComEd Gears Up for a Distributed Energy Boom, Greentech Media (July 1, 2016).

It's Not Just About Energy Anymore: Utilities Add Roles, Omaha World-Herald, Sept. 10, 1998.

Maryland Utility Proposes $44.2M Pilot for Public Purpose Microgrids, Microgrid Knowledge (Oct. 3, 2017).

MidAmerican Does Real Estate, Electricity Daily (Apr. 10, 1998).

NGC/Destec Merger Latest in BTU Convergence, Oil & Gas J. (Feb. 24, 1997).

NRG Energy's GenOn Unit Files for Bankruptcy, Reuters (June 14, 2017).

Our Beaker is Starting to Boil, N.Y. Times (July 17, 2017).

Oncor, S&C and Schneider Electric Complete a Unique Four-Part Microgrid, Greentech Media (Apr. 7, 2015).

Pepco's Power Outages Infuriate Washingtonians, Washington Examiner (July 27, 2010).

PowerSecure Becomes Microgrid Implementation Provider for New Innovative Energy Joint Venture Compass Energy Platform LLC, PR Newswire (May 17, 2019).

PSEG and Exelon Announce Termination of Proposed Utility Merger; Companies Cite Insurmountable Gaps with New Jersey Board of Public Utilities, Bus. Wire (Sept. 14, 2006).

Schneider Electric to Help Enable Energy Resiliency at USMC Base, PowerGrid Int'l (Mar. 14, 2017).

Sempra Bests Berkshire with $9.45 Billion Offer for Oncor, Bloomberg (Aug. 21, 2017).

Some of FirstEnergy's Power-Generation Businesses File for Bankruptcy, Wall St. J. (Apr. 1, 2018).

Southern California Edison Unveils Smart Neighborhood Electricity Circuit, T&D World (Oct. 24, 2007).

Southern's PowerSecure Contracts with Bloom for Fuel Cell + Storage Solution, Util. Dive (Oct. 26, 2016).

Structure of Equality, The, New Yorker (Dec. 31, 2018).

Texas Fight Could Ripple Across U.S. Grid, E&E News (July 10, 2019).

Texas Regulators Reject $18B NextEra-Oncor Deal, Util. Dive (Apr. 13, 2017).

Troubled Calpine Files Bankruptcy, N.Y. Times (Dec. 21, 2005).

'They Were Conned': How Reckless Loans Devastated a Generation of Taxi Drivers, N.Y. Times (May 19, 2019).

Ways to Put the Boss's Skin in the Game, N.Y. Times (Mar. 21, 2015).

What's the Path Forward for DC's Grid Mod? After Nearly a Year of Study, the City is Still Finding Out, Util. Dive (June 10, 2019).

You're Not Going to Change Your Mind, N.Y. Times (May 27, 2017).

REPORTS AND OTHER SOURCES

21st Century Power Partnership, Nat'l Renewable Energy Lab, *An Introduction to Retail Electricity Choice in the United States* (2017).

Am. Inst. of Certified Pub. Accts., *U.S. GAAP Financial Statements: Best Practices in Presentation and Disclosure* (67th ed. 2013).

Buffet, Warren E., *Berkshire Hathaway Inc., 2018 Annual Report* (2019).

Energy Info. Admin., U.S., *The U.S. Electric System is Made up of Interconnections and Balancing Authorities* (2016).

Gov't Accountability Office, U.S., *Key Issues: Disposal of High Level Nuclear Waste.*

Guidelines on the Assessment of Non-Horizontal Mergers Under the Council Regulation on the Control of Concentrations Between Undertakings, 2008 O.J. (C 265).

Fed. Reserve Bank, *Living Wills (or Resolution Plans).*

Feinstein, Richard, Fed. Trade Comm'n, *Negotiating Merger Remedies* (2012).

Filipink, Eric, Harrison Inst. for Pub. Law, *Serving the "Public Interest": Traditional vs. Expansive Utility Regulation* (2009).

Financial Accounting Standards Bd., *Accounting Standards Update: Intangibles— Goodwill and Other (Topic 350)* (2019).

Gov't Accountability Office, U.S., *Public Utility Holding Company Act: Opportunities Exist to Strengthen SEC's Administration of the Act* (2005).

Hempling, Scott, *No Anticompetitive Conduct, No Unearned Advantage: Effective Competition Depends on Merit* (2018).

Hempling, Scott, *Regulatory Expense: Is Asymmetry Inevitable?* (2015).

Hempling, Scott & Strauss, Scott H., *Pre-Approval Commitments: When And Under What Conditions Should Regulators Commit Ratepayer Dollars to Utility-Proposed Capital Projects?* (Nat'l Regulatory Research Inst. 2008).

Hill, Stephen G., *Private Equity Buyouts of Public Utilities: Preparation for Regulators* (Nat'l Regulatory Research Inst. 2007).

ICF Int'l & Nat'l Ass'n of Energy Serv. Cos., *Introduction to Energy Performance Contracting* (2007).

Kemp, William, Presentation to the International Association for Energy Economics: Economies of Scale and Scope in Electric Utility Mergers (Oct. 10, 2011).

Kranz, Johann J. & Picot, Arnold, *Toward an End-to-End Smart Grid: Overcoming Bottlenecks to Facilitate Competition and Innovation in Smart Grids* (Nat'l Regulatory Research Inst. 2011).

Kwoka, John E., Jr. & White, Lawrence, American Antitrust Inst., *Public Comment: AAI Criticizes Surface Transportation Board's Railroad Merger Guidelines* (2000).

Lesieutre, Bernard C. & Eto, Joseph H., *Electricity Transmission Congestion Costs: A Review of Recent Reports* (Lawrence Berkeley Nat'l Lab. 2003).

Lichtenberg, Sherry, *Smart Grid Data: Must There Be Conflict Between Energy Management and Consumer Privacy?* (Nat'l Regulatory Research Inst. 2010).

Moody's Investors Service, *A Rating Agency Perspective on the Utility Industry* (2012).

Moody's Investors Service, *Moody's Reviews Exelon and Exelon Generation for Possible Downgrade; Affirms Constellation, Outlook Positive* (2011).

Moody's Investors Service, *Oncor Electric Delivery Company LLC: Exploring the Limits of Parent Company Leverage, Again* (2015).

Morris, Derek, *Dominant Firm Behaviour Under UK Competition Law*, presented to Fordham Corporate Law Institute, Thirtieth Annual Conference on International Antitrust Law and Policy (Oct. 23–24, 2003).

Nat'l Regulatory Research Inst., *Effective Regulation: Guidance for Public-Interest Decisionmakers* (2009).

Nat'l Research Council, Bd. on Sci., Tech., and Econ. Policy, *Investing for Productivity and Prosperity* (1994).

New York Stock Exchange, *Listed Company Manual*.

Nuclear Regulatory Comm'n, U.S., *Backgrounder: Radioactive Waste* (2019).

PJM Learning Center, *Markets for Electricity*.

PJM Stakeholder Affairs Dep't, *PJM Manual 34: PJM Stakeholder Process* (2019).

Regulatory Assistance Project, *Revenue Regulation and Decoupling: A Guide to Theory and Application* (2016).

Simeone, Christina, *PJM Governance: Can Reforms Improve Outcomes?* (Kleinman Ctr. for Energy Policy 2017).

Smart Elec. Power Alliance, *Final Report v1.0 of the MEDSIS Stakeholder Working Groups* (2019).

Standard & Poor's, *Research Update: Ratings Are Affirmed on Exelon Companies on News It Will Merge with Constellation; Constellation Is on CW Positive* (2011).

Tabors Caramanis & Associates, *Horizontal Market Power in Wisconsin Electricity Markets: A Report to the Public Service Commission of Wisconsin* (2000).

Index